FACHWÖRTERBUCH

Neue Informations- und Kommunikationsdienste

Deutsch-Englisch
Englisch-Deutsch

FACHWÖRTERBUCH

Neue Informations- und Kommunikationsdienste

Deutsch - Englisch
Englisch - Deutsch

Mit etwa 13.500 Wortstellen und 8 Tabellen

Herausgegeben von
Horst E. von Renouard

Hüthig Buch Verlag Heidelberg

Eingetragene Gebrauchsmuster, Warenzeichen oder Patente sind in diesem Wörterbuch nicht besonders gekennzeichnet. Das Fehlen eines solchen Hinweises bedeutet jedoch nicht, daß solche Bezeichnungen frei sind oder frei benutzt werden können.

In this dictionary, registered trade marks, utility models or patents are not identified as such. The absence of such reference does not, however, imply that these terms are not so protected.

CIP-Titelaufnahme der Deutschen Bibliothek

Renouard, Horst E. von:
Fachwörterbuch neue Informations- und Kommunikationsdienste : deutsch - englisch, englisch - deutsch / hrsg. von Horst E. von Renouard. - Heidelberg : Hüthig, 1990
    ISBN 3-7785-1801-1
NE: HST

© 1990 Hüthig Buch Verlag GmbH, Heidelberg
Printed in Germany

Vorwort

Alle sich mit der Fernmeldetechnik befassenden Wörterbücher streifen die von dieser Technik vermittelten Dienstleistungen nur am Rande, wenn überhaupt. Mit der rasanten Entwicklung dieser Dienste - man denke nur an Telefax, den Bildschirmtext, den Mobilfunk und das Satellitenfernsehen - sind aber aus den dafür entwickelten nationalen und internationalen Normen auch viele neue Wortprägungen entstanden, die jetzt erstmalig zusammenfassend in der vorliegenden Terminologiesammlung festgehalten worden sind. Diese Sammlung, die mit Hinblick auf den europäischen Anwendungsbereich auf der englischsprachigen Seite insbesondere aus dem Britischen schöpft (die wesentlichsten US-Begriffe dabei aber nicht außer Acht läßt und auch nicht lassen könnte), wendet sich damit an Fachübersetzer und Nachrichtentechniker, aber auch an Diensteanbieter und Bedarfsträger sowie die Berichterstatter über diese Technik.

Mit dieser Zielgebung sind mit einem beim ISDN liegenden Schwerpunkt die verschiedenen Schlüsselbegriffe über den Rahmen der üblichen Sachgebietsverweise hinausgehend mit Hinweisen auf die einschlägigen Normen und mit technischen Angaben ergänzt worden, um, wo nötig, tiefergehende Definitionen zu vermitteln und Beziehungen zwischen verschiedenen Einzelbegriffen herzustellen. Im Anhang sind Tabellen der wichtigsten I-, V- und X-Empfehlungen des CCITT sowie der Temex-Struktur, der wesentlichen ISDN-bezogenen NET-Normen, der europäischen Videotexsysteme und der Schichten des ISO-Referenzmodells zu finden. Nebenbei enthält diese Wortliste auch Ausdrücke, die mir während meiner Tätigkeit als Übersetzer auf diesem Gebiet als nützlich oder ungewöhnlich ins Auge gefallen sind.

Von den deutsch- und englischsprachigen Fach- und Firmenschriften, vom Rotbuch des CCITT bis zum Postbuch sind alle verfügbaren Quellen bei der Erarbeitung der Termini in gründlicher und sorgfältiger Sichtungsarbeit ausgeschöpft worden. Diese, ohne Personal Computer nicht realisierbare Arbeit dürfte durch den bevorstehenden europäischen Binnenmarkt und die damit verbundenen erweiterten internationalen Kommunikationsbedürfnisse noch zusätzlich an Bedeutung gewinnen, nicht zuletzt als Informationsquelle.

Für die Benutzung dieses Wörterbuches sind gewisse Sprachkenntnisse die Vorbedingung, und es werden daher außer dem Geschlecht der deutschen Substantiva keine grammatischen Hinweise gegeben. Alle Abkürzungen, voll alphabetisch als Suchbegriff eingegliedert, sind, soweit sich diese nicht auf derselben Seite befinden, zusammen mit ihren deutschen und englischen Entsprechungen aufgeführt, womit sich das bei Weiterverweisungen so lästige Hin- und Herblättern erübrigt. Das trifft auch auf die in den kursiven Erklärungen erscheinenden Abkürzungen zu, die ebenfalls als Suchbegriff wiederzufinden sind, nicht in einer separaten, beispielsweise am Anfang stehenden Liste (*GB* und *US* verweisen, wie üblich, auf den jeweiligen Sprachraum).

Es sei an dieser Stelle allen mein besonderer Dank ausgesprochen, die mir bei der Fertigstellung dieser Wortsammlung Beistand geleistet haben, im Verlag, im FTZ, bei BTRL, im Ausland und zuhause, Kollegen, Freunden und freundlichen Fremden, und allen voran meiner Familie für ihr tolerantes Verständnis, ohne das das Buch nie zustande gekommen wäre! Hinweise und Verbesserungsvorschläge, die gegebenenfalls in einer zukünftigen Ausgabe berücksichtigt werden können, bitte ich an den Verlag zu richten.

London, im Frühjahr 1990   *H. v. Renouard*

Preface

There are many excellent technical dictionaries covering the various aspects of telecommunications, but the services provided by means of these technologies are not usually given much space. In recent years, however, these services have expanded at a tremendous rate which has, in turn, been matched by the speed with which new terms have been created, e.g. in the relevant national and international standards. It is these terms which are being presented here comprehensively for the first time and which have been collected from fields as diverse as telefax, videotex, mobile radio and satellite communications. The emphasis is on British terminology as the intended area of use of this dictionary is Europe, but essential US terms have not been excluded.

Where necessary in order to provide a more detailed definition, explanations are given and references to relevant standards like the CCITT V, X and I Recommendations, NET standards, European videotex systems and ISO Reference Model layers are included, tables of which are appended at the back of the book which thus also serves as a source of up-to-date reference information.

Users of this dictionary are assumed to have a basic knowledge of the languages involved and, apart from the genders of German nouns, no grammatical references are, therefore, given. All abbreviations, included alphabetically in the main listing, are rendered with their corresponding equivalents unless these are located on the same page, when they are referred to in the usual manner by 's.'. This also applies to abbreviations appearing in the explanations in italics, which will be found in the main list, not in a separate list e.g. at the beginning of the text (*GB* and *US* still refer to usage, as elsewhere).

My special thanks go to all those who have assisted me in the compilation and completion of this book. Any suggestions for improvements, corrections or additions will be gratefully received, with a view to inclusion in a future edition, and should be addressed to the Publisher.

London, Spring 1990   *H. v. Renouard*

Deutsch - Englisch

A

AA (allgemeine Amtsabfrage *f*) unassigned (exchange line) answer
AAE (Anrufbeantwortungs-Einrichtung *f*) answering equipment
abarbeiten process; run *(program)*, execute *(program steps)*; service
a/b-Schnittstelle *f* a/b interface *(tel. copper interface)*
Abbau *m* release *(data line)*, clear-down *(connection)*
abbauen reduce; release, disconnect
   Verbindung *f* **a.** clear a connection *(VC)*
Abbereitung *f* splitting up *(carrier frequency technique)*; demultiplexing
Abbild *n* image; capacity *(e.g. of system)*; equivalent circuit; waveform *(pulses)*
Abbildspannung *f* representative voltage *(of a current)*
Abbildung *f* imaging; mapping *(logical association of values like addresses in one network with values like devices in another network)*
Abbildungsweg *m* imaging path *(FO)*
abbrechen abandon, disconnect, abort
   Ruf a. cancel the call
Abbruchverfahren *n* abortion procedure *(access control)*
ABE (Aufbereitungseinrichtung *f*) processing equipment
abfahren shut down *(process)*; trace *(cables, tracks)*
Abfall *m* drop, dip *(voltage)*, slope *(characteristic)*, tilt *(pulse)*
Abfallverzögerung *f* releasing *or* drop-out delay *(relay)*; hangover *(PS)*
abfangen compensate, correct *(errors)*; clamp *(signal)*; intercept
Abfertigung *f* **von Belegungen** handling of calls *(tel. sys.)*
Abfertigungsrate *f* dispatch rate *or* block dispatch rate *(transmitter, PCM speech channel)*
Abfertigungsreihenfolge *f* queue discipline *(delay system)*
Abfertigungszeit *f* service time
Abfrage *f* answering, interrogation *(tel.)*; retrieval, query, enquiry, inquiry *(data)*; interrogation, polling *(data)*; reading *(values)*; scanning *(signalling, keyboard)* sensing, examination *(HW)*;
   A. und Auskunftsystem *n* interrogation and information system
   A. und Speicherglied *n* sample and hold circuit
   A. von Internrufen answering internal calls *(PBX)*
Abfrageapparat *m* operator's telephone set, inquiry set
Abfragebetrieb *m* delivery *(message)*, retrieval mode; transmission on demand *(TC)*; direct trunking; ring down junction
Abfrageeinrichtung *f* **für Telefonanschlüsse mit Datenverkehr** (AED) polling unit for telephone connections with data service *(FTZ)*
Abfragefolge *f* Inquiry sequence
Abfrageklinke *f* answering jack *(tel.)*
abfragen challenge *(identify)*; interrogate, scan *(addresses, keys, signalling)*; accept a call, answer *or* interrogate a calling subscriber *(tel. exchange)*; retrieve *(message)*; read *(values)*
Abfragen *n* polling *(terminals, telefax stations)*; answering *(calls)*
   Find *(user in MHS nameserver)*
Abfragesender *m* challenger
Abfragestelle *f* attendant's station; extension *(tel.)*; scanning point *(dig. exchange)*
Abfragetaste *f* speaking key, answering key *(PABX)*; request key
Abfragezusatz *m* answering equipment
Abgang *m* outgoing section
abgeben feed, provide, output, emit, deliver
abgefragte Verbindung *f* outgoing call, call answered
abgehend outgoing *(call)*
   a. Ruf *m* call request
   a. Zugang m outgoing access *(from a network to a subscriber in another network, CCITT)*
abgemeldete Endeinrichtung *f* de-affiliated terminal *(tel.)*
abgeschaltete Leitung *f* dead line

abgesetzt: vom Amt a. remotely located
abgesichert fused
abgleichen tune *(frequency)*; adjust, balance *(circuit)*
abhängen off-hook, remove the handset
abhängiger Wartebetrieb *m* normal disconnected mode
Abhängigkeiten *fpl* circuit conditions
abheben off-hook, remove the handset
Abhörsicherheit *f* listening protection, privacy *(tel.)*
Ablage *f* tray *(HW)*; deviation, error *(frequency)*
Ablageposition *f* stored position
Ablauf *m* run *(program)*; sequence *(process)*; procedure; supply *(cable, tape)*; expiry *(timer)*
Ablaufdiagramm *n* timing chart; structogram, flowchart
ablaufen elapse *(time)*; time-out *(timer)*; run *(program)*
ablauffähig executable *(program)*
Ablauffehler *m* procedure error
Ablaufgeschwindigkeit *f* sweep speed *(CRO)*
Ablaufsteuerung *f* sequence control *(exch.)*
Ablaufüberwachung *f* sequence supervisor, monitor
Ablaufunterbrechung *f* exception condition
Ablaufverfolgung *f* monitoring, tracing
Ablaufzeit *f* period *(delay element)*
Ablegebetrieb *m* (message) recording mode *(tel.)*
ablehnen disregard *(a call, tel.)*
ableiten derive; bypass, earth, bleed
    Daten a. drop data *(in MUX)*
    Strom a. return *or* bypass current *(to earth)*
    Takt a. extract clock, timing
Ableitung(sbelag *m*) *f* leakage *(cable, in kohm/km)*
Ableitungspunkt *m* earthing point
Ableitwiderstand *m* leakage resistance
Ablenkung *f* deflection *(TV)*, sweep *(CRO)*
abliefern transmit, forward
abmelden de-affiliate
    sich a. sign off, log off; go on-hook
Abnahmeprüfung *f* acceptance test
Abnehmer *m* serving line, output line *(PCM data/speech)*
    belegter A. busy server *(tel.sys.)*
    Verbindungs-A. communication server (CS) *(LAN gateway)*
Abnehmerbündel *n* serving trunk group *(tel.sys.)*
Abnehmerleitung *f* serving trunk, server *(tel.sys.)*

Abrechnen *n* billing; invoicing, accounting
abriegeln isolate
Abriegeln *n* **der Sprechwege** DC isolation of the speech paths
Abruf *m* polling *(fax)*; proceed-to-send signal; retrieval *(messages)*
Abrufdienst *m* conversational service
abrufen recall, request *(messages in E-mail)*; poll; call up, call in, fetch *(from storage)*
abrufgesteuerte Kanalzuteilung *f* demand assignment (DA)
absaugen filter out *(frequencies)*
Abschaltebereich *m* range of faulty operation *(signalling link)*; security unit *(area of devices in exch.)*
abschalten switch off, turn off *(device)*; detach *(terminal)*; disconnect *(subscriber)*
Abschalteschwelle *f* failure threshold *(signalling link)*
Abschaltkette *f* shutdown sequence *(process)*
Abschaltung *f* disconnection *(of the subscriber)*
abschließen terminate
Abschluß *m* termination
abschneiden clip *(signal)*
Abschnitt *m* section; slot *(time slot)*
Abschnittsrahmenkopf *m* section overhead *(STM-1, CCITT G.70x)*
abschnittweise link by link *(SS7 network)*
absetzen transmit *(signal)*
absichern support *(results)*
Absichtserklärung *f* letter of intent
Absorberraum *m* anechoic chamber
Abstand *m* distance, spacing, separation, gap; range, proximity, clearance, interval; difference, ratio
    Leistungspegel-A. power level difference
    Nebenzipfel-A. side-lobe attenuation *or* gain *(antennas)*
    Rausch-A. signal/noise ratio (SNR)
    Rauschleistungs-A. (RLA) noise power ratio (NPR)
    Signal-Geräusch-A. (SGA) signal/noise ratio (SNR, S/N)
abstimmen align *(transmit/receive data synchronization)*; tune *(receiver)*; syntonize *(frequencies)*
Abstimmung *f* alignment; syntonization; tuning

abstützen: auf etwas a. reference to something *(values)*
absuchen scan *(sat.)*
Abtastabstand *m* sampling interval
abtasten scan, sweep *(analog)*; sample *(digital)*; trace *(mechanical)*
Abtaster *m* scanner, reader; sample and hold circuit *(ADC)*
Abtastfeld *n* raster
Abtastfrequenz *f* sampling rate
Abtast/Halteschaltung *f* sample and hold circuit
Abtastimpuls *m* sampling pulse, strobe (pulse)
Abtastraster *n* sampling pattern
Abtastsystem *n* sampled-data system
Abtasttakt *m* scanning *or* sampling cadence *(tel.)*
Abtasttheorem *n* sampling theorem, Nyquist theorem
Abtastumschaltung *f* sample and hold circuit
Abtastwert *m* (AW) sample
Abteilung *f* section *(in an organisation)*
Abwahl *f* deselection
Abwärtsstrecke *f* down-link *(sat.)*
Abwärtsumsetzer *m* downconverter *(VSAT)*
Abwärtsverbindung *f* down-link *(RT, basemobile)*
Abweichung *f* deviation, variation
Abweiseinrichtung *f* rejection device *(traffic control)*
Abwerfen *n* lock-out; shedding *(calls)*
Abwesenheitsauftrag *m* absent-subscriber job *(tel.)*
abwickeln handling *(of traffic, tel.)*
ACD (automatische Anrufverteilung *f*) automatic call distribution *(ISDX)*
Achterkreis *m* double-phantom circuit
ACK (Bestätigung *f*, Quittung *f*) acknowledgement
ADaM (Automatischer Datenmeßsender *m*) automatic data signal generator
Adapter *m* adapter
Peripherie-A. peripheral interface adapter (PIA)
Adaptionszeit *f* adjustment period *(echo canceller)*
adaptiv:
  a. Deltamodulation *f* adaptive delta modulation (ADM) *(MAC audio, CCITT Rep. 953)*; continuously variable slope delta modulation (CVSD) *(voice mail processing code, CCITT Rec. G.721)*
  a. Differenz-PCM *f* adaptive differential PCM (ADPCM)
  a. Quantisierung *f* adaptive quantisation (AQ)
  a. Teilbandcodierung *f* (ATBC) adaptive subband coding (ASC)
  a. Transformationscodierung *f* adaptive transformation coding (ATC) *(data reduction)*
  a. Transversalentzerrer *m* adaptive transversal equalizer *(sat.)*
ADC (Analog-/Digital-Umsetzer *m* (ADU)) analog/digital converter
Ader *f* wire, conductor *(cable)*
Adernvertauschung *f* reversed wires
Aderplus *n* surplus wire
ADF (Stapelbetrieb *m*) automatic document feed *(fax)*
ADM s. adaptive Deltamodulation *f*
ADMA (Vielfachzugriff *m* im Amplitudenbereich) amplitude domain multiple access
ADMD (öffentlicher MHS-Versorgungsbereich *m*) administrative management domain
ADo (Anschlußdose *f*) junction *or* connection box, wall socket
ADONIS Soviet E-mail system
ADoS8 (8-poliger Anschlußdosenstecker *m*) 8-pin connector plug *(ISDN, X interface)*
ADPCM s. adaptive Differenz-PCM *f*
adressierbarer Multiplexer *m* digital cross connect (DCC) *(multiplexer, ATM)*
ADS (Betriebs- und Datenserver *m*) administration and data server *(ISDN)*
ADU (Analog-Digitalumsetzer *m*) analog/digital converter (ADC, A/D converter)
AE (Anschlußeinheit *f*) line unit (LU)
AED (Abfrageeinrichtung *f* für Telefonanschlüsse mit Datenverkehr) polling unit for telephone connections with data service
AEK (Anschalteinheit *f* Kartentelefon) phonecard telephone access unit
AF s. alternative Frequenzen *fpl*
AFNOR (Association Francaise de Normalisation) French Standardisation Institute
AG s. Amt *n* gehend belegen
AIS s. Alarm-Indikationssignal *n*
aktiv active, on-line
aktivieren activate, enable; bring on-line
Aktivierung *f* Awake Indication (AWI) *(HW)*
Aktiv-Verkehr *m* calling subscribers
Akustikkoppler *m* acoustic coupler *(modem)*
akustisch acoustic, sonic, audible
  a. Alarm *m* audible alarm (signal)
  a. Bedienerführung *f* voice guidance

akustisch 4

(public card phone)
a. Oberflächenwellen *fpl* (AOW) surface acoustic waves (SAW) *(filter)*
a. signal sound signal
a. Telegramme *npl* voice mail
Akzentuierung *f* preemphasis
AL s. **Amtsleitung** *f*
Alarmauswertung *f* alarm evaluator
Alarmdatenschnittstelle *f* alarm data interface (ADI) *(TC)*
Alarmgabe *f* alarm signal *(TC)*
Alarm-Indikations-Signal *n* (AIS) alarm indication signal *(PCM data, ISDN D channel, TC)*
Alarmwächter *m* alarm monitor *(TC)*
allgemein:
  a. Amtsabfrage *f* (AA) unassigned (exchange line) answer
  a. Fernsprechwählnetz *n* General Switched Telephone Network (GSTN) *(CCITT Rec. V.25 bis)*
  a. Nachtschaltung *f* (universal) night service (extension) *(tel.)*
Allgemeinzulassung *f* general type approval *(FTZ)*
Aliasfrequenz *f* aliasing frequency
ALOHA *n* ALOHA *(sat., RMA method of the University of Hawaii)*
Alphageometrie *f* alphageometry *(vtx standard, CEPT profile 1)*
alternativ:
  a. Bündel *n* alternative routing, second- etc. choice routing
  a. Frequenzen *fpl* (AF) Alternative Frequencies (list) (AF) *(RDS)*
AMI (bipolare Schrittinversion *f*) alternate mark inversion *(pseudoternary PCM, redundant binary line code, ISDN D channel)*
amplitudenstabil amplitude-stabilized; constant-amplitude
Amplituden-Phasenumtastung *f* amplitude phase shift keying (APK) *(hybrid modulation, sat.)*
Amplitudenumtastung *f* amplitude shift keying (ASK)
AMPS (Funktelefon-System *n*) Advanced Mobile Phone Service *(US)*
Amt *n* exchange, office *(US)*; station, centre
  A. gehend belegen (AG) seize outgoing exchange line
  bemanntes A. attended exchange
  besetztes A. attended exchange
  betriebsführendes A. controlling exchange
  fernes A. remote station

ferngespeistes A. power-fed *or* dependent station
internationales A. international exchange
selbstgespeistes A. non-power-fed *or* independent station
Amtsabfrage *f* answer, exchange line answer
  allgemeine *or* **offene A.** unassigned (exchange line) answer
Amtsanlassung *f* exchange line access *or* seizure *(PBX)*
Amtsanruf *m* exchange line call; external *or* outside call *(PBX)*
Amtsbatterie *f* station battery, central battery
Amtsbelegung *f* exchange line seizure *(PBX)*
amtsberechtigt unrestricted *(extension)*
Amtsberechtigung *f* exchange access; trunk-barring level *(tel.)*
Amtsbündel *n* exchange line group *(PABX)*
Amtsgespräch *n* external *or* outside call
Amtsgruppe *f* exchange group
Amtskennziffer *f* exchange identification code
Amtskonferenz *f* exchange-line conference
Amtsleitung *f* (AL) exchange line, circuit; local loop; outside line *(PBX)*
Amtsrufweiterleitung *f* (ARW) exchange line transfer
Amtstakt *m* exchange clock pulse
Amtsteilnehmer *m* outside caller *(PBX)*
Amtston *m* dialling tone
Amtsübertragung *f* (AUe) exchange line interface *(PBX)*
Amtsverbindung *f* external *or* outside call
Amtsverbindungsnetzbetreiber *m* Interexchange Carrier (IEC) *(US)*
Amtsverbindungssatz *m* (AVS) exchange-line connector set
Amtsverdrahtung *f* station wiring
Amtswähler *m* code selector, office selector
An-/Abschaltung *f* **des Teilnehmers** connection/disconnection of subscriber
Analog-/Digital-Umsetzer *m* (ADU) -**Wandler** *m* analog/digital converter(ADC), A/D converter
Analog-/Digital-Zeichenumsetzer *m* (SAD) Signalling converter, Analog/Digital
Analogverfahren *n* analog *(time- and value-continuous)* method
Anbieten *n* offering *(marking of the serving trunks or paths available for setting up the call; also offering a call after breaking in on an existing call)*
Anbieterschnittstelle *f* service provider interface *(TEMEX)*
Anbindung *f* interworking *(of networks)*
andere Programme *npl* Other Networks (ON)

(service information) (RDS)
ändern n update; alter (class of service)
aneinandergereiht cascaded, chained; concatenated (SW)
Anforderung f request; call instruction (PCM speech)
Anfangsfeld n starting delimiter (FDDI)
Anfangssatz m start record (PCM data)
Anfangston m: **Ansage-A.** quote tone
Anfrage f enquiry, inquiry
Anfrageruf m inquiry call
Angebot n offered load (traffic intensity of offered traffic, tel.sys.)
angebotene Belegung f offered call
angeklopft call waiting
angeschlossen connected; on line
Angriffsrichtung f starting direction (pulse)
Anhalt m preference
anhalten inhibit (clock)
Anhaltesignal n break signal
anhängen replace the handset
Ankertechnik f anchoring technique (data network)
Ankerpunkt m anchor point, point of entry (data network)
Anklopfen n call waiting; offering (tel.); sending call waiting tone (interception indicating that a third party is requesting connection)
Anklopfmeldung f call waiting indication
Anklopfschutz m intrusion protection
Anklopfton m call waiting tone
Anklopfverbindung f call waiting connection
ankommend incoming (call)
Ankommender Ruf m INcoming Call (INC) (V.25 bis); Ring Indicator (RI) (V.24/RS232C, s. Table VI)
Ankopplung f coupling device (bus, ring)
Anlage f installation, plant, system, station
Anlagenberechtigung f installation, system barring level
anlagenunabhängige Systemdaten npl general system data (i.e. data not connected with a specific system)
anlassen start, initiate (process);
  Amtsleitung a. seize exchange line
Anlauffeld n initial section (power feeding)
Anlaufschritt m start signal, start bit (TC)
Anlaufverzögerung f start delay
anlegen apply (a voltage)

anmelden book, affiliate
  Gespräch a. book a call
  sich a. log on, sign on; go off-hook (tel.)
annullieren cancel (number)
Anordnung f arrangement, disposition, layout, configuration, assembly, structure
  Koppelanordnung switching network (tel.sys.)
Anpaßglied n matching pad (testing)
Anpaßmöglichkeit f matching option
Anpassung f adaptation, interface; matching pad (testing)
  Papier-A. paper alignment (fax.)
Anpassungseinrichtung f (ANPE) switching equipment (sat., DFS local switch); modem (transmission on analog lines); matching unit
Anpassungsprotokoll n convergence protocol
Anpassungsrechner m front-end processor (FEP)
Anpassungsschaltung f interface circuit
ANPE s. Anpassungseinrichtung f
Anregungspulse mpl excitation pulses
Anreiz m alerting signal
anreizen alert
Anreizerkennung f off-hook detection
Anreiztelegramm n initiation message (TC)
Anruf m call
  gleichzeitiger A. dual seizure
  nicht zur Verbindung führender A. lost call
  unbeantworteter A. no-reply call
Anrufablehnungsbefehl m disregard incoming call (DIC) (V.25 bis)
Anrufbeantworter m answering machine (to BS 6789, 6301, 6305)
Anrufbeantwortung f answering
Anrufbeantwortungseinrichtung f (AAE) answering equipment
Anrufblockierung f call congestion
Anrufidentifizierung f calling line identification
Anrufklinke f calling jack
Anrufliste f traffic list; log of incoming calls, call log
Anrufmelder m pager (mobile RT)
Anruforgan n calling or answering equipment
Anrufreihung f call queuing
Anrufrelais n ringing relay
Anrufschema n call (allocation) plan (PBX)
Anrufschutz m incoming-call protection
Anrufsignalisierung f call indicator (tel.)

Anrufsucher *m* line finder
　erster A. primary line switch, subscriber's line finder
　zweiter A. secondary line switch, second line finder
Anruftaste *f* call button *(telex)*
Anrufticker *m* call progress ticking *(PBX)*
Anrufton *m* ringing tone *(tel.)*
Anrufübernahmegruppe *f* call acceptance group *(team, tel.)*
Anrufumlegung *f* call forwarding
Anrufumleitung *f* call diversion, diversion service
Anrufverlegung *f* call transfer
Anrufverteiler *m* traffic distributor
Anrufverteilung *f* call distribution system, queuing system
Anrufweiterschalter *m* (GEDAN) device for (decentralized) call forwarding *(tel.)*
Anrufweiterschaltung *f* call forwarding
Anrufwiederholung *f* camp-on-busy; callback *(service feature, to camp-on to a busy subscriber)*; repertory dialling *(f. tel.)*
Ansage-Anfangston *m* quote tone *(tel.)*
Ansagedienst *m* recorded announcement service
Ansage-Endton *m* unquote tone *(tel.)*
Ansagegerät *n* recorded announcement equipment *(tel.)*
Anschalteeinheit *f* **Kartentelefon** (AEK) phonecard telephone access unit *(exch., DOV)*
　Endgeräte-A. medium attachment unit (MAU) *(transmit/receive unit)*
Anschalteeinrichtung *f* access equipment *(vtx)*
Anschaltekoppler *m* connecting matrix
Anschaltepegel *m* interconnection level
Anschalterelais *m* connecting relay *(tel.)*
Anschaltesatz *m* access circuit; connector
Anschaltezustand *m* connected/disconnected status
Anschaltfeld *n* interconnection panel
Anschaltstelle *f* interface
Anschaltung *f* connection, transfer; insertion, access
　funktionelle A. an das System affiliation *(tel.)*
　GS-Anschaltung *f* DC connection
Anschlagen *n* push-fitting *(cable)*
Anschluß *m* connection; extension *(tel.)*; feedpoint *(antenna)*; interface *(DC)*; link *(computer)*; outlet *(PS)*; port *(MUX)*; terminal *(component)*; termination *(permanent connection)*
　A. Belegt Connection Busy (CB) *(local DCE busy, V.25 bis)*
　A. für Datenkanal terminal for data channel
　gebührenfreier A. non-chargeable subscriber
Anschlußanordnung *f* pin configuration (IC)
Anschlußbedingungen *fpl* supply conditions; terminal conditions
Anschlußbelegung *f* terminal or pin assignment or connections
Anschlußberechtigung *f* class of service
Anschlußbereich *m* (Asb) exchange area, service area *(tel.)*
Anschlußbox *f* access unit *(vtx - ISDN)*
Anschlußdaten *npl* subscriber terminal data
Anschlußdienstmerkmal *n* access-related service attribute
Anschlußdose *f* (ADo) junction or connection box, wall socket
Anschlußeinheit *f* (AE) line unit (LU) *(PCM data)*; terminating unit *(tel.)*; access unit (AU) *(CCITT Rec. X.400, gateway to telematic services)*
　A. für digitale Übertragungssysteme digital interface unit
　A. für physikalische Zustellgeräte physical delivery access unit *(e.g. printer, CCITT Rec. X.400)*
Anschlußerkennung *f* line verification
Anschlußfaser *f* pigtail, fibre tail (FO)
Anschlußgruppe *f* line trunk group
Anschlußkennung *f* station answerback *(telex)*
　A. gerufene Station called line identification (CLI)
　A. rufende Station calling line identification (CLI)
Anschlußklasse *f* class of line
Anschlußlasche *f* terminal clip
Anschlußleistung *f* connected load
Anschlußleitung *f* (Asl) subscriber line, branch line, junction line *(tel.)*
　A. Belegt Connection Busy (CB) *(V.25 bis)*
Anschlußmöglichkeit *f* interconnection option
Anschlußpunkt *m* terminal *(network)*
　A. zu anderen Netzen network access point (NAP)
Anschlußrufnummer *f* call number *(tel.)*; network user address (NUA) *(ISDN)*
Anschlußschaltung *f* termination circuit

Anschlußsperre f service denial (tel.); terminal restriction data
Anschlußstation f (AS) terminal station (sat.)
Anschlußstelle f access point; terminal device (IEC)
Anschlußverteiler m terminal block
Ansichtsplan m layout drawing
ansprechen: einen TLN a. address a subscriber (direct listening, f. tel.)
Ansprechschutz m loudspeaker intrusion protection (dig. f. tel.)
Ansprechwert m operating threshold (circuit)
Ansprechzeit f response time; operate time, operating time (relay)
Anspruch m: **Priorität f in A. nehmen** invoke priority
Leistungsmerkmal n in A. nehmen access a facility
anstehen be present, applied, available; be queued (up), be waiting (messages, calls)
Ansteuerfolge f switching sequence
Ansteuerlogik f access logic
ansteuern select (addresses), access, gate, drive; trigger; control, activate (switching point)
Fernplatz a. route the B operator
Ansteuerungssatz m access circuit
anstoßen activate, trigger
Antenne f aerial (GB, radio); antenna (TV, sat.)
Antennenanschluß m (antenna) feedpoint
Antennendiagramm n radiation pattern
Antennencharakteristik f radiation pattern
Antennenöffnung f (antenna) aperture
Antennenschwerpunkt m (antenna) radiation centre
Antennenspiegel m (antenna) reflector
Antennenweiche f combiner, diplexer, multicoupler
Antext m lead-in (character) (PCM data)
Antiope (acquisition numérique et télévisualisation d'images organisées en pages d'ecriture) videotex standard in France (CEPT Profile 2, s. Table VIII)
Antragstellung f: **Zeitpunkt der A.** subscription time (service)
Antwortblock m response block (PCM)
Antwortkanal m return control channel (trunking)
Antwortton m answer tone
Antwortverzug m response time
Antwortzeit f round-trip delay (sat.) (= 2 x signal transit time);

response time (modem)
Anwahl f dial up, selection (tel., vtx)
Anwahlzeilen und -punkte select lines and poke points (VDU)
Anweisungsstelle f accounts (checking and clearing) office (ZZF)
Anwender-Anwender-Protokoll n user-to-user protocol (CCITT I.112)
anwenderfreundlich user-friendly, user-oriented
Anwenderprogramm n user program
Anwenderteil m **für Fernsprechen** telephone user part (TUP) (SS7, CCITT Rec. Q.721 - 725)
Anwenderzugriff m user (network) access (CCITT I.112)
Anwendungsbeschreibung f application note
Anwendungsebene f application layer (layer 7, OSI 7-layer reference model)
Anwendungskennung f operation mode indication (transmission signal)
Anwendungsprogrammschnittstelle f application program interface (API)
Anzeige f display, indicator, indication
Rufnummern a. (calling) number identification (ISDN)
Anzeigeleiste f display strip
anzeigepflichtig subject to notification (e.g. RF equipment, ZZF)
AOW (akustische Oberwellen fpl) surface acoustic waves (SAW) (filter)
AP (Aufputz-...) surface mounting (HW)
APC (ADPCM f mit Leitfrequenzsteuerung) ADPCM with primary frequency control
APC-MLQ (adaptive prädiktive Codierung f mit Maximum-Likelihood-Quantisierung) adaptive predictive coding with maximum-likelihood quantization (speech codec)
APD (Lawinen-Fotodiode f) avalanche photo diode (FO)
Aperturunsicherheit f jitter (ADC)
APK (Amplituden-Phasenumtastung f) amplitude phase shift keying (hybrid modulation, sat.)
A-Platz m A position, A operator
Apothekermodem m series D20P-A DBP modem (appr. 15000 sold to German pharmacies (1987 status))
Apothekerschaltung f switching from door intercom to telephone mode (f.-tel.)
Apparateverzerrung f characteristic distortion, inherent distortion
Apparatewiderstand m handset resistance (tel.)
APT (automatische Bildübertragung f) automatic picture transmission (radio-

facsimile)
AQ (adaptive Quantisierung *f*) adaptive quantisation
äquivalente isotrop abgestrahlte Sendeleistung *f* equivalent isotropically radiated power (EIRP) *(sat., in dBW)*
arbeitsfähig operable, functional
Arbeitsfeldsteuerwerk *n* (AST) section control unit *(ESS)*
Arbeitsfrequenz *f* operating frequency
Arbeitsgruppe *f* Study Group (SG) *(CCITT)*
Arbeitslage *f* operating state *(of a trigger circuit)*
Arbeitsschritt *m* (AS) step
Arbeitsspeicher *m* main memory
Arbeitstakt *m* clock pulse; operating cycle
arbeitsunfähig inoperable
Architekturmodell *n* architectural model *(OSI RM)*
ARHC appels reduits a l'heure chargée *(unit of traffic intensity, 1/30 Erl resp. VE)*
ARI (Autofahrer-Rundfunk-Informationssystem *n*) broadcast information service for drivers *(in Germany)*
ARM (Spontanbetrieb *m*) asynchronous responce mode
ARQ (automatische Wiederholung *f*) automatic repeat request *(PCM data)*
ARR (automatische Wiederholung *f*) automatic retransmission request *(PCM data)*
ARTHUR (Verkehrs-Notfunksystem *n* für mobilen Einsatz) Automatic Radiocommunication for Traffic emergency situations on Highways and Urban Roads *(vehicle-vehicle system including digital cellular network and satellite)*
ARW (Amtsrufweiterleitung *f*) exchange line transfer
AS (Anschlußeinheit *f*) terminal station *(sat.)*
AS s. Arbeitsschritt *m*
AS (Aufschalten *n*) trunk offering
AS (Aufschalteschutz *m*) intrusion protection
ASCII (amerikanischer Standardcode *m* für Datenaustausch) American Standard Code for Information Interchange
ASIC (anwendungsspezifische IC) application-specific IC
ASK (Amplitudenumtastung *f*) amplitude shift keying
Asl (Anschlußleitung *f*) subscriber line *(FTZ)*, main line
Assoziativspeicher *m* content-addressable memory (CAM)
AST s. Arbeitsfeldsteuerwerk *n*

asynchron asynchrononous, out of phase
 a. Übertagungsmodus *m* asynchronous transfer mode (ATM) *(FO, PCM data, CCITT Rec. I.121, 'asynchronous' relating to the information, not the bit synchronisation)*
 a. Zeitvielfachtechnik *f* asynchronous time division multiplex (ATD,ATM) *(ATM)*
ATBC (adaptive Teilbandcodierung *f*) adaptive subband coding
ATC (adaptive Transformationscodierung *f*) adaptive transformation coding
ATD s. asynchrone Zeitvielfachtechnik *f*
A-Teilnehmer *m* calling subscriber, A party
ATM s. asynchroner Übertragungsmodus *m*
ATM s. asynchrone Zeitvielfachtechnik *f*
AU (Anschlußeinheit *f*) access unit
Audiotex (Sprachspeicher- und ausgabedienst *m*) Audiotex voice mail service
AUe-g/-k (Amtsübertragung *f* gehend/kommend) exchange line interface outgoing/incoming
Aufbau *m* arrangement, configuration *(system)*; mechanical design; structure *(field, frame)*
 establishing communication *(bearer service)*; setting up *(call)*
aufbereiten condition *(signal, measurement)*; edit *(data)*
Aufbereitung *f* regeneration *(pulses)*; encoding *(AMI)*
 Bild-A. display generation *(monitor)*
 Speisespannungs-A. supply voltage conversion *(system)*
Aufbereitungseinrichtung *f* (ABE) processing equipment *(ISDN vtx)*
aufbewahren hold, retain
Aufenthaltsbereich *m* location area *(GSM)*
Aufenthaltsnetz *n* visited network *(mobile RT)*
Aufenthaltsregistrierung *f*:
 Aktualisierung der A. location update *(GSM)*
auffächern fan out *(signal demux)*
auffangen latch *(signal)*
Auffangen *n* **des Anrufers bei böswilligem Anruf** malicious call tracing
Auffang-Flipflop *m* latch *(signal)*
Aufforderung *f* invitation, request
Aufforderungsbetrieb *m* normal response mode (NRM) *(HDLC)*
Aufgabe *f* function, job, task
Aufgabenstellung *f* objectives; terms of reference
aufgelaufene Gebühren *fpl* accrued charges
aufgeschaltet external call connected
aufhängen on-hook; replace, hang up

(handset)
aufheben cancel; disconnect *(subscriber equipment)*
auflegen (go) on-hook; replace, hang up *(handset)*
auflösen resolve, demultiplex *(signals)*
  Kollisionen a. resolve collisions
  Rahmen a. separate the channels in the frame
  Zellen a. disassemble cells *(ATM)*
Auflösung f resolution
  Modul n der A. index of cooperation (IOC) *(fax)*
Auflösungsvermögen n resolution, resolving capability, definition *(TV)*
Aufmerksamkeitston m attention tone *(PABX)*
Aufnahme f: **Verbindungs-A.** building up a connection
aufnehmen: Verbindung a. set up a connection
  Verbindungswünsche a. receive requests for connection
aufprüfen test *(a wire for e.g. seizure)*
Aufputz-... (AP) surface mounting *(socket)*
Aufreih-Klemmenleiste f channel-mounted terminal block
Aufrufbetrieb m polling/selecting mode
aufrufen invoke *(code)*
Aufrufverfahren n polling
Aufschalteanforderung f intrusion request, break-in request
Aufschalteeinrichtung f intrusion device, conferencing device
aufschalten offer, connect *(ext. call)*, intrude *(PBX)*; feed forward; enter, cut in *(stand-by generator)*; connect (to); add-on *(device)*
Aufschalten n offering, trunk offering, intrusion, breaking-in *(on a busy connection, e.g. for offering a call)*, entering, busy override; monitoring
Aufschalteschutz m monitoring protection, intrusion protection *(tel.)*
Aufschalteton m intrusion tone; call waiting tone, (trunk-)offering tone
Aufschalteverbindung f intrusion-type connection, call waiting connection
Aufschaltezeichen n offering signal
Aufschaltezeit f switching time, setting-up time
Aufsetzpunkt m checkpoint
Aufsynchronisieren n acquiring lock; synchronizing to *(e.g. access status)*; lock to, lock on to *(signal, clock)*
Aufteilungskabel n exchange cabling
Auftragdienst m absent-subscriber service

(tel.)
Auftraggeber m (AG) principal; contracting authority
Auftragnehmer m (AN) supplier; contractor
Auftrennweiche f separating filter
Aufwärtsstrecke f up-link *(sat.)*
Aufwärtsumsetzer m up-converter *(VSAT)*
Aufwärtsverbindung f up-link *(RT, mobile-base)*
aufweisen: einen Verlauf aufweisen follow a curve
Augendiagramm n eye pattern *(PCM phase, on oscilloscope)*
Augenwahrscheinlichkeitsdichte f eye pattern probability density *(PCM transmission)*
Ausbau m upgrading, extension; configuration
Ausbaumöglichkeiten fpl upgrading options
Ausbaustufe f stage of completion *(HW)*; update level *(SW)*
  End-A. final capacity stage
  Erst-A. initial capacity stage
ausblenden extract *(signal)*; strobe; mask out, eliminate *(jitter)*; gate out *(digital circuit)*; blank out *(analog circuit)*; skip *(program records)*
Ausblendimpuls m gate or strobe (pulse)
Ausbreitungslaufzeit f propagation delay *(of packets)*
Ausfallabstand m: **mittlerer A.** mean time between failures (MTBF)
ausfallbeständig fault-tolerant
ausfallsicher failure-proof, fail-safe
Ausfallzeit f downtime
  mittlere A. mean time to failure (MTTF)
ausfügen delete *(characters)*
Ausführung f model, version, design
ausgabebereit ready to send
Ausgang m output, port
Ausgangsadresse f original address
Ausgangsdaten base-line data, raw data
Ausgangsdrehwähler m rotary out-trunk or outgoing selector
Ausgangsgröße f initial value or parameter
Ausgangspunkt m starting point, point of origin, basic point
Ausgangsschwingung f output frequency *(as a signal)*, emission signal *(FO)*
Ausgangssignal n output (signal)
Ausgangswert m default value
ausgefüllter Kreis m solid circle *(display)*
ausgelastet: voll a. used to full capacity
ausgewähltes Bitmuster n (Signalisierungsgelegenheitsmuster n) signalling opportunity pattern (SOP)

Ausgleichsknick

Ausgleichsknick *m* **nach innen** surplus length bent inwards *(wire link)*
aushängen off-hook
Aushängeprogramm *n* off-hook program
Auskoppeldämpfung *f* coupling attenuation *(direct coupler, sat.)*
Auskoppelfeld *n* outgoing *or* absorbing switching network
Auskunft *f* inquiry *(tel.)*
Auskunftsdienst *m* directory inquiry service
Auslandsamt *n* international exchange
Auslandsverbindung *f* international call
Auslastung *f* load, utilization (rate of capacity)
    Kanal-A. channel usage (factor)
Auslastungsfaktor *m* duty factor *(in %) (PCM speech)*
Auslaufteil *n* discontinued item
Auslenkung *f* deflection *(pointer)*, excursion; deviation
Ausleseadressierung *f* read addressing
Ausleuchtzone *f* coverage, footprint *(sat.)*
    Rand *m* **der A.** edge of coverage (EOC)
Auslösebestätigung *f* Release Complete *(SS7 SCCP)*
auslosen choose at random
auslösen trigger, release, actuate, initiate; trip *(relay)*
    Verbindung a. clear (down)
Auslösezeichen *n* clear-forward signal *(after A party goes on-hook)*; clear-back signal *(after B party goes on-hook)*
Auslösezeitüberwachung *f* disconnect time-out
Auslösung *f* clearing, cleardown *(of the call)*; disconnection; release *(for transfer)*
Ausnahmeanschluß *m* remote *(ISDN)* access *(at non-ISDN exchange)*; foreign exchange line *(tel.)*
Ausrastbereich *m* pull-out range *(signal lock)*
ausrasten drop lock
ausregeln compensate, correct
Aussagefähigkeit *f* information content
ausschalten open *(switch)*, trip *(breaker)*; break *(current)*; disconnect *(module)*; interrupt *(line)*; turn off *(component)*
Ausschalteton *m* disabling tone
Ausschreibung *f* request for quote (RFQ); invitation of tender
außen: nach a. weitergeben externalize *(a signal etc.)*

Außenstation *f* terminal *(TC)*
Außerband-Signalisierung *f* out-band signalling
außer Betrieb out of service
Außerbetriebnahme *f* decommissioning; transition to idle state *(D channel)*
Aussetzbetrieb *m* intermittent operation
aussparen notch out, mask out *(bits)*
Ausstattung *f* equipment (level)
Aussteuerbereich *m* dynamic range
Aussteuergrenze *f* peak code *(PCM)*
Ausstrahlungsradius *m* radius of propagation *(sat.)*
austasten gate off, blank
Austastsignal *n* extraction signal *(pulses)*
Austauschen *n* interchanging *(files)*; replenishment *(image coding)*
Austritt *m* withdrawal *(from conference, tel.)*
Auswahl *f* selection; dialling out
    Netz-A. dial-out
Auswahllogik *f* selector logic
Auswandern *n* drift *(out of range, sat.)*
auswerten evaluate, interpret, analyse *(GB)*, analyse *(US)*, recognize, decode
autark:
    a. Dienstmerkmal *n* network-independent service attribute
    a. System *n* autonomous system
AUTEX (automatische Telex-Teletex-Auskunft *f*) automatic telex/teletex directory service *(DBP)*
automatisch:
    a. Antwort *f* auto answer
    a. Datenmeßsender *m* (ADaM) automatic data signal generator
    a. Herunterschalten *n* automatic fallback *(modem)*
    a. Meßablauf *m* automatic measurement program *(test set)*
    a. Pegelregelung *f* automatic level control (ALC) *(sat. TWTA)*
    a. Rechnungserstellung *f* automatic billing
    a. Rückruf *m* (RRUF) automatic call-back
    a. Rufnummernanzeige *f* automatic number identification (ANI) *(ISDN)*
    a. Schrittgeschwindigkeitserkennung *f* automatic Baud (rate) recognition (ABR)
    a. Stapelbetrieb *m* automatic document feed (ADF) *(fax)*
    a. Teilnehmer *m* test call generator
    a. Verbindungsaufbau *m* autodialling
    a. Verbindungswiederherstellung *f* automatic call restoration
    a. Wähleinrichtung *f* für Datenübertra-

gung (AWD) automatic dialling facility for data transmission *(V.24/RS232C)*
a. Wahlmöglichkeit *f* automatic calling facility
a. Wähl- und Ansagegerät *n* (AWAG) automatic dialling and recorded announcement equipment
a. Wiederholung *f* automatic repeat request (ARQ), automatic retransmission request (ARR)
Automatisierungsstufe *f* automation level
Autotelefon *n* in-car telephone *(mobile RT)*
A-Vermittlungsstelle *f* (A-VSt.) originating exchange
AVS (Amtsvermittlungssatz *m*) exchange-line connector set *(tel.)*
A-VSt s. A-Vermittlungsstelle *f*
AW (Abtastwert *m*) sample
AWAG s. automatisches Wähl- und Ansagegerät *n*
AWD s. automatische Wähleinrichtung *f* für Datenübertragung
AWGN-Kanal *m* AWGN channel, channel with additive white Gaussian noise
A-wertig priority A, with priority A *(AIS, fault signal)*
AXE (automatische digitale Vermittlungseinrichtung *f*) Automatic digital Exchange Equipment *(Ericsson, S)*

B

BA s. Basisanschluß *m*
BA (Betriebsart *f*) operating mode
BABT (Britische Zulassungsbehörde *f* für Fernmeldetechnik) British Approvals Board for Telecommunications
Babyruf *m* babyphone feature *(f. tel.)*
BA-Konzentrator *m* (BAKT) basic access concentrator, basic acces multiplexer (BAMX) *(ISDN)*
BAKT s. BA-Konzentrator *m*
BAMX s. Basisanschlußmultiplexer *m*
Bandabstand *m* band gap, energy gap *(FO)*
BAP s. Basisanschlußpunkt *m*
BAPT (Bundesamt Post und Telekommunikation) Federal (German) Post and Telecommunications Office *(from 1990)*
Bargeldautomat *m* automatic cash dispenser; automatic teller machine (ATM) *(US)*
BAS-Signal *n* (Bild-, Austast- u. Synchronsignal) composite video signal *(TV, Mon.)*
BASA (Bundesbahn-Selbstanschlußsystem *n*) subscriber-dialling telephone network of the Federal Railways *(Austrian)*
Basisanschluß *m* (BA) basic access *(ISDN S_0, CCITT Rec. I.420, 192 kbit/s, B_{64}+ B_{64}+D_{16} channels)*; base terminal
Basisanschlußkanal *m* basic access (channel) *(ISDN)*
Basisanschlußmultiplexer *m* (BAMX) basic access multiplexer *(ISDN)*
Basisanschlußpunkt *m* (BAP) basic access point *(ISDN)*
Basisbandeinheit *f* baseband unit (BBU)
Basiskanal *m* basic access channel *(ISDN)*
Basisprozessor *m* base processor *(exch.)*
Basisstation *f* base station *(CT2)*
Basisstationssystem *n* base station system (BSS) *(GSM)*
Basisstationswechsel *m* handover *(cellular RT)*
Batton-Paß-Bus *m* batton-passing bus
BAV (Breitbandanschlußvermittlung *f*) broadband access switch *(VBN, FO)*
Baueinheit *f* structural unit; constructional unit
Bauelement *n* (BE) component
Bauform *f* model, type, style
  niedrige B. low profile
  schmale B. slim design
Baugröße *f* frame size
Baugruppe *f* circuit board; component block *(inside an IC)*; module; subassembly *(inside a module)*
Baugruppenrahmen *m* module frame
Baugruppenträger *m* subrack
Baugruppenziehwerkzeug *n* module extractor
Bauleistung *f* design rating
Bauschaltplan *m* wiring diagram
Baustein *m* chip *(IC)*
  Koppel-B. switching module
Baustufenverordnung *f* regulation relating to the stages of construction *(DBP)*
Bauteil *n* component
BB (Betriebsbereitschaft *f*) hot standby
BB (Breitband *n*) wideband, broadband
BBV (Breitbandvermittlungsstelle *f*) broadband switching centre *(VBN, FO)*
BCD (binär codierte Dezimalzahl *f*) binary coded decimal
BCH Bose-Chandhuri-Hoequenghem *(code)*
Bd Baud, baud
BDE (Betriebsdatenerfassung *f*) operating data acquisition *or* entry *(unit)*
BDG s. Bediengerät *n*
BDSG (Bundesdatenschutzgesetz *n*) Federal (German) Data Protection Act
BDV (Breitbanddurchgangsvermittlung *f*) broadband transit switch *(VBN, FO)*
BE s. Bauelement *n*
Beanspruchung *f*: **punktuelle B.** localized stress
Beantwortungszeit *f* response time
beaufschlagen subject, load, force, charge, apply; act upon
  Zeitkanal mit einem Signal b. inject a signal into a time slot
BECR (Bitfehlerkorrekturrate *f*) bit error correction rate
bedarfsgesteuerte Kanalzuteilung *f* oder **Kanalzuweisung** *f* demand assignment (DA) *(VSAT)*
Bedarfsträger *m* user (organisation) *(service radio)*; interested party
Bedarfswartung *f* corrective maintenance
bedienen control, operate *(HW)*; process, handle *(signal)*

Bediener *m* server *(network gateway function, sat.)*
Bedienerführung *f* menu prompt(ing), operator prompt
  akustische B. voice guidance *(public cardphone)*
Bedieneroberfläche *f* operator interface; terminal operating elements
Bedienfeld *n* operating panel; unit front; keypad *(tel.)*
Bediengerät *n* (BDG) control unit
Bedienhörer *m* handset *(RT)*
Bedienpersonal *n* operating personnel
Bedienplatz *m* workstation *(comp.)*; operator's station *(tel.)*
Bedienstation *f* service station, server *(network gateway function, sat.)*
  B. mit unendlich vielen Bedienern infinite server *(network gateway function, sat.)*
bedient attended *(terminal)*, manned
Bedientableau *n* keyboard tablet
Bedienung *f* operation
Bedienungs- und Wartungsfeld *n* operating and maintenance panel
Bedienungsfeld *n* control panel
Bedienungshandbuch *n* operator manual
Bedienungsgang *m* operating aisle *(rack)*
bedienungslos unattended, automatic
  b. Wählunteranlage *f* (WU-Anl.) PABX, dependent PABX
Bedienungsrechner *m* (BR) service computer; operating system *(tel.)*
Bedienungsteil *n* control section
Bedienungsvorschrift *f* operating instructions
Bedienzeit *f* serving delay *(network gateway function)*
bedingtes Austauschen *n* conditional replenishment *(image coding)*
  b. Genauigkeit *f* reduced accuracy
beeinflußbare Bündelsuche *f* alterable trunk group search
beeinflussend:
  b. Feld *n* interfering field
  b. Kenngröße *f* influencing characteristic
Beeinflussung *f* interference, induction *(as in electromagnetic interference)*
Befehl *m* command, instruction; request *(a primitive from a higher to a lower layer)*
Befestigungsteile *npl* mounting hardware
befristeter Zählvergleich *m* temporary meter comparison
Beginnabgleich *m* handshaking

beginnen start, turn on
  Betrieb b. set the mode
  Ruf b. originate a call
Beginn-Flagge *f* opening flag *(SS7)*
Beginnzeichen *n* answer signal *(from called station)*
Beginnzustand *m* off-hook state, answer state *(tel.)*
Begleitton *m* sound component *(TV)*
Begrenzungszeichen *n* flag *(ISDN)*
behaftet:
  fehlerb. faulty, defective *(HW)*
  kontaktb. with contacts
  kurzschlußb. affected by a short (circuit)
  lückenb. gapped *(PCM clock)*
  verlustb. lossy
beheimateter Funkteilnehmer *m* registered mobile subscriber
Behinderung *f* blocking; congestion *(route)*
Beidraht *m* additional wire
beidseitig at both ends *(cable)*
Beistellgerät *n* adapter *(domestic TV decoder)*; add-on or TV-top unit *(dom. sat. receiver)*
BEL (Batterie- und Erdschleife *f*) battery and earth loop *(tel.)*
Bel s. Belegung *f*
Belag *m* quantity per unit length
  Stromb. electric loading
Belastbarkeit *f* maximum load *(transmission link)*
belasteter Kondensator *m* RC smoothing circuit
belästigter Teilnehmer *m* molested subscriber
Belastung *f* load of traffic carried *(traffic intensity of traffic handled)*
Belastungsmessung *f* load measurement
belegen allocate *(pins)*; assign, program *(keys)*; load *(memory area)*; seize *(line)*
belegt seized, held, busy; occupied *(line)*
  b. Abnehmer *m* busy server *(tel.sys.)*
  homogen b. Apertur *f* uniformly illuminated aperture *(sat.)*
  vierfach b. has four function allocations, four-function-... *(keyboard)*
Belegtzustand *m* busy/idle status *(tel. system)*
Belegung *f* (Bel) loop closure on a/b wires *(tel.)*; activity, seizure *(line, channel)*; arrangement *(panel)*; distribution; assignment, allocation, connections

(pins, contacts); illumination *(antenna)*
call *(using the server)*;
contents *(data field)*;
state of occupancy, loading *(bus)*;
usage,loading *(channel)*;
B. nach Bedarf demand assignment multiple access (DAMA) *(VSAT)*
angebotene B. offered call *(tel.sys.)*
einfallende B. call arriving *(tel.)*
gleichzeitige B. dual seizure*(tel.)*
verarbeitete B. carried call *(tel.sys.)*
wartende B. waiting *or* delayed call
Belegungsabbild *n* busy/idle status image
Belegungsangebot *n* number of incoming calls
Belegungsannahmeintervall *n* call acceptance interval
belegungsbereit idle (signal) *(tel.)*
Belegungsdauer *f* call duration; holding time *(uninterrupted busy time of server, tel.sys.)*
Belegungsdichte *f* call density *(number of calls per km² which can be simultaneously set up, CT2)*
Belegungsfaktor *m* usage factor
Belegungsintensität *f* call intensity *(tel.sys.)*
Belegungskennzeichen *n* holding signal *(tel.)*
Belegungsliste *f* equipment list *(rack)*
Belegungsplan *m* (Blp) routing assignment
Belegungsrate *f* usage rate, call rate
Belegungsspeicher *m* call-count store
Belegungsspektrum *n* call mix *(tel. sys.)*
Belegungs-Steuerblock *m* token *(supervisory frame controlling access to a token ring network)*
belegungsunabhängig load-invariant
Belegungsverkehr *m* equipment usage
Belegungsversuch *m* call attempt
  B. in der HVStd busy hour call attempt (BHCA)
Belegungszahl *f* number of seizures
Belegungszeit *f* holding time *(telecontrol)*
Belegungszustand *m* (**frei** *oder* **belegt**) busy/idle status *(system)*
Beleuchtungsstärke *f* illumination (level), illuminance *(FO, in lx or ft.c)*
Bemessungsunterlagen *fpl* design charts *(tel.sys.)*
Bemessungsvorschrift *f* dimensioning specification
Benachrichtigungsdienst *m* message service
Benutzer *m* user; user agent (UA) *(MHS SW, CCITT Rec. X.400)*

Benutzerführung *f* user prompting, user prompts, user instructions
benutzergesteuerte Präsentation *f* user-individual presentation control
Benutzerklasse *f* user class of service
Benutzermittel *n* (Box in TELEBOX) user agent (UA) *(MHS SW, CCITT Rec. X.400)*
Benutzeroberfläche *f* user interface; terminal operating elements
Benutzerschnittstelle *f* man-machine interface
benutzungsrechtliche Vorraussetzungen *fpl* compliance with conditions of use *(ZZF)*
Beobachtung *f* monitoring
Beobachtungsplatz *m* observational switchboard
BER (Bitfehlerhäufigkeit, -rate *f*) bit error rate
berechtigt unrestricted *(subscriber)*
nichtamtsb. exchange barred, fully restricted
Berechtigung *f* authorisation *(of users)*; class of service; authentication
  Nicht-Amts-B. trunk barring level
  Nicht-Anlagen-B. installation barring level
Berechtigungen *fpl* class-of-service data
Berechtigungscode *m* access code *(vtx)*
Berechtigungskarte *f* phonecard *(BT, tel.)*
Berechtigungsklasse *f* class of service, class of access level *(tel.)*
Berechtigungsmittel *n* means of authentication
Berechtigungsprüfung *f* class-of-service check
Berechtigungsstufe *f* barring level
Berechtigungsumschaltung *f* access level selection
Berechtigungsweitergabe *f* token passing *(LAN)*
Bereichsendwert *m* full scale range (FSR) *(% FSR; ADC)*
Bereichskennung *f* (BK) Area Identification signal *(RDS)*
bereichsprädiktive Code-Modulation *f* band predictive code modulation (BPCM) *(signal analyzer)*;
range predictive code modulation *(range of predicted values, image encoding)*
bereichsübergreifend cross-office *(US)*
Bereichsüber-/ unterschreitung *f* violation of range limits
Bereichsumschaltung *f* (BU) range switching
Bereichsverstärker *m* band amplifier
Bereichswechsel *m* roaming *(cellular RT)*

Bereitschaftskriterium 16

Bereitschaftskriterium *n* ready criterion *(ESS)*
Bereitschaftssystem *n* standby system, fallback system
bereitstellen designate *(code)*
Berichtszeitraum *m* period under review
Berkom (Berliner Kommunikationssystem *n*) Berlin communications system *(FO, B-ISDN test network, 140 MHz)*
berührungssensitiv touch sensitive
  b. Anzeige *f* touch display
  b. Eingabeeinrichtung *f* touch input device (TID)
Beschallungsanlage *f* audio system; PA system, public address system
beschalten wire
Beschaltung *f* load; wiring, cabling
Beschaltungseinheit *f* line unit (LU)
Beschaltungsliste *f* wiring list
Beschaltungswiderstand *m* circuit resistor
Beschaltwerkzeug *n* wiring tool
Bescheidansage *f* intercept announcement
Bescheiddienst *m* intercept service; changed-number interception
Bescheidverkehr *m* intercept service
Bescheidzeichen *n* information tone
Beschriftung *f* lettering
Besetztanzeige *f* busy signal
Besetztlampe *f* engaged lamp
Besetztprüfung *f* busy testing
Besetztton *m* engaged tone (ET) *(V.25 bis)*
Besetztzeichen *n* (BZT) busy signal *(tel.)*
Besetztzustand *m* busy state
  Wege-B. congestion
bespult loaded *(line, trunk)*
Bestandsfähigkeit *f* validity
Bestätigung *f* acknowledgement (ACK)
bestehende Verbindung *f* call in progress
bestimmungsgemäßer Betrieb *m* normal use
Bestimmungs-Netzknoten *m* destination node (DN) *(data network)*
Bestrahlungsstärke *f* irradiance *(FO, in W/cm^2)*
bestromen apply current
Bestückung *f* complement *or* options *(equipment)*; layout, component layout
  Mischb. mixed configuration *(rack)*
Bestückungsplan *m* component layout
Bestückungsseite *f* component side *(PCB)*
Bestückungsvariante *f* version
Besucherdatei *f* visitor location register (VLR) *(GSM)*
Betreff *m* subject
Betriebsanzeige *f* pilot lamp
Betriebsart *f* (BA) mode, operating mode

Betriebsbereitschaft *f* ready status Data Set Ready (DSR) *(V.24/RS232C, s. Table VI)*
in B stehen on hot standby
Betriebsdämpfung *f* composite loss *(PCM)*; transmission loss
Betriebsdatei *f* service file
Betriebsdaten *npl* operational *or* operating data; ratings
Betriebsdatenerfassung *f* (BDE) operating data acquisition *or* entry *(unit)*
Betriebsdauer *f* operating time, uptime
Betriebsdienst *m* Operation and Maintenance (O&M service); traffic section *(tel.)*
Betriebsdienstplatz *m* technical service position
Betriebserde *f* system earth; Signal Ground (GND) *(V.24/RS232C, s. Table VI)*
Betriebserfahrungen *fpl* practical results, (operating *or* field) experience
Betriebsfrequenz *f* power system frequency; operating *or* working frequency
betriebsführende Leitung *f* controlling line
Betriebsführungs- und überwachungszentrale *f* (BÜZ)- operating and monitoring centre
Betriebsfunk *m* service radio *(PMR)*
Betriebsgesellschaft *f* recognized private operating agency (RPOA)
Betriebsgrenze *f* overload level *(data sheet)*
Betriebsgüte *f* grade of service
Betriebshandbuch *n* operating manual
Betriebskanal *m* (BK) operating channel *(radio link)*; service channel (SC) *(CF)*
Betriebskanalnetz *n* (BK-Netz) service channel network
Betriebslebensdauer *f* useful life, operating life
Betriebsmessung *f* in-service test
Betriebsmittel *npl* resources; facility, equipment
Betriebsmittelengpaß *m* congestion
Betriebspegel *m* service level *(data transmission)*
Betriebsprotokoll *n* event log
Betriebsspannung *f* working voltage (WV)
Betriebssteuereinrichtung *f* (BSE) station control equipment *(sat.)*
Betriebsstörung *f* accident, breakdown
Betriebstechnik *f* operating hardware *(PBX)*

betriebstechnische Aufgabe f operational task
Betriebsüberwachung f in-service monitoring (ISM)
Betriebs- und Datenserver m administration and data server (ADS) *(ISDN)*
Betriebsversuch m test in the field, field test
Betriebszeit f operating time, uptime
Betriebszustand m operating condition; regime *(system)*; power-up mode *(HW)*
Beugung f diffraction *(FO)*
Bevorrechtigung f priority
bewählte Amtsleitung f selected exchange line *(exchange line dialled onto)*
beweglich mobile
  b. Leitung f temporary line
  b. Flugfunkdienst m aeronautical mobile service
  b. Landfunkdienst m land mobile service
  b. Seefunkdienst m maritime mobile service
Bewegtbild n full-motion picture *(WB video)*, moving picture
  B.-Dienst m videophone teleservice *(CCITT)*
  B.-Übermittlung f videophone transmission *(ISDN, 64 kb/s)*
Bewertungsfaktor m weighting factor
bezeichnen designate; identify
Bezeichner m identifier *(DP)*
Beziehung f relation *(e.g. signalling relation in the network)*
Bezirksnetz n short-haul network *(tel.)*
Bezugsdämpfung f reference equivalent *(PCM)*
Bezugs-Funkkonzentrator m leading base station *(mobile RT)*
Bezugspunkt m reference point *(CCITT Rec. I.112)*
Bezugspunktkonfiguration f reference configuration *(CCITT Rec. I.112)*
Bezugsverbindung f hypothetical reference connection (HRC)
BFH s. Bitfehlerhäufigkeit f
BHCA (Belegungsversuch m in der HVStd) busy hour call attempt
BIGFON (breitbandiges integriertes Glasfaser-Fernmelde-Ortsnetz n) local wideband integrated glass-fibre telephone network *(DBP)*
Bildaufbereitung f display generation *(monitor)*
Bildcodierung f picture-signal encoding
Bildelement n picture element, pixel *(TV)*
  B.-Wiederholfrequenz f refresh rate *(monitor)*
Bilderkennung f connectivity analysis *(video encoding)*
Bildfernsprecher m videotelephone, videophone
Bildfunk m facsimile radio
Bildinhalt m screen content *(monitor)*
Bildner m: **Summen-B.** sum-forming circuit, sum former
Bildnutzbandbreite f useful video bandwidth *(TV)*
Bildplatte f video disk, laser video disk
Bildpunkt m picture element, pixel *(TV)*
Bildschirmtext m (BTX, Btx) videotex, two-way videotext, viewdata *(CEPT Profile 1, s. Table VIII)*
  B.-Leitzentrale f (Btx-LZ) videotex service centre
  B.-Telex-Dienst m videotex-telex service *(DBP service providing telex access to videotex users)*
  B.-Telex-Umsetzer m (BTU) videotex-telex converter
  B.-Vermittlungsstelle f (Btx-VSt) videotex switching centre
  B.-Zentrale f (BTZ) videotex computer centre
Bildspeicher m frame store *(vtx)*
Bildspeicherdienst m picture mail
Bildtelefon n videophone *(ISDN 64 kbit/s)*; image phone, picture-phone
Bildtelegramm n facsimile message, fax
Bildübertragungsnetz n facsimile network
Bildungsgesetz n coding law *(line code)*
Bild(wechsel)frequenz f frame rate, vertical frequency *(TV)*; refresh rate *(monitor)*
binär binary
  b. codiert binary coded, converted to binary code
  b. codierte Dezimalzahl f binary coded decimal (BCD)
  b. Phasenumtastung f binary phase shift keying (BPSK)
  b.-synchrone Übertragungssteuerung f binary synchronous communication, 'bisync' (BSC)
Binärcode m binary code
BIP-8 bit-interleaved parity 8 *(code, STM-1)*
Bipolaritätserkennungsschaltung f bipolar detection circuit
Bipolartastung f bipolar operation
BIS (Breitbandinformationssystem n) broadband information system *(DBP, FO)*
Bis, bis *(Appended to a CCITT network*

standard, it identifies its second version, e.g. V.25 bis)
B-ISDN (Breitband-ISDN *n*) broadband ISDN (FO, 140 - 565 Mbit/s)
Bitbündel *n* burst
Bitdauer *f* bit period
BITE (eingebaute Prüfeinrichtung *f*) built-in test equipment
Bitel (Bildtelefon *n*) multifunctional vtx terminal *(Siemens, no modem)*
Bitfehlerhäufigkeit *f* (BFH) bit-error rate (BER) *(PCM data)*
Bitfehlerkorrekturrate *f* bit-error correction rate (BECR)
Bitfehlerrate *f* (BFH) bit-error rate (BER) *(PCM data)*
Bitgleichlauf *m* bit synchronism
Bitmitte *f* midpoint of bit
Bittakt *m* bit clock, bit timing
Bittiefe *f* resolution in bits, bit scaling, word length *(video encoding, e.g. 8 bits/pixel)*
Bitübertragungsdienst *m* physical (transmission) service *(ISO)*
Bit-Übertragungsschicht *f* physical layer *(CCITT I.430, layer 1, OSI 7-layer reference model)*
Bit-Unversehrtheit *f* bit integrity
Bitversatz *m* skew
Bit-Vielfachfehler *m* multiple bit error
Bitvollgruppe *f* envelope *(octet + status and framing bit)*
BK (Bereichskennung *f*) Area Identification signal *(RDS)*
BK (Betriebskanal *m*) service channel
BK (Bürokommunikation *f*) office communication
B-Kanal *m* B channel *(ISDN, 64 kbit/s)*
B-Kanal Schicht 1 (B1) layer 1 B channel protocol *(ISDN)*
BK-Anlage s. Breitband-Kabelanlage *f*
BKN (Breitband-Koppelnetz *n*) broadband switching network
BK-Netz (Betriebskanal-Netz *n*) service channel network;
BK-Netz (Breitband-Kommunikationsnetz *n*) broadband communications network
BKS (Bundesverband Kabel und Satellit) Federal Cable and Satellite Association
Blendenerde *f* module handle earth
BIFH s. Blockfehlerhäufigkeit *f*
Blindstecker *m* dummy plug
Blindverkehr *m* waste traffic
Block *m* block *(tel)*; set *(PCM frame)*; cell *(ATM time slot, incl. header and user signal)*

Informations-B. *m* information frame *(ISDN)*
Steuer-B. supervisory frame *(transmission control)*
Blockaufzeichnung *f* matrix scan recording *(VTR)*
Blockfehlerhäufigkeit *f* (BlFH) block error rate (BLER) *(CD)*
Blockfehlerrate *f* block error rate (BLER) *(PCM)*
blockiert blocked; disabled *(keyboard)*
Blockierung *f* blocking; congestion *(channel)*; interlocking; disabling *(keyboard)*
Anrufb. call congestion
blockierungsfrei nonblocking *(matrix)*
Blockierungswahrscheinlichkeit *f* blocking probability *(trunks)*
Blockkennung *f* block code
Blockkopf *m* header *(TDM, ATM)*
Blockprüfung *f* longitudinal redundancy check (LRC)
Blockprüfzeichenfolge *f* frame checking sequence (FCS) *(HDLC)*
Blocksicherung *f*: zyklische B. cyclic redundancy check (CRC)
Blocksicherungszeichen *n* block check character (BCC) *(DLC protocol)*
Blockwahl *f* en-bloc dialling
Blockwahlziffern-Wählverfahren *n* en-bloc signalling
Blp (Belegungsplan *m*) routing assignment
B-MAC *n* (Variante B von MAC) B-Mac (variant B of MAC) *(525/625 lines, US/Australian TV sat. transmission standard, CCITT Rep. 1073)*
BMFT (Bundesministerium *n* für Forschung und Technologie) Federal (German) Ministry for Research and Technology
BMI (Bundesministerium *n* des Inneren) Federal (German) Ministry of the Interior
Bodenschiene *f* bottom rail, floor bar *(rack)*
Bodenstation *f* earth station, ground station *(sat.)*
Bodenstelle *f* earth station, ground station *(sat.)*
B. mit sehr kleinem Öffnungswinkel very-small aperture terminal (VSAT) *(sat.)*
Bodenstreifen *m* swath *(sat. earth observation)*
Bootstrap-Fähigkeiten *fpl* bootstrap facilities
BORSCHT (Schleifenstromeinspeisung, Überspannungsschutz, Rufstromeinspeisung,

Kennzeichengabe, Signalcodierung *(A/D, D/A conversion)*, Gabelschaltung, Leitungsmessung) Battery feeding, Overvoltage protection, Ringing, Signalling, Coding, Hybrids, Testing *(exchange/telephone interface functions in digital telephone network)*
Botenruf *m* messenger call *(executive tel.)*
BPCM (bereichsprädiktive Code-Modulation *f*) band predictive code modulation *(signal analyzer)*
B-Platz *m* B position, B operator, trunk position
BPM (Bundespostministerium *n*) Federal Ministry for Post and Telegraphs
bps (Bit/s) bits per second
BPSK (binäre Phasenumtastung *f*) binary phase shift keying
BR (Bedienungsrechner *m*) operating system
BRD (Rückkanal *m* Empfangsdaten) Back Receive Data *(V.24/RS232C, s. Table VI)*
Brechung *f* refraction *(FO)*
Breitband *n* (BB) wideband *(gen. analog signals)*, broadband *(gen. dig. signals)*
  B.-Anschlußvermittlung *f* (BAV) broadband access switch *(FO, VBN)*
  B.-Durchgangsvermittlung *f* broadband transit switch *(FO, VBN)* (BDV)
  B.-Informationskanal *m* (H-Kanal) H channel, high-speed user information channel *(ISDN)*
  B.-Informationssystem *n* (BIS) broadband information system *(DBP, FO)*
  B.-ISDN *n* (B-ISDN) broadband ISDN *(FO, 140 - 565 Mbit/s)*
  B.-Kabelanlage *f* (BK-Anlage) wideband cable system *(TV)*
  B.-Kanal *m* high-speed channel *(ISDN H channel)*
  B.-Koppelfeld *n* broadband switching matrix *(FO, VBN)*
  B.-Koppelnetz *n* broadband switching network
  B.-Koppelstelle *f* wideband switching point (WSP) *(digital mobile RT)*
  B.-Paketvermittlung *f* fast packet switching *(supports voice and data)*
  B.-Vermittlungsstelle *f* (BBV) broadband switching centre *(FO, VBN)*
  B.-Verteilnetz *n* (BVN) wideband distribution network *or* system *(TV)*
  B.-Vorläufernetz *n* (BVN) pilot broadband network *(DBP, FO, 565 Mb/s)*
Breitbildformat *n* wide screen *or* letterbox format *(16:9, HDTV)*
Briefkasten *m*: **elektronischer B.** electronic mailbox; user agent (UA) *(X.400)*
BRTS (Rückkanal Sendeteil einschalten) Back Request To Send *(V.24/RS232C, s. Table VI)*
Brücke *f* link, jumper, strap; bridge *(betw. LANs)*; vertical (unit) *(crossbar switch)*
Brückenfunktion *f* relay *(between layers, GSM)*
BS (Rundfunksatellit *m*) broadcast satellite
BSB British Satellite Broadcasting *(DBS, D MAC)*
BSC (binär-synchrone Übertragungssteuerung *f*) binary synchronous communication, 'bisync'
BSE (Betriebssteuereinrichtung *f*) station control equipment *(sat.)*
BSI (Britisches Normen-Institut *n*) British Standards Institution
BTD (Rückkanal Sendedaten) Back Transmit Data *(V.24/RS232C, s. Table VI)*
B-Teilnehmer *m* called subscriber, B party
BTU (Bildschirmtext-Telex-Umsetzer *m*) videotex-telex converter
BTV (Industriefernsehen *n*) business television
BTX,Btx (Bildsschirmtext *m*) videotex, two-way videotext, viewdata *(GB)*, Prestel *(BT)*
  Btx-Anschlußbox *f* videotex access unit *(to ISDN)*
  Btx-ISDN-Anschluß *m* videotex-ISDN access *(BA, later PA)*
  Btx-LZ (Bildschirmtext-Leitzentrale *f*) videotex service centre
  Btx-Mitteilungsdienst *m* videotex E-mail *or* message handling service (MHS)
  Btx-Tx (Bildschirmtext-Telex-Dienst *m*) videotex-telex-service
  Btx-VSt (Bildschirmtext-Vermittlungsstelle *f*) videotex switching centre
BTZ (BTX-Zentrale *f*) videotex computer centre
BU (Bereichsumschaltung *f*) range switch
BU s. Buchstabenumschaltung *f*
Buchsenleiste *f* socket strip
Buchstabenumschaltung *f* (BU) letter shift *(telex)*
Bündel *n* trunk group *(tel.sys., grouping of transmission paths of a given route)*; trunk *(PMR channels)*; group *(of lines)*
  Abnehmer-B. *n* serving trunk group
  Bit-B. burst
  Kanal-B. channel block *(data)*; trunked channels *(PMR)*

Zellen-B. cluster of cells *(cellular RT)*
Zubringer-B. *n* offering trunk group
Bündelburst *m* main traffic burst (MTB) *(sat.)*
Bündelfehler *m* error burst *(e.g., of 20 bits)*
Bündelfreimarkierungsrelais *n* route-idle-marking relay
Bündelführung *f* trunk group layout *(tel.)*
Bündelfunk *m* trunking, radio trunking *(PMR, 460 MHz, DTI standard MPT1327 signalling system)*
Bündelfunknetz *n* trunked mobile radio network
bündeln combine *(PCM)*; multiplex *(FO)*; trunk *(PMR channels or frequencies)*; focus *(light)*
Bündelnetz *n* trunking system *(PMR)*
B.-Steuerung *f* trunking system control (TSC)
Bündelschlüsselgerät *n* trunk coding equipment *(tel.)*
Bündelsperrzähler *m* congested-route counter
Bündelstärke *f* number of transmission channels
Bündelstörung *f* noise burst
Bündelsuche *f*: **beeinflußbare B.** alterable trunk group search
Bündelung *f* concentration *(of data channels)*; trunking *(mobile frequencies)*
Bündelzieltaste *f* (BZT) **für Amtsleitungen** (AL) route name key for exchange lines
Bundesbahn-Selbstanschlußsystem *n* (BASA) subscriber-dialling telephone network of the Federal Austrian Railways
Bundesdatenschutzgesetz *n* (BDSG) Federal German Data Protection Act *(Jan. 1977)*
Bundespostministerium *n* (BPM) Federal (German) Ministry of Posts and Telecommunications
Bürofernschreiben *n* (Teletex) teletex *(2.4 kb/s, conforms to OSI 7-layer reference model)*
Bürokommunikation *f* (BK) office communication
Bürokommunikationsprotokoll *n* technical and office protocol (TOP) *(OSI)*
Büro-Nebenstellenanlage *f* key system *(tel.)*
Burst-Übertragung *f* burst mode transmission *(TCM or ping pong method, sat.)*
Busabschlußgerät *n* bus terminator
Busanforderung *f* bus request *(DCE; network user)*
Busanschaltung *f* bus access unit
Busanspruch *m* bus claim *(DCE in queue)*
Busbesetzt-Signal *n* bus busy signal *(with bus request)*
Busbewilligung *f* bus approval *(with bus request)*
Busgerät *n* communication unit
Buskoppler *m* bus coupler; transceiver
Buslaufzeit *f* bus transit time, bus delay
Busvergabe *f* bus arbiter, arbitration *(DCE)*
Buswettbewerb *m* bus contention
Buszuteiler *m* bus arbiter
Buszuteilung *f* bus assignment *(DCE)*
Buszutritt *m* bus access *(DCE; network user)*
BÜZ (Betriebsführungs- und überwachungszentrale *f*) operating and monitoring centre
BVN (Breitbandverteilnetz *n*) wideband distribution network *or* system *(TV)*
BVN (Breitbandvorläufernetz *n*) pilot broadband network *(DBP)*
B-Vermittlungsstelle *f* (B-VSt) destination exchange
B-VSt s. B-Vermittlungsstelle *f*
Bytetakt *m* byte timing *(CCITT X.21)*, octet timing
BZ (Besetztzeichen *n*) busy signal
BZT (Besetztzeichen *n*) busy signal
BZT s. Bündelzieltaste *f* für Amtsleitungen
B1 (B-Kanal Schicht 1) layer 1 B channel protocol *(ISDN)*

C

CAC (Konferenzschaltungs-Zugangssteuerung *f*) conferencing access controller
CAI (universelle Luftschnittstelle *f*) common air interface *(DTI cellular RT protocol for CT2)*
CAM (Kommunikationszugriffmethode *f*) communication access method
CAM (inhaltsadressierbarer Speicher *m*, Assoziativspeicher *m*) content-addressable memory
CA-SE (computergestützte Software-Entwicklung *f*) computer-aided software development
CAW (rechnergestützte Verdrahtung *f*) computer-aided wiring
CB (11-Meter-Band, CB-Band *n*, Jedermannfunk *m*) Citizen's Band *(27 MHz communication channel)*
CB (Anschluß belegt) Connection Busy *(local DCE busy, V.25 bis)*
C-Band *n* C band *(4/6 GHz down-/uplink, sat.)*
CBS (gemeinsame Basisstation *f*) common base station *(radio trunking)*
CCI (kontaktlose Chipkarten-Schnittstelle *f*) contactless chip card interface *(ISO 7816)*
CCIR (Comité Consultatif International des Radiocommunications) International Consultative Committee for Radio Communication
CCITT (Comité Consultatif International Téléphonique et Télégraphique) International Consultative Committee for Telephony and Telegraphy
CCM s. Crossconnect-Multiplexer *m*
CCS *(Verkehrseinheit)* Cent Call Seconds *(traffic unit, = 1/36 Erl or TU)*
CD (Empfangssignalpegel *m*) Carrier Detect *(V.24/RS232C, s. Table VI)*
CD (Kollisionserkennung *f*) collision detect *(PCM data)*
CD (Compact-Disk *f*, Digitalschallplatte *f*, Laserplatte *f*) compact disk
CD-DA (digitale Audio-CD *f*) compact disk digital audio
CD-I (interaktive CD *f*) compact disk interactive *(ADPCM coding)*
CDMA (Vielfachzugriff *m* im Codemultiplexverfahren) code division multiple access *(tel., VSAT)*
CD-R (bespielbare CD *f*) compact disk recordable
CD-ROM (CD-Datenspeicher *m*) CD ROM *(ADPCM coding)*
CD-ROM XA (erweiterter CD-Datenspeicher *m*) CD ROM extended architecture
CD-V (Video-CD *f*) compact disk video
CeBIT *f* (Centrum *n* für Büro, Information und Telekommunikation) Centre for Office, Information and Telecommunications *(German IT exhibition)*
CEBus (UE-Bus *m*) consumer electronics bus *(EIA, conforms to OSI RM, US)*
CEE (Commission Internationale de Réglementation en Vue de l'Approbation de l'Equipement Electrique) International Commission on Rules for the Approval of Electrical Equipment
CEE-Stecker *m* shock-proof plug
CEN (Comité Européen de Normalisation) European Committee for Standardisation
CENELEC (Comité Européen de Normalisation Electrotechniques) European Committee for Electrotechnical Standardisation
Centel-100 BT centrex service
Centrex-Vermittlung *f* central office exchange service (CENTREX) *(central exchange switch for private networks)*
CEPT (Conférence Européenne des Administrations des Postes et des Télécommunications) European Conference of Postal and Telecommunications Administrations
Cept-Profil *n* (1...3) CEPT Profile *(vtx presentation standards, s. Table VIII)*
Cept-Tel, Ceptel Cept-Telefon *n* Ceptel *(DBP, low-cost vtx terminal, includes modem, with optional telephone function, now "Multikom-Gerät")*
CF (Trägerfrequenz *f*) carrier frequency
CF (Farb-Bildbegrenzung *f*) colour framing *(TV studio)*
CFI (erfolgloser Verbindungsaufbau *m*) Call Failure Indication *(V.25 bis)*
CFIET (erfolgloser Verbindungsaufbau *m*, Besetztton *m*) Call Failure Indication, Engaged Tone
CFINT (erfolgloser Verbindungsaufbau, kein

Ton) Call Failure Indication, No Tone
Chef-Sekretär-Anlage f manager/secretary station *(tel.)*
Chef-Sekretär-Funktion f manager/secretary function *(tel.)*
Chef-Telefonanlage f executive telephone system
Chiffrat n enciphered text
CHILL (Höhere CCITT Programmiersprache f) CCITT High Level Language *(ISDN)*
Chipkartenleser m chip card reader *(mobile RT)*
C/I (Träger/Störungsverhältnis n) carrier/interference ratio *(sat.)*
CIF (gemeinsames Zwischenformat n) Common Intermediate Format *(videophone codec, 156,064 pixels, 288 lines, 8 1/3 Hz frame rate)*
CIRC Cross-Interleaved Reed Solomon Code *(error correction code, sat.)*
Cityruf m (Stadtfunkrufdienst m (SFuRD)) regional radio-paging service *(DBP, to POCSAG standard; GB: "Europage")*
C-MAC n (Variante C von MAC) C-Mac (variant C of MAC) *(TV sat. transmission standard; FM video, PM digital audio, 8 audio channels)*
CMI s. codierte Schrittinversion f
CMRR (Gleichtaktunterdrückungsverhältnis n) common mode rejection ratio
CN (Verbindung f) connection *(CCITT Rec. I.112)*
C/N (Träger/Rausch-Verhältnis n) carrier/noise ratio *(sat.)*
CNET (Nationales Zentrum n für Telekommunikationsstudien) Centre National d'Etudes des Télécommunications (National Centre for Telecommunication Studies)
C-Netz C network *(cellular radiotelephone network, 450 MHz)*
CNR (DÜE nicht betriebsbereit) Controlled Not Ready *(loop testing)*
C/N-Verhältnis (Träger/Rausch-Verhältnis n) carrier/noise ratio *(sat.)*
Code-Aussteuerung f:
   maximale C. peak code *(PCM)*
CODEC m coder/decoder
Codeelement n digit
Codemultiplex n code division multiplex
Codemultiplexzugriff m code division multiplex access (CDMA) *(VSAT)*
Coderate f code rate *(error correction)*
Coderegel f coding rule
Coderegelverletzung f code violation
Code-Spreizung f interleaving *(sat.)*
Codesteuerzeichen n code extension character *(DP)*
Code-Umschaltung f escape (ESC) *(DLC protocol)*
Codevorschrift f code instructions
Codierer m encoder, coding unit
Codierer/Decodierer m codec
Codierstecker m coding plug
Codierungskennlinie f encoding law, companding law
codierte Schrittinversion f coded mark inversion (CMI)
Combo (Kombinationsschaltung f) combined ADC/PCM coding chip *(digital PBX)*
Computer-Graphikschnittstelle f computer graphics interface (CGI) *(ISO DIS)*
Computersatz m desk-top publishing (DTP)
Comtel (Siemens-Multitel n) multifunctional vtx terminal *(no modem)*
CP HDLC checkpoint mode *(ARQ procedure, sat.)*
CPC (zyklisch vertauschter Binärcode m) cyclically permuted code
CPDFSK (kontinuierliche Phasen-Frequenzumtastung f) continuous phase differential FSK
CPE (Teilnehmereinrichtung f) customer premises equipment
CPM (kontinuierliche Phasenmodulation f) continuous phase modulation
cps (Zeichen pro Sekunde (ZPS)) characters per second *(printers)*
CPSK (kohärente Phasenumtastung f) coherent phase shift keying
CR (Verbindungsanforderung f) Connection Request *(SS7 UP)*
CRC (CRC-Prüfung, zyklische Blockprüfung f) cyclic redundancy check *(ARQ procedure)*
CRI (Wahlbefehl m) Call Request with Identification *(V.25 bis)*
Crossconnect-Multiplexer m cross connect multiplexer (CCM) *(computer-controlled switching network with integrated multiplexing functions)*
CS (Durchschaltevermittlung f) circuit switch *(DC)*;
CS (Verbindungsabnehmer m) communication server *(LAN gateway)*
CSC (zentraler Zeichenkanal m (ZZK)) common signalling channel
CSDC (leitungsvermitteltes digitales Leistungsmerkmal n) circuit-switched digital capability *(BOC service, AT&T, 56 Kb/s Accunet)*
CSMA (Vielfachzugriff m mit Trägererkennung) carrier sense multiple access *(LAN)*

CSMA/CD (Vielfachzugriff *m* mit Trägererkennung und Kollisionserkennung) carrier sense multiple access with collision detection *(LAN)*
CSPDN (leitungsvermitteltes öffentliches Datennetz *n*) circuit switched public data network
CT (schnurloses Telefon *n*) cordless telephone
  CT1 (Telefon-HAs mit schnurlosem Zusatzgerät) CT1 *(BT, to BS 6301)*
  CT2 (schnurloses Telefon *n* der zweiten Generation) CT2 *(BT standard for digital Telepoint system, 864-868 MHz, FDMA, public cordless telephones of the second generation, to BS 6301, 6833)*
  CT3 (schnurloses Digitaltelefon *n*) CT3 *(GSM DECT)*
CT (Uhrzeit und Datum) clock time
CTS (Sendebereitschaft *f*) Clear To Send *(V.24/RS232C, s. Table VI)*
CUG (geschlossene Benutzergruppe *f* (GBG)) closed user group
CVSD (adaptive Deltamodulation *f*) continuously variable slope delta modulation *(voice mail processing code, CCITT Rec. G.721)*

D

DA (abrufgesteuerte Kanalzuteilung *f*) demand assignment *(sat.)*
Da (Daten *npl*) data
DAA (Datenzugriffsanordnung *f*) Data Access Arrangement *(CERMETEC modem interface)*
Dab (abgehende Daten *npl*) data out *(test loop)*
DAB (digitaler Hörfunk *m*) digital audio broadcasting
DAC (Digital-Analogumsetzer *m*) digital/analog converter
Dachleistung *f* maximum power, peak power
DAE s. Datenanpassungseinrichtung *f*
DAG s. Datenanschaltgerät *n*
DAG(t) s. Datenanschlußgerät *n*
D-Alarm *m* (Dringend) urgent alarm (signal) *(TC)*
DAM (DFS-Anschlußmodul *n*) DFS access module
DAMA (Belegung *f* nach Bedarf) demand assignment multiple access *(VSAT)*
Dämpfungsausgleich *m* attenuation equalization
Dämpfungsbelag *m* attenuation coefficient *(FO)*
Dämpfungsbetrag *m* attenuation, attenuation constant *(PCM)*
Dämpfungseinbruch *m* attenuation dip; dip *(in signal level etc.)* due to additional losses
Dämpfungsflanke *f* attenuation skirt *(sat.)*
Dämpfungskonstante *f* attenuation coefficient *or* constant
Dämpfungsplan *m* transmission plan *(telephone network)*
Dämpfungswert *m* transmission loss
Dan (ankommende Daten *npl*) data in *(test loop)*
DAN s. Datenanpassungseinheit *f*
DAN (Teilnehmernetz *n*) domestic area network
Darstellungselemente *n* graphical primitives *(set of instruction codes defining basic graphical shapes (circle, line etc.), vtx)*
Darstellungsschicht *f* presentation layer *(layer 6, OSI 7-layer reference model)*
Darstellungsstandard *m* presentation standard *(for vtx terminals, CEPT Profile 1...3)*
DAT (digitales Tonband *n*) digital audio tape
Datagramm *n* datagram (DG)
Dateibediener *m* file server *(SW gateway for LANs)*
Dateiübertragungsprotokoll *n* file transfer protocol (FTP)
Dateiübertragungs- und Zugriffsverfahren *n* file transfer and access method (FTAM)
Datel data telecommunication *(all BT public data services: data telecommunication, data telephone, data telegraphy)*
Datenanpassungseinheit *f* (DAN) data adapter *(a modem)*
Datenanpassungseinrichtung *f* (DAE) data converter *(teletex)*
Datenanschaltgerät *n* (DAG) data connecting unit *(TEMEX)*
Datenanschlußgerät *n* (DAG(t)) data interface unit *(TEMEX)*
Datenaustausch- u. Übertragungssteuerwerk *n* (DTÜ) data transfer control unit
Datenbankrechner *m* data base processor *(vtx)*
Datenbanksystem *n* data base system (DBS)
Datenblock *m* data block; frame *(transm.)*; batch *(POCSAG code)*
Datendirektverbindung *f* (DDV) direct data link
Datendurchsatz *m* data throughput *or* rate
Datenendeinrichtung *f* (DEE) data terminal equipment (DTE)
Datenendgerät *n* (DEG(t)) data terminal (equipment) (DTE)
Datenerfassungsgerät *n* data entry terminal
Datenfeld *n* data field
Datenfernschaltgerät *n* (DFG(t)) remote data switching unit *(sat.)*
Datenfernübertragung *f* (DFÜ) remote data transmission
Datenfernübertragungssteuerung *f* remote data communications controller
Datenfernverarbeitung *f* (DFV) remote data processing
Datenfestnetz *n* dedicated circuit data network *(packet switching)*
Datenfunk *m* radio data transmission
Datengesamtheit *f* ensemble *(transmission)*

Datenkanal *m* data channel (DC)
Datenkanalschnittstelle *f* data channel interface (DCI)
Datenkonzentrator *m* (DKZ) data concentrator; input-output controller *(mobile RT base)*
Datenkopf *m* header; data transmission control *(multiplexer)*
Datenmeßsender *m* data signal generator
Datennetz *n* data network *(includes all facilities for establishing data links between DTEs)*
Datennetzkennung *f* data network identification code (DNIC)
Datennetzsignalisierung *f* (DNS) data network signalling *(TEMEX)*
Datenpaket *n* packet; data burst *(transm.)*
Datenpaket-Leitung-Schnittstelle *f* packet/circuit interface (PCI)
Datenrate *f* data (signalling) rate
Datenrichtungsauswahleinheit *f* data route selector
Datensammeldienst *m* multipoint-to-point service *(VSAT)*
Datensammler *m* data collection platform (DCP) *(sat.)*
Datenschlüsselgerät *n* data encryption unit
Datenschutz *m* data protection, data privacy
Datenschutzgesetz *n* (BDSG) Federal German Data Protection Act *(FRG)*; Data Surveillance Act *(GB)*; Federal Privacy Act *(US)*
Datenschutzverbindung *f* protected-privacy call, intrusion-protected call *(PBX)*
Datensenke *f* data sink *(the data terminal equipment)*
Datensicherheit *f* data integrity
Datensicherung *f* data locking *(transmission link)*; data protection *(system failure)*
Datensichtgerät *n* (DSG) video terminal; video display unit (VDU)
Datensignalzeichen *n* data signal element
Datenstation *f* (DST,Dst) data station *(DTE + DCE, FTZ 118)*
Datenstau *m* data congestion
Datenstelle *f* code position *(connector)*
Datenstrecke *f* data link *(two associated data channels operated in two-way mode)*
Datenstrom *m* data stream
Datentaste *f* (DT) data key *(on telephone set, FTZ)*
Datentelegramm *n* data message
Datenträger *m* data medium
Datenübermittlungsdienst *m* bearer service *(CCITT Rec. I.210)*

Datenübertragungsblock *m* data transmission block; block; frame
Datenübertragungseinrichtung *f* (DÜE) data circuit-terminating equipment (DCE) *(i.e. modem for RS232C connections, network access and PS nodes for X.25 connections)*
Datenübertragungsgeschwindigkeit *f* data rate
Datenübertragungssteuerung f data link control (protocol) (DLC)
Datenumsetzer *m* (DU) data converter; modem *(for analog mode)*; interface adapter *(for digital mode)*
D.-Einrichtung *f* (DÜE) data converter *(dig. PBX modem)*
Datenverarbeitung *f* (DV) data processing (DP)
Datenverarbeitungsanlage *f* (DVA) data processing system
Datenvermittlungsanlage *f* data switching system
Datenvermittlungsstelle *f* (DVSt) data switching centre
Datenweiche *f* data selector *(multiplexer)*
Datenwiedergewinnung *f* data retrieval
Datenwortsicherung *f* data word protection
Datex (Wählnetz *n* für Datenaustausch (Dx)) switched data exchange (network) *(DBP service)*
Datexfernschaltgerät *n* (DXG) Datex remote control unit *(TEMEX)*
Datex-L (leitungsvermitteltes Datennetz *n* (Dx-L)) circuit-switched data exchange (network)
Datex-Netzabschlußgerät *n* (DXG) datex terminating unit *(DBP)*
Datex-P (paketvermitteltes Datennetz *n* (Dx-P)) packet-switched data exchange (network) *(X.25, corresponds to PSS, GB)*
Datex-P10H (Datex-P10-Hauptanschluß *m*) synchronous X.25 data link *(DBP, 2.4 - 48 kb/s)*
Datex-P20F (Datex-P20-Wählanschluß *m*) asynchronous dial-up data link via telephone network *(DBP X.28, 300 - 1200 kb/s)*
Datex-P20H (Datex-P20-Hauptanschluß *m*) asynchronous dial-up data link via tieline *(DBP, 300 - 1200 kb/s)*
Datex-S (vermittelnde Satelliten-Datenverbindung *f*) switched satellite data link *(DBP, 1.92 Mb/s)*
DAU (Digital-Analog-Umsetzer *m*) digital/analog converter
Dauerbelastung *f* continuous test *(FO)*

Dauereinssignal *n* continuous train of ones
Dauernullsignal *n* continuous train of zeros
Dauerschwund *m* long-term fading
D-Bit (Übergabe-Bestätigungsbit *n*) D bit, delivery confirmation bit *(ISDN NUA)*
DBP (Deutsche Bundespost *f*) German Federal Post Office *(now divided into the three POSTDIENST, POSTBANK, TELEKOM services)*
DBS (Datenbanksystem *n*) data base system
DBS (Rundfunksatellit *m*) direct broadcasting satellite
DBT-03-Schnittstelle *f* ISDN videotex terminal/telephone network interface *(DBP, 1200/75 Bd)*
DCD (Empfangssignalpegel *m*) Data Carrier Detect *(V.24/RS232C, s. Table VI)*
DCDM (digital gesteuerte Deltamodulation *f*) digital controlled delta modulation
DCPC (PCM *f* mit Differenzcodierung und Synchrondemodulation) differential coherent pulse code modulation
DCPSK (differential kohärente Phasenumtastung *f*) differentially coherent phase shift keying
DCT (diskrete Cosinus-Transformation *f*) discrete cosine transformation *(video codec)*
D/D (Digital-Digital-Geschwindigkeitsanpassung *f*) bit rate adaptation (digital/digital)
DDCMP (Nachrichtenprotokoll *n* für digitale Datenübertragung) digital data communications message protocol *(DEC)*
DDV (Datendirektverbindung *f*) direct data link
DECT (D-Netzstandard *m*) Digital European Cordless Telephone *(EC and CEPT supported GSM standard for CT3 telephones, TDMA)*
DEE (Datenendeinrichtung *f*) data terminal equipment (DTE)
DEE betriebsbereit Data Terminal Ready (DTR) *(V.24/RS232C, s. Table VI)*
definiert starten initialize *(microprocessor)*
DEG(t) (Datenendgerät *n*) data terminal (equipment) (DTE)
DEGt-E (Einbau-DÜE *f*) built-in DTE *(ZZF)*
Dehner *m* expander *(PCM)*
dekadische Impulswahl *f* decimal pulsing or pulse action *(tel.)*
Dekoder-Identifizierung *f* (DI) Decoder Identification *(RDS)*
Deltamodulation *f* delta modulation (DM)

Demontage *f* disassembly
DEMUX (Demultiplexer *m*) demultiplexer
DEPAK s. Depaketierer *m*
Depaketierer *m* (DEPAK) packet disassembly facility *(PCM data)*
Depotstreifen *m* strip, panel for depositing, storing plugs
dezentrale Steuerung *f* non-centralized control
df (FS-Verbindung hergestellt) you are in communication with the called subscriber *(CCITT Rec. F.60)*
DFB-Laser *m* distributed-feedback laser
DFF (D-Flipflop *m*) D-type flip flop
DFG (Deutsche Forschungsgemeinschaft *f*) German Research and Development Authority
DFG(t) (Datenfernschaltgerät *n*) remote data switching unit
DFN (Deutsches Forschungsnetz *n*) German Scientific Network *(MHS, X.400)*
DFS (Deutscher Fernmeldesatellit *m*) *(Kopernikus, 23.5°E)* German communications satellite
DFS-Anschlußmodul *n* DFS access module
DFT (diskrete Fourier-Transformation *f*) discrete Fourier transform *(codec)*
DFÜ (Datenfernübertragung *f*) remote data transmission
DFV (Datenfernverarbeitung *f*) remote data processing
DFVLR (Deutsche Forschungs- und Versuchsanstalt *f* für Luft- und Raumfahrt) German Aerospace Research Establishment *(now DLR)*
DG (Durchschaltegitter *n*) through-connection gate *(PCM, tel.)*
DI (Dekoder-Identifizierung *f*) Decoder Identification *(RDS)*
Diagnose *f* diagnostic analysis
Dialog *m* conversational mode
Dialogfähigkeit *f* dialog or interactive capability
dialoggeführte Bedienung *f* interactive operation
DIANE (europäisches Datennetz *n* für Informationsdienste) Direct Information Access Network for Europe
DIC (Anrufablehnungsbefehl *m*) Disregard Incoming Call (DIC) *(V.25 bis)*
DICE (TDMA-Direktanschluß *m*) direct-interface CEPT equipment *(sat.)*
Dienstaufbau *m* establishing communication *(bearer service)*
Dienstekennung *f* service indicator *(ISDN)*
Dienstelement *n* (DIN) primitive *(elemen-*

tary interlayer message)
Dienst-Erstanforderungssignal *n* initial service request message (ISRM)
Dienstewechsel *m* changing services, swap *(e.g. telephone to telefax, ISDN)*
Dienstgüte *f* grade of service *(tel.)*; quality of service (QOS)
diensthabend on duty
Dienstinformationskanal *m* service information channel (SIC)
Dienstkanal *m* (DK) service channel
Dienstkanaleinheit *f* service channel unit (SCU)
Dienstkennung *f* service indicator octet (SIO) *(SS7 MTP)*
Dienstkonfiguration *f* communication configuration *(bearer service)*
Dienstleistungen *fpl* services *(layer-layer)*
Dienstleistungsanbieter *m* service provider *(vtx, cellular RT, Temex)*
Dienstleistungsnetz *n* value-added network (VAN) *(ISDN)*
Dienstleistungsnetzdienste *mpl* value-added network services (VANS)
Dienstleistungsrechner *m* host computer *(SS7 UP)*; server
Dienstleitung *f* traffic circuit *(tel.)*
Dienstmeldungen *fpl* call progress signals
Dienstmerkmal *n* service attribute; supplementary service, *(SS7, CCITT Rec. I.451)*, facility
  D.-Anforderung *f* facility request (FRQ)
  D. durchführen provide a supplementary service
  D.-Indikator *m* facility indicator *(SS7 UP)*
dienstneutral service-independent
Dienstnutzung *f* information transfer capability *(bearer service)*
dienstorientiert service-related
Dienstplatz *m* manual answering service (ISDN)
Dienstsignal *n* service signal/code, (call) progress signal *(TTY)*; call progress signal *(ISDN)*
Dienstträger *m* service provider
Dienstübergang *m* intercommunication between service attributes *(bearer service)*; service intercommunication
Dienstunterbrechungsdauer *f* loss-of-service time
Dienstzugriffspunkt *m* service access point (SAP) *(SS7 layer access)*
Dienstzugriffspunktkennung *f* service access point identifier (SAPI)
differenzcodierte QPSK *f* differential QPSK (DQPSK)

Differenz-Pulscodemodulation *f* differential pulse code modulation (DPCM)
Differenz-Zähler *m* difference meter *(reset monthly, tel.)*
Digital-/Analog-Umsetzer *m* (DAU) digital/analog converter (DAC, D/A converter)
Digital-/Analog-Zeichenumsetzer *m* Signalling converter, Digital/Analog (SDA)
digital:
  d. Datenkanal *m* digital signal channel (DSC)
  D.-Digital-Geschwindigkeitsanpassung *f* digital/digital bit rate adaptation (D/D)
  d. Fernvermittlung *f* (DIVF) digital trunk exchange
  d. Funkfernsprechnetz *n* (D-Netz) digital radiotelephone and data network
  d. Funkfernsprechnetz *n* Digital European Cordless Telephone (DECT)
  d. gesteuerte Deltamodulation *f* digitally controlled delta modulation (DCDM)
  d. Hörfunk *m* digital audio broadcasting (DAB) *(Eureka project)*
  d. Kreuzschienenverteiler *m* digital cross connect (multiplexer) (DCC), addressable multiplexer
  d. Leitungsabschluß *m* Digital Line Termination (DLT) *(BT ISDN)*
  d. Leitungsendeinrichtung *f* (DLE) digital line equipment *or* unit (DLU)
  d. Nahbereichsfunk *m* digital short-range radio (DSRR) *(mobile RT, 933-935 MHz)*
  d. Ortsnetz *n* (DIGON) digital local network of the DBP
  d. Ortsvermittlung *f* (DIVO) digital local exchange
  d. Richtfunk-System *n* (DRS) digital radio link system *(sat.)*
  d. Satelliten-Hör(rund)funk *m* digital satellite radio (DSR)
  d. Signal *n* digital *or* discrete signal
  d. Sprachinterpolation *f* digital speech interpolation (DSI)
  d. Sprechstelle *f* digital voice terminal (DVT)
  d. Teilnehmerschleife *f* digital subscriber loop (DSL) *(2-wire ISDN connection)*
  d. Tonband *n* digital audio tape (DAT)
  d. Vermittlung *f* (DIV) digital switching centre; digital PABX
  d. Videosystem *n* (DVS) digital video system *(Eureka project, 12.5 - 20 Mb/s, FO)*
Digitalanschluß *m* digital access *(ISDN)*
Digital-Grundleitungsabschnitt *m* (DSGLA) digital line section

Digitalsignal *n* digital signal
  D.-Grundleitung *f* (DSGL) digital line path
  D.-Prozessor *m* digital signal processor (DSP)
  D.-Verbindung *f* (DSV) digital path
Digitalsignalverteiler *m* digital cross connect (DCC) (equipment) *(switching station on transmission link)*
Digitalverfahren *n* digital (time- and value-discrete) method
DIGON s. digitales Ortsnetz *n*
DIN (Deutsches Institut *n* für Normung) German Institute for Standardisation
DIN-Entwurf *m* draft DIN standard
Direktanschluß *m* direct access
Direktansprechen *n* direct addressing *(via loudspeaker, digital f. tel.)*
Direktantworten *n* direct answering *(via microphone, digital f. tel.)*
Direktbündel *n* direct trunk group
Direktruf *m* direct call; hot line, tie line *(tel.)*
Direktrufnetz *n* data/telephone network for fixed connections
Direktrufverordnung *f* (DirRufv.) Ordinance Concerning Fixed Connections of the DBP *(superceded by the TKO)*
direktstrahlender Satellit *m* direct broadcasting satellite (DBS)
Direktwahl *f* direct dialling; direct distance dialling (DDD)
Direktwahlnetz *n* direct distance dialling (DDD) network
Direktweg *m* high-usage route
DirRufv s. Direktrufverordnung *f*
DIS (Internationaler Normenentwurf *m*) Draft International Standard *(FTZ, ISO)*
diskontinuierlicher Bitstrom *m* bursty traffic
diskrete Cosinus-Transformation *f* discrete cosine transformation (DCT) *(video codec)*
  d. Fourier-Rücktransformation *f* inverse discrete Fourier transform (IDTF)
  d. Fourier-Transformation *f* discrete Fourier transform (DFT) *(IT)*
dispersionsverschoben dispersion-shifted *(FO)*
Disposition *f* arrangement, layout
Distanzadresse *f* displacement address
Distanzrelais *n* distance relay
DIV s. digitale Vermittlung *f*
DIVF s. digitale Fernvermittlung *f*
DIVO s. digitale Ortsvermittlung *f*
DIVO(ISDN) (ISDN-fähige digitale Ortsvermittlung *f*) digital local exchange *(with ISDN capability)*
DIVF(ISDN) (ISDN-fähige digitale Fernvermittlung *f*) digital trunk exchange *(with ISDN capability)*
DK (Datenkanal *m*) data channel (DC) *(TC)*
DK (Dienstkanal *m*) service channel (SC)
DK (Durchsagekennung *f*) Traffic Announcement (TA) identification *(RDS)*
D-Kanal *m* D channel *(ISDN BA, $D_{16}=16$ kb/s, SS7)*
D-Kanal-Kennzeichengabe *f* (DKZE) D-channel signalling *(ISDN PBX)*
DKZ (Datenkonzentrator *m*) data concentrator
DKZE s. D-Kanal-Kennzeichengabe *f*
DLC (Datenübertragungssteuerung *f*) data link control (protocol)
DLE (digitale Leitungsendeinrichtung *f*) digital line equipment *or* unit (DLU)
DLR (Deutsche Forschungsanstalt *f* für Luft und Raumfahrt) German Aerospace Research Establishment *(formerly DFVLR)*
DLT (digitaler Leitungsabschluß *m*) Digital Line Termination *(BT ISDN)*
DM (Deltamodulation *f*) delta modulation
Dm (Multiplex-D-Kanal *m*) multiplexed D channel *(ISDN)*
D-MAC *n* (Variante D von MAC) D-Mac (variant D of MAC) *(TV transmission protocol, 12 MHz bandwidth, 8 audio channels)*
  D2-MAC duo-binary MAC *(TV transmission protocol, 8 MHz bandwidth, 4 audio channels)*
D-Netz (digitales Funkfernsprechnetz *n*) digital radiotelephone network; Digital European Cordless Telephone (DECT) *(GSM standard)*
DNIC (Datennetzkennung *f*) data network identification code
DNS (Datennetzsignalisierung *f*) data network signalling *(TEMEX)*
Dokumentenarchitektur *f* Office Document Architecture *(ISO DIS 8613)*; Open Document Architecture (ODA) *(ISDN, CCITT Rec. I.410)*
Dokumenten-Austauschformat *n* Office Document Interchange Format (ODIF) *(ISDN, CCITT Rec. I.415, ISO DIS 8613)*
Dokumentenübertragung und -bearbeitung *f* (DTAM) Document Transfer And Manipulation *(ISDN, CCITT Rec. I.430)*
Domotik *f* domotics *(encompasses all domestic electrical/electronic equipment; from Fr. "domotique")*
DOM-Prägung *f* domed embossing *(membra-*

ne keypad)
Doppelader *f* pair *(tel.)*
Doppeldruck *m* repeat printing *(fax)*
Doppelkontakt *m* twin contact
Doppelraster *m* interleaved channel arrangement *(RT)*
Doppelring *m* dual ring *(token ring structure, LANs)*
Doppelstromtastung *f* bipolar operation
doppeltgerichtet two-way *(serving trunk, tel.)*
DOV (dem Sprachband überlagerte Datenübermittlung *f*) data over voice *(Centrex service attribute, data rate typically 19.2 kb/s; at 40 kHz carrier frequency in DBP TEMEX and public phonecard telephones)*
DOVE (DOV-Einrichtung *f*) data-over-voice equipment
Downstream: im D. zum Teilnehmer downstream to the user, in the downstream link to the user
DP (Vorschlagsentwurf *m*) draft proposal
DPC (Zielpunkt(code) *m*) destination point code *(SS7 MTP)*
DPCM (Differenz-Pulscodemodulation *f*) differential PCM
dpi (Punkte pro Zoll) dots per inch *(facsimile resolution)*
dpn 100 packet-switched system *(Sweden)*
DPSK (Phasendifferenzumtastung *f*) differential phase shift keying
DQPSK (differenzcodierte QPSK) differential quaternary phase shift keying
dr (-draht) wire
  2-dr (zweidraht-) 2-wire
Drahtfernmeldeanlage *f* wired telecommunications installation
drahtgebundenes Fernsehen *n* closed-circuit TV
drahtloses Telefon *n* cordless telephone *(f.-tel.)*
Drahtnetz *n* public switched telephone network (PSTN)
  Selbstwählfernsprech-D. public switched telephone network (PSTN)
Drahtwickeltechnik *f* wirewrap method
DRAW (direkt lesen nach beschreiben) direct read after write *(recordable video disk)*
DRCS (dynamisch neu definierbarer Zeichensatz *m*) dynamically redefinable character set *(VDU, vtx)*
Dreieckgenerator *m* triangular-wave generator
Dreierverbindung *f* three-party call

Dreiklang-Tonruf *m* three-tone ringing *(tel.)*
Drei-Ton-Ruf *m* three-tone caller *(f. tel.)*
dreiwertige Differenz-Phasenumtastung *f* three-level differential PSK (TDPSK)
Drosselungseinrichtung *f* flow control device
DRS (digitales Richtfunk-System *n*) digital radio link system *(sat.)*
Druckknopf *m* press button *(connector)*
Druckprotokoll *n* printout
DS64K (Digitalsignal *n* mit 64 kbit/s) 64-kbit/s digital signal
DSA (verzeichnisorientierter Systemteil *m*) Directory Service Agent *(CCITT X.500)*
DSC (digitaler Datenkanal *m*) digital signal channel
  DSC34COD DSC 3 channels 64 kbit/s codirectional
DSCR (Entwürfler *m*) descrambler *(FO data channel)*
DSG (Datensichtgerät *n*) video terminal
DSGL (Digitalsignal-Grundleitung *f*) digital line path
DSGLA (Digital-Grundleitungsabschnitt *m*) digital line section
DSI (digitale Sprachinterpolation *f*) digital voice interpolation
DSIF (Weltraum-Meßanlage *f*) Deep Space Instrumentation Facility *(JPL, US)*
DSN (Weltraum-Funkverbindungsnetz *n*) Deep Space Network *(world-wide network of JPL DSIF ground stations)*
DSP (Digitalsignalprozessor *m*) digital signal processor
DSR (Betriebsbereitschaft *f*) Data Set Ready *(V.24/RS232C, s. Table VI)*
DSR (digitaler Satelliten-Hörrundfunk *m*) digital satellite radio
DSRR (digitaler Nahbereichsfunk *m*) digital short-range radio
DSSS (Vermittlungsteilsystem *n* für digitale Teilnehmeranschlüsse) Digital Subscribers Switching Subsystem *(BT ISDN)*
DST,Dst (Datenstation *f*) data communication terminal *(DTE + DCE)*
D-Steckverbinder *m* D connector *(25 pins)*
DSV (Digitalsignalverbindung *f*) digital path
DT (Datentaste *f*) data key *(on telephone set, FTZ)*
DTAM s. Dokumentenübertragung und -bearbeitung *f*
DTC (zentrale Prüfstelle *f* für Datenein-richtungen) data test centre
DTE (Datenendeinrichtung *f* (DEE)) data

terminal equipment *(user device)*
DTMF (Mehrfrequenzverfahren *n* (MFV)) dual-tone multifrequency (dialling method)
DTP (Desktop-Publishing n) desk-top publishing
DTR (Endgerät *n* betriebsbereit) Data Terminal Ready *(V.24/RS232)*
DTÜ (Datenaustausch- und Übertragungssteuerwerk *n*) data transfer control unit
DU (Datenumsetzer *m*) data converter; modem *(for analog mode)*; interface adapter *(for digital mode)*
DUA (verzeichnisorientierter Endbenutzer-Systemteil *m*) Directory User Agent *(CCITT Rec. X.500)*
Dualcode *m* binary code
DUE (Datenumsetzer-Einrichtung *f*) data converter
DÜE (Datenübertragungseinrichtung *f*) data communication equipment (DCE)
dunkelsteuern blank *(monitor)*
Dunkeltastung *f* blanking *(videotex monitor)*
Duplex *n* (DX) duplex *(modem)*
durchführen: ein Dienstmerkmal d. provide a supplementary service *(SS7)*
Durchgang *m* pass *(sat.)*
Durchgangsamt *n* transit exchange *(links local exchanges)*, tandem exchange
Durchgangsdämpfung *f* transmission loss *(FO, tel.)*
Durchgangshäufigkeit *f* transmission frequency *(signals)*
Durchgangsmischer *m* transmissive mixer *(FO)*
Durchgangsnetz *n* transit network
Durchgangsverkehr *m* transit traffic
Durchgangsvermittlung *f* (DV) transit switching
Durchgangsvermittlungsstelle *f* transit exchange; tandem exchange
Durchgangswahl *f* tandem dialling *(tel.)*
Durchgangswellenleiter *m* transmissive waveguide *(FO)*
durchgehende Signalisierung *f* end-to-end signalling
durchgeschaltet patched through
Durchlaßbetrieb *m* forward-biased operation *(FO)*
Durchlaßdämpfung *f* pass-band attenuation *(filter)*
durchlässig transparent *(network, generally with out-band signalling)*
d. **steuern** enable *(circuit)*
Durchlauf *m* pass *(program, tape)*, run; cycle; sweep *(frequency)*

Durchlaufen *n* **einer Periode** cycling
Durchlaufprinzip *n* feed-through principle *(storage procedure, e.g. first-in-first-out (FIFO))*
Durchlaufspeicher *m* transit store
Durchlaufspeicherung *f* **der gewählten Ziffer** cyclic storage *(of digits)*
Durchlaufzeit *f* turnaround time *(for a job, DP)*
Durchsagekennung *f* (DK) Traffic Announcement (TA) identification *(RDS)*
Durchsatzrate *f* throughput *(packets/sec.)*
Durchschalteeinheit *f* switching unit (SWU) *(ISDN)*
Durchschaltegitter *n* (DG) through-connection gate *(PCM, tel.)*
durchschalten connect through, switch through *(tel.)*; turn on *(HW)*
Durchschalteprüfsignal *n* connection test signal
Durchschalteprüfung *f* connection testing *(network)*
Durchschalteschnittstelle *f* circuit switching interface *(FO)*
Durchschaltevermittlung *f* circuit switch (CS), circuit *or* line switching
Durchschaltevermittlungseinheit *f* switching system
Durchschaltung *f* connection; through-connection
Durchschlag *m* Carbon Copy *(remote screen dump program, PC-PC test)*
durchschleifen bypass *(in MUX)*; loop through
durchstellen put through *(call)*
durchsteuern turn on *(semiconductor)*
mehr d. turn on harder
Durchstrahlungsmodus *m* transmission mode *(antenna)*
Durchwahl *f* direct dialling-in (DDI) *(GB)*, direct (inward, outward) dialling (DID, DOD) *(US)*
Durchwahlsatz *m* (DS) direct inward dialling (DID) circuit
DV (Datenverarbeitung *f*) data processing (DP)
DV s. Durchgangsvermittlung *f*
DVA (Datenverarbeitungsanlage *f*) data processing system
DVI (interaktive Video-CD *f*) digital video interactive *(video CD ROM, IBM)*
DVPDC (Programm-Zustellungssteuerungssystem *f* für Heim-Videorecorder) Domestic Video Programme Control system *(TV broadcast service)*
DVS (digitales Videosystem *n*) digital

video system *(Eureka project)*
DVSt (Datenvermittlungsstelle *f*) data switching centre
DVT (digitale Sprechstelle *f*) digital voice terminal
DX s. Duplex *n*
DXG (Datexfernschaltgerät *n*) Datex remote control unit *(TEMEX)*
DXG (Datex-Netzabschlußgerät *n*) datex terminating unit
Dx-L-HAs (Hauptanschluß im leitungsvermittelten Datendienst) main station in the circuit-switched data service

Dx-P (paketvermitteltes Datennetz *n* (Datex-P)) packet-switched data exchange (network)
dynamisch neu definierbarer Zeichensatz *m* dynamically redefinable character set (DRCS) *(VDU)*
D1 (D-Kanal Schicht 1) layer 1 D channel protocol *(ISDN)*
D1 (D-Netz der DBP) digital mobile RT network *(to GSM DECT standard)*
D2 (D-Netz für private Anbieter) digital PMR network *(to GSM DECT standard)*

E

E (Teileinheit *f* (TE)) unit (of width) *(rack, 1 E = 0.2")*
E (Empfänger *m*) receiver
E (Erlang) erlang
EA (Einzelanschluß *m*) main station line
EACW (Ein-/Ausgabe-Codewandler *m*) input/output code converter *(EDS)*
E/A-Port (Ein-/Ausgabeport *n*) I/O port
EB (elektronische Berichterstattung *f* electronic news gathering (ENG) *(TV)*
EBCDIC (erweiterter BCD-Code für Datenübertragung) extended binary coded decimal (BCD) interchange code
Ebene *f* plane *(matrix)*; level *(software, network)*; layer *(in the OSI 7-layer reference model (RM))*
   Meß-E. test interface
EBHC *(Verkehrswerteinheit)* Equated Busy Hour Call *(unit of traffic intensity, = 1/30 Erl. bzw. VE)*
EBIT (europäischer Breitbandverbundnetz-Versuch *m*) European Broadband Interconnection Trial *(RACE, 2 Mb/s)*
EBR-Codec *m* EBR codec *(image reduction)*
EBU (Union Europäischer Rundfunkanstalten) European Broadcasting Union
EC (externer Rechner *m* (ER)) external computer *(vtx information provider)*
Echobedingung *f* echo suppression requirement
Echokanal *m* echo channel, back channel
Echokompensation *f* echo cancellation
Echolaufzeit *f*: **einfache E.** one-way propagation time *(PCM)*
   gesamte E. round-trip delay *(PCM)*
Echolöscher *m* echo canceller *(ping pong method)*
Echorestabstand *m* residual error ratio *(echo canceller)*
Echosperre *f* echo suppressor
Echounterdrückung *f* echo compensation
Echtzeit-Ablaufverfolgung *f* real-time monitoring
Echtzeitkern *m* real-time kernel *(control software)*
echtzeitnah near instantaneous, near real-time
   e. kompandiertes Tonfrequenz-Multiplex *n* near-instantaneously companded audio multiplex (NICAM) *(digital stereo TV sound system, GB)*
   e. Kompandierung *f* near-instantaneous companding (NIC) *(A/D quantisation)*
Echtzeituhr *f* real-time clock (RTC)
Eckdaten *npl* characteristic data
Eckfrequenz *f* limit frequency *(FO)*; cut-off *or* cross-over frequency *(filter)*
Eckkanal *m* band-edge channel
Eckwert *m* corner value, limit, cut-off
ECM (Fehlerkorrekturverfahren *n*) error correction mode *(fax)*
ECMA (Vereinigung *f* der Europäischen Computerhersteller) European Computer Manufacturers' Association
ECS (europäischer Kommunikationssatellit *m*) European Communications Satellite
EDC (Fehlererkennung und Korrektur *f*) error detection and correction
EDD (elektronisches Datensichtgerät *n*) electronic data display
Edelmetallmotordrehwähler *m* (EMD) uniselector with gold-plated contacts
EDF (Ein-Kanal-Datenübertragungssystem *n* mit Frequenzmultiplex) single-channel FDM data transmission system *(telex)*
EDI (standardisierter Datenaustausch *m*) Electronic Data Interchange *(a VAS)*
EDIFACT (Elektronischer Datenaustausch *m* für Verwaltung, Wirtschaft und Transportwesen) Electronic Data Interchange for Administration, Commerce and Transport *(ISO IS 9735)*
EDP (elektronische Datenverarbeitung *f*) electronic data processing
EDTV (Fernsehen *n* mit erhöhter Auflösung) extended definition TV *(US)*
EDV (elektronische Datenverarbeitungsanlage *f*) electronic data processing system
EDVA (zentrale EDV-Anlage *f*) EDP centre
EDV-gerecht EDP-compatible
EE (Endeinrichtung *f*) terminal *or* terminating equipment (TE)
EEMA European Electronic Mail Association *(affiliated to the EMA)*
effektive Leistungszahl *f* gain/noise temperature ratio (G/T) *(sat.)*
EFT (elektronische Geldüberweisung *f*) electronic funds transfer

EFuRD (Europäischer Funkrufdienst *m*)
European radio paging system
EFuSt (Erdfunkstelle *f*) earth *or* ground station *(sat.)*
EGB (elektrostatisch gefährdete Bauteile *npl*) electrostatically sensitive components
EGN (Einzelgebührennachweis *m*) detailed record of charges *(ISDN)*
EHKP s. einheitliches höheres Kommunikationsprotokoll *n*
Eichleitung *f* variable attenuator *(FO, tel.)*
eigen own, self, inherent, intrinsic, internal, auto-, local
 e. **Einrichtung** *f* own facility
 e. **Telegramm** *n* local message
 e. **Vermittlungsstelle** *f* home exchange
Eigenanwendung *f* In-House application (IH) *(RDS)*
Eigenbildmonitor *m* split-screen monitor *(video conference)*
Eigennachführung *f* autotracking *(sat.)*
Eigenprüfung *f* self-check
Eigenrauschen *n* internal, inherent noise *(device)*
Eigenschaften *fpl* properties, characteristics
 Netz-E. network capabilities
Eigentest *m* internal test, selftest
Eigenwahl *f* own-number dialling *(PBX)*
Eigenzeit *f* operating time *(relay)*
Einader- unbalanced *(signalling)*
Einarbeitungshilfe *f* learning tool
Ein-/Auseffekt *m* on/off colour effect *(membrane keypad)*
Ein-/Ausgabe-Codewandler *m* (EACW) input/output code converter *(EDS)*
Ein-/Ausgabeport *n* (E/A-Port) I/O port
Ein-/Auskoppler *m* input/output coupler
Ein-/Ausschaltung *f* **der Vermittlung** connection/disconnection of switching system
Einbaubuchse *f* panel jack
Einbau-DÜE *f* (DFGt-E) built-in DTE
Einbauplatz *m* mounting *or* plug-in location, slot, position
Einbausatz *m* mounting adapter; slide-in unit
Einbauteilung *f* installation pitch
einblenden inject, insert *(signal, PCM)*; apply *(trunk offering tone)*; stuff *(bits, flags)*; superimpose *(signal, FO)*
Einbinden *n* integrating; tieing-in *(subscribers)*
Einbruch *m* fall, dip
 Spannungse. dip in voltage level
einfacher Startschritt *m* single-length start element
Einfachklammer *f* single-sided clamp *(rack)*
Einfachstromtastung *f* unipolar operation
Einfachzählung *f* single metering
Einfallabstand *m* inter-arrival time *(delay system)*
einfallende Belegung call arriving *(tel.)*
Einfallzeit *f* incidence time *(PS)*
Einfügungsdämpfung *f* insertion loss
Einführungskonzentrator *m* (EKT) growth concentrator
Eingabeeinrichtung *f* : berührungssensitive E. touch input device (TID)
Eingang *m* input, port
Eingangsleistungsflußdichte *f* input power flux density (IPFD) *(sat.)*
Eingangssignalabstand *m* **vom Sättigungspunkt** input backoff *(TWT, in dB)*
eingebaute Prüfeinrichtung *f* built-in test equipment (BITE)
eingelagert nested
eingerastet locked
eingeregelter Zustand *m* steady-state condition
eingeschrieben loaded *(buffer store, PCM data)*
eingeschwungener Zustand *m* steady-state condition
eingreifend invasive
Einhängeminus *n* on-hook pulse (negative) *(tel.)*
Einhängeplus *n* on-hook pulse (positive) *(tel.)*
einheitlich:
 e. **Fernmeldesteckdose** *f* universal telecommunication socket *(ISDN)*
 e. **höheres Kommunikationsprotokoll** *n* (EHKP) standard high-level communications protocol *(BMI videotex transport protocols)*
Einheitskurzrufnummer *f* (EKR) standard abbreviated call number
Einheitsschrittlänge *f* unit interval
Ein-Kanal-Datenübertragungssystem *n* **mit Frequenzmultiplex** (EDF) single-channel FDM data transmission system *(telex)*
Einkanal-Niederfrequenzverfahren *n* single-channel voice frequency (SCVF) *(telex signalling)*
Ein-Kanal-pro-Träger-System *n* single channel per carrier (SCPC) *(sat.)*
Ein-Kanal-pro-Transponder-System *n* single channel per transponder (SCPT) *(sat.)*
einkoppeln insert, launch *(FO)*
Einlaufverhalten *n* stabilisation

characteristic
einleiten initiate *(process)*; originate *(call)*
einlesen write in, copy *(into memory)*
einmal Beschreiben, mehrfach Lesen write once, read many (WORM)
einmessen commission *(a route)*
Einmodenfaser f monomode fibre *(FO)*
einordnen insert *(into a sequence or queue, PCM data, speech)*
einpendeln settle *(oscillator)*
Einphasenblinken n synchronized flashing *(videotex monitor)*
einpolig miteinander verbunden connected at a single terminal *or* pin
einrasten (auf) lock on (to) *(a carrier)*, acquire lock
einreihen insert *(into a sequence or queue, PCM data, speech)*
einrichten adjust; set up, install *(a function, program)*; connect *(an extension, tel.)*
Einrichtung f unit, equipment, facility;
 bei E. at subscription time *(service)*
 durchgeführte E. completed setting up *(of function)*
Einrichtungssuchspeicher m device search store
Einsatz m inset
Einsatzfeld n inset section
Einsatzplatz m (EPL) inset location *(rack)*
Einsatzspannung f turn-on voltage; turn-off, cut-off voltage; threshold voltage
Einsbit n mark
Einschaltdämpfung f insertion loss
Einschaltdauer f operating time
 relative E. duty cycle
einschalten close *(switch)*; make *(breaker, circuit)*; connect, switch on *(unit)*; turn on *(component)*
Einschaltrückstellung f power-on reset
Einschub m slide-in unit
Einschubplatz m (EP) unit location *(rack)*
Einschubtechnik f: **in E.** as a plug-in device
Einschwingen n transient; recovery *(transients)*
einschwingende Spannung f recovery voltage
Einschwingverhalten n transient response
Einschwingzeit f transient response time; rise time; response time *(tel., MF)*; pull-in period *(PLL)*; synchronisation time
Einseitenband n (ESB) single sideband

(SSB)
Einseitenbandmodulation f (EM) single-sideband modulation (SSB)
einseitig single-sided, unilateral; single-ended
 e. Einspeisung f feeding from one end *(cables)*; single-ended feeding *(equipment)*
 e. geerdet single-ended, outer conductor grounded, unbalanced
 e. Verzerrung f bias distortion
Einsetzseite f (E-Seite) component side (PCB)
einspeichern store, write in
einspeisen inject
einspielen inject, play *(music)*
Einspringberechtigung f takeover priority (TC)
Einspringschaltung f takeover circuit (TC)
Einspringzähler m changeover counter (TC)
Einsprungverbindung f single-hop link *(VSAT star network)*
einstecken slot in, insert
Einsteckseite f (E-Seite) component side (PCB)
einstellbar selectable *(addresses)*
Einstellbefehl m setting instruction
Einsteller m (EN) controller, network controller
Einstellfunktion f control function, control operation
Einstellregler m adjustable potentiometer
Einstieg m entry point *(into a program)*
Einstrahlungsstörfestigkeit f immunity to radiation-induced interference
Einströmungsstörfestigkeit f immunity to line-induced interference
eintakten clock in *(a signal)*
Eintaktsignal n simplex signal *(data transmission)*
eintasten key in; gate on
Eintreteaufforderung f operator recall
Eintreten n cut-in
Einwahl f dialling in
 Netz-E. dial-in
Einwählvorgang m access via switched lines *(to packet network)*
Einwegdienst m one-way service *(e.g. teletext or radiopaging)*
Einzelanruf m selective ringing *(party line)*
Einzelanschluß m single line; main station line
Einzeldienstendgerät n service-specific terminal *(ISDN)*

Einzelendgeräte-Anschluß 36

Einzelendgeräte-Anschluß *m* single-terminal access
Einzelgesprächsnachweis *m* itemized charge accounting, detailed call record
Einzelgesprächszählung *f* single-fee metering
Einzelkanalburst *m* single channel per burst (SCPB) *(sat.)*
Einzelkanalsignalisierung *f* channel-associated signalling
Einzelkonfiguration *f* single-terminal configuration
Einzelmeldung *f* single message *(telefax protocol)*
Einzelstecker *m* banana plug
Einzelwahlziffern-Wahlverfahren *n* overlap signalling *(SS7 MTP)*
Einzelzulassung *f* individual type approval (ZZF)
EIRP (äquivalente isotrop abgestrahlte Sendeleistung *f*) equivalent isotropically radiated power *(sat.)*
EKR (Einheitskurzrufnummer *f*) standard abbreviated directory number
ELA-Anlage *f* public address (PA) system
elektromagnetisch:
  e. Beeinflussung *f* electromagnetic interference (EMI)
  e. Impuls *m* electromagnetic pulse (EMP) *(nuclear)*
  e. Verträglichkeit *f* (EMV) electromagnetic compatibility (EMC)
elektromechanische Vermittlungstechnik *f* electromechanical distribution frame (EMDF)
elektronisch:
  e. Adreßbuch *n* electronic directory *(CCITT X.500)*
  e. Anschlagtafel *f* electronic bulletin board *(MHS)*
  e. Bankverkehr *m* electronic banking, telebanking, home banking
  e. Berichterstattung *f* (EB) electronic news gathering (ENG) *(TV)*
  e. Briefkasten *m* electronic mailbox; user agent (UA) *(CCITT Rec. X.400)*
  e. Datenaustausch *m* electronic data interchange (EDI)
  e. Datensichtgerät *n* electronic data display (EDD)
  e. Datenverarbeitung *f* electronic data processing (EDP)
  e. Datenverarbeitungsanlage *f* (EDVA) electronic data processing system (EDP)
  e. Datenvermittlungssystem *n* electronic data switching system (EDS)
  e. Geldüberweisung *f* electronic funds transfer (EFT)
  e. Mitteilungsübermittlungs-System *n* electronic messag(ing) system (EMS) *(CCITT X.400)*
  e. Namensverzeichnis *n* name server *(CCITT Rec. X.400)*
  e. Notizbuch *m* electronic notebook *(tel.)*
  e. Post *f* (TELEBOX) electronic mail (E-mail, MHS) *(CCITT Rec. X.400, generic name for noninteractive communication of text, data, images or voice messages between a sender and designated recipient(s) by systems utilizing telecommunication links (EMA definition))*
  e. Postamt *n* message transfer agent (MTA) *(CCITT Rec. X.400)*
  e. Schalter *m* solid-state switch
  e. Störaustastung *f* (ESA) muting *(FM radio)*
  e. Telefonbuch *n* (ETB) electronic directory *(vtx attribute)*
  e. Verzeichnissystem *m* name server system *(CCITT Rec. X.400)*
  e. Wählsystem *n* (EWS) electronic switching system (ESS)
  e. Wählsystem *n*, **analog** (EWSA) analog electronic switching system
  e. Wählsystem *n*, **digital** (EWSD) digital electronic switching system
  e. Wählsystem *n*, **Fernverkehr** (EWSF) electronic switching system for long-distance traffic
  e. Wählsystem *n*, **Ortsverkehr** (EWSO) electronic switching system for local traffic
  e. Zahlungsverkehr *m* electronic funds transfer (EFT)
elektrostatisch gefährdete Bauteile *npl* (EGB) electrostatically sensitive components
Elementarnachricht *f* primitive *(elementary inter-layer message, OSI)*
EM (Einseitenbandmodulation *f*) single-sideband modulation (SSB)
EMA Electronic Mail Association *(Washington, DC, US)*
E-mail (elektronische Post *f*) electronic mail *(CCITT Rec. X.400)*
EMC s. elektromagnetische Verträglichkeit *f*
EMD (Edelmetallmotordrehwähler *m*) uniselector with gold-plated contacts
EMDF (elektromechanische Vermittlungstechnik *f*) electromechanical distribution frame
EMI s. elektromagnetische Beeinflussung *f*

EM-L (Ingenieurmodell *n* Lebensdauerprüfung) engineering model - life (test) *(ESA)*
EMP s. elektromagnetischer Impuls *m*
Empfangsadresse *f* receive identifier *(PCM data)*
Empfangsband *n* downlink band *(sat.)*
Empfangsbaustein *m* receive module *(PCM)*
empfangsbereit sein keep watch
Empfangsbereitschaft *f* receive ready (rr) *(videotex)*
   keine E. receive not ready (rnr) *(videotex)*
Empfangsbezugdämpfung *f* receiving level equivalent *(FO, tel.)*
Empfangsdaten Receive Data (RD) *(V.24/RS232C, s. Table VI)*
Empfangsdiode *f* detector diode *(FO)*
Empfangssendgerät *n* receive terminal (RT)
Empfangsgüte Signal Quality detect (SQ) *(V.24/RS232C, s. Table VI)*
Empfangsschrittakt Receive Clock (RC) *(V.24/RS232C, s. Table VI)*
Empfangssignalpegel Data Carrier Detect (DCD) *(V.24/RS232C, s. Table VI)*
Empfangsstelle *f* head end *(community antenna)*
Empfangsumsetzer *m*: **rauscharmer E.** low noise converter (LNC) *(sat.)*
Empfangszeit *f* time of reception (TOR)
Empfangszug *m* receiving channel
Empfangszweig *m* receive path
EMS s. elektronisches Mitteilungsübermittlungs-System *n*
E-MUX (Ethernet-Multiplexer *m*) Ethernet multiplexer *(switched broadband network)*
EMV s. elektromagnetische Verträglichkeit *f*
EN (Einsteller *m*) controller, network controller
Endamt *n* terminating exchange (TE); terminal exchange (TX), terminal office
Endausbau *m* final capacity stage
Endebedingungen *fpl* terminating criteria
Endeflagge *f* closing flag *(SS7 frame)*
Endeinrichtung *f* (EE) terminal or terminating equipment (TE);
   customer premises equipment (CPE)
Endesatz *m* end record *(PCM data)*
Endgerät *n* terminal device;
   E. betriebsbereit Data Terminal Ready (DTR) *(V.24/RS232C, s. Table VI)*
Endgeräteanpassung *f* terminal adapter (TA) *(ISDN, for non ISDN TE)*
Endgeräte-Anpassungseinheit *f* terminal adapter unit (TAU) *(dig. PBX, US)*
Endgeräte-Anschalteeinheit *f* medium attachment unit (MAU) *(transmit/receive unit)*
Endgeräte-Anschlußsteuerung *f* media access control (MAC) *(FDDI subprotocol to IEEE 802, supplements LLC)*
endgeräteautark network-independent
Endgeräte-Endpunktkennung *f* terminal endpoint identifier (TEI)
Endgerätewechsel *m* change of terminals *(ISDN)*
Endgestell *n* terminating rack
Endregenerator *m* terminal regenerator
Endpunkt *m* endpoint, connection endpoint *(SAP, logical connection)*
Endstelle *f* terminal station *(PCM data, speech)*
Endstellenleitung *f* (EndStLtg.) terminal line; in-house wiring
EndStLtg. s. Endstellenleitung *f*
End-Systemteil *m* user agent (UA) *(CCITT X.400)*
Endteilnehmer *m* terminating subscriber
Endton *m*: **Ansage-E.** unquote tone
Endverkehr *m* terminating traffic
Endvermittlungsstelle *f* (EVSt) terminal exchange (TX) *(DBP)*
Endverschluß *m* termination
Endverzweiger *m* (EVz) terminal box, distribution point (DP)
Endwert *m* full-scale deflection (FSD) *(meter)*;
   full scale *(ADC)*
ENG (elektronische Berichterstattung *f* (EB)) electronic news gathering *(TV)*
ENQ (Stationsaufforderung *f*) enquiry *(DLC protocol)*
Entdämpfung *f* de-attenuation *(PBX)*
entgegennehmen: einen Anruf e. answer (a call)
entschachteln demultiplex, *(signals)*
entscheiden decide; detect *(repeater)*
Entscheider *m* decision circuit
entscheidungs-rückgekoppelter Entzerrer *m* decision feedback equalizer (DFE) *(cellular mobile RT)*
Entspannungsbogen *m* strain relief *(cable)*
entsperren reconnect
entstopfen extract *(PCM signal)*; destuff *(TDM bits)*
Entstörfilter *m* interference suppression filter
Entstörstelle *f* maintenance centre
Entstörung *f* fault clearance
Entstörungsdienst *m* fault clearance service
Entstörungsstelle *f* maintenance centre
Entwürfler *m* descrambler (DSCR) *(sat.)*

entzerren equalize, correct, eliminate distortion
Entzerrer *m* equalizer
ENV (europäische Vornorm *f*) European Preliminary Standard *(NET)*
Envelope *n* envelope *(data byte + status and framing bit)*
EOM (Mitteilungsende *n*) End Of Message *(signal)*
EOT (Übertragungsende *n*) End Of Transmission *(signal)*
EP (Einschubplatz *m*) unit location *(rack)*
EPL (Einsatzplatz *m*) inset location *(rack)*
ER (externer Rechner *m*) external computer (EC) *(videotex information provider)*
Erdefunkstelle *f* s. Erdfunkstelle
Erderkundungs-Satellitendienst *m* earth exploration satellite service (EES) *(CCIR)*
Erdfunkstelle *f* (EFuSt) earth *or* ground station *(sat.)*
Erdschluß *m* earth fault, line-to-earth fault
Erdschlußkompensation *f* earthing through a Petersen coil
erdsymmetrisch balanced to earth
erdsynchrone Umlaufbahn *f* geosynchronous orbit *(approx. 35,900 km orbital altetude, for 'stationary' satellites (22,300 mi))*
Erdtaste *f* (ET) earth (recall) key *or* button, grounding *or* earthing key *(tel.)*
Erdtastenzeit *f* earth recall time *(f.tel.)*
erfassen acquire *(signal, data)*; capture, register, cover; detect; accept; intercept *(radar)*; record, sense, measure
  die mit einem Stecker e.-ten Löcher the holes engaged by one plug
Erfassung *f* acquisition *(signal, data)*
erfolglos ineffective, unsuccessful *(call attempt)*
  e. Verbindungsaufbau *m* Call Failure Indication (CFI) *(V.25 bis)*
  e. Verbindungsaufbau *m* **Besetztton** Call Failure Indication, Engaged Tone (CFIET)
  e. Verbindungsaufbau *m* **kein Ton** Call Failure Indication, No Tone (CFINT)
erfolgreich: nicht e. Verbindung *f* call failure
erkennen monitor, detect
Erkennung *f* **durch laufende Mehrheitsentscheidung** running majority vote detection (RMVD)

Erl s. Erlang
Erlang *n* (Erl, E) *(Einheit für den Verkehrswert)* erlang *(dimensionless traffic intensity unit, 1 Erl = 1 continuously busy trunk)*
Erlaubnis *f* authorization (access control)
ERMES (europäisches Funkmitteilungssystem *n*) European Radio Messaging System *(EC CEPT radio paging, will supersede Euromessage 1993)*
Erprobungszulassung *f* trial approval *(FTZ)*
erregter Verkehr *m* originated traffic
erreichbar obtainable *(subscriber)*
Erreichbarkeit *f* availability *(tel.sys.)*
Ersatzangebot *n* equivalent offered load *(tel.sys.)*
Ersatzbaugruppe *f* replacement module *or* assembly
Ersatzbetrieb *m* standby operation
Ersatzrechner *m* alternate computer
Ersatzschaltbild *n* equivalent circuit; equivalent network diagram
Ersatzschalteeinrichtung *f* (ESE) changeover unit *(exchange, PCM data)*
Ersatzschaltekontakt *m* changeover-to-standby contact
Ersatzschaltung *f* changeover to standby; standby operation; equivalent network circuit
Ersatzspannung *f* equivalent voltage
Ersatzteil *n* (ET) spare part
Erstanlage *f* primary (master) station *(conference circuit)*
Erstausbau *m* initial capacity stage
erstellen create
Erstnebenstellenanlage *f* primary *or* master station *(tel.)*
Erstwahlbündel *n* direct route, first-choice route
Erwartungsfunktion *f* expectation function *(video encoding)*
Erwartungsmenge *f* set of expected values *(video encoding)*
Erwartungswert *m* expected value *(video encoding)*
erweiterter BCD-Code *m* **für Datenübertragung** extended binary coded decimal interchange code (EBCDIC)
erweiterter Sonderkanalbereich *m* (ESB) extended special-channel band *(TV, s.a. "Hyperband")*
Erweiterungsschritt *m* expansion stage
ES (Externsatz *m*) interexchange circuit
ESA (elektronische Störaustastung *f*) muting *(FM radio)*
ESA (Europäische Weltraumorganisation *f*)

European Space Agency
ESB (Einseitenband *n*) single side band (SSB)
ESB s. erweiterter Sonderkanalbereich *m*
ESC (Codeumschaltung *f*) escape *(DLC protocol)*
ESD-Schutz *m* (Schutz gegen elektrostatische Entladung) protection against electrostatic discharge (ESD) *(membrane keypad)*
ESE s. Ersatzschalteeinrichtung *f*
E-Seite *f* (Einsetz-, Einsteckseite) component side *(PCB)*
ESPRIT European Strategic Programme for Research and Development in Information Technologies
ET (Besetztton *m*) Engaged (*or* busy) Tone *(V.25 bis)*
ET s. Erdtaste *f*
ET s. Ersatzteil *n*
ETACS (erweitertes TACS *n*) extended TACS *(cellular mobile RT, GB)*
Etage *f* subrack
19"-Etage *f* 19" subrack, shelf
Etagenverdrahtungsprüfautomat *m* automatic shelf-wiring tester
ETB (elektronisches Telefonbuch *n*) electronic directory *(vtx attribute)*
Ethernet *(local-area network to IEEE standard 802.3, 10 Mb/s CSMA/CD baseband transmission)*
ETSI (europäisches Institut *n* für Telekommunikationsnormen) European Telecommunications Standards Institute
ETX (Textende *n*) End of TeXt
Eu-95 Eureka 95 *(Eureka HDTV project, incl. HD Mac)*
Euler-Diagramm *n* Venn diagram *(statistics)*
EUREKA (Europäische Organisation *f* für Zusammenarbeit in der Forschung) European Research Cooperation Agency *(study group of 18 European countries to set up a framework programme for promoting collaborative hi tech projects, e.g. HDTV, RACE, Archimedes' exclamation 'eureka' (I have found it!) being symbolic of success in research)*
EUROCOM (Europäische Kommunikationsnormen *fpl*) European FM communication standards *(NATO, for tactical FM systems)*
Eurocrypt (europäische Verchlüsselungsnorm *f*) European satellite TV *(MAC)* encryption standard
Euromessage (Europäischer Funkrufdienst *m*) European messaging service *(Interconnection of Europage (GB), Alphapage (FR), Teldin (I), Cityruf (FRG), March 1990, precursor to Ermes)*
EURONET *n* (Europäisches wissenschaftliches Datennetz *n*) Euronet *(packet-switched EEC network for scientific and technical databases of member countries, conforms to TRANSPAC)*
EuroOSInet *n* European OSI test network
Europabauform *f* Eurocard design
Europäisches Funkmitteilungssystem *n* European Radio Messaging System (ERMES) *(EC radio paging)*
Europäischer Funkrufdienst *m* (EFuRD) European radio-paging system; Pan European Paging service (PEP)
Europäische Vornorm *f* European Preliminary Standard (ENV)
Europiep s. Eurosignal *n*
Eurosignal *n* (Europäischer Funkrufdienst *m* (EFuRD)) European radio-paging service *(FRG, Switzerland, France)*
Eutelsat (europäische Nachrichtensatelliten-Organisation *f*) European Telecommunications Satellite Organisation
EVA (elektronischer Verkehrslotse *m* für Autofahrer) electronic traffic pilot for drivers *(Bosch)*
EVSt (Endvermittlungsstelle *f*) terminal exchange *(DBP)*
EVz (Endverzweiger *m*) distribution point (DP)
EWS (elektronisches Wählsystem *n*) electronic switching system (ESS) *(Siemens)*
EWSA (EWS für analoge Raummultiplexübertragung) electronic switching system with analog space division multiplex switching, (EWS mit Analogtechnik) analog electronic switching system
EWSD (EWS für Zeitmultiplexübertragung mit Digitalwähltechnik) electronic switching system with digital time division multiplex switching, (EWS mit Digitaltechnik) digital electronic switching system
EWSF (EWS für Fernverkehr) electronic switching system for long-distance *or* trunk traffic
EWSO (EWS für Ortsverkehr) *(VSt)* local network electronic switching system
EWSP (EWS mit Paketvermittlung) electronic switching system with packet switching
EWSP-V (EWS mit Paketvermittlung für Verbindungsunterstützung) electronic switching system with packet switching for interconnection support *(for*

VASs)
Exemplarstreuung *f* component spread
extern:
   e. Leitungszeichengabe *f* interexchange signalling
   e. Rechner *m* (ER) information provider database *(vtx)*
   e. Umschalten *n* intercell handoff *(mobile RT)*
Externsatz *m* (ES) interexchange circuit
Externverkehr *m* interexchange traffic

F

fachliche Voraussetzung f technical qualification *(of applicant for type approval ZZF)*
FAG (Fernmeldeanlagengesetz n) telecommunication systems law
Fähigkeiten fpl: **Bootstrap-F.** bootstrap facilities
Fahrgastinformationssystem n (FIS) train tannoy *(GB) or* PA system
falsch wrong, false, faulty. erroneous, incorrect
  f. Zustand m false state *(logic)*
Falschanruf m wrong-number call
Falschwahl f faulty selection
Faltungscode m convolution code *(FEC)*
Familientelefonanlage f (FTA) domestic telephone system
Fangberechtigung f call identification class of service
Fangbereich m locking-in *or* capture range *(e.g. PLL)*
Fangdaten npl malicious call identification data *(tel.)*
Fangeinrichtung f call intercept equipment *(tel.)*
Fangen n call tracing *(tel.)*
Fangmeldung f call identification report *(tel.)*
Fangtastenwahlempfänger m (FTE) push-button dialling receiver for malicious call identification *(tel.)*
Fangwunsch m call identification request *(tel.)*
Fangzustand m malicious call hold, call hold condition *(tel.)*
Farbart, Bild-(Luminanz-)**Signal, Austastung, Synchronsignal** (FBAS) composite colour signal *(TV)*
Farbschwindeffekt m on/off colour effect *(membrane keypad)*
Faserdämpfung f fibre loss *(FO)*
Faseroptik f fibre optics (FO)
faseroptische Berichterstattung f fibre-optic news gathering (FONG)
faßbare Schnittstelle f standard accessible interface *(FTZ 118)*
faxen fax, send by fax *(documents etc.)*
Fax-Gruppe 1,2 fax group 1,2 *(analog telefax machines, page transmission 6 - 2 min.)*
Fax-Gruppe 3,4 fax group 3,4 *(digital telefax machines, page transmission 1 min. - 10 sec.)*
Faxmaschine f fax machine, telefax machine, telecopier
Fax-Steuerfeld n fax control field (FCF) *(fax control character)*
FBAS s. Farbart, Bild-(Luminanz-)Signal, Austastung, Synchronsignal
FBAZ (zentrale Fernbedienungsanlage f) central remote control system *(sat.)*
FBBZ (Fernmeldebaubezirk m) telephone construction district
FBP (fischbißgeschützt) fish bite protected *(TAT8, FO)*
FBO (Fernmeldebauordnung f) planning regulations for telecommunications equipment *(DBP)*
FCF s. Fax-Steuerfeld n
FCS (Blockprüfzeichenfolge f) frame checking sequence *(HDLC)*
FCS (Rahmenprüfzeichen n) frame checking sequence *(SS7 CRC)*
FDDI (Datenanschluß m mit Signalverteilung über Glasfaser) Fiber Distributed Data Interface *(ANSI AXC X3T9.5, 100 Mb/s token ring LAN to IEEE 802.2, 802.5; 2 km transmission distance)*
FDDI-Schnittstelle f FDDI interface *(IEEE 802.3, CSMA/CD)*
FDM (Frequenzmultiplex n, Frequenzgetrenntlageverfahren n) frequency division multiplex
FDMA (Vielfachzugriff m im Frequenzmultiplex) frequency division *or* domain multiple access *(tel.)*
FDS (Funkdatensteuerung f) base station control unit
FDX (voll duplex) full duplex
Fe (Fernsprech-/en n) telephone ...
FEAD (Fernsprechauftragsdienst m) customer service
FeAp (Fernsprechapparat m) telephone set *(FTZ)*
FeAsl (Fernsprech-Anschlußleitung f) telephone subscriber line
FEC (Vorwärts-Fehlerkorrektur f) forward error correction

Feder *f* clip *(female connector)*
Federklammer *f* clip *(female connector)*
Federkontakt *m* pressure contact
Federleiste *f* female contact *or* connector strip;
socket, receptacle (strip)
federnd:
  f. Kontaktstifte *mpl* spring contact pins
  f. Taste *f* spring-loaded key
FeE (Fernsprechentstörung *f*) telephone fault clearance
FeHA (Fernsprechhauptanschluß *m*) main station
Fehlabschluß *m* mismatch
Fehlanruf *m* false signal
Fehlbedienung *f* operating error
Fehler *m* fault *(HW)*; error *(SW, data etc.)*
fehlerbehaftet faulty, defective *(HW)*
Fehlererkennung und Korrektur *f* error detection and correction (EDC)
fehlerfrei error-free, correct *(HW)*; faultless, valid *(HW)*
fehlerhaft defective, faulty, inoperable *(HW)*;
invalid, incorrect, errored, erroneous *(data, blocks etc.)*
flawed, faulty *(data, blocks etc.)*
  f. Zeichen *n* error character
Fehlerkorrekturverfahren *n* error correction mode (ECM) *(fax)*
Fehlerlokalisierung *f* fault locating, finding
Fehlermeldung *f* fault signal *(AIS)*
Fehlernormal *n* standard mismatch *(testing)*
Fehlerortung *f* fault location
Fehlerortungseinheit *f* fault location unit (FLU) *(tel.)*
Fehlersammelmeldung *f* error list signal
Fehlerschutzbit *n* error control bit
fehlersicher faultless
Fehlersicherung *f* error control, error protection
Fehlersicherungsverfahren *n* error control procedure
Fehlersuche *f* faultfinding *(HW)*, debugging *(SW)*
Fehlertelegramm *n* fault signal *(service channel)*
Fehlerüberwachung *f* error control procedure
Fehlerüberwachungseinheit *f* error control unit
Fehlerverdeckung *f* error masking
Fehlerverhalten *n* error performance *(PCM)*
Fehlfunktionstest *m* malfunction test
Fehlsekunde *f* errored second *(CCITT G.821)*

Fehlstrom *m* non-operate current; offset current
Fehlverbindung *f* wrong connection, wrong-number call
Feinschutz *m* secondary protection (circuit)
feinstufig verändern vary gradually
Feld *n* array *(LEDs)*;
block *(terminals, pins)*;
field *(data)*;
panel, cubicle, section *(rack)*;
section *(repeater)*
Feldfernkabel *n* (FFK) long-distance field cable *(NATO)*
feldgebunden field guided *(wave)*
FEP (Anpassungsrechner *m*) front-end processor
fern remote, distant, tele-
  f. Teilnehmer *m* distant caller
Fernabfrage *f* polling *(telefax)*;
remote replay *(tel. answering machine)*
Fernabruf *m* polling *(fax)*
Fernamt *n* regional centre (RC); trunk exchange, toll office *(US)*
fernamtsberechtigter Teilnehmer *m* trunk unrestricted subscriber
Fernamtsleitung *f* long-distance exchange trunk
Fernamtstechnik *f* long-distance switching system
Fernanschluß *m* trunk subscriber's line
Fernanzeige *f* remote signalling;
bivalent teleindication *(yes/no, good/bad, to CCITT V.31 bis, TEMEX)*
Fernberechtigung *f* trunk access (level)
fernbesetzt trunk busy
Fernbetriebseinheit *f* communication control
Fernecho *n* far-end echo
Fernerkundung *f* remote sensing *(sat.)*
Ferngesprächsdienst *m* message telephone service (MTS) *(official US designation)*
Fernknotenamt *n* trunk junction exchange
Fernkopierer *m* telecopier, telefax machine, fax machine
Fernladen *n* downloading *(comp.)*
Fernleitung *f* toll trunk; trunk circuit
Fernmelde- (Fm) telecommunication, communication
  F.-Abschluß *m* trunk terminating unit
  F.-Kontrollnetz *n* telecommunications management network (TMN) *(CCITT)*
  F.-Schema *n* trunking scheme
Fernmeldeanlagengesetz *n* (FAG) Telecommunication Installation Act *(DBP)*
Fernmeldebaubezirk *m* (FBBZ) telephone construction district

Fernwirken

Fernmeldebauordnung f (FBO) planning regulations for telecommunications equipment (DBP)
Fernmeldegebührenvorschriften fpl (FGV) Telecommunications Charges Schedules (DBP)
Fernmeldegeheimnis n secrecy of telecommunications
Fernmeldemechaniker m lineman
Fernmeldemeßkoffer m portable VF test set
Fernmeldeordnung f (FO) Telecommunications Regulations (DBP, superceded by the TKO)
Fernmelderechnungsdienst m (FRD) telephone accounts service (DBP)
Fernmeldesatellit m telecommunications satellite
Fernmeldeschutzschalter m circuit breaker
Fernmeldesteckdose f telecommunication socket (ISDN)
Fernmeldetechnisches Zentralamt n (FTZ) Telecommunication Engineering Centre (DBP, corresponds to BTRL)
Fernmeldeübertrager m line transformer
Fernmeldeunterhaltungsbezirk m (FEUBZ) telecommunications maintenance district
Fernmeldeunternehmen n common carrier (in US, e.g BOCs); telecommunication company (in FRG, e.g. Siemens)
Fernmeldeverwaltung f common carrier (PTT)
Fernmeldewesen n communications, telecommunication
Fernmeldezeugamt n Telecommunication Supply Office (DBP)
Fernmeßeinrichtung f telemetry equipment
Fernnebensprechen n far-end crosstalk (tel.)
Fernnetz n long-haul network (tel.)
Fernplatz m B operator, B position, trunk position
Fernschalten n bivalent remote switching (off/on, to CCITT V.31 bis, TEMEX); telecommanding (TEMEX)
Fernschreib- (Fs) teletype ...
Fernschreiben n (FS) telex, teletype (TTY); telewriting (ISDN)
Fernschreiber m teleprinter
Fernschreibmaschine f teleprinter
Fernsehempfangsstation f TV receive only (TVRO) station (sat.)
Fernsehtext m teletext (txt) (TV broadcast service)
fernspeisbar power-fed
Fernspeise- (FSP) power-feeding ... (RPF) (Tel.)
Fernsperre f toll restriction

Fernsprech- (Fe) telephone ...
 F.-**Anschlußleitung** f (FeAsl) telephone subscriber line
 F.-**Fernverkehr** m wide-area telephone service (WATS) (US, corresponds to International 0800 (GB))
Fernsprechapparat m (FeAp) telephone set (FTZ)
Fernsprechauftragsdienst m (FEAD) absent-subscriber service; customer service (tel.)
Fernsprechbuch n telephone directory
fernsprechen telephone, phone
Fernsprechentstörung f (FeE) telephone fault clearance
Fernsprecher m telephone set
 F. **für Impulswahl** dial-pulse telephone
 F. **für Mehrfrequenzwahl** tone-dialling telephone
 F. **für Tastwahl** pushbutton telephone
Fernsprechhauptanschluß m (FeHA) subscriber's main station
Fernsprechnetz n telephone network
Fernsprechnummer f subscriber's directory number
Fernsprechübertragung f telephony
Fernsprechvermittlungsstelle f central office (US), telephone exchange
Fernstation f distant station
Fernübertragung f external (long distance) call
Fernübertragungseinheit f (FÜ) telecommunication equipment (TC)
Fernüberwachung f remote supervision (system)
Fernverkehr m long-distance (or toll) traffic or communication (PCM, tel.)
Fernverkehrmodem m long-haul modem (s.a. LDM)
Fernverkehrsdienst m **zu Ortsgebühren** extended area service
Fernverkehrsnetz n wide area network (WAN), long-haul network (FO)
Fernvermittlung f (FVSt) long-distance (or trunk) exchange
Fernverwaltung f remote (circuit) management (conference circuit)
Fernvorabfrage f remote screening (tel. answering machine)
Fernwahlleitung f trunk circuit with dialling facility
Fernwähltechnik f direct distance dialling (DDD)
Fernwirken n (FW) telecontrol; teleaction (TEMEX service; features: remote monitoring with telemetry and

Fernwirk- (Fw) teleaction ... (TEMEX)

teleindication, and telecommanding with remote adjustment and remote switching; NTG Rec.2001)
Fernwirk- (Fw) teleaction ... *(TEMEX)*
  F.-Dienstanbieter *m* teleaction service provider
  F.-Endeinrichtung *f* (FwEE) teleaction terminal equipment *(TEMEX)*
  F.-Endgerät *n* (FwEG) teleaction terminal *(TEMEX)*
  F.-Leitstelle *f* (FwLSt) teleaction master station *(TEMEX)*
  F.-Stelle *f* (FwSt) teleaction station *(TEMEX)*
  F.-System *n* (FW) telecontrol system
  F.-Unterstation *f* remote (telecontrol) terminal unit (RTU)
  F.-Verbindung *f* teleaction link *(TEMEX)*; supervisory control system *(general)*
Fernzeichnen *n* telescript; telepictures, telewriting *(ISDN)*
ferroelektrisches Flüssigkeitskristall *n* ferroelectric liquid crystal (FLC) *(FO switch)*
fest fixed, permanent, stationary, solid
  f. eingebaut built-in; permanently installed
  f. geschaltete Verbindung *f* permanent circuit; fixed *or* dedicated *or* non-switched *or* point-to-point connection
Festanschluß *m* permanent connection, tie line; private circuit
Festfrequenzen *fpl* spot frequencies *(testing)*
festhalten: eine Anzeige f. hold a display
Festkörperansteuerung *n* solid-state drive (SSD)
Festkörperrelais *n* solid-state relay (SSR)
Festnetz *n* dedicated circuit network
Feststation *f* base station *(general mobile RT)*; fixed station *(PMR, trunking)*
Festverbindung *f* (FV) dedicated connection, tie line
Festverstärker *m* fixed-gain amplifier
Festzeichen *n* permanent echo *(FO)*
Festzeitverbindung *f* fixed-time call
FeTAp83 (Fernsprechapparat 83) telephone model 83 of the DBP
FEUBZ (Fernmeldeunterhaltungsbezirk *m*) telecommunications maintenance district
FEWAS (Fernwirken *n* auf der Telefonanschlußleitung) telecontrol (*or* teleaction) on the telephone line *(DBP pilot project for TEMEX)*
FFK (Feldfernkabel *n)* long-distance field cable

FFSK (schnelle Frequenzumtastung *f*) fast FSK
FGV (Fernmeldegebührenvorschriften *fpl*) Telecommunications Charges Schedules
FH (Frequenzhüpfer-) frequency hopping (circuit)
FH-DPSK (DPSK *f* mit Frequenzsprung) frequency-hopped DPSK
FID (Fülldaten-Eingabevorrichtung *f*) fill input device
FIFO (Durchlaufprinzip *n*, Siloprinzip *n*) first-in-first-out *(storage procedure)*
Fingerführung *f* (finger) locating ridges *(membrane keypad)*
FIR-Filter *n* finite impulse response filter *(digital audio coding)*
FIS (Fahrgastinformationssystem *n*) train tannoy *(GB)* or PA system
fischbißgeschützt fish bite protected (FBP) *(TAT8, FO)*
Fixpunkttechnik *f* checkpointing
FKTG (Fernseh- und Kinotechnische.Gesellschaft e.V. *f*) Television and Cinematographic Association
Flachbett-Scanner *m* flatbed scanner *(OCR)*
Flächenkabelrost *n* planar cable shelf *(rack)*
Flächenrauschen *n* granular noise *(DPCM video encoding)*
Flächenwiderstand *m* resistance per unit area; surface impedance
Flachkabel *n* ribbon cable
Flagge *f* flag *(indicator bit)*
Flankensteilheit *f* edge slope; Q factor *(filter)*; slope rate, rise time *(pulse)*
Flankenwechsel *m* edge transition
Flankenzählung *f* transition count
Flashtaste *f* (FT) flash key *or* button (PBX)
FLC s. ferroelektrisches Flüssigkeitskristall *n*
fliegende Verdrahtung *f* loose wiring
FLU (Fehlerortungseinheit *f*) fault location unit
Flugfunkdienst *m*:
  beweglicher F. aeronautical mobile service
FM, Fm (Fernmelde-) communication, telecommunication
FMS (Funkmeldesystem *n*) radio signalling system
FO (Faseroptik *f*) fibre optics
FO (Fernmeldeordnung *f*) Telecommunications Regulations
FOF (Verlustrate *f*) freeze-out fraction

Folge *f* sequence; stream *(bits)*, train *(pulses)*
Gesprächsf. order of calls
Prüff. test signal
Folgemeldung *f* secondary alarm
Folgefrequenz *f* repetition frequency
Folgekennzeichen *n* successor signal
Folgepaket-Anzeige *f* 'More Data' mark
Folgesteuerung *f* secondary *(function of communication control)*; sequencing
Folgesteuerungsstation *f* secondary station (HDLC)
Folgezeit *f* repetition period *(pulses)*
Folientastatur *f* membrane keypad
FONG (faseroptische Berichterstattung *f*) fibre-optic news gathering
Formatsteuerzeichen *n* format effector; layout character
Former *m* shaper *(response curve shaper)*
fortschalten increment, step, advance *(counter)*
Fortschaltimpuls *m* stepping pulse
Fourier-Transformation *f* (FT) Fourier transform (FT)
FRD (Fernmelderechnungsdienst *m*) telephone accounts service
frei idle *(channel, trunk)*; unoccupied, available *(line)*
 f. halten keep clear
 f. Vorzug *m* optional priority
Freigabe *f* clearing, cleardown *(of the call)*; reconnection *(of a subscriber line)*; release *(for transfer)*, disconnection
freigeben clear *(shift reg.)*; discharge *(capacitor)*; enable, strobe *(gate, divider)*; release *(signal, connection)*
Freileitung *f* overhead line *(el.)*; open-wire circuit *or* line
Freileitungszustand *m* idle-circuit condition
Freimeldesignal *n* idle status indication signal
Freimeldung *f* idle status indication
Freischalten *n* isolation of equipment; clearing *(line)*; clear-down *(exchange)*
Freischreiben *n* erasing
Freisprecheinrichtung *f* hands-free voice input device *(mobile telephone dialling)*
Freisprechen *n* (FS) hands-free talking *or* operation *(f. tel.)*
Freisprechtaste *f* hands-free talk key *(f. tel.)*
Freiton *m* (F-Ton) ringing signal *or* tone

Freizeichen *n* call connected signal *(TTY)*
freizügige Zuordnung *f* flexible allocation
Freizustand *m* idle condition *(transmission channel)*
Freizustandssignal *n* idle-status signal
-fremd non-
Fremdanschluß *m* remote access *(to ISDN exchange at non-ISDN exchange)*
Fremdnetz *n* visited network *(mobile RT)*
Fremdspannung *f* unweighted noise voltage, foreign potential *(transmission channel)*
Fremdtakt *m* external(ly driven) clock
Frequenzabstand *m* frequency spacing
Frequenzabstimmung *f* frequency tuning; syntonisation *(matching frequencies)*
Frequenzbandmultiplex *n* wavelength division multiplex (WDM) *(FO)*
frequenzbewertet frequency-weighted
Frequenzgang *m* frequency response *(filter)*
Frequenzgenauigkeit *f* frequency stability
Frequenzgetrenntlageverfahren *n* frequency division multiplex method (FDM) *(tel., carrier frequency)*
Frequenzgleichlageverfahren *n* common-frequency method
Frequenzhüpfer-(FH-)Schaltung *f* dehopper *(receiver)*; frequency hopper *(transmitter)*; frequency hopping circuit *(spread spectrum technique)*
Frequenzintervall *n* frequency step
Frequenzkontrolle *f* frequency check *or* monitoring; frequency comparison unit
Frequenzlage *f*: **in hoher F.** at high frequencies
Frequenzmultiplex *n* frequency division multiplex (FDM) *(tel., carrier frequency)*
Frequenznachziehschaltung *f* frequency control circuit
Frequenzraster *m* spacing, frequency spacing
Frequenzspringen *n* hopping
Frequenzsprungempfänger *m* dehopper
Frequenzsprungmodulation *f* frequency shift keying (FSK)
Frequenzsprungsender *m* frequency hopper, hopper
Frequenzumtastung *f* frequency shift keying (FSK)
Frequenzvergleich *m* frequency comparison; syntonisation *(matching frequencies)*
Frequenzversatz *m* frequency shift, offset, error
Frequenzweiche *f* diplexer (antenna); cross-over network *(LF)*
-freundlich compatible with, -optimised

-freundlich 46

anwenderf. user-oriented
Frittspannung f fritting or wetting voltage
FS (Fernschreiben n)telex, teletype (TTY)
Fs (Fernschreib-) teletype ...
FS (Feststation f) base station *(general mobile RT)*; fixed station *(PMR, trunking)*
FS s. Freisprechen n
FSK s. Frequenzumtastung f
FSP (Fernspeisung f) remote power feeding (RPF) *(tel.)*
FT (Flashtaste f) flash key or button *(PBX)*
FT (Fourier-Transformation f) Fourier transform
FTA (Familientelefonanlage f) domestic telephone system
FTAM (Dateiübertragungs- und Zugriffsverfahren n) file transfer and access method *(ISO IS 8571)*
FTE (Fangtastenwahlempfänger m) push-button dialling receiver for malicious call identification *(tel.)*
F-Ton (Freiton m) ringing signal or tone
FTP (Dateiübertragungsprotokoll n) file transfer protocol
FTZ (Fernmeldetechnisches Zentralamt n) Telecommunication Engineering Centre *(DBP, corresponds to BTRL)*
FÜ (Fernübertragungseinheit f) telecommunication equipment *(TC)*
Fühlerschaltung f scanning circuit, scanner *(PCM data)*
Fühler- und Geberschaltungen fpl scanning and distribution circuits *(PCM data)*
Führung f guidance, control
 Bediener-F. operator prompt(ing)
 Benutzer-F. user prompt(ing)
 Leitungsf. conductor arrangement
 Signal-F. signal transmission
Führungsformer m reference shaper *(reg.)*
Führungsrechner m master computer
Führungsstift m alignment pin *(FO)*
Führungswinkel m propagation angle *(FO)*
FuKo s. Funkkonzentrator m
Füllbefehl m dummy instruction
Füllbit n justification bit *(PCM)*; stop bit or element *(bit rate adaptation)*
Fülldaten-Eingabevorrichtung f fill input device (FID)
füllen fill; justify *(PCM)*
Füllinformation(sbit) n justification service bit
Füllschritt m padding (stop) element *(bit rate adaptation)*
Füllstand m loading *(memory)*

Füllwort n stuffing word *(PCM)*
Füllzeichen n filler bit; filler; pad (character) *(preceding and following a data block - leading and trailing pad, resp.)*
Funkanschlußpunkt m radio access point (RAP) *(tel.)*
Funkblock m message block *(mobile RT)*
Funkdatensteuerung f (FDS)base station control unit *(mobile RT)*
Funkdienst m radio communication service
Funkentstörung f radio interference suppression
Funkfax n radio telefax, radiofax
Funkfeld n radio hop, link section
Funkfelddämpfung f path loss *(sat.)*
Funk-Fernschaltsystem n radio teleswitching *(GB; TC off-peak power switching)*
Funkfernschreiben n radioteletype (RTTY)
Funkfernsprechdienst m radiotelephone service
Funkfernsprechen n radiotelephony (RT) *(PLMN and PMR)*
Funkfernsprecher m personal portable telephone (PPT) *(UK)*
Funkfernsprechnetz n public land mobile network (PLMN)
Funkfeststation f mobile base station *(general mobile RT, incl. cellular)*
Funkkanal m radio (telephony) channel
Funkkanalwechsel m handover *(cellular mobile RT)*
Funkkontroll-Meßstelle f radio checks/measurements office
Funkkonzentrator m (FuKo) mobile (radio) concentrator *(cellular RT)*, base station *(mobile RT)*
Funkmeldesystem n (FMS) radio signalling system
Funk-Nebenstellenanlage f radio PBX
Funkprozessor m traffic processor *(PMR, trunking)*
Funkruf m paging (PAG) *(RDS)*; bleep *(GB, colloquial)*
Funkrufdienst m radio paging service *("air-call bleep", GB)*
Funkrufempfänger m pager, bleeper *(GB)*
Funkrufvermittlungsstelle f (FuRVSt) radio paging switching centre
Funkschutzbestimmungen fpl RF interference (RFI) regulations
Funkstörspannung f conducted interference
Funkstörung f radio frequency interference (RFI)
Funkteilnehmer m mobile subscriber, mobile RT service user

beheimateter F. registered mobile subscriber
Funktelefon n cordless or radio telephone, mobile telephone
Funktelefondienst m mobile telephone service
Funktionsablauf n sequence of operations
Funktionsbeschreibung f description of operation
Funktionsdauer f operating period
mittlere F. mean time to failure
Funktionseinheit f functional unit, element
Funktionserde f signal ground
funktionsfähig operable, viable
Funktionsfähigkeit f operability
Funktionsprüfung f performance check
Funktionsschalter m mode selection switch
funktionssicher functionally dependable, reliable
Funktionstaste f function key, control key
Funktionsteil n functional section, device
funktionstüchtig operable, viable
Funküberleitstelle f radio relay (switching centre) *(cellular mobile RT)*
Funküberwachung f radio supervisor (RSV)
Funkverbindungsnetz n ground station network *(DSN or MSFN)*
Funkverbindungsprotokoll n radio link protocol (RLP) *(GSM)*
Funkvermittlung f radio relay (station)
Funkvermittlungsstelle f (FVSt) mobile switching centre (MSC) *(DBP Cellular mobile RT)*
Funkzelle f cell,, base station area *(mobile RT)*
FuRVSt s. Funkrufvermittlungsstelle f
FV (Festverbindung f) dedicated connection, tie line
F-Vermittlung f, **unsymmetrische Zeichengabe** F exchange, unbalanced signalling (FXU)
FVSt s. Funkvermittlungsstelle f
FW (Fernwirksystem n) telecontrol, supervisory control system *(general)*
Fw (Fernwirk-) teleaction ... *(TEMEX)*
FwEE (Fernwirkendeinrichtung f) teleaction terminal equipment *(TEMEX)*
FwEG (Fernwirkendgerät f) teleaction terminal *(TEMEX)*
FwLSt (Fernwirkleitstelle f) teleaction master station *(TEMEX)*
FXU s. F-Vermittlung f, unsymmetrische Zeichengabe
FZ (Freizeichen n) clear signal *(tel.)*
FZA (Fernmeldetechnisches Zentralamt n) Telecommunication Engineering Centre of the Federal Austrian Post Office

G

GA (Gemeinschaftsantenne *f*) master antenna
GAA (Geldausgabeautomat *m*) automatic cash dispenser *(GB)*, automatic teller machine (ATM) *(US)*
GaAs (Galliumarsenid *n*) gallium arsenide
Gabel *f* cradle *(HW)*; hybrid circuit *(tel.)*
   G.-Nachbildung *f* building-out network, hybrid termination
Gabelschaltung *f* hybrid network *(tel.)*
Gabelübergang *m* hybrid transition *(tel.)*
Gabelübergangsdämpfung *f* transhybrid loss, hybrid transformer loss; echo balance return loss *(PCM)*
Gabelumschalter *m* (GU) cradle *or* hook switch *(tel.)*
Gang *m* cycle; response *(frequency)*, path *(optical)*
   G. einer Uhr rate of a clock *(in ns/d, atomic clock)*
   Temperatur-G. variation due to temperature
Gangkonstante *f* propagation coefficient
Ganglinie *f* curve
Ganzseitenabtastung *f* whole-page scanner *(fax)*
GAS (Gemeinschaftsanschluß *m*) two-party line
GAS (Grundadressenspeicher *m*) base address store
gassenbesetzt all trunks busy (ATB)
Gateway *m* gateway *(conceptual or logical protocol-converting interconnection between networks, nodes or devices)*
Gatternetzwerk *n* logic array
Gaußsche Mindestwertumtastung *f* Gaussian Minimum Shift Keying (GMSK) *(cellular digital RT)*
GBG (geschlossene Benutzergruppe *f*) closed *(network)* user group (CUG)
GBW s. Gebührenweiche *f*
GEB s. Gebühren *fpl*
Gebäudeverteiler *m* building (services) distributor *or* distribution board *(PBX)*
Geber *m* generator, transmitter
Geber und Fühler *mpl* scanning and distribution circuits *(dig.tel.)*
Gebilde *n* structure *(cable)*
gebohrt pre-drilled *(chassis, PCB)*

Gebrauchsfehler *m* operating error
Gebrauchsunterlage *f* technical information
Gebühren *fpl* (GEB) charges *(tel.)*
Gebührenanzeige *f* subscriber's check meter *(tel.)*
Gebührenbefreiung *f* exemption from charges
Gebührendaten *npl* call-charge data *(tel.)*
Gebühreneinheit *f* charge unit
Gebührenerfassung *f* call costing, charge metering, call charge registration *(tel.)*
Gebührenfernsehen *n* pay TV, pay-per-view TV *(US)*
gebührenfreier Anschluß *m* non-chargeable subscriber
Gebührenimpuls *m* metering pulse, charge pulse
Gebührenimpuls-Einspeisesatz *m* charge-pulse injection circuit
Gebührenpflicht *f* chargeable time
Gebührenrechnungsstellung *f* billing
Gebührenstand *m* charge meter position
Gebührentakt *m* meter clock pulse
Gebührenübernahme *f* reverse charging
   G. durch B-Teilnehmer freephone service *(ISDN)*
Gebührenweiche *f* (GBW) injector circuit
Gebührenzähler *m* (call) charge meter, subscriber's meter
Gebührenzone *f* charge area, charge band *(GB)*
Gebührenzuschreibung *f* call unit statement *(BT, TTY)*
gebündelt grouped, bundled, bunched; focussed, collimated *(FO)*
   g. auftretende Daten *npl* data occurring in bursts, "bursty" data
   g. Funkkanäle *mpl* trunked radio channels *(PMR)*
gebunden:
   drahtg. Fernsehen *n* closed-circuit TV
   feldg. field guided *(wave)*
   kanalg. channel-associated
   leiterg. line connected *(network)*
   leitungsg. line conducted *(signal)*
   sprechkreisg. channel-associated
   systemg. system-linked, system-inherent
   taktg. clocked
GEDAN (Gerät *n* zur dezentralen Anrufweiter-

gedruckte Rückverdrahtung 50

schaltung) equipment for decentralized call forwarding *(DBP, tel.)*
gedruckte Rückverdrahtung f (GRV) printed backplane *(rack wiring)*
gefächerter Sprung m multi-address branching *(ESS)*
Gefahr! Sehr Dringend! (GSD) Danger! Extremely Urgent! *(priority 1 in TTY, immediate break-in priority)*
Gefahrenmeldung f alarm signalling
geführt carried, conducted, controlled, fed, guided
  stromrichterg. current-converter-fed
Gegenamt n distant exchange
Gegenbelegzeichen n opposite-seizing signal *(tel.)*
Gegenbetrieb m duplex transmission
Gegenfrequenzbetrieb m reverse frequency operation *(trunking, fixed station)*
Gegenkontakt m mating contact *(connector)*
Gegenlauf m negative phase relationship *(filter, phase)*
Gegenschreiben n full duplex *(TTY)*
Gegenseite f distant station
Gegensprechanlage f intercom system
Gegensprechen n duplex *(tel.)*
Gegenstation f secondary station *(HDLC)*
Gegenstelle f distant station, distant end *(PCM)*
Gegentaktsignal n duplex signal *(data transmission)*
gehaltene Verbindung f held call, call on hold *(tel.)*
Gehäuse n case *(module)*; housing, cabinet; shell *(connector)*
Geheimhaltung f privacy
Geheimnummer f unlisted number *(tel.)*
gehend outgoing
  g. Satz m (GS) outgoing circuit
  g. Sperre f outgoing-call barring facility *(tel.)*
  g. Verbindung f outgoing call, call answered
gekreuzt reversed polarity *(tel. current feed)*
Gelbdruck m yellow-paper edition *(DIN)*
Gelbe Post f (POSTDIENST) the postal services branch of the DBP *(now independent of TELEKOM and POSTBANK)*
Geldausgabeautomat m (GAA) automatic cash dispenser *(GB)*, automatic teller machine (ATM) *(US)*
Geldautomat m s. Geldausgabeautomat
Geldüberweisung f: **elektronische G.** electronic funds transfer (EFT)
gemeinsame Basisstation f common base station *(trunking)*
g. Signal n composite signal *(CCITT Rec. G.703)*
Gemeinschaftsanschluß m (GAS) two-party line, shared line *(tel.)*
Gemeinschaftsantenne f (GA) community antenna, master antenna *(radio)*
Gemeinschaftsantennenanlage f master antenna TV (MATV) system
Gemeinschaftseinrichtung f shared-line equipment
Gemeinschaftsleitung f party-line *(tel.)*
gemischtes Signal n composite signal *(TV)*
Genehmigung f licence *(ZZF)*
Generaladresse f all-station *or* global address
Gentex (Telegrammwähldienst m) gentex (general telegraph exchange) *(telegram service of the DBP telex network)*
Geradeausempfang m straight-through reception *(FO)*
gerade Parität f even parity
Gerätefehler m device *or* hardware fault
Geräteklinke f equipment jack
Geräteschutzsicherung f (G-Sicherung) miniature fuse
Gerätetechnik f hardware
Geräteübersicht f equipment list
gerecht:
  EDV-g. EDP-compatible
  verkehrsg. to suit traffic conditions
Gerechtigkeit f fairness *(in bus allocation)*
gerichtet directional, guided; one-way *(tel.)*
  doppeltg. two-way *(tel.)*
geringe Steigung f gradual slope *(of a curve)*
Gesamtlaufzeit f overall delay
Gesamtverbindung f end-to-end connection
Gesamtverzerrung f signal/total distortion ratio
geschalteter virtueller Kanal m switched virtual channel (SVC) *(Datex-P)*
geschlossen:
  g. Benutzergruppe f (GBG) closed user group (CUG)
  g. Codierung f composite encoding *(dig. TV)*
geschützte Kleinspannung f protected extra low voltage (PELV) *(tel.)*
Geschwindigkeitsanpassung f bit rate adaptation *or* adaptor (D/D) *(CCITT Rec. V.110)*; rate adaption (RA) *(GSM)*
Geschwindigkeitsumsetzung f data rate conversion

gesichert acknowledged *(connection, SS7)*; error-corrected, -protected *(link)*; protected, fail-safe, secure
gesperrt restricted *(extension)*
Gespräch *n* conversation; call
  G. mit Herbeiruf messenger call
  G. mit Voranmeldung personal call
  internes G. intra-office call
gesprächsbegleitend while speaking *(dig. PBX, using other service)*
Gesprächsbelegung *f* channel loading *(mobile RT)*
Gesprächsdatenerfassung *f* (GEZ) call data acquisition *(dig. PBX)*
Gesprächsdauer *f* duration of call
Gesprächsdichte *f* calling rate
Gesprächsklirrfaktor *m* distortion (factor) of voice channel
Gesprächsmessung *f* call timing
Gesprächsumleitung *f* call diversion
Gesprächsweitergabe *f* roaming *(cellular RT)*
Gesprächszustand *m* voice *(e.g. 'voice is established')*; call in progress
gesteckt connected
Gestellbelegung *f* rack equipment; rack face *or* front layout *or* plan
Gestellholm *m* upright *(rack)*
Gestellrahmen *m* (GR) rack frame
Gestellreihe *f* rack row, suite
Gestellreihenfuß *m* rack row base
Gestellrost *m* rack shelf
Gestellsockel *m* rack base
gestört out of order *(connection)*; faulty *(transmission)*; errored *(data)*
  g. Leitung *f* faulty line
  stark g. Sekunden *fpl* severely errored seconds *(CCITT G.821)*
gestreckte Gruppierung *f* straight-through trunking scheme
getaktet clocked, cycled; pulsed
getastet gated, pulsed
geteilte Zentralstation *f* shared hub *(VSAT)*
Getrenntlageverfahren *n* grouped-frequency operation *(transmit and receive signals transmitted at different frequencies)*
Gewinn *m* gain (factor) *(TASI)*
Gewinner *m* successful DCE, winner *(in bus allocation)*
GEZ s. Gesprächsdatenerfassung *f*
gezielte Abfrage *f* selective answering
  g. Belegen *n* designated seizure *(tel.)*
GFK s. Glasfaserkabel *n*
GGA s. Groß-Gemeinschaftsantenne *f*
Glasfaserkabel *n* (GFK) fibre optic cable
Gleichanteil *m* DC component

gleichberechtigter Spontanbetrieb *m* asynchronous balanced mode; balanced mode
  g. Zugriff *m* contention mode
Gleichkanalbeeinflussungen *fpl* co-channel interference
Gleichkanalfunk *m* common-channel radio
Gleichlageverfahren *n* duplex channel method *(ISDN B channel transmission method with echo cancellation, signals transmitted at the same time and frequency)*; common-frequency method
Gleichlauf *m* co-routing *(cables)*; synchronism *(signals)*; tracking *(of component characteristics)*
Gleichlaufsteuerung *f* clocking
Gleichlichtanteil *m* CW light component *(FO)*
Gleichsignal *n* mean signal
Gleichspannung *f*: **unterlegte G.** DC bias *(FO)*
Gleichspannungstastung *f* (GT) DC keying
Gleichstrom *m* (GS) direct current (DC)
Gleichstromfehlerortung *f* DC fault location *(PCM data)*
gleichstromfrei AC only, floating; DC-balanced *(PCM transmission signal)*
Gleichstromleitungssatz *m* DC trunk circuit
Gleichstromtastung *f* (GT) DC keying
Gleichtaktdämpfung *f* common-mode attenuation
Gleichtaktsignal *n* common-mode signal; in-phase signal
Gleichtaktunterdrückungsverhältnis *n* common-mode rejection ratio (CMRR)
Gleichwelle *f* common wave
Gleichwellenfunk *m* common-frequency radio
Gleichwellenstörungen *fpl* common-channel interference *(mobile RT)*
gleichzeitig simultaneous
  g. Anruf *m* dual seizure
  g. Belegung *f* dual seizure
GMSK (Gaußsche Mindestwertumtastung *f*) Gaussian Minimum Shift Keying
GND (Betriebserde *f*) Signal Ground *(V.24/ RS232C, s. Table VI)*
Golay-Methode *f* Golay method *(alphanumeric and voice signalling method for radio paging, Motorola)*
GOU (Erde o. offener Kreis unsymmetrisch) ground or open unbalanced *(signalling)*
gpm (Gruppen/Minute) groups per minute *(TTY)*
GPS (weltweites Navigationssystem *n*) Global Positioning System *(navigation, sat.)*
GR s. Gestellrahmen *m*
Gradient *m* gradient, rate of change

Gradientenglasfaser 52

Gradientenglasfaser f graded-index fibre *(FO)*
Grenzfrequenz f cut-off frequency, critical frequency
Grenzwellenlänge f cut-off wavelength *(FO)*
Grenzwert m **nach Datenblatt** upper specification limit
Griffblende f handle
Grobschutz m primary protection (circuit)
größere Datenmengen fpl bulk data
Groß-Gemeinschaftsantenne f (GGA) community antenna television system (CATV); Community Authority TV (CATV)
Großmodul n module group
Großplattenspeicher m large-capacity disk storage unit
Großrahmen m rack, 19" rack
großräumiges Personenrufsystem n wide area radio paging *(cellular RT)*
Großraumspeicher m bulk store
Großrechner m host *(computer)*
Grundadressenspeicher m (GAS) base address store
Grundausbau m basic configuration
Grunddämpfung f insertion loss; pass-band loss *or* attenuation *(filter)*; residual attenuation *(FO)*
Grunddatenspeicher m (GRUSPE) basic data store of the DBP
Grundfehler m intrinsic error *(PCM)*
Grundfolge f forcing configuration *(data transmission)*
Grundgeräusch n idle-channel noise *(tel.)*
Grundlänge f fundamental period *(signal)*
Grundleitung f main route
  Digitalsignal-G. (DSGL) digital line path
Grundstücknetz n local area network (LAN)
Gruppe f group; array *(ant.)*
Gruppenkoppler m group switch
Gruppenrahmen m combining fame *(rack)*
Gruppenschalter m (GS) group selector *(fax)*
Gruppensteuerung f group processor;
cluster controller *(equipment cluster)*
gruppentechnischer Begriff m trunking term *(tel. system)*
Gruppenwahl f group hunting
gruppenweise Nummernsuche f group hunting
Gruppensperrerde f group blocking ground
Gruppierung f trunking arrangement *(tel. system)*
GRUSPE s. Grunddatenspeicher m
GRV (gedruckte Rückverdrahtung f) printed backplane *(rack wiring)*
GS (gehender Satz m) outgoing circuit
GS (Gleichstrom m) direct current (DC)
GS-Anschaltung f DC connection
GSD (Gefahr! Sehr Dringend!) Danger! Extremely Urgent!
G-Serie f **der CCITT-Empfehlungen** G-series of CCITT Recommendations *(relates to PCM considerations)*
G-Sicherung (Geräteschutz-Sicherung f) miniature fuse
GSM (Sondergruppe f Mobilfunk) Groupe Special Mobile *(CEPT study group for digital cellular mobile radio, DECT)*
GSTN (allgemeines Fernsprechwählnetz n) General Switched Telephone Network *(ref. CCITT Rec. V.25 bis)*
GS-Zeichen n (geprüfte Sicherheit f) 'safety-tested' mark *(TÜV, HW)*
GT (Gleichstrom-/Gleichspannungstastung f) DC keying
G/T-Verhältnis n (Gewinn/Rauschtemperaturverhältnis n) G/T (gain/noise temperature) ratio *(sat., in dB/K)*
GU (Gabelumschalter m) cradle *or* hook switch *(tel.)*
Gültigkeit f Valid (VAL) *(V.25 bis message)*
Güte f. quality; Q factor *(filter)*
  Dienstg. grade of service
  Betriebsg. grade of service
Gütekriterium n performance index *(reg.)*
Gutquittung f acknowledgement positive

H

HA s. Handapparat *m*
Haftspeicher *m* non-volatile memory; latch
HAG (Hinweisansagegerät *n*) intercept announcement unit
HAK s. Hauptanschlußkennzeichen *n*
halbamtsberechtigt semirestricted *(extension)*
Halbamtsberechtigung *f* indirect exchange access
Halbduplex *n* (HDX) half duplex *(modem)*, two-way alternate
halbgesperrt semirestricted *(extension)*
halbgraphische Symbole *npl* semigraphic symbols *(display)*
Halbklammer *f* single-sided clamp *(rack)*
Haltebereich *m* hold-in *or* locked *or* tracking range *(VCO)*
halten: Leitung *f* **auf "H" h.** clamp the line to "H"
Haltespeicher *m* latch; control memory; hold latch *(tel.sys.)*
Halte- und Entnahmekreis *m* sample and hold circuit *(ADC)*
Hamming-Abstand *m* Hamming distance *(FEC)*, signal distance *(in two binary words of the same length, compared bit by bit, the number of positions having different bits, DIN 44300)*
Hamming-Distanz *f* Hamming distance *(FEC)*
Handapparat *m* (HA) handset *(tel.)*
handelsüblich standard
Handfunke *f* walkie-talkie
Handfunksprechgerät *n* walkie-talkie; handheld cordless telephone
Handgerät *n* handset *(mobile tel.)*
Händlerarbeitsplatz *m* broker's *or* trading facility, station *(ITS)*
Handruf *m* manual calling, manual ringing *(tel.)*
Handsender *m* Keyboard transmitter
Handstecker *m* cable plug
Handtelefon *n* ("Handy") handheld *or* cordless telephone (transceiver) *(RT)*
handvermittelt manual mode, operator-switched
Handvermittelung *f* operator-assisted calls
Hardware *f* (HW) hardware
Hardwareschicht *f* physical layer *(layer 1, OSI RM; FDDI)*

HAs s. Hauptanschluß *m*
Hashing *n* hashing *(binary bit search)*
HAsl s. Hauptanschlußleitung *f*
Hauptanlage *f* primary *or* master station *(PBX)*; primary exchange
Hauptanschluß *m* (HAs) main station, subscriber's main station; network termination point (NTP)
H. für Direktruf *or* **Direktverbindung** (HfD) main station for fixed connections *or* tie lines *(DBP Datex)*
H. im leitungsvermittelten Datendienst (Dx-L-HAs) main station in the circuit-switched data service
H.-Kennzeichen *n* (HAK,HKZ) main station identification (code) *(tel., for non-DDI)*
H.-Kennzeichengabe *f* loop signalling *(SS7 UP)*
H.-Leitung *f* (HAsl) local (exchange) line
Hauptapparat *m* master set, subscriber's main station
Hauptinformation *f* primary information
Hauptkanal *m* forward channel
Hauptleitung *f* concentrator trunk
Hauptrahmen *m* basic frame *(PCM)*
Hauptstelle *f* primary exchange, main station; main *(PBX or centrex facility to which other PBXs are connected)*
Hauptverkehrsstunde *f* (HVStd) busy (busiest) hour *(tel.)*
Hauptvermittlung *f* parent exchange
Hauptvermittlungsstelle *f* (HVSt) main exchange (MX)
Hauptverteiler *m* (HV,HVt) main distribution frame (MDF) *(tel.)*
Hauptverteilergestell *n* (HV,HVT) main distribution frame (MDF) *(tel.)*
Hausanschluß *m* subscriber's line
Hausanschlußkabel *n* drop cable *(CATV)*
hauseigenes Netz *n* domestic area network (DAN) *(video conference etc.)*; in-house *or* private network
Hausnetz *n* in-house *or* private network
Havarie *f* accident, failure, breakdown
Havariefeld *n* emergency control panel
havarieren: einen defekten Verstärker h. replace a defective amplifier
Havarie-Verstärker *m* back-up amplifier

Havarie-Weg m back-up path
H-Bus m bus system in TEMEX line termination *(EIA RS485)*
HCS *(Verkehrswerteinheit)* Hundred Call Seconds *(unit of traffic intensity, = 1/36 Erl)*
HDB3 high-density bipolar *(3-level code, CCITT Rec. G.703, Annex A)*
HDLC (bitorientiertes Übertragungssteuerungsverfahren n) High-level Data Link Control *(synchronous PSDN protocol, ISO 3309, 4335, DIN 66221)*
HD-Mac (hochauflösendes Mac n) high definition MAC *(HDTV standard)*
HDPCM (Hybrid-DPCM f) hybrid DPCM *(HD Mac)*
HDTV s. Hochzeilenfernsehen n
HDX (halbduplex) half duplex *(modem)*
HE s. Höheneinheit f
Heimatdatei f home location register (HLR) *(GSM)*
Heimtelefonanlage f (HTA) domestic telephone system
helligkeitsabhängig intensity-dependent *(FO)*
Helltastung f unblanking *(videotex monitor)*
HEMT (Transistor m mit hoher Elektronenbeweglichkeit) high electron mobility transistor
heranholen call pick-up *(f. tel.)*
herausfallen fall outside *(range)*
herausgezogen remotely located *(HW)*
herausschalten disconnect
Herbeiruf m recall
Hermaphrodit-Kupplung f hermaphrodite or hermaphroditic (sexless) connector
Herrschaft f mastership *(in bus arbitration)*
herstellen: Verbindung hergestellt carried call
Herstellerwartung f für Eigen- und Fremdsysteme third-party maintenance (TPM)
Herunterschalten n switching down; fallback *(modem)*
hervorheben embolden *(videotex monitor)*
HfD s. Hauptanschluß m für Direktruf
HF-dichte Tür f RF-screened door
HF-Verteilungsmatrix f (HVM) RF distribution matrix *(RF transmitter)*
HH-(Hochspannungs-Hochleistungs)-**Sicherung** f high-voltage HRC-type fuse
Hierarchieebene f hierarchical level *(process)*
Hierarchiestufe f: **4. H.** 4th order *(PCM)*
hierarchische Codierung f embedded coding

(PCM speech)
Hilbert-Transformator m Hilbert transformer *(splits VF frequency mixture into 2 part-signals: 1 containing all sine and 1 containing all cosine components of the input signal)*
Hilfsbit n auxiliary bit
Hilfskanal m backward channel
 H. Empfangsdaten Secondary Receive data (SRCV) *(V.24/RS232C, s. Table VI)*
 H. Sendedaten Secondary Transmit data (SXMT) *(V.24/RS232C, s. Table VI)*
hineinhören: in den Kanal h. listen before and while transmitting *(PCM)*
hinterlegen back, mix *(videotex monitor)*
Hinweis m indication; reference
Hinweisansagegerät n (HAG) intercept announcement unit
Hinweisdienst m intercept service
Hinweisgabe f service code *(BT, TTY)*
Hinweismarke f pointer
Hinweiston m intercept tone
H-Kanal m (Breitband-Informationskanal m) high-speed user information channel *(ISDN, H_0 = 384 kb/s, H_{11} = 1.536 Mb/s, H_{12} = 1.92 Mb/s, H_2 = 30 - 40 Mb/s, H_4 = 120 - 140 Mb/s)*
HKZ (Hauptanschluß-Kennzeichen n) main station identification
HKZ-Schnittstelle f user-telephone network non-DDI interface for PBX
Hochfrequenzabriegelung f RF block
Hochfrequenz-Verteilungsmatrix f (HVM) RF distribution matrix *(RF transmitter)*
Hochgeschwindigkeitsstation f high-capacity station *(LAN)*
hochgespannter Strom m current under high tension
hochlegen: ein Signal h. set a signal to High
hochohmig highly resistive; high-resistance; high-impedance
hochratig high-speed *(link)*
 h. Modulation f high-bit-rate modulation
höchstwertiges Bit n most significant bit (MSB)
hochtasten key on *(transmitter)*
Hochzeilenfernsehen n (HDTV) high definition TV *(Eu-95, 1250 lines, aspect ratio 16:9, progressive 1:1 scanning)*
Hohe Übertragungsgeschwindigkeit Einschalten Data Signalling Rate selector *(V.24, RS232C, s. Table VI)*
Höheneinheit f (HE) rack unit (U) *(rack, 1 U = 1 3/4")*
homogen belegte Apertur f uniformly illu-

minated aperture *(sat. antenna)*
hörbares Signal *n* audible signal, sound signal
Hörbarkeit *f* audibility, intelligibility *(tel.)*
Hörbeziehung *f* listening relationship *(tel.)*
Hörer *m* handset; listener *(test instr.)*
  H. anhängen, auflegen replace the handset
  Ruhezustand des H. listener idle state (LIDS) *(tel.)*
Hörkapsel *f* receiver capsule, earphone *(tel.)*
Hörmuschel *f* earpiece
Hörtöne *mpl* audible tones; call progress tones *(tel.)*
Hörzeichentoleranz *f* audible signal tolerance
HPA (Hochleistungsverstärker *m*) high power amplifier *(sat.)*
HTA (Heimtelefonanlage *f*) domestic telephone system
Hub *m* deviation *(FM)*; shift *(FSK,PSK)*; range, rise, excursion *(voltage,signal)*; stroke, travel, lift *(mech.)*;

swing *(measurement, logic)*; sweep *(CRO)*; width *(channel)*
Huffmann-Code *m*: **modifizierter H.** modified Huffmann code *(a redundancy-reducing source encoding method, fax)*
HUL (Querleitungsbündel *n* (Ql)) high-usage line *(network)*
Hülse *f* ferrule *(cable)*
HV (Hauptverteiler *m*) main distribution frame (MDF)
HVM s. Hochfrequenz-Verteilungsmatrix *f*
HVSt (Hauptvermittlungsstelle *f*) main exchange
HVStd (Hauptverkehrsstunde *f*) busy hour
HVt (Hauptverteiler *m*) main distribution frame (MDF)
HW (Hardware *f*) hardware
HX (Halbduplex *n*) half duplex *(modem)*
Hybrid-DPCM *f* hybrid DPCM (HDPCM) *(HD Mac)*
Hybridstation *f* combined station, balanced station
Hyperband *n* (ESB) cable TV band *(302-446 MHz, 12 MHz channel spacing, for D2-MAC signal, DBP)*

I

IA (Abfrage f von Internrufen) answering internal calls
IA (Instandsetzungsauftrag m) repair order
IA (konzentrierte Abfrage f von Internrufen) concurrent answering of internal calls
IAOG (Internationale Verwaltungsgruppe f von Betreibern im Versorgungsbereich) International Administrative management domain Operators Group (of PTTs to administer E-mail protocol X.400)
Iasnet Soviet packet-switched X.25 network (DNIC 2501)
iAWD (integrierte automatische Wähleinrichtung f für Datenübertragung) integrated automatic dialling facility
IA5 (internationales (Telegraphen-) Alphabet n Nr.5) International Alphabet No.5
IBC (integrierte Breitbandkommunikation f) Integrated Broadband Communications (RACE project)
IBC (Internationale Rundfunk-Konvention f) International Broadcasting Convention
IBFN (integriertes Breitbandfernmeldenetz n) integrated broadband telecommunication network of the DBP (FO)
IBS s. Inbetriebsetzung f
IBS (Intelsat-Geschäftsdienst m) Intelsat Business Service (to IESS 309)
IBU (Welt-Rundfunkunion f) International Broadcasting Union
ICM (Internverkehrvielfach n) internal communication matrix
ICS (ISDN-Kommunikationssystem n) ISDN communication system (up to 70 ports)
IDN (integriertes Text- und Datennetz n) Integrated Digital Network (without digital subscriber connection)
IDTF (diskrete Fourier-Rücktransformation f) inverse discrete Fourier transform
IEC (Internationale Elektrotechnische Kommission f) International Electrotechnical Commission
IEEE (Verband m der Elektroingenieure und -techniker) Institute of Electrical and Electronic Engineers (US network standards IEEE 802.x)
IFRB (Internationaler Ausschuß m für Frequenzregistrierung) International Frequency Registration Board
IFU (Internationale Fernmeldeunion f) International Telecommunications Union (ITU)
Igelprint f experimental PCB
IH (Eigenanwendung f) In-House application (RDS)
I+K-Geräte (Informations- und Kommunikationsgeräte npl) information and communications equipment
I-Kanal m in-phase channel (FO, homodyne receiver)
IKZ s. Impulskennzeichen n
IKZ-Schnittstelle f user-telephone network interface for PBX pulse dialling
ILC (ISDN-Übertragungssteuerung f) ISDN link controller
ILD s. Injektionslaser m
IM (unabhängige Wartung f) independent maintenance
IMA (Intermodulationsabstand m) intermodulation ratio
Imband-Signalisierung f in-band signalling; in-slot signalling
IM/DD (Intensitätsmodulation f mit Direktdetektion) intensity modulation with direct detection (FO)
Impulsfolge f pulse train
Impulskennzeichen n (IKZ) pulse signal (tel., for DDI)
Impulslaufzeit f pulse time delay (cable)
Schleifen-I. loop delay (circuit)
Impulsmuster n bit pattern
Impulsnebensprechen n intersymbol interference (FO)
Impulsreihe f pulse train
Impulsserie f pulse train
Impulsstoß m impulse hit (tel.)
Impulswahl f decimal pulsing, pulse dialling
Impulswählverfahren n (IWV) pulse dialling or loop (disconnect) dialling (LD) method (tel.)
Impulsweiche f separating filter
Impulszittern n jitter
Impulszug m pulse train
Imvierernahnebensprechdämpfung f in-quad near-end crosstalk attenuation

Imvierernebensprechen n in-quad or intra-quad crosstalk
IM3 (Intermodulationspegel m 3. Ordnung) 3rd-order intermodulation product *(CT1, in dBm)*
IN (Transitknoten m) intermediate node *(PCM data)*
inaktivieren deactivate, take off-line; disable
Inband inband
Inbetriebnahme f commissioning *(networks)*; putting into service *(equipment)*; cutover *(initial switch-on)*
Inbetriebnahmesystem n hardware check system
Inbetriebsetzung f (IBS) commissioning
INC (ankommender Ruf m) INcoming Call *(V.25 bis)*
index-sequentiell indexed sequential
INDI-VSt (VSt für INformation und DIalogdienste) videotex switching centre for information and interactive services
Industriefernsehen n business television (BTV) *(US)*; closed-circuit television (CCTV)
Informatik f informatics, information technology (IT), information science
Informatiker m information specialist or technologist
Informationen fpl information items; signals
Informationsanbieter m information provider (IP) *(videotex)*
Informationsblock m information frame *(ISDN)*
Informationsdienstmerkmal n information-related service attribute
Informationseinheit f protocol data unit (PDU) *(videotex; ISO, a data packet exchanged between two network entities)*
Informationskanal m user information channel
Informationstechnik f information technology (IT), informatics
Inforuf m radio paging information service *(DBP, one-way service)*
Ingenieurmodell n **Lebensdauerprüfung** engineering model - life (test) (EM-L) *(ESA)*
Inhalt m contents *(memory, register)*
inhaltsadressierbarer Speicher m content-addressable memory (CAM)
Injektionslaser m (-diode f) injection laser diode (ILD) *(FO)*
INMARSAT (Internationale Seefunk-Satelliten-Organisation f) International Maritime Satellite Organisation
Innenübertragung f local call; connecting path, circuit
Innenverbindungskabel n exchange wiring
Innenweiche f diplexer
Inneramtssignalisierung f intra-exchange signalling *(tel.)*
Inselamtsbetrieb m isolated-exchange operation *(tel., fault mode)*
Inselnetz n subnetwork, isolated network; separate system
Instandsetzungsauftrag m (IA) repair order
Instanz f entity
instanzieren particularize *(e.g. a logic state with 'H' or 'L')*
Integrierintervall n integrating period
integriert:
  i. automatische Wähleinrichtung f **für Datenübertragung** (iAWD) integrated automatic dialling facility
  i. Breitbandfernmeldenetz n (IBFN) integrated wideband telephone network of the DBP *(FO)*
  i. Breitbandkommunikation f Integrated Broadband Communications (IBC)
  i. Modem m built-in modem *(ISDX)*
  i. optische Schaltung f integrated optical circuit (IOC)
  i. Text- und Datennetz n Integrated Digital Network (IDN) *(telephony, text and data network with access by analog means, BT definition, X.21)*
INTELSAT (Internationale Gesellschaft f für den Betrieb von Nachrichtensatelliten) International Telecommunications Satellite Organisation
Intensitätsmodulation f (IM) intensity modulation *(FO)*
  I. mit Direktdetektion intensity modulation with direct detection (IM/DD) *(FO)*
Interferenzfestigkeit f interference immunity *(FO, sat., in dB)*
Intermodendispersion f multimode dispersion *(FO)*
Intermodulationsabstand m (IMA) intermodulation ratio
international:
  I. Ausschuß m **für Frequenzregistrierung** International Frequency Registration Board (IFRB)
  I. Elektrotechnische Kommission f International Electrotechnical Commission (IEC)
  i. Kopfamt n international gateway exchange
  I. Normenentwurf m Draft International

Standard (DIS) *(FTZ, ISO)*
I. Organisation *f* **für Normung** International Organisation for Standardisation (ISO)
i. (Telegraphen-) Alphabet *n* International Alphabet (IA)
I. Vermittlungsamt *n* International Switching Centre (ISC) *(international gateway)*
internes Umschalten *n* intracell handoff *(mobile RT)*
Internsatz *m* intra-exchange circuit
Internverkehrvielfach *n* internal communication matrix (ICM)
interpersonelle Mitteilungen *fpl* interpersonal messages (IPM)
Interphonanlage *f* interphone, door intercom
Intritt-fallen *n* pulling into lock
INV (Ungültigkeit *f*) INValid *(V.25 bis)*
IOC (Modul *n* der Auflösung) index of cooperation *(fax)*
IOC s. integrierte optische Schaltung *f*
IOT (Prüfung *f* im Orbit) in-orbit test *(sat., prior to commissioning)*
IP (Informationsanbieter *m*) information provider *(videotex)*
IPFD (Eingangsleistungsflußdichte *f*) input power flux density *(sat.)*
IPM (interpersonelle Mitteilungen *fpl*) interpersonal messages
IPM-Dienst *m* IPM service *(CCITT Rec. X.400)*
IPM-Übermittlungsdienst *m* IPM transfer service *(CCITT Rec. X.400, P2; level 7 OSI model)*
IRT (Institut *n* für Rundfunktechnik) Institute for Radio Engineering *(FRG)*
IS (internationale Norm *f*) International Standard *(ISO)*
ISC (Internationales Vermittlungsamt *n*) International Switching Centre *(international gateway)*
ISDN (diensteintegrierendes Digitalnetz *n*) Integrated Services Digital Network *(IDN with access by digital means, BT definition)*
ISDN-Anwenderteil *m* ISDN user part (ISDN UP) *(SS7, CCITT Q.761...764)*
ISDN-Bilddienste *mpl* ISDN image transmission

ISDN-Echolöscher *m* ISDN echo canceller
ISDN-Kommunikationssystem *n* ISDN communication system (ICS)
ISDN-Nebenstellenanlage *f* ISDN PBX (ISDX, ISPBX)
ISDN-Übertragungssteuerung *f* ISDN link controller (ILC)
ISDN-UP (ISDN-Anwenderteil *m*) ISDN user part *(SS7, CCITT Q.761 ...764)*
ISDX (ISDN-Nebenstellenanlage *f*) ISDN PBX
I-Serie *f* **der CCITT-Empfehlungen** I series of CCITT Recommendations *(relates to ISDN, s. Table III)*
ISM (Betriebsüberwachung *f*) in-service monitoring
ISO (Internationale Organisation *f* für Normung) International Organisation for Standardisation
ISO8877 ISO standard for ISDN connector
isochron isochronous *(real-time)*
Isolation *f* insulation; isolation, separation
Kanal-I. interchannel signal/crosstalk ratio
Isolationsabstand *m* signal/crosstalk ratio *(switching matrix, in dB)*
Isolationsspannung *f* rated working voltage *(FO)*
ISPBX (Telekommunikationsanlage *f*) ISDN PBX
Ist-Aufnahme *f* actual status
ISUP s. ISDN-Anwenderteil *m*
IT (Informationstechnik *f*) information technology
Iterationsregister *n* successive approximation register (SAR)
ITG (Informationstechnische Gesellschaft *f* im VDE) communications engineering standards body *(formerly NTG)*
ITU (Internationale Fernmeldeunion *f* (IFU)) International Telecommunication Union
IuK (Information und Kommunikation *f*) information and communications
IuK-Technik *f* information and communications technology
IWS (Übergangsdienst *m*) interworking service
IWV (Impulswählverfahren *n*) pulse dialling *or* loop (disconnect) dialling (LD) method

J

J.17 audio preemphasis for C MAC/packet and D2 MAC/packet *(CCITT Rec. J.17)*
Jedermannfunk *m (11-Meter-Band)* Citizen's Band (CB) *(27 MHz communication channel)*
Jitterfestigkeit *f* jitter tolerance *(PCM)*
JPL Jet Propulsion Laboratories *(Cal., US)*

K

KA s. Kabelabschluß *m*
KA (Knotenamt *n*) main center office *(US)*
KAA (konzentrierte Amtsabfrage *f*) concurrent (exchange line) answering
Ka-Band *n* Ka band *(sat., 20 - 30 GHz)*
Kabelabschluß *m* (KA) cable (installation) termination
Kabelanlage *f* cable plant; cable system, cable network
Kabelbrunnen *m* jointing manhole, cable pit
Kabelbuchse *f* cable bush
Kabeldämpfung *f* cable attenuation, cable loss
 K. in Km kilometric cable attenuation
Kabeldurchführung *f* cable entrance, cable bushing
Kabel-Endschrank *m* cable terminal cabinet
Kabelendverschluß *m* cable termination
Kabelfernsehen *n* cable television (CATV, CTV)
Kabelform *f* formboard *(for cable forming)*
Kabelformbrett *n* formboard *(for cable forming)*
Kabelformgarn *n* lacing cord, thread or string
Kabelführungsplan *m* cabling diagram
Kabelkasten *m* cable terminating box
Kabel(lage)plan *m* cable layout plan
Kabellaufzeit *f* cable delay
Kabelmeßgerät *n* cable tester
Kabelraster *n* channel spacing *(cable TV, 7/12 MHz)*
Kabelrost *m* cable runway or trough
Kabelschacht *m* manhole, cable runway
Kabelschelle *f* cable clamp
Kabelschrank *m* cable (terminal) cabinet
Kabelschuh *m* cable terminal or lug
Kabelseite *f* line side
Kabeltrasse *f* cable route
Kabelverbinder *m* adapter, connector, coupler
Kabelverbindung *f* joint; route
Kabelverzweiger *m* (KVZ) cable distributor; cross connection point (CCP)
Kalman-Filter *n* Kalman filter *(state predictor)*
Kammerkabel *n* slotted-core cable *(FO)*
Kampagne *f* field trip, workshop
Kanal *m* channel, port

Kanalabstand *m* channel spacing
Kanalauslastung *f* channel usage *(factor)*
Kanalbelegungsdichte *f* channel loading density
Kanalbündel *n* channel block *(data)*; trunked channels *(PMR)*
kanalgebunden channel-associated
 k. Signalisierung *f* common channel signalling (CCS)
Kanalhub *m* channel width, channel frequency deviation *(sat.)*
Kanalisolation *f* interchannel signal/crosstalk ratio
Kanallücke *f* interchannel gap
Kanalnebensprechen *n* interchannel crosstalk
Kanalraster *n* channel separation (TV); channel spacing
Kanalschaltung *f* (KS) channel switching *(PCM)*
Kanalstörung *f* co-channel interference
Kanalwechsel *m* handover *(cellular RT)*
Kanalweiche *f* channel branching filter
Kanal-Zeitlage *f* time-slot pattern
K-Anlage (Kommunikationsanlage *f*) digital PBX
Karenzzeit *f* call acceptance waiting time
Kartenbaugruppe *f* (KBG) PCB module
Kartentelefon *n* (KartTel) phonecard phone *(BT)*
KartTel s. Kartentelefon *n*
Kassenterminal *n* point of sale (POS) terminal *(telebanking)*
katastrophenberechtigt with emergency priority
Kathodenstrahl-Oszillograph *m* or **-Oszilloskop** *n* (KO) cathode ray oscilloscope (CRO)
K.Bel. s. Keine Belegung *f*
K-Bereich *m* short-wave band
KBG s. Kartenbaugruppe *f*
KE (Konzentratoreinheit *f*) concentrator *(VSAT user interface multiplexer)*
Keine Belegung *f* (K.Bel.) no loop closure on a/b wires
 k. Empfangsbereitschaft *f* receive not ready (rnr) *(videotex)*
Kelch *m* barrel *(crimp contact)*
Kennblatt *n* data sheet

Kenndaten *npl* system specification
Kennfeld *n* set of curves
Kennfrequenz *f* code frequency *(for ones and zeroes, TTY)*; assigned frequency; characteristic frequency
Kennhülse *f* ferrule *(cable)*
Kennlinienknick *m* kink
Kennschritt *m* parity check bit *(TC)*
Kennummer *f*: **persönliche K.** personal identification number (PIN) *(electronic banking)*
Kennung *f* identification code *(message header)*; selection code *(SS7 MTP)*
Kennungsbit *n* code bit *(TC)*
Kennungsgeber *m* answerback unit *(telex)*
Kennwort *n* keyword; password; alignment signal *(data transmission)*
Kennzahl *f* code number
Kennzeichen *n* switching signals *(tel.)*; signalling code *(PCM)*; signal *(SS7)*; identification (code); flag
Kennzeichenabschnitt *m* signalling data link
Kennzeicheninformation *f* signalling data *(PCM)*
Kennzeichenkanal *m* signalling channel
Kennzeichennachricht *f* signalling message *(SS7)*
Kennzeichenumsetzer *m* (KZU) signalling converter *(tel. signalling)*
Kennzeichenwort *n* signalling time slot
Kennzeichnung *f* flag *(SW)*; identification, marking
Kanal-K. channel coding *(GSM)*
Kennziffer *f* identification code *(exch.)*
Kennzustand *m* significant condition *or* state *(TTY)*
Kettengespräch *n* automatic sequence call
Kettenverstärker *m* distributed amplifier *(LNA)*; transmission line amplifier *(tel.)*
Kettung *f* chaining *(of messages)*
KF (Koppelfeld *n*) switching network
KG (Koppelgruppe *f*) switching unit
KGABST (Koppelgruppen-Steuerteile *npl* für Koppelgruppen AB) control units for switching units AB
KI (künstliche Intelligenz *f*) artificial intelligence (AI)
kilometrische Kabeldämpfung *f* kilometric cable attenuation
kippen switch, change state *(flip flop)*; trigger; pull out of synchronism
Kippsicherheit *f* stability
Kippverstärker *m* sweep amplifier *(CRO)*
Kippwahl *f* sweep range *(CRO)*

Klammer *f* double-sided clamp *(rack)*
Klasse *f* line category
Kleinstation *f* very small aperture terminal (VSAT), micro earth station (MES) *(Ku band)*
Kleinzelle *f* microcell *(cellular RT)*
Klemmenbaustein *m* terminal module
Klemmenbrücke *f* terminal link
Klemmenkasten *m* terminal box
Klemmenleiste *f* terminal strip
Klingelstörer *m* nuisance caller *(tel.)*
Klingelzeichen *n* bell signal
Klinkenfeld *n* jack panel, jackfield *(panel)*
Klinkenstecker *m* phone plug, jack plug
Klirrdämpfung *f* harmonic ratio
Klirrfaktor *m* total harmonic distortion (THD); distortion factor *(voice channel)*
Klirrgeräusch *n* intermodulation noise
Klirrproduktion *f* (generation of) harmonics *(EMC)*
Klirrverzerrung *f* harmonic distortion
Knacken *n* clicking *(voice channel)*
Knackschutz *m* click suppressor
Knoten *m* junction *(network)*
Knotenamt *n* (KA) main center office *(US)*
Knoteneinrichtung *f* nodal equipment
Knotennetz *n* multipoint network
Knotenpunkt *m* crosspoint *(passive signal matrix)*
Knotenstation *f* concentrator *(TC)*
Knotenvermittlung *f* (KnV) tandem switching
Knotenvermittlungsstelle *f* (KVSt) nodal switching centre; regional exchange (RX); toll centre *(DBP mobile radio)*
KnV (Knotenvermittlung *f*) tandem switching
KO s. Kathodenstrahl-Oszillograph *m*
kohärente Phasenumtastung *f* coherent phase shift keying (CPSK)
Kollisionsauflösung *f* collision resolution *(access control)*
Kollisionserkennung *f* collision detect (CD) *(PCM data)*
kollisionsfreier Vielfachzugriff *m* conflict-free multiaccess (CFMA) *(sat.)*
Kombinationsdiversität *f* combining diversity
kombiniertes S-Band *n* unified S-band (USB) *(sat.)*
Kombiverschraubung *f* screw assembly *(cable couplings)*
komfortabel user-friendly
Komfortabilität *f* comfort level
Komfortmerkmal *n* added feature *(tel.)*
Komforttelefon *n* (K.-Tel.) feature telephone; added-feature telephone

Komfortzusatz m convenience attachment (tel.)
kommend incoming (call)
Kommunikationsanlage f (K-Anlage) digital PBX
Kommunikationsprotokoll n gateway protocol (international vtx, e.g. EHKP for FRG, Prestel for GB, Teletel for FR)
Kommunikationsrechner m (KR) gateway computer (vtx)
Kommunikationssteuerungsschicht f session layer (layer 5, OSI 7-layer reference model)
K.-Dienst m session service (SS)
Kommunikationszugriffmethode f communication access method
Kompandergesetz n companding or encoding law
kompandierte FM f companded FM (CFM) (sat.)
Kondensator m capacitor
  belasteter K. RC smoothing circuit
konfektionierte Leitung f cable assembly
Konferenzbrücke f conference bridge (tel.)
Konferenzführer m controller, initiator, chairman (tel.)
Konferenzsatz m conference circuit
Konferenzschaltungs-Zugangssteuerung f conferencing access controller (CAC)
Konferenzteilnehmer m conferee, party (tel.)
Konfetti n chad (PT)
Konflikt m contention (bus access)
Konformitätserklärung f statement of compliance
Konformitätsprüfung f conformance testing
Konkurrenzbetrieb m contention mode
Konstanz f stability (frequency)
Konstruktionsteil n structural part
Konsumelektronik f consumer electronics
kontaktlose Chipkarten-Schnittstelle f contactless chip card interface (CCI) (C2 card, ISO 7816)
kontinuierliche Phasen-Frequenzumtastung f continuous phase differential FSK (CPDFSK)
kontinuierliche Phasenmodulation f continuous phase modulation (CPM)
Kontrolllampe f pilot lamp, warning lamp
Kontrollbitgenerator m check bit generator
Kontrollschritt m check bit (TC)
Kontrollsuchlauf m check search
Konverter m:
  rauscharmer K. low noise converter (LNC) (sat.)
Konzentrator m concentrator; multiplexer

K.-Einheit f concentrator (VSAT user interface multiplexer)
mittlerer K. (MKT) medium-sized concentrator
konzentrierte Abfrage f von Internrufen (IA) concurrent answering of internal calls (PBX)
Koordinatenschalter m crossbar switch
Koordinatenschalteramt n crossbar (selector) exchange (XB) (analog)
K., unsymmetrische Zeichengabe crossbar exchange, unbalanced signalling (XBU)
Koordinatenstecker m matrix plug (signal distributor)
Koordinatenwähler m crossbar switch
Koordinationszähler m semaphore or semaphore counter
Kopfamt m: **internationales K.** international gateway exchange or centre
Kopfstation f head station (cable TV)
Kopfstelle f head station (cable TV)
Kopfteil m overhead (TDM)
Koppelanordnung f switching network (tel. sys.)
Koppelbaustein m switching module
Koppeleinrichtung f switching network
  K. für Mehrfachnutzung multi-role switch (MRS)
Koppelfeld n (KF) switching network or stage; switching array, matrix
  rechnergestütztes K. digital cross connect (DCC)
Koppelfeldscheibe f matrix plane (ATM)
Koppelgruppe f (KG) switching unit (tel.)
Koppelgruppen-Steuerteile npl für **Koppelgruppen AB** (KGABST) control units for switching units AB
Koppelnavigation f dead-reckoning navigation, compound navigation
Koppelnetz n switching network
Koppelortung f (EVA) compound navigation system (updated by RDS)
Koppelpunkt m crosspoint (passive signal matrix, crosspoint matrix); switching element, switching point (active signal matrix)
Koppelscheibe f matrix plane (ATM node)
Koppelstelle f connecting point, switching point, interface (PBX/exch. line)
Koppelvielfachreihen C-Steuerteile npl (KVRCST) switching matrix row C control units
Kopplung f: **Rechner-K.** computer link
Kopplungsausgleich m balancing (cable)
Kopplungsgrad m transmission coefficient (FO); coupling coefficient, degree of

coupling
Kopplungswiderstand *m* transfer impedance *(cable)*
Korrelationszähler *m* (KOR) correlation counter (COR)
korrespondieren communicate *(computers)*
Kostenstelle *f* cost centre
KR s. Kommunikationsrechner *m*
Kreditverfahren *n* credit procedure *(PCM data block transmission)*
Kreisfrequenz *f* angular frequency
Kreuzglied *n* lattice filter *(digital audio)*
Kreuzkabel *n* modem eliminator *(direct DTE-DTE connection)*
Kreuzklemme *f* four-wire connector
Kreuzpolarisationsentkopplung *f* cross polarisation discrimination (XPD) *(sat.)*
Kreuzschiene *f* (KS) crossbar *(video matrix)*
Kreuzschienenverteiler *m* crossbar distributor, matrix *(audio, video)*; matrix distribution panel
Kreuzschienenwähler *m* crossbar selector
KRN s. Kurzrufnummer *f*
KS (Kanalschaltung *f*) channel switching *(PCM)*
KS ("kein Signal") "no signal" signal
KS s. Kreuzschiene *f*
K.-Tel. (Komforttelefon *n*) feature telephone; added-feature telephone
Ku-Band *n* Ku band *(11/14 GHz down-/uplink, sat.)*
Kühlflansch *m* component case *(semiconductor)*
Kühlkörper *m* heat sink *(semiconductor)*
kundenspezifisches Anwenderprogramm *n* customized user program
künstliche Intelligenz *f* (KI) artificial intelligence (AI)
Kunststofflichtwellenleiter *m* (KWL) all-plastic fibre *(FO)*
Kurvenform *f* waveshape *(of a signal)*
Kurvenschar *f* family of curves
Kurzdistanz *f* limited distance *(modem)*
Kurzrufnummer *f* (KRN) abbreviated directory number *(tel.)*
kurzschlußbehaftet affected by a short (circuit)
Kürzung *f* clipping *(of talkspurts) (PCM speech, packet switching)*
 K. von Sprachblockanfängen front-end clipping (FEC) *(packet switching)*
Kurzwahl *f* (KW) abbreviated address *(f. tel.)*; compressed or abbreviated dialling, shortcode dialling *(f. tel.)*
Kurzwahlplatz *m* shortcode dialling position *(f. tel.)*
Kurzwegdurchschaltung *f* short-path switching
kurzzeitig short-time; transient *(peaks)*
 k. Geräusch *n* impulsive noise, clicks
KVRCST s. Koppelvielfachreihen C-Steuerteile *npl*
KVSt (Knotenvermittlungsstelle *f*) toll centre *(DBP mobile radio)*;
KVSt (Knotenvermittlungsstelle *f*) nodal exchange
KVZ (Kabelverzweiger *m*) cable distributor
KW s. Kurzwahl *f*
KWL s. Kunststofflichtwellenleiter *m*
KZU (Kennzeichenumsetzer *m*) signalling converter

L

Lage f position; disposition, layout; topology (IC); layer (winding)
  hohe Frequenzl. high frequency
  NF-L. VF level
  Raumlagenvielfach n space division multiplex (SDM); space switch (ESS)
  Zeitl. time slot
Lagebeziehung f topology (IC)
LAK (Leitungsanpassung f für das Koppelnetz) line termination for the switching network (VBN)
Lampenfeld n lamp array
Lampenkontrolle f lamp test
LAN (Ortsnetz n (ON)) local area network
Landeskennzahl f national code, country code
Landfunkdienst m land (mobile) radio service
  satellitengestüzter L. land mobile satellite service (LMSS)
Länge f: **Übertragungs-L.** distance, transmission distance
Längenindikator m length indicator (LI) (SS7)
längenmoduliert width modulated (pulse)
Langrufnummer f directory number, normal call number, regular directory number (f. tel.)
langsame störsichere Logik f high noise immunity logic (HNIL)
Längsholm m longitudinal support
Längsprüfung f longitudinal redundancy check (LRC)
Längsspannungsbeeinflussung f longitudinal induced voltage (tel.)
Langstreckennetz(werk) n wide area network (WAN)
Längswiderstand m (LW) series resistance
Langzeitverbindung f nailed connection (NC) (auxiliary service channel, ISDN)
LAP (Übertragungssteuerungsverfahren n, Leitungszugangsverfahren n) link access procedure (ISDN)
  LAPB (LAP für gleichberechtigten Spontanbetrieb) LAP for balanced mode (X.25 LAP, ISO 6256, DIN 66222 Part 1)
  LAPD (LAP für ISDN-D-Kanal) LAP for ISDN D channel (X.32, X.75 LAP, CCITT Rec. I.440,441, FTZ 1R6D)
  LAPM (LAP für Modem-Fehlerüberwachung) LAP for modem error control (based on CCITT LAPD, V.42, includes MNP)
Laserabschaltung f (LSA) laser shutdown (FO)
laseraktualisierbare Speicherkarte f (Recallcard) Recallcard (BT, with WORM drive)
Laserplatte f compact disk (CD)
Laserstartsignal n laser turn-on signal (FO)
Lastabwehr f overload protection; flow control (traffic)
Lastenheft n requirement specifications or catalog(ue)
Lastleitwert m load conductance (FO)
Lastrückschaltung f change-back of traffic (after link restoration)
Lastsprung m step load change
Lastteilung f load sharing
Lastübernahme f rerouting of traffic
Latenzzeit f latency (DP, includes waiting time)
Lauf m run; travel
laufend:
  l. Digitalsumme f running digital sum (RDS)
  l. Gespräch n call in progress
  l. Mehrheitsentscheidung f running majority vote
Laufnummer f sequence number (SS7)
Laufwerk n drive (unit)
Laufzeit f transit time, propagation time (of packets)
Laufzeitverzerrung f delay distortion, envelope distortion; delay variation with frequency (fax, in microsec.)
Lautform f phoneme
Lauthöreinrichtung f loudspeaker facility (tel.)
Lauthören n open or direct listening; loudspeaker monitoring (f. tel.)
Lauthörtaste f open or direct listening key (f. tel.)
Lautsprechen n loudspeaking (f. tel.)
LE (Leitungsempfänger m) line terminating equipment or unit (LTU)
LE (Leitungsendeinrichtung f) line termi-

Lebensdauer 68

nating equipment *or* unit (LTU)
Lebensdauer *f* service life *(of a component)*
lebensdauerbeeinflußt deteriorating
Lebenslauf *m* history *(of an item)*
Leckleitung *f:* **Übermittlung über L.** leaky feeder signal transmission *(mobile RT)*
Leckwelle *f* leaky *or* tunnelling mode *(FO)*; leaky wave *(cables)*
Leerbit *n* dummy bit
Leerblock *m* dummy cell *(ATM)*
Leergriff *m* ineffective access
leerlaufende Leitung *f* open-ended line
Leerlaufspannung *f* open-circuit voltage
Leerruf *m* (LR) idle call; no-operation call *(cellular mobile RT)*
Leertelegramm *n* substitute message *(transmission link)*
Leerzählen *n* emptying the counter
Leerzelle *f* dummy cell *(ATM)*
Leistung *f* power; output, capacity, performance, efficiency
Leistungsaufnahme *f* power consumption *or* rating *(in W)*
Leistungsbeschreibung *f* statement of services provided *(tender)*
Leistungsdichtespektrum *n* power density spectrum *(sat.)*
Leistungsfähigkeit *f* traffic capacity *(tel. sys.)*
Leistungsmaß *n* performance criterion
Leistungsmerkmal *n* (LM) service feature; facility, user facility *(tel.)*;
   L. in Anspruch nehmen access a facility
Leistungspegelabstand *m* power level difference
Leistungsverzeichnis *n* (LV) tender specifications
Leistungszahl *f:* **effektive L.** gain/noise temperature ratio (G/T) *(sat.)*
leiten route *(signalling)*
Leiterabgang *m* outgoing conductor section *(membrane keypad)*
Leitererdspannung *f* conductor-to-earth voltage
leitergebunden line connected *(network)*
Leiterplatte *f* printed circuit board (PCB)
Leiterprüfung *f* continuity test *(of wires)*
Leitfrequenzsteuerung *f* primary frequency control
Leitimpuls *m* master pulse, strobe (pulse)
Leitkleber *m* conductive adhesive
Leitprogramm *n* main program
Leitseite *f* leading *or* routing page *(vtx.)*
Leitstation *f* control station
Leitstelle *f* (LSt) master station *(TEMEX)*

Leitsteuerung *f* primary *(function of communication control)*
Leitsteuerungsstation *f* primary station (HDLC)
Leitsystem *n* supervisory control system; management system
Leitung *f* bus *(one or more conductors used as common link between two or more circuits, IEEE)*; highway *(PCM)*; line *(circuit between subscriber's telephone and exchange)*, circuit; trunk *(one communication channel between 2 ranks of switching equipment in the same exchange, or between two exchanges)*
   abgeschaltete L. dead line
   betriebsführende L. controlling line
   gestörte L. faulty line
   verkabelte L. cable line
Leitungsabschluß *m* line termination (LT)
   teilnehmerseitiger L. network termination (NT)
   vermittlungsseitiger L. exchange termination (ET)
Leitungsanpassung *f* matching network; line termination (LT) *(ISDN)*
   L. für das Koppelnetz (LAK) line termination for the switching network *(VBN)*
Leitungsanschlußeinheit *f* line jack unit (LJU) *(BS 6506 for PBX, corresponds to DBP TAE)*
Leitungsanschlußkarte *f* (LAK) line card *(VBN, 140 Mb/s)*
Leitungsanschlußmodul *n* line access module (LA)
Leitungsausfall *m* circuit outage
Leitungscode *m* line code *(transmission, 4B3T, 2B1Q)*
Leitungsdämpfung *f* line loss, line attenuation;
   standard cable equivalent *(in Standard Cable Miles)*
Leitungsempfänger *m* (LE) line terminating equipment *or* unit (LTU)
Leitungsendeinrichtung *f* (LE) line termination (LT) *(ISDN)*;
   line terminating equipment *or* unit (LTU)
Leitungsendgerät *n* line terminating unit (LTU)
Leitungsführung *f* cable route
leitungsgebunden conducted *(interference)*, line conducted *(signal)*
leitungskodiert line coded *(data stream)*
Leitungsmuster *n* conductor pattern *(PCB)*
Leitungsnachbildung *f* equivalent line,

line balance, artificial line; line building-out network
Leitungsnetz n loop plant
Leitungsplan m wiring diagram
Leitungsschnittstelle f line interface (ISDN)
Leitungsseite f track side (PCB)
Leitungssicherung f line error control (sat.)
Leitungsstörung f line hit (PCM)
Leitungstreiber m line driver
Leitungsumschaltung f rerouting
leitungsvermittelt circuit switched
 l. **Datennetz** n (Datex-L,Dx-L) circuit switched data exchange (network)
 l. **öffentliches Datennetz** n circuit-switched public data network (CSPDN)
Leitungsverstärker m line amplifier (sat.)
Leitungswähler m (LW) line selector (tel.)
Leitungszeichengabe f: externe L. interexchange signalling
Leitungszug m conductor or wiring run
Leitungszugangsverfahren n link access procedure (LAP) (ISDN)
Leitungszugname m line designation
Leitvermittlungsstelle f routing centre
Leitweg m route
Leitwegführung f routing
Leitweglenkung f automatic alternate routing; routing (SS7)
Leitwegzuteilung f route allocation (tel.)
Leitzentrale f service centre (videotex); communication controller (remote data transmission)
Leitziffer f routing digit
Letztquerweg m (LQW) final high-usage route
Letztweg m (LW) last-choice route
Leuchtdichte f luminous density, luminance (FO, in cd/m²)
Leuchtschalter m illuminated switch
LI (Längenindikator m) length indicator (SS7)
Lichtempfänger m light sensor (FO)
Lichtleiteranschluß m fibre-optic link (FO)
Lichtleiterbus m fibre-optics bus (FO)
Lichtleitung f light transmission (FO)
Lichtstärke f light intensity, emissivity (FO, in cd)
Lichtwellenleiter m (LWL) optical waveguide (OWG) (FO)
Lichtzeicheneinrichtung f (LZE) light signal equipment
LIM (Vermittlungsschrank m) line interface module (DFS ground station)

linear linear; flat (response characteristic)
 l. **Datenbits** npl video data bits (digital TV)
 l. **Prädiktions-Codierung** f linear predictive coding (LPC)
Liniennetz n serial network (TC); subscriber line network (tel.)
Linienstromschnittstelle f current loop (TTY)
linientechnische Einrichtung f line equipment
Linienzug m trace (recorder); route (tel.)
linkszirkulare Polarisation f left-hand circular polarisation (LHCP)
Listenplatz m buffer location
LKL s. Lochkartenleser m
LL s. lokaler Laser m
LLC s. logische Übertragungssteuerung f
LM (Leistungsmerkmal n) service feature, facility (tel.)
LMK-Signal (Lang-, Mittel-, Kurzwellensignal n) long-, medium-, short-wave signal (sound broadcasting)
LNA (rauscharmer Verstärker m) low noise amplifier
LNB (rauscharmer Blockwandler m) low noise block converter (sat.)
LNC (rauscharmer Empfangsumsetzer m or Konverter m) low noise converter (sat.)
Lochkartenleser m (LKL) punched-card reader
Lochrasterplatte f matrix board
Lochstreifen m (LS) punched tape, paper tape (TTY)
Lochstreifenleser m punched-tape reader, (paper) tape reader (PTR) (TTY)
Lochstreifenlocher m tape punch (TTY)
Lochstreifenstanzer m tape punch (TTY)
Lockruf m polling call
Logikadapter m level matching circuit
logische Übertragungssteuerung f logical link control (LLC) (layer 2 protocol in LANs, IEEE 802.2)
logische Verbindung f logical channel or connection (ISDN)
lokal off-line (TTY operation), local
 l. **Laser** (LL) m local laser (optical heterodyne receiver, FO)
 l. **Netz** n local area network (LAN)
 l. **Uhrzeit** f local time offset (LTO) (VPT, = local time - UTC)
löschen delete (data), erase (tape, disk), reset, clear (memory, register);
Löschen n Drop (user O/R name from MHS name server)

Löschen

L. von Berechtigungen cancelling class-of-service data
Lötfahne *f* solder tag *(DIN)*
Lötöse *f* solder lug *(DIN)*
Lötseite *f* soldering side *(PCB)*
Lötstift *m* signal tag
LPC s. lineare Prädiktions-Codierung *f*
L-profiliger Gestellholm *m* L-shaped upright *(rack)*
LQW (Letztquerweg *m*) final high-usage route
LR (Leerruf *m*) no-operation call *(cellular mobile RT)*
LRC (Blockprüfung *f*, Längsprüfung *f*) longitudinal redundancy check
LS (Lautsprechen *n*) loudspeaking
LS s. Lochstreifen *m*
LSA (Laserabschaltung *f*) laser shutdown
LSB (niedrigstwertiges Bit *n*) least significant bit
L-Seite (Leiter-, Lötseite *f*) track side, soldering side *(PCB)*
LSt (Leitstelle *f*) master station *(TEMEX)*

LTO s. lokale Uhrzeit *f*
LTU (Leitungsendgerät *n*) line terminating unit
lückenbehaftet gapped *(PCM clock)*
Lückentakt *m* gapped clock *(PCM data)*
Lückenveränderung *f* gap change *(packet switching)*
luftdicht hermetically sealed
Luftschnittstelle *f* radio interface *(tel.)*
universelle L. common air interface (CAI) *(DTI cellular RT and CT2 protocol)*
LV (Leistungsverzeichnis *n*) tender specifications
LW (Längswiderstand *m*) series resistance
LW (Leitungswähler *m*) line selector
LW (Letztweg *m*) last-choice route
LWL (Lichtwellenleiter *m*) optical waveguide *(FO)*
LX (Ortsvermittlungsstelle *f* (OVSt)) local exchange
LZE (Lichtzeicheneinrichtung *f*) light signal equipment

M

M.1020 CCITT recommendation for international leased telephone tie lines
MAC (gemultiplexte Analog-Komponenten *fpl*) Multiplexed Analog Components *(TV transmission protocol, CCITT Rep. 1073)*
Mächtigkeit *f* capacity, size *(memory, channel)*
Magnetbandaufzeichnung *f* (MAZ) video tape recording (VTR)
Mailbox *f* E-mail service *(AT&T)*
makeln
  hold toggle,
  trade *(tel., switching between two existing connections)*
Makeln *n* broker's call,
  call *(stock)* hold, brokering
Makleranlage *f* broker's facility, station; trading system
MAN (Stadtnetz *n*) metropolitan area network *(1 - 200 Mb/s, IEEE 802.6, ANSI X3T9.5)*
Manchester-Code *m* Manchester code *(Ethernet, IEEE 802.3)*
Marke *f* label *(DP)*
Markierung *f* marking; flag *(SW)*
MAS (Mobilfunk-Anschlußsystem *n*) mobile access system *(to network)*
MASCAM *(s. Mithörschwelle)* masking pattern adapted subband coding and multiplexing *(sound coding procedure)*
Maschennetz *n* meshed network
Maskierer *m* masking sound *(digital audio)*
MAZ (Magnetbandaufzeichnung *f*) video tape recording (VTR)
maschinenlesbar machine-readable
Massendaten- bulk data ... *(sat. transm.)*
maximale Codeaussteuerung *f* peak code *(PCM)*
  m. Gruppenlaufzeitverzerrung *f* maximum group delay distortion *(symbol: Tg)*
MC (Messen, Steuern, Regeln *n* (MSR)) measurement & control
MCMI (modifizierte codierte Schrittinversion *f*) modified coded mark inversion *(FO)*
MDNS (Netzdienst *m* für Managementdaten) management data network service
MDT (mittlere Datentechnik *f*) office computers
Medien-Anschlußeinheit *f* medium attachment unit (MAU) *(receive/transmit unit, LAN)*
Medienbruch *m* medium discontinuity *(data transmission)*
Medienpark *m* teleport *(building (complex) with provision of interconnected telematics services for the lessees)*
Medien-Schnittstelle *f* medium-dependent interface *(LAN)*
Mehrbelastung *f* surplus load
mehrbenutzbar shareable *(SW)*
Mehrdeutigkeit *f* ambiguousness
Mehrdienstterminal *n* multifunction or multi-services terminal *(tel.)*; integrated voice/data terminal (IVDT) *(US)*
Mehrfachabruf *m* multiple polling *(fax)*
Mehrfachanschluß *m* multi-access line or point
Mehrfachendgeräte-Anschluß *m* multi-terminal installation
  M.-Anschlußeinheit *f* multistation access unit (MAU) *(LAN)*
Mehrfachgebührenerfassung *f* repetitive metering *(tel.)*
Mehrfachkommunikation *f* multi-service communication
Mehrfachrahmen *m* multiframe (MF) *(TDM)*
  M.-Rahmenkennwort *n* (M-RKW) multiframe (MF) frame alignment signal
  M.-Synchronisierung *f* multiframing
Mehrfach-Steuereinheit *f* cluster controller (CC) *(multiplexer for several terminals)*
  M.-TN-Anschluß *m* line grouping *(tel.)*
Mehrfachzugriff *m* multiple access
Mehrfrequenz-Code (MFC) multifrequency code *(PCM signalling)*
  M.-Code-Zeichen *n* multifrequency code signalling *(PCM signalling)*
  M.-Empfänger *m* (MFE) multifrequency receiver *(tel.)*
  M.-Sender *m* (MFS) multifrequency transmitter
  M.-Verfahren *n* (MFV) dual-tone multifrequency (DTMF) method
  M.-Wahl *f* (MF-Wahl) dual-tone multifre-

quency dialling (DTMF)
Mehrheitsentscheidung *f* : Erkennung durch laufende M. running majority vote detection (RMVD)
Mehrleistungs-Datendienst *m* value-added data service (VADS)
Mehrpunkt-Konferenzeinrichtung *f* (MKE) multipoint conference system
Mehrpunktverbindung *f* multidrop *(MUXs, common channel shared by multiple devices)*; multi-endpoint connection
M. mit zentraler Steuerung central multi-endpoint connection
Mehrwege-Fading *n* multipath fading *(RT)*
Mehrwegeführung *f* multiple routing
Mehrwertdienst *m* value-added service (VAS) *(ISDN)*
Mehrwertnetz *n* value-added network (VAN)
Meldekanal *m* signal channel *(TC)*
Meldekennzeichen *n* answering signal *(tel.)*
Meldelampe *f* pilot lamp, pilot light, warning lamp
melden: sich m. answer *(tel.)*
Meldespeicher *m* indication store *(TC)*
Meldetelegramm *n* indication message *(TC)*
Meldeverkehr *m* control traffic
Meldeverzug *m* answering delay
Meldewort *n* (MW) service word *(PCM data)*
Meldezeichen *n* offering signal *(from the exchange)*
Meldung *f* indication *(telecontrol)*; message, report, signal, information; primitive *(from a lower to a higher OSI layer)*; response *(HDLC)*
Meldungsverkehr *m* control traffic
Mensch-Maschine-Kommunikation *f* (MMK) man/machine interface (MMI)
Menü *n* menu *(user interface for program selection)*
Merker *m* flag
Merkmal *n* feature
  Dienstm. service attribute *(ISDN, CCITT Rec. I.112)*
Merkmalsattribut *n* service attribute *(CCITT X.32)*
MESFET metal semiconductor FET
Meßablauf *m*: **automatischer M.** automatic measurement program *(test set)*
Meßbus *m* instrumented van *(DLR)*
Meßdekoder *m* monitoring decoder *(RDS)*
Meßebene *f* test interface
Meßempfänger *m* selective decoder *(radio link)*; monitoring decoder *(RDS)*; monitoring detector *(radio paging)*

Messen, Steuern, Regeln *n* (MSR) measurement & control (MC)
Messen und Regeln *n* (MR) measurement & control (MC)
Messerkontakt *m* blade contact *(connector)*
Messerleiste *f* contact *(or* connector) strip, *(male)* plug *(connector)*
Meßfeld *n* test panel
Meßgröße *f* measured value; measurand
Meßinstrument *n* meter
Meßkampagne *f* recording field trip *or* programme
Meßkoffer *m* portable test set
Meßkoppler *m*: **Sende- und M.** (SMK) transmission test equipment connecting matrix
Meßplatz *m* test set *or* set-up *or* rig *or* position; test assembly *or* desk *or* rack
Meßsender *m* signal generator
Meßspanne *f* signal range
Meßstreifen *m* recording chart
Meßtonempfänger *m* (MTE) test tone receiver
Meßungenauigkeit *f* measuring error
Meßwert *m* measured value, measurand
Meßwertaufbereitung *f* signal conditioning
Meßzeit *f* response time
Meßzubehörkoffer *m* test accessories (kit *or* set)
MF (Mehrfachrahmen *m*, Überrahmen *m*) multi-frame
MFC (Mehrfrequenz-Code *m*) multifrequency code
MFE (Mehrfrequenz-Empfänger *m*) multifrequency receiver *(tel.)*
MFLOPS million floating point operations per second
MFS (Mehrfrequenz-Sender *m*) multifrequency transmitter *(tel.)*
MFV (Mehrfrequenzverfahren *n*) dual tone multifrequency (DTMF) method
MF-Wahl (Mehrfrequenzwahl *f*) dual-tone multifrequency (DTMF) dialling
MHS s. Mitteilungsdienst *m*
Mietleitung *f* leased line *or* circuit, tie line
Mikrobefehl *m* microinstruction
Mikrowellen-Videoverteildienst *m* microwave video distribution service (MVDS) *(GB)*
Mindestwertumtastung *f* minimum shift keying (MSK)
Minitel *n* videotex terminal for Teletel *(France)*
Mischbestückung *f* mixed configuration *(rack)*
Mischkommunikation *f* mixed-services communication

Mischung f grading *(servers/offering subgroups interconnecting scheme; tel.sys.)*
Norm-M. standard grading *(tel. sys.)*
mischungsfrei free of gradings
Mischungsverhältnis n (Q) mean interconnecting number *(tel.sys.)*
Mitbewerber m competitor *(bus assignment)*
mithören listen in
Mithörschwelle f masking pattern (threshold) *(s. MASCAM, dig. sat. voice channel)*
Mithörsicherheit f privacy *(tel.)*
Mithörton m side tone *(tel.)*
Mitlauf m positive phase relationship *(filter, phase)*
mitlaufende Überwachung f synchronous supervision
Mitlauffilter n tracking filter
Mitlaufgebührenanzeiger m **für Hausanschluß** subscriber's check (or private) meter
mitlesen monitor *(channel)*
Mitrechner m coupled computer, parallel computer
Mitschnitt m recording, copying
Mitschrieb m recording, trace
Mitschrift f trace *(recorder)*
mitteilen signal
Mitteilungsaustausch-Systemteil m message transfer agent (MTA) *(MHS SW, CCITT Rec. X.400)*
Mitteilungsdienst m message handling service (MHS) *(CCITT Rec. X.400, F.400, ISO 10021-x (MOTIS))*
Mitteilungsende n End Of Message (EOM) *(signal)*
mitteilungsfähiger Dienst m message handling service (MHS)
Mitteilungssignalisierung f message oriented signalling (MOS)
Mitteilungsspeicher m message store (MS) *(CCITT Rec. X.413, ISO 10021-5)*
Mitteilungs-Transfer-Dienst m message transfer service *(CCITT Rec. X.411, ISO 10021-4, P1, OSI layer 7)*
M.-Übermittlung f messaging *(CCITT Rec. X.400)*
M.-Übermittlungs-System n message handling system (MHS) *(CCITT Rec. X.400, F.400, ISO 10021-x)*
Mittelpunktspeisung f centre feed *(ant.)*
mittelratige Sprachcodierung f medium-rate speech coding (MSC) *(dig. audio, US)*
Mittelstück n adaptor *(FO connector)*
Mittelungsfaktor m averaging factor *(mobile concentrator)*

Mittelwertbildner m averaging circuit or unit
Mittelwertverfahren n mean value analysis *(math.)*
Mittenverstärkung f mean gain
mittlere(r):
  m. Ausfallabstand m mean time between failures (MTBF)
  m. Ausfallzeit f mean time to failure (MTTF)
  m. Beurteilungs-Punktestand m mean opinion score (MOS) *(audio, subjective)*
  m. Funktionsdauer f mean time to failure *(MTTF)*
  m. Konzentrator m (MKT) medium-sized concentrator
  m. Reparaturzeit or **Reparaturdauer** f mean time to repair (MTTR)
  m. Übertragungsgeschwindigkeit f intermediate data rate (IDR) *(Intelsat service)*
  m. Zeit f **bis zur (ersten) Störung** mean time to failure (MTTF)
Mitzieheinrichtung f frequency pulling equipment
MKE (Mehrpunkt-Konferenzeinrichtung f) multipoint conference system
MKT s. mittlerer Konzentrator m
MMI (Mensch-Maschine-Kommunikation f) man-machine interface
MMK (Mensch-Maschine-Kommunikation f) man-machine interface (MMI)
MMS43-Code m modified monitored sum code *(DBP BA line code, 43 = 4B3T coding)*
MNP (Microcom-Netzverbindungsprotokoll n) Microcom Networking Protocol *(modems, V.42)*
Mobilanschluß-Funkgerät n mobile access radio (MAR)
mobile Nebenstellenanlage f radio PABX
m. Satelliten-Funkdienst m mobile satellite service (MSS) *(CCIR)*
Mobilfunk m mobile radio; private mobile radio (PMR)
M.-Anschlußsystem n mobile access system (MAS)
Mobilfunkzellennetz n cellular mobile radio network
Mobilkommunikations-Vermittlungsstelle f mobile switching centre (MSC) *(GSM)*
Mobilstation f (MS) mobile station *(cellular mobile RT)*
Modem m (Modulator-Demodulator m) modem (modulator/demodulator)
  M.-Eliminator m modem bypass, modem eliminator *(direct DTE-DTE connection)*

Modem

M. für begrenzte Leitungslänge limited distance modem (LDM), short-haul modem
Modul *n* **der Auflösung** index of cooperation (IOC) *(telefax drum diameter/line spacing ratio)*
Modulationsleitung *f* programme line, programme circuit *(broadcasting)*
Modulo-N *n* modulo N *(a number N, e.g. of messages or frames, which can be incremented before a counter is reset or an acknowledgement is required)*
Möglichkeit *f* option
Montagesatz *m* installation kit
Montageschaltbild *m* wiring diagram
Montageschaltplan *m* wiring diagram
Montageschiene *f* mounting channel
MOS s. mittlerer Beurteilungs-Punktestand *m*
MOS (Mitteilungssignalisierung *f*) message-oriented signalling
MOSFET metal oxide silicon FET *(semiconductors)*
MPJ-Formel *f* modified Palm Jacobus (MPJ) formula
MPLPC s. Multipuls-LPC *n*
MPS (Satellit *m* mittlerer Sendeleistung) medium power satellite
MPX s. Multiplex *n*
MR (Messen und Regeln *n*) measurement & control (MC)
MRJE (verschachtelte Jobfernverarbeitung *f*) multileaving remote job entry
M-RKW (Mehrfachrahmen-Rahmenkennungswort *n*) MF frame alignment word
MRS (Koppeleinrichtung *f* für Mehrfachnutzung) multi-role switch
MS (Mitteilungsspeicher *m*) message store
MS s. Mobilstation *f*
MS (Musik-/Sprache-Umschaltung *f*) music/speech switching *(RDS)*
MS (Nachrichtenspeicher *m*) message store *(CCITT Rec. X.400)*
MSB (höchstwertiges Bit *n*) most significant bit
MSC (C-Netz-Funkvermittlungsstelle *f*) mobile switching centre
MSFN (Funkverbindungsnetz *n* für die bemannte Raumfahrt) Manned Spaceflight Network *(JPL-operated world-wide network of ground stations)*
MSK (Mindestwertumtastung *f*, Minimum-Frequenzumtastung *f*) minimum shift keying
MSR (Messen, Steuern, Regeln *n*) measuring & control (MC)
MSS s. mobiler Satelliten-Funkdienst *m*
MSU (Nachrichten-Zeicheneinheit *f*) message signal unit *(SS7)*

MTA (elektronisches Postamt *n*) message transfer agent *(CCITT X.400)*
MTBF (mittlerer Ausfallabstand *m*) mean time between failures
MTC (Sprachausblendung *f*) mid-talkspurt clipping
MT-Dienst (Mitteilungs-Transfer-Dienst *m*) message transfer service *(CCITT X.400, ISO 10021-4)*
MTE (Meßtonempfänger *m*) test tone receiver
MTP (Nachrichtenübertragungsteil *m*) message transfer part *(SS7)*
MTS (MT-Dienst *m*) message transfer service *(CCITT X.411, ISO 10021-4)*
MTTF s. mittlere Funktionsdauer *f*
MTTR s. mittlere Reparaturzeit *f*
MULDEX s. Multiplexer/Demultiplexer *m*
Multiframe-Rahmenkennwort *n* (M-RKW) multiframe (MF) frame alignment signal
Multifrequenz(wähl)**verfahren** *n* (MFV) dual tone multi-frequency (DTMF) (dialling) method *(CCITT Yellow Book Vol. VI.1 Recommendation Q.23)*
Multikom-Gerät *n* (formerly Ceptel) multifunctional communication device *(vtx terminal with optional telephone function)*
Multiplex *n* (MPX) multiplex
Multiplexanschluß *m* primary rate access (ISDN S$_{2M}$)
Multiplexbildung *f* multiplexing
Multiplex-D-Kanal *m* (Dm) multiplexed D channel *(ISDN)*
multiplexen multiplex, assemble
Multiplexer *m* multiplexer (MUX)
Multiplexer/Demultiplexer *m* multiplexer/demultiplexer (MULDEX)
Multiplexierung *f* multiplexing
Zellen-M. cell interleaving *(ATM)*
Multiplexzentrale *f* central multiplexer section
Multipuls-LPC *f* multipulse linear predictive coding
Multitel (multifunktionelles Btx-Telefon *n*) multifunctional telephone *(DBP, does not include modem)*
Münzer *m* coin-operated telephone, coinbox telephone
Muse Multiple Sub-Nyquist Sampling Encoding *(NHK HDTV coding method)*
Musikeinspielung *f* music injection, music on hold (MOH) *(tel.)*
Musik-/Sprache-Umschaltung *f* (MS) music/speech switching *(RDS)*
Musterbau *m* prototype construction
Mutteruhr *f* master clock

MUX s. Multiplexer *m*

MW (Meldewort *n*) service word

N

NA (Netzanschaltung *f*) network access (unit) *(radio paging, Cityruf)*
nach außen weitergeben externalize *(a signal etc.)*
Nachbarkanalbetrieb *m* adjacent channel operation *(radio link)*
Nachbarverbindung *f* direct line, tie line
Nachbarzeichenstörung *f* intersymbol interference
Nachbilddämpfung *f* balance loss
Nachbildfehler *m* balance return
Nachbildimpedanz *f* balancing (network) impedance
Nachbildung *f* (Nb) balance, (line) balancing network; functional equivalent
Gabel-N. building-out network
Netz-N. artificial (mains) network
Nachfolgeschaltkennzeichen *n* successor switching signal
nachführen update *(file, display)*; control *(frequency)*
Nachführgenauigkeit *f* tracking accuracy *(sat.)*
Nachführgeschwindigkeit *f* slew rate *(IC)*
nachgeführt:
  n. Quarz-Oszillator *m* voltage-controlled crystal oscillator
  n. Signal *n* signal tracking the input voltage, follow-up signal
Nachlauf- tracking, trailing
Nachläufer *m* undershoot *(pulse)*
Nachlegeliste *f* modification wiring list
nachregeln correct
Nachricht *f* message, signal, information, communication
Nachrichtenabfragebetrieb *m* delivery *(message)*, retrieval mode; direct trunking; ring-down junction
Nachrichtenablegebetrieb *m* message recording mode *(tel.)*
Nachrichtenaufnehmer *m* listener *(test instrument, tel.)*
Nachrichtenaustausch *m* information exchange
Nachrichtenendezeichen *n* end-of-message (EOM) signal
Nachrichtenkopf *m* label, routing label; message header *or* preamble
Nachrichtenprotokoll *n* für digitale Datenübertragung digital data communications message protocol (DDCMP) *(DEC)*
Nachrichtensatellit *m* telecommunications satellite
Nachrichtenspeicher *m* message store (MS) *(CCITT Rec. X.400)*
Nachrichtentheorie *f* communication theory, informatics
Nachrichtentransferteil *m* message transfer part (MTP) *(SS7, CCITT Rec. Q.701 - 707)*
Nachrichtenübermittlung *f* message transmission
Nachrichtenübermittlungseinrichtung *f* telecommunication facility; message transmission facility
Nachrichtenübertragungssystem *n* message handling system (MHS) *(CCITT Rec. 400, F.400. ISO 10021-x)*
Nachrichtenübertragungsteil *m* message transfer part (MTP) *(SS7, CCITT Rec. Q.701 - 707)*
Nachrichtenunterscheidung *f* message discrimination *(SS7 layer 3)*
Nachrichtenverbindung *f* transmission link
Nachrichtenverkehr *m* message traffic
nachrichtenvermitteltes System *n* message-switched system *(SF circuit switching)*
Nachrichtenvermittlung *f* message switching *(TWX, telex)*
Nachrichtenverteiler *m* message buffer *(digital exchange)*; router *(LAN)*
Nachrichtenweiterleitgerät *n* router *(LAN)*
Nachrichtenzeicheneinheit *f* message signal unit (MSU) *(SS7)*
Nachruf *m* forward-transfer signal
nachrufen forward transfer; call back *(tel.)*
nachschalten connect to the output of ...
Nachschwinger *m* pulse tail
Nachsendung *f* retransmission
Nachstellkorrelator *m* correlator *(transmission)*
nachsteuern retune *(filter)*
Nachtabfragestelle *f* night service extension
nachtgeschaltete NStA *f* night service extension

Nachtschalter

Nachtschalter *m* night service key
Nachtschaltung *f.* **allgemeine N.** (universal) night service (extension) *(tel.)*
Nachverarbeitungsmodus *m* processable mode (PM) *(teletex, X.200)*
Nachvermittlungsplatz *m* manual trunk operator position
Nachwahl *f* dialling a suffix digit, suffix dialling *(f. tel.)*
N. 2. Amt 2nd-exchange redialling *(DTMF exchanges only, tel.)*
Nachwahlnummer *f* suffix (digit)
nachweisen confirm, verify, detect
Nachwirkzeit *f* hangover (time) *(opposite of response time, modem)*
nachziehen control, pull *(frequency)*
NACK (negative Bestätigung *f*) negative acknowledgement
Nadelspitzen *fpl* spikes *(noise on pulse)*
nahbearbeitbares Studiosignal *n* contribution-quality signal *(TV in ISDN, 135 Mb/s)*
Nahbereichsnetz *n* local area network (LAN)
Nahbus *m* local bus
Nahe Prüfschleife einschalten loopback *(not standardized, V.24, s. Table VI)*
Nahecho *n* near-end echo
Nahnebensprechen *n* near-end crosstalk (NEXT)
Nahtstellenbaustein *m* interface module
Nahwählverbindung *f* extended-area call *(tel.)*
N-Alarm *m* (Nicht-Dringend-Alarm) non-urgent alarm (signal) *(TC)*
Namensverzeichnis *n* name server *(MHS SW)*
Namentaste *f* name key *(f. tel.)*
Namentaster *m* repertory dialler *(tel.)*
NAMUR (Normenausschuß *m* für Meß- und Regelungstechnik) German standards committee for measurement and control techniques
Namursignal *n* NAMUR signal *(8-Volt signal present when initiators drop out)*
NAP (Anschlußpunkt *m* zu anderen Netzen) network access point *(to other networks)*
Natel C (Nationales Autotelefon-System *n*) national in-car telephone system *(Swiss, 900 MHz)*
natürlicher Erdradius *m* true earth radius
Nb (Nachbildung *f*) balance, (line) balancing network; functional equivalent
NBP s. Nebenbedienungsplatz *m*
NC (Langzeitverbindung *f*) nailed connection *(auxiliary service channel)* *(ISDN)*
NCP (Netzsteuerprogramm *n*) network control program
NCP (Netzsteuerprotokoll *n*) network control protocol
NCU (Netzsteuereinheit *f*) network control unit *(VSAT)*
Nebenanschluß *m* extension
Nebenapparat *m* parallel (telephone) set
Nebenbedienungsplatz *m* (NBP) secondary operator's console
Nebeninformation *f* secondary information
Nebenrechner *m* back-up computer
Nebenschlußbügel *m* shunt bracket
Nebensprechdämpfung *f* crosstalk attenuation
Nebensprechen *n* crosstalk
Nebenstelle *f* (NSt) extension
N.-Anschluß m (NStA) extension *(tel.)*
N.-Anschlußleitung *f* PBX main line
N.-Teilnehmer *m* extension user
Nebenstellenanlage *f* (NStAnl) private branch exchange (PBX); private automatic branch exchange (PABX) *(with dialling capability)*
N.-Computer-Schnittstelle *f* PBX-to-Computer Interface (PCI) *(US)*
N. mit Digitalanschluß digitally connected PBX (DCPBX)
Nebenviernebensprechen *n* inter-quad crosstalk
Nebenzipfelabstand *m* side-lobe attenuation *or* gain *(antennas)*
negativ female *(connector)*
n. Bestätigung *f* negative acknowledgement (NACK)
Neigung *f* inclination; canting *(precipitation, sat. transm.)*
NEMP (nuklearer elektromagnetischer Impuls *m*) nuclear electromagnetic pulse
Nennbereich *m* rated range
Nenndämpfung *f* nominal loss
Nennfrequenz *f* characteristic frequency
Nennlast *f* conventional load *(link test)*
NET (Europäische Telekommunikationsnorm *f*) Norme Européenne de Telecommunication, CEPT standard *(s. Table II)*
Netzabschluß *m* network termination (NT) *(ISDN, CCITT Rec. I.112)*
N.- und Meßstelle *f* Network Termination and Test Point (NTTP) *(BT)*
Netzabschlußeinheit *f* Network Terminating Unit (NTU) *(BT ISDN)*
Netzabschlußeinrichtung *f* Network Terminating Equipment (NTE) *(BT ISDN)*
Netzanpassung *f* AC mains (*or* line) adapter
Netzanschaltung f (NA) network access (unit) *(radio paging, Cityruf)*

Netzanschluß *m* power connection
N.-Rufnummer *f* network user address (NUA) *(packet switching)*
Netzarchitektur *f* network architecture *(vtx)*
Netz-Ausfallbetrieb *m* power failure mode
Netzbetreiber *m* network operator, carrier
Netzdienst *m* network service
  N. für Managementdaten management data network service (MDNS)
  N.-Zugriffspunkt *m* network service access point (NSAP) *(SS7, CCITT Rec. Q. 761 - 764)*
Netzebene *f* network level
Netzeigenschaften *fpl* network capabilities
Netzersatzschaltung *f* standby power system switching; network change-over system
Netzfilter *n* (NFI) mains *or* line filter
Netzführungsrechner *m* network management processor (NMP)
Netzführungssystem *n* supervisory network control system
netzgestütztes Dienstmerkmal *n* network-dependent service attribute
Netzinstanz *f* network entity
Netzknoten *m* network node *(an exchange)*, node
Netzknotensteuerung *f* terminal node controller (TNC) *(PR)*
Netzkontrolleinrichtung *f* network management system
Netzkontrollrelais *n* (NK-Relais) mains control relay *(PBX)*
Netzkontrollzentrale *f* (NKZ) network control centre (NCC)
Netzkoppler *m* gateway
Netzleittechnik *f* supervisory control in networks
netzlos mains-independent *(PS)*
Netzmeldung *f* call progress signal, service signal
Netz-Nachbildung *f* artificial (mains) network
Netzrückkehr *f* AC power restoration
Netzschnittstelleneinheit *f* network interface unit (NIU) *(LAN)*
Netzschnittstellenkarte *f* network interface card (NIC)
Netz-Sprachübertragungsprotokoll *n* network voice protocol (NVP)
Netzsteuereinheit *f* network control unit (NCU) *(VSAT)*
Netzsteuerprogramm *n* (NCP) network control program
Netzsteuerprotokoll *n* (NCP) network control protocol
Netzträger *m* carrier
Netzübergang *m* (NÜ) network gateway (NG) *(for terminals)*; gateway (between networks); network interworking (unit)
Netzüberlastung *f* network congestion (NC) *(service signal)*
Netzverbindung *f* networking
Netzverbund *m* network interconnection
Netzvorsatz *m* AC mains *(or* line) adapter
netzweite Erreichbarkeit *f* anywhere call pickup *(mobile RT)*
Netzwerkebene *f* network layer *(CCITT I.450 and I.451, layer 3, OSI 7-layer reference model)*
Netzwerkrechner *m* (NR) information provider *(videotex)*
Netz-Zustandsanzeige *f* network status display
neu:
  N. Leitung *f* New Line *(V.25 bis)*
  n. Paketmodus *m* additional packet mode *(CCITT)*
  n. rufen recall
  n. wählen redial
Neubelegung *f* new call
Neueinrichtung *f* installation *(of subscriber equipment)*
Neuformierung *f* restart *(program)*
Neuruf *m* recall
Neutralisation *f* balancing out *(cables)*
Neuwahl *f* rerouting
NF s. Niederfrequenz *f*
NF-Lage *f* VF level
NFM (Schmalband-FM *f*) narrow-band FM
NFI s. Netzfilter *n*
NFR s. Normalfrequenz(-Einsatz *m*) *f*
NG s. Netzübergang *m* (NÜ)
NHK (japanische Rundfunkgesellschaft *f*) Japan Broadcasting Corporation
NIC s. Netzschnittstellenkarte *f*
nicht:
  n. amtsberechtigt fully restricted; exchange-barred
  N.-Amtsberechtigung *f* trunk-barring level
  n. angeschlossen off line *(TTY)*
  N.-Anlagenberechtigung *f* installation-barring level
  N.-Beantworten *n* **eines Anrufs** Disregard Incoming Call (DIC) *(V.25 bis)*
  n. betriebsbereit controlled not ready (CNR) *(X.21)*
  n. betriebsfähig uncontrolled not ready (UCNR) *(X.21)*

N.-Dringend-Alarm *m* (N-Alarm) urgent alarm (signal) *(TC)*
n. erfolgreiche Verbindung *f* call failure
n.-fallend non-decreasing *(function)*
n.-flüchtiger Direktzugriffsspeicher *m* non-volatile RAM (NVRAM)
n. gesteckt disconnected *(TE)*
n. navigatorischer Ortungsfunkdienst *m* radiolocation service
n.-öffentlicher beweglicher Landfunk *m* (nöbL) private mobile radio (PMR)
n.-öffentlicher mobiler Landfunk *m* (nömL) private mobile radio (PMR) *(usually simplex, includes CUG and trunked schemes)*
n.-wachsend non-increasing *(function)*
n. unterbrechende Priorität *f* non-preemptive priority
n. verschlüsselt non-secure
n. wählfähig non-dialling
Niederfrequenz *f* (NF) voice frequency (VF) *(tel.)*
niedrigratig low speed *(link)*
niedrigstwertiges Bit *n* least significant bit (LSB)
nivellieren equalize
NIU (Netzschnittstelleneinheit *f*) network interface unit *(LAN)*
NK-Relais (Netzkontroll-Relais *n*) mains control relay *(PBX)*
NKZ (Netzkontrollzentrale *f*) network control centre (NCC)
NL s. Neue Leitung *f*
NMT 450, 900 Nordic *(cellular)* Mobile Telephone system *(450, 900 MHz)*
nöbL s. nichtöffentlicher beweglicher Landfunk *m*
nömL s. nichtöffentlicher mobiler Landfunk *m*
Normalfrequenzeinsatz *m* (NFR) standard frequency inset
Normalteilnehmer *m* ordinary subscriber
Normalton *m* reference tone
Normgerechtigkeitsbescheinigung *f* Certificate of Conformance to Standard
normieren normalize; reset
Normmischung *f* standard grading *(tel. sys.)*
NOS (Übertragung *f* im Netz gestört) network out of service *(loop testing)*
Not-Aus-Druckknopf *m* emergency pushbutton, "panic button"
Notizblockfunktion *f* notepad facility *(f.tel.)*
Notrufdienst *m* emergency call service
notspeiseberechtigt entitled to operate in restricted powering conditions
Notspeisung *f* restricted powering *(power feeding)*
Notstromversorgung *f* restricted powering *(power feeding)*
NPR (Rauschleistungsdichteabstand *m* (RLA) noise power ratio
N-PSK (N-Phasenumtastung *f*) N phase shift keying *(cellular digital RT)*
N-QAM (N-Quadratur-Amplitudenmodulation *f*) N quadrature amplitude modulation *(cellular digital RT)*
NR (Netzwerkrechner *m*) information provider
NRM (Aufforderungsbetrieb *m*) normal response mode *(HDLC)*
NRZ(C) (Richtungsschrift *f*) non-return to zero (change) *(PCM code)*
NRZ(M,I) (Wechselschrift *f*) non-return to zero (mark, inverted)
nsa s. Nummernschalter-Arbeitskontakt *m*
NSAP (Netzdienst-Zugriffspunkt *m*) network service access point *(SS7)*
nsi s. Nummernschalter-Impulskontakt *m*
nsr s. Nummernschalter-Ruhekontakt *m*
NSt (Nebenstelle *f*) extension
NStA (Nebenstellenanschluß *m*) extension
NStAnl (Nebenstellenanlage *f*) private automatic branch exchange (PABX)
NT (Keine Antwort) No (answer) Tone detected *(V.23 signal)*
NT (Netzabschluß *m*) network termination *(ISDN)*
NT1 NT with layer-1 functions *(OSI RM)*
NT2 NT with layer 1-3 functions *(OSI RM)*
NT12 NT1 + NT2
NTG (Nachrichtentechnische Gesellschaft *f* im VDE) communications engineering standards body *(now ITG)*
NU (Nummer unbeschaltet) number unobtainable
NÜ (Netzübergang *m*) network gateway (NG)
NUA (Netzanschluß-Rufnummer *f*) network user address *(X.25)*
NUI (Teilnehmerkennung *f*) network user identification *(DBP DATEX-P)*
nuklearer elektromagnetischer Impuls *m* nuclear electromagnetic pulse (NEMP)
Nullabgleich *m* nulling
Nulldurchgang *m* zero transition, zero crossing
Nullmodem *m* (0-Modem) modem bypass, modem eliminator *(direct DTE-DTE connection)*
Nullpunktabweichung *f* drift
Nullzeichen *n* null character

Numerierungs- und Adressierungskennung *f* numbering and addressing plan identifier (NAPI) *(ISDN, CCITT I.451)*
Numeris French ISDN (RNIS)
Nummer *f* **der Verbindungskennung** call reference number *(ISDN)*
Nummernschalter *m* dial (switch) *(tel.)*
  N.-Arbeitskontakt *m* (nsa) normally-open dial contact *(tel.)*
  N.-Impulskontakt *m* (nsi) dial pulse contact *(tel.)*
  N.-Ruhekontakt *m* (nsr) normally-closed dial contact *(tel.)*
Nummernschaltwahl *f* rotary dialling *(tel.)*
Nummer unbeschaltet (NU) number unobtainable (NU)
Nur-Empfang *m* receive-only (RO) *(sat. TV)*
Nur-Ton-Empfänger *m* pager, bleeper *(GB)*, beeper *(US)*
NU-Ton *m* number unobtainable (NU) tone
Nutzband *n* wanted band
Nutzbit *n* data bit, information bit, program bit
Nutzbitrate *f* bit rate of user information; net bit rate *(transmission)*
Nutzdaten *npl* user data
Nutzdatenrate *f* data rate of user packets *(in bytes/packet)*

Nutzerschnittstelle *f* user interface *(TEMEX)*
Nutzinformation *f* tributary bits *(TDM)*; user information
Nutzkanal *m* message channel; service channel; user information channel
Nutzkanalverbindung *f* user information (channel) connection
Nutzkanalverkehr *m* user traffic
Nutzlast *f* payload *(useful signal section of PCM frame, ATM; sat. HW)*
Nutzleistung *f* signal power
Nutzpegel *m* signal level
Nutzsignal *n* useful signal, service signal; wanted signal; user (information) signal
Nutzung *f* information transfer capability *(bearer service)*
Nutzungsgrad *m* utilization ratio *(PCM)*
Nutzungszeit *f* airtime *(cellular RT)*
Nutzwert *m* efficiency
Nutzzellen/Leerzellen-Verhältnis *n* burstiness factor *(ATM)*
NVP (Netz-Sprachübertragungsprotokoll *n*) network voice protocol
NVRAM (nichtflüchtiger Direktzugriffsspeicher *m*) non-volatile RAM

O

OB (Ortsbatterie f) local or station battery
Oberer Sonder(kanal)bereich m (OSB) upper special-channel band (CATV, 230-286 MHz)
Oberfläche f: **Bediener-, Benutzer-O.** operator, user interface; terminal operating elements
Oberflächenmontagetechnik f surface mounting technology (SMT)
oberflächenmontiert surface-mounted
  o. Bauelement n surface-mounted device (SMD)
  o. Vorrichtung f surface-mounted device (SMD)
Oberpostdirektion f (OPD) regional postal district administration (DBP)
öbL s. öffentlicher beweglicher Landfunk m
OBN s. optisches Breitbandnetz n
Ö-Btx s. öffentliches Btx-Terminal n
OC-1 (optischer Kanal m) optical channel (50 Mb/s, SONET standard)
ODA (Dokumentenarchitektur f) Open Document Architecture or Office Document Architecture
ODIF (Dokumenten-Austauschformat n) Office Document Interchange Format
OE s. optischer Empfänger m
OEIC (optoelektronische Schaltung f) optoelectronic IC (FO)
OEM-Hersteller m original manufacturer (of equipment for OEMs)
offen:
  o. Amtsabfrage f unassigned (exchange line) answer
  o. Ausschreibung f open competitive tender
  O. Kommunikation f Open System Interconnection (OSI) (ISO DIS 8613, US network standard, s. Table I)
  O. Netzarchitektur f Open Network Architecture (ONA) (FCC)
öffentlich:
  ö. beweglicher Landfunk m (öbL) public access mobile radio (PAMR)
  ö. BTX-Terminal n public videotex terminal (DBP)
  ö. Datennetz n public data network (PDN)
  ö. Fernsprechwählnetz n general or public switched telephone network (GSTN, PSTN)
  ö. Kartentelefon n (ÖKartTel) public phonecard phone (BT)
  ö. Kartentelefon n **für internationale Kreditkarten** (ÖKartlnKa) public card phone for international credit cards
  ö. Landfunknetz n public land mobile network (PLMN)
  ö. mobiler Landfunk m (ömL) public access mobile radio (PAMR)
  ö. (Post-)Netz n public switched telephone network (PSTN)
  ö. rechtlich (under)public law
  ö. rechtliche Rundfunkanstalt f public-service broadcast station
  ö. Schlüssel m public key (chipcard encryption)
Öffnung f window (gate)
Öffnungsimpuls m enable pulse, strobe (pulse)
Öffnungszeit f aperture time (ADC)
ofKnV s. ortsfeste Knotenvermittlung f
OG s. Ortungsgerät n
OgK s. Organisationskanal m
ohne Wahl: Verbindung o. W. dedicated connection
OIC s. optischer Baustein m
OIC s. optoelektronische Schaltung f
ÖKartlnKa s. öffentliches Kartentelefon n für internationale Kreditkarten
ÖKartTel s. öffentliches Kartentelefon n
Oktett n octet (8-bit byte)
ömL s. öffentlicher mobiler Landfunk m
O-Modem (Null-Modem m) modem eliminator, modem bypass
ON (andere Programme npl) Other Networks (service information, RDS)
ON s. Ortsnetz n
ONA s. Offene Netzarchitektur f
Ö-Netz (Österreichisches digitales Breitbandnetz n) Austrian digital broadband network
OPD s. Oberpostdirektion f
Operatorruf m **bedingt/unbedingt** conditional/unconditional operator request
OPLL s. optischer Phasenregelkreis m
ONP (Richtlinien fpl für offene Netze) Open Network Provision (EC)
optisch:
  o. Baustein m optical IC (OIC) (FO)

optisch 84

o. **Breitbandnetz** n (OBN) optical broadband network
o. **Empfänger** m (OE) optical receiver (FO)
o. **Phasenregelkreis** m optical phase-locked loop (OPLL)
o. **Raster** m optical grating
o. **Rufsignalisierung** f visual call signalling (f.tel.)
o. **Sender** m (OS) optical transmitter (FO)
o. **Überlagerungsempfänger** m optical heterodyne receiver (FO)
optoelektronische Schaltung f optoelectronic IC (OIC) (FO)
Organisationskanal m (OgK) control channel (cellular mobile RT, PMR, trunking)
Originalgerätehersteller m original equipment manufacturer (OEM)
O/R-Name m originator/recipient name (CCITT Rec. X.400, MHS)
Ortsanschlußleitung f local loop
Ortsbatterie -(OB-)**Apparat** m local-battery set (tel.)
Ortscode m local code
ortsfeste Knotenvermittlung f permanent switch or node (ofKnV)
Ortsfunkstelle f fixed radio station
ortsgebunden localized
Ortsmultiplex n space division multiplex (SDM)

Ortsnetz n (ON) local network (tel.); local area network (LAN) (data)
Ortsnetzbetreiber m local exchange carrier (LEC)
Ortsruf B m regional radio-paging service (Switzerland, to POCSAG standard)
ortsveränderlich transportable, movable
Ortsverbindungsleitung f (Ovl) local junction line (tel.)
Ortsvermittlungsstelle f (OVSt) local exchange (LX)
Ortswählverbindung f local call (tel.)
Ortungsgerät n (OG) fault-locating unit (tel.)
Ortungsfunkdienst m radiodetermination service
  nichtnavigatorischer O. radiolocation service
OS s. optischer Sender m
OSB (Oberer Sonder(kanal)bereich m) upper special-channel band (CATV, DBP)
OSI (Offene Kommunikation f) Open Systems Interconnection
OSITOP-Anwendervereinigung f international association of OSI users (OSI + TOP)
Oszilloreg n recording oscilloscope
Outband-Signalisierung f out-band signalling
Ovl s. Ortsverbindungsleitung f
OVSt s. Ortsvermittlungsstelle f

P

PA (Primärmultiplexanschluß *m* (PMXA)) primary rate access *(ISDN)*
paarverseilt twisted-pair
PAD s. Paketierer/Depaketierer *m*
PAG (Funkruf *m*) paging *(RDS)*
Pager *m* pager *(radio-paging service)*, bleeper *(GB, colloquial)*
PAK s. Paketierer *m*
Paket *n* burst *(sat.)*; packet *(data)*
  Schaltp. switching stack *(membrane keypad)*
  Spulenp. coil assembly
  Wicklungsp. winding assembly
Paketblock *m* packet stream
Paketbündel *n* packet group
Paket-DEE *f* packet-mode DTE
Paketierer *m* (PAK) packet assembly facility
Paketierer/Depaketierer *m* packet assembly/disassembly facility (PAD) *(DTE which interfaces non-X.25 terminals to an X.25 network. PAD protocol-related standards are X.3, X.28 and X.29)*
Paketkopfinformation *f* overhead information
Paketlänge *f* **in Bit** packet length in bits (PLB)
Paketnutzungsgrad *m* packet utilization ratio
paketorientiert packet-oriented; packet mode
Paketradio *n* packet radio (PR) *(packet-switched radio service, AX25 - amateur X.25, VHF)*
Paketradioeinheit *f* packet radio unit (PRU)
Paketrate *f* (PR) packet rate *(packets/sec.)*
Paketreihung *f* packet sequencing
Paketrumpf *m* packet body
Paketsteuerung *f* packet handler (PH) *(ISDN)*
Paketteilnehmer *m* packet-terminal customer
Paketverlust *m* dropped packet
Paketverluste *mpl* packet losses
Paketverlustrate *f* (PVR) packet loss rate
paketvermittelt packet switched
  p. Dateldienst *m* Packet Switch Stream (PSS) *(BT)*
  p. Datennetz *n* (Datex-P, Dx-P) packet-switched data network (PSDN)
  p. öffentliches Datennetz *n* packet-switched public data network (PSPDN)
  p. Sprachendgerät *n* packet voice terminal (PVT)
Paketvermittlung *f* packet switch (PS) *(US)*
Paketvermittlungsnetz *n* (PV-Netz) packet switching network
paketweise packet-oriented
  p. verschachtelt packet interleaved
Paketwiederholung *f* packet retransmission
PAM (Pulsamplitudenmodulation *f*) pulse amplitude modulation
Papieranpassung *f* paper alignment *(fax.)*
Papiertransport *m* paper feed *(printer)*
P/AR (Spitze-Mittelwert-Verhältnis *n*) peak/average ratio *(analog transmission line test)*
Parallel-Ein-/Ausgabe *f* parallel Input/output (PIO) *(port)*
paralleler Ein-/Ausgabebus *m* (PEAB) parallel input/output (I/O) bus
Parallelweg *m* backup path
Paritätsbit *n* parity bit, balancing bit *(transmission signal)*
Paritätskontrolle *f* parity check
Parken *n* parking, queuing *(a call, tel.)*
Parkierung *f* parking, holding *(a call)*
Parkstellung *f*: **aus P.** from parked position *(tel.)*
Partnerbeziehung *f* traffic relation *(ISDN)*
Partnerinstanz *f* peer entity *(OSI)*
Passagiertelefondienst *m* aeronautical mobile telephone and data (fax) service *('Airphone' (US), 'Skyphone' (GB), 'Aircom' (SITA) - INMARSAT supported)*
passiv inactive
  p. übermittelndes optisches Netz *n* passive optical network (PON) *(FO)*
passivieren deactivate, take off-line *(DTE)*
Passiv-Verkehr *m* called subscribers
Paßteil *n* locating part *(connector)*
Paßwort *n* password
Pauschaltarif *m* flat rate
Pausenblock *m* silence *(PCM speech)*
Pausenblocklänge *f* silence duration
Pausenlänge *f* silence period
Pausenmeldung *f* pause indication *(ESS)*
Pausenmodulation *f* gap modulation *(PCM*

Pausenmusik 86

speech)
Pausenmusik *f* music while you wait, music on hold (MOH) *(tel.)*
Pausenzustand *f* tone-off condition
PCI (Datenpaket-Leitung-Schnittstelle *f*) packet/circuit interface
PCM (Pulscodemodulation *f*) pulse code modulation
PCM *f* mit Differenzcodierung und Synchrondemodulation differential coherent pulse code modulation (DCPC)
PCM30 (Primärmultiplexsystem *n*) primary rate TDM system *(DBP, 2 Mb/s, 30 channel capacity)*
PCR (vorbeugende zyklische Wiederholung *f*) preventative cyclic retransmission *(SS7 error correction procedure)*
PDAU (Anschlußeinheit *f* für physikalische Zustellung) physical delivery access unit *(e.g. printer, letter post, CCITT X.400)*
PDC (Programm-Zustellungssteuersystem n) Programme Delivery Control system *(TV broadcast service)*
PDM (Pulsdauermodulation *f*) pulse duration modulation
PDS (Postsystem *n*) physical delivery system *(IPM)*
PDU (Informationseinheit *f*) protocol data unit *(videotex)*
PE (Programmsteuereinheit *f*) program control unit *(EDS)*
PEAB s. paralleler Ein-/Ausgabebus *m*
Pegelsende- und Meßeinrichtung *f* (PSME) transmission test equipment
Pegelverlauf *m* level response
Pegelsprung *m* amplitude hit *(CCITT Rec. 0.95, PCM)*
PEL (fotografisches Element *n*) photographic element *(fax.)*
PELV (geschützte Kleinspannung *f*) protected extra low voltage *(tel.)*
PEP (europäischer Funkrufdienst *m*) Pan European Paging service *(now Euromessage)*
PEP (Protokoll *n* für die paketierte Datengesamtheit) Packetized Ensemble Protocol *(data compression protocol for high-speed modems)*
Perilex-Stecker *m* shock-proof plug
periodischer Ruf *m* interrupted ringing signal
Peripherie-Adapter *m* peripheral interface adapter (PIA)
Personenruf *m* paging
Personenrufempfänger *m* pager

Personenrufendgerät *n* pager
persönliche Erdfunkstelle *f* personal earth station (PES) *(VSAT)*
p. Kennummer *f* personal identification number (PIN) *(Telepoint system, telebanking)*
p. Kennummer/Transaktionsnummer *f* personal identification number/transaction number (PIN/TAN) *(telebanking password code)*
PES s. persönliche Erdfunkstelle *f*
PETRUS (Protokoll-Entwicklungs- und Test-Rechner-Universal-System *n*) test system for communication protocols *(ZZF)*
Pfadkopfteil *m* path overhead (POH) *(TDM)*
Pfeifen *n* singing *(tel.)*; howl *(radio)*
Pfeifsicherheit *f* stability
Pflichtenheft *n* requirement specification
PFM (Pulsfrequenzmodulation *f*) pulse frequency modulation
Phasenabweichung *f* phase shift, phase displacement
phasenangeschnitten phase-angle controlled *(PS)*
Phasenaugendiagramm *n* eye pattern of phase *(PCM)*
Phasenbereich *m* phase region *(PCM)*
Phasendifferenzmodulation *f* differential two-phase modulation
Phasendifferenzumtastung *f* differential phase shift keying (DPSK)
Phasendrehung *f* phase shift
Phasenfläche *f* phase front *(FO)*
Phasenisolation *f* phase segregation
Phasenjitter *m* phase jitter *(data transm.)*
Phasenlage(nabstand *m*) *f* phase angle
Phasenmodulation *f* phase modulation (PM)
Phasenraum *m* phase space *(PCM)*
Phasensprung *m* phase hit *(CCITT Rec.0.95)*; phase shift
phasenstarr locked in phase
Phasensteilheit *f* rate of phase change
Phasenumtastung *f* phase shift keying
Phasenverschiebung *f* phase shift, phase displacement
phasenverschoben out of phase, asynchronous
Phasenzittern *n* phase jitter
Phonepoint *m* (öffentliche Funktelefon-Feststation *f*) public CT2 telepoint base station *(BT, 860 MHz, 200 m range, also name of BT telepoint service, not DECT compatible)*
physikalisch:
 p. Schicht *f* physical layer *(CCITT I.430; layer 1, OSI reference model)*
 p. Zustellgerät *n* physical delivery de-

vice *(e.g. printer, CCITT Rec. X.400)*
PI (Programmketten- *oder* Senderkennung *f* (SK)) Programme Identification *(RDS)*
PIA s. Peripherie-Adapter *m*
Piepser *m* bleeper *(colloquial)*
Piepserl *m* regional radiopaging service *(Austria, colloquial)*
Piktogramm *n* icon *(PC)*, pictogram
PIN s. persönliche Kennummer *f*
PIN (Programm-Reihenfolge *f*) Programme Identification Number *(RDS)*
Ping-Pong-Verfahren *n* ping pong method *(full duplex time division method, direction of high-speed data transmission changes, e.g., at 8-kHz rate)*
PIN/TAN s. persönliche Kennummer/Transaktionsnummer *f*
PIO (Parallel-Ein-/Ausgabe *f*) parallel input/output *(port)*
PIO (programmierbare Ein-/Ausgabe *f*) programmable input/output
Pixel *n* pixel, picture element *(TV)*
PKI Philips Kommunikations-Industrie
Plattenspeicher *m* (PSP) disk storage unit
Platz *m* position; operator *(tel.)*
Platzherbeiruf *m* operator recall
Platzkraft *f* operator *(tel.)*
   P.-Unterstützungssystem *n* (PLUS) operator support system *(radio paging, Cityruf)*
Plausibilitätskontrolle *f* validity check
PLB (Paketlänge *f* in Bit) packet length in bits (PLB)
plesiochron plesiochronous *(free-running)*
PLUS s. Platzkraft-Unterstützungssystem *n*
PM s. Phasenmodulation *f*
PM (Nachverarbeitungsmodus *m*) processable mode *(teletex, CCITT Rec. X.200, ISO 7498)*
PMP-Netz (Punkt-zu-Multipunkt-Netz *n*) point-to-multipoint network *(VSAT)*
PMXA s. Primärmultiplexanschluß *m*
PN (Pseudozufallsfolge *f*) pseudo noise *(code)*
POH s. Pfadkopfteil *m*
Pointel *n* proposed French Telepoint system *(public mobile RT)*
Polarisationsweiche *f* orthomode transducer, orthogonal mode transducer (OMT) *(sat.)*
Polarisator *m* polarizer *(ant.)*
-polig -channel *(data link)*,
   -core *(cable)*,
   -pin, -contact *(plug)*,
   -position *(switch)*,
   -terminal *(terminal block)*,
   zweip. Verbinder *m* twin connector, two-pin connector

Polklemme *f* terminal clip
Polteilung *f* interpin space *(connector)*
Polungskeil *m* locating wedge *(connector)*
Polvorgabe *f* network terminal selection *(in circuit design)*
Polygonzug *m* progression, broken line, polygonal course *(vectors)*
Port *n*: **E/A-P.** I/O port
Porty *n* portable *(cellular mobile RT transceiver, colloquial)*
POS (Kassenterminal *n*) point of sale *(telebanking)*
positiv male *(connector)*
Postamt *n*: **elektronisches P.** message transfer agent (MTA) *(CCITT Rec. X.400)*
POSTBANK *f* the banking services branch of the DBP *(now independent of POSTDIENST and TELEKOM)*
POSTDIENST *m* ('Gelbe Post') the postal services branch of the DBP *(now independent of TELEKOM and POSTBANK)*
posteigene Stromwege *mpl* PTT-owned circuits
Postnetz *n* public switched telephone network (PSTN)
Postsystem *n* physical delivery system (PDS) *(IPM)*
Posttechnisches Zentralamt *n* (PTZ) Postal Engineering Centre *(DBP)*
Postverwaltung *f* Postal, Telegraph and Telephone (PTT) (administration), common carrier
potentialfrei floating (input connection)
Potentialverlauf *m* potential profile
Potenzierer *m* exponentiating circuit
pph (Seiten pro Stunde) pages per hour *(printer)*
PPM (Pulsphasenmodulation *f*) pulse phase modulation
PR (Paketradio *n*) packet radio
PR (Paketrate *f*) packet rate (PR) *(packets/sec.)*
PR s. privat
Prädiktionswert *m* predicted *or* estimated value *(video encoding)*
Präsentationsebene *f* presentation layer *(layer 6, OSI 7-layer reference model)*
Praxis *f*: **in der P.** in practice, in the field
Preisangebotsanforderung *f* request for price quotation (RPQ)
Prestel videotex standard in Britain, Belgium *(Cept Profile 3, s. Table VIII)*
Primärgruppenverbindung *f* group link *(modems)*
Primärmultiplexanschluß *m* (PMXA) primary

Primärratenanschluß 88

rate access (PA) *(ISDN S_{2M}, 2 Mb/s, 30 x B_{64} + D_{64} channels capability, CCITT Rec. I.421)*
Primärratenanschluß *m* primary rate access (PA) *(ISDN S_{2M})*
Primitive *n* primitive *(SS7 elementary inter-layer message, basic unit of machine instruction)*
Prinzip *n* concept
Print *n* module, PC board (PCB)
Printplatte *f* board, printed circuit board (PCB)
Prinzipaufbau *m* basic structure
priorisieren prioritize, assign priority
priorisierte Anforderung *f* high-priority call instruction
Priorität in Anspruch nehmen invoke priority
Prioritätsstaffelung *f* priority grading
Prioritätsstufe *f* priority level
Prioritäts-Unterbrechung *f* pre-emption
Prioritätsverkehr *m* pre-emption *(tel.)*
Prioritätswechsel *m* change of priority level
Prioritätsziffer *f* priority number *(mobile radio)*
privat private (PR) *(tel.)*
  p. Bildschirmtext *m* in-house videotex system
  p. Fernsprech NStAnl *f* privately owned PBX
  p. MHS-System *n* private management domain (PRMD)
  p. MHS-Versorgungsbereich *m* private management domain (PRMD) *(CCITT Rec. X.400)*
  p. Schlüssel *m* private key (chipcard encryption)
  p. Telefax-Nutzung *f* homefax
  p. TK-Anlage *f* private digital exchange (PDX)
  p. transatlantisches Telefonkabel *n* private transatlantic telephone cable (PTAT)
PRMD s. privater MHS-Versorgungsbereich *m*
Probebetrieb *m* proving
Profil *n* profile, contour; section
  Widerstandsp. resistance characteristic
Programmartenkennung *f* Programme TYpe (PTY) *(RDS)*
programmierbare Ein-/Ausgabe *f* programmable input/output (PIO)
Programmkettenkennung *f* Programme Identification (PI) *(RDS)*
Programmname *m* Programme Service (PS) *(RDS)*

Programm-Programm-Verbindung *f* program-to-program communication (PPC)
Programm-Reihenfolge *f* Programme Identification Number (PIN) *(RDS)*
Programmsteuereinheit *f* (PE) program control unit *(EDS)*
Programmvorschau-Seite *f* index *or* menu page *(teletext)*
Programmzuführungskabel *n* trunk cable *(CATV)*
Programm-Zustellungssteuersystem *n* **für Heim-Videorecorder** Domestic Video Programme Delivery Control system (DVPDC, PDC) *(TV broadcast service)*
Projektierung *f* planning
projekt-spezifisch user-specific
Protokoll *n* log *(DP, fax)*; protocol *(set of data transmission rules)*
Protokollausgabe *f* hardcopy output
Protokolldifferenzierung *f* protocol discriminator *(ISDN)*
Protokollgerät *n* recording *or* listing *or* logging device
Protokollkennung *f* protocol discriminator *(SS7)*
Protokoll-Übertragungsablaufsteuerung *f* protocol communications controller (PCC)
Prozedur *f* procedure code *(f.tel. programming)*
PRU (Paketradioeinheit *m*) packet radio unit
Prüfautomat *m* automatic tester
Prüfbit *n* check bit
Prüfbuchse *f* test jack
prüfen test, verify, check
Prüffeld *n* test room
Prüfling *m* component under test; unit under test (UUT)
Prüfsatz *m* test circuit
Prüfschleife *f* loopback, interface loopback
Prüfstandversuch *m* bench test
Prüfstellung *f* test position *(IEC)*
Prüfsumme *f* checksum
Prüftechnik *f* testing
Prüfvorbereitung *f* test planning
Prüfzeilenmeßplatz *m* insertion signal test set *(TV)*
Prüfzeilenmeßsignal *n* vertical interval test signal *(TV)*
Prüfzustand *m* test indicator *(not standardized, V.24, s. Table VI)*
PS s. Programmname *m*
Pseudobefehl *m* dummy command
Pseudozufallsfolge *f* (PZF) pseudo-random noise (PRN)

P.-Generator *m* pseudo-noise (PN) generator
PSK (Phasenumtastung *f*) phase shift keying
PSM s. Pulsstufenmodulation *f*
PSME (Pegelsende- und Meßeinrichtung *f* transmission test equipment
PSP (Plattenspeicher *m*) disk storage unit
PTAT (privates transatlantisches Telefonkabel *n*) private transatlantic telephone cable
PTP (Punkt-zu-Punkt) point-to-point *(connection)*
PTR (Lochstreifenleser *m*) paper tape reader
PTT (Postverwaltung *f*) Postal, Telegraph and Telephone *(administration)*, common carrier
PTY (Programmart *f*) Programme TYpe *(RDS)*
PTZ (Posttechnisches Zentralamt *n*) Postal Engineering Centre *(DBP)*
Pufferspeicher *m* buffer (memory)
Pulsamplitudenmodulation *f* pulse amplitude modulation (PAM)
Pulsbreitenmodulation *f* pulse width modulation (PWM)
Pulscodemodulation *f* pulse code modulation (PCM)
Pulsdauermodulation *f* pulse duration modulation (PDM)
Pulsfehlerortung *f* pulse fault location *(PCM data)*

Pulsfolge *f* pulse train
Pulsfrequenzmodulation *f* pulse frequency modulation (PFM)
Puls-Pause-Verhältnis *n* make-break ratio *(tel.)*, mark-space ratio
Pulsphasenmodulation *f* pulse phase modulation (PPM)
Pulsplan *m* timing diagram
Pulsstufenmodulation *f* pulse step modulation (PSM)
Pumpen *n* hunting *(oscillator)*
Punktraster *m* dot matrix
punktuell localized
Punkt-zu-Mehrpunkt point-to-multipoint *(connection)*
Punkt-zu-Mehrpunkt-Netz *n* point-to-multipoint network *(VSAT)*
Punkt-zu-Punkt back-to-back *(connection, MUXs)*; point-to-point (PTP) *(connection)*
Pupinkabel *n* loaded cable, coil-loaded cable
Pupinspule *f* loading coil
Putzen *n* debugging *(program)*; row/column clearance *(switching)*
PV-Netz (Paketvermittlungsnetz *n*) packet switching network
PVR (Paketverlustrate *f*) packet loss rate
PVT (paketvermitteltes Sprachendgerät *n*) packet voice terminal
PWM s. Pulsbreitenmodulation *f*
PZF s. Pseudozufallsfolge *f*

Q

QAM s. Quadratur-Amplitudenmodulation *f*
QASK s. Quadratur-Amplitudenumtastung *f*
Q-Bit (Unterscheidungsbit *n*) Q bit, qualifier bit *(ISDN NUA)*
Q-CIF (gemeinsames Zwischenformat *n* mit Viertel-Pixelzahl) Quarter Common Intermediate Format *(CCITT videophone standard, 38,016 pixels)*
Ql s. Querleitungsbündel *n*
QMF s. Quadratur-Spiegelfilter *n*
QPSK s. Quadratur-Phasenumtastung *f*
QPSK (Vierphasen-Modulation *f*) quaternary PSK *(sat.)*
QSAM s. Quadratur-Seitenbandamplitudenmodulation *f*
Q-Serie *f* **der CCITT-Empfehlungen** Q-series of CCITT Recommendations *(relates to Signalling System No.7)*
Quadbit-Codierung *f* quad bit coding *(2^4 = 16 bits, QAM)*
Quadratur *f* quadrature
  Q.-Amplitudenmodulation *f* quadrature amplitude modulation (QAM)
  Q.-Amplitudenumtastung *f* quadrature amplitude shift keying (QASK)
  Q.-Phasenumtastung *f* quadrature phase shift keying
  Q.-Seitenbandamplitudenmodulation *f* quadrature sideband amplitude modulation (QSAM)
  Q.-Spiegelfilter *n* quadrature mirror filter (QMF) *(digital audio subband filter)*
  Q.-Phasenumtastung *f* quadrature phase-shift keying (QPSK)
Quadratwurzelbildner *m* square-root calculator
quanteln quantize
Quantisierung *f* quantization, discretization, signal scaling
Quantisierungspegel *m* quantizing level *(speech coding)*
Quantisierungsrauschabstand *m* signal/quantization noise ratio (SQNR)
Quantisierungsstufe *f* quantization size

quarzgenau crystal calibrated
quarzstabilisiert crystal controlled
quasivollkommene Erreichbarkeit *f* quasi-full availability
Quasizufallsfolge *f* (QZF) quasi-random *(bit)* sequence; quasi-random noise (QRN)
Quasizufallsgenerator *m* (QZG) noise generator
Quellensystem *n* source node (SN)
Quellstation *f* source station, originator
quer: Signal l q. barred, negated: l barred
Querbügel *m* cross rail *(rack)*
querdruckfest crush resistant
Querholm *m* transverse support *(rack)*
Querleitungsbündel *n* (Ql) high-usage line (HUL) *(network)*
Querprüfung *f* vertical redundancy check (VRC)
Querruf *m* inter-network call
Querschnittswandler *m* optical waveguide transition *(FO)*
Querverbinder *m* terminal link *(connector)*
Querverbindung(sleitung) *f* direct line, tie line, tie trunk *(between private branch exchanges)*; interoffice trunk *(US)*
Querverkehr *m* internet traffic
Querweg *m* (QW) high-usage route
Querwegführung *f* alternative routing
Quintbit-Codierung *f* quint bit coding *(2^5 = 32, HS modems)*
Quittungsbetrieb *m* handshake procedure *(bus)*
quittungsgesteuert controlled by acknowledgement signals
Quittungsmeldung *f* acknowledgement
Quittungston *m* audible acknowledgement signal
Quittungsverfahren *n* handshaking method *(PCM data, speech)*
QW s. Querweg *m*
QZF s. Quasizufallsfolge *f*
QZG s. Quasizufallsgenerator *m*

R

RACE Research and development for Advanced Communications in Europe *(Eureka project, FO network, HDTV)*
Radaus *f* Radio Austria AG *(VAS of Austrian PTT)*
Radiocom 2000 *n* cellular mobile telephone system *(France, 200 and 400 MHz)*
Radio-Datensystem *n* radio data system (RDS) *(EBU specification document Tech. 3244-E)*
Radiotext *m* radio text (service) *(RDS)*
Rahmen *m* frame *(PCM)*; block *(transmission)*
Rahmenabgleich *m* frame alignment
Rahmenaufbau *m* frame structure (PCM)
Rahmenbildung *f* framing *(PCM)*
Rahmengleichlauf *m* frame alignment
Rahmenkennwort *n* frame alignment signal
Rahmenkontrollfeld *n* frame control field *(FDDI)*
Rahmenprogramm *n* main program
Rahmenprüfzeichen *n* frame check sequence (FCS) *(SS7 CRC)*
Rahmenstart *m* framing; frame timing *(X.21)*
Rahmensynchronisierung *f* frame alignment *(PCM data)*
Rahmentakt *m* frame cycle *or* interval
Rahmen-TL *m* (Technischer Leitfaden *m*) Basic Technical Requirements
Rahmenvermittlung *f* frame switching *(CCITT X.31)*
Rahmenversatz *m* frame delay
Rahmenweiterleitung *f* frame relaying *(CCITT X.31)*
Rangierdraht *m* jumper wire
Rangieren *n* jumpering, patching, strapping; switching, routing *(signals, channels)*
Rangierfeld *n* distribution panel
RAP (Funkanschlußpunkt *m*) radio access point *(to network)*
Rastblock *m* latching block *(X.21, ISO 4903)*
Raster *m* pitch *(connector pins)*; raster, scanning pattern *(display)*; spacing *or* pattern *(frequency, clock (pulse))*; timing *(samples)*; spacing, separation *(channels)*; grid *(wiring)*; grating *(optical)*;
Doppelr. interleaved channel arrangement
Punktr. dot matrix

Signalr. signal quantization *(video encoding)*
Zeichnungsr. coordinate system
Zellenr. cell spacing *(ATM, e.g. 69 bytes)*
19"-Raster-Modul 19" rack size module
Rasterbildprozessor *m* raster image processor (RIP) *(DTP)*
Rasterkennwort *n* pattern *or* (multi)frame alignment signal *(line testing)*
Rastermaß *n* matrix spacing; grid spacing (NC); resolution *(fax)*
Rasteroszillator *m* spectrum oscillator
Rasterschalter *m* resolution selector *(fax)*
Rasterung *f* scanning pattern *(video display)*; timing pattern *(pulse)*; quantization, signal scaling
Rasterverzerrung *f* timing error *(ESS)*
Rastkontakt *m* detent contact *(connector)*
Rastteil *n* locking part *(connector)*
rauhe Bedingungen *fpl* severe conditions
Raumkoppelelement *n* space division multiplex (SDM) switching element
Raumkoppelnetz *n* space division (switching) network *(for each call, a separate physical path is set up through the switching centre)*
Raumlagenvielfach *n* space division multiplex (SDM); space division multiplexer, SDM multiplexer, space switch *(ESS)*
Raummultiplex *n* space division multiplex (SDM)
Raumstufe *f* space (division multiplex (SDM)) stage
Raumstufenmodul *m* space switch module
Raumvielfach *n* s. Raumlagenvielfach
Raumvielfachkoppelnetz *n* space division multiplex (SDM) switching network
Rauschabstand *m* signal/noise ratio (SNR)
rauscharm:
  r. Blockwandler *m* low noise block converter (LNB) *(sat.)*
  r. Empfangsumsetzer *m* low noise converter (LNC) *(sat.)*
  r. Konverter *m* low noise converter (LNC) *(sat.)*
  r. Vorverstärker *m* low noise amplifier (LNA) *(sat.)*

Rauschklirrmessung 94

Rauschklirrmessung f intermodulation noise measurement
Rauschleistungs(dichte)abstand m (RLA) noise power ratio (NPR)
Rauschsender m noise generator
Rauschverhältnis n signal/noise ratio (SNR)
Rauschzahl f gain/noise temperature (G/T) *(sat.)*
Rautentaste f lozenge or hash key *(tel.)*
RB (Rückkehr f zur Grundmagnetisierung, zum Ausgangszustand) return to bias *(data recording method, PCM)*
RBOC Regional Bell Operating Company *(US)*
RC (Empfangsschritttakt m) Receive Clock *(V.24/RS232C)*
RC (Fernamt n) regional centre
RD (Empfangsdaten npl) Receive Data *(V.24/RS232C)*
RDS (Radio-Datensystem n) radio data system
RDS (laufende Digitalsumme f) running digital sum
Reaktionszeit f response time
Realisierung f execution, implementation
Recheneinheit f arithmetic (and logic) unit (ALU)
rechnergesteuertes Koppelfeld n digital cross connect (DCC)
rechnergestützt or -**unterstützt** automatic, automated, computer-assisted or -aided, computerized, machine-assisted or -aided
 r. Entwurf m computer-aided design (CAD)
 r. Fertigung f computer-aided manufacturing (CAM)
 r. Konstruktion f computer-aided design (CAD)
 r. Übersetzung f machine-assisted translation (MAT)
 r. Verdrahtung f computer-aided wiring (CAW)
rechnerintegrierte Geschäftsabwicklung f computer integrated business (CIB)
Rechnerkopplung f computer link
Rechnerverbund m computer link-up or network *(vtx)*
Rechtsbehelfsbelehrung f information on available legal remedies
Rechtsmittelbelehrung f information on available legal remedies
rechtszirkulare Polarisation f right-hand circular polarisation (RHCP) *(sat.)*
Redundanz f redundancy
reell resistive *(impedance)*
Referat n section *(organisation)*

Referenzmodell n reference model (RM) *(7-layer OSI model, s. Table I)*
Referenz-Nummer f call reference *(SS7)*
Reflexionsdämpfung f return loss
Reflexionsmischer m reflective mixer *(FO)*
Regelung f closed-loop control
 vorläufige R. preliminary regulation
Regelverstärker m gain-controlled amplifier
Regelwerk n Standards and Codes; rule system *(AI)*
Regendämpfung f rain attenuation *(sat., microwave)*
Regeneratorfeld n regenerator section *(tel.)*
Regenintensität f rainfall rate *(sat., microwave)*
regionales Fernnetz n short-haul network
Register n: **Termin-R.** notepad *(f. tel.)*
Registereintragung f directory entry *(tel.)*
Registersuchermarkierer m (RSM) register finder marker
Registerzeichen n interregister signal *(dig. tel.)*
Registrieren n Install *(user in MHS name server)*
Registrieroszillograph m recording oscilloscope
Regler m variable attenuator; controller
Reihe f: **der Block ist an der R.** the block has reached the head of the queue
Reihen n sequencing
Reihenanlage f series telephones; intercom *(tel.)*
Reihenfolgenummer f (RFN) sequence number *(of blocks, sat.)*
Reihenfolgetreue f correct sequencing, sequence conformity *(of blocks, sat.)*
Reihenklemme f terminal block
Reihenordner m queuing device, call storage device
Reihung f: **Paketr.** packet sequencing
rein:
 r. digital all digital
 r. Wartesystem n proper delay system
 r. Zufallsverkehr m pure-chance traffic
relative Anrufblockierung f call congestion ratio
 r. Einschaltdauer f duty cycle
RELP-Codierung f residual excited linear predictive coding
Reparaturdauer f: **mittlere R.** mean time to repair
Reparaturdienstzentrale f Repair Service Centre (RSC) *(BT IDA)*

Reparaturzeit f: **mittlere R.** mean time to repair (MTTR)
Reserve f margin; standby
Reserveprozessor m backup or standby processor
Reserveschaltfeld n emergency control panel
Reserveschaltung f automatic reserve/back-up activation
Reserveverstärker m backup amplifier
reservieren booking *(lines)*
Reservierungsverfahren n reserved-access method *(PCM speech)*
Restdämpfung f residual or overall attenuation; insertion loss, net loss *(US)*; overall loss
Restdämpfungsverzerrung f loss/frequency distortion
Restfehlersatz m residual error rate *(%)*
Restseitenbandmodulation f (RM) residual sideband modulation (RSB)
RF-CSM (Hochfrequenz-Kommunikationssystem-Überwachung f) RF Communication System Monitoring *(DBP, sat.)*
RFI (Antrag m auf Auskunftserteilung) Request for Information *(prior to purchase)*
RFN s. Reihenfolgenummer f
RFRA (Rückfrage f) enquiry; call hold *(tel.)*
R-Gespräch n collect call *(tel.)*
Rheinfunkdienst m Rhine radio-telephone service *(international)*
Rhythmus m cadence *(e.g. 1 s ON, 250 ms OFF, 1 s ON)*
   im R. der/des ... in time with ...; locked to...
   im 10-mS-R. at a 10-ms rate
RI (Ankommender Ruf) Ring Indicator *(V.24/RS232C)*
Richtfunk m (RiFu) radio relay
Richtfunkabschnitt m radio relay section
Richtfunknetz n radio relay system
Richtfunkstrecke f radio (relay) link; microwave link
Richtig/Falsch-Bewertung f Go/No-Go evaluation
Richtkoppler m directional coupler *(sat.)*
Richtlinien fpl **für offene Netze** Open Network Provision *(EC)*
Richtstrom m rectified current *(TDM, mobile RT)*
Richtung f route *(tel. sys.)*
Richtungsabgriff m route tap *(zoner)*
Richtungsausscheidung f route segregation
Richtungsbetrieb m simplex or one-way transmission

richtungsindividueller Speicher m individual-route store
Richtungsschrift f non return to zero (change) (NRZ(C)) code *(PCM)*
Richtungstaktschrift f phase modulation (PM), phase encoding
Richtungsumwertung f route translation
Richtverbindung f (RV) radio (relay) link
Richtwerte mpl norms
Riegelwanne f shell *(connector)*
RiFu s. Richtfunk m
Ringleitungssystem n loop network *(FO)*
RIP (Rasterbildprozessor m) raster image processor *(DTP)*
RISC (Computer m mit verringertem Befehlsvorrat) reduced-instruction set computer
RKM-Code m resistor coding *(e.g. 4R7,47K, 4M7)*
RKW (Rahmenkennungswort n) frame alignment signal *(PCM)*
RLA (Rauschleistungsabstand m) noise power ratio (NPR)
RM (Referenzmodell n) reference model *(7-layer OSI model)*
RM s. Restseitenbandmodulation f
RMA (zufallsmäßiger Vielfachzugriff m) random multiple access *(sat. access method, e.g. ALOHA)*
RNG (Rufnummerngeber m) automatic dialler *(PBX)*
RNIS (ISDN n) Réseau Numérique à Intégration des Services ("numeris") *(French ISDN)*
rnr (keine Empfangsbereitschaft f) receive not ready *(videotex)*
Rohrleitung f conduit, duct *(cables)*
Rollkugel f tracker ball *(VDU)*
Rost m cable rack or shelf, rack shelf; runway
Roststütze f runway support
RPOA (anerkannte private Betriebsgesellschaft f) recognized private operating company
rr (Empfangsbereitschaft) receive ready *(videotex)*
RRUF (automatischer Rückruf m) automatic call-back
RS232 *EIA standard for serial data communication; interfaces up to 20 kb/s and NRZ signalling (0 = +3 to 25V, 1 = -3 to -25V, adopted in CCITT Recommendations V.24, V.28 and DIN 66020, see Tables IV and VI)*
RS232A *RS232 interface with 20mA current loop*
RS232C *RS232 interface with 5V voltage source drive, s. Table VI*

RS232D *RS232 revision to match V.24/V.28*
RS422, RS423 *corresponds to RS232 logic for high data rate and long-range traffic*
RS485 *corresponds to RS422, as bus system*
RSA-Verfahren *n* Rivest Shamir Adleman (RSA) method *(chipcard encryption)*
RSB (Restseitenband *n*) residual sideband *(TV)*
RS-Code *m* Reed Solomon code *(error corr.)*
RSE (Ruf- und Signaleinrichtung *f*) ringing and signalling generator
RSM (Registersuchermarkierer *m*) register finder marker
RT (Radiotext *m*) radio text (service) *(RDS)*
RTC (Echtzeituhr *f*) real time clock
RTS (Sendeteil *n* Einschalten) Request To Send *(V.24/RS232C)*
RTTY (Funkfernschreiber *m*) radio teletype
RTU (Fernwirk-Unterstation *f*) remote terminal unit *(telecontrol)*
Rückdämpfung *f* front-to-back ratio *(antenna)*
Rückflußdämpfung *f* return loss *(distributor, FO)*
Rückfrage *f* check-back signal *(ISDN)*; consultation call; (RFRA) enquiry; call hold *(tel.)*
Rückfragebetrieb *m* transmission with negative acknowledgement *(telecontrol)*
rückfragen hold for inquiry *(tel.)*
Rückführung *f* double-ended control *(synchronization)*; rerouting *(after link restoration)*
rückholen retrieve *(a transferred call)*
Rückhören *n* side-tone *(tel.)*
   R. im eigenen Kanal echo, inchannel echo
Rückhörbezugsdämpfung *f* return loss, side-tone reference equivalent *(tel.)*
Rückkanal *m* back channel *(sat.)*; echo channel
   R. Empfangsdaten Secondary Received data (SRCV) *(V.24/RS232C, s. Table VI)*
   R. Sendedaten Secondary Transmit data (SXMT) *(V.24/RS232C, s. Table VI)*
   R. Sendeteil Einschalten Back Request To Send (BRTS) *(V.24/RS232C, s. Table VI)*
Rückkehr *f* return; resetting *(relay)*; recovery *(power)*
   R. nach Null return to zero (RZ) *(PCM code)*
   R. zum Ausgangszustand return to bias (RB) *(data recording method, PCM)*
   R. zur Grundmagnetisierung return to bias (RB) *(data recording method, PCM)*

Rückmeldung *f* feedback, acknowledgement *(message)*; signalling
Rücknahme *f* removal *(TEI assignment)*
Rückpolung *f* reversal to normal polarity *(tel.)*
Rückruf *m* call-back, recall *(from operator)*; return call *(by called subscriber)* camp-on to a busy subscriber, camp-on-busy *(waiting for the line to become available)*
   R. bei Besetzt completion of call on meeting busy
Rückruftaste *f* camp-on-busy button or key *(f.tel.)*
rücksetzen reset
Rücksetzen *n* **einer Verbindung** resynchronisation (of a connection) *(ISDN)*
rückspulen rewind *(PTR)*
rückstellen reset; clear *(counter)*
Rückwand *f* back panel; backplane
Rückwandleiterplatte *f* backplane (circuit board)
rückwärts auslösen forced release
Rückwärtskanal *m* backward channel
Rückwärtskennzeichen *n* backward call indicator *(SS7 UP)*
Rückwärtszeichen *n* backward signal *(signal transmitted against the direction of call setup)*
Rückwechsel *m* changeback *(after change of service, ISDN)*
Rückwirkungsüberlagerung *f* superimposed feedback
Rückzugspunkt *m* recovery point, checkpoint, save point
Ruf *m* call; ringing signal *(tel.)*
   R. ablehnen disregard a call
   R. beginnen originate a call
   R. einleiten originate a call
Ruf- und Signaleinrichtung *f* (RSE) ringing and signalling generator
Rufabschaltung *f* ring tripping
Rufannahme *f* call acceptance
Rufanschaltung *f* connection of ringing tone
Rufaufbau *m* call set-up
Rufbeantwortung *f* call response
Rufbereich *m* cell *(cellular RT)*
Rufbereichswechsel *m* roaming *(cellular RT)*
Rufbetrieb *m* manual operation *(exchange)*
Rufdatennachverarbeitung *f* post-processing of call data
Rufende *n* signal end *(PCM data, speech)*
Ruferkennung *f* ringing tone detector
Rufgenerator *m* ringing generator
Rufleitung *f* ringdown line

Rufnummer f address signal *(data)*, directory number *(tel.)*
Rufnummernanzeige f (calling) number identification *(ISDN)*
Rufnummerngeber m (RNG) call sender; automatic dialler *(tel.)*
Rufnummernregister n call number directory
Rufnummernumsetzung f number or call number conversion *(directory numbers)*
Rufrhythmus m ringing cadence *(tel.)*
Rufstromquelle f ringing (current) source
Ruftakt m ringing cadence; ringing cycle
Rufton m ringing tone *(tel.)*; signal tone *(data)*
Rufumlegung f call transfer
Rufumleitung f call diversion *(f. tel.)*
Rufverteilung f call allocation *(tel.)*
Rufverzug m post-dialling delay
Rufwegelenkung f call routing
Rufweiterleitung f (RWL) call forwarding, call transfer; call redirection
Rufweiterschaltung f call forwarding, call transfer; call redirection
Rufzeit f ringing time
Rufzeitüberwachung f ringing time supervision *(SS7)*
Rufzone f (RZo) call zone *(radio paging)*
Rufzuschaltung f follow me (mode) *(call diversion pick-up)*
Ruhe f idle condition
R. vor dem Telefon Do-Not-Disturb feature
Ruhebitrate f zero-movement bit rate *(video encoding)*
Ruhecodewort n idle code word *(PCM)*

Ruhegeräusch n idle-channel noise *(tel.)*, weighted noise *(PCM)*; background noise
Ruheschleife f loop in idle condition
Ruhestellung f normal state *(flip flop)*
Ruhestrom m zero-signal current
Ruhezustand m idle condition *(transmission channel)*, idle state; quiescent state *(ESS)* power-down mode *(HW)*
Ruhezyklus m idle cycle
Rumpf m: **Paket-R.** packet body
Rundfunk m broadcast(ing)
Rundfunksatellit m broadcasting satellite (BS), direct broadcasting satellite (DBS)
Rundfunksatellitendienst m broadcasting satellite service (BSS) *(CCIR)*
Rundgabe f broadcast(ing), multi-address *(data)*
Rundschreiben n broadcast(ing), multi-address *(TTY)*
Rundsendeeinrichtung f multi-addressing device
Rundsenden n broadcast(ing); sequence calling *(ISDN tel.)*, multi-address calling *(tel.)*; multi-address service *(data)*
RV (Richtverbindung f) radio (relay) link
RWL s. Rufweiterleitung f
RX (Knotenvermittlungsstelle f (KVSt)) regional exchange
RZ (Rückkehr f nach Null) return to zero *(PCM code)*
RZo s. Rufzone f

S

S (Sender *m*) transmitter
Sachmittel *npl* materials
SAD (Analog-/Digital-Zeichenumsetzer *m*) Signalling converter, Analog/Digital
SAF (Speichervermittlung *f*) store-and-forward (S&F)
S-ALOHA (segmentiertes ALOHA *n*) slotted ALOHA
Sammelanschluß *m* collective line, collective number *(tel.)*; line group *(PABX)*; hunt group
Sammelbefehl *m* broadcast command *(TC)*
Sammelbitrate *f* aggregate bit rate
Sammeldienst *m* nultipoint-point service *(VSAT)*
Sammelgruppe *f* hunt group *(tel.)*
Sammelkabel *n* bus cable
Sammelnachtstelle *f* common night extension *(tel.)*
Sammelrichtung *f* inbound *(VSAT)*
Sammelruf *m* group hunting
Sammelrufnummer *f* group number; hunt group
Sammelschiene *f* bus *(data)*; bus-bar *(el.)*
SAP (Dienstzugriffspunkt *m*) service access point *(SS7, CCITT Rec. Q.761...764)*
SAPI (Dienstzugriffspunktkennung *f*) service access point identifier *(SS7)*
  p-SAPI (SAPI *f* für Paketdaten) SAPI for packet data
  s-SAPI (SAPI *f* für Signalisierungsdaten) SAPI for signalling data
SARCOM (Seenotfunknetz *n*) search and rescue communication system
Satellitenempfangsantenne *f* receive only satellite (ROS) *(antenna)*
Satellitenkommunikations-Empfangseinrichtung *f* (SKE) satellite communications receiving facility *(DFS)*
Satellitenkommunikationsprotokoll *n* satellite link protocol
Satellitenstromweg *m* satellite circuit
satellitenvermittelter TDMA *m* satellite switched TDMA (SSTDMA)
Satelliten-Verteildienst *m* satellite data distribution service *(X.25, DBP VSAT)*
Sat-Kom (Satelliten-Kommunikation *f*) satellite communications
Satz *m* circuit, circuit group *(tel.)*; record *(data)*; set *(PCM frame)*
Satzübertrager *m* repeater *(tel.)*
Saugkreis *m* series resonant circuit
SB s. Schmalband *n*
SB-Terminal (Selbstbedienungs-T. *n*) self service terminal *(vtx, telebanking)*
SB-Videoterminal (Schmalband-Videoterminal *n*) compressed-video terminal *(with codec-compressed bandwidth)*
SCCP (Steuerteil *m* für Zeichengabeverbindungen) signalling connection control part *(SS7)*
Schaltbrücke *f* switchable link *(DIP FIX switch)*
Schaltbuchse *f*: **koaxiale S.** switched coaxial jack
Schaltdraht *m* hook-up wire
Schalteinrichtung *f* switching device
Schaltelement *n* jumper module
schalten switch, connect, patch; gate *(digital)*; interrupt *(line)*
Schaltfeld *n* connector panel, control panel
Schaltgefühl *n* switching response *or* action *(membrane keypad)*
Schaltkabel *n* terminating cable
Schaltkennzeichen *n* switching signal *(exchange)*
Schaltknackfilter *n* key click filter
Schaltmultiplexer *m* cross connect multiplexer (CCM) *(network management)*
Schaltnetz *n* combinational circuit
Schaltnetzteil *n* switched-mode power supply (SMPS)
Schaltpaket *n* switching stack *(membrane keypad)*
Schaltstation *f* cross connect equipment *(for standby network switching)*
Schaltstecker *m* connecting plug *(signal distributor)*
Schaltteil *n* switch (element)
Schaltunterlage *f* engineering data
Schaltverstärker *m* switching amplifier
Schaltwähler *m* access switch
Schaltweg *m* switched path, contact travel
Schaltwerk *n* switch(ing) mechanism *or* device *or* unit; logic circuit *(with delay elements)*; processor
Schaltwert *m* switching value; residual

Schätzwert 100

parameter
Schätzwert *m* estimated *or* predicted value *(video encoding)*
Scheibe *f* plate; disc, disk
Koppel(feld)sch. matrix plane
Zeitsch. time slice
Scheinverkehr *m* traffic padding
Schema *n* mask *(on CRO or VDU screen, to CCITT G.712 or others)*
Schicht *f* layer *(in the OSI 7-layer reference model* (RM), *s. Table I)*
  S.-3 Signalisierungsprotokoll *n* layer 3 signalling protocol
Schichtenprotokoll *n* layer protocol *(ISDN)*
Schichtverteiler *m* stacked terminal block
Schichtwellenleiter *m* planar waveguide *(FO)*
Schieflage *f* skew *(clock alignment)*
Schieflauf *m* skew *(fax.)*
Schiene *f* rail *(PS);* bus(bar) *(HW);* beam, feed, channel *(sat.)*
  Supermultiplexsch. super-multiplex highway *(transm.)*
Schildträger *m* label mounting
Schirmdämpfung *f* shielding efficiency
Schlaglänge *f* pitch *(FO);* length of lay *(cable)*
Schlagtaste *f* impact button
Schlagtaster *m* emergency button, panic button *(colloquial)*
schlecht poor quality *(channel)*
Schlechtquittung *f* negative acknowledgement
Schleifenbefehl *m* loop-back command *(NT)*
Schleifenbildung *f* looping
Schleifenimpulslaufzeit *f* loop delay
Schleifenschluß *m* loop closure *(tel.)*
Schleppy *n* portable transceiver *(cellular mobile RT, colloquial)*
Schloßtaste *f* lock switch *or* key
schlüsselfertiges System *n* turnkey system
Schlüsselschalter *m* key-operated switch; keylock switch
Schlüsselwechsel *m* code change
Schlußtaste *f* clear key *or* button *(TTY)*
Schlußzeichen *n* clear back signal; clearing, disconnect signal
Schlußzustand *m* on-hook state *(tel.,* indicates replacement of handset in the backward direction)
schmale Bauform *f* slim design
Schmalband *n* (SB) narrow-band (NB)
  S.-FM *f* narrow-band FM (NFM)
  S.-Fernsehen *n* slow scan TV (SSTV)
Schmelzeinsatz *m* fusible cartridge
Schnappfeder *f* snap disc *(membrane keypad)*

schnelle Frequenzumtastung *f* fast frequency shift keying (FFSK) *(PMR, 1200 Bd)*
Schnellrückmeldung *f* priority return information
Schnellverschluß *m* snap *or* quick-action closure
Schnittstelle *f* interface
Schnittstellenanpassung *f* interface adapter
Schnittstellendämpfung *f* interface attenuation
Schnittstellenelement *n* primitive *(elementary inter-layer message)*
Schnittstellenkabel *n* interconnecting cable
Schnittstellenleitung *f* interchange circuit *(DIN 44302)*
schnurlos cordless
  s. Telefon *n* cordless telephone (CT)
Schnurverteiler *m* jackfield distributor
Schrägspuraufzeichnung *f* helical scan recording *(VTR)*
Schrank *m* cabinet
Schraubstutzen *m* threaded ferrule *(cable)*
Schreiber-Mitschrift *f* recorder trace
Schreibfunk *m* radio teletype
Schreibstation *f* printer terminal
Schriftzeichen *n* graphic character *(DP)*
Schritt *m* signal element; bit *(in the case of binary modulation)*
  84-S.-Telegramm *n* 84-bit message
Schrittdauer *f* pulse period, bit period
Schrittfehler *m* symbol error *(transmission)*
Schrittfolgefrequenz *f* symbol rate *(bit stream)*
Schrittgeschwindigkeit *f* modulation rate, Baud rate; data rate stepping speed *(relay)*
Schritthaltende Wahl *f* direct dialling
schritthaltend gesteuertes System *n* stage-by-stage control system
Schrittlänge *f* step length; unit interval
Schrittpuls *m* clock pulse
Schrittrate *f* modulation rate; symbol rate *(transmission)*
Schritttakt *m* line clock *(transmission);* signal element timing *(X.21)*
Schrittweite *f* step size
Schrittweitenbestimmung *f* signal scaling, quantization *(video encoding)*
Schrotrauschen *n* shot(-effect) noise *(FO)*
Schrumpfschlauch *m* heat shrink
Schuko-Steckdose *f* 2-pin/3-wire power outlet *(HW)*
Schuldnerdaten *npl* outstanding charge data
Schutzabstand *m* guard band *(adjacent channel)*

Schutzart f protection class
Schutzerde f protective ground, frame (V.24/RS232C, s. Table VI)
Schutzmaßnahmen fpl safety precautions (data sheet)
Schutzzeit f buffer period (between transmission bursts, sat.)
Schwankung f fluctuation, variation
schwarzes Brett n bulletin board (MHS)
Schwebung(sfrequenz) f beat (frequency)
Schwenkrahmenbauweise f hinged-frame construction (rack)
Schwenkrahmenfeld n hinged-frame panel (rack)
Schwerpunkt m centre of gravity; radiation centre (sat. antenna)
Schwingung f oscillation, frequency
  Ausgangsschw. output frequency
SCPB (Einzelkanalburst m) single channel per burst (sat.)
SCPC (Ein-Kanal-pro-Träger-System n) single channel per carrier (sat.)
SCPT (Ein-Kanal-pro-Transponder-System n) single channel per transponder (sat.)
SCVF (Einkanal-Niederfrequenz-Verfahren n) single-channel voice frequency (telex signalling)
SCU (Unternetz-Steuereinheit f) subnetwork control unit (VSAT)
SDA (Digital-/Analog-Zeichenumsetzer m) Signalling converter, Digital/Analog
SDH- (Synchron-Digital-Hierarchie-)**Bitrate** f SDH bit rate (155 Mbit/s, radio link)
SDLC (synchrone Übertragungssteuerung f) synchronous data link control
SDM (Raummultiplex n) space division multiplex
SDS (Sonder(dienst)satz m) special-service circuit
SE (Speichereinheit f) storage unit (EDS)
S/E (Sender/Empfänger m) transceiver (transmitter/receiver)
Seefunk m maritime radio (INMARSAT)
Seefunkdienst m public maritime radio service
  beweglicher S. maritime mobile service
Seekabel n submarine or undersea cable
Seenavigationsfunkdienst m maritime radionavigation service
Seenotfunknetz n search and rescue communication system (SARCOM) (German maritime FM radio service)
Seele f core (cable)
Segment n slot (time slot)
segmentiertes ALOHA n slotted ALOHA (S-ALOHA) (sat. RMA method of the University of Hawaii)
Seitengestaltung f page layout (videotex monitor)
Seiten pro Stunde pages per hour (pph) (printer)
Seitentabelle f table of pages (TOP) (vtx)
Seitenteil n lateral section
Seitenumkehrfunktion f flip page function (fax)
Seitenverhältnis n aspect ratio (TV)
SEL (Übertragungsgeschwindigkeit f) SELect data signal rate (V.24/RS232C)
Selbstbedienungsterminal n (SB-Terminal) self-service terminal (vtx, telebanking)
Selbsteinschreiben n **von Betriebsmöglichkeiten** subscriber-activated service features
selbstgespeistes Amt n non-power-fed station
selbststeuerndes Koppelnetz n self-routing switching network (ATM)
selbsttätige optische Wegermittlung f automatic optical path selection
Selbsttest m self-test
Selbstumschaltung f subscriber-activated change-over
Selbstwahl f manual calling
Selbstwählferndienst m (SWFD) subscriber trunk dialling (STD); direct distance dialling (DDD)
Selbstwählfernsprech-Drahtnetz n public switched telephone network (PSTN)
Selbstwähl-Funktelefonsystem n mobile automatic telephone system (MATS)
Selbstwählteilnehmer m DDI subscriber
Selbstwählverkehr m subscriber dialling (tel.)
Selbstwählvorrichtung f autodialler (vtx)
Selektivabfrage f selective polling
selektive Wiederholungsaufforderung f selective repeat (SR) (ARQ procedure, sat.)
Selektivruf m selective calling (tel.)
Selektivrufeinrichtung f selective call facility (SELCALL)
SEM signalling converter, E&M
Semaphor n semaphore or semaphore counter
Sendeadresse f transmit identifier (PCM data)
Sendeaufforderung f polling call
Sendeaufruf m polling
Sendeberechtigungsmarke f token (token ring network)
Sendebereitschaft Clear To Send (CTS) (V.24/RS232C, s. Table VI)

Sendebezugsdämpfung *f* sending reference equivalent *(FO)*
Sendedaten Transmit Data (TD) *(V.24/RS 232C, s. Table VI)*
Sendefrequenz select transmit frequency *(V.24/RS232C, s. Table VI, 200-Baud modem)*
Sendeleistung *f* equivalent isotropically radiated power (EIRP) *(sat., in dBW)*
Sendemodus *m* originate mode
Senderechte *npl* right to transmit *(PCM data blocks)*
Sender/Empfänger *m* (S/E) transceiver *(transmitter/receiver)*
Senderkennung *f* (SK) Programme Identification (PI) *(RDS)*
Sendeschrittakt transmit clock (TC) *(from DTE, from DCE; V.24/RS232C, s. Table VI)*
sendeseitige Taktzentrale *f* transmit clock (TC)
Sendesperre *f* transmit block
Sendestation *f* master station
Sendestop *m* end of transmission (EOT)
Sendeteil einschalten Request To Send (RTS) *(V.24/RS232C, s. Table VI)*
Sendeterminal *n* (ST) send terminal *(DC)*
Sendeumsetzer *m* modulator *(dig. TV)*
Sende- und Meßkoppler *m* (SMK) transmission test equipment connecting matrix
Sendezeit *f* time of origin (TOO)
Sendungsvermittlung *f* message switching
Senke *f* sink *(data)*, load
Sequentialisierung *f* sequencing *(ISO, dividing the user message into frames, sets or packets with sequence number)*
sequenzgesicherte Protokollklasse *f* sequenced protocol class *(SS7)*
seriell:
  s. Ein-/Ausgabe *f* serial input/output (SIO) *(port)*
  s. Information *f* bit-serial information
serienmäßig standard
Serientakt-Unterdrückungsmaß *n* series mode rejection range (SMRR)
Servicegerät *n* (SG) service unit (SU) *(FO service channel)*
Servicerechner *m* (SVR) service processor *(vtx)*
Service 130 freephone service of the DBP *(subscriber trunk dialling at local rates, dialling code 0130+; corresponds to International 0800 (GB), International 800, WATS (US), International Toll Free (AUS), numero vert (FR))*
SF (Speichervermittlung *f*) store-and-forward (switching)

SFuRD (Stadtfunkrufdienst *m* (Cityruf)) regional radio paging service *(DBP)*
SG s. Servicegerät *n*
SG s. Sichtgerät *n*
SGA s. Signal-Geräuschabstand *m*
SHF (superhohe Frequenz *f*) super high frequency *(sat., 3-30 GHz)*
SIC (S-Schnittstellenschaltung *f*) S-interface circuit *(ISDN)*
sicher secure; safe; reliable; dependable
Sicherheitsabstand *m* guard band *(between frequency bands)*; safety margin
Sicherheitsrückruf *m* secure dial-back
Sicherheitsstufe *f* security level
sichern save *(data, messages)*; protect *(transmission)*
Sicherung *f* : **Daten-S.** data locking *(transmission link)*, data protection *(system failure)*
Sicherungsausschalter *m* automatic cutout
Sicherungsautomat *m* automatic cutout
Sicherungsdienst *m* data link service
Sicherungsschicht *f* data link layer *(CCITT Rec. I.440 and I.441, layer 2, OSI reference model)*
Sicherungssignal *n* data protection signal
Sicherungsteil *m* data protection section *(of a message)*
Sichtanzeige *f* visual display (unit)
sichtbar unblanked *(videotex monitor)*
  nicht s. blanked *(videotex monitor)*
Sichtgerät *n* (SG) video display unit (VDU)
Signalader *f* signalling wire *(TC)*
Signalaufbereitung *f* signal processing or conditioning
Signalausbreitung *f* signal distribution *(TV broadcasting)*
Signalausfall *m* dropout
Signalbelegung *f* signal levels
Signalerde *f* signal ground (GND) *(V.24/RS232C, s. Table VI)*
Signalfeld *n* alarm signal panel; control and alarm panel
Signalform *f* signal (wave)shape
Signalformung *f* signal processing, conditioning *(meas.)*; shaping *(transm.)*
Signalgabe *f* signalling
Signalgeber *m* signal generator
Signalgemisch *n* noise
Signal-Geräuschabstand *m* (SGA) signal/ noise ratio (SNR, S/N)
Signalgeschwindigkeit *f* signal speed *(transmission, in microsec./km)*
Signalisierung *f* signalling
  S. außerhalb des Bandes outband signalling

S. außerhalb der Zeitlagen out-slot signalling
S. innerhalb der Zeitlagen in-slot signalling
S.-Gelegenheitmuster *n* signalling opportunity pattern (SOP)
S.-Kanal *m* signalling channel
S.-Multiplexer *m* (SMUX) signalling multiplexer *(DC)*
S.-Prozessor *m* (SPROZ) signalling processor *(DC)*
S.-Rahmenkennungswort *n* multiframe alignment signal *(PCM)*
S.-Umsetzer *m* signalling converter *(DC)*
S.-Zentrale *f* central signalling section
Signallaufzeit *f* signal delay; signal transit time *(2 x = round trip delay)*
Signalraster *m* signal quantization, signal scaling
Signal/Nebensprechverhältnis *n* signal/crosstalk ratio *(in dB)*
Signal/Rausch-Abstand *m* (SRA) signal/noise ratio (SNR)
Signalspeicher *m* latch
Signalstauchung *f* signal crushing *(CATV, black level)*
Signalsynchronisierung *f* acquisition of signal (AOS) *(sat.)*
Signaltiefe *f* signal quantization, signal resolution (in bits) *(video encoding, e.g. 8 bits/pixel)*
Signalumformung *f* signal conditioning
Signalumsetzer *m* signalling converter
Signalverfahren *n* signalling system
Signalverlauf *m* signal flow, path, signal trace *(CRO)*, signal variation *or* shape *or* change
Signalverlust *m* loss of signal (LOS) *(sat.)*
Signalverteiler *m* signal distributor *(audio, video)*
Signalweg *m* signal path
Signalzeichen *n* signal element
Signalzuführung *f* signal contribution *(TV studios)*
Signalzug *m* signal flow diagram, signal path
Signalzustand "Eins" marking condition
Signalzustand "Null" spacing condition
Silikon *n* silicone
Silizium *n* silicon
Siloprinzip *n* first-in-first-out (FIFO) *(storage procedure)*
Simplex *n* (SX) simplex *(modem)*
Simultanwahl *f* simplex dialling *(PBX)*
SINAD (Störabstand *m* einschließlich Verzerrungen) Signal to Noise and Distortion (ratio)
Sinus-Standard *m* CT1 standard of the DBP
SIO (Dienstindikator *m*, Dienstkennung *f*) service indication octet *(SS7 MTP)*
SITA Société Internationale Telecommunication Aeronautique *(international data network for airlines)*
Sitzungsaufbau *m* session establishment
Sitzungsdienst *m* session service (SS)
Sitzungsebene *f* session layer *(layer 5, OSI 7-layer reference model)*
SK (Senderkennung *f*) Programme Identification (PI) *(RDS)*
SK (Sprachkanal *m*) voice channel (VC)
Skalenfaktor *m* step size control *(ADM, CCITT Rep.953)*
SKE (Satellitenkommunikations-Empfangseinrichtung *f*) satellite communications receiving facility *(DFS)*
SLA (Speicherleitungsanschluß *m*) storage bus interface unit
SLC (Teilnehmersatz *m* (TS)) subscriber line circuit
SLIC (Teilnehmeranschluß-Schnittstellenbaustein *m*) subscriber line interface circuit *(tel., digital PBX)*
SMD (oberflächenmontiertes Bauelement *n*) surface mounted device
SMK (Sende- und Meßkoppler *m*) transmission test equipment connecting matrix
SMP-Bus (Siemens-Mikroprozessor-Bus *m*) Siemens microprocessor bus
SMRR (Serientakt-Unterdrückungsmaß *n*) series mode rejection range
SMS (Satelliten-Mehrdienstsystem *n*) Satellite Multiservice System *(Eutelsat)*
SMT (Oberflächenmontagetechnik *f*) surface mounting technology
SMUX (Signalisierungsmultiplexer *m*) signalling multiplexer *(DC)*
SN (Quellensystem *n*) source node
SNA (SNA-Architektur *f*) Systems Network Architecture *(IBM)*
S₀-Schnittstelle *f* S₀ interface *(S interface, ISDN BA)*
Sockelzapfen *m* base pin *(rack)*
Sofortverkehr *m* demand traffic
Softtaste *f* softkey *(programmable key)*
Sollwert *m* reference signal *(CRO)*; setpoint *(control)*
Sonder(dienst)satz *m* (SDS) special-service circuit
Sonderfernsprecher *m* special-purpose telephone
Sonderkanal *m* special channel *(CATV,*

Sondernetz 104

7 MHz bandwidth)
Sondernetz *n* dedicated network
Sondersatz *m* (SDS) special-service circuit
Sondertaste *f* special-purpose key
SP (Zeichengabepunkt *m*) signalling point *(node in SS7 network)*
SPADE (Vielfachzugriff *m* im Frequenzmultiplex mit Kanalzuteilung nach Bedarf) Single channel per carrier PCM multiple Access Demand assignment Equipment *(sat.)*
SPAG (Arbeitsgruppe *f* zur Förderung und Anwendung von Standards) Standards Promotion and Applications Group *(in the EC Esprit programme)*
Spaltensperre *f* column barring
Spaltfrequenz *f* split frequency *(testing)*
Spannarm *m* tension arm *(PTR)*
Spannungsabhängigkeit *f* voltage coefficient
Spannungseinbruch *m* dip in voltage level
spannungsgesteuerter Quarzoszillator *m* voltage-controlled X-tal oscillator (VCXO)
Spannungshub *m* voltage excursion, voltage swing
Spannungssteilheit *f* rate of voltage change
Spannungssteuerung *f* voltage source drive *(RS232)*
Spannungswiderstand *m* voltage resistance level
Sparschalter *m* power down switch *(RT)*
SPC s. speicherprogrammierbare Steuerung *f*
SPC-Code *m* single parity check code *(error correction code with 1 bit redundancy)*
SPE (synchrone Nutzlast-Bitvollgruppe *f*) synchronous payload envelope *(TDM)*
SPEC (Kommunikation *f* mit Sprachprädiktionscodierung) Speech Predictive Encoding Communication
Speicher *m* store *(generally: an auxiliary data storage device)*;
memory *(usually describes an internal computer data store. Where an external device is referred to as memory unit, the internal device is the main memory)*
Arbeits-Sp. main memory *(s. above)*
Speicherdienst *m* message service
Speichereinheit *f* (SE) storage unit *(EDS)*
Speicherfüllstand *m* memory loading
Speicherfüllung *f* memory content
Speicherkarte *f* smart card
Speicherleitungsanschluß *m* (SLA) storage bus interface unit
speichern store, save *(data)*; latch *(signal)*

speicherprogrammierbare Steuerung *f* (SPS) stored-program control (SPC)
Speicherraum *m* storage space
Speichertakt *m* storage cycle
Speichervermittlung *f* store and forward (S&F) switching
Speicherwähleinrichtung *f* repertory dialler *(f. tel.)*
Speisereichweite *f* range of power supply *(power feeding, in ohm)*
Speisespannungsaufbereitung *f* supply voltage conversion *(tel.sys.)*
Speisung *f* power feeding *(of terminal equipment)*
speisungslos non-power-fed, independently powered;
sound-powered *(maritime mobile RT)*
Spektrallinienabstand *m* line spectrum
Sperrbereich *m* stop band *(filter)*
Sperre *f* block; (access) restriction *(tel.)*
Sp. im gehenden Verkehr block of outgoing traffic *(tel.)*
16-Hz-Sp. 16-Hz meter pulse blocking *(tel.)*
sperren bar *(telephones)*;
block *(faulty devices)*;
deactivate *(file)*; disable *(gate)*;
disconnect *(subscriber)*;
inhibit *(data, pulses)*;
lock out *(keyboard)*; restrict *(access)*;
turn off *(transistor)*
Sperren *n* call barring
Sperrerde *f* blocking ground *(PCM data)*
Sperrkriterium *n* blocking criterion
Sperrschloß *n* disabling lock *(HW, dig. PBX)*; call barring lock *(f.tel.SW)*
Sperrschritt *m* stop signal, stop bit
Sperrspannung *f* reverse voltage
Sperrtaste *f* make-busy key
Sperrtiefe *f* stop-band attenuation
Sperrwiderstand *m* backward resistance *(semiconductor)*
Sperrziffer *f* call-barring number *(tel.)*
spezifische Kabeldämpfung *f* cable attenuation coefficient
Spiel *n* cycle; tolerance, clearance
Spitze-Mittelwert-Verhältnis *n* peak/average ratio (P/AR)
Spitzigkeitsfaktor *m* peakedness factor *(stat.)*
SpK s. Sprechkanal *m*
Spleißen *n* splicing, jointing *(FO)*
Spontanbetrieb *m* asynchronous response mode (ARM) *(HDLC)*
Sprachaktivität *f* speech activity

sprachähnliche Belastung *f* white noise loading
Sprachansagen *fpl* prompts *(in voice mail)*
Sprachausblendung *f* mid-talkspurt clipping *(PCM voice)*
Sprachausgabegerät *n* audio response unit
Sprachausgabepuffer *m* voice output buffer
sprachbegleitend while speaking, with speech *(dig. PBX, using another service)*
Sprachblock *m* talkspurt *(PCM voice)*
Sprachblocklänge *f* talkspurt duration *(PCM voice)*
Sprachblockstauchung *f* talkspurt compression *(PCM voice)*
Sprachbox *f* electronic telephone mailbox; voice mail
Sprach-/Datenspeicher *m* voice/data mailbox
Sprachdetektor *m* speech detector
Spracheingabe *f* voice input *(mobile tel., hands-free dialling)*
Sprachendeinrichtung *f:* **digitale S.** digital voice terminal
Sprachinformationsserver *m* voice mail server *(dig. PBX)*
Sprachkanal *m* (SK) voice channel (VC); traffic channel *(trunking)*
Sprachmelodie *f* intonation
Sprachpaketsender *m* (SPS) voice packet transmitter
Sprachpausennutzung *f* speech interpolation *(TASI)*
Sprachspeicherdienst *m* *(AUDIOTEX)* voice mail service, voice messaging service
Sprachterminal *n* voice terminal *(dig. PBX)*
Sprachübertragung *f* voice transmission
Sprachverschlüsselung *f* speech encoding
Sprechader *f* speech wire *(tel.)*
Sprechadern *fpl* speaking pair *(tel.)*
Sprechfunk *m* radio telephony
Sprechkanal *m* (SpK) voice channel *(cellular mobile RT)*
Sprechkreis *m* speaking *or* talking circuit, speech circuit; voice circuit *or* channel
sprechkreisgebundene Zeichengabe *f* channel-associated signalling *(CCITT Rec. I.112)*
Sprechmaschine *f* synthetic speech generator
Sprechstelle *f* extension; audio station *(intercom)*, telephone station, subscriber's station
   S. für Paketvermittlung packet voice terminal (PVT)
Sprechverkehr *m* voice communication
Sprechweg *m* VF path; speech path

Sprechwegeführung *f* voice circuit
Sprechzustand *m* conversation state
Spreizspektrum-Verfahren *n* spread spectrum *(frequency hopping)* technique
Spreizspektrumzugriff *m* spread spectrum multiple access (SSMA) *(VSAT)*
SPROZ (Signalisierungsprozessor *m*) signalling processor *(DC)*
Sprung *m* step change, discontinuity
Sprunganregung *f* step-function excitation *(FO)*
sprunghaft discontinuous
Sprungwert *m* level-change value
SPS (speicherprogrammierbare Steuerung *f*) stored-program control
SPS s. Sprachpaketsender *m*
Spule *f* reel *(tape)*; coil *(winding)*
Spürgas *n* tracer gas *(cables)*
SQ (Empfangsgüte *f*) Signal Quality (detect) *(V.24/RS232C)*
SQNR (Quantisierungsrauschabstand *m*) signal/quantization noise ratio *(ADC)*
S/Q(-Verhältnis) *n* signal/quantizing distortion (ratio) *(ADC)*
S/R-Leistungsdichte-Verhältnis *n* signal/noise-density ratio
SR selective repeat *(ARQ procedure) (sat.)*
SRA (Signal-Rausch-Abstand *m*) signal/noise ratio
SRCV (Hilfskanal-Empfangsdaten *npl*) Secondary ReCeiVed data *(V.24/RS232C)*
SRV (Signal-Rausch-Verhältnis *n*) signal/noise ratio (SNR)
SS (Zeichengabesystem *n* (ZGS)) Signalling System
SS7 (Zeichengabesystem Nr.7) Signalling System No.7 *(ISDN)*
S-Schnittstelle *f* S-interface circuit (SIC) *(user-network interface, 4-wire line, ISDN)*
SSMA s. Spreizspektrumzugriff *m*
SSO (ungewollte Abschaltung *f*) spurious switch-off *(sat.)*
SSR (selektive serielle Wiederholung *f*) selective serial repeat *(ARQ)*
SSTDMA (TDMA *m* mit Vermittlung im Satelliten) satellite switched TDMA *(sat.)*
SSTV (Schmalband-Fernsehen *n*) slow scan TV
ST (Sendeterminal *n*) send terminal *(DC)*
Stadtfunkrufdienst *m* (Citycall) regional radio-paging service
Stadtnetz *n* metropolitan area network (MAN)
Staffelspeicher *m* tandem memory
Staffelzeit *f* queuing time

Stammelement n primitive
Stammkreis m side circuit *(PCM data, voice)*
Stammleitung f bus
Stammnetz n distribution network *(CATV)*
Stammverstärker m distribution amplifier
Stand m error, reading, state *(clock)*; setting, timing (difference *(DFVLR)*)
Standablage f time deviation *(clock comparison)*
standardisierter Datenaustausch m electronic data interchange (EDI)
s. **Dienst** m teleservice (telecommunication service) *(CCITT Rec. I.112, I.210)*
Standardwert m default value
Standbild n freeze frame *(NB video communications)*
Standleitung f leased line *(DIN 44302)*; point-to-point circuit *(RT)*; tie line; dedicated line or circuit
Standverbindung f point-to-point link, communication
Stanzabfall m chad *(PT)*
Stapelbetrieb m automatic document feed (ADF) *(fax)*; batch mode *(PCM data)*
stark gestörte Sekunden fpl severely errored seconds *(CCITT G.821)*
Stärke f **des Verkehrs** density of the traffic
starr rigid, solid
  phasenst. locked in phase
Startbit n start element
Start-/Stopp-DEE f asynchronous, non-packet-mode DTE *(with start and stop bit)*
stationäre Besetzung f steady-state distribution *(FO)*
Stationsaufforderung f enquiry (ENQ) *(DLC protocol)*; interrogation
statischer Verständigungsbereich m (SVB) static communication area *(SW)*
statistischer Multiplexer m (STDM) statistical time division multiplexer
Statusabfrage f status request
Stau m congestion *(data)*
Stauchung f compression *(data)*; crushing *(signal)*
STD (synchrone Zeitvielfachtechnik f) synchronous time division multiplex *(STM)*
STDM s. statistischer Multiplexer m
Steckbrücke f plug-in jumper
Steckdose f socket, outlet
Steckerdepot n plug storage or panel *(matrix plugs)*
Steckfehler m patching error *(matrix)*

Steckgerät n plug-in device
Steckplatz m slot, location *(subrack)*
Steckverbinder m (plug-in) connector
Steckzunge f FASTON tab *(connector)*
stehenlassen: die Leitung s. leave the connection up
Steigung f slope *(characteristic)*, gradient
Steilheit f slope *(curve)*; steepness *(pulse)*; transconductance, gain, sensitivity *(amplifier)*; rate of change *(value, e.g. voltage)*
Steilheitsverzerrung f non-linear distortion
Stelle f position *(DP)*
Stellenkomplement n diminished (radix) complement
Stellreserve f spare control capacity
Sternnetz n star-type network
steuerbarer Teiler m variable attenuator
Steuerblock m supervisory frame *(transmission control)*
Steuerfeld n control field *(SS7 frame)*
Steuerfrequenz f master frequency
Steuerkugel f tracker ball *(VDU)*
Steuerleitung f control trunk
steuern control; route *(signal)*
Steuerprogramm n handler *(packets)*
Steuertakt m control bit *(TC)*
Steuerteil n control unit *(exchange)*
Steuerung f open-loop control; controller, control system
Steuerwerk n control unit, processor
Stichleitung f feeder cable *(CATV)*
Stiftenwalze f sprocket wheel *(PTR)*
Stift- und Federleiste f pin-contact and receptacle strip
stimmhaft voiced
stimmlos unvoiced
STM (synchroner Übertragungsmodus m) synchronous transfer mode *(FO PCM)*
STM-1 (synchroner Transportmodul m) synchronous transport module *(pulse frame, CCITT Rec. G.70X)*
stochastisches Rauschen n random noise
Stockwerkverteiler m floor (services) distributor or distribution board *(tel.)*
stoffschlüssig surface-bonded or -connected, integral
stopfbar stuffable *(PCM data)*
Stopfbit n justification bit *(PCM)*; stop bit
stopfen inject, insert *(signal)*, stuff *(PCM)*, pad *(characters, ESS)*
Stopfschritt m padding (stop) element

(bit rate adaptation)
Stopfwort *n* stuffing word *(PCM)*
Stoppschritt *m* stop element *(bit rate adaptation)*
Störabstand *m* signal/noise ratio (SNR)
S. einschließlich Verzerrungen Signal/Noise and Distortion (SINAD) ratio
Störanteil *m* noise component
Störanzeige *f* false indication *or* reading
Störbeeinflussung *f* interference; rate of impairment *(ISDN)*
Störbefreiung *f* regeneration *(of signals)*
Störbelag *m* impairments
störend unwanted
Störmeldung *f* fault signal
Störphasenmodulation *f* **durch ein stetiges Signal** deterministic modulation
Störsignal *n* fault signal
Störspektrum *n* noise spectrum
Störstelle *f* fault location
Störstrahlung *f* radiated interference
Störtor *n* noise window *(shielding characteristic)*
Störung *f* failure *(termination of the ability of an item to perform a required function, IEEE definition)*; malfunction; disturbance; fault; interference; disruption *(connection)*; trouble; hit *(PCM)*
 ein Signal von S.en befreien clean up a signal
Störungserkennung *f* error detection
störungsfrei error-free
Störungsmeldung *f* service alarm signal *(PCM data, CCITT Rec. G.704)*; fault report
Störungsspitze *f* hit *(PCM)*
Störungsstelle *f* fault clearance office
Störverkehr *m* traffic padding
Stoßantwort *f* unit pulse response *(r(t))*
Stoßdämpfung *f* reflection loss
stoßfrei free of hits, discontinuities
Stoßspannung *f* surge voltage
Stoßstelle *f* reflection point
Strahldichte *f* radiance, brightness *(in N)*
Strahlendiagramm *n* signal space diagram
Strahlennetz *n* radial network
Strahlstärke *f* radiant intensity *(FO, in W/sr)*
Strang *m* string *(of drives)*; phase *(el.)*; line *(of racks)*
STRV s. Stromversorgung *f*
Strecke *f* route, line, link
Streckenabschnitt *m* route section
Streckenbilanz *f* link budget *(sat.)*
Streckenmanagement *n* link management

(SS7 MTP)
Streckenmessung *f* end-to-end test *(tel.)*
Streifenaufnahme *f* tape take-up system *(PTR)*
Streifenbehälter *m* tape bin *(PTR)*
Streifenbreite *f* swath width *(sat. earth observation)*
Streifenzug *m* tape tension *(PTR)*
Streit *m* contention *(bus allocation, e.g. lost contention of a channel)*
streiten contend *(bus allocation)*
Streubereich *m* zone of dispersion *(FO)*; spread
Streubreite *f* scatter band
Streulicht *n* scattered light *(FO)*
Streuung *f* dispersion, scatter, spread, variance, variation
Streuwert *m* variance coefficient *(traffic)*
Streuwertverfahren *n* traffic variance method
Strichcode *m* bar code
Stromableitung *f* current return
Stromaufnahme *f* current drain or consumption; input current
Strombelastung *f* current rating
stromerfüllter Schritt *m* current bit *(TC)*
Stromlaufplan *m* circuit diagram
stromlos:
 s. Schritt *m* no-current bit *(TC)*
 s. Sperrschritt *m* spacing stop bit *(TC)*
Stromrauschen *n* current noise; noise level
stromrichtergeführt current converter-fed
stromschlüssig with circuit continuity
Stromschnittstelle *f* current loop interface
Stromversorgung *f* (STRV, SV) power supply (unit) (PS, PSU)
Stromweg *m* circuit *(tel.)*
Stufenkippen *n* state switching
Stufung *f* grading *(relays)*; discretization, quantization *(video encoding)*
Stummschaltung *f* muting
Stummtaste *f* mute key *(f.tel.)*
Stützblech *n* support plate
Stützpunkt *m* discrete point *(on a signal curve)*; interpolation point *(mathem.)*
Stützspannung *f* back-up voltage *(for memory)*
SU (Servicegerät *n*) service unit
Suchbrücke *f* outletbar *(to a free connecting path/circuit)*
Suchvorgang *m* search operation
Suffix *m* suffix (digit) *(f. tel.)*
sukzessiv gradual, progressive
Summator *m* summing integrator *(discrete analog of the integrator)*

Summenalarm *m* summation alarm
Summenbildner *m* sum former, sum-forming circuit
Summenbitrate *f* aggregate bit rate *(e.g. 2.043 Mb/s for basic access, ISDN)*
Summenentkopplungskondensator *m* overall decoupling capacitor
Summenerfassung *f* bulk registration *(tel.)*
Summengebührenzählung *f* summation call metering *(tel.)*
Summengeschwindigkeit *f* aggregate data rate *(total channel rate)*
Summengesprächszählung *f* summation call metering *(tel.)*
Summenkurve *f* composite curve
Summenpegel *m* aggregate level
Summenverkehr *m* composite traffic *(tel. sys.)*
Summenverkehrswert *m* total traffic intensity *(incoming and outgoing)*
Summenzähler *m* summation meter
Summer *m* buzzer
Summierer *m* summing circuit
Supermultiplexschiene *f* super-multiplex highway *(transm.)*
SV s. Stromversorgung *f*
SVB (statischer Verständigungsbereich *m*) static communication area *(SW)*
SVC (geschalteter virtueller Kanal *m*) switched virtual channel *(Datex-P)*
SVR (Servicerechner *m*) service processor *(vtx)*
S/W (schwarz/weiß) black/white *(display)*
SW s. Synchronwort *n*
SWFD (Selbstwählferndienst *m*) subscriber trunk dialling (STD), direct distance dialling (DDD)
SWU (Vermittlungseinheit *f*) switching unit *(ISDN)*
SX (Simplex *n*) simplex *(modem)*
SXMT (Hilfskanal Sendedaten) Secondary X-mit *(transmit)* data *(V.24/RS232C)*
SXS (Schrittschaltsystem *n*) Step-by-Step (selector) exchange *(analog)*
Symmetrie *f* symmetry *(PCM encoder)*; balance *(line, circuit)*
synchron:
  s. **Nutzlast-Bitvollgruppe** *f* synchronous payload envelope (SPE) *(TDM)*
  s. **Transportmodul** *m* synchronous transport module (STM-1) *(pulse frame, CCITT Rec. G.70X)*
  s. **Übertragungsmodus** m synchronous transfer mode (STM) *(circuit-switched PCM data transmission, FO, 'synchronous' relating to the information, not the bit synchronisation)*
  s. **Übertragungssteuerung** *f* synchronous data link control (SDLC)
  s. **Zeitvielfachtechnik** *f* synchronous time division (STD) multiplex *(STM)*
Synchronfalle *f* sync (character) trap *(TC)*
Synchronisation *f* synchronisation; alignment *(frames)*, framing
  S. durch das Netz network timing
Synchronisierbit *n* framing bit, alignment bit
Synchronisiereinheit *f* timing generator
Synchronisierschaltung *f* frame aligner *(PCM)*
Synchronisierung *f* synchronisation, alignment, pacing, timing
Synchronisierungsausfall *m* loss of lock *or* synchronism; loss of signal (LOS) *(sat.)*
Synchronisierungsfehler *m* loss of lock *or* synchronism
Synchronisierungssignal *n* framing signal *(ISDN)*
Synchronismus *m* lock *(signal)*, frame alignment *(PCM)*
Synchronwort *n* synchronisation word (SW)
Synchronzeichen *n* synchronizing character *(TC)*
Synchronzustand *m* synchronism, lock
System X *n* digital switching system *(Plessey, GB)*
Systemaufforderung *f* prompt
Systemdaten *npl*: **anlagenunabhängige S.** general system data *(i.e. not connected with a specific system)*
Systemempfindlichkeit *f* (G/T) system sensitivity *(sat., in dB/K)*
systemgebunden system-linked, system-inherent
Systemverband *m* system complex
Systemverklemmung *f* system deadlock *(network node)*
Systemwertmessung *f* figure-of-merit measurement *(sat.)*
S$_{2M}$-Schnittstelle *f* S$_{2M}$ interface *(S interface for ISDN PA)*

T

TA (Endgeräteanpassung *f*) terminal adapter *(ISDN)*
TA (Verkehrsdurchsagekennung *f*) Traffic Announcement *(RDS)*
Tableau *n* tablet *(e.g. for telepictures)*
  Bedient. keyboard tablet
  Zeichent. drawing tablet *(for telepictures)*
TAE (Telekommunikations-Anschluß-Einheit *f*) telecommunication line unit (TLU) *(FTZ, corresponds to BT LJU)*
Tafel *f* page *(vtx)*
TAG (Teilnehmeranschlußgerät *n*) user terminal
Takt *m* cycle; clock, clock pulse, timing (signal)
  T. halten keep time
  Im T. des/der ... in synchronism with ...
  Rahmen-T. frame cycle, frame interval
Taktablauf *m* cycling
Taktableitung *f* clock *or* timing extraction
Taktanpassung *f* clock alignment
Taktdiagramm *n* timing diagram
Takten *n* clocking, cycling, timing
taktgebunden clocked
taktgesteuert clocked, timed
Taktgehalt *m* timing information
Taktgeschwindigkeit *f* transmission speed *(TC)*
Taktimpuls *m* clock pulse, strobe (pulse)
Taktloch *n* feed hole *(PTR)*
Taktnormal *n* clock frequency standard
Taktpause *f* clock pulse space
Taktraster *m* clock (pulse) spacing
Taktrückgewinnung *f* clock recovery
taktsynchron clocked
Taktung *f* timing *(PCM data)*
Taktweiche *f* clock selector *(PCM data)*
Taktzeit *f* clock cycle, period *(PCM data)*; pulse spacing
Taktzentrale *f* **S** central transmit clock
TAM (Teilnehmeranschlußmodul *n*) user module
TAN (Transaktionsnummer *f*) transaction number
TAS (Teilnehmeranschlußschaltung *f*) user line circuit
Taschentelefon *n* handheld telephone
TASI (zeitmultiplexierte Sprachübertragung *f*) time-assigned speech interpolation *(VC)*
Tastatur *f* keypad *(tel.)*, keyboard *(terminal etc.)*
Tastatur(ton)wahl *f* touch-tone dialling *(tel.)*
Tasteingabevorrichtung *f* touch input device (TID) *(VDU)*
Tastenfeld *n* key array, keyboard *(VDU)*; touch panel *(membrane keypad)*
Tastensperre *f* key lock
Tastenwahl *f* touch-tone dialling *(tel.)*
Taster *m* key switch
Tastfernsprecher *m* key-operated telephone, push-button telephone
Tastfilter *n* keying filter
Tastfläche *f* touch area *(on key)*
Tastfunk *m* radio telegraphy
Tastgefühl *n* tactile response *(membrane keypad)*
Tastkodierschalter *m* touch-sensitive coding switch
Tastspeicher *m* sample and hold circuit
Tastung *f* keysending
Tastverhältnis *n* (pulse) duty factor *or* ratio
Tastwahl *f* push-button dialling *(tel.)*
Tastwahlblock *m* (TWB) keypad *(tel.)*
Tastwahlzeichen *n* push-button signal
TAT-x (transatlantisches Telefonkabel *n* Nr. x) Transatlantic Telephone cable No. x
TAU (Engeräteanpassungseinheit *f*) terminal adapter unit *(dig. PBX, US)*
TAU-P terminal adapter unit for PCs
TAU-T terminal adapter unit for telephone
TB (Teilnehmerbaugruppe *f*) subscriber module
TBC s. Teilbandcodierung *f*
TBETSI (Technischer Beirat *m* für Normungsfragen des ETSI) German advisory committee to ETSI
TBP (TEMEX-Bedienplatz *m*) workstation
TC (Sendeschritttakt) Transmit Clock *(V.24/RS232C)*
TC (Transformationscodierung *f*) transformation coding *(dig. audio)*
TCM (Zeitkompressionsmultiplex *n*) time com-

pression multiplex *(ping pong)* method, burst mode transmission
TD (Sendedaten *npl*) Transmit Data *(V.24/ RS232C)*
TDC (Datenkanal *m*) Data Channel *(RDS)*
TDD (Zeitduplex *n*, Zeitgetrenntlageverfahren *n*) time division duplex *(tel., ping pong transmission method, ISDN B channel)*
TDM (Zeitmultiplex *n*) time division multiplex
TDMA (Vielfachzugriff *m* im Zeitmultiplex, Zeitvielfachzugriff *m*) time division or domain multiple access *(VSAT)*
TDMA-Direktanschluß *m* direct interface CEPT equipment (DICE) *(sat.)*
TDPSK (dreiwertige Differenz-Phasenumtastung *f*) three-level differential PSK
TE (Endeinrichtung *f*) terminal *or* terminating equipment *(ISDN, CCITT Rec. I.112)*
TE1 (ISDN-Endeinrichtung *f*) ISDN terminal equipment
TE2 (Endeinrichtung *f* ohne ISDN-Schnittstelle) non-ISDN terminal equipment *(requires TA for ISDN access)*
TE s. Teileinheit *f* für die Breite
Technik *f* engineering; technique; design; technology; hardware
technisches Fangen *n* line lockout *(subscriber line status after off-hook status has remained static for a predetermined time)*
t. Geräusch *n* man-made noise
T. Leitfaden *m* (TL) Technical Requirements
T. Lieferbedingungen *fpl* (TL) Equipment Specifications *(DBP)*
TEE s. Teilnehmerendeinrichtung *f*
TEI (Endgeräte-Endpunktkennung *f*) terminal endpoint identifier
Teilband *n* half of the band *(radio link)*
Teilbandcodierung *f* (TBC) subband coding *(digital audio)*
Teilberechtigung *f* partial authorisation; (sub)class of service access level
teilbewählt partially selected *(line, PBX)*
Teileinheit *f* **für die Breite** (TE) *(1 TE = 5.08 mm)* width unit (E) *(1 E = 0.2", rack)*
Teiler *m*: **steuerbarer T.** variable attenuator
Teilfunktionsprüfung *f* functional test of subassemblies
Teilgruppe *f* subgroup *(tel. sys.)*
Teilhaber *m* on-line (system) user
Teilnachricht *f* message segment *(PCM data, voice)*

Teilnehmer *m* (TN,TLN) subscriber, party, user *(tel)*; caller
time sharing user *(network)*;
mobile station *(mobile RT)*;
partner *(conference)*;
system user *(off-line, data channel)*
automatischer T. test call generator
belästigter T. molested subscriber
Paket-T. packet-terminal customer
Teilnehmeranschlußeinrichtung *f* (TAE) telecommunication line unit (TLU) *(in connector)*; user connection device; line jack unit (LJU) *(GB, BS6506, for PBX)*
Teilnehmeranschlußgerät *n* (TAG) user terminal *(DBP BIGFON)*
Teilnehmeranschlußmodul *n* (TAM) user module *(DBP BIGFON)*
Teilnehmeranschlußsatz *m* exchange termination (ET) *(ISDN)*
Teilnehmeranschlußschaltung *f* (TAS) user line circuit; subscriber line circuit
Teilnehmeraushängeprogramm *n* subscriber off-hook program
Teilnehmerbaugruppe *f* (TB) subscriber module
Teilnehmerbetriebsklasse *f* closed user group (CUG)
teilnehmerbezogene Dienstmerkmale *npl* supplementary services *(SS7)*
t. Anwenderprogramm *n* customized user program *(CCITT X.32)*
Teilnehmerdienstmerkmale *npl* supplementary services
Teilnehmerdoppeleinbindung *f* double tieing-in of subscribers *(tel.)*;
multi-homing *(tel.)*
Teilnehmereinrichtung *f* customer premises equipment (CPE);
subscriber installation
T.-NStAnl. *f* key (telephone) system (KTS)
T.-Verdrahtung *f* inside wiring
Teilnehmerendeinrichtung *f* (TEE) subscriber terminal *(FTZ)*
Teilnehmergerät *n* (TG) mobile station *(RT)*
Teilnehmerkennung *f* network user identification (NUI) *(DBP DATEX-P)*
Teilnehmerklasse *f* subscriber line category
Teilnehmerkonzentrator *m* line concentrator
Teilnehmerleitungsnetz *n* loop plant
Teilnehmermeldung *f* called party's answer
Teilnehmermodul *n* exchange termination (ET) *(ISDN)*
Teilnehmernetz *n* domestic area network (DAN) *(video conferencing etc.)*
Teilnehmer-Netz-Schnittstelle *f* user/net-

work interface (UNI)
Teilnehmerrechner *m* (TR,TNR) access computer *or* local *or* regional computer (RC) *(videotex)*
Teilnehmersatz *m* (TS) subscriber line circuit (SLC)
Teilnehmerschnittstelle *f* S_0 user-network interface *(ISDN)*
Teilnehmerschutz *m* line protection
Teilnehmervermittlungsstelle *f* (TVSt) access exchange *(ISDN packet switching)*
Teilnehmerwahl *f.* **nach T.** on demand *(bearer service)*
Teilnetz *n* subnetwork
Teilsteuerwerk *n* intermediate-level processor
Teilstrecke *f* section, line section
Teilstreckendämpfung *f* section attenuation
Teilstreckenvermittlung *f* store-and-forward (SF,SAF,S&F) switching, section-by-section switching
Teilung *f* spacing *(connector)*
Teilverkehre *mpl* traffic components *(tel. sys.)*
Teilvermittlungsstelle *f* dependent exchange, sub-centre
teilzentral intermediate-level *(exchange)*
t. Ebene intermediate level *(exchange)*
TELEBOX *f* (Textspeicherdienst *m*) electronic mail (E-mail) service of the DBP *(Telecom Gold (BT), DIALCOM (US), KEY-LINK-D (AUS); MHS to CCITT Rec. X.400, F.400, ISO 10021-x)*
Telefaxmaschine *f* telefax machine, telecopier
Telefon-Leitungs-Nachbildung *f* (TLN) artificial telephone line *(FTZ)*
Telefonseelsorge *f* Samaritans' call service
Telefonsprachdienst *m* telephone voice service
Telegramm *n* message *(TEMEX)*
telegrammloser Zustand *m* no-message state
Telegrammwähldienst *m* (Gentex) gentex (general telegraph exchange) *(telegram service of the DBP telex network)*
Telekarte *f* PMR chip card *(DBP)*
TELEKOM *f* the telecommunications services branch of the DBP *(now independent of POSTDIENST and POSTBANK)*
Telekommunikation *f* (TK) telecommunications
 T.-Anlage *f* (TK-Anl.) ISDN PBX (ISPBX); (private) digital exchange
 T.-Anschlußeinheit *f* (TAE) telecommunication line unit (TLU) *(FTZ; 6,8 or 12 pin connector, ISO standard IS 8877)*,

user connection device *(DBP plug-in connector, ISDN, corresponds to BT LJU)*
 T.-Ordnung *f* (TKO) Telecommunications Regulation *(BPM, in force Jan. 1988)*
Telematikdienste *mpl* telematics services *(text communications, remote data processing, video conferencing, TV etc., from FR télématique)*
Telemetriedaten *npl* telemetry data
Telepoint *m* (öffentliches Funktelefon-System *n*) public CT2 system *(BT, comprises handset, home base station and access to public 'phonepoint', not compatible with DECT)*
Teleport *m* teleport *(building (complex) with provision of interconnected telematics services for the lessees)*
Teleskopschiene *f* telescopic rail
Teletel videotex service of France *(CEPT Profile 2, s. Table VIII)*
Teletex *n* (Bürofernschreiben *n* (Ttx)) teletex *(2400 bit/s, circuit or packet switched, to OSI standards)*
 T.-Telex-Umsetzer *m* (TTU) teletex/telex converter (TTC)
Telex *n* (Tx) telex *(teleprinter exchange, ASCII)*
TEMEX telemetry exchange *(telecontrol service of the DBP, carried in telephone network, DOV, 40 kHz carrier, and in ISDN D channel; NTG 2001, SW protocol to DIN 19244; s. Table VII)*
 T.-Bedienplatz *m* (TBP) workstation *(in the TEMEX exchange)*
 T.-Hauptzentrale *f* (THZ) main exchange *(of the TEMEX service)*
 T.-Konzentrator *m* (TK) concentrator *(of the TEMEX service)*
 T.-Netzabschluß *m* (TNA) network termination *(of the TEMEX service)*
 T.-Schnittstelle *f* (TSS) interface *(of the TEMEX service)*
 T.-Übertragungsbaugruppe *f* (TÜB) transmission module *(of the TEMEX service)*
 T.-Übertragungseinheit *f* (TÜE, now TÜ) line termination *(of the TEMEX service)*
 T.-Vermittlungsrechner *m* (TVR) switching processor *(of the TEMEX service)*
 T.-Zentrale *f* (TZ) exchange, front-end processor *(of the TEMEX service)*
Temperaturgang *m* variation due to temperature, variation with temperature
Ter, ter *(Appended to CCITT network interface standard, identifies its third version, e.g. V.27 ter)*
Terko-Steckdose *f* 3-wire power outlet

(rack)
Terminal betriebsbereit *(DIN 66020, S1.2)* Data Terminal Ready (DTR) *(V.24/RS232C, s. Table VI)*
Terminalisierung *f* equipping with terminals *(colloquial)*
Termineinrichtung *f* appointments facility, engagement diary *(dig. PBX)*
Terminregister *n* notepad *(f. tel.)*
ternär ternary *(having three discrete values)*
Testumgebung *f* test environment *(program)*
Tetrade *f* 4-bit word, nibble
Textende *n* end of text (EOT, ETX) *(PCM data)*
Text-Fax-Server *m* (TFS) text/fax server *(ISDN)*
Textspeicherdienst *m* (TELEBOX) electronic mail (E-mail) service *(MHS, CCITT Rec. X.400)*
Textzeiger *m* cursor *(display)*
TF s. Trägerfrequenz *f*
TF (Transportfunktionsteil *m* *(FTZ)*) signalling connection control part (SCCP)
TF-Übertragung *f* carrier frequency line circuit *(tel. signalling)*
TF+DL-Gerät (Trägerfrequenz/Dienstleistungs-Gerät *n*) FDM/SC unit *(RT terminal station)*
TFS s. Text-Fax-Server *m*
TG (Teilnehmergerät *n*) mobile station *(RT)*
Tg s. maximale Gruppenlaufzeitverzerrung *f*
THZ s. TEMEX-Hauptzentrale *f*
Tickerzeichen *n* ticking tone *(progress tone)*
TID (Tasteingabevorrichtung *f*) touch input device *(VDU)*
Tiefe *f* depth
 Bitt. word length, resolution in bits *(video encoding, e.g. 8 bits/pixel)*
 Signalt. signal resolution in bits *(video encoding, e.g. 8 bits/pixel)*
 Sperrt. stop-band attenuation *(filter)*
tieflegen: ein Signal t. set a signal to Low
Tischablage *f* desk-top base *(f.tel.)*
Tischansteuerungssatz *m* (TAS) desk access circuit
Tischapparat *m* table set
TK s. Temex-Konzentrator *m*
TK-Anl. s. Telekommunikationsanlage *f*
TKO s. Telekommunikationsordnung *f*
TL (Technischer Leitfaden *m*) Technical Requirements
TL (Technische Lieferbedingungen *fpl*) Equipment Specifications *(DBP)*

TLN (Teilnehmer *m*) subscriber, party *(tel)*
TLN (Telefon-Leitungs-Nachbildung *f*) artificial telephone line *(FTZ)*
TLN-Netz-Schnittstelle *f* user/network interface (UNI); I420 interface *(GB ISDN)*
TN (Teilnehmer *m*) subscriber, party *(tel)*
TNA s. TEMEX-Netzabschluß *m*
TNC (Netzknotensteuerung *f*) terminal node controller *(PR)*
Token *m* token *(supervisory frame controlling access to a token ring network)*
T.-Bus-Schnittstelle *f* token bus interface *(IEEE 802.4)*
T.-Ring-Netz *n* token ring network *(one in which a token providing access is passed sequentially from station to station; LAN to IEEE 802.5)*
Toleranzschlauch *m* tolerance band *(cable)*
tonfrequent voice-frequency
Tonfrequenz *f* voice frequency
Tonruf *m* ringing, ringer *or* tone caller *(tel.)*
Tonruflautstärke *f* ringer *or* tone caller volume
Tonschreiber *m* sound recorder
Ton-Zweiersatz *m* (TZS) tone/two-party circuit
TOO (Sendezeit *f*) time of origin
TOP (Bürokommunikationsprotokoll *n*) technical and office protocol *(OSI)*
TOP (Programmvorschau-Seitentabelle *f*) table of (preview) pages *(vtx, 'Fasttext' (GB))*
TOR (Empfangszeit *f*) time of reception
Torruf *m* door (intercom) call *(tel.)*
Torsprechanlage *f* door *or* gate interphone, door *or* gate intercom system
Torsprechstelle *f* door (intercom) extension *or* station, door *or* gate interphone *(tel.)*
Totalausfall *m* total failure, fatal fault
TP (Verkehrsfunkkennung *f*) Traffic Programme (identification) *(RDS)*
TPM (Herstellerwartung *f* für Eigen- und Fremdsysteme) third-party maintenance
TR (Teilnehmerrechner *m*) information provider
Trägerdienst *m* bearer service *(GSM)*
Trägerfrequenz *f* (TF) carrier frequency (CF)
Trägerpaket *n* burst *(VSAT)*
Träger/Rausch-Verhältnis *n* carrier/noise ratio (C/N) *(sat., in dB)*
Träger/Störung-Verhältnis *n* carrier/interference ratio (C/I) *(sat.)*
Trägerumtastverfahren *n* carrier shift keying *(testing)*

Tragorgan *n* suspension strand *(cable)*
Tragschiene *f* mounting rail
Transaktionsnummer *f* (TAN) transaction number
Transcom International ISDN link between France and USA
Transfergeschwindigkeit *f* data transfer rate
Transformationscodierung *f* (TC) transformation coding
Transitamt *n* transit exchange
Transitknoten *m* intermediate node (IN) *(PCM data)*
TRANSPAC packet-switched French data network *(supports X.25, X.3, X.28 and X.29 DCEs and DTEs, 72 kb/s channels)*
transparent transparent *(generally with out-band signalling)*
Transponder *m* transponder (txp) *(sat.)*
Transportdienst *m* bearer service *(ATM)*
Transportebene *f* transport layer *(layer 4, OSI 7-layer reference model)*
Transportfunktionsteil *m* (TF) signalling connection control part (SCCP) *(SS7, CCITT Rec. Q.711...714, FTZ)*
Transportprotokoll *n* transport protocol *(ISO, sat.)*
Transportuhr *f* travelling clock *(clock synchronisation)*
Transportverbindung *f* transport *or* transparent connection
Transversalfilter *n* transversal filter *(transmissions)*
Trasse *f* route
Treffunsicherheit *f* setting accuracy *(test instrument)*
Trennbuchse *f* splitting jack *(tel.)*
Trenndiode *f* isolating diode
trennen disconnect *(channel)*
Trenn-Fernmeldesteckdose *f* disconnect socket
Trennfrequenz *f* space frequency
Trennrelais *n* disconnecting relay
Trennsteckverteiler *m* terminal disconnect patchboard
Trenntaste *f* cut-off button *or* key *(f.tel.)*
Trennweiche *f* separating filter *(CATV)*
Treppenstufenmodulation *f* pulse step modulation (PSM)

Treppen(stufen)generator *m* stairstep generator *(TV)*
-treue conformity
Trog *m* tray *(battery)*
T-Serie *f* **der CCITT-Empfehlungen** T-series of CCITT Recommendations *(relates to Group 1,2,3 facsimile, telematic, teletex, telex and videotex services)*
TS (Teilnehmersatz *m*) subscriber line circuit (SLC)
TSC (Bündelnetzsteuerung *f*) trunking system control
TSS s. TEMEX-Schnittstelle *f*
TTU (Teletex-Telex-Umsetzer *m*) teletex/telex converter
Ttx (Teletex) teletex
TTY (Fernschreiben *n* (FS)) teletype
TU (Verkehrseinheit *f* (VE)) Traffic Unit (= 1 Erl)
TÜ s. TEMEX-Übertragungseinheit *f*
TÜB s. TEMEX-Übertragungsbaugruppe *f*
TÜE s. TEMEX-Übertragungseinheit *f*
TUP (Anwenderteil *m* für Fernsprechen) telephone user part *(SS7)*
Türfreisprechanlage *f* door release/intercom system *(f. tel.)*
Türsprechanlage *f* door interphone, door intercom (system)
Türsprechstelle *f* door (intercom) extension *or* station, door interphone
TVR s. TEMEX-Vermittlungsrechner *m*
TVSt (Teilnehmervermittlungsstelle *f*) access exchange *(ISDN)*
TWB (Tastwahlblock *m*) keypad *(tel.)*
TWT (Wanderfeldröhre *f*) travelling wave tube *(sat.)*
Typenprüfung *f* type *or* qualification test
Typisierung *f* standardisation
tx (Telex *n*) telex
TX (Endvermittlungsstelle *f* (EVSt)) terminal exchange
txp Transponder *m* transponder *(sat.)*
txt (Fernsehtext *m*) teletext
TZ s. TEMEX-Zentrale *f*
tZGT (temporäre Zeichengabetransaktion *f*) temporary signalling transaction *(SS7, CCITT Rec. Q.711...714)*
TZS (Ton-Zweiersatz *m*) tone/two-party circuit

U

U (Höheneinheit f (HE)) rack unit
(1 U = 1 3/4")
Ü s. Überwachung f
UA (Benutzer m) user agent *(CCITT Rec. X.400)*
UART (universeller asynchroner Empfänger/Sender m) universal asynchronous receiver/transmitter
überbrücken strap, bypass
Überdimensionierung f oversized
übereinanderfallen coincide *(curves)*
Überflug m pass *(sat.)*
Übergabe f delivery *(MHS)*
  Ü.-Bestätigungsbit n (D-Bit) delivery confirmation bit, D bit *(ISDN NUA)*
Übergabeseite f access page *(vtx, access to ECs)*
Übergabestelle f interchange point, interface *(tel.)*;
  (formerly TAE) user connection device, telecommunication line unit (TLU) *(ISDN plug-in connector, corresponds to LJU)*
Übergabesystemteil m delivery agent *(MHS)*
Übergabetransformator m coupling transformer
Übergang m transition; adapter *(waveguide)* gateway *(e.g. to telephone network)*; intercommunication *(between services)*; interworking *(network)*
Übergangsdämpfung f joint loss *(FO)*
Übergangsdienst m interworking service (IWS)
Übergangsprotokoll n internet protocol *(OSI layer 3 and above)*
Übergangsstelle f interface
Übergangsstück n adapter *(HW)*
Übergangsverkehr m transition traffic
Übergangszone f junction *(semiconductor)*
übergreifend cross-office
Überhang m hangover *(of talkspurts)*
überkoppeln transfer *(light)*
Überlagerung f mixing, heterodyning *(frequencies)*;
  multiplication *(pulse modulation)*;
  addition *(of noise)*
  unsymmetrische Ü. unbalanced interference
Überlagerungsempfänger m superheterodyne receiver *(RF)*

optischer Ü. optical heterodyne $(f_{IF} > 0)$ or homodyne $(f_{IF} = 0)$ receiver *(FO)*
Überlagerungskanal m superaudio or data-over-voice (DOV) channel *(TEMEX, Centrex, phonecard phone)*
Überlast f overload
Überlastabwehr f flow control *(SS7)*; overload protection
Überlastbarkeit f overload capability
Überlastung f congestion *(traffic)*
Überlaufbelegung f overflow call *(tel. sys., offered call overflowing to other serving trunk groups)*
Überlaufverkehr m overflow traffic *(tel. sys.)*
Überleiteinrichtung f (ÜLE) mobile switching centre (MSC) *(mobile RT)*; gateway *(networks)*
Überleitungsamt n transfer exchange *(tel.)*
Überleitungseinrichtung f transfer facility
überlesen skip
Übermittlung f communication *(source-sink information transport, NTG 1203)*
Übermittlungsabschnitt m data link
Übermittlungsdienst m bearer service (ISDN)
Übermittlungsvorschrift f link protocol
Übernahmetaste f enter key
Überrahmen m superframe, multiframe *(PCM)*
Überrahmensynchronisierung f multiframe alignment *(PCM)*
überregional supraregional
  ü. Fernnetz n long-haul network
Überschreiten n **der Einstellbereiche** violation of range limits
Überschreitungswahrscheinlichkeit f :
  Wartezeit-Ü. delay-exceeding probability *(delay system)*
Überschwingen n slope overload *(DPCM video encoding)*
Übersichtsplan m layout diagram; trunking diagram *(exchange)*
Übersichtsstromlauf m functional circuit diagram
Übersichtsschaltplan m functional circuit diagram
überspielen copy *(MTR)*; transfer *(data)*
Übersprechdämpfung f crosstalk attenuation
Übersprechimpuls m cross-coupled signal

(antenna)
überspringen skip
überstreichen: einen Bereich ü. cover a range *(VCO)*
Übertrager *m* transformer; repeating coil *(tel.)*
Übertragung *f* transfer, transmission; line circuit *(tel. signalling)*
Ü. im Netz gestört network out of service (NOS) *(loop testing)*
Übertragungsablaufsteuerung *f* communications controller; (UEAS) transmission sequence control *(EDS)*
Übertragungsbereich *m* transmission bandwidth
Übertragungseingang *m* AC-coupled input
Übertragungsende *n* End Of Transmission (EOT) *(signal)*
Übertragungsfenster *n* spectral window *(FO)*
Übertragungsgeschwindigkeit *f* data signalling rate; equivalent bit rate; SELect data signal rate (SEL) *(V.24/RS 232, s. Table VI)*
Übertragungsgüte *f* grade of transmission performance
Übertragungskapazität *f* transmission capacity; bit rate
Übertragungskopfteil *m* transport overhead *(TDM)*
Übertragungslänge *f* transmission distance
Übertragungsleitung anschalten connect data set to line *(no RS232C specifications; V.24, s. Table VI)*
Übertragungsmaß *n* propagation constant *(cables)*
Übertragungsrate *f* information transfer rate *(bearer service)*
Übertragungssteuerung *f* transmission control (TC)
Übertragungssteuerungsprotokoll *n* transmission control protocol (TCP) *(layer 4, DARPA)*
Übertragungssteuerungsverfahren *n* link access procedure (LAP) *(ISDN)*
Übertragungssteuerzeichenfolge *f* supervisory sequence
Übertragungsstrecke *f* link; trunk
übertragungstechnischer Kabelanschluß *m* transmission line termination *(ISDN U interface)*
Übertragungsweg *m* transmission path
Übertragungszeichenfolge *f* information message
Überwachung *f* policing *(bit rate, ATM)*; (Ü) supervision *(PCM unit or equipment)*; supervisory function
Ü. ohne Betriebsunterbrechung in-service *or* on-line monitoring
zeitliche Ü. timing
Überwachungsabschnitt *m* monitored section
Überwachungsaufgabe *f* supervisory function
Überwachungseinrichtung *f* watchdog *(computers)*
Überwachungseinsatz *m* supervision threshold
Überwachungsrahmen *m* supervisory frame
Überwachungssatz *m* supervision circuit
Überwachungstor *n* expectancy window *(mobile RT)*
Überweisungsverkehr *m* transfer traffic *(PBX)*
UC *(Verkehrseinheit)* Unit Call *(unit of traffic intensity, = 1/36 Erl)*
UCNR (DÜE nicht betriebsfähig) uncontrolled not ready *(loop testing)*
UE s. Unterhaltungselektronik *f*
UEAS s. Übertragungsablaufsteuerung *f*
U-Elektronik *f* s. Unterhaltungselektronik *f*
UER (Union *f* Europäischer Rundfunkanstalten) European Broadcasting Union (EBU)
Uhrengang *m* clock rate
Uhrenstand *m* clock timing *or* reading, state; setting
Uhrenvergleich *m* clock synchronisation
Uhrzeitprogramm *n* time-of-day program
Uhrzeit und Datum clock time (CT)
UIC (U-Schnittstelle *f*) U-interface circuit *(2-wire, ISDN)*
U$_{ko}$-Schnittstelle *f* U$_{ko}$ interface *(U interface for ISDN BA copper circuit to local ISDN exchange)*
ÜLE (Überleitungseinrichtung *f*) transfer facility, mobile switching centre (MSC)
Umbuchen *n* cell change *(mobile RT)*
Umgebung *f* background *(monitor)*; environment *(program)*
umgeleitet diverted *(call)*
Umkehrgruppierung *f* reversed trunking scheme
Umkehrverstärker *m* inverting amplifier, inverter
Umlauf *m* orbit, revolution *(sat.)*
Umlaufbahn *f* orbit *(sat.)*
Umlaufzeit *f* round-trip time
umlegen transferring a call *(f. tel.)*
Umleitung *f* redirection *(call)*
Umlenkung *f* rerouting *(traffic)*
umpolen reverse polarity
Umrüstzeit *f* change-over time
Umschalten *n* reversal *(trunk barring lev-*

els); handoff *(mobile RT)*
Umschalter *m* changeover unit *(CATV)*
Umschaltezeit *f* line turnaround *(RS232C connection, half duplex)*
Umsetzer *m* transducer, converter, modem; translator *(exch.)*
Umsetzerstufen *fpl* modulator and demodulator stages
umspeichern dump, copy *(data)*
Umstecken *n* replugging of terminals *(at the bus)*
umsteuern reroute *(signal)*
Umwegsteuerung *f* rerouting *(PCM data, voice)*
Umwerter *m* converter, translator *(signalling)*
Umwertespeicher *m* translator *(for route determination, ATM)*
unabhängig:
  u. getaktet plesiochronous mode
  u. TN-Suche *f* follow me; independent subscriber search
  u. Wartebetrieb *m* asynchronous disconnected mode
  u. Wartung *f* independent maintenance (IM)
unbeantworteter Anruf *m* no-reply call
unbeaufsichtigt unattended *(distant station)*
unbelegt unassigned, free
  u. Buchse *f* unused jack
  u. Kanal *m* idle channel
unbeschaltet: Nummer u. (NU) number unobtainable
unbesetzt unoccupied, idle *(channel)*
unbespulte NF-Leitung *f* unloaded VF line
unbestätigt negatively acknowledged (N-ACK)
unbewählt unselected *(line, PBX)*
ungeneigt uncanted *(precipitation, sat. transmission)*
ungestörte Übermittlung *f* correct transmission
ungewollte Abschaltung *f* spurious switch-off (SSO) *(sat.)*
Ungültigkeit *f* Invalid (INV) *(V.25 bis message)*
UNI (Teilnehmer-Netz-Schnittstelle *f*) user/network interface
unipolare Leitfähigkeit *f* unilateral conductivity *(cables)*
Unipolartastung *f* unipolar operation *(NTG 1203)*
Universalanschluß *m* telecommunication line unit (TLU), universal telecommunication socket *(ISDN)*

Universalgestell *n* miscellaneous apparatus rack (MAR)
universell:
  u. asynchroner Empfänger/Sender *m* universal asynchronous receiver/transmitter (UART)
  u. Luftschnittstelle *f* common air interface (CAI) *(DTI CT2 protocol, to CCITT Rec. G.721)*
  u. synchroner/asynchroner Empfänger/Sender *m* universal synchronous/asynchronous receiver/transmitter (USART)
  u. Transaktionsmonitor *m* universal transaction monitor (UTM) *(vtx, DP SW)*
unkonfektionierte Faser *f* unconnectorized fibre *(FO)*
unsichtbar blanked *(videotex monitor)*
Unstetigkeit *f* discontinuities
Unstetigkeitsstellen *fpl*: **Signale mit U.** signals which change abruptly with time
Unsymmetriedämpfung *f* longitudinal balance *(PCM data)*; longitudinal conversion loss *(cable, interface)*
unsymmetrische Überlagerung *f* unbalanced interference *(PCM data)*
Unterabtastverfahren *n* sub-nyquist sampling method *(image coding)*
Unterband *n* lower (half) band *(mobile RT)*
unterbrechende Priority *f* preemptive priority
Unterbrechungsankündigungston *m* preemption tone
unterbrechungsfreie Stromversorgung *f* (USV) uninterruptible power supply (UPS)
unterdrücken reject *(frequencies)*
Unteres Seitenband *n* (USB) lower sideband
Unterer Sonder(kanal)bereich *m* (USB) lower special-channel band *(CATV, 111-174 MHz)*
Unterhaltung *f* maintenance
Unterhaltungselektronik *f* (UE) consumer *or* leisure electronics
Unterkanal *m* subchannel
unterlagerter Betriebskanal *m* service channel below message
unterlegte Gleichspannung *f* DC bias *(FO)*
Unternetz-Steuereinheit *f* subnetwork control unit (SCU) *(VSAT)*
Unterscheidungsbit *n* (Q-Bit) qualifier bit, Q bit *(ISDN NUA)*
unterschreiten underrun *(time)*
Unterstation *f* (US) remote terminal unit (RTU) *(telecontrol)*; outstation *(TEMEX)*
untersynchron subsynchronous

unverlierbar: u. Schraube f captive screw
Unversehrtheit f: **Bit-U.** bit integrity
unzulässig unauthorized, illegal, unwanted, inadmissable
 u. Ströme mpl fault currents
 u. Zeichen n invalid character
UP (Anwenderteil m) user part *(SS7)*
ÜPlan80 (Übertragungstechnische Planung 80) transmission system design *(DBP, FTZ 1TR800)*
U$_{P0}$-Schnittstelle f U$_{P0}$ interface *(U interface for ISDN BA 2-wire circuit, for ping pong transmission to/from local exchange)*
UPS s. unterbrechungsfreie Stromversorgung f
Upstream m: **im U. vom TLN** in the upstream link from the user
Urheber m originator *(of a call)*
Ursprungsvermittlung f originating exchange
Urstart m initial start *(ESS)*
USART s. universeller synchroner/asynchroner Empfänger/Sender m
USB (kombiniertes S-Band n) unified S-band *(sat.)*
USB (oberes Seitenband n) upper sideband
USB s. Unterer Sonder(kanal)bereich m
USB s. Unteres Seitenband n
U-Scheibe (Unterlegscheibe f) washer
U-Schnittstelle f U-interface circuit (UIC) *(network-side interface for 2-wire circuit, ISDN)*
USOC (US-Steckdose f) US socket (standard)
USRT (universeller synchroner Empfänger/Sender m) universal synchronous receiver/transmitter
USV s. unterbrechungsfreie Stromversorgung f
UT Universal Time *(= GMT)*
UTC (Weltzeit f) Universal Time Coordinated
UTM s. universeller Transaktionsmonitor m
UTP (unabgeschirmte verdrillte Doppelleitung f) unshielded twisted pair
U$_{2M}$-Schnittstelle f U$_{2M}$ interface *(network-side U interface for ISDN PA)*

V

VADS (Mehrleistungs-Datendienst *m*) value-added data service *(an MDNS)*
VAG s. Verbindungsaufbau gehend
VAK s. Verbindungsaufbau kommend
VAL (Gültigkeit *f*) Valid *(V.25 message)*
VAN (Dienstleistungsnetz *n*) value-added network *(ISDN)*
VANS (Dienstleistungsnetzdienste *mpl*) value-added network services *(ISDN)*
VAP (Videotex-Anschlußpunkt *m*) videotex access point *(international vtx)*
variabler Quantisierungspegel *m* variable quantizing level *(speech coding, nom. 32 kb/s)*
VAS (vermittlungsseitige Anschlußschaltung *f*) exchange line circuit
VAS (Mehrwertdienst *m*) value-added service *(ISDN)*
VBN (vermittelndes Breitbandnetz *n*) switched broadband network *(DBP)*
VBN (Vorläufer-Breitbandnetz *n*) pilot broadband network *(DBP)*
VC (virtueller Kanal *m*) virtual channel *(sat.)*
VC (Sprechkanal *m*) voice channel
VC (Videokonferenz *f*) video conference
VC-Teilnehmer *m* video conference party
VDE (Verband *m* Deutscher Elektrotechniker) Association of German Electrotechnical Engineers
VDI (Verein *m* Deutscher Ingenieure) Association of German Engineers
VDMA (Verband *m* Deutscher Maschinenbauanstalten) Association of German Engineering Institutions
vdr (vierdraht ...) four-wire ...
VDU (Sichtgerät *n* (SG)) video display unit
VE (Verkehrseinheit *f*) traffic unit (TU)
VE (Vermittlungseinrichtung *f*) switching equipment
Vektorquantisierung *f* (VQ) vector quantization
Veranstalter *m* programme organiser *(broadcast services)*
verarbeiten process *(a call)*
verarbeitete Belegung *f* carried call *(tel. sys.)*
   v. Verkehr *m* traffic carried
Verarbeitung *f* **des Verkehrs** handling of traffic
Verarbeitungsrechner *m* host computer
Verarbeitungsschaltwerk *n* processor *(exch.)*
Verarbeitungsschicht *f* application layer *(layer 7, OSI 7-layer reference model)*
Verästelung *f* ramification *(network)*
verbinden connect, patch through
Verbinder *m* connector, adapter
   zweipoliger V. twin connector, two-pin connector
verbindlich vereinbart mandatory
Verbindung *f* link; call, connection, interconnection; communication
   V. abbauen clear a connection *(VC)*
   V. aufnehmen set up a connection
   V. auslösen clear (down)
   V. hergestellt carried call
   V. herstellen set up a connection
   V. ohne Wahl dedicated connection
Verbindungsabbau *m* call clear-down
Verbindungsabnehmer *m* communication server (CS) *(LAN gateway)*
Verbindungsabweisung *f* call rejection
Verbindungsabwicklung *f* connection procedure
Verbindungsanforderung *f* call request with identification (CRI) *(V.25 bis)*; connection request (CR) *(SS7)*
Verbindungsaufbau *m* call set-up; link establishment
   V. gehend (VAG) outgoing call set-up *(cellular mobile RT network)*
   V. kommend (VAK) incoming call set-up *(cellular mobile RT)*
   V.-Meldung *f* setup message *(ISDN)*
   V.-Zeit *f* link establishment time (LET) *(trunking)*
   V. ohne Sprechkanal off-air call set-up *(DBP 'C-Netz' feature)*
   erfolgloser V. call failure indication (CFI) *(V.25 bis)*
Verbindungsaufnahme *f* building up a connection
Verbindungsdaten *npl* call data *(tel.)*
Verbindungsdauer *f* call time, circuit time, line holding time
Verbindungsdienstmerkmal *n* connection-related service attribute
Verbindungsendpunkt *m* connection endpoint (SS7)

Verbindungsidentifikation 120

Verbindungsidentifikation *f* connection identity
Verbindungsleitung *f* (Vl) junction line; trunk; interexchange trunk *(system)*
V.-Netz *n* trunk network
paketorientierte V. (VI-P) packet-oriented interexchange trunk
Verbindungsliste *f* list of circuit connections
verbindungsloser Dienst *m* connectionless service *(SS7)*
Verbindungsmatrix *f* call control matrix *(PBX)*
Verbindungsmerkmal *n* connection attribute *(ISDN)*
Verbindungssatz *m* connector set
Verbindungsschicht *f* data link layer *(OSI RM layer 2; FDDI)*
Verbindungsstecker *m* link plug, connecting plug *(matrix)*
Verbindungssteuerungsverfahren *n* call control procedure
Verbindungs- und Verteildose *f* (VVD) multi-joint box (MJB) *(tel.)*
Verbindungsunterstützungseinrichtung *f* (VU-E) interconnection support equipment
Verbindungsunterstützungssystem *n* (VU-S) *(EWSP-V)* interconnection support system *(DBP, CCITT Rec. X.400, supports telex, teletex, TELEBOX & vtx E-mail, packet-switched VASs)*
Verbindungswiederherstellung *f* call restoration
Verbindungswunsch *m* (= angebotene Belegung) offered call *(requiring a server)*; request for connection *(tel.sys.)*
Verbindungswünsche *mpl* aufnehmen receive requests for connection
Verbindungszeit *f* call time, circuit time, line holding time
Verbraucher *m* load *(el.)*; sink *(data)*
Verbraucheranschluß *m* load input *(el.)*
Verbund *m* interconnection *(network)*
Videotex-V. videotex interworking (VI)
Verbundensignal *n* call connected signal
Verbundkommunikation *f* mixed *(data/voice)* communication
Verbundnetz *n* combined *or* mixed network
Verbundrechner *m* (VR) network computer *(videotex)*
verdecken cover; mask
verdeckte Numerierung *f* closed numbering
Verdeckung *f* masking *(digital audio)*
verdrahtete UND-Verknüpfung *f* wired-AND
Verdrahtung *f*: **fliegende V.** loose wiring

verdrahtungsprogrammiert hard-wired program
Verdrahtungsprüfautomat *m* automatic wiring tester
Verdrahtungsraster *m* wiring grid
Verdrahtungsraum *m* wiring compartment *(rack)*
Vereinbarkeitsfeststellung *f* verification of compliance *(type approval)*
Vereinbarung *f* protocol
Verfalldatum *n* expiry date
verfälschen corrupt *(bits)*, mutilate *(characters)*; invalidate *(record)*
Verfälschung *f* aliasing *(frequency response, spectrum)*
verflachen flatten out *(curve)*
Verfolgung *f* monitoring, tracing
Verfügbarkeitszeit *f* uptime, operating time *(network, computer)*
Vergabe *f* assignment
Vergleichbarkeit *f* reproducibility *(QA)*
Vergleichssignal *n* reference signal
verkabelte Leitung *f* cable line
verkämmen interleave *(TDM)*
Verkehrsangebot *n* offered load
Verkehrsart *f* traffic mode
Verkehrsaufkommen *n* traffic volume
Verkehrsausscheidungszahl *f* trunk prefix *(national = 0, international = 00 (D), 010 (GB))*
Verkehrsausscheidungsziffer *f* traffic discrimination code, prefix
Verkehrsbereich *m* cell *(cellular RT)*
Verkehrsbereichswechsel *m* roaming *(cellular RT)*
Verkehrsdurchsagekennung *f* Traffic Announcement (TA) *(RDS)*
Verkehrseinheit *f* (VE) traffic unit (TU) *(= 1 Erl)*
Verkehrselemente *npl* traffic components
Verkehrsführung *f* traffic routing
Verkehrsfunkkennung *f* Traffic Programme identification (TP) *(RDS)*
verkehrsgerecht to suit traffic conditions
Verkehrsgüte *f* grade of service *(tel. sys.)*
Verkehrslast *f* traffic intensity
Verkehrsleistung *f* traffic handling capacity
Verkehrslenkung *f* **mit Zielsuche** saturation routing
Verkehrsmanagement *n* traffic management *(SS7)*
Verkehrs(rund)funk *m* (VRF) traffic (broadcast) programme
Verkehrsstärke *f* traffic density *(tel. sys.)*

Verkehrssteuerung f traffic control, flow control
Verkehrsumfang m traffic load, traffic volume
Verkehrsweg m traffic channel
Verkehrswegeschaltbild n trunking diagram
Verkehrswert m traffic intensity *(dimensionless, in Erlang)*; traffic load *(general)*
verkettet chained together; concatenated *(SW)*
Verknüpfbarkeit f connectivity
Verknüpfung f relation, combination, function, logic
  verdrahtete V. wired-AND
Verknüpfungsstelle f combinatorial point, gate
verkoppeln lock (together)
Verlauf m curve, progress, shape, behaviour, variation (in), change *(signal)*, course, characteristic, response; profile *(potential)*
  einen V. aufweisen follow a curve
Verlaufsbeziehung f characteristic *(of a number of signals)*
verlustbehaftet lossy
Verlustbelegung f *(zu Verlust gehender Verbindungswunsch)* lost call *(tel. sys.)*
Verlustgerät n expendable equipment
Verlustleistung f power loss, power dissipation
Verlustprinzip n lost-call principle
Verlustrate f freeze-out fraction (FOF) *(TASI)*
Verlustregler m dissipative regulator
verlustreich lossy
Verlustspannung f (dissipation) loss voltage
Verlustsystem n loss system *(exchange, offered call rejected when blocking occurs)*
Verlustverkehr m lost traffic *(tel. sys.)*
Verlustwärme f heat loss *or* dissipation; waste heat
Verlustzeit f lost time
verminderte Dienstgüte f degraded service
vermittelndes Breitbandnetz n (VBN) switched broadband network *(DBP, FO, (FTZ RL 141R50, 140 Mbit/s aggregate bit rate, from 1989)*
Vermittlung f switching system; exchange; switch, office *(US)*
Vermittlungsabschluß m exchange termination (ET) *(ISDN)*
Vermittlungsamt n telephone exchange; central office *(US)*

Vermittlungseinheit f switching unit (SWU) *(ISDN)*
Vermittlungseinrichtung f (VE) switching equipment
Vermittlungsendeinrichtung f exchange termination (ET) *(ISDN)*
Vermittlungsgüte f grade of switching performance, grade of service
Vermittlungsinstanz f network entity
Vermittlungsknoten m switching node
Vermittlungsplatz m manual switching position (MSP); switchboard position, operator's position *(PBX)*
Vermittlungsrechner m (VR) switching system *or* processor
Vermittlungsschicht f network layer *(CCITT I.450 and I.451, layer 3, OSI reference model)*
Vermittlungsschrank m line interface module (LIM) *(DFS ground station)*
vermittlungsseitige Anschlußschaltung f (VAS) exchange line circuit
Vermittlungsstelle f (VSt) switching centre, exchange
  V.-Leitungsabschluß m exchange termination (ET)
Vermittlungstechnik f switching
vermittlungstechnisch call processing
  v. Aufgabe f switching task
Vermittlungsteilsystem n **für digitale Teilnehmeranschlüsse** Digital Subscribers Switching Subsystem (DSSS) *(BT ISDN)*
Vermittlungsterminal n switch terminal
Vermittlungstisch m switchboard
vernetzen connect into a network
Vernetzung f networking
vernetzt interconnected; networked
Verordnung f **für den Fernschreib- und den Datexdienst** (VFsDx) regulation relating to the teletype and the data exchange service *(DBP)*
verriegeln interlock; latch *(a signal or an output)*
Versatz m offset
  Bit-V. skew(ing)
  Frequenz-V. frequency shift, offset, error
  Rahmen V. frame delay
  Signal-V. skew(ing)
verschachtelte Jobfernverarbeitung f multileaving remote job entry (MRJE)
  v. Signale npl interleaved signals (TDM)
Verschachtelung f interleaving *(of packets)*; multiplexing
Verschaltung f interconnection

Verschleierung *f* masking
verschlüsselt encrypted, secure
Verschlüsselung *f* encryption *(data)*
verseucht polluted *(with noise)*
Versorgung *f* coverage *(of a network)*
Versorgungsbereich *m* coverage *(of a network)*; domain, management domain *(MHS)*; service area *(TV)*
Versorgungsinstanz *f* management entity
versorgungsunabhängig independently powered
Verständigungsprotokoll *n* peer protocol *(within OSI layers)*
Verständlichkeit *f* intelligibility *(speech)*
Verstärker *m* amplifier, repeater *(PBX)*
Verstärkeramt *n* repeater station
Verstärkerfeld *n* repeater section
Verstärkerstelle *f* repeater station
Verstärkungslänge *f* gain length *(laser)*
verstümmeln corrupt *(data)*
Versuchszulassung *f* prototype approval
vertauschen interchange, reverse *(phases)*, cross *(wires)*
Verteildienst *m* distribution service *(sat.)*
Verteileinrichtung *f* data distributor; fan-out unit *(LAN)*
Verteiler *m* splitter *(CATV)*; distributor, matrix; buffer *(dig. exchange)*; router *(LAN)*; terminal block *(rack)*
V. 1. Ordnung level-1 distributor *(electronic or active distributor)*
V. 2. Ordnung level-2 distributor *(electro-mechanical or passive distributor)*
V. 3. Ordnung level-3 distributor *(jackfield distributor)*
Verteilerleiste *f* terminal strip
Verteilertafel *f* distribution panel
Verteilfeld *n* distribution matrix *(CATV)*
Verteil-Koppelnetz *n* switched distribution network
Verteilnetz *n* distribution network or system *(TV)*; point-to-multipoint network *(VSAT)*
Verteilrichtung *f* outbound *(SATV)*
Verteilsystem *n* distributive system *(ISDN)*
verteilte Übertragung *f* burst mode transmission *(TCM or ping pong method)*
Verteilung *f* distribution; allocation *(calls)*
Verteilungsrauschen *n* partition noise *(FO)*
verteilvermittelter Dienst *m* switched-distribution service *(TV etc)*
Verteilvermittlung *f* point-to-multipoint switch
vertikale Verständigung *f* vertical communication *(between OSI layers)*
Vertikalprüfung *f* vertical redundancy checking (VRC)
Vertraulichkeit *f* privacy
Vertretungsschaltung *f* (secretarial) function transfer or night-service switch *(tel., executive-secretary system)*
Verwaltung *f* administration *(telecom.)*; management *(data, programs)*
Verweilzeit *f* turnaround time
Verwischungsspannung *f* dispersal voltage *(MAC baseband carrier frequ. dispersal)*
Verwürfler *m* scrambler
verzeichnisorientierter Endbenutzer-Systemteil *m* Directory User Agent (DUA) *(CCITT X.500)*
v. Systemteil *m* Directory Service Agent (DSA) *(CCITT X.500)*
verzögert:
 v. Alarm *m* deferred alarm
 v. Weitersendung *f* delayed delivery, mail box
Verzögerungseinrichtung *f* delay section; timer
Verzögerungskette *f* chain of delay elements
Verzoner *m* zoner *(exchange)*
Verzonung *f* zoning *(exchange)*
Verzweigungskabel *n* (VzK) distribution cable
VF (Niederfrequenz *f*) voice frequency
VF s. Videofrequenz *f*
VFsDx s. Verordnung *f* für den Fernschreib- und den Datexdienst
VFT (Wechselstrom-Telegraphie *f*) voice-frequency telegraphy
VHSIC very high-speed IC
VI s. Videotex-Verbund *m*
Videodat data transmission in the video signal *(WDR, serial, 300-38400 Bd)*
Videofrequenz *f* (VF) video frequency
Videokommunikationsanlage *f* (VKA) video communication system
Videokonferenz *f* (VK) video conference (VC)
Videokonferenzdienst *m* video teleconferencing service *(CCITT Rec. H.261, 41.920 Mb/s)*
Videokonferenzraum *m* (VKR) video conference room
Video-Programm-System *n* (VPS) videorecorder programming system *(TV broadcast service)*
Videorecorder-Programmierung *f* mit Fern-

sehtext (VPT) videorecorder programming by teletext *(TV broadcast service)*
Videostörabstand *m* video signal/noise ratio *(symbol = A)*
Videotex *n* (Vtx) videotex, viewdata *(interactive videotext, international, Prestel-based, s. Table VIII)*
Videotex-Anschlußpunkt *m* videotex access point (VAP)
Videotext *m* teletext *(non-interactive videotext in broadcast TV)*
Videotexverbund *m* videotex interworking (VI) protocol *(international vtx)*
Video-Verteilverstärker *m* video distribution amplifier (VDA) *(TV)*
Vielfach *n* matrix, multiplex, multiple; multiplexer, switch *(e.g. space switch)*
Vielfachanruf *m* multi-call
Vielfachleitung *f* highway *(exchange)*
Vielfachsystem *n* matrix system *(AF, VF)*
Vielfachzugriff *m* multiple access
  V. im Codemultiplexverfahren code division multiple access (CDMA) *(tel.)*
  V. im Frequenzmultiplex frequency division multiple access (FDMA) *(tel.)*
  V. im Frequenzmultiplex mit Kanalzuteilung nach Bedarf Single channel per carrier PCM multiple Access Demand assignment Equipment (SPADE)
  V. im Zeitmultiplex time division (or domain) multiple access (TDMA)
  V. mit Trägerkennung carrier-sense (or domain) multiple access (CSMA) *(LAN)*
  V. mit Trägerkennung und Kollisionserkennung carrier-sense multiple access with collision detection (CSMA/CD) *(LAN)*
Vielsprecher *m* high-calling-rate subscriber
Vielstrahlbedeckung *f* multibeam coverage *(sat.)*
vierdraht ... (vdr) four-wire ...
viererverseilt twisted quad
Vierfachschalter *m* four-section switch
Vierphasen-Modulation *f* quaternary PSK (QPSK) *(sat.)*
V-Impuls (Verkopplungsimpuls *m*) locking pulse *(PCM data)*
virtuell:
  v. Kanal *m* virtual channel, logical channel *(sat.)*
  v. Verbindung *f* (VV) virtual circuit (VC) *(PSN)*
  v. Vernetzungsdienst virtual networking service (VNS) *(private networking)*
Visualisierung *f* visual display
VITS (Prüfzeilenmeßsignal *n*) vertical (blanking) interval test signal *(TV)*

VK s. Videokonferenz *f*
VKA s. Videokommunikationsanlage *f*
VI-P (paketorientierte Verbindungsleitung *f*) packet-oriented interexchange trunk
VMS (Sprachinformationsserver *m*) voice mail server *(ISPBX)*
VOCODER voice code to recreate
Vollamtsberechtigung *f* direct *or* trunk exchange access
voll ausgelastet used to full capacity
vollduplex full duplex (FDX); two-way simultaneous
Vollhubfolie *f* full travel membrane (FTM) *(membrane keypad)*
Vollsperre *f* all calls barred
Vollstörung *f* total failure
Volumen-Datenübertragung *f* bulk data transmission *(sat.)*
Voranhebung *f* preemphasis
Vorbelastungswiderstand *m* bleeder resistor
Vorbereitende Anschaltung Data Terminal Ready (DTR) *(V.24/RS232C, s. Table VI)*
Vorbereitungsbetrieb *m* initialization mode *(modem)*
vorbeugende zyklische Wiederholung *f* preventative cyclic retransmission (PCR) *(error correction, SS7)*
Vordämpfung *f* input attenuation
voreilend:
  v. Impulsflanke *f* leading edge
  v. Kontakt *m* leading contact *(switch)*
  v. Stifte *mpl* pre-mating pins *(connector)*
Vorfeld *n*: **im V. des ...** as a forerunner to ...
Vorfeldeinrichtung *f* out-of-area equipment; remote (ISDN) equipment
Vorführzulassung *f* demonstration approval *(ZZF)*
Vorgaben *fpl* constraints; default values
vorgeschaltet front-end *(computer)*; series-connected, preceding *(component)*
vorgezogener Konzentrator *m* remote concentrator *(for remote access)*
Vorhaltezeit *f* lead time
Vorkreis *m* input circuit, series circuit
Vorläufer *m* overshoot *(pulse)*
  V.-Breitbandnetz *n* (VBN) pilot broadband network *(DBP, FO, 140 Mbit/s, before 1989)*
vorläufig:
  v. Empfehlung *f* provisional recommendation *(CCITT)*
  v. Spezifikation *f* tentative *or* draft specification
Vorlaufzeit *f* lead time *(with long codes, PCM)*

Vorleistung 124

Vorleistung *f* advance provisioning
vormerken: eine Leitung v. book a line
Vornorm *f* tentative standard *(DIN)*
Vorrang *m* priority, precedence
V.-Handhabungssystem *n* precedence handling system
Vorrangstufe *f* precedence level
Vorrechner *m* front-end processor
Vorsatzweiche *f* input filter *(CATV)*
Vorschaltrechner *m* front-end processor
Vorschlagsentwurf *m* draft proposal (DP) *(ISO)*
Vorteiler *m* prescaler *(synthesizer)*
vorverschieben advance *(phase shift)*
Vorverzerrung *f* preemphasis
Vorwahlkennzahl *f* dialling code, area code, preselection code
Vorwahlstufe *f* preselection stage *(exchange)*
Vorwärts-Fehlerkorrektur *f* forward error correction (FEC) *(PCM)*
vorwärtsgesteuerte Adaption *f* forward-controlled adaptation
Vorwärtskanal *m* forward channel; forward control channel (trunking)
Vorwärtskennzeichen *n* forward call indicator *(SS7 UP)*
Vorwärtssteuerung *f* forward supervision *(DIN 44302)*
Vorwärtszeichen *n* forward signal *(transmitted in the direction of call set-up)*
Vorzimmeranlage *f* executive-secretary system *(PBX)*
Vorzugswert *m* default value *(comp.)*
VPS (Video-Programm-System *n*) videorecorder programming system *(TV broadcast service)*
VPT (Videorecorder-Progammierung *f* mit Fernsehtext) video-recorder programming by teletext *(TV broadcast service)*

VQ (Vektorquantisierung *f*) vector quantization
VR (Verbundrechner *m*) network computer
VR (Vermittlungsrechner *m*) switching processor *or* system
VRC (Querprüfung *f*, Vertikalprüfung *f*) vertical redundancy checking
VRF (Verkehrsrundfunk *m*) traffic (broadcast) programme
VSAT (Bodenstelle *f* mit sehr kleinem Öffnungswinkel, Kleinstation *f*) very-small aperture termminal *(sat., Ku band, Hughes)*
V-Serie *f* **der CCITT Empfehlungen** V-series of CCITT Recommendations *(relates to telephone networks, s. Table IV)*
VSt (Vermittlungsstelle *f*) exchange; switching centre
VSt-Leitungsabschluß *m* exchange termination (ET)
VTR (Magnetbandaufzeichnung *f* (MAZ)) video tape recording
Vtx (Videotex *n*) videotex *(interactive videotext)*
Vtx-GA (Btx-Grundsystem *n*) basic videotex computer system
Vtx-Verbund *m* videotex interworking (VI) (protocol)
VU-E (Verbindungsunterstützungseinrichtung *f*) interconnection support equipment
VU-S (Verbindungsunterstützungssystem *n*) interconnection support system *(DBP, VASs)*
VV (virtuelle Verbindung *f*) virtual circuit (VC) *(packet switching)*
VVD (Verbindungs- und Verteildose *f*) multi-joint box (MJB)
VzK (Verzweigungskabel *n*) distribution cable

W

Wachempfänger *m* watch receiver *(mar.)*
WACK Wait before positive ACKnowledgement
WAD s. Wählautomat *m* für Datenverbindungen
Wagenrücklauf *m* carriage return (CR) *(printer)*
Wägeprogramm *n* weighting program
WaH s. Wählen *n* mit aufgelegtem Handapparat
Wahl *f* **bei aufliegendem Hörer** (WaH) on-hook dialling *(f. tel., direct listening key)*
Wählanlage *f* (W-Anlage) PBX with dialling capability, switch
Wählanschluß *m* dial-up connection *or* port; switch *(PBX)*
   W. der Gruppe L (Datex-L) circuit-switched connection *(DBP)*
   W. der Gruppe P (Datex-P) packet-switched connection *(DBP)*
   W. der Gruppe S (Datex-S) switched satellite connection *(DBP)*
Wahlaufforderungszeichen *n* proceed to dial signal *(tel.)*
Wahlaufnahme *f* digit input
Wahlaufnahmerelais *n* dialling relay *(tel.)*
Wahlaufnahmesatz *m* (WAS) digit input circuit
Wählautomat *m* **für Datenverbindungen** (WAD) automatic dialling facility for data transmission *(FTZ)*
Wahlbefehl *m* Call Request with Identification (CRI) *(V.25 bis)*
Wahlbereitschaft *f* dialling standby (status) *(PBX)*
Wählbetrieb *m* circuit switching
Wahlblock *m* keypad
   12er W. 12-button keypad
Wahlempfangssatz *m* digit input circuit
Wählen *n* **mit aufgelegtem Handapparat** (WaH) dialling with the handset replaced, on-hook dialling *(direct listening key)*
Wahlendezeichen *n* end-of-pulsing signal *(forward signal)*; end-of-selection signal *(backward signal)*
Wahlendezeit *f* end-of-address time *(SS7 UP)*

Wähler *m* selector *(exchange)*
   Crossbar-W. crossbar (XB) selector
   Step-by-Step-W. step-by-step (SXS) selector
wählfähig dialling
Wahlfrequenz *f* pulse speed *(tel.)*
Wahlhilfe *f* operator assistance
Wahlimpuls *m* dial pulse
Wahlkontrolle *f* barred-code check *(dig. PBX)*
Wählkorrektur *f* dial pulse correction *(tel.)*
Wählleitung *f* switched circuit
Wahlnachsendesatz *m* (WNS) digit output circuit
   W. für Impulskennzeichen (WNSI) digit output circuit, pulse signalling
   W. für Schleifenkennzeichen (WNSS) digit output circuit, loop signalling; loop output circuit
Wählnebenstellenanlage *f* private branch exchange (PBX)
Wählnebenstellendienst *m*: **zentralisierter W.** central office exchange service *(centrex)*
Wählnetz *n* automatic network, switched network
   W. für Datenaustausch (Datex, Dx) switched data exchange (network) *(DBP service)*
Wählpause *f* interdigital pause *(f.tel.)*
Wählprüfnetz *n* subscriber line testing network
Wahlsatz *m* (WS) signalling set, digit circuit
   W. für Nummernschalterwahl (WSN) digit circuit for rotary dialling
   W.-Tastenwahlempfänger *m* (WTE) pushbutton signal receiver for digit circuits
Wählscheibe *f* dial *(tel.)*
Wahlspeicher *m* dialling register
Wahlsperre *f* dialling restriction *(mobile RT)*
Wählsternanschluß *m* concentrator line
Wählsternschalter *m* line concentrator *(tel.)*
Wahlstufe *f* selector; switching stage *(tel.)*
Wähltastatur *f* dialling keyboard

Wählton m (W-Ton) dial tone
Wähltonempfänger m (WTE) dial tone receiver (PBX)
Wähltonverzug m dialling delay
Wahlumsetzer m (WU) dial converter (tel.)
Wählunteranlage f (WU-Anlage) private branch exchange (PBX) **bedienungslose W.** (dependent) PABX
Wählverbindung f (WV) switched or dial-up connection (service attribute)
Wahlvorbereitung f call preparation
Wahlwiederholung f last-number (automatic) redialling (f. tel.); repeat last call
Wahlzeichen n selection signal (X.21)
Wählzeichen npl dialling pulses (tel.), dialling signals
Wahlziffer f dial digit
WAN (Weitverkehrnetz n, Langstreckennetz n) wide area network
Wanderfeldröhre f travelling wave tube (TWT)
Wanderfeldröhrenverstärker m travelling wave tube amplifier (TWTA) (sat.)
Wandern n roaming (change of base station area, mobile RT)
WAN-Konformitätsprüfungsdienste mpl Wide-Area Networks Conformance Testing Services (WAN-CTS) (EC, testing centres for X.21, X.25 and ISDN terminals)
W-Anlage (Wählanlage f) PBX with dialling capability, switch
WARC World Administrative Radio Conference
Wartebelastung f waiting traffic
Wartebetrieb m disconnected mode
Wartedauer f delay
Wartemusik f music-while-you-wait, music on hold (MOH)
Warten n **auf Abfragen** operator's answering delay
  w. auf Freiwerden (einer Leitung) camp on busy (line)
wartende Belegung f waiting or delayed call (tel. sys.)
Warteordner m queuing device, call storage device
Wartepuffer m queuing buffer
Warteschaltung f holding circuit (ESS)
Warteschlange f queue (PCM data, voice)
Warteschlangenbetrieb m queuing
Warteschlangennetz n queuing network (PCM data, voice)
Warteschleife f waiting loop
Wartestation f passive station
Wartesystem n delay system (exchange, offered call queued when blocking occurs)
Warteton m progress tone (ticking tone)

Wartevermittlung f camp-on switching
Wartewahrscheinlichkeit f probability of delay
Wartezeit f queuing delay, delay, hold period, latency
Wartezustand m camp-on
Wartungsfeld n maintenance panel
WAS (Wahlaufnahmesatz m) digit input circuit
WB (Breitband n (BB)) wideband
WDM s. Wellenlängenmultiplex n
WD-Multiplex s. Wellenlängenmultiplex n
Wechselbetrieb m half duplex transmission
Wechselbiegung f flexing (cable)
Wechselleistung f variance (of the quantization error, ADC)
Wechselschrift f non return to zero inverted (NRZI) code (PCM); non return to zero (mark) (NRZ(M)) code (PCM)
wechselseitig betriebene Leitungen fpl two-way trunks
Wechselsprechen n simplex (tel.)
Wechselstrom-Telegraphie f (WT) voice frequency telegraphy (VFT)
Wechselstromübertragung f alternating-current line circuit (tel. signalling)
Wechseltaktschrift f two-frequency recording (magnetic stripe card)
Weckdienst m alarm call service
Weckeinrichtung f telephone ringer; wake-up facility
Weckruf m wake-up call (tel.)
Wecksignal n wake-up signal (HW activation)
Weckzeit f time of the wake-up call (tel.)
Wegeführung f circuit
Wegelenkung f routing
Wegemanagement n route management (SS7 MTP)
Wegermittlung f path selection, path finding
Wegesuche f path selection
wegfaxen send by fax (colloquial)
Wegführung f conduit (cable)
Weglänge f travel (switch)
Weglenkung f routing
Wegpunkt m position point (navigation)
Weiche f filter; gating circuit; combining/separating filter, combiner (ant.)
  Datenw. data selector
  Frequenzw. diplexer (ant.); cross-over network (LF)
  Gebührenw. injector circuit (tel.)
  Impulsw. separating filter
  Kanalw. channel branching filter or

network
Taktw. clock selector *(PCM)*
Trennw. separating filter
Weichendämpfung *f* branching network loss
Weichumtastung *f* silent reversal *(of line polarities, tel.)*
Weißdruck *m* white-paper edition *(DIN)*
Weitergabe *f* transfer
weitergeben: nach außen w. externalize *(a signal etc.)*
weiterleiten forward *(a call)*; insert *(data in MUX)*
Weiterleit-/Endmultiplexer *m* drop and insert multiplexer
weiterreichen hand-over *(tel.)*
Weiterruf *m* periodic ringing
weiterschalten forward, transfer *(a call)*
Weitverkehrsnetz *n* long-range communications network; wide-area network (WAN)
Weitverkehrsschleife *f* long-distance loop (LDL)
weitverzweigt highly ramified
Wellendämpfung *f* attenuation constant *(cable, in dB/km)*
Wellenlängenmultiplex *m* (WD-Multiplex) wavelength division multiplex (WDM) *(multi-laser FO application)*
wellenrichtig abschließen terminate in characteristic impedance
Wellenwiderstand *m* characteristic impedance
Wellenzug *m* wave train
W.-frequenz *f* group frequency
weltweites Navigationssystem *n* Global Positioning System (GPS) *(navigation, sat.)*
Wenigsprecher *m* low-calling-rate subscriber
Wer da Who-are-you (WRU)
Wettbewerb *m* contention *(DC, bus, trunking)*
Wettbewerbsverfahren *n* competitive-access method *(PCM data)*
Wickelanschluß *m* wirewrap connection
Widerstandsbelag *m* resistance per unit length *(cable, ohm/km)*
Widerstandsprofil *n* resistance characteristic
Wiederanruf *m* call-back, return call, recall
W. nach Zeit timed redialling
Wiederaufprüfung *f* restoral attempt *(sat.)*
Wiederbelegungsentfernung *f* repeat or reuse distance *(mobile radio)*
wiedereingliedern reassign *(subscriber in queue)*
Wiedereinschreiben *n* re-storing
Wiederherbeiruf *m* recall
Wiederherstellung *f* recovery procedure

W. der Verbindung restoration of the connection *or* call
Wiederholdauer *f* repetition *or* cycle period
Wiederholgenauigkeit *f* reproducibility
Wiederholung *f* recirculating, retransmission *(packets)*; retry
Wiederholungsaufforderung *f* reject
Wiederholungsprüfung *f* persistence check *(PCM data; a bit-by-bit test of receive data)*
Wiederholungssendung *f* retransmission *(PCM)*
Wiederkehrfehler *m* repeatability error
Winkel *m* bracket *(rack)*
Winkelschiene *f* angle bar *(rack)*
Wirkanteil *m* real component
wirkliche Leitung *f* physical, actual line
Wirkrechner *m* active processor
Wirkungsgrad *m* efficiency
Wirtschaftlichkeit *f* (economic) efficiency
Wischer *m* transient
wissensbasiertes System *n* knowledge-based-system (KBS) *(AI)*
WNSI (Wahlnachsendesatz *m* für Impulskennzeichen) digit output circuit, pulse dialling
WNSS (Wahlnachsendesatz *m* für Schleifenkennzeichen) digit output circuit, loop signalling; loop output circuit
Wobbelgenerator *m* sweep generator
Wobbelsender *m* sweep generator
WORM (einmal beschreiben, mehrmals lesen) write once, read many *(CD-R, storage disk)*
Wortaufbereitung *f* word synthesis *(PCM transmitter)*
Wortbreite *f* word length
Worttakt *m* octet timing *(TE)*
wortweise Verschachtelung *f* word interleaving
Wrapfeld *n* wire-wrap block
WRU (Wer da) Who-are-you *(telex)*
WS (Wahlsatz *m*) digit circuit
WSN (Wahlsatz *m* für Nummernschaltwahl) digit circuit for rotary dialling
WSP (Breitband-Koppelstelle *f*) wideband switching point *(D network)*
WT (Wechselstrom-Telegraphie *f*) voice frequency telegraphy (VFT)
WTE (Wahlsatz-Tastenwahlempfänger *m*) push-button signal receiver for digit circuit
WTE (Wähltonempfänger *m*) dial tone receiver *(PBX)*
W-Ton (Wählton *m*) dial tone

WU (Wahlumsetzer *m*) dial converter *(tel.)*
WU-Anlage (Wählunteranlage *f*) private branch exchange (PBX)
   bedienungslose W. (dependent) PABX

WV (Wählverbindung *f*) switched connection
WW (Wahlwiederholung *f*) redialling
WYSIWYG what-you-see-is-what-you-get *(DTP method)*

X

XB (Koordinatenschalteramt *n*) crossbar (selector) exchange *(analog)*

XBU (Koordinatenschalteramt *n*, unsymmetrische Zeichengabe) crossbar exchange, unbalanced signalling

X/OPEN RARE (Reseaux Associés pour la Récherche Européenne) Association of Networks for European Research

X-Schnittstelle *f* X interface *(8-wire ISDN connection device between telephone set and ancillary equipment, analog)*

X-Serie der CCITT-Empfehlungen X-series of CCITT Recommendations *(relates to data networks, s. Table V)*

Y

Y-Schnittstelle f Y interface *(4-wire ISDN connection device between telephone set and ancillary equipment, digital)*

Y-Verzweigung f Y junction, three-port coupler *(FO)*

Z

ZA (zentrale Anzeigeeinrichtung *f*) central display (unit *or* equipment)
Zähler *m* counter; meter *(charges)*
Zählstörung *f* metering fault
Zählung *f* metering *(tel.)*
Zählvergleich *m* meter comparison
Zählverhinderungsrelais *n* non-metering relay
Zählwerkprotokoll *n* meter status log
ZB (Zentralbatterie *f*) station battery *(exchange)*
ZBBeo (zentrale Beobachtung *f*) central service observation
ZC s. Zeitcode *m*
ZC (Zonenzentrum *n*) zone centre *(exchange)*
ZD (Zeitmultiplex-Datenübertragung *f*) TDM data transmission
zdr. (zweidraht ...) two-wire
ZE (Zentraleinheit *f*) central processing unit (CPU)
ZE (Zugangseinheit *f*) access unit *(to the LAN from FDDI network)*
Zeichen *n* character *(WP)*; signal *(signalling)*
Zeichenbildung *f* character alignment *(DIN 44302)*
Zeicheneinheit *f* signal unit *(SS7 MTP frame)*
Zeichenfehlerhäufigkeit *f* character error rate
Zeichenfrequenz *f* mark frequency *(TC)*
Zeichengabe *f* signalling *(CCITT Rec. I.112)*
  Z. außerhalb der Zeitlagen out-slot signalling
  Z. innerhalb der Zeitlagen in-slot signalling
Zeichengabekanal *m* signalling data link *(SS7 MTP)*
Zeichengabepunkt *m* signalling point (SP) *(node in SS7 network)*
Zeichengaberechner *m* (ZGR) signalling processor *(VBN, FO)*
Zeichengabestrecke *f* signalling link *(SS7 MTP)*
  Z.-Bündel *n* signalling link set *(SS7 MTP)*
  Z.-Kennung *f* signalling link selection code *(SS7 MTP)*
Zeichengabesystem *n* (ZGS) signalling system (SS) *(CCITT Rec. Q.700 ff, FTZ RL 1TR6)*
Zeichengabesystem Nr.7 (ZGS 7) Signalling System No.7 (SS7) *(CCITT Rec. Q.701 - 764, FTZ RL 1R7)*
Zeichengabetransaktion *f*: **temporäre Z.** (tZGT) temporary signalling connection *(SS7 MTP)*
Zeichengabeübertragungsstrecke *f* signalling data link
Zeichengabewegebündel *n* signalling route set *(SS7)*
Zeichengeschwindigkeit *f* printing speed
Zeichenimpedanz *f* (ZZ) character (line) impedance (Z_{CO}) *(tel.)*
Zeichenlänge *f* signal duration *(tel.)*
Zeichenplan *m* bit allocation table *(signalling)*
Zeichenschritt *m* mark, signal element *(TC)*
Zeichen/Sekunde (Z/s) characters/second
Zeichenstrecke *f* signalling link
Zeichenstrom *m* signalling current *(tel.)*
Zeichentableau *n* drawing tablet *(for telepictures)*
Zeichentakt *m* byte timing
Zeichentonumsetzer *m* (ZTU) signal/tone converter
Zeichenumsetzer *m* **(Analog-/Digital)** Signalling converter, Analog/Digital (SAD)
Zeichenverzerrung *f* signal distortion
Zeichnungsraster *m* coordinate system
Zeile *f* row *(matrix)*
Zeilendichte *f* scanning density *(fax)*
Zeilenhintergrund *m* line backing *(videotex monitor)*
Zeilensperrkontakt *m* row blocking contact
Zeilensummenmarkierung *f* row rest-condition marking
Zeilenumordnung *f* line shuffling *(HDTV scanning technique, Eu-95)*
-zeilig: **12-z.** 12-row
Zeitabschnitt *m* time interval, time slot
Zeitansage *f* speaking clock service *(tel.)*, time announcement
Zeitbasis *f* gate time *(counter)*
zeitbegrenzt with time-out, timed
  z. Zuf *m* timed ringing signal
Zeitbezug *m* time reference, time correlation

Zeitcode 134

Zeitcode *m* (ZC) time code (TC)
Zeitduplex *n* time division duplex (TDD) *(tel.)*
Zeitentscheider *m* time discriminator
Zeitgeber *m* timer
zeitgerecht at the correct time, with correct timing, in the correct time relationship
Zeitgetrenntlageverfahren *n* time division method *(generally)*; burst operation; time division duplex (TDD) *(ping pong type transmission technique for local loops, ISDN B channel)*
Zeitkanal *m* time slot *(octet or multiples thereof)*
   Z. mit einem Signal beaufschlagen inject a signal into a time slot
Zeitkompressionsmultiplex *n* time compression multiplex (TCM); burst mode transmission *(ping pong type technique involving alternating transmission of high-speed data bursts)*
Zeitkoppelfeld *n* TDM switching matrix
Zeitlage *f* timing relationship *(PCM)*; time slot
   Kanal-Z. time-slot pattern
   Signalisierung f außerhalb/innerhalb der Z.en out-slot/in-slot signalling
Zeitlagenvielfach *n* time division multiplex (TDM); time division multiplexer, TDM multiplexer, time switch *(ESS)*
zeitlich as a function of time; over time, with respect to time
   z. Änderung *f* rate of change
   z. erfaßt timed
   z. gesteuert *or* **überwacht** timed
   z. Verlauf *m* time characteristic
Zeitmarke *f* time stamp
Zeitmessung *f* time measurement, timing
Zeitmultiplex *n* time division multiplex (TDM) *(bit- or byte-interleaving of a number of user data streams in a serial communications channel)*
   Z.-Datenübertragung *f* (ZD) TDM data transmission
Zeitmultiplexer *m* TDM multiplexer
zeitmultiplexierte Sprachübertragung *f* time-assigned speech interpolation (TASI)
Zeitmultiplexleitung *f* highway
Zeitmultiplexzugriff *m* time division multiple access (TDMA)
Zeitprogramm *n* timing program *(exchange)*
Zeitraster *m* time(-slot) *or* timing pattern
   im 10-ms-Z. at a 10-ms rate
Zeit-Raum-Raum-Zeit-Struktur *f* time-space-space-time structure *(switching system)*

Zeitrückhalt *m* time reserve
Zeitscheibe *f* time slice *(subset of total computing time in multitasking)*
Zeitscheibenteilung *f* time division multiplex (TDM)
Zeitschlitz *m* time slot
Zeitschwelle *f* threshold period
Zeitsperre *f* timeout
Zeitsperrung *f* time congestion *(tel. sys.)*
Zeittakt *m* clock, clock pulses
Zeittaktgeber *m* clock, timer
Zeittaktzähler *m* time pulse *or* clock pulse counter
Zeitüberwachung *f* timer, time supervision *(HW)*; time-out *(SW)*
Zeitverlauf *m* time characteristic
Zeitvielfach *n* s. Zeitlagenvielfach
Zeitvielfachzugriff *m* time division multiple access (TDMA)
Zeitweichensteuerung *f* burst control
Zeitzählung *f* metering *(tel.,DC)*
Zelle *f* cell *(ATM timeslot, incl. header and user signal)*
Zellenbündel *n* cluster (of cells) *(cellular mobile RT)*
Zellenfunk *m* cellular radio *(mobile RT)*
Zellenmultiplexierung *f* cell interleaving *(ATM)*
Zellenraster *m* cell spacing *(ATM, e.g. 69 bytes)*
Zellkopf *m* header *(ATM)*
zellulares Funkfernsprechnetz *n* cellular mobile radio telephony network *(usually duplex)*
zentral central, centralized
   z. Anlagendatei *f* central exchange file
   z. Anzeigeeinrichtung *f* (ZA) central display *(unit, equipment)*
   z. (Betriebs-)Beobachtung *f* (ZBBeo) central service observation *(unit, equipment)*
   z. (Betriebs-)Beobachtung *f* (ZBBeo) transmission surveillance center *(optical transmission)*
   z. EDV-Anlage *f* (EDVA) EDP centre
   z. Einrichtungen *fpl* common equipment, units *(tel.sys.)*
   z. Fernbedienungsanlage *f* (FBAZ) central remote control system *(sat.)*
   z. Fernsteuerkanal *m* (ZFK) central telecontrol channel *(VBN)*
   z. Kontrollstation *f* central controller
   z. Prüfstelle *f* für Dateneinrichtungen data test centre (DTC) *(FTZ)*
   z. Rechnereinheit *f* (ZRE) central processor (CPU)

z. Reservierungsplatz *m* central booking station *(VBN)*
z. Signalisierungskanal *m* common signalling channel (CSC)
z. Steuerwerk *n* central *or* common processor *or* control unit
z. Zeichenkanal *m* (ZZK) common signalling channel (CSC)
Zentralamt *n* **für Mobilfunk** (ZfM) DBP Central Mobile Radio Office
Zentralamt *n* **für Zulassungen im Fernmeldewesen** (ZZF) DBP Central Approval Office for Telecommunications *(corresponds to BABT in GB)*
Zentralbatterie *f* (ZB) station battery *(exchange)*
Zentrale *f* central station
Zentraleinheit *f* central processing unit (CPU) *(comp.)*; central station *(tel.)*
zentralgesteuert centrally controlled *(exch.)*
Zentralkanal-Zeichengabesystem *n* common-channel signalling system (CCSS) *(ISDN, CCITT Rec. I.112)*
Zentralstation *f* hub *(VSAT network)*
Zentralsteuerwerk *n* (ZST) central processor; common control unit *(tel.)*
Zentralvermittlungsstelle *f* (ZVSt) tertiary exchange
zentrisch erregt concentrically illuminated *(sat. antenna)*
zerlegen dismantle *(equipment)*
ZFK s. zentraler Fernsteuerkanal *m*
ZfM s. Zentralamt *n* für Mobilfunk
ZGS (Zeichengabesystem *n*) signalling system (SS)
ZGS-Nr.7 (Zeichengabesystem *n* Nr.7) signalling system No.7 (SS7) *(ISDN)*
Zi s. Ziffernumschaltung *f*
Ziehwerkzeug *n* module extractor tool
Zielpunkt(code) *m* destination point code (DPC) *(SS7 MTP)*
Zielrufnummer *f* designational number *(f. tel.)*
Zieltaste *f* name key *(f. tel.)*
Zielvermittlungsstelle *f* (B-VSt) destination exchange
Zielwahl *f* speed dialling *(with name keys, to external subscriber, tel.)*
Ziffer *f* digit *(DP)*
Ziffernmodus *m* numeric mode *(ESS)*
Ziffernumschaltung *f* (Zi) figure shift *(telex)*
Ziffernumwertung *f* digit translation
Ziffernzuschaltung *f* figure shifting *(telex)*

Zittermatrix *f* dither matrix *(digital video processing)*
Zonenzentrum *n* zone centre (ZC) *(exchange)*
Zonephone (öffentlicher Funktelefondienst *m*) public CT2 service *(GB, Ferranti telepoint system)*
ZPS (Zeichen *npl* pro Sekunde) characters per second (cps) *(printers)*
ZR (Rückhörimpedanz *f*) zero sidetone (line) impedance (Z$_{SO}$) *(tel., CCITT Rec. P.10)*
ZRE s. zentrale Rechnereinheit *f*
ZRP s. zentraler Reservierungsprozessor *m*
Z/s (Zeichen/Sekunde) characters/second
ZSB s. Zweiseitenband *n*
Z-Schnittstelle *f* Z interface *(at the telephone terminal, e.g. X.21, S$_0$, ISDN)*
ZST s. Zentralsteuerwerk *n*
ZTU (Zeichentonumsetzer *m*) signal/tone converter
Zubringer *m* feeding line, input line
Zubringerbündel *n* offering trunk group
Zubringerleitung *f* offering trunk
Zubringersystem *n* **für Richtfunk** radio relay station cable network
Zufallsgenerator *m* random-number generator
zufallsmäßiger Rundruf *m* random broadcast
z. Vielfachzugriff *m* random multiple access (RMA) *(sat. access method, incl. ALOHA)*
Zufallsverkehr *m* pure-chance traffic
Zuführung *f* supply, feed; contribution *(TV programme signal)*
Zug *m* pull, tension *(mech.)*; train *(of waves, pulses)*
   Empfangsz. receiving channel
   Impulsz. pulse train
   Leitungsz. conductor *or* wiring run *(HW)*
   Linienz. trace *(recorder)*; route *(tel.)*
   Wellenz. wave train
   Wellenz.-Frequenz *f* group frequency
Zugangsberechtigung *f* authorization *(of users)*
Zugangseinheit *f* (ZE) access unit *(to the LAN from FDDI nework)*
Zugangskoppler *m* cross connect matrix *(ATM node)*
   Z. für Steuerleitungen connecting matrix for control trunks
Zugangspfad *m* link *(PAD)*
Zugangs-Steuerblock *m* token *(supervisory frame controlling access to a token ring network)*
Zugorgan *n* strain-relief element *(cable)*
zugreifen auf access
Zugriffsberechtigung *f* access barring

Zugriffs-Clipping 136

level; access authorization
Zugriffs-Clipping *n* competitive clipping, "freeze-out" *(of packets)*
Zugriffskapazität *f* access capability *(CCITT Rec. I.112)*
Zugriffspunkt *m* access point, point of entry *(data network)*
Zugriffssteuerung *f* access control, resolution of access contentions
Zulassung *f* type approval *(FTZ)*
Zulassungsnummer *f*: **DBP-Z.** type approval number *(FTZ)*
zulassungspflichtig subject to permit *or* approval
Zuordner *m* translator *(NTG 0902)*
Zuordnungsspeicher *m* assignment store
zurückgebildeter Abtastwert *m* reconstructed sample
Zurückregelung *f* gain reduction
Zurückstellungsdienst *m* quarantine service
Zusammenarbeit *f* interoperation *(between system sections)*; intercommunication *(between services)*
zusammengefaßtes Daten- und Textnetz *n* (IDN) integrated data and text network
zusammenhängend coherent *(signal)*; contiguous *(memory areas)*
Zusammenschaltung *f* interconnection
zusammensetzen s. zusammenstellen
zusammenstellen assemble, multiplex *(TDM)*
Zusammenstoß *m* collision *(bus)*
Zusammenwirken *n* interworking
Zusatz *m* feature
Zusatzaufwand *m* overhead *(control)*
Zusatzdämpfung *f* additional losses *(additional to fixed section losses, PCM)*
Zusatzdienste *mpl* supplementary service attributes
Zusatzeinrichtung *f* ancillary equipment *(TE in main station or ISPBX)*
Zusatzgerät *n* attachment
Zusatzschaltung *f* supplementary circuit
Zustandsbeschreibung *f* status description *(ARQ)*
Zustellgerät *n* delivery device *(e.g. printer, CCITT Rec. X.400)*
Zustopfen *n* blocking *(of RF receivers)*
ZV s. Zwischenverteiler *m*
ZVEI (Zentralverband *m* der Elektrotechnischen Industrie)
ZVSt (Zentralvermittlungsstelle *f*) tertiary exchange
ZW (Zielwahl *f*) speed dialling *(with name keys)*
Zwangsauslösung *f* automatic cleardown *(tel.)*

Zwangsbelüftung *f* forced ventilation (system)
Zweidrahtleitung *f* two-wire trunk
Zweieranschluß *m* two-party subscriber *or* line, shared line
Zweig *m* path
Zweigruppentelegramm *n* double group message *(TC)*
Zweikanalüberwachung *f* dual watch *(maritime radio)*
zweipoliger Verbinder *m* twin connector, two-pin connector
Zweipunktverbindung *f* point-to-point link *(e.g. RS232)*
Zweiseitenband *n* (ZSB) double sideband
Zweisprungverbindung *f* double-hop link *(networked VSATs, one- or two-way links)*
Zweit-, Dritt-, Viert- *usw.* **anlage** *f* second *(third, fourth etc.)* station *(conference circuit)*
Zweitanruf *m* secondary call *(tel.)*; re-call *(f. tel.)*
zweites digitales Mobilfunknetz *n* (D2) second digital mobile RT network
Zweitnebenstellenanlage *f* secondary *or* slave station *(tel.)*
zweitorig two-port
Zweitweg *m* alternative routing, second etc. choice routing
Zweiwegdienst *m* two-way service *(e.g. videotex)*
Zweiwegeführung *f* dual routing
Zwillingsleitung *f* flat twin flexible cord *(DIN)*
Zwischengenerator *m* repeater *(tel.)*
Zwischenleitung *f* link
Zwischenleitungsbündel *n* link group
Zwischenregenerator *m* (ZWR) regenerative repeater *(tel., ISDN BA)*
Zwischenschaltzeit *f* intervening time
Zwischenspeicher *m* buffer store, buffer; message buffer *(exch.)*
zwischenspeichern buffer
Zwischenspeicherung *f* temporary storage, buffer storage;
store and forward (switching) *(MHS)*
Zwischenstelle *f* repeater station *(transmission link)*
Zwischenverteiler *m* (ZV) intermediate distributor *(exchange)*
Zwischenverteilergestell *n* intermediate distribution frame (IDF) *(tel.)*
Zwischenwahlzeit *f* interdigital pause *(tel.)*
Zwitterkupplung *f* hermaphrodite *or* hermaphroditic *or* sexless connector, adapter *(cable)*

ZWR s. Zwischenregenerator *m*
zyklisch :
  z. Blockprüfung *f* s. z. Blocksicherung
  z. Blocksicherung *f* cyclic redundancy check (CRC)
  z. vertauschter Binärcode *m* cyclically permuted code, reflected code
  z. Zuteilungsverfahren *n* polling method *(access control)*
zyklusführende Haupt-Z-Station *f* cycle-initiating *or* polling primary centre
ZZ (Zeichenimpedanz *f*) character (line) impedance (Z_{CO}) *(tel.)*
ZZF (Zentralamt *n* für Zulassungen im Fernmeldewesen) Central Approval Office for Telecommunications *(corresponds to BABT in GB)*
ZZK (zentraler Zeichenkanal *m*) common signalling channel (CSC) *(ISDN)*

Englisch - Deutsch

A

A operator A-Platz *m (Tel.)*
A party A-Teilnehmer *m (Tel.)*
A position A-Platz *m (Tel.)*
a/b interface a/b-Schnittstelle f (Tel.-Kupferschnittstelle)
abbreviated address Kurzadresse f *(EWS)*; Kurzwahlzeichen *n* (KW) *(K.-Tel.)*
  a. dialling Kurzwahl f (KW)
  a. directory number Kurzrufnummer f (KRN) *(Tel.)*
abortion procedure Abbruchverfahren *n (Zugriffssteuerung)*
ABR (Automatic Baud (rate) Recognition) automatische Schrittgeschwindigkeitserkennung f
absent subscriber job Abwesenheitsauftrag *m (Tel.)*
  a.-subscriber service Auftragdienst *m*, Fernsprechauftragsdienst *m* (FEAD)
absorbing switching network Auskoppelfeld *n*
AC (advance calling) Vorauswählen *n*
AC (alternating current) Wechselstrom *m*
AC-coupled input Übertragungseingang *m*
AC mains adapter Netzanpassung f, Netzvorsatz *m (SV)*
AC only gleichstromfrei
AC power restoration Netzrückkehr f
accept annehmen, aufnehmen; erfassen
  a. a call abfragen *(Tel.-Verm.)*
acceptance test Abnahmeprüfung f
access zugreifen (auf); Anschaltung f, Zugang *m*, Zugriff *m*
  a. a facility Leistungsmerkmal *n* in Anspruch nehmen
  a. barring level Zugriffsberechtigung f
  a. card Berechtigungskarte f *(ÖKartTel)*
  a. capability Zugriffskapazität f *(CCITT Rec. I.112)*
  a. circuit Anschaltesatz *m*, Ansteuerungssatz *m*
  a. code Berechtigungscode *m (Vtx.)*
  a. computer Teilnehmerrechner *m* (TR, TNR) *(Vtx.)*
  a. control Zugriffssteuerung f
  a. equipment Anschalteeinrichtung f *(Vtx.)*
  a. exchange Teilnehmervermittlungsstelle f (TVSt) *(ISDN-Paketvermittlung)*
  a. level selection Berechtigungsumschaltung f
  a. logic Ansteuerlogik f
  a. page Übergabeseite f *(Vtx., Zugriff auf ER)*
  a. point Anschlußstelle f
  a.-related service attribute Anschlußdienstmerkmal *n*
  a. switch Schaltwähler *m*
  a. unit (AU) Anschlußbox f *(Vtx.-ISDN)*; Anschlußeinheit f *(CCITT Rec. X.400, Übergang zu Telematik-Diensten)*
  a. via switched lines Einwählvorgang *m (zum Paketnetz)*
accessible interface faßbare Schnittstelle f
AccessLine BT-Analog-Festverbindung f *(2-/4-drahtig, NF-Bereich)*
accident Betriebsstörung f, Havarie f
accrued charges aufgelaufene Gebühren fpl
Accunet digitaler Datennetzdienst *m* von AT&T *(1,544 MB/s, auf terrestrischer und Satelliten-Basis, mit DDS, Paketvermittlung)*
ACD (automatic call distribution) automatische Anrufverteilung f *(ISDX)*
ACFA (advanced CMOS frame aligner) fortgeschrittene CMOS-Rahmensynchronisierschaltung f *(ISDN)*
ACIA (asynchronous communications interface adapter) E/A-Schnittstelle f für serielle Anschlüsse
ACK s. acknowledgement
acknowledged gesichert *(Verbindung, ZGS.7)*
acknowledgement (ACK) Bestätigung f, Quittungsmeldung f, Rückmeldung f
  a. positive Gutquittung f
acoustic akustisch
  a. coupler Akustikkoppler *m (Modem)*
acquire erfassen *(Signal, Daten)*
acquiring lock Aufsynchronisieren *n*, Einrasten *n*
acquisition Beschaffung f; Erfassung f *(Signal, Daten)*
  a. of signal (AOS) Signalsynchronisierung f *(Sat.)*
activate aktivieren, ansteuern; anstoßen, auslösen
active processor Wirkrechner *m*

activity Aktivität *f*; Belegung *f (Leitung, Kanal)*
actual line wirkliche Leitung *f*
a. status Ist-Zustand *m*; Ist-Aufnahme *f*
actuate auslösen, betätigen, ansteuern
A/D converter Analog-/Digital-Umsetzer *m* (ADU) *oder* -Wandler *m*
adapter, adaptor Kabelverbinder *m*, Übergangsstück *n*; Mittelstück *n (FO Verbinder)*; Adapter *m* Vorsatz *m*; Zwischenstecker *m*; Anpassungseinheit *f*; Beistellgerät *n (TV-Decoder)*
adaptive adaptiv
 a. delta modulation (ADM) adaptive Deltamodulation *f (MAC-Audio, CCITT Rep. 953)*
 a. differential PCM (ADPCM) adaptive Differenz-PCM *f (CCITT Rec. G.721)*
 a. quantisation (AQ) adaptive Quantisierung *f*
 a. subband coding (ASC) adaptive Teilbandcodierung *f* (ATBC)
 a. transformation coding (ATC) adaptive Transformationscodierung *f (Datenreduktion)*
 a. transversal equalizer adaptiver Transversalentzerrer *m (Sat.)*
ADC (analog/digital converter) Analog-/Digital-Umsetzer *m* (ADU) *oder* -Wandler *m*
ADCCP (Advanced Data Communications Control Procedure) fortgeschrittene Datenübermittlungs-Steuerungsprozedur *f (ANSI, FIPS PUB 71,78)*
add-on aufschalten *(Geräte)*
 a.-on unit Beistellgerät *n (Sat.-Heimempfänger)*
added-feature telephone Komforttelefon *n*
addition Überlagerung *f (von Rauschen)*
additional losses Zusatzdämpfung *f (zusätzlich zur festen Teilstreckendämpfung, PCM)*
 a. packet mode neuer Paketmodus *m (CCITT)*
address signal Rufnummer *f (Daten)*
addressable multiplexer (DCC) digitaler Kreuzschienenverteiler *m*
ADF (automatic document feed) Stapelbetrieb *m (Fax.)*
ADI s. alarm data interface
adjacent-channel operation Nachbarkanalbetrieb *m (Funkstrecke)*
adjustable potentiometer Einstellregler *m*
adjustment period Adaptionszeit *f (Echosperre)*
ADM s. adaptive delta modulation

ADMA (amplitude domain multiple access) Vielfachzugriff *m* im Amplitudenbereich *(Sat.)*
ADMD s. administrative management domain
administration Verwaltung *f (Fernmeldewesen)*
 a. and data server (ADS) Betriebs- und Datenserver *m (ISDN)*
administrative management domain (ADMD) öffentlicher MHS-Versorgungsbereich *m (TELEBOX, CCITT Rec. X.400)*
ADPCM s. adaptive differential PCM
ADS s. administration and data server
advance fortschalten *(Zähler)*; vorverschieben *(Phasenverschiebung)*, Phasenvoreilwinkel *m*
 a. provisioning Vorleistung *f*
advanced-feature telephone multifunktionales Komforttelefon *n (BT)*
AEA American Electronics Association
AEEC Airlines Electronic Engineering Committee
aeronautical mobile service beweglicher Flugfunkdienst *m*
 a. mobile telephone and data (fax.) service Passagiertelefondienst *m*
AES Audio Engineering Society *(US)*
AF s. Alternative Frequencies (list)
affected by a short (circuit) kurzschlußbehaftet *oder* -beeinflußt
affiliate anmelden, anschließen
affiliation funktionelle Anschaltung *f* an das System *(Tel.)*
AFNOR (Association Francaise de Normalisation) französische Standardisierungsgesellschaft *f*
AFSK (audio FSK) Tonfrequenzumtastung *f*
aggregate data rate Summengeschwindigkeit *f (Gesamtbitrate für den Kanal)*
 a. bit rate Sammelbitrate *f*, Summenbitrate *f (z.B. 2,043 MB/s für Basisanschluß, ISDN)*
aggregate level Summenpegel *m*
AI (artificial intelligence) künstliche Intelligenz *f* (KI)
air-call bleep Funkrufdienst *m (GB)*
Aircom Aircom-Passagiertelefondienst *m (SITA, INMARSAT-unterstützt)*
Airphone Airphone-Passagiertelefondienst *m (US, INMARSAT-unterstützt)*
airtime Nutzungszeit *f (Mobilfunk)*
AIS s. alarm indication signal
alarm Alarmsignal *n*
 a. call service Weckdienst *m*
 a. data interface (ADI) Alarmdatenschnittstelle *f (FW)*
 a. evaluator Alarmauswertung *f*

a. indication signal Alarm-Indikations-Signal *n* (AIS) *(PCM, ISDN D-Kanal)*
a. monitor Alarmwächter *m (FW)*
a. signal Alarmsignal *n*, Alarm *m*; Alarmgabe *f (FW)*
a. signal panel Signalfeld *n*
a. signalling Gefahrenmeldung *f*
ALC (automatic level control) automatische Pegelregelung *f (Sat.)*
alert warnen; anreizen
alerting signal Anreiz *m*
aliasing Verfälschung *f (Frequenzgang, Spektrum)*
   a. frequency Aliasfrequenz *f*
align abstimmen *(Sende-/Empfangsdatensynchronisation)*; justieren, ausrichten
alignment Abgleichung *f*; Synchronisierung *f (PCM)*
   a. bit Synchronisierbit *n*
   a. pin Führungsstift *m (FO HW)*
   frame a. Rahmengleichlauf *m (PCM)*
all calls barred Vollsperre *f*
   a. digital rein digital
   a.-plastic fibre Kunststofflichtwellenleiter *m* (KWL) *(FO)*
   a.-station address Generaladresse *f*
   a. trunks busy (ATB) gassenbesetzt
allocate belegen *(Stifte, Kontakte)*
allocation Belegung *f (Stifte, Kontakte)*; Verteilung *f (Anrufe, NStAnl.)*
ALOHA Aloha-Verfahren *n (Sat., RMA-Verfahren der University of Hawaii)*
alphageometry Alphageometrie *f (Vtx-Standard, CEPT-Profil 1, s. Tabelle VIII)*
alter ändern *n (Berechtigung)*
alterable trunk group search beeinflußbare Bündelsuche *f*
alternate computer Ersatzrechner *m*
   a. mark inversion (AMI) bipolare Schrittinversion *f (pseudoternäre PCM, redundanter binärer Leitungscode, ISDN D-Kanal)*
alternating current, voltage Wechselstrom *m*, -spannung *f*
   a.-current line circuit Wechselstromübertragung *f (Tel.-Signalisierung)*
Alternative Frequencies (list) (AF) alternative Frequenzen *fpl* (AF) *(RDS)*
   a. routing alternatives Bündel *n*; Zweitweg *m*
   a. voice/data (AVD) Alternativ-Sprache/Daten-Verfahren *n (Multiplexer)*
ALU (arithmetic (and logic) unit) Recheneinheit *f*
AMI s. alternate mark inversion
amplitude domain multiple access (ADMA)

Vielfachzugriff *m* im Amplitudenbereich *(Sat.)*
   a. hit Pegelsprung *m (CCITT Rec. 0.95, PCM)*
   a. phase shift keying (APK) Amplituden-Phasenumtastung *f (hybride Modulationsart, Sat.)*
   a. shift keying (ASK) Amplitudenumtastung *f*
   a.-stabilized amplitudenstabil
AMPS (Advanced Mobile Phone Service) AMPS-Funktelefon-System *n (US)*
AMSS (Aeronautical Mobile Satellite Service) Satellitengestützter Flug-Mobilfunk *m (über INMARSAT-Satelliten)*
analog method Analogverfahren *n (zeit- und wertkontinuierlich)*
   a./digital converter (ADC, A/D converter) Analog-/Digital-Umsetzer *m* (ADU), -Wandler *m*
   a. electronic switching system elektronisches Wählsystem *n*, analog (EWSA)
Analogue Private Network Signalling System (APNSS) Zeichengabesystem *n* für analoge Privatnetze *(BT, entspricht DPNSS1)*
anchor point Ankerpunkt *m (Datennetz)*
anchoring technique Ankertechnik *f (Datennetz)*
ancillary equipment Zusatzeinrichtung *f (DEE in HA oder in TK-Anl.)*
anechoic chamber Absorberraum *m*
angle bar Winkelschiene *f (Gestell)*
angular frequency Kreisfrequenz *f*
ANI (automatic number identification) automatische Rufnummernanzeige *f (ISDN)*
ANSI (American National Standards Institute) Nationales Amerikanisches Normeninstitut *n*
answer Amtsabfrage *f*;
   (**a** call) sich melden; einen Anruf entgegennehmen, beantworten *(Tel.)*
   a. a calling subscriber abfragen *(Tel.-Vermittlung)*
   a. key Abfragetaste *f (PBX)*
   a. signal Beginnzeichen *n (von gerufener Station)*
   a. state Beginnzustand *m (Tel.)*
   a. tone Antwortton *m*
answerback unit Kennungsgeber *m (Tx.)*
answering Abfrage *f*, Anrufbeantwortung *f*
   a. delay Meldeverzug *m*
   a. equipment Abfragezusatz *m*, Anruforgan *n*, Anrufbeantwortungs-Einrichtung *f* (AAE)
   a. internal calls Abfrage *f* von Intern-

rufen (IA) *(NStAnl.)*
  a. **jack** Abfrageklinke *f (Tel.)*
  a. **machine** Anrufbeantworter *m (nach BS 6789, 6401, 6305)*
  a. **sequence** Abfragefolge *f*
  a. **signal** Meldekennzeichen *n*
antenna Antenne *f (Rundf., TV, Sat. usw.)*
  a. **aperture** Antennenöffnung *f*
  a. **feedpoint** Antennenanschluß *m*
  a. **radiation centre** Antennenschwerpunkt *m*
  a. **radiation pattern** Antennencharakteristik *f*
  a. **reflector** Antennenspiegel *m*, Reflektor *m*
Antiope (Acquisition numérique et télévisualisation d'images organisées en pages d'écriture) Antiope-Videotextstandard *m* in Frankreich *(CEPT-Profil 2, s. Tabelle VIII)*
anywhere call pickup netzweite Erreichbarkeit *f (Mobilfunk)*
AOS (acquisition of signal) Signalsynchronisierung *f (Sat.)*
APC (ADPCM with primary frequency control) ADPCM *f* mit Leitfrequenzsteuerung
APC-MLQ (adaptive predictive coding with maximum-likelihood quantization) adaptive prädiktive Codierung *f* mit Maximum-Likelihood-Quantisierung *(Sprachcodec)*
APD (avalanche photo diode) Lawinen-Fotodiode *f (FO)*
aperture Öffnung *f*, Öffnungswinkel *m (Antenne)*
  a. **time** Öffnungszeit *f (ADU)*
API s. application program interface
APK s. amplitude phase shift keying
APNSS s. Analogue Private Network Signalling System
APPC (advanced program-to-program communication) höhere Programm-Programm-Kommunikation *f (IBM)*
application layer Anwendungsebene *f*, Verarbeitungsschicht *f (Schicht 7, OSI 7-Schicht-Referenzmodell)*
  a. **note** Anwendungsbeschreibung *f*
  a. **program interface** (API) Anwendungsschnittstelle *f (PC X.25, X.75 HDLC)*
apply anwenden; anlegen *(Spannung)*; einblenden *(Aufschalteton)*
  a. **current** Strom *m* anlegen, bestromen
appointments facility Termineinrichtung *f (TK-Anl.)*
APT (automatic picture transmission) automatische Bildübertragung *f (Funkfax)*

AQ (adaptive quantisation) adaptive Quantisierung *f*
AQAP (Allied Quality Assurance Publications) NATO-Qualitätssicherungsdokumente *npl*
architectural model Architekturmodell *n (OSI-RM)*
area code Vorwahlkennzahl *f*
  a. **identification signal** Bereichskennung *f* (BK) *(RDS)*
ARHC appels réduits à l'heure chargée *(Verkehrswerteinheit, 1/30 Erl bzw. VE)*
arithmetic (and logic) unit (ALU) Recheneinheit *f*
ARM s. asynchronous response mode
ARPANET (Advanced Research Projects Agency network) Daten-Verbundnetz *n* der ARPA *(US DoD-Agentur für Spitzenforschungsprojekte)*
ARQ (automatic repeat request) automatische Wiederholung *f*
ARR (automatic retransmission request) automatische Wiederholung *f*
arrangement Anordnung *f*, Aufbau *m*; Belegung *f (Anzeigefeld)*
array Feld *n (LEDs)*; Gruppe *f (Antenne)*
artificial intelligence (AI) künstliche Intelligenz *f* (KI)
  a. **line** Leitungsnachbildung *f*
  a. **(mains) network** Netz-Nachbildung *f*
  a. **telephone line** Telefon-Leitungs-Nachbildung *f* (TLN) *(FTZ)*
AS s. audio station
ASC (adaptive subband coding) adaptive Teilbandcodierung *f*
ASCII (American Standard Code for Information Interchange) amerikanischer Standardcode *m* für Datenaustausch
ASIC (application-specific IC) anwendungsspezifische IC *f*
ASK (amplitude shift keying) Amplitudenumtastung *f*
aspect ratio Seitenverhältnis *n (TV)*
assemble zusammenstellen, zusammensetzen, multiplexen *(PCM)*
assembly Baugruppe *f*, Anordnung *f*, Einrichtung *f*
assign belegen *(Tasten, Stifte, Kontakte)*, zuordnen
assignment Belegung *f (Tasten, Stifte, Kontakte)*, Vergabe *f*, Zuordnung *f*
  a. **store** Zuordnungsspeicher *m*
AST s. audio station
asynchronous asynchron
  a. **balanced mode** gleichberechtigter Spontanbetrieb *m*
  a. **communications interface adapter**

(ACIA) E/A-Schnittstelle *f* für serielle Anschlüsse
a. disconnected mode unabhängiger Wartebetrieb *m*
a. response mode (ARM) Spontanbetrieb *m* (HDLC)
a. time division multiplex (ATD, ATM) asynchrone Zeitvielfachtechnik *f (ATM)*
a. transfer mode (ATM) asynchroner Übertragungsmodus *m (FO, PCM-Daten, CCITT Rec. I.121, wobei 'asynchron' auf die Information und nicht die Bitsynchronisierung bezogen ist)*
a. DTE Start-/Stopp-DEE *f (mit Start- und Stoppbit)*
AT&T American Telephone & Telegraph Company
ATB (all trunks busy) gassenbesetzt
ATC (adaptive transformation coding) adaptive Transformationscodierung *f*
ATD s. asynchronous time division multiplex
ATM s. asynchronous time division multiplex
ATM s. asynchronous transfer mode
ATM s. automatic teller machine
attachment Zusatz *m*, Zusatzgerät *n*
attendant's station Abfragestelle *f (PBX)*
attended bedient *(Terminal)*
   a. exchange bemanntes *oder* besetztes Amt *n*
attention tone Aufmerksamkeitston *m (NStAnl.)*
attenuation Dämpfung *f*, Dämpfungsbetrag *m*
   a. coefficient Dämpfungsbelag *m (FO)*, Dämpfungskonstante *f*
   a. constant Dämpfungsbetrag *m (PCM)*, Dämpfungskonstante *f*; Wellendämpfung *f (Kabel, dB/km)*
   a. dip Dämpfungseinbruch *m*
   a. equalization Dämpfungsausgleich *m*
   a. skirt Dämpfungsflanke *f (Sat.)*
AU (access unit) Anschlußeinheit *f*
audible hörbar
   a. acknowledgement signal Quittungston *m*
   a. alarm (signal) akustischer Alarm *m*
   a. signal tolerance Hörzeichentoleranz *f*
   a. tones Hörtöne *mpl*
audio response unit Sprachausgabegerät *n*
audio station (AS,AST) Sprechstelle *f (Gegensprechanlage)*
audio system Beschallungsanlage *f*, Lautsprecheranlage *f*
Audiotex Audiotex-Dienst *m (Sprachspeicher- und -ausgabedienst)*

authentication: means of a. Berechtigungsmittel *n*
authorization Berechtigung *f*, Zugangsberechtigung *f (für Benutzer)*; Erlaubnis *f (Zugriffssteuerung)*
autoanswer automatische Antwort *f*
autodialler Selbstwählvorrichtung *f (Vtx.)*
auto-dialling automatischer Verbindungsaufbau *m*
automated rechnergestützt *oder* -unterstützt
automatic automatisch; bedienungslos *(NStAnl)*; rechnergestützt *oder* -unterstützt
   a. alternate routing Leitweglenkung *f*
   a. Baud (rate) recognition (ABR) automatische Schrittgeschwindigkeitserkennung *f*
   a. billing automatische Rechnungserstellung *f*
   a. call-back automatischer Rückruf *m* (RRUF)
   a. call restoration automatische Verbindungswiederherstellung *f*
   a. calling facility automatische Wahlmöglichkeit *f*
   a. cash dispenser Bargeldautomat *m*, Geldausgabeautomat *m* (GAA), Geldautomat *m*
   a. cleardown Zwangsauslösung *f (Tel.)*
   a. data signal generator automatischer Datenmeßsender *m* (ADaM)
   a. dialler Rufnummerngeber *m (Tel.)*
   a. dialling and recorded announcement equipment automatisches Wähl- und Ansagegerät *n* (AWAG)
   a. dialling facility for data transmission automatische Wähleinrichtung *f* für Datenübertragung (AWD) *(V.24/RS232C)*, Wählautomat *m* für Datenverbindungen (WAD) *(FTZ)*
   a. document feed (ADF) *(Fax.)* automatischer Stapelbetrieb *m*, Stapelbetrieb *m*
   a. fallback automatisches Herunterschalten *n (Modem)*
   a. level control (ALC) automatische Pegelregelung *f (Sat.-TWT)*
   a. measurement program automatischer Meßablauf *m (Meßplatz)*
   a. network Wählnetz *n*
   a. number identification (ANI) automatische Rufnummernanzeige *f (ISDN)*
   a. optical path selection selbsttätige optische Wegermittlung *f*
   a. picture transmission (APT) automatische Bildübertragung *f (Funkfax)*
   a. repeat request (ARQ) automatische Wiederholung *f (PCM-Daten)*

automatic

a. reserve/backup activation Reserveschaltung *f*
a. retransmission request (ARR) automatische Wiederholung *f (PCM-Daten)*
a. sequence call Kettengespräch *n*
a. shelf-wiring tester Etagenverdrahtungsprüfautomat *m*
a. telex/teletex directory service automatische Telex-Teletex-Auskunft *f* (AUTEX) *(DBP)*
a. teller machine (ATM) *(US)* Bargeldautomat *m*, Geldautomat *m*, Geldausgabeautomat *m* (GAA)
a. tester Prüfautomat *m*
a. wiring tester Verdrahtungsprüfautomat *m*
automation level Automatisierungsstufe *f*
autonomous system autarkes System *n*

autotracking Eigennachführung *f (Sat.)*
auxiliary bit Hilfsbit *n*
available verfügbar, frei *(Leitung)*
availability Erreichbarkeit *f (TelAnl.)*
AVD (alternative voice/data) Alternativ-Sprache/Daten-Verfahren *n*
averaging factor Mittelungsfaktor *m (Mobilfunk-Konzentrator)*
a. circuit Mittelwertbildner *m*
Awake Indication (AWI) Aktivierung *f (HW)*
AWGN (additive white Gaussian noise) additives Gaußsches Rauschen *n*
AWI s. Awake Indication
AXE (Automatic Exchange Equipment) automatische digitale Vermittlungseinrichtung *f (Ericsson, S)*

B

B channel B-Kanal *m (ISDN, 64 kB/s)*
B-ISDN (broadband ISDN) Breitband-ISDN *n*
B-MAC (variant B of MAC) B-MAC *n* (Variante B von MAC) *(525/625 Zeilen, US/Australischer TV Sat.-Übertragungsstandard, CCITT Rep. 1073)*
B operator Fernplatz *m (Tel.)*
B party B-Teilnehmer *m (Tel.)*
B position B-Platz *m*, Fernplatz *m (Tel.)*
B Series of CCITT Recommendations B-Serie *f* der CCITT-Empfehlungen *(betrifft Telekommunikationsbegriffe und -definitionen)*
BA s. basic access
BABT British Approvals Board for Telecommunications *(entspricht dem ZZF)*
babyphone feature Babyruf *m (K.-Tel.)*
back hinterlegen *(Vtx. Monitor)*
　b. channel Rückkanal *m (Sat.)*
　b.-off current Kompensationsstrom *m*
　b.-off voltage Gegenspannung *f*
　input b.-off Eingangssignalabstand *m* vom Sättigungspunkt *(TWT, in dB)*
　b. panel Rückwand *f*
　B. Receive Data (BRD) Rückkanal Empfangsdaten *(V.24/RS232C)*
　B. Request To Send (BRTS) Rückkanal Sendeteil einschalten *(V.24/RS232C)*
　b.-to-back Punkt-zu-Punkt *(Verbindung, MUX)*
　B. Transmit Data (BTD) Rückkanal Sendedaten *(V.24/RS232C)*
　b.-up amplifier Havarie-Verstärker *m*, Reserveverstärker *m*
　b.-up computer Nebenrechner *m*
　b.-up path Havarie-Weg *m*, Parallelweg *m*
　b.-up processor Reserveprozessor *m*
　b.-up voltage Stützspannung *f (für Speicher)*
background Hintergrund *m*; Umgebung *f (Mon.)*
　b. noise Ruhegeräusch *n*
backplane Rückwand *f*
　b. circuit board Rückwandleiterplatte *f*
backward call indicator Rückwärtskennzeichen *n (ZGS.7-UP)*
　b. channel Rückwärtskanal *m*, Hilfskanal *m*
　b. resistance Sperrwiderstand *m (Halbleiter)*
　b. signal Rückwärtszeichen *n (entgegengesetzt zur Verbindungsaufbaurichtung übertragenes Zeichen)*
balance kompensieren; abgleichen *(Satz)*; Nachbildung *f* (Nb); Symmetrie *f (Leitung, Satz)*
　b. loss Nachbilddämpfung *f*
　b. return Nachbildfehler *m*
balanced mode gleichberechtigter Spontanbetrieb *m (Modem)*
　b. station Hybridstation *f*
　b. to earth erdsymmetrisch
balancing Kopplungsausgleich *m (Kabel)*
　b. bit Paritätsbit *n (Übertragungssignal)*
　b. network Nachbildung *f* (Nb)
　b. (network) impedance Nachbildimpedanz *f*
　b. out Neutralisation *f (Kabel)*
BAMX s. basic access multiplexer
banana plug Einzelstecker *m*
band amplifier Bereichsverstärker *m*
　b.-edge channel Eckkanal *m*
　b. gap Bandabstand *m (FO)*
　b. predictive code modulation (BPCM) bereichsprädiktive Code-Modulation *f (Signalanalyse)*
BAP s. basic access point
bar sperren *(Sprechstellen)*
barred-code check Wahlkontrolle *f*
barrel Kelch *m (Quetschanschluß, Kabel)*
barring level Berechtigungsstufe *f*
base address store Grundadressenspeicher *m* (GAS)
　b.-line data Ausgangsdaten *npl*
　b. pin Sockelzapfen *m (Gestell)*
　b. station Feststation *f* (FS) *(Mobilfunk,* Funkkonzentrator *m* (FuKo) *(C-, D-Netz)*; Basisstation *f* (CT2)
　b. station area Funkzelle *f (Mobilfunk)*
　b. station control unit Funkdatensteuerung *f* (FDS) *(Mobilfunk)*
　b. station system (BSS) Basisstationssystem *n* (GSM)
　b. terminal Basisanschluß *m*
baseband unit (BBU) Basisbandeinheit *f*
basic access Basisanschluß *m* (BA) *(ISDN-S_0, CCITT Rec. I.420, 192 kB/s, Kapazität B_{64}- + B_{64}- + D_{16}-Kanal)*

b. access (channel) Basisanschlußkanal m; Basiskanal m *(ISDN)*
b. access concentrator BA-Konzentrator m (BAKT), Basisanschlußmultiplexer m *(ISDN)*
b. access multiplexer (BAMX) Basisanschlußmultiplexer m, BA-Konzentrator m (BAKT) *(ISDN)*
b. access point Basisanschlußpunkt m (BAP) *(ISDN)*
b. configuration Grundausbau m
b. data store (of the DBP) Grunddatenspeicher m (GRUSPE)
b. frame Hauptrahmen m *(PCM)*
b. point Ausgangspunkt m *(Diagramm)*
b. structure Prinzipaufbau m
B. Technical Requirements Rahmen-TL m *(Technischer Leitfaden)*
b. videotex computer system Btx-Grundsystem n (Vtx-GA)
batch Datenblock m *(POCSAG-Code)*
b. mode Stapelbetrieb m *(PCM-Daten)*
battery and earth loop (BEL) Batterieund Erdschleife f *(Tel.)*
batton-passing bus Batton-Paß-Bus m
Baud rate Schrittgeschwindigkeit f
BBD (bucket brigade device) Eimerkettenvorrichtung f *(Halbleiter)*
BBU s. baseband unit
BCC s. block check character
BCD s. binary coded decimal
BCH Bose-Chandhuri-Hoequenghem *(Code)*
Bd (Baud) Baudot-Code m
beam Strahl m; Keule f, Schiene f *(Sat.)*
bearer service Transportdienst m *(ATM)*, Datenübermittlungsdienst m, Übermittlungsdienst m *(ISDN, CCITT Rec. I.210)*, Trägerdienst m *(GSM)*
beat (frequency) Schwebung(sfrequenz) f
BECR s. bit error correction rate
beeper s. bleeper
BEL s. battery and earth loop
bell signal Klingelzeichen n
bench test Prüfstandversuch m
BER s. bit error rate
BHCA (busy hour call attempt) Belegungsversuch m in der Hauptverkehrsstunde
BHCA value BHCA-Wert m *(Anzahl Wahlvorgänge/Zeiteinheit)*
bias distortion einseitige Verzerrung f
billing Gebührenrechnungsstellung f
binary binär, dual
b. code Dualcode m, Binärcode m
b. coded decimal (BCD) binär codierte Dezimalzahl f
b. phase shift keying (BPSK) binäre

Phasenumtastung f
b. synchronous communication (BSC) binär-synchrone Übertragungssteuerung f
bipolar detection circuit Bipolaritätserkennungsschaltung f
b. operation Bipolartastung f, Doppelstromtastung f
BIP 8 code s. bit-interleaved parity 8 code
Bis,bis *(einem CCITT-Netzstandard nachgefügt, wird damit seine zweite Version identifiziert, z.B. V.25 bis)*
BIS (broadband information system) Breitbandinformationssystem n
bisync (BSC) binär-synchrone Übertragungssteuerung f
bit Bit n, Element n, Schritt m
b. allocation table Zeichenplan m *(Zeichengabe)*
b. clock Bittakt m
b. error correction rate (BECR) Bitfehlerkorrekturrate f
b. error rate (BER) Bitfehlerhäufigkeit f (BFH), Bitfehlerrate f (BFR) *(PCM-Daten)*
b. integrity Bit-Unversehrtheit f
b.-interleaved parity 8 (BIP 8 code) BIP-8-Code m *(STM-1)*
b. pattern Impulsmuster n
b. period Bitdauer f, Schrittdauer f
b. rate Bitrate f; Übertragungskapazität f
b. rate adaptation oder **adaptor** Geschwindigkeitsanpassung f *(D/D, CCITT Rec. V.110)*
b. rate of user information Nutzbitrate f
b.-serial information serielle Information f
b. synchronism Bitgleichlauf m
b. timing Bittakt m
84-b. message 84-Schritt-Telegramm n
BITE (built-in test equipment) eingebaute Prüfeinrichtung f
bits per second (bps) Bit pro Sekunde (Bit/s)
bivalent teleindication zweiwertige Fernanzeige f *(ja/nein, ein/aus, TEMEX, nach CCITT V.31 bis)*
b. remote switching Fernschalten n *(ein/aus, TEMEX, nach CCITT V.31 bis)*
black/white schwarz/weiß (S/W) *(Monitor)*
blade contact Messerkontakt m *(Verbinder)*
blank dunkelsteuern *(TV)*, austasten
b. out ausblenden *(Analogschaltung)*
blanked nicht sichtbar, unsichtbar *(Vtx.-Monitor)*
blanking Dunkeltastung f *(Vtx.-Monitor)*

bleeder resistor Vorbelastungswiderstand *m*
bleep Funkruf *m (GB)*
bleeper Funkrufempfänger *m*, Pager *m (GB)*, Nur-Ton-Empfänger *m ('Piepser')*
BLER s. block error rate
block Block *m (Tel., Datenübertragung)*, Feld *n (Klemmen, Stifte)*; Sperre *f (Zugang)*; sperren *(fehlerhafte Geräte)*
  b. check character (BCC) Blocksicherungszeichen *n (DLC-Protokoll)*
  b. code Blockkennung *f*
  b. dispatch rate Abfertigungsrate *f*
  b. error rate (BLER) Blockfehlerhäufigkeit *f* (BIFH) *(CD)*, Blockfehlerrate *f (PCM)*
  b. of outgoing traffic Sperre *f* im gehenden Verkehr *(Tel.)*
  channel b. Kanalbündel *n*
blocking Zustopfen *n (HF-Empfänger)*, Blockierung *f (Kanal)*; Behinderung *(Verkehr)*
  b. criterion Sperrkriterium *n*
  b. ground Sperrerde *f (PCM-Daten)*
  b. probability Blockierungswahrscheinlichkeit *f (Leitungen)*
  16-Hz meter pulse b. 16-Hz-Sperre *f (Tel.)*
BOC Bell Operating Company *(US)*
book anmelden, reservieren
  b. a line eine Leitung *f* vormerken
booking Buchung *f*; Reservierung *f (Leitungen)*
  b. station Reservierungsplatz *m (VBN)*
bootstrap facilities Bootstrap-Fähigkeiten *fpl*
BORSCHT (Battery feeding, Overvoltage protection, Ringing, Signalling, Coding, Hybrids, Testing) Schleifenstromeinspeisung, Überspannungsschutz, Rufstromeinspeisung, Kennzeichengabe, Signalcodierung *(A/D, D/A)*, Gabelschaltung, Leitungsmessung *(HAs-VSt-Schnittstellenfunktionen im digitalen Fernsprechnetz)*
bottom rail Bodenschiene *f (Gestell)*
BPCM (band predictive code modulation) bereichsprädiktive Code-Modulation *f*
BPON (broadband passive optical network) passiv übermittelndes optisches Breitbandnetz *n (FO, BT)*
bps s. bits per second
BPSK (binary phase shift keying) binäre Phasenumtastung *f*
bracket Winkel *m (Gestell)*
branching network loss Weichendämpfung *f*
BRD (Back Receive Data) Rückkanal Empfangsdaten *(V.24/RS232C)*

break unterbrechen, ausschalten *(Strom)*
breakdown Betriebsstörung *f*, Havarie *f*
breaking-in Aufschalten *n*
  b.-in on a busy line auf eine belegte Leitung *f* aufschalten
brightness Strahldichte *f (in N)*
bring on-line aktivieren
broadband Breitband *n* (BB) *(meist digital)*
  b. access switch Breitbandanschlußvermittlung *f* (BAV) *(VBN, FO)*
  b. communications network Breitband-Kommunikationsnetz *n* (BK-Netz)
  b. information system Breitbandinformationssystem *n* (BIS) *(DBP, FO)*
  b. ISDN Breitband-ISDN *n* (B-ISDN) *(FO, 140 - 565 MB/s)*
  b. switching centre Breitband-Vermittlungsstelle *f* (BBV) *(FO, VBN)*
  b. switching matrix Breitband-Koppelfeld *n (FO, VBN)*
  b. switching network Breitband-Koppelnetz *n* (BKN)
  b. transit switch Breitbanddurchgangsvermittlung *f* (BDV) *(FO, VBN)*
broadcast(ing) Rundgabe *f (Daten)*, Rundsenden *n*, Rundspruch *m (Tel.)*, Rundschreiben *n (FS)*; Rundfunk *m*
  b. command Sammelbefehl *m (FW)*
  b. satellite (BS) Rundfunksatellit *m*
  b. satellite service (BSS) Rundfunksatellitendienst *m (CCIR)*
broken line Polygonzug *m (Vektor)*
broker's call Makeln *n*
  b. facility *oder* **station** Maklerangläge *f*, Händlerarbeitsplatz *m (ITS)*
brokering makeln
BRTS (Back Request To Send) Rückkanal Sendeteil einschalten *(V.24/RS232C)*
BS (British Standard) Britische Norm *f*
BS6312 plug Telefon-Anschlußstecker *m (GB)*
BS s. broadcast satellite
BSB British Satellite Broadcasting Ltd. *(britischer DBS 'Marcopolo', D-MAC)*
BSC (binary synchronous communication) binär-synchrone Übertragungssteuerung *f*
BSI (British Standards Institution) Britisches Normen-Institut *n*
BSS (base station system) Basisstationssystem *n (GSM)*
BSS s. broadcast satellite service
BT British Telecom
BTD (Back Transmit Data) Rückkanal Sendedaten *(V.24/RS232C)*
BTI British Telecom International
BTMC British Telecom Mobile Communica-

tions
BTNR (British Telecom Network Requirement) BT-Netzerfordernis *n (BT-Spezifikationen)*
BTRL British Telecom Research Laboratories *(entspricht dem FTZ)*
BTV s. business television
bucket brigade device (BBD) Eimerkettenvorrichtung *f (Halbleiter)*
buffer zwischenspeichern; Pufferspeicher *m*, Zwischenspeicher *m*
 b. location Listenplatz *m*
 b. period Schutzzeit *f (zwischen Trägerpaketen, Sat.)*
 b. store Zwischenspeicher *m*
building-out network Gabel-Nachbildung *f*
 b. (services) distributor Gebäudeverteiler *m*
 b. up a connection Verbindungsaufnahme *f*
built-in fest eingebaut
 b.-in DTE Einbau-DEE *f* (DFGt-E)
 b.-in modem integrierter Modem *m (ISDX)*
 b.-in test equipment (BITE) eingebaute Prüfeinrichtung *f*
bulk data größere Datenmengen *fpl*
 b. data transmission Massendatenübertragung *f (Sat.)*
 b. store Großraumspeicher *m*
 b. transmission Bitbündelübertragung *f*
bulletin board schwarzes Brett *n (MHS)*
bunched gebündelt *(Kabel)*
bundled gebündelt
burst Stoß *m*; Paket *n*, Trägerpaket *n (Sat.)*; Bitgruppe *f*
 b. control Zeitweichensteuerung *f*
 b. mode transmission Burst-Übertragung *f*, verteilte Übertragung *f*, Zeitkompressionsverfahren *n (TCM oder Ping-Pong-Verfahren*
 b. transmission stoßweise Übertragung *f*, Bitbündelübertragung *f*
 data b. Datenpaket *n*
 error b. Fehlerhäufung *f*
burstiness factor Nutzzellen/Leerzellen-Verhältnis *n (ATM)*
bursty data gebündelt auftretende Daten *npl*
 b. traffic diskontinuierlicher Bitstrom *m*
bus Stammleitung *f*, Bus *m*, Leitung *f (als gemeinsame Übertragungsstrecke zwischen zwei oder mehr Schaltkreisen benutzte Leiter, IEEE)*, Vielfachleitung *f*; Sammelschiene *f*
 b. access Buszutritt *m (DÜE; Netzbenutzer)*, Buszugriff *m*
 b. access unit Busanschaltung *f*
 b. approval Busbewilligung *f (bei Busanforderung)*
 b. arbiter Buszuteiler *m*; Busvergabe *f*
 b. arbitration Busvergabe *f (DÜE)*
 b. assignment Buszuteilung *f (DÜE)*
 b. busy signal Busbesetzt-Signal *n (bei Busanforderung)*
 b. cable Sammelkabel *n*
 b. claim Busanspruch *m (DÜE in Warteschlange)*
 b. contention Buswettbewerb *m*
 b. coupler Buskoppler *m*
 b. delay Buslaufzeit *f*
 b. request Busanforderung *f (DÜE; Netzbenutzer)*
 b. terminator Busabschlußgerät *n*
 b. transit time Buslaufzeit *f*
bushing Durchführung *f (Kabel)*
business computer Bürorechner *m*
 b. television (BTV) Industriefernsehen *n (US)*
busy belegt *(Leitung)*
 b. (busiest) hour Hauptverkehrsstunde *f* (HVStd) *(Tel.)*
 b./idle status Belegungszustand *m* (frei *oder* belegt), Belegtzustand *m (Tel.-Anl.)*
 b./idle status image Belegungsabbild *n*
 b. hour Hauptverkehrsstunde *f* (HVStd)
 b. hour call attempt (BHCA) Belegungsversuch *m* in der Hauptverkehrsstunde
 b. server *(Tel.-Anl.)* belegter Abnehmer *m*
 b. signal Besetztanzeige *f*, Besetztzeichen *n* (BZ, BZT) *(Tel.)*
 b. testing Besetztprüfung *f*
buzzer Summer *m*
bypass überbrücken; umleiten, ableiten; durchschleifen *(in MUX)*
byte timing Bytetakt *m (CCITT X.21)*; Zeichentakt *m*

C

C band C-Band *n (6/4 GHz, Sat.)*
C-MAC (variant C of MAC) Variante C von MAC *(TV-Übertragungsprotokoll - FM-Video, PM-Digitalaudio, 8 Tonkanäle)*
C/A code (course/acquisition code) C/A-Code *m (GPS)*
cabinet Schrank *m*, Gehäuse *n*
cable Kabel *n*, Leitung *f*
  c. attenuation Kabeldämpfung *f*
  c. attenuation coefficient spezifische Kabeldämpfung *f*
  c. delay Kabellaufzeit *f*
  c. distributor Kabelverzweiger *m* (KVZ)
  c. entrance Kabeldurchführung *f*
  c. (installation) termination Kabelabschluß *m* (KA)
  c. layout plan Kabel(lage)plan *m*
  c. line verkabelte Leitung *f*
  c. loss Kabeldämpfung *f*
  c. network Kabelanlage *f*, Kabelnetz *n*
  c. pit Kabelbrunnen *m*
  c. plant Kabelanlage *f*
  c. plug Handstecker *m*
  c. rack Kabelgerüst *n*, Rost *m*
  c. route Kabeltrasse *f*; Leitungsführung *f*
  c. runway Kabelschacht *m*, Kabelrost *m*
  c. shelf Rost *m*
  c. system Kabelanlage *f*
  c. television (CATV,CTV) Kabelfernsehen *n*
  c. terminal cabinet Kabelabschlußschrank *m*, Kabel-Endschrank *m*
  c. terminating box Kabelabschlußkasten *m*
  c. termination Kabelendverschluß *m*
  c. tester Kabelmeßgerät *n*
  c. trough Kabelrost *m*
  c. TV (CATV,CTV) Kabelfernsehen *n*
  c. TV band Hyperband *n (302-446 MHz, 12 MHz-Raster, für D2-MAC-Signal, DBP)*
cabling Verkabelung *f*, Verdrahtung *f*, Beschaltung *f*
  c. diagram Kabelführungsplan *m*
CAC (conferencing access controller) Konferenzschaltungs-Zugangssteuerung *f*
CAD (computer-aided design) rechnergestützter Entwurf *m*
cadence Rhythmus *m (z.B. 1 S EIN, 250 mS AUS, 1 S EIN)*
CAI (common air interface) universelle Luftschnittstelle *f*
call Anruf *m*, Gespräch *n*, Ruf *m (Tel.)*, Verbindung *f*; Belegung *f (über Bediener)*
  c. acceptance Rufannahme *f*
  c. acceptance group Anrufübernahmegruppe *f*
  c. acceptance interval Belegungsannahmeintervall *n*
  c. acceptance waiting time Karenzzeit *f*
  c. answered abgefragte Verbindung *f*, gehende Verbindung *f*
  c. arriving einfallende Belegung *f*
  c. attempt Belegungsversuch *m*
  c.-back Anrufwiederholung *f (Dienstmerkmal, Rückruf)*; Nachruf *m*, Wiederanruf *m*, Rückruf *m*
  c. barring Sperren *n*
  c. barring lock Sperrschloß *n (K.-Tel. SW)*
  c. button Ruftaste *f*, Anruftaste *f (Tx.)*
  c.-charge data Gebührendaten *npl (Tel.)*
  c.-charge registration Gebührenerfassung *f*
  c. clear-down Verbindungsabbau *m*
  c. congestion Anrufblockierung *f*
  c. connected signal Verbundensignal *n*; Freizeichen *n (FS)*
  c. control matrix Verbindungsmatrix *f (NStAnl.)*
  c. control procedure Verbindungssteuerungsverfahren *n*
  c. costing Gebührenerfassung *f (Tel.)*
  c. data Verbindungsdaten *npl*
  c. data acquisition Gesprächsdatenerfassung *f (GEZ) (TK-Anl.)*
  c. distribution system Anrufverteilung *f*
  c. distributor Anrufverteiler *m*
  c. diversion Anrufumleitung *f*, Gesprächsumleitung *f*, Rufumleitung *f (K.-Tel.)*
  c. duration Belegungsdauer *f*
  c. failure nicht erfolgreiche Verbindung *f*
  C. Failure Indication (CFI) erfolgloser Verbindungsaufbau *m (V.25 bis)*
  C. Failure Indication, Engaged Tone (CFIET) erfolgloser Verbindungsaufbau *m*, Besetztton
  C. Failure Indication, No Tone (CFINT) erfolgloser Verbindungsaufbau *m*, kein

call 150

Ton
c. forwarding Anrufumlegung f, Anrufweiterschaltung f, Rufweiterleitung f (RWL), Rufweiterschaltung f
c. held condition Fangzustand m
c. hold Rückfrage f (RFRA) *(Tel.)*
c. identification class of service Fangberechtigung f
c. identification report Fangmeldung f *(Tel.)*
c. identification request Fangwunsch m *(Tel.)*
c. in abrufen; aufrufen *(Programmteil)*
c. in progress laufendes Gespräch n, Gesprächszustand m
c. indicator Anrufsignalisierung f *(Tel.)*
c. instruction Anforderung f *(PCM-Sprache)*
c. intensity Belegungsintensität f *(Tel.-Anl.)*
c. intercept equipment Fangeinrichtung f *(Tel.)*
c. log Anrufliste f
c. number Rufnummer f, Anschlußnummer f
c. number conversion Rufnummernumsetzung f
c. number directory Rufnummernregister n
c. on hold gehaltene Verbindung f *(Tel.)*
c. pick-up heranholen *(K.-Tel.)*
c. preparation Wahlvorbereitung f
c. progress signal Dienstsignal n *(ISDN)*; Netzmeldung f
c. progress signals Dienstmeldungen fpl
c. progress tones Hörtöne mpl *(Tel.)*
c. queuing Anrufreihung f
c. redirection Rufweiterleitung f (RWL), Rufweiterschaltung f
c. reference Referenz-Nummer f *(ZGS.7)*
c. reference number Nummer f der Verbindungskennung *(ISDN)*
c. rejection Verbindungsabweisung f
c. request abgehender Ruf m
C. Request with Identification (CRI) Verbindungsanforderung f *(V.25 bis)*, Wahlbefehl m *(V.25 bis)*
c. response Rufbeantwortung f
c. restoration Verbindungswiederherstellung f
c. routing Rufwegelenkung f
c. sender Rufnummerngeber m *(Tel.)*
c. set-up Rufaufbau m, Verbindungsaufbau m
c. storage device Reihenordner m, Warteordner m
c. time Verbindungszeit f, Verbindungsdauer f
c. timing Gesprächsmessung f
c. tracing Fangen n
c. transfer Anrufverlegung f, Rufweiterleitung f (RWL), Rufweiterschaltung f ; Rufumlegung f
c. unit statement Gebührenzuschreibung f *(BT, TTY)*
c. up abrufen, aufrufen; anrufen
c. waiting angeklopft, Anklopfen n *(Tel., Hinweis auf den Verbindungswunsch eines dritten Teilnehmers)*
c. waiting connection Anklopfverbindung f, Aufschalteverbindung f
c. waiting indication Anklopfmeldung f
c. waiting tone Anklopfton m, Aufschalteton m
c. zone Rufzone f (RZo) *(Cityruf)*
called line identification (CLI) Anschlußkennung f gerufene Station
c. party's answer Teilnehmermeldung f
c. subscriber B-Teilnehmer m
c. subscribers Passiv-Verkehr m
calling line identification (CLI) Anrufidentifizierung f; Anschlußkennung f rufende Station
c. equipment Anruforgan n
c. jack Anrufklinke f
c. subscriber A-Teilnehmer m
c. subscribers Aktiv-Verkehr m
CAM (communication access method) Kommunikationszugriffmethode f
CAM (computer-aided manufacturing) rechnergestützte Herstellung f
CAM (content-addressable memory) inhaltsadressierbarer Speicher m, Assoziativspeicher m
camp-on Wartezustand m
c.-on-busy Anrufwiederholung f *(Dienstmerkmal, Rückruf)*
Rückruf m *(auf Freiwerden der Leitung warten)*
c.-on busy button Rückruftaste f *(K.-Tel.)*
c.-on busy (line) warten auf Freiwerden *(einer Leitung)*
c.-on switching Wartevermittlung f
c.-on to a busy subscriber Rückruf m
cancel löschen; aufheben; zurücknehmen; annullieren *(Nummer)*
c. the call Ruf abbrechen
cancelling class-of-service data Löschen n von Berechtigungen
capacity Kapazität f, Mächtigkeit f *(Speicher, Kanal)*;
Leistung f, Leistungsfähigkeit f;

Abbild *n (z.B. der Anlage)*
c. utilization Auslastung *f*
captive screw unverlierbare Schraube *f*
capture einfangen; erfassen
   c. range Fangbereich *m (PLL)*
Carbon Copy Durchschlag *m (Fernabzug des Schirmbildinhalts, PC-Programm)*
carriage return (CR) Wagenrücklauf *m (Drucker)*
carried geführt
   c. call verarbeitete Belegung *f (Tel.-Anl.)*, Verbindung *f* hergestellt
carrier Netzbetreiber *m*, Netzträger *m*
   c. frequency (CF) Trägerfrequenz *f* (TF)
   c. frequency line circuit TF-Übertragung *f (Tel.-Signalisierung)*
   c./interference ratio (C/I) Träger/Störungsverhältnis *n (Sat.)*
   c./noise ratio (C/N) Träger/Rausch-Verhältnis *n (Sat., in dB)*
   c./noise temperature ratio (C/T) Träger/Rauschtemperatur-Verhältnis *n (Sat., in dB/K)*
   c.-sense (*oder* **domain**) **multiple access** (CSMA) Vielfachzugriff *m* mit Trägerkennung *(LAN)*
   c.-sense multiple access with collision detection (CSMA/CD) Vielfachzugriff *m* mit Trägerkennung und Kollisionserkennung *(LAN)*
   c. shift keying Trägerumtastverfahren *n (Prüfung)*
CAS (Communication Application Specification) CAS-Kommunikationsprotokoll *n*
cascaded aneinandergereiht; in Kaskade *f* geschaltet
CASE (computer-aided software engineering) computergestützte Software-Entwicklung *f*
cathode ray oscilloscope (CRO) Kathodenstrahl-Oszillograph *m oder* -Oszilloskop *n* (KO)
CATV (cable TV) Kabelfernsehen *n*
CATV (community antenna TV system *oder* Community Authority TV) Groß-Gemeinschaftsantennenanlage *f* (GGA), Gemeinschaftsantenne *f* (GA)
CAW (computer-aided wiring) rechnergestützte Verdrahtung *f*
CB (Citizen's Band) CB-Band *n*, 11-Meter-Band *n*, Jedermannfunk *m*
CB (Connection Busy) Anschluß belegt (V.25 bis)
CBS (common base station) gemeinsame Basisstation *f*
CC (channel coding) Kanal-Kennzeichnung *f* (GSM)

CC (cluster controller) Mehrfach-Steuereinheit *f*
CCI (contactless chip card interface) kontaktlose Chipkarten-Schnittstelle *f*
CCIR (Comité Consultatif International des Radiocommunications) Internationaler Beratender Ausschuß *m* für den Funkdienst
CCITT (Comité Consultatif International Téléphonique et Télégraphique) Internationaler Beratender Ausschuß *m* für den Fernsprech- und den Fernschreibdienst
CCM (cross connect multiplexer) Cross-connect-Multiplexer *m*, Schaltmultiplexer *m*; Zugangskoppler *m*
CCP (cross-connection point) Kabelverzweiger *m* (KVz)
CCS (Cent Call Seconds) *(Verkehrseinheit, =1/36 Erl oder VE)*
CCSS (common-channel signalling system) Zentralkanal-Zeichengabesystem *n (ISDN)*
CCTV (closed-circuit TV) Industriefernsehen *n*, drahtgebundenes Fernsehen *n*
CD (Carrier Detect) Empfangssignalpegel *m (V.24/RS232C)*
CD (collision detect) Kollisionserkennung *f*
CD-I (compact disk interactive) interaktive CD *f (ADPCM-codiert)*
CD-R (compact disk recordable) bespielbare CD *f*
CD-ROM CD-Datenspeicher *m (ADPCM-codiert)*
CD-ROM XA (CD ROM extended architecture) erweiterter CD-Datenspeicher *m*
CD-V (compact disk video) Video-CD *f*
CDLC s. cellular data link control
CDMA (code division multiple access) Vielfachzugriff *m* im Codemultiplexverfahren
CEBus (Consumer Electronics Bus) UE-Bus *m (EIA, entspricht dem OSI-RM)*
CEE (Commission Internationale de Reglementation en Vue de l'Approbation de l'Equipment Electrique) Internationale Kommission *f* für die Konformitätsprüfung elektrotechnischer Erzeugnisse
cell Zelle *f*, Block *m (ATM-Zeitkanal einschließlich Zellkopf und Nutzsignal)*; Funkzelle *f*, Verkehrsbereich *m (Mobilfunk)*
   c. change Umbuchen *n (Mobilfunk)*
   c. interleaving Zellenmultiplexierung *f (ATM)*
   c. spacing Zellenraster *m (ATM, z.B. 69 Byte)*
Cellnet *(Britisches nichtöffentliches mobiles Funkzellennetz, 450 MHz, entspricht*

cellular 152

C-Netz)
cellular data link control (CDLC) Zellen-Datenübertragungssteuerungsverfahren *n (Racal, GB, Protokoll für mobile Datenübermittlung)*
c. mobile radio network Mobilfunkzellennetz *n*, zellulares Funkfernsprechnetz *n (gewöhnlich Duplex, einschl. CT1, CT2, C-Netz)*
c. radio Zellenfunk *m (Mobilfunk)*
CEN (Comité Européen de Normalisation) Europäisches Normungskomitee *n*
CENELEC (Comité Européen de Normalisation Electrotechniques) Europäisches Komitee *n* für elektrotechnische Normung
Centel 100 BT-Centrex-Dienst *m*
central zentral
 c. battery Amtsbatterie *f*
 c. booking station zentraler Reservierungsplatz *m (VBN)*
 c. booking processor zentraler Reservierungsprozessor *m* (ZRP) *(SK)*
 c. control unit zentrales Steuerwerk *n*, Zentralsteuerwerk *n*
 c. controller zentrale Kontrollstation *f*
 c. display (unit *oder* equipment) zentrale Anzeigeeinheit *oder* Einrichtung *f* (ZA)
 c. exchange file zentrale Anlagendatei *f*
 c. multiplexer section Multiplexzentrale *f*
 c. office Fernsprechvermittlungsstelle *f*, Vermittlungsamt *n (US)*
central office exchange service (centrex) Centrex-Vermittlung *f*, zentralisierter Wählnebenstellendienst *m (Amtsvermittlungsdienst für Privatnetze, DOV)*
 c. processing unit (CPU) Zentraleinheit *f (Computer)*
 c. processor (CPU) zentrales Steuerwerk *n*, Zentralsteuerwerk *n* (ZST) *(Tel.)*; zentrale Rechnereinheit *f* (ZRE)
 c. remote control system zentrale Fernbedienungsanlage *f* (FBAZ) *(Sat.)*
 c. service observation (unit, equipment) zentrale (Betriebs-)Beobachtung *f* (ZBBeo)
 c. signalling section Signalisierungszentrale *f (DK)*
 c. station Zentrale *f*; Zentraleinheit *f (Tel.)*
 c. telecontrol channel zentraler Fernsteuerkanal *m* (ZFK) *(VBN)*
 c. transmit clock Taktzentrale *f* S
centralized zentral
 c. multi-endpoint connection Mehrpunktverbindung *f* mit zentraler Steuerung

centrally controlled zentralgesteuert
centre Zentrale *f*, Amt *n*
 c. feed Mittelpunktspeisung *f (Antenne)*
 sub-c. Teilvermittlungsstelle *f*
centrex s. central office exchange service
Centronics interface Centronics-Schnittstelle *f (für parallele Datenkommunikation mit 25-poligem D-Verbinder, z.B. für Druckausgabe)*
CEPT (Conférence Européenne des Administrations des Postes et des Télécommunications) Europäische Konferenz *f* der Verwaltungen für das Post- und Fernmeldewesen
CEPT profile Cept-Profil *n* (1...3) *(Vtx Darstellungsstandards, s. Tabelle VIII)*
Ceptel Cept-Tel, Ceptel, Cept-Telefon *n (DBP, Vtx-Terminal, umfaßt Modem, mit Telefonoption, heute:* Multikom-Gerät*)*
Certificate of Conformance to Standard Normgerechtigkeitsbescheinigung *f*
CF (carrier frequency) Trägerfrequenz *f* (TF)
CF (colour framing) Farb-Bildbegrenzung *f (TV-Studio)*
CFI (Call Failure Indication) erfolgloser Verbindungsaufbau *m (V.25 bis)*
CFIET (Call Failure Indication, Engaged Tone) erfolgloser Verbindungsaufbau *m*, Besetztton
CFINT (Call Failure Indication, No Tone) erfolgloser Verbindungsaufbau *m*, kein Ton
CFM (companded FM) kompandierte FM *f*
CFMA (conflict-free multiaccess) kollisionsfreier Vielfachzugriff *m*
CGI (Computer Graphics Interface) Computer-Grafikschnittstelle *f*
chad Stanzabfall *m*, Konfetti *n*
chain of delay elements Verzögerungskette *f*
chained together verkettet, verknüpft
chaining Kettung *f (von Telegrammen)*
chairman Konferenzführer *m*
challenge abfragen *(Sendeaufforderung)*
challenger Abfragesender *m*
change-back Rückwechsel *m (nach Dienstewechsel, ISDN)*
 c.-back of traffic Lastrückschaltung *f (nach Verbindungswiederherstellung)*
 c. of priority level Prioritätswechsel *m*
 c. of terminals Endgerätewechsel *m (ISDN)*
c.-over counter Einspringzähler *m (FW)*
c.-over time Umrüstzeit *f*

c.-over to standby Ersatzschaltung f
c.-over-to-standby contact Ersatzschaltekontakt m
c.-over unit Ersatzschalteeinrichtung f (ESE) (Verm., PCM-Daten); Umschalter m (GGA)
c. state Zustand m ändern; kippen (Flipflop)
changed-number interception Bescheiddienst m
changing services Dienstewechsel m (z.B. Telefon zu Telefax, ISDN)
channel Kanal m; -polig (Dataverbindung)
c.-associated kanalgebunden; sprechkreisgebunden
c.-associated signalling Einzelkanalsignalisierung f; sprechkreisgebundene Zeichengabe f (CCITT Rec. I.112)
c. block Kanalbündel n
c. branching filter Kanalweiche f
c. coding (CC) Kanal-Kennzeichnung f (GSM)
c. frequency deviation Kanalhub m
c. loading Gesprächsbelegung f (Mobilfunk); Kanalbelegung f
c. spacing Kanalabstand m, Kabelraster m (Kabel TV, 7/12 MHz); Kanalhub m (Sat.)
c. switching Kanalschaltung f (KS) (PCM)
c. timeslot Kanalzeitlage f, Zeitkanal m
c. usage (factor) Kanalauslastung f
c. width Kanalbreite f; Kanalhub m (Sat.)
character alignment Zeichenbildung f (DIN 44302)
c. error rate Zeichenfehlerhäufigkeit f
characteristic Verlauf m (Kurve), Kennlinie f; Verlaufsbeziehung f (einer Anzahl Signale)
c. data Eckdaten npl
c. distortion Apparateverzerrung f
c. frequency Nennfrequenz f
c. impedance Wellenwiderstand m
resistance c. Widerstandsprofil n
characters/second (cps) Zeichen/Sekunde (Z/s) (Drucker)
charge area oder band Gebührenzone f
c. meter Gebührenzähler m
c. meter position Gebührenstand m.
c. metering Gebührenerfassung f
c.-pulse injection circuit Gebührenimpuls-Einspeisesatz m
chargeable time Gebührenpflicht f
charges Gebühren fpl (GEB) (Tel.)
charging unit Gebühreneinheit f

check-back signal Rückfrage f (ISDN)
c. bit Kontrollschritt m (FW); Prüfbit n
c. bit generator Kontrollbitgenerator m
c. search Kontrollsuchlauf m
checkpoint Rückzugspunkt m (Programm)
c. mode (CP) Kontrollpunktverfahren n (HDLC)
checkpointing Fixpunkttechnik f
checksum Prüfsumme f
CHILL (CCITT High Level Language) Höhere CCITT-Programmiersprache f (ISDN)
chip Chip n, Baustein m (IC)
c. card reader Chipkartenleser m (Mobilfunk)
choose at random auslosen
C/I (carrier/interference ratio) Träger/Störung-Verhältnis n (Sat.)
CIB (computer integrated business) rechner-integrierte Geschäftsabwicklung f
CIF (Common Intermediate Format) gemeinsames Zwischenformat n (Bildtelefonstandard mit 152064 Pixeln, Bildfrequenz 8 1/3 Hz)
CIRC Cross-Interleaved Reed Solomon Code (Fehlerkorrekturcode, Sat.)
circuit Schaltkreis m; Verbindung f; Stromweg m; Wegeführung f, Satz m (Tel.);
c. board Baugruppe f
c. breaker Fernmeldeschutzschalter m
c. conditions Abhängigkeiten fpl
c. diagram Stromlaufplan m
c. group Satz m, Leitungsbündel n (Tel.)
c. outage Leitungsausfall m
c. resistor Beschaltungswiderstand m
c. switch (CS) Durchschaltevermittlung f (DK)
c. switched leitungsvermittelt
c.-switched connection Wählanschluß m der Gruppe L (Datex-L) (DBP)
c. switched data exchange (network) leitungsvermitteltes (DBP-)Datennetz n (Datex-L,Dx-L)
c.-switched digital capability (CSDC) leitungsvermitteltes digitales Leistungsmerkmal n (BOC-Dienste, AT&T, 56kB/s-Accunet)
c.-switched public data network (CSPDN) leitungsvermitteltes öffentliches Datennetz n
c. switching Wählbetrieb m, Durchschaltevermittlung f
c. switching interface Durchschalteschnittstelle f (FO)
c. time Verbindungszeit f, Verbindungsdauer f

circuit 154

with c. continuity stromschlüssig
Citizen's Band (CB) Jedermannfunk *m (11- Meter-Band, 27 MHz)*
clamp klemmen; abfangen *(Signal)*
  c. the line to "H" Leitung *f* auf "H" halten
class of access (level) Berechtigungsklasse *f*
  c. of line Anschlußklasse *f*
  c. of service Anschlußberechtigung *f*, Berechtigung *f*, Berechtigungsklasse *f*
  c.-of-service check Berechtigungsprüfung *f*
  c.-of-service data Berechtigungen *fpl*
clean up a signal ein Signal *n* von Störungen befreien
clear löschen *(Speicher, Register)*; freigeben *(Schieberegister)*; rückstellen *(Zähler)*;
  c. a connection Verbindung *f* abbauen *(SK)*
  c. back signal Schlußzeichen *n*, Auslösezeichen *n (nach Aufhängen des B-TN)*
  c. (down) Verbindung *f* auslösen
  c.-down Abbau *m*, Auslösung *f (der Verbindung)*, Freigabe *f*; Freischalten *n (Vermittlung)*
  c.-forward signal Auslösezeichen *n (nach Aufhängen des A-TN)*
  c. key *oder* **button** *(FS)* Schlußtaste *f*
  c. signal Freizeichen *n* (FZ) *(Tel.)*
Clear To Send (CTS) Sendebereitschaft *(V.24/RS232C)*
clearing Auslösung *f (der Verbindung)*, Freigabe *f (der Leitung)*; Freischalten *n (Vermittlung)*; Schlußzeichen *n*
  c. time Ausschaltzeit *f (Fehlerbeseitigung)*
CLI (called line identification) Anschlußkennung *f* gerufene Station
CLI (calling line identification) Anschlußkennung *f* rufende Station
click suppressor Knackschutz *m*
clicking Knacken *n (Sprachkanal)*
clicks kurzzeitiges Geräusch *n*
clip Feder *f*, Federklammer *f (Federleiste)*; abschneiden *(Signal)*
clipping Kürzung *f (von Sprachblöcken, PCM-Sprachpaketvermittlung)*
clock Takt *m*, Zeittakt *m*; Zeittaktgeber *m*
  c. alignment Taktanpassung *f*
  c. cycle Taktzeit *f (PCM-Daten)*
  c. extraction Taktableitung *f*
  c. frequency standard Taktnormal *n*
  c. in eintakten *(ein Signal)*
  c. period Taktzeit *f (PCM-Daten)*

  c. pulse Arbeitstakt *m*, Schrittpuls *m*
  c. pulse counter Zeittaktzähler *m*
  c. pulses Taktimpulse *mpl*, Zeittakt *m*
  c. (pulse) spacing Taktraster *m*
  c. reading Uhrenstand *m*
  c. recovery Taktrückgewinnung *f*
  c. selector Taktweiche *f (PCM-Daten)*
  c. synchronisation Uhrenvergleich *m*
  c. time (CT) Uhrzeit und Datum
  c. timing Uhrenstand *m*
clocked getaktet, taktgebunden, taktgesteuert; taktsynchron
clocking Takten *n*; Gleichlaufsteuerung *f*
close einschalten *(Schalter)*
closed-circuit TV (CCTV) Industriefernsehen *n*, drahtgebundenes Fernsehen *n*
  c.-loop control Regelung *f*
  c. numbering verdeckte Numerierung *f*
  c. user group (CUG) geschlossene Benutzergruppe *f* (GBG); Teilnehmerbetriebsklasse *f*
closing flag Endeflagge *f (ZGS.7-Rahmen)*
cluster Zellenbündel *n (C-Netz)*
  c. controller (CC) Mehrfach-Steuereinheit *f (Multiplexer für mehrere Terminals)*; Gruppensteuerung *f (Gerätegruppe)*
CMI s. coded mark inversion
CMRR s. common mode rejection ratio)
CN (connection) Verbindung *f (ISDN)*
C/N (carrier/noise ratio) Träger/Rauschverhältnis *n (Sat.)*
CNET (Centre National d'Etudes des Télécommunications) Nationales Zentrum *n* für Telekommunikationsstudien
CNR (Controlled Not Ready) DÜE nicht betriebsbereit
co-routing Gleichlauf *m (Kabel)*
co-channel interference Kanalstörung *f*; Gleichkanalbeeinflussungen *fpl*
code bit Kennungsbit *n (FW)*
  c. change Schlüsselwechsel *m*
  c. division multiplex Codemultiplex *n*
  c. division multiplex access (CDMA) Codemultiplexzugriff *m (VSAT)*; Vielfachzugriff *m* im Codemultiplexverfahren *(Tel.)*
  c. extension character Codesteuerzeichen *n (DV)*
  c. frequency Kennfrequenz *f (FS, für Einsen und Nullen)*
  c. instructions Codevorschrift *f*
  c. number Kennzahl *f*
  c. position Datenstelle *f (Verbinder)*
  c. rate Coderate *f (Korrekturcode: Verhältnis von Informationsbits zu übertragenen Bits)*

c. selector Amtswähler *m*
c. violation Coderegelverletzung *f*
codec Codierer/Decodierer *m*
coded mark inversion (CMI) codierte Schrittinversion *f (PCM-Code)*
coded orthogonal FDM (COFDM) codiertes Orthogonal-FDM *n (DAB-Übertragung)*
coder/decoder (CODEC) CODEC *m*
coding Codierung *f*, Verschlüsselung *f*; Kennzeichnung *f (Kanäle, GSM)*
c. law Bildungsgesetz *n (Leitungscode)*
c. plug Codierstecker *m*
c. rule Coderegel *f*
COFDM s. coded orthogonal FDM
coherent phase shift keying (CPSK) kohärente Phasenumtastung *f*
coil Spule *f (Wicklung)*
c. assembly Spulenpaket *n*
c.-loaded cable Pupinkabel *n*
coin-operated telephone Münzfernsprecher *m*, Münzer *m*
coinbox telephone Münzfernsprecher *m*, Münzer *m*
collect call R-Gespräch *n (Tel.)*
collective line Sammelanschluß *m (Tel.)*
c. number Sammelanschluß *m (Tel.)*
collision Zusammenstoß *m*, Kollision *f*
c. detect (CD) Kollisionserkennung *f (PCM-Daten)*
c. resolution Kollisionsauflösung *f (Zugriffssteuerung)*
column barring Spaltensperre *f (Koppelvielfach)*
combinational circuit Verknüpfungsschaltung *f*, Schaltnetz *n*
combinatorial point Verknüpfungsstelle *f*
combine bündeln *(PCM)*
combined network Verbundnetz *n*
c. station Hybridstation *f*
combiner Antennenweiche *f*
combining diversity Kombinationsdiversität *f*
c. frame Gruppenrahmen *m (Gestell)*
c./separating filter Weiche *f (Antenne)*
Combo (combined ADC/PCM coding chip) Kombinationsschaltung *f (K-Anlage)*
comfort level Komfortabilität *f*
commission einmessen *(eine Strecke)*
commissioning Inbetriebnahme *f (Netze)*; Inbetriebsetzung *f* (IBS)
common gemeinsam, zentral; gemeinsame Leitung *f*, Rückleitung *f*
c. air interface (CAI) universelle Luftschnittstelle *f (DTI, CT2-Zellenfunksprech- und Telepoint-Protokoll, ADPCM, nach CCITT Rec. G.721)*
c. base station gemeinsame Basisstation

f (Bündelfunk)
c. carrier Fernmeldeverwaltung *f*, Postverwaltung *f* (PTT); Netzbetreiber *m (US, z.B. BOCs)*
c.-channel radio Gleichkanalfunk *m*
c.-channel interference Gleichwellenstörungen *fpl (Mobilfunk)*
c. channel signalling (CCS) kanalgebundene Signalisierung *f*
c.-channel signalling system (CCSS) Zentralkanal-Zeichengabesystem *n (ISDN, CCITT Rec. I.112)*
c. control unit Zentralsteuerwerk *n*, zentrales Steuerwerk *n (Vermittlung)*
c. equipment zentrale Einrichtungen *fpl (Tel.-Anl.)*
c.-frequency operation Frequenzgleichlageverfahren *n*, Gleichlageverfahren *n*
c.-frequency radio Gleichwellenfunk *m*
c.-mode attenuation Gleichtaktdämpfung *f*
c.-mode rejection ratio (CMRR) Gleichtaktunterdrückungsverhältnis *n*
c.-mode signal Gleichtaktsignal *n*
c. night extension Sammelnachtstelle *f (Tel.)*
c. processor Zentralsteuerwerk *n*, zentrales Steuerwerk *n (Vermittlung)*
c. signalling channel (CSC) zentraler Zeichenkanal *m* (ZZK); zentraler Signalisierungskanal *m*
c. TDMA terminal equipment (CTTE) gemeinsame TDMA-Stationseinrichtung *f (VSAT)*
c. units zentrale Einrichtungen *fpl (Tel.-Anl.)*
c. wave Gleichwelle *f*
communicate mitteilen, übertragen; verkehren, korrespondieren, s. verständigen
communication Übermittlung *f (Informationsbeförderung Quelle-Senke, NTG 1203)*; Fernmelde- (FM, Fm); Verbindung *f*, Kommunikation *f*
c. access method Kommunikationszugriffmethode *f*
C. Application Specification (CAS) CAS-Kommunikationsprotokoll *n (G3-telefaxkompatible PC-KommuniKation, Intel)*
c. configuration Dienstkonfiguration *f (Transportdienst)*
c. control Fernbetriebseinheit *f*
c. link Übermittlungsabschnitt *m*, Nachrichtenverbindung *f*
c. satellite Nachrichtensatellit *m*
c. server (CS) Verbindungsabnehmer *m (LAN-Übergang)*
c. theory Nachrichtentheorie *f*
c. unit Busgerät *n*

communication 156

vertical c. vertikale Verständigung *f* *(zw. OSI-Schichten)*
voice c. Sprechverkehr *m*, Sprechverbindung *f*
communications controller Übertragungsablaufsteuerung *f*; Leitzentrale *f (DFÜ)*
community antenna Gemeinschaftsantenne *f* (GA) *(Rundfunk)*
  c. antenna television system (CATV) Gemeinschaftsantennenanlage *f* (GA), Groß-Gemeinschaftsantenne *f* (GGA)
  C. Authority TV system (CATV) Groß-Gemeinschaftsantennenanlage *f* (GGA)
compact disk (CD) Laserplatte *f*, Compact-Disk *f*
companded FM (CFM) kompandierte Frequenz-Modulation *f (Sat.)*
companding law Kompandergesetz *n*, Codierungskennlinie *f*
compatible (with) kompatibel (zu); -freundlich
  EDP-c. EDV-gerecht
compensate kompensieren, ausgleichen; abfangen *(Fehler)*, ausregeln
competitive-access method Wettbewerbsverfahren *n (PCM-Daten)*
  c. clipping Zugriffs-Clipping *n (von Paketen)*
competitor Mitbewerber *m (Buszuteilung)*
complement Bestückung *f (Geräte)*
completion of call on meeting busy Rückruf *m* bei Besetzt
  stage of c. Ausbaustufe *f (HW)*
complex: system c. Systemverband *m*
compliance Konformität *f*
  statement of c. Konformitätserklärung *f*
component Bauelement *n* (BE), Bauteil *n*; Komponente *f*
  c. block Baugruppe *f (in einer IC)*
  c. case Kühlflansch *m (Halbleiter)*
  c. layout Bestückungsplan *m*; Bestückung *f*
  c. side Bestückungsseite *f*, Einsetzseite *f* (E-Seite), Einsteckseite *f* (E-Seite) *(Leiterplatte)*
  c. spread Exemplarstreuung *f*
composite zusammengesetzt, gemischt
  c. colour signal Farbart, Bild- (Luminanz-)Signal, Austastung, Synchronsignal (FBAS) *(TV)*
  c. curve Summenkurve *f*
  c. encoding geschlossene Codierung *f (Dig.-TV)*
  c. loss Betriebsdämpfung *f (PCM)*
  c. signal gemeinsames Signal *n (CCITT Rec. G.703)*;

gemischtes Signal *n*, Signalgemisch *n (TV)*
  c. traffic Summenverkehr *m (Tel.-Anl.)*
compound navigation system Koppelortung *f (EVA, aktualisiert mit RDS)*
compressed dialling Kurzwahl *f* (KW)
  c.-video terminal SB-Videoterminal *n (mit Codec-komprimierter Bandbreite)*
computer-aided *oder* **-assisted** rechnergestützt *oder* -unterstützt
  c.-aided design (CAD) rechnergestützter Entwurf *m*; rechnergestützte Konstruktion *f*
  c.-aided manufacturing (CAM) rechnergestützte Fertigung *f*
  c.-aided software engineering (CASE) computergestützte Software-Entwicklung *f*
  c.-aided wiring (CAW) rechnergestützte Verdrahtung *f*
  C. Graphics Interface (CGI) Computer-Grafikschnittstelle *f (ISO DIS)*
  c. integrated business (CIB) rechnerintegrierte Geschäftsabwicklung *f*
  c. link Rechnerkopplung *f*
  c. link-up Rechnerverbund *m (Vtx.)*
  c. network Rechnerverbund *m (Vtx.)*
computerized rechnergestützt *oder* -unterstützt
COMSAT Communications Satellite Corp. *(US)*
concatenated aneinandergereiht; verkettet, gekettet *(SW)*
concentration Bündelung *f (von Datenkanälen)*
concentrator Konzentrator *m* (TEMEX, ISDN), Wählstern *m (Tel.)*; Konzentratoreinheit *f* (KE) *(VSAT-Teilnehmeranschlußmultiplexer)*
  c. line Wählsternanschluß *m*
  c. station Knotenstation *f (FW)*
  c. trunk Hauptleitung *f*
concentrically illuminated zentrisch erregt *(Sat.-Antenne)*
concept Prinzip *n*
concurrent (exchange line) answering konzentrierte Amtsabfrage *f* (KAA)
  c. answering of internal calls konzentrierte Abfrage *f* von Internrufen (IA) *(NStAnl.)*
condition konditionieren; vorverarbeiten, aufbereiten *(Signal, Meßwert)*
conditional replenishment bedingtes Austauschen *n (Bildcodierung)*
  c./unconditional operator request Operatorruf *m* bedingt/unbedingt
conducted leitungsgebunden *(Störung)*; geführt
  c. interference Funkstörspannung *f*
conductive adhesive Leitkleber *m*

conductor Ader *f (Kabel)*; Leiter *m*
  c. arrangement Leitungsführung *f*
  c. pattern Leitungsmuster *n (Leiterplatte)*
  c. run Leitungszug *m*
  c.-to-earth voltage Leitererdspannung *f*
conduit Wegführung *f*, Rohrleitung *f*, Schutzrohr *m (Kabel)*
conference bridge Konferenzbrücke *f (Tel.)*
  c. circuit Konferenzsatz *m*
conferencing access controller (CAC) Konferenzschaltungs-Zugangssteuerung *f*
  c. device Konferenzeinrichtung *f*, Aufschalteeinrichtung *f*
conferee Konferenzteilnehmer *m (Tel.)*
configuration Aufbau *m*, Bestückung *f*, Ausbau *m*; Anordnung *f*
confirm bestätigen, nachweisen
conflict-free multiaccess (CFMA) kollisionsfreier Vielfachzugriff *m (Sat.)*
conformance Normentsprechung *f*, Konformität *f*
  c. testing Konformitätsprüfung *f*
conformity -treue, -gerechtigkeit *f*
congested-route counter Bündelsperrzähler *m*
congestion Blockierung *f*, Behinderung *f (Verkehr)*; Stau *m (Daten)* Besetztzustand *m*, Wegebesetztzustand *m*; Betriebsmittelengpaß *m*
  network c. (NC) Netzüberlastung *f (Netzmeldung)*
connect einschalten *(Gerät)*, verbinden, anschließen
  c. data set to line Übertragungsleitung anschalten *(V.24, nicht RS232C-Spez.)*
  c. external call Amtsanruf *m* aufschalten
  c. into a network vernetzen
  c. through durchschalten
  c. to anschließen an; aufschalten auf *(Tel.)*
  c. to the output of nachschalten
connected gesteckt, geschaltet
  c. at a single terminal *oder* **pin** einpolig miteinander verbunden
  c. load Anschlußleistung *f*
  c./disconnected status Anschaltezustand *m*
connecting Verbindungsherstellung *f*
  c. box Anschlußdose *f* (ADo) *(Tel.)*
  c. circuit Innenübertragung(sweg) *m*
  c. matrix Anschaltekoppler *m*
  c. matrix for control trunks Zugangskoppler *m* für Steuerleitungen
  c. path Innenübertragung(sweg) *m*

  c. plug Schaltstecker *m (Signalverteiler)*; Verbindungsstecker *m*
  c. point Koppelstelle *f*, Anschaltstelle *f (NStAnl./AL)*
  c. relay Anschalterelais *m (Tel.)*
connection Anschaltung *f*, Anschluß *m*, Durchschaltung *f*; (CN) Verbindung *f (CCITT Rec. I.112)*
  c. attribute Verbindungsmerkmal *n (ISDN)*
  C. Busy (CB) Anschluß Belegt, Anschlußleitung Belegt *(V.25 bis)*
  c./disconnection of subscriber An-/Abschaltung *f* des Teilnehmers
  c./disconnection of switching system Ein-/Ausschaltung *f* der Vermittlung
  c. endpoint Verbindungsendpunkt *m (ZGS.7)*
  c. identity Verbindungsidentifikation *f*
  c. of ringing tone Rufanschaltung *f*
  c. procedure Verbindungsabwicklung *f*
  c.-related service attribute Verbindungsdienstmerkmal *n*
  c. request (CR) Verbindungsanforderung *f (ZGS.7 UP)*
  c. test signal Durchschaltprüfsignal *n (Netz)*
  c. testing Durchschalteprüfung *f (Netz)*
  wrong c. Fehlverbindung *f*
connectionless service verbindungsloser Dienst *m (ZGS.7)*
connectivity Verknüpfbarkeit *f*
  c. analysis Bilderkennung *f (Bildcodierung)*
connector Verbinder *m*, Steckverbinder *m*; Anschlußstecker *m*; Anschaltesatz *m (Tel.)*
  c. panel Schaltfeld *n*
  c. set Verbindungssatz *m (Vermittlung)*
  c. strip plug Messerleiste *f (Verbinder)*
constant-amplitude amplitudenstabil
constraints Zwangs- *oder* Nebenbedingungen *fpl*; Vorgaben *fpl*
constructional unit Baueinheit *f*
consultation call Rückfrage *f*
consumer electronics Konsumelektronik *f*, Unterhaltungselektronik *f*, U-Elektronik *f* (UE)
contact Kontakt *m* Anschluß *m*; -polig *(Stecker)*
  c. strip plug Messerleiste *f (Verbinder)*
  c. travel Schaltweg *m (HW)*
contactless chip card interface (CCI) kontaktlose Chipkarten-Schnittstelle *f (C2-Karte, ISO 7816)*
contacts: with c. kontaktbehaftet

contend streiten *(Buszuteilung)*
content-addressable memory (CAM) Assoziativspeicher *m*; inhaltsadressierbarer Speicher *m*
contention Streit *m (Buszuteilung, z.B. verlorener Wettbewerb um einen Kanal),* Wettbewerb *m,* Konflikt *m (DK, Bus, Bündelfunk)*
  c. mode Konkurrenzbetrieb *m*; gleichberechtigter Zugriff *m*
contents Inhalt *m (Speicher, Register),* Belegung *f (Datenfeld)*
contiguous zusammenhängend *(Speicherbereiche)*
continuity test Leiterprüfung *f,* Durchgangsprüfung *f*
  with circuit c. stromschlüssig
continuous phase differential FSK (CPDFSK) kontinuierliche Phasendifferenz-Frequenzumtastung *f*
  c. (controlled) phase frequency shift keying (CPFSK) phasenkonstante Frequenzumtastung *f*
  c. phase modulation (CPM) kontinuierliche Phasenmodulation *f*
  c. test Dauerbelastung *f (FO)*
  c. train of ones Dauereinssignal *n*
  c. train of zeros Dauernullsignal *n*
continuously variable slope delta modulation (CVSD) adaptive Deltamodulation *f (Voice-Mail-Verarbeitungscode, CCITT Rec. G.721)*
contracting authority Auftraggeber *m* (AG)
contractor Auftragnehmer *m* (AN)
contribution-quality signal nahbearbeitbares Studiosignal *n (TV im ISDN, 135 MB/s)*
control Steuerung *f,* Regelung *f,* Führung *f,* Bedienung *f;* Überwachung *f;* steuern, regeln; nachführen, nachziehen *(Frequenz)*
  c. and alarm panel Signalfeld *n*
  c. bit Steuerbit *n,* Steuertakt *m (FW)*
  c. channel Organisationskanal *m* (OgK) *(nömL, Mobilfunkzellennetz)*
  c. field Steuerfeld *n (ZGS.7 Rahmen)*
  c. function Einstellfunktion *f*
  c. key Funktionstaste *f*
  c. memory Haltespeicher *m*
  c. operation Einstellfunktion *f*
  c. panel Bedienungsfeld *n,* Schaltfeld *n*
  c. section Bedienungsteil *n*
  c. station Leitstation *f,* Leitstelle *f*
  c. system Kontrollsystem *n,* Steuerung *f*
  c. traffic Meldeverkehr *m*
  c. trunk Steuerleitung *f*

  c. unit Steuerwerk *n*; Bediengerät *n* (BDG)
  c. units for switching units Koppelgruppen-Steuerteile *mpl*
controlled by acknowledgement signals quittungsgesteuert
C. Not Ready (CNR) DÜE nicht betriebsbereit *(X.21, Schleifenprüfung)*
controller Einsteller *m* (EN); Konferenzführer *m (Tel.)*; Steuerung *f,* Steuergerät *n*; Regler *m*
controlling exchange betriebsführendes Amt *n*
  c. line betriebsführende Leitung *f*
convenience attachment Komfortzusatz *m (Tel.)*
conventional load Nennlast *f (Streckenprüfung)*
conversation state Sprechzustand *m*
conversational mode Dialog *m*
  c. service Abrufdienst *m*
converted to binary code binärcodiert
converter Umwerter *m (Signalisierung);* Umsetzer *m,* Wandler *m*
convolution code Faltungscode *m (FEC)*
coordinate system Zeichnungsraster *m*
copy umspeichern, einlesen *(Computer);* überspielen *(MAZ)*
copying Mitschnitt *m*
COR s. correlation counter
cordless schnurlos
  c. telephone drahtloses *oder* schnurloses Telefon *n (K.-Tel.);* Funktelefon *n*
core Seele *f (Kabel);* -polig
correct ausregeln, nachregeln, abfangen *(Fehler);* entzerren; fehlerfrei *(HW)*
  c. sequencing Reihenfolgetreue *f (von Blöcken, Sat.)*
  c. transmission ungestörte Übermittlung *f*
  with c. timing zeitgerecht
corrective maintenance Bedarfswartung *f*
correlation counter (COR) Korrelationszähler *m* (KOR)
correlator Nachstellkorrelator *m (Übertragung)*
corrupt verfälschen *(Bit),* verstümmeln *(Daten)*
COS Corporation for Open Systems *(US)*
COSINE (Cooperation of Open Systems Interconnection Networking in Europe) Arbeitsgemeinschaft *f* für OSI-Vernetzung in Europa
cost centre Kostenstelle *f*
counter Zähler *m (Gebühren)*

country code Landeskennzahl f
coupled computer Mitrechner m
coupling attenuation Auskoppeldämpfung f *(Direktkoppler, Sat.)*
  c. coefficient Kopplungsgrad m
  c. device Ankopplung f *(Bus, Ringnetz)*
  c. transformer Übergabetransformator m
course Weg m; Verlauf m
  c./acquisition code (C/A code) C/A-Code m, *(GPS, Zyklusdauer 1 ms)*
cover a range einen Bereich überstreichen
coverage Ausleuchtzone f *(Sat.)*; Versorgung f, Versorgungsbereich m *(eines Netzes)*
CP (HDLC checkpoint mode) HDLC-Kontrollpunktverfahren n *(ARQ-Prozedur, Sat.)*
CPC (cyclically permuted code) zyklisch vertauschter Binärcode m
CPDFSK s. continuous phase differential FSK
CPE (customer premises equipment) Teilnehmereinrichtung f; Endeinrichtung f
CPFSK (continuous (controlled) phase frequency shift keying) phasenkonstante Frequenzumtastung f
CPM (continuous phase modulation) kontinuierliche Phasenmodulation f
cps (characters per second) Zeichen pro Sekunde (ZPS)
CPSK (coherent phase shift keying) kohärente Phasenumtastung f
CPU (central processing unit) Zentraleinheit f
CR (carriage return) Wagenrücklauf m
CR (Connection Request) Verbindungsanforderung f *(ZGS.7)*
cradle Gabel f *(HW)*
  c. switch Gabelumschalter m (GU) *(Tel.)*
CRC (cyclic redundancy check) CRC-Prüfung f, zyklische Blockprüfung f
credit procedure Kreditverfahren n *(PCM-Datenblockübertragung)*
CRI (Call Request with Identification) Wahlbefehl m *(V.25 bis)*
critical frequency Grenzfrequenz f
CRO (cathode ray oscilloscope) Kathodenstrahl-Oszillograph m oder -Oszilloskop n (KO)
cross connect equipment Schaltstation f *(für Ersatznetzschaltung)*; Zugangskoppler m *(ATM-Knoten)*
  c. connect multiplexer (CCM) Cross-connect-Multiplexer m, Schaltmultiplexer m *(Netzmanagement)*
  c. connection point (CCP) Kabelverzweiger m

  c.-office (bereichs)übergreifend *(US)*
  c.-over frequency Eckfrequenz f *(Filter)*
  c.-over network Frequenzweiche f *(NF)*
  c. polarisation discrimination (XPD) Kreuzpolarisationsentkopplung f *(Sat.)*
  c. rail Querbügel m *(Gestell)*
crossbar (XB) Kreuzschiene f (KS) *(Video-Verteiler)*
  c. distributor Kreuzschienenverteiler m
  c. exchange, unbalanced signalling (XBU) Koordinatenschalteramt n, unsymmetrische Zeichengabe
  c. matrix Kreuzschienenverteiler m
  c. selector Crossbar-Wähler m; Kreuzschienenwähler m
  c. (selector) exchange (XB) Koordinatenschalteramt n *(analog)*
  c. switch Koordinatenschalter m
crosspoint Knotenpunkt m *(passiver Signalverteiler)*; Koppelpunkt m *(aktiver Signalverteiler)*
crosstalk Nebensprechen n, Übersprechen n
  c. attenuation Nebensprechdämpfung f, Übersprechdämpfung f
  far-end c. Fernnebensprechen n
  near-end c. Nahnebensprechen n
crystal calibrated quarzgenau
  c. controlled quarzstabilisiert
CS (circuit switch) Durchschaltevermittlung f
CS (communication server) Verbindungsabnehmer m *(Ortsnetz-Übergang)*
CSC (common signalling channel) zentraler Zeichenkanal m (ZZK)
CSD Communications Systems Division *(BT)*
CSD code (canonical signed digit code) CSD-Code m *(digitale DV)*
CSDC (circuit-switched digital capability) leitungsvermitteltes digitales Leistungsmerkmal n
CSMA (carrier sense multiple access) Vielfachzugriff m mit Trägererkennung *(LAN)*
CSMA/CD (carrier sense multiple access with collision detection) Vielfachzugriff m mit Trägererkennung und Kollisionserkennung *(LAN)*
CSPDN (circuit switched public data network) leitungsvermitteltes öffentliches Datennetz n
C/T (carrier/noise temperature ratio) Träger/Rauschtemperatur-Verhältnis n *(Sat.)*
CT (clock time) Uhrzeit f und Datum n
CT (cordless telephone) schnurloses Telefon n
CT1 (cordless telephone 1) schnurloses

Telefon *n* der ersten Generation *(DBP "Sinus"-Geräte, Analog-Hauptanschluß mit schnurlosen Zusatzgeräten)*
CT2 (cordless telephone 2) schnurloses Telefon *n* der zweiten Generation *(BT-Standard für das digitale Telepoint-System, 864-868 MHz, FDMA; nach BS 6301, 6833)*
CT3 (cordless telephone 3) schnurloses Telefon *n* der dritten Generation *(digital, entspricht dem GSM DECT-Standard)*
CTTE (common TDMA terminal equipment) gemeinsame TDMA-Stationseinrichtung *f (Sat.)*
CTS (Clear To Send) Sendebereitschaft *f (V.24/RS232C)*
CTV (cable TV) Kabelfernsehen *n*
CUG (closed user group) geschlossene Benutzergruppe *f* (GBG); Teilnehmerbetriebsklasse *f*
current Strom *m*
  c. bit stromerfüllter Schritt *m (FW)*
  c. consumption Stromaufnahme *f*, Stromverbrauch *m*
  c. converter-fed stromrichtergeführt
  c. drain Stromaufnahme *f*
  c. loop Linienstromschnittstelle *f (FS)*
  c. loop interface Stromschnittstelle *f*
  c. noise Stromrauschen *n*
  c. rating Strombelastung *f*
  c. return Stromableitung *f*
  c. under high tension hochgespannter Strom *m*
cursor Textzeiger *m*, Schreibmarke *f*, Cursor *m (Anzeige)*
curve Kurve *f*, Ganglinie *f*, Kennlinie *f*, Verlauf *m*
customer premises equipment (CPE) Endeinrichtung *f*, Teilnehmereinrichtung *f*
c. service Fernsprechauftragsdienst *m* (FEAD)
customized user program kundenspezifisches *oder* teilnehmerbezogenes Anwenderprogramm *n*
cut-in Eintreten *n*; Aufschalten *n (Ersatzgenerator)*
  c.-off button Trenntaste *f (K.-Tel.)*
  c.-off frequency Eckfrequenz *f*, Grenzfrequenz *f*
  c.-off voltage Sperrspannung *f*, Einsatzspannung *f*
  c.-off wavelength Grenzwellenlänge *f (FO)*
cutover Inbetriebnahme *f (Ersteinschaltung)*; Überschneiden *n (Frequenzen)*
CVSD (continuously variable slope delta modulation) adaptive Deltamodulation *f*
CW light component Gleichlichtanteil *m (FO)*
cycle Zyklus *m*, Durchlauf *m*, Gang *m*, Spiel *n*, Takt *m*
  c.-initiating primary centre zyklusführende Haupt-Z-Station *f*
  c. period Wiederholdauer *f*
cycled getaktet
cyclic redundancy check (CRC) zyklische Blockprüfung *f oder* Blocksicherung *f (ARQ-Prozedur)*
  c. storage Durchlaufspeicherung *f* der gewählten Ziffer
cyclically permuted code zyklisch vertauschter Binärcode *m*
cycling Durchlaufen *n* einer Periode; Takten *n*; Taktablauf *m*

D

D bit D-Bit *n*, Übergabebestätigungsbit *n* *(ISDN NUA)*
D channel D-Kanal *m (ISDN, D_{16} = 16 kB/s, ZGS.7)*
D channel signalling D-Kanal-Kennzeichengabe *f* (DKZE) *(ISDX)*
D-MAC (variant D of MAC) Variante D von MAC *(GB-TV-Übertragungs-Protokoll, Bandbreite 12 MHz, 8 Tonkanäle)*
D-type flip flop D-Flipflop *m* (DFF)
D1 (layer 1 D channel protocol) D-Kanal Schicht 1 *(ISDN)*
D2-MAC (duo-binary MAC) Variante D2-MAC von MAC *(DBP-TV-Übertragungs-Protokoll, Bandbreite 8 MHz, 4 Tonkanäle)*
DA (demand assignment) abrufgesteuerte Kanalzuteilung *f (Sat.)*
DAA (Data Access Arrangement) Datenzugriffsanordnung *f (CERMETEC Modem-Schnittstelle)*
DAB (digital audio broadcasting) digitaler Hörfunk *m*
DAC (digital/analog converter) Digital-Analog-Umsetzer *m* (DAU)
DAMA (demand assignment multiple access) Belegung *f* nach Bedarf *(VSAT)*
DAN (domestic area network) Teilnehmernetz *n*
Danger! Extremely Urgent! Gefahr! Sehr Dringend! (GSD) *(Prioritätsstufe 1 bei FS, sofortige Unterbrechung)*
DARPA Defense Advanced Research Projects Agency *(US)*
DARPANET (DARPA communications network) DARPA-Kommunikationsnetz *n (US)*
DASS (demand assignment signalling and switching unit) Zeichengabe- und Durchschalteeinheit *f* für abrufgesteuerte Kanalzuweisung *(Sat.)*
DASS (Digital Access Signalling System) Digitalanschluß-Zeichengabesystem *n*
DASS1 (Digital Access Signalling System 1) Digitalanschluß-Zeichengabesystem *n* Nr.1 *(BT ISDN, BA, 80 kB/s)*
DASS2 (Digital Access Signalling System 2) Digitalanschluß-Zeichengabesystem *n* Nr.2 *(BT ISDN, PA, 2 MB/s ZZK, entspricht BTNR 190)*
DAT (digital audio tape) digitales Tonband *n*
data Angaben *fpl*; Daten *npl* (Da)
d. adapter Datenanpassungseinheit *f* (DAN) *(ein Modem)*; Datenanpassungseinrichtung *f* (DAE)
d. base processor Datenbankrechner *m (Vtx.)*
d. base system (DBS) Datenbanksystem *n*
d. bit Nutzbit *n*
d. burst Datenpaket *n*
D. Carrier Detect (DCD) Empfangssignalpegel *m (V.24/RS232C)*
d. channel (DC) Datenkanal *m* (DK) *(FW)*
d. channel interface (DCI) Datenkanalschnittstelle *f*
d. circuit-terminating equipment (DCE) Datenübertragungseinrichtung *f* (DÜE) *(d.h. Modem für RS232C-Verbindungen, Netzanschluß und PV-Netzknoten für X.25-Verbindungen)*
d. collection platform (DCP) Datensammler *m (Sat.)*
d. communication terminal Datenstation *f* (DST,Dst) *(DEE+DÜE)*
d. concentrator Datenkonzentrator *m* (DKZ)
d. congestion Datenstau *m*
d. connecting unit Datenanschaltgerät *n* (DAG) *n (teletex)*; Datenanschlußgerät *n* (DAG(t)) *(TEMEX)*
d. converter Datenanschaltgerät *n*; Datenumsetzer *m* (DU) *(Modem, für Analogbetrieb)*
d. distributor Verteileinrichtung *f*
d. encryption unit Datenschlüsselgerät *n*
d. entry terminal Datenerfassungsterminal *n*
d. field Datenfeld *n*
d. in ankommende Daten *npl* (Dan) *(Prüfschleife)*
d. interface unit Datenanschlußgerät *n* (DAG(t)) *(TEMEX)*
d. integrity Datensicherheit *f*
d. key Datentaste *f* (DT) *(am Telefongerät, FTZ)*
d. link Übermittlungsabschnitt *m*; Datenstrecke *f (zwei wechselseitig betriebene einander zugeordnete Datenkanäle)*
d. link control (protocol) (DLC) Daten-

übertragungssteuerung *f*
d. link layer Sicherungsschicht *f*
(CCITT Rec. I.440 und I.441, Schicht 2, OSI Referenzmodell); Verbindungsschicht *f (Schicht 2, OSI-RM, FDDI)*
d. locking Datensicherung *f (Übertragungsstrecke)*
d. medium Datenträger *m*
d. message Datentelegramm *n*
d. network Datennetz *n (umfaßt alle zum Verbindungsaufbau zwischen DEEn benötigten Einrichtungen)*
d. network for fixed connections Direktrufnetz *n*
d. network identification code (DNIC) Datennetzkennung *f*
d. network signalling (DNS) Datennetzsignalisierung *f (TEMEX)*
d. occurring in bursts gebündelt auftretende Daten *npl*
d. out abgehende Daten *npl (Dab) (Prüfschleife)*
d. over voice (DOV) dem Sprachband überlagerte Datenübermittlung *f (Centrex-Dienstmerkmal, typische Datenrate 19,2 kB/s, auch bei DBP-TEMEX und ÖKartTel mit Trägerfrequenz 40 kHz)*
d.-over-voice channel Überlagerungskanal *m (Centrex, Telepoint, ÖKartTel, TEMEX)*
d.-over-voice equipment (DOVE) DOV-Einrichtung *f (BT, Datelnet 500)*
d. processing Datenverarbeitung *f* (DV)
d. processing system Datenverarbeitungsanlage *f* (DVA)
d. protection Datensicherung *f (Systemausfall)*
d. protection section Sicherungsteil *m (einer Nachricht)*
d. protection signal Sicherungssignal *n*
d. rate Schrittgeschwindigkeit *f;* Übertragungsgeschwindigkeit *f;* Datenrate *f,* Datendurchsatz *m*
d. rate conversion Geschwindigkeitsumsetzung *f*
d. rate of user packets Nutzdatenrate *f (in Byte/Paket)*
d. reduction Datenreduktion *f,* Datenverdichtung *f*
d. retrieval Datenwiedergewinnung *f*
d. route selector Datenrichtungsauswahleinheit *f*
d. selector Datenweiche *f (Multiplexer)*
D. Set Ready (DSR) Betriebsbereitschaft *(V.24/RS232C)*
d. sheet Kennblatt *n*
d. signal element Datensignalzeichen *n*
d. signal generator Datenmeßsender *m*
d. signalling rate Übertragungsgeschwindigkeit *f*; Datenrate *f*
D. Signalling Rate selector Hohe Übertragungsgeschwindigkeit einschalten *(V.24/RS232C)*
d. sink Datensenke *f (die Datenendeinrichtung)*
d. station Datenstation *f (DEE + DÜE, FTZ 118)*
d. stream Datenstrom *m*
D. Surveillance Act Datenschutzgesetz *n (GB)*
d. switching centre Datenvermittlungsstelle *f* (DVSt)
d./telephone network for fixed connections Direktrufnetz *n*
d. terminal (equipment) (DTE) Datenendeinrichtung *f* (DEE), Datenendgerät *n* (DEG(t)) *(Benutzergerät)*
D. Terminal Ready (DTR) Terminal betriebsbereit, Vorbereitende Anschaltung, DEE betriebsbereit, Endgerät betriebsbereit *(V.24/RS232C)*
d. test centre (DTC) zentrale Prüfstelle *f* für Dateneinrichtungen *(FTZ)*
d. throughput Datendurchsatz *m*
d. transfer control unit Datenaustausch- und Übertragungssteuerwerk *n* (DTÜ)
d. transfer rate Transfergeschwindigkeit *f*
d. transmission block Datenübertragungsblock *m*
d. transmission control Datenkopf *m (Multiplexer)*
d. word protection Datenwortsicherung *f*
datagram (DG) Datagramm *n (unabhängiges Datenpaket mit eigenen Wegeleitinformationen, Übertragung typisch ohne durchgehenden Sitzungsaufbau)*
Dataphone digital service (DDS) Dataphone-Digitaldienst *m (AT&T BA, 56 kB/s im Telefonnetz)*
datel (data telecommunication) Datel *n*
Datelnet 500 (datel network) Datel-Netz *n (BT-DOV-Einrichtung, bis 19,2 kB/s)*
datex network Datex-Netz *n*
d. terminating unit Datexnetzabschlußgerät *n (DBP)*
DATV (digitally assisted TV) digital gestütztes Fernsehsignal *n (HD-MAC)*
DBS (data base system) Datenbanksystem *n*
DBS (direct broadcasting satellite) direktstrahlender Satellit *m,* Rundfunksatellit *m*
DC (data channel) Datenkanal *m* (DK)
DC (direct current) Gleichstrom *m* (GS)

D/C (downconverter) Abwärtsumsetzer *m*
DC-balanced gleichstromfrei *(PCM-Übertragungssignal)*
DC bias unterlegte Gleichspannung *f (FO)*
DC component Gleichanteil *m*
DC connection GS-Anschaltung *f*
DC fault location Gleichstromfehlerortung *f (PCM-Daten)*
DC isolation of the speech paths Abriegeln *n* der Sprechwege
DC keying Gleichstrom-/Gleichspannungstastung *f* (GT)
DC trunk circuit Gleichstromleitungssatz *m*
DCC (digital cross connect (multiplexer)) digitaler Kreuzschienenverteiler *m*
DCD (Data Carrier Detect) Empfangssignalpegel *m (V.24/RS232C)*
DCDM (digitally controlled delta modulation) digital gesteuerte Deltamodulation *f*
DCE (data circuit-terminating equipment) Datenübertragungseinrichtung *f* (DÜE)
DCI (data channel interface) Datenkanalschnittstelle *f*
DCP (data collection platform) Datensammler *m (Sat.)*
DCPBX (digitally connected PBX) Nebenstellenanlage *f* mit Digitalanschluß
DCPC (differential coherent pulse code modulation) PCM *f* mit Differenzcodierung und Synchrondemodulation
DCPSK (differential coherent phase shift keying) Phasenumtastung *f* mit Differenzcodierung und Synchrondemodulation
DCT (discrete cosine transformation) diskrete Cosinus-Transformation *f (VK)*
D/D (digital/digital bit rate adaptation) Digital-Digital-Geschwindigkeitsanpassung *f*
DDCMP (digital data communications message protocol) Nachrichtenprotokoll *n* für digitale Datenübertragung
DDD (direct distance dialling) Fernwähltechnik *f*, Selbstwählferndienst *m* (SWFD)
DDI (direct dialling-in) Durchwahl *f (GB)*
DDI subscriber Selbstwählteilnehmer *m*
DDS s. Dataphone digital service
de-affiliate abmelden
de-affiliated terminal abgemeldete Endeinrichtung *f (Tel.)*
deactivate abschalten; passivieren *(DEE)*; sperren *(Datei)*
dead line abgeschaltete Leitung *f*
   d.-reckoning navigation Koppelnavigation *f*
deadlock: system d. Systemverklemmung *f*

(Netzknoten)
deattenuation Entdämpfung *f (NStAnl.)*
debugging Entstörung *f*, Fehlersuche *f*, Putzen *n (Programm)*
decimal pulsing dekadische Impulswahl *f*, Impulswahl *f (Tel.)*
decision circuit Entscheider *m*
   d. feedback equalizer (DFE) entscheidungsrückgekoppelter Entzerrer *m (zellularer Mobilfunk))*
decoder identification Dekoder-Identifizierung *f* (DI) *(RDS)*
decommissioning Außerbetriebnahme *f*
DECT (Digital European Cordless Telephone) digitales europäisches Funkfernsprechnetz *n*
dedicated circuit Standleitung *f*
   d. circuit data network Datenfestnetz *n (Paketvermittlung)*
   d. connection Verbindung *f* ohne Wahl, Festverbindung *f*
   d. line Standleitung *f*
   d. network Sondernetz *n*
Deep Space Network (DSN) Weltraum-Funkverbindungsnetz *n (weltweites Netz der JPL-DSIF-Bodenstellen)*
default value Vorzugswert *m (Comp.)*; Vorgabe *f*; Standardwert *m*, Ausgangswert *m*
defective fehlerhaft *(HW)*, gestört
deferred alarm verzögerter Alarm *m*
definition Auflösungsvermögen *n (TV etc.)*
degraded minutes beeinträchtigte Minuten *fpl (CCITT Empf. G.821)*
   d. service verminderte Dienstgüte *f*
degree of coupling Kopplungsgrad *m*
dehopper Frequenzhüpfer-(FH-)Schaltung *f (Empfänger)*; Frequenzsprungempfänger *m*
delay Laufzeit *f*, Verzögerung *f*, Wartedauer *f*
   d. distortion Laufzeitverzerrung *f*
   d.-exceeding probability Wartezeit-Überschreitungswahrscheinlichkeit *f (Wartesystem)*
   d. system Wartesystem *n (Vermittlung, eine angebotene Belegung wird bei Blockierung aufrechterhalten, kann warten)*
   d. variation with frequency Laufzeitverzerrung *f (Fax., in Mikro-Sek.)*
delayed call wartende Belegung *f (Tel.-Anl.)*
   d. delivery verzögerte Weitersendung *f*
delete löschen *(Daten)*, ausfügen *(Zeichen)*
delivery Abfragebetrieb *m*, Nachrichtenabfragebetrieb *m*; Übergabe *f*
   d. agent Übergabe-Systemteil *m (MHS)*
   d. confirmation bit (D bit) Übergabebe-

delivery 164

stätigungsbit *n* (D-Bit) *(ISDN NUA)*
d. device Zustellgerät *n (z.B. Drucker, CCITT Rec. X.400)*
delta modulation (DM) Deltamodulation *f*
demand assignment (DA) abrufgesteuerte *oder* bedarfsgesteuerte Kanalzuteilung *f oder* Kanalzuweisung *f (VSAT)*
   d. assignment multiple access (DAMA) Belegung *f* nach Bedarf *(VSAT)*
   d. assignment signalling and switching unit (DASS) Zeichengabe- und Durchschalteeinheit *f* für abrufgesteuerte Kanalzuweisung *(Sat.)*
   d. traffic Sofortverkehr *m*
on d. nach Teilnehmerwahl *f (Netzträgerdienst)*
demonstration approval Vorführzulassung *f (ZZF)*
demultiplex entschachteln, auflösen *(TDM)*, abbereiten *(TF-Technik)*
DEMUX (demultiplexer) Demultiplexer *m*
denial Sperre *f (Tel.)*
   service d. Anschlußsperre *f*
density of the traffic Stärke *f* des Verkehrs
dependable (betriebs)sicher
dependent exchange Teilvermittlungsstelle *f*
   d. PABX bedienungslose Wählunteranlage *f* (WU-Anl.) *(veraltet)*
   d. station ferngespeistes Amt *n*
DES (Data Encryption Standard) Datenverschlüsselungsnorm *f (IBM, ANSI)*
descrambler (DSCR) Entwürfler *m (Sat., FO-Datenkanal)*
description of operation Funktionsbeschreibung *f*
deselection Abwahl *f*
design Konstruktion *f*, Technik *f*, Ausführung *f*
   d. charts Bemessungsunterlagen *fpl (Tel.-Anl.)*
   d. margin Auslegungsreserve *f*
   d. rating Bauleistung *f*
designate bezeichnen; bereitstellen (Code)
designated seizure gezielte Belegung *f*
designational number Zielrufnummer *f*
desk access circuit Tischansteuerungssatz *m* (TAS)
   d. top publishing (DTP) Desktop-Publishing *n*; Computersatz *m*
destination exchange B-Vermittlungsstelle *f* (B-VSt), Zielvermittlungsstelle *f*
   d. node (DN) Bestimmungs-Netzknoten *m (Datennetz)*
   d. point code (DPC) Zielpunkt(code) *m (ZGS.7-MTP)*

destuff entstopfen *(TDM-Bits)*
detach abschalten *(Terminal)*
detect entscheiden *(Verstärker)*, erfassen, erkennen
detector diode Signalgleichrichter *m*; Empfangsdiode *f (FO)*
detent contact Rastkontakt *m (Verbinder)*
deteriorating sich verschlechternd; lebensdauerbeeinflußt
deterministic modulation Störphasenmodulation *f* durch ein stetiges Signal
deviation Ablage *f (Frequenz)*; Hub *m (FM)*
device fault Gerätefehler *m*
   d. for (decentralized) call forwarding Anrufweiterschalter *m* (GEDAN) *(Tel.)*
   d. search store Einrichtungssuchspeicher *m*
df (You Are In Communication With The Called Subscriber) FS-Verbindung hergestellt *(CCITT Rec. F.60)*
DFE (decision feedback equalizer) entscheidungsrückgekoppelter Entzerrer *m*
DFT (discrete Fourier transform) diskrete Fourier-Transformation *f (Bildcodec)*
DG (datagram) Datagramm *n*
DGS (digital group selector) digitaler Gruppenschalter *m*
diagnostic analysis Diagnose *f*
dial Nummernschalter *m*, Wählscheibe *f*
   d. converter Wahlumsetzer *m* (WU)
   d. digit Wahlziffer *f*
   d.-in Einwahl *f*, Netzeinwahl *f*
   d.-out Auswahl *f*, Netzauswahl *f*
   d. pulse Wahlimpuls *m*
   d. pulse correction Wählkorrektur *f*
   d.-pulse telephone Fernsprecher *m* für Impulswahl
   d. switch Nummernschalter *m*
   d. tone Wählton *m* (W-Ton)
   d. tone receiver Wähltonempfänger *m* (WTE)
   d. up Anwahl *f (Dienst)*
   d.-up port Wählanschluß *m*
   secure d.-back Sicherheitsrückruf *m*
DIALCOM Textspeicherdienst *m (US-MHS nach CCITT Rec. X.400, entspricht TELEBOX)*
dialling wählfähig
   d. a suffix digit Nachwahl *f (K.-Tel.)*
   d. code Vorwahlkennzahl *f*
   d. delay Wähltonverzug *m*
   d. keyboard Wähltastatur *f*
   d. pulses Wählzeichen *npl (Tel.)*
   d. relay Wahlaufnahmerelais *n (Tel.)*
   d. register Wahlspeicher *m*
   d. restriction Wahlsperre *f (Mobilfunk)*

d. **signal** Wählzeichen *n (Verm.)*
d. **standby (status)** Wahlbereitschaft *f*
d. **tone** Amtston *m*
d. **with the handset replaced** Wählen *n* mit aufgelegtem Handapparat (WaH), Wahl *f* bei aufliegendem Hörer *(Lauthörtaste)*
dialog capability Dialogfähigkeit *f*
DIANE (Direct Information Access Network for Europe) europäisches Datennetz *n* für Informationsdienste
DIC (Disregard Incoming Call (DIC)) Anrufablehnungsbefehl *m (V.25 bis)*
DICE (direct-interface CEPT equipment) TDMA-Direktanschluß *m*
DID (direct (inward) dialling) Durchwahl *f*
difference Differenz *f*; Abstand *m*
d. **meter** Differenz-Zähler *m (Tel.)*
differential coherent pulse code modulation (DCPC) PCM *f* mit Differenzcodierung und Synchrondemodulation
d. **coherent phase shift keying** (DCPSK) Phasenumtastung *f* mit Differenzcodierung und Synchrondemodulation
d. **phase shift keying** (DPSK) Phasendifferenzumtastung *f*
d. **pulse code modulation** (DPCM) Differenz-Pulscodemodulation *f*
d. **quaternary phase shift keying** (DQPSK) differenzcodierte QPSK *f*
diffraction Beugung *f (FO)*
digit Stelle *f*; Codeelement *n*, Ziffer *f*
d. **circuit for rotary dialling** Wahlsatz *m* für Nummernschalterwahl (WSN)
d. **circuit** Wahlsatz *m*
d. **input** Wahlaufnahme *f*
d. **input circuit** Wahlaufnahmesatz *m* (WAS), Wahlempfangssatz *m*
d. **output circuit** Wahlnachsendesatz *m* (WNS)
d. **translation** Ziffernumwertung *f*
digital digital *(zeit- und wertdiskret)*
D. **Access Signalling System** (DASS) Digitalanschluß-Zeichengabesystem *n (BT ISDN)*
d./**analog converter** (DAC, D/A converter) Digital-/Analogumsetzer *m* (DAU)
d. **audio broadcasting** (DAB) digitaler Hörfunk *m (Eureka-Projekt EU-147)*
d. **audio tape** (DAT) digitales Tonband *n*
d. **cross connect** (DCC) adressierbarer Multiplexer *m (Multiplexer, ATM)*; digitaler Kreuzschienenverteiler *m*, Digitalsignalverteiler *m (Schaltstation auf Übertragungsstrecke)*; digitales *oder* rechnergesteuertes Koppelfeld *n*

d. **data communications message protocol** (DDCMP) Nachrichtenprotokoll *n* für digitale Datenübertragung *(DEC)*
d./**digital bit rate adaptation** (D/D) Digital-Digital-Geschwindigkeitsanpassung *f*
d. **electronic switching system** elektronisches Wählsystem *n*, digital (EWSD)
D. **European Cordless Telephone** (DECT) digitales europäisches Funkfernsprechnetz *n (EG- u. CEPT-unterstützter Industriestandard für schnurlose Telefone der dritten Generation, TDMA)*
d. **exchange** Telekommunikationsanlage *f* (TK-Anlage)
d. **group selector** (DGS) digitaler Gruppenschalter *m*
d. **interface unit** Anschlußeinheit *f* für digitale Übertragungssysteme
d. **line equipment** digitale Leitungsendeinrichtung *f* (DLE)
d. **line path** Digitalsignal-Grundleitung *f* (DSGL)
d. **line section** Digital-Grundleitungsabschnitt *m* (DSGLA)
D. **Line Termination** (DLT) digitaler Leitungsabschluß *m (BT ISDN)*
d. **line unit** (DLU) digitale Leitungsendeinrichtung *f* (DLE) *(BT ISDN)*
d. **local exchange** digitale Ortsvermittlung *f*
d. **local network** digitales Ortsnetz *n* (DIGON)
d. **method** Digitalverfahren *n*
d. **multiplexed interface** digitaler Multiplexanschluß *m (US-PMXA-Standard mit D-Kanal-Zeichengabe für PCI-Kommunikation)*
d. **PABX** digitale Nebenstellenanlage *f*, digitale Vermittlung *f*, TK-Anlage *f*
d. **path** Digitalsignalverbindung *f* (DSV)
d. **PBX** Kommunikationsanlage *f* (K-Anlage)
d. **radio link system** digitales Richtfunk-System *n* (DRS) *(Sat.)*
d. **radiotelephone and data network** digitales Funkfernsprechnetz *n* (D-Netz)
d. **radiotelephone network** digitales Funkfernsprechnetz *n*
d. **satellite radio** (DSR) digitaler (Satelliten-)Hör(rund)funk *m*
d. **short-range radio** (DSRR) digitaler Nahbereichsfunk *m (Mobilfunk, 933-935 MHz)*
d. **signal** digitales Signal *n*, Digitalsignal *n*
d. **signal channel** (DSC) digitaler Datenkanal *m*
d. **signal processor** (DSP) Digitalsig-

digital 166

nalprozessor *m*
d. speech interpolation (DSI) digitale Sprachinterpolation *f*
d. subscriber loop (DSL) digitale Teilnehmerschleife *f (2-dr.-ISDN-Anschluß, Philips)*
D. Subscribers Switching Subsystem (DSSS) Vermittlungsteilsystem *n* für digitale Teilnehmeranschlüsse *(BT ISDN)*
d. switching centre digitale Vermittlung *f* (DIV)
d. trunk exchange digitale Fernvermittlung *f*
d. video system digitales Videosystem *n* (DVS) *(Eureka-Projekt, 12,5-20 MB/s, FO)*
d. voice interpolation digitale Sprachinterpolation *f* (DSI)
d. voice terminal (DVT) digitale Sprachendeinrichtung *f*, digitale Sprechstelle *f*
digitally assisted TV (DATV) digital gestütztes Fernsehsignal *n (HD-Mac-Technik, Eu-95)*
d. connected PBX (DCPBX) Nebenstellenanlage *f* mit Digitalanschluß *(BT IDA)*
d. controlled delta modulation (DCDM) digital gesteuerte Deltamodulation *f*
dilution of precision Präzisionsverringerung *f (Navigation)*
dimensioning specification Bemessungsvorschrift *f*
diminished (radix) complement Stellenkomplement *n*
DIP (document image processing) Dokumentbildverarbeitung *f (EDI)*
dip due to additional losses Dämpfungseinbruch *m (im Signalpegel usw.)*
d. in voltage level Spannungseinbruch *m*, Spannungsabfall *m*
diplexer Innenweiche *f;* Antennenweiche *f;* Frequenzweiche *f*
direct access Direktanschluß *m*
d. addressing Direktansprechen *n (über Lautsprecher, dig. K.-Tel.)*
d. answering Direktantworten *n (über Mikrofon, dig. K-Tel.)*
d. broadcasting satellite (DBS) Rundfunksatellit *m*, direktstrahlender Satellit *m*
d. call Direktruf *m (Tel.)*
d. data link Datendirektverbindung *f* (DDV)
d. dialling (DDD) Schritthaltende Wahl *f*, Direktwahl *f*
d. dialling-in (DDI) *(GB)* Durchwahl *f*
d. distance dialling (DDD) Selbstwählferndienst *m* (SWFD), Direktwahl *f*, Fernwähltechnik *f*
d. distance dialling network Direktwahlnetz *n*
d. interface CEPT equipment (DICE) TDMA-Direktanschluß *m (Sat.)*
d. (inward, outward) dialing (DID,DOD) Durchwahl *f (US)*
d. inward dialling circuit Durchwahlsatz *m* (DS)
d. line Nachbarverbindung *f,* Querverbindung(sleitung) *f (zw. nichtöffentlichen Vermittlungsstellen)*
d. listening Lauthören *n*
d. listening key Lauthörtaste *f*
d. exchange access Vollamtsberechtigung *f*
d. route Erstwahlbündel *n*
d. trunk group Direktbündel *n*
d. trunking Abfragebetrieb *m,* Nachrichtenabfragebetrieb *m*
directional gerichtet
d. coupler Richtkoppler *m (Sat.)*
directory entry Registereintragung *f (Tel.)*
d. inquiry service Auskunftsdienst *m*
d. number Langrufnummer *f,* Rufnummer *f*
D. Service Agent (DSA) verzeichnisorientierter Systemteil *m (CCITT X.500)*
D. User Agent (DUA) verzeichnisorientierter Endbenutzer-Systemteil *m (CCITT X.500)*
DIS (Draft International Standard) Internationaler Normenentwurf *m*
disable sperren *(Gatter),* abschalten
disabled blockiert *(Tastatur)*
disabling lock Sperrschloß *n (TK-Anl.)*
disassemble cells Zellen auflösen *(ATM)*
disassembly Demontage *f*
discharge entladen, freigeben *(Kondensator)*
disconnect herausschalten *(Gerät);* ausschalten *(Modul);* abschalten, sperren (TLN), trennen *(Kanal);* aufheben *(TLN-Einrichtung)*
d. signal Schlußzeichen *n*
d. socket Trenn-Fernmeldesteckdose *f*
d. time-out Auslösezeitüberwachung *f*
disconnected nicht gesteckt *(TE)*
d. mode Wartebetrieb *m*
disconnecting relay Trennrelais *n*
disconnection Abschaltung *f (des TLN),* Auslösung *f;* Ausschaltung *f (Verm.),* Freigabe *f*
discontinued item Auslaufteil *n*
discontinuities Sprünge *mpl,* Sprungstellen *fpl;* Unstetigkeit *f (Signal)*

discontinuous sprunghaft, unstetig
discrete cosine transformation (DCT) diskrete Cosinus-Transformation *f (Video-Codec)*
   d. Fourier transform (DFT) *(IT)* diskrete Fourier-Transformation *f (Bildcodec)*
   d. point Stützpunkt *m (auf einer Signalkurve)*
   d. signal digitales Signal *n*
discretization Diskretisierung *f*, Stufung *f (Signalquantisierung)*
disk storage unit Plattenspeicher *m* (PSP)
dispatch rate Abfertigungsrate *f*
dispersal Zerstreuung *f*
   d. voltage Verwischungsspannung *f (MAC-Basisband-Trägerfrequenz-Verwischung)*
dispersion Ausbreitung *f*; Streuung *f*
   d.-shifted dispersionsverschoben *(FO)*
displacement address Distanzadresse *f*
display generation Bildaufbereitung *f (Monitor)*
   d. strip Anzeigeleiste *f*
disposition Lage *f*, Anordnung *f*
disregard a call Ruf *m* ablehnen
Disregard Incoming Call (DIC) Nichtbeantworten *n* eines Anrufs, Anrufablehnungsbefehl *m (V.25 bis)*
disruption Störung *f (Verbindung)*
dissipative regulator Verlustregler *m*
distance Übertragungslänge *f*
   d. relay Distanzrelais *n*
   Hamming d. Hamming-Distanz *f (FEC)*
distant caller ferner Teilnehmer *m*
   d. end Gegenstelle *f (PCM)*
   d. exchange Gegenamt *n*
   d. station Fernstation *f*; Gegenstelle *f (PCM)*
distortion (factor) of voice channel Gesprächsklirrfaktor *m*
distributed amplifier Kettenverstärker *m (LNA)*
   d.-feedback laser DFB-Laser *m (FO)*
distribution Verteilung *f*, Belegung *f*
   d. amplifier Stammverstärker *m*
   d. cable Verzweigungskabel *n* (VzK)
   d. frame Verteiler *m (Tel.)*
   d. matrix Verteilfeld *n (GGA)*
   d. network Verteilnetz *n (TV)*; Stammnetz *n (GGA)*
   d. panel Verteilertafel *f*, Rangierfeld *n*
   d. point (DP) Endverzweiger *m* (EVz) *(Tel.)*
   d. service Verteildienst *m (Sat.)*
   d. system Verteilsystem *n (ISDN)*; Verteilnetz n *(TV)*
   floor d. board Stockwerkverteiler *m (Tel.)*

distributor Verteiler *m*, Verzweiger *m (Signal)*
disturbance Störung *f*
dither matrix Zittermatrix *f (dig. Video-Verarbeitung)*
diversion service Anrufumleitung *f*
DLC (data link control (protocol)) Datenübertragungssteuerung *f*
DLE (digital line equipment *oder* unit (DLU)) digitale Leitungsendeinrichtung *f*
DLT (Digital Line Termination) digitaler Leitungsabschluß *m*
DLU (Digital Line Unit) digitale Leitungsendeinrichtung *f* (DLE)
DM (delta modulation) Deltamodulation *f*
DMI (digital multiplexed interface) digitaler Multiplexanschluß *m*
DN (destination node) Bestimmungs-Netzknoten *m*
DNIC (data network identification code) Datennetzkennung *f*
DNS (data network signalling) Datennetzsignalisierung *f (TEMEX)*
Do-Not-Disturb (feature) Ruhe *f* vor dem Telefon
document image processing (DIP) Dokumentbildverarbeitung *f (EDI)*
Document Transfer And Manipulation (DTAM) Dokumentenübertragung und -bearbeitung *f (ISDN, CCITT Rec. I.430)*
DOD (direct outward dialing) Durchwahl *f (US, NStAnl.)*
domestic area network (DAN) hauseigenes Netz *n*, Teilnehmernetz *n (Videokonferenz)*
   d. telephone system Familientelefonanlage *f* (FTA), Heimtelefonanlage *f* (HTA)
   D. Video Programme Delivery Control system (DVPDC, PDC) Programmzustellungssteuersystem *n* für Heim-Videorecorder *(TV-Rundfunkdienst)*
domotics Domotik *f (umfaßt alle Elektro-/Elektronikheimgeräte; FR "domotique")*
door (intercom) call Türruf *m (Tel.)*
   d. (intercom) extension *oder* **station** Türsprechstelle *f (Apothekerschaltung)*
   d. interphone Türsprechanlage *f*
   d. release/intercom system Türfreisprechanlage *f (K.-Tel.)*
dot matrix Punktraster *m (TV)*
double-ended control Rückführung *f (Synchronisierung)*
   d. group message Zweigruppentelegramm *n* (FW)
   d.-hop link Zweisprungverbindung *f (vernetzte VSATs, Ein- u. Zweiwegverbindung)*

double 168

d.-phantom circuit Achterkreis *m*
d. sideband Zweiseitenband *n* (ZSB)
d.-sided clamp Klammer *f (Gestell)*
d. tieing-in of subscribers Teilnehmerdoppeleinbindung *f (Tel.)*
DOV (data over voice) dem Sprachband überlagerte Datenübermittlung *f*
DOV channel Überlagerungskanal *m*
DOVE (data-over-voice equipment) DOV-Einrichtung *f*
downconverter (D/C) Abwärtsumsetzer *m (VSAT)*
downlink Abwärtsstrecke *f (Sat.)*, Abwärtsverbindung *f (Mobilfunk, Feststation-Mobilstation)*
d. band Empfangsband *n (Sat.)*
downloading Fernladen *n (Computer)*
downstream to the user im Downstream zum Teilnehmer *(Sat.)*
downtime Ausfallzeit *f*, Störungszeit *f*
DP s. distribution point
DP s. draft proposal
DPC (destination point code) Zielpunkt(code) *m*
DPCM (differential PCM) Differenz-Pulscodemodulation *f*
dpi (dots per inch) Punkte pro Zoll *(Faksimile-Auflösung)*
dpn 100 *(paketvermitteltes System, Sweden)*
DPNSS (Digital Private Network Signalling System) Zeichengabesystem *n* für digitale private Datennetze *(BT IDA, für Querverkehr zwischen TK-Anlagen, entspricht DASS2, DPNR 190)*
DPSK (differential phase shift keying) Phasendifferenzumtastung *f*
DQPSK (differential QPSK) differenzcodierte QPSK *f*
draft DIN standard DIN-Entwurf *m*
D. International Standard (DIS) Internationaler Normenentwurf *m (FTZ, ISO)*
d. proposal (DP) Vorschlagsentwurf *m (ISO)*
d. specification vorläufige Spezifikation *f*
DRAW (direct read after write) direkt Lesen nach Beschreiben *(einmal beschreibbare Bildplatte)*
drawing tablet Zeichentableau *n (zum Fernzeichnen)*
DRCS (dynamically redefinable character set) dynamisch neu definierbarer Zeichensatz *m*
drift Nullpunktabweichung *f*; Auswandern *n (aus dem Bereich, Sat.)*
drive (unit) Laufwerk *n*

Drop Löschen *n (Benutzer-O/R-Namen im MHS-Namenverzeichnis)*
d. and insert multiplexer Weiterleit- und Endmultiplexer *m*
d. (cable) Hausanschlußkabel *n (Kabel-TV)*
d. data Daten ableiten *(in MUX)*
d. lock ausrasten
dropped packet Paketverlust *m*
DSA (Directory Service Agent) verzeichnisorientierter Systemteil *m*
DSC (digital signal channel) digitaler Datenkanal *m*
DSC34COD (DSC 3 channels 64 kbit/s codirectional) kodirektionaler 3-Kanal-64-kBit/s-Digitalsignalkanal *m*
DSCR (descrambler) Entwürfler *m*
DSI (digital speech interpolation) digitale Sprachinterpolation *f*
DSIF (Deep Space Instrumentation Facility) Weltraum-Meßanlage *f (JPL, US)*
DSL (digital subscriber loop) digitale Teilnehmerschleife *f*
DSN (Deep Space Network) Weltraum-Funkverbindungsnetz *n*
DSP (digital signal processor) Digitalsignalprozessor *m*
DSR (Data Set Ready) Betriebsbereitschaft *f (V.24/RS232C)*
DSR (digital satellite radio) digitaler Satelliten-Hörrundfunk *m*
DSRR (digital shortwave radio) digitaler Kurzwellenfunk *m*
DSSS (Digital Subscribers Switching Subsystem) Vermittlungsteilsystem *n* für digitale Teilnehmeranschlüsse *(BT ISDN)*
DTAM (Document Transfer And Manipulation) Dokumentenübertragung und -bearbeitung *f*
DTC (data test centre) zentrale Prüfstelle *f* für Dateneinrichtungen
DTE (data terminal equipment) Datenendeinrichtung *f* (DEE) *(Benutzergerät)*
DTF s. dynamic tracking filter
DTI Department of Trade and Industry *(GB)*
DTMF s. dual-tone multifrequency (dialling method)
DTP (desk-top publishing) Desktop-Publishing *n*; Computersatz *m*
DTR (Data Terminal Ready) Endgerät *n* betriebsbereit *(V.24/RS232)*
DUA (Directory User Agent) verzeichnisorientierter Endbenutzer-Systemteil *m*
dual ring Doppelring *m (Token-Ring-Struktur, LANs)*
d. routing Zweiwegeführung *f*

d. seizure gleichzeitiger Anruf *m*, gleichzeitige Belegung *f*
d.-tone multi-frequency dialling (DTMF) Mehrfrequenzwahl *f* (MF-Wahl)
d. tone multi-frequency (dialling) method (DTMF) Mehrfrequenzverfahren *n* (MFV), Multifrequenz(wähl)verfahren *n* *(CCITT Gelbbuch-Band VI.1 Empfehlung Q.23)*
d. watch Zweikanalüberwachung *f (Seefunk)*
dummy bit Leerbit *n*
d. cell Leerzelle *f*, Leerblock *m (ATM)*
d. command Pseudobefehl *m*
d. plug Blindstecker *m*
dump umspeichern
duplex Duplex *n* (DX) *(Modem)*; Gegensprechen *n (Tel.)*
d. channel method Gleichlageverfahren *n (ISDN B-Kanal, gleichzeitige und gleichfrequente Übertragung von Sende- und Empfangssignalen mit Echokompensation)*

d. signal Gegentaktsignal *n (Datenübertragung)*
d. transmission Gegenbetrieb *m*
duration of call Gesprächsdauer *f*
duty cycle Tastverhältnis *n (Impulse)*; relative Einschaltdauer *f*
d. factor Tastverhältnis *n (Impulse)*; Auslastungsfaktor *m (PCM-Sprache, in %)*
d. ratio Tastverhältnis *n (Impulse)*
DVI (digital video interactive) interaktive Video-CD *f (Video-CD-ROM, IBM)*
DVT (digital voice terminal) digitale Sprechstelle *f*
DX s. duplex
dynamic range Aussteuerbereich *m*
d. tracking filter (DTF) dynamisches Mitlauffilter *n*
dynamically redefinable character set (DRCS) dynamisch neu definierbarer Zeichensatz *m (Monitor)*

E

E (unit of width) Teileinheit *f* (TE) *(Gestell, 1 TE = 0.2", 5,08 mm)*
E-mail (electronic mail) elektronische Post *f*, Textspeicherdienst *m (CCITT Rec. X.400)*
E Series of CCITT Recommendations E-Serie *f* der CCITT-Empfehlungen *(betrifft Telefondienste und ISDN-Numerierung)*
E-TACS (Extended TACS) erweitertes TACS *n (GB)*
earphone Hörkapsel *f (Tel.)*
earpiece Hörmuschel *f (Tel.)*
earth exploration satellite service (EES) Erderkundungs-Satellitendienst *m (CCIR)*
e. **fault** Erdschluß *m*
e. **(recall) button** Erdtaste *f* (ET) *(Tel.)*
e. **station** Bodenstelle *f*, Erdfunkstelle *f (Sat.)*
system e. Betriebserde *f*
earthing point Ableitungspunkt *m*
e. **through a Petersen coil** Erdschlußkompensation *f*
EBCDIC (extended binary coded decimal interchange code) erweiterter BCD-Code *m* für Datenübertragung
EBHC Equated Busy Hour Call *(Verkehrswerteinheit, = 1/30 Erl. bzw. VE)*
EBIT (European Broadband Interconnection Trial) europäischer Breitbandverbundnetz-Versuch *m (RACE, 2 MB/s)*
EBR codec EBR-Codec *m (Bildreduktion)*
EBU (European Broadcasting Union) Union *f* Europäischer Rundfunkanstalten
EC (external computer) externer Rechner *m* (ER)
ECB s. electronic code book
echo Echo *n*; Rückhören *n* im eigenen Kanal
e. **balance return loss** Gabelübergangsdämpfung *f (PCM)*
e. **cancellation** Echokompensation *f*
e. **canceller** Echolöscher *m (Ping-Pong-Methode)*
e. **channel** Echokanal *m*, Rückkanal *m*
e. **compensation** Echounterdrückung *f*
e. **suppression requirement** Echobedingung *f*
e. **suppressor** Echosperre *f*
ECM (error correction method) Fehlerkorrekturverfahren *n (Fax.)*

ECMA (European Computer Manufacturers' Association) Vereinigung *f* der Europäischen Computerhersteller
ECS (European Communications Satellite) europäischer Kommunikationssatellit *m*
ECSA Exchange Carriers Standards Association *(US)*
EDC (error detection and correction) Fehlererkennung und Korrektur *f*
EDD s. electronic data display
edge of coverage Rand *m* der Ausleuchtzone (EOC) *(Sat.)*
e. **slope** Flankensteilheit *f*
e. **transition** Flankenwechsel *m*
EDI s. Electronic Data Interchange
EDIFACT Electronic Data Interchange for Administration, Commerce and Transport *(ISO IS 9735, EDI)*
edit aufbereiten, editieren *(Daten)*
EDP s. electronic data processing
EDP centre zentrale EDV-Anlage *f* (EDVA)
EDP-compatible EDV-gerecht
EDS s. electronic data switching system
EDTV (extended definition TV) Fernsehen *n* mit erhöhter Auflösung *(US)*
EEMA European Electronic Mail Association *(an die EMA angeschlossen)*
EES s. earth exploration satellite service
efficiency Wirkungsgrad *m*, Leistung *f*, Wirtschaftlichkeit *f*; Nutzwert *m*
EFT s. electronic funds transfer
EIA Electronic Industries Association *(US)*
EIRP (equivalent isotropically radiated power) Sendeleistung *f*
electromagnetic elektromagnetisch
e. **compatibility** (EMC) elektromagnetische Verträglichkeit *f* (EMV), elektromagnetische Kompatibilität *f*
e. **interference** (EMI) elektromagnetische Beeinflussung *f*
e. **pulse** (EMP) elektromagnetischer Impuls *m (nuklear)*
electromechanical distribution frame (EMDF) elektromechanische Vermittlungstechnik *f*, elektromechanisches Verteilergestell *n (Verm.)*
electronic elektronisch
e. **banking** elektronischer Bankverkehr *m*
e. **bulletin board** elektronische An-

electronic 172

schlagtafel f *(MHS)*
e. **code book** (ECB) elektronische Code-(übersetzungs)tabelle f *(DES)*
e. **data display** (EDD) elektronisches Datensichtgerät n
E. **Data Interchange** (EDI) standardisierter Datenaustausch m *(ein VAS)*
e. **data processing** (EDP) elektronische Datenverarbeitung f
e. **data processing system** elektronische Datenverarbeitungsanlage f (EDV)
e. **data switching system** (EDS) elektronisches Datenvermittlungssystem n *(einschließlich Telex- und Datexnetze)*
e. **directory** elektronisches Adreßbuch n *(CCITT X.500)*; elektronisches Telefonbuch n (ETB) *(Vtx-Attribut)*
e. **drive circuit** *oder* unit Ansteuerelektronik f
e. **funds transfer** (EFT) elektronische Geldüberweisung f, elektronischer Zahlungsverkehr m *(ein VAS)*
e. **mail** (E-mail, MHS) elektronische Post f (TELEBOX) *(CCITT Rec. X.400; siehe EMA-Definition, D/E-Teil)*
e. **mail service** Textspeicherdienst m (TELEBOX) *(MHS, CCITT Rec. X. 400)*
e. **message system** (EMS) elektronisches Mitteilungsübermittlungs-System n *(CCITT X.400)*
e. **news gathering** (ENG) elektronische Berichterstattung f (EB) *(TV)*
e. **notebook** elektronisches Notizbuch m *(Tel.)*
e. **switching system** (ESS) *(AT&T)* elektronisches Wählsystem n (EWS)
e. **telephone mailbox** Sprachbox f
e. **traffic pilot for drivers** elektronischer Verkehrslotse m für Autofahrer (EVA) *(Bosch)*
electrostatic discharge (ESD) elektrostatische Entladung f
electrostatically sensitive components elektrostatisch gefährdete Bauteile npl (EGB)
element Element n; Funktionseinheit f
eliminate ausblenden *(Jitter)*
e. **distortion** entzerren
EM-L (engineering model - life (test)) Ingenieurmodell n Lebensdauerprüfung *(ESA)*
EMA Electronic Mail Association *(Washington, DC, US)*
embedded coding hierarchische Codierung f *(PCM-Sprache)*
embolden hervorheben *(Vtx.-Monitor)*

EMC s. electromagnetic compatibility
EMDF s. electromechanical distribution frame
emergency call service Notrufdienst m
e. **control panel** Havariefeld n, Reserveschaltfeld n
e. **pushbutton** Not-Aus-Druckknopf m with e. **priority** katastrophenberechtigt
EMI s. electromagnetic interference
emission signal Ausgangsschwingung f *(FO)*
emissivity Lichtstärke f *(FO, in cd)*
EMP s. electromagnetic pulse
emptying the counter Leerzählen n
EMS s. electronic message system
en-bloc dialling Blockwahl f
e.-**bloc signalling** Blockwahlziffern-Wahlverfahren n
enable durchlässig steuern, freigeben, öffnen *(Gatter, Teiler)*; aktivieren
enciphered text Chiffrat n
encoder Codierer m
encoding Codierung f; Aufbereitung f *(AMI)*
e. **law** Codierungskennlinie f, Kompandergesetz n
encrypted verschlüsselt
encryption Verschlüsselung f *(Daten)*
end: at both ends beidseitig *(Kabel)*
e.-**of-address time** Wahlendezeit f *(ZGS. 7 UP)*
E. **Of Message** (EOM) Mitteilungsende n *(Signal)*
e.-**of-message signal** Nachrichtenendezeichen n
e.-**of-pulsing signal** Wahlendezeichen n *(Vorwärtssignal)*
e.-**of-selection signal** Wahlendezeichen n *(Rückwärtssignal)*
e. **of text** (EOT, ETX) Textende n *(PCM-Daten)*
E. **Of Transmission** (EOT) Übertragungsende n *(Signal)*, Sendestop m
e. **record** Endesatz m *(PCM-Daten)*
e.-**to-end connection** Gesamtverbindung f
e.-**to-end measurement** Streckenmessung f
e.-**to-end signalling** durchgehende Signalisierung f
endpoint Endpunkt m *(ZGS.7, SAP, logische Verbindung)*
energy gap Bandabstand m *(FO)*
ENG s. electronic news gathering
engaged lamp Besetztlampe f
e. **tone** (ET) Besetztton m *(V.25 bis)*
engineering Technik f
e. **data** Schaltunterlage f
e. **model - life (test)** (EM-L) Ingenieurmodell n Lebensdauerprüfung *(ESA)*

ENQ/ACK (enquiry/acknowledge) Handshakeverfahren n für Peripheriegeräte (HW)
enquiry (ENQ) Abfrage f (Daten); Stationsaufforderung f (DLC-Protokoll); Rückfrage f (RFRA)
ensemble Datengesamtheit f (Übertragungsprotokoll)
enter key Übernahmetaste f
entering aufschalten
entitled to operate in restricted powering conditions notspeiseberechtigt
entity Instanz f
entry point Einstieg m (in ein Programm)
ENV (European preliminary standard) europäische Vornorm f (NET)
envelope Bitvollgruppe f, Envelope n (Oktett + Status- und Synchronisierbit)
    e. distortion Laufzeitverzerrung f
EOC (edge of coverage) Rand m der Ausleuchtzone (Sat.)
EOM s. End Of Message
EOT, ETX s. End of Text
EOT s. End Of Transmission
equalize ausgleichen, nivellieren
equalizer Entzerrer m, Korrekturfilter m
equipment Ausstattung f, Einrichtung f; Betriebsmittel n
    e. jack Geräteklinke f
    e. level Ausstattung f
    e. list Belegungsliste f (Gestell), Geräteübersicht f
    E. Specifications Technische Lieferbedingungen fpl (TL)
    e. usage Belegungsverkehr m
equivalent gleichwertig, entsprechend; Abbild-
    e. bit rate Übertragungsgeschwindigkeit f
    e. circuit Ersatzschaltbild n
    e. isotropically radiated power (EIRP) Sendeleistung f (in dBW)
    e. line Leitungsnachbildung f
    e. network circuit Ersatzschaltung f
    e. network diagram Ersatzschaltbild n
    e. offered load Ersatzangebot n (Tel.-Anl.)
    e. voltage Ersatzspannung f
ER (earth recall) Erdtaste f (K.-Tel.)
erasing Freischreiben n (Speicher), Löschen n (Magnetband)
Erl s. erlang
erlang Erlang n (dimensionslose Verkehrswerteinheit, 1 Erl = 36 CCS = 1 dauerbelegte Übertragungsstrecke)
ERMES (European Radio Messaging System) europäisches Funk-Mitteilungssystem n (EG, Funkruf, Einführung 1992 geplant, CEPT-Weiterentwicklung von Euromessage)
erroneous fehlerhaft (Daten usw.)
    e. block fehlerhaft empfangener Datenblock m
error Fehler m (SW, Daten usw.), Ablage f (Frequenz), Stand m (Uhr)
    e. burst Bündelfehler m (z.B., von 20 Bit)
    e. character fehlerhaftes Zeichen n
    e. control Fehlersicherung f
    e. control bit Fehlerschutzbit n
    e. control procedure Fehlersicherungsverfahren n, Fehlerüberwachung f
    e. control unit Fehlerüberwachungseinheit f
    e.-corrected gesichert (Strecke)
    e. correction method (ECM) Fehlerkorrekturverfahren n (Fax.)
    e. detection Störungserkennung f
    e. detection and correction (EDC) Fehlererkennung und Korrektur f
    e.-free fehlerfrei (HW), störungsfrei
    e. list signal Fehlersammelmeldung f
    e. masking Fehlerverdeckung f
    e. performance Fehlerverhalten n (PCM)
    e.-protected gesichert (Strecke)
    e. protection Fehlersicherung f
errored fehlerhaft (Daten usw.); gestört (Übertragung)
    e. second Fehlsekunde f (CCITT G.821)
    severe e. seconds stark gestörte Sekunden fpl (CCITT G.821)
ESA (European Space Agency) Europäische Weltraumorganisation f
ESC s. escape
escape (ESC) Codeumschaltung f (DLC-Protokoll, Tastatur)
ESD (electrostatic discharge) elektrostatische Entladung f (Klassen nach IEC-801-2)
ESPRIT European Strategic Programme for Research and Development in Information Technologies
ESS (electronic switching system) (AT&T) elektronisches Wählsystem n (EWS)
establishing communication Verbindungsaufbau m, Dienstaufbau m (Transportdienst)
ET (Engaged (oder busy) Tone) Besetztton m (V.25 bis)
ET s. exchange termination
ETACS (extended TACS) erweitertes TACS n (zellularer Mobilfunk, GB)
Ethernet (lokales Netz, nach IEEE-Standard 802.3, 10 MB/s, CSMA/CD Basisbandübertragung)

ETS (European Temporary Standard) europäischer Interim-Standard *m (ETSI)*
ETSI (European Telecommunications Standards Institute) europäisches Institut *n* für Telekommunikationsnormen
ETX (End of TeXt) Textende *n*
EUREKA (European Research Cooperation Agency) Europäische Organisation *f* für Zusammenarbeit in der Forschung *(Arbeitsgruppe zur Aufstellung eines Rahmenprogramms zur Förderung von Projekten wie HDTV, RACE; der Ausruf 'heureka' von Archimedes ist symbolisch für den Forschungserfolg)*
Eu-95 Eureka-95 *(HDTV-, HD-Mac-Projekt)*
Eu-147 Eureka-147 *(DAB-Projekt)*
Eurocard design Europabauform *f*
EUROCOM Europäische Kommunicationsnormen *fpl (NATO, für taktische FM-Systeme)*
Eurocrypt (European satellite TV (MAC) encryption standard) europäische Verschlüsselungsnorm *f*
Euromessage (European Messaging) europäischer Funkrufdienst *m (Zusammenschaltung von Europage (GB), Alphapage (FR), Teledin (I), Cityruf (BRD), März 1990, Vorläufer zu ERMES)*
EURONET Europäisches wissenschaftliches Datennetz *n (paketvermitteltes EG-Netz, entspricht TRANSPAC)*
EuroOSInet (European OSI test network) europäisches OSI-Netz *n*
Europage britischer Funkrufdienst *m (entspricht DBP-Cityruf)*
European Broadcasting Union (EBU) Union *f* Europäischer Rundfunkanstalten (UER)
European radio-paging system Europäischer Funkrufdienst *m* (EFuRD), Europiep *m*, Eurosignal *n*
Eutelsat (European Telecommunications Satellite Organisation) europäische Nachrichtensatelliten-Organisation *f*
even parity gerade Parität *f*
event log Betriebsprotokoll *n*
examination Untersuchung *f*; Abfrage *f (HW)*
exception condition Ablaufunterbrechung *f*
exchange Vermittlung *f*, Vermittlungsstelle *f* (VSt); TEMEX-Zentrale *f* (TZ)
  e. **access** Amtsberechtigung *f (Tel.)*
  e. **area** Anschlußbereich *m* (Asb)
  e.-**barred** nichtamtsberechtigt
  e. **cabling** Aufteilungskabel *n*
  e. **circuit** Amtsleitung *f* (AL)
  e. **clock pulse** Amtstakt *m*
  e. **group** Amtsgruppe *f*
  e. **line access** Amtsanlassung *f (NStAnl.)*
  e. **line** Amtsleitung *f* (AL)
  e. **line answer** Amtsabfrage *f*
  e. **line circuit** vermittlungsseitige Anschlußschaltung *f* (VAS)
  e. **line group** Amtsbündel *n (NStAnl.)*
  e. **line seizure** Amtsbelegung *f*, Amtsanlassung *f (NStAnl.)*
  e. **line transfer** Amtsrufweiterleitung *f* (ARW)
  e. **termination** (ET) Teilnehmeranschlußsatz *m*, Teilnehmermodul *n*; Vermittlungsabschluß *m*, VSt-Leitungsabschluß *m*, vermittlungsseitiger Leitungsabschluß *m*; Vermittlungsendeinrichtung *f (ISDN)*
  e. **wiring** Innenverbindungskabel *n*
excitation pulses Anregungspulse *mpl*
excursion Auslenkung *f*; Hub *m (Spannung, Signal)*
executable ablauffähig *(Programm)*
execute ausführen *(Programm)*; abarbeiten *(Programmschritte)*
execution Realisierung *f*, Ausführung *f*
executive-secretary system Chef-Sekretär-Anlage *f*, Vorzimmeranlage *f*
  e. **telephone system** Chef-Telefonanlage *f*
exemption from charges Gebührenbefreiung *f*
expander Dehner *m (PCM)*
expectancy window Überwachungstor *n (Mobilfunk)*
expected value Erwartungswert *m (Bildcodierung)*
expendable equipment Verlustgerät *n*
expiry Ablauf *m (eines Zeitgebers)*
  e. **date** Verfalldatum *n*
exponentiating circuit Potenzierer *m*
extendable erweiterungsfähig, ausbaubar
extended-area call Nahwählverbindung *f (Tel.)*
  e.-**area service** Fernverkehrsdienst *m* zu Ortsgebühren
  e. **binary coded decimal interchange code** (EBCDIC) erweiterter BCD-Code *m* für Datenübertragung
  e.-**definition TV** (EDTV) Fernsehen *n* mit erhöhter Auflösung *(US)*
  e. **special-channel band** erweiterter Sonderkanalbereich *m* (ESB) *(TV)*
extension Ausbau *m*; Anschluß *m*, Nebenanschluß *m*; Abfragestelle *f (Tel.)*, Nebenstelle *f* (NSt), Nebenstellenanschluß *m* (NStA); Sprechstelle *f (Gegensprechanlage)*
  e. **user** Nebenstellenteilnehmer *m*

external (long distance) call Fernübertragung *f*
 e. call Amtsanruf *m*, Amtsgespräch *n*, Amtsverbindung *f*
 e. call connected (Amtsanruf) aufgeschaltet
 e. computer (EC) externer Rechner *m* (ER) *(Vtx-Informationsanbieter)*
externalize nach außen weitergeben *(ein Signal usw.)*
external(ly driven) clock Fremdtakt *m*

extract ausblenden *(Signal)*, entstopfen *(PCM-Signal)*
 e. clock, timing Takt ableiten
extraction signal Austastsignal *n (Pulse)*
eye pattern Augendiagramm *n (PCM-Phase, auf Oszillograph)*
 e. pattern of phase Phasenaugendiagramm *n (PCM)*
 e. pattern probability density Augenwahrscheinlichkeitsdichte *f (PCM-Übertragung)*

F

F exchange, unbalanced signalling (FXU) F-Vermittlung *f*, unsymmetrische Zeichengabe
F Series of CCITT Recommendations F-Serie *f* der CCITT-Empfehlungen *(betrifft Telefax, Teletex und Telex)*
f. tel. s. feature telephone
facility Einrichtung *f*; Betriebsmittel *n*; Dienstmerkmal *n*, Leistungsmerkmal *n*
   f. indicator Dienstmerkmal-Indikator *m* *(ZGS.7 UP)*
   f. request (FRQ) Aufforderung *f* zur Durchführung eines Dienstmerkmals *(ZGS. 7 UP)*; Dienstmerkmal-Anforderung *f*
facsimile s. fax
   f. network Bildübertragungsnetz *n*
   f. radio Bildfunk *m*
fail-safe ausfallsicher, gesichert
failure Ausfall *m*, Havarie *f*, Störung *f*
   f.-proof ausfallsicher
   f. threshold Abschaltschwelle *f (Zeichenstrecke)*
fairness Gerechtigkeit *f (bei Buszuteilung)*
fall Einbruch *m (im Signal)*
   f. outside herausfallen *(Bereich)*
fallback Herunterschalten *n (Modem)*
   f. system Bereitschaftssystem *n*
false indication *oder* **reading** Störanzeige *f*
   f. signal Fehlanruf *m*
family of curves Kenn(linien)feld *n*, Kurvenschar *f*
fan out auffächern *(Demux)*
   f.-out factor Ausgangslastfaktor *m (IC)*
   f.-out unit Verteileinrichtung *f (LAN)*
far-end crosstalk Fernnebensprechen *n (Tel.)*
   f.-end echo Fernecho *n*
fast FSK (FFSK) schnelle Frequenzumtastung *f (1200 Bd, nömL)*
   f. packet switching Breitband-Paketvermittlung *f (unterstützt Sprache sowie Daten)*
FASTON tab Steckzunge *f (Verbinder)*
fault Fehler *m*, Fehlerstelle *f*; Störung *f*
   f. clearance Entstörung *f*
   f. clearance office Störungsstelle *f*
   f. clearance service Entstörungsdienst *m*
   f. currents unzulässige Ströme *mpl*
   f. finding Fehlerlokalisierung *f*

   f. locating Fehlerlokalisierung *f*
   f. location Fehlerortung *f*, Störstelle *f*
   f. location unit (FLU) Fehlerortungseinheit *f*, Ortungsgerät *n* (OG) *(Tel.)*
   f. report Störungsmeldung *f*
   f. signal Fehlermeldung *f (AIS)*, Fehlertelegramm *n (Dienstkanal)*; Störmeldung *f*, Störsignal *n*
   f.-tolerant ausfallbeständig
fatal f. Totalausfall *m*
faultfinding *(HW)* Fehlersuche *f*
faultless fehlerfrei *(HW)*, fehlersicher
faulty fehlerhaft *(HW)*, gestört *(Übertragung)*
   f. line gestörte Leitung *f*
fax Fax *n*, Telefax *n*; Fernkopie *f*, Bildtelegramm *n*;
faxen, wegfaxen *(Dokumente, Grafik)*
   f. control field (FCF) Fax-Steuerfeld *n (Fax-Steuerzeichen)*
   f. group 1,2 Fax-Gruppe 1,2 *(analoge Telefaxmaschinen, Seitenübertragung 6 - 2 Min.)*
   f. group 3,4 Fax-Gruppe 3,4 *(digitale Telefaxmaschinen, Seitenübertragung 1 Min. - 10 Sek.)*
   f. machine Telefaxmaschine *f*, Telekopierer *m*, Fernkopierer *m*
FBP (fish bite protected) fischbißgeschützt *(TAT8, FO)*
FCC Federal Communications Commission *(US)*
FCF s. fax control field
FCFS first-come-first-served *(Warteprotokoll)*
FCS (frame checking sequence) Blockprüfzeichenfolge *f (HDLC)*; Rahmenprüfzeichen *n*
F/D (focal length/diameter) F/D-Verhältnis *n (Brennweite/Antennendurchmesser, Sat.)*
FDDI s. Fiber Distributed Data Interface
FDDI interface FDDI-Schnittstelle *f (IEEE 802.3, CSMA/CD)*
FDM (frequency division multiplex) Frequenzmultiplex *n*, Frequenzgetrenntlageverfahren *n*
FDM/SC unit TF+DL-(Trägerfrequenz/Dienstleistungs)-Gerät *n (Mobilfunk-Endgerät)*
FDMA (frequency division *oder* domain mul-

tiple access) Vielfachzugriff *m* im Frequenzmultiplex
FDX (full duplex) Gegenschreiben *n*; vollduplex
feature Merkmal *n*, Zusatz *m*
   f. telephone Komforttelefon *n*
FEC (forward error correction) Vorwärts-Fehlerkorrektur *f (PCM-Daten)*
FEC (front-end clipping) Kürzung *f* von Sprachblockanfängen *(PV)*
fed gespeist
   current converter-f. stromrichtergeführt
Federal Information Processing Standard (FIPS) Bundes-Informationsverarbeitungsnorm *f (US)*
Federal Privacy Act Datenschutzgesetz *n (US, 1974)*
feed forward aufschalten *(NStAnl.)*
   f. hole Taktloch *n (LSL)*
   f.-through principle Durchlaufprinzip *n (Speicherung, z.B- FIFO)*
feedback Rückmeldung *f (Nachricht)*
feeder cable Stichleitung *f (Kabel-TV)*
feeding from one end einseitige Einspeisung *f*
   f. line Zubringer *m*
feedpoint Anschluß *m (Antenne)*
female aufnehmend, negativ *(Verbinder)*
   f. connector strip Federleiste *f*
   f. contact Mutterkontakt *m*
FEP (front-end processor) Anpassungsrechner *m*
FER (frame erasure rate) Rahmenlöschrate *f (GSM, Sprachcodierung)*
ferroelectric liquid crystal (FLC) ferroelektrisches Flüssigkeitskristall *n (FO-Schalter)*
ferrule Hülse *f*, Kennhülse *f (Kabel)*; mit Hülse *f* versehen
fetch abrufen *(aus dem Speicher)*
FFSK s. fast FSK
FH (frequency hopping) Frequenzhüpfen *n*; Frequenzspringen *n*
FH-DPSK (frequency hopped DPSK) DPSK *f* mit Frequenzsprung
Fibre Distributed Data Interface (FDDI) Datenanschluß *m* mit Signalverteilung über Glasfaser *(ANSI ASC X3T9.5, 100 MB/s, Token-Ring nach IEEE 802.2, 802.5; max. Übertragungslänge 2 km, US)*
   f. loss Faserdämpfung *f (FO)*
   f. optic cable Glasfaserkabel *n (GFK)*
   f.-optic link Lichtleiteranschluß *m (FO)*
   f.-optic news gathering (FONG) faseroptische Berichterstattung *f*

   f. optics Faseroptik *f* (FO)
   f.-optics bus Lichtleiterbus *m (FO)*
   f. tail Anschlußfaser *f*
FID s. fill input device
field Feld *n (Daten)*
   f. experience Betriebserfahrungen *fpl*
   f. test Betriebsversuch *m*
   f. trip Meßkampagne *f*
   in the f. in der Praxis *f*
FIFO s. first-in-first-out
figure-of-merit measurement Systemwertmessung *f*
   f. shift Ziffernumschaltung *f* (Zi) *(Tx.)*
   f. shifting Ziffernzuschaltung *f (Tx.)*
file server Dateibediener *m (SW-Übergang für LANs)*
   f. transfer and access method (FTAM) Dateiübertragungs- und Zugriffsverfahren *n (ISO IS 8571)*
   f. transfer protocol (FTP) Dateiübertragungsprotokoll *n*
fill input device (FID) Fülldaten-Eingabevorrichtung *f*
filler Füllzeichen *n*
   f. bit Füllzeichen *n*
filter out ausfiltern, aussieben; absaugen *(Frequenzen)*
final capacity stage Endausbau *m*
   f. high-usage route Letztquerweg *m* (LQW)
Find Abfragen *n (Benutzer im MHS-Namensverzeichnis)*
finger locating ridges Fingerführung *f (Folientastatur)*
finite impulse response filter FIR-Filter *n (digitale Audiocodierung)*
FIPS (Federal Information Processing Standard) Bundes-Informationsverarbeitungsnorm *f (US)*
FIR filter s. finite impulse response filter
first choice route Erstwahlbündel *n*
   f.-in-first-out (FIFO) Durchlaufprinzip *n*, Siloprinzip *n (Register-Speicherverfahren)*
fish bite protected (FBP) fischbißgeschützt *(TAT8, FO)*
fixed connection festgeschaltete Verbindung *f*, Festverbindung *f*, Festanschluß *m*
   f.-gain amplifier Festverstärker *m*
   f. satellite service (FSS) fester Satelliten-Funkdienst *m (CCIR)*
   f. station Feststation *f* (FS) *(Bündelfunk, nömL)*
   f.-time call Festzeitverbindung *f (HfD)*
flag Flagge *f (Kennungsbit)*; Begrenzungszeichen *n (ISDN)*; Merker *m*, Markierung *f*

flash button Flashtaste *f* (FT) *(Tel.)*
flat rate Pauschaltarif *m*
  f. twin flexible cord Zwillingsleitung *f* *(DIN)*
flatbed scanner Flachbett-Scanner *m (OCR)*
flatten out verflachen *(Kurve)*
flawed fehlerhaft *(Daten, Blöcke usw.)*
FLC s. ferroelectric liquid crystal
flexible allocation freizügige Zuordnung *f*
flexing Wechselbiegung *f (Kabel)*
flip page function Seitenumkehrfunktion *f (Fax.)*
floating gleichstromfrei, potentialfrei
FLOF (full level one features) Merkmale *npl* der vollen Ebene 1 *(GB-Txt, entspr. TOP)*
floor bar Bodenschiene *f (Gestell)*
  f. (services) distribution Stockwerkverteiler *m (Tel.)*
  f. (services) distributor Stockwerkverteiler *m (Tel.)*
flow control Verkehrssteuerung *f*; Überlastabwehr *f (ZGS.7)*
  f. control device Drosselungseinrichtung *f (Verkehrsfluß)*
  f.-soldered onto aufgeschwallt auf
FLU (fault location unit) Fehlerortungseinheit *f*, Ortungsgerät *n* (OG)
FOF s. freeze-out fraction
follow a curve einen Verlauf *m* aufweisen
  f. me unabhängige TN-Suche *f*; Rufzuschaltung *f (Heranholen der Rufumleitung, Tel.)*
  f.-up signal nachgeführtes Signal *n*
FONG s. fibre-optic news gathering
footprint Ausleuchtzone *f (Sat.)*
forced release rückwärts auslösen
  f. ventilation Zwangsbelüftung *f (Tel.-Anl.)*
forcing configuration Grundfolge *f (DFÜ)*
foreign exchange line Ausnahmeanschluß *m*
foreign potential Fremdspannung *f (Übertragungskanal)*
format effector Formatsteuerzeichen *n*
formboard Kabelform *f*, Kabelformbrett *n*
forward abliefern *(Signal)*, weiterleiten *(Ruf)*; weiterschalten
  f.-biased operation Durchlaßbetrieb *m (FO)*
  f. call indicator Vorwärtskennzeichen *n (ZGS.7 UP)*
  f. channel Vorwärtskanal *m*, Hauptkanal *m*
  f. control channel Vorwärtskanal *m (Bündelfunk)*
  f.-controlled adaptation vorwärtsgesteuerte Adaption *f*
  f. error correction (FEC) Vorwärts-Fehlerkorrektur *f (PCM)*

  f. signal Vorwärtszeichen *n (in Verbindungsaufbaurichtung übertragen)*
  f. supervision Vorwärtssteuerung *f (DIN 44302)*
  f. transfer nachrufen *(Tel.)*
  f.-transfer signal Nachruf *m*
four-section switch Vierfachschalter *m*
  f.-wire ... vierdraht ... (vdr)
  f.-wire connector Kreuzklemme *f*
Fourier transform (FT) Fourier-Transformation *f* (FT)
frame Rahmen *m (PCM)*; Datenübertragungsblock *m*
  f. aligner Synchronisierschaltung *f (PCM)*
  f. alignment Rahmensynchronisierung *f*, Synchronismus *m*, Rahmengleichlauf *m (PCM-Daten)*
  f. alignment signal Rahmenkennwort *n* (RKW) *(PCM-Daten)*
  f. check sequence (FCS) Rahmenprüfzeichen *n (ZGS.7 CRC)*
  f. checking sequence (FCS) Blockprüfzeichenfolge *f (HDLC)*
  f. control field Rahmenkontrollfeld *n (FDDI)*
  f. cycle Rahmentakt *m*
  f. delay Rahmenversatz *m*
  f. ground Schutzerde *f (V.24/RS232C)*
  f. interval Rahmentakt *m*
  f. rate Bild(wechsel)frequenz *f*
  f. relaying Rahmenweiterleitung *f (CCITT X.31)*
  f. size Baugröße *f*, Bildformat *n (TV)*
  f. store Bildspeicher *m (Vtx.)*
  f. structure (PCM) Rahmenaufbau *m*
  f. timing Rahmenstart *m (X.21)*, Rahmenraster *m*
  f. switching Rahmenvermittlung *f (CCITT X.31)*
framing Rahmenbildung *f (PCM)*, Rahmenstart *m (X.21)*; Bildbegrenzung *f (Monitor)*
  f. bit Synchronisierbit *n*
  f. signal Synchronisierungssignal *n (ISDN)*
free of discontinuities stoßfrei *(Datensignal)*
  f. of gradings mischungsfrei
  f. of hits stoßfrei
freephone service Gebührenübernahme *f* durch B-Teilnehmer *(ISDN)*
freeze frame Standbild *n (Schmalbandvideo)*
  f.-out Zugriffs-Clipping *n (von Paketen, PV)*
  f.-out fraction (FOF) Verlustrate *f (TASI)*
frequency Schwingung *f*, Frequenz *f*, Häufigkeit *f*

frequency 180

f. check Frequenzkontrolle *f*
f. comparison Frequenzvergleich *m*
f. comparison unit Frequenzkontrolle *f*
f. control circuit Frequenznachziehschaltung *f*
f. dehopper Frequenzhüpfer-(FH-)Schaltung *f (Empfänger)*, Frequenzsprungempfänger *m*
f. division *oder* **domain multiple access** (FDMA) Vielfachzugriff *m* im Frequenzmultiplex *(Tel.)*
f. division multiplex (FDM) Frequenzmultiplex *n*, Frequenzgetrenntlageverfahren *n (Tel., TF-Technik)*
f. error Frequenz-Versatz *m*
f. hopper (FH) Frequenzhüpfer-Schaltung *f (Sender)*, Frequenzsprungsender *m*
f. hopping circuit Frequenzhüpfer-(FH-)-Schaltung *f*, Frequenzsprungschaltung *f (Speizspektrumverfahren)*
f. monitoring Frequenzkontrolle *f*
f. offset Frequenz-Versatz *m*
f. pulling equipment Mitzieheinrichtung *f*
f. response Frequenzgang *m (Filter)*
f. shift Frequenzversatz *m*
f. shift keying (FSK) Frequenzsprungmodulation *f*, Frequenzumtastung *f*
f. spacing Frequenzabstand *m*, Frequenzraster *m*
f. stability Frequenzgenauigkeit *f*, Frequenzkonstanz *f*
f. step Frequenzintervall *n*
f. tuning Frequenzabstimmung *f*
f.-weighted frequenzbewertet
fritting voltage Frittspannung *f*
front-end vorgeschaltet *(Computer)*
f.-end clipping (FEC) **(of talkspurts)** Kürzung *f* von Sprachblockanfängen *(Paketvermittlung)*
f.-end processor (FEP) Anpassungsrechner *m*, Vorrechner *m*, Vorschaltrechner *m*
f. layout Gestellbelegung *f*

f.-to-back ratio Rückdämpfung *f (Antenne)*
FRQ (facility request) Aufforderung *f* zur Durchführung eines Dienstmerkmals *(ZGS. 7 UP)*, Dienstmerkmal-Anforderung *f*
FSD s. full scale deflection
FSK s. frequency shift keying
FSR s. full scale range
FSS (fixed satellite service) fester Satelliten-Funkdienst *m*
FT (Fourier transform) Fourier-Transformation *f*
FTAM (file transfer and access method) Dateiübertragungs- und Zugriffsverfahren *n*
FTP (file transfer protocol) Dateiübertragungsprotokoll *n*
full duplex (FDX) Gegenschreiben *n*; vollduplex
f.-motion picture Bewegtbild *n (Breitbandvideo)*
f. scale Endwert *m (ADU)*
f.-scale deflection (FSD) Endwert *m (Meter)*
f. scale range (FSR) Bereichsendwert *m (ADU)*
fully restricted nicht amtsberechtigt
functional circuit diagram Übersichtsschaltplan *m*, Übersichtsstromlauf *m*
f. device Funktionsteil *n*
f. element Funktionseinheit *f*
f. equivalent Nachbildung *f*
f. section Funktionsteil *n*
f. test of subassemblies Teilfunktionsprüfung *f*
f. unit Funktionseinheit *f*
functionally dependable funktionssicher
fundamental period Grundlänge *f (Signal)*
fused abgesichert
fusible cartridge Schmelzeinsatz *m*
FXU (F exchange, unbalanced signalling) F-Vermittlung *f*, unsymmetrische Zeichengabe

G

G Series of CCITT Recommendations
G-Serie f der CCITT-Empfehlungen *(betrifft PCM)*
G.703 *(betrifft physikalische/elektrische Eigenschaften hierarchischer digitaler Schnittstellen (CCITT))*
G.712 *(die Leistung von NF-PCM-Kanälen betreffende CCITT-Empfehlung)*
G.821 *(betrifft Fehlerverhalten einer digitalen ISDN-Verbindung (CCITT))*
GaAs s. gallium arsenide
gain Verstärkung f; Steilheit f *(Verstärker)*; Gewinn m *(TASI, Antenne)*
  g.-controlled amplifier Regelverstärker m
  g. length Verstärkungslänge f *(Laser)*
  g./noise temperature ratio (G/T) effektive Leistungszahl f *(Sat., in dB/K)*
  g. reduction Zurückregelung f
gallium arsenide (GaAs) Galliumarsenid n
gap change Lückenveränderung f *(Paketvermittlung)*
  g. modulation Pausenmodulation f *(PCM-Sprache)*
gapped lückenbehaftet *(PCM-Takt)*
  g. clock Lückentakt m *(PCM-Daten)*
gate ansteuern, schalten *(digital)*; Gatter n, Tor n
  g. (intercom) extension oder **station** Torsprechstelle f *(Apothekerschaltung)*
  g. interphone Torsprechanlage f
  g. off austasten
  g. on eintasten, auftasten
  g. out ausblenden *(Digitalkreis)*
  g. time Zeitbasis f *(Zähler)*
gated getastet
gateway Gateway m *(konzept- oder protokollwandelnde Zusammenschaltung von Netzen, Netzknoten oder Einrichtungen)*, Übergang m *(z.B. zum Telefonnetz)*, Netzübergang m *(zwischen Netzen)*; Netzkoppler m, Überleiteinrichtung f *(Netz-HW)*
  g. computer Kommunikationsrechner m (KR) *(Vtx.)*
  g. protocol Kommunikationsprotokoll n *(internationales Vtx, z.B. EHKP für BRD, Prestel für GB, Teletel für FR,*

s. Tabelle VIII)
gating circuit Verknüpfungskreis m; Weiche f *(Daten)*
Gaussian Minimum Shift Keying (GMSK) Gaußsche Mindestwert-Umtastung f *(Code, zellularer digitaler Mobilfunk)*
GBN s. Go-Back-N
GDN s. Government Data Network
General Switched Telephone Network (GSTN) allgemeines Fernsprechwählnetz n *(CCITT Rec. V.25 bis)*, öffentliches Fernsprechwählnetz n
  g. system data anlagenunabhängige Systemdaten npl
  g. type approval Allgemeinzulassung f *(FTZ)*
generator Geber m, Generator m
gentex (general telegraph exchange) Telegrammwähldienst m (Gentex) *(Telegrammdienst des DBP-Telexnetzes)*
geostationary orbit (GSO) erdsynchrone oder geostationäre Umlaufbahn f *(Sat.)*
  g. transfer orbit (GTO) Transferbahn f *(in die Synchronbahn, Sat.)*
geosynchronous satellite Synchronsatellit m *(Sat.)*
global address Generaladresse f
  g. mobile phone standard (GMP) Welt-Funktelefonnorm f
  G. Positioning System (GPS) weltweites Navigationssystem n *(Navigation, Sat., 1,57/1,22 GHz)*
GMP s. global mobile phone standard
GMSK s. Gaussian Minimum Shift Keying
GND (signal GrouND) Betriebserde f *(V.24/RS232C)*
Go-Back-N (GBN) *(ARQ-Protokoll, Sat.)*
Go/No-Go evaluation Richtig/Falsch-Bewertung f
go off-hook abhängen, sich anmelden *(Tel.)*
go on-hook aufhängen, sich abmelden *(Tel.)*
Golay method Golay-Methode f *(alphanumerische and Sprach-Signalisierungsmethode für Funkruf, Motorola)*
GOSIP (Government OSI Profile) Regierungsprofil n für OSI *(Benutzernorm)*
GOU s. ground or open unbalanced
Government Data Network (GDN) Regierungsdatennetz n *(privaten Benutzern*

zugängliches paketvermitteltes X.25-Netz, Racal, GB)
GPS s. Global Positioning System
grade of service Betriebsgüte *f*, Dienstgüte *f*; Verkehrsgüte *f (Tel.-Anl.)*
  g. of switching performance Vermittlungsgüte *f*
  g. of transmission performance Übertragungsgüte *f*
graded-index fibre Gradientenglasfaser *f (FO)*
gradient Gradient *m*, Steigung *f*
grading Mischung *f (Abnehmer/Zubringer-Teilgruppen-Verbindungsschema; Tel.-Anl.)*
gradual stufenweise, sukzessiv
  g. slope geringe Steigung *f (einer Kurve)*
granular noise Flächenrauschen *n (DPCM-Video-Codierung)*
graphic character Schriftzeichen *n (DV)*
graphical primitives Darstellungselemente *npl (Kreise, Linien usw., Vtx.)*
graphics tablet Grafiktableau *n (Fernzeichnen)*
grating Gitter *n*; Raster *m (optisch)*
grid Gitter *n*; Raster *m (Verdrahtung)*
  g. spacing Rastermaß *n*
ground or open unbalanced (GOU) Erde oder offener Kreis unsymmetrisch *(Signalisierung)*
  g. station Bodenstelle *f*, Erdfunkstelle *f (Sat.)*
grounding *oder* **earthing key** Erdtaste *f*

group blocking ground Gruppensperrerde *f*
  g. frequency Wellenzugfrequenz *f*
  g. hunting Gruppenwahl *f*, gruppenweise Nummernsuche *f*, Sammelruf *m*
  g. link Primärgruppenverbindung *f (Modem)*
  g. number Sammelrufnummer *f*
  g. (of lines) Bündel *n*
  g. processor Gruppensteuerung *f*
  g. selector Gruppenschalter *m* (GS) *(Fax.)*
  g. switch Gruppenkoppler *m*
grouped gebündelt *(Frequenzen)*
  g.-frequency operation Getrenntlageverfahren *n (Sende- und Empfangssignale werden mit unterschiedlichen Frequenzen übertragen)*
groups per minute (gpm) Gruppen/Minute *(FS)*
growth concentrator Einführungskonzentrator *m* (EKT)
GSM (Groupe Special Mobile) Sondergruppe *f* Mobilfunk *(CEPT-Arbeitsgruppe für digitalen zellularen Mobilfunk, DECT)*
GSO s. geostationary orbit
GSTN s. General Switched Telephone Network
G/T (gain/noise temperature ratio) effektive Leistungszahl *f (Sat.)*
GTO s. geostationary transfer orbit
guard band Schutzabstand *m*, Sicherheitsband *n (Nachbarkanäle)*
guidance Leitung *f*, Führung *f*
guided geführt, gerichtet

H

H channel (high-speed user information channel) H-Kanal *m*, Breitbandinformationskanal *m (ISDN)*
H Series of CCITT Recommendations H-Serie *f* der CCITT-Empfehlungen *(betrifft Breitband-Gruppenverbindungen)*
half duplex Halbduplex *n* (HDX, HX) *(Modem)*
  h. duplex transmission Wechselbetrieb *m*
  h. of the band Teilband *n (Richtfunk)*
Hamming distance Hamming-Abstand *m (FEC, in zwei stellenweise verglichenen Binärwörtern gleicher Länge, die Stellenzahl mit unterschiedlichen Bitzeichen, DIN 44300)*, Hamming-Distanz *f (FEC)*
hand over weiterreichen *(Tel.)*
handheld cordless telephone Handfunksprechgerät *n*
  h. telephone Handtelefon *n* ("Handy"), Taschentelefon *n*
handle Handgriff *m*, Griffblende *f (Gestell)*
handler Steuerprogramm *n (z.B. Paketsteuerung)*
handling Bedienen *n (HW)*, Handhaben *n*
  h. of calls Abfertigung *f* von Belegungen *(Tel.-Anl.)*
  h. of traffic Verarbeitung *f* des Verkehrs, Verkehr *m* abwickeln
handoff Umschalten *n (Mobilfunk)*
handover Basisstationswechsel *m*, Funkkanalwechsel *m*, Kanalwechsel *m (C-Netz)*
hands-free voice input device Freisprecheinrichtung *f (Funkfernsprechwahl)*
  h.-free talking Freisprechen *n* (FS) *(K.-Tel.)*
  h.-free talk key Freisprechtaste *f (K.-Tel.)*
handset Bedienhörer *m (Mobilfunk)*, Handapparat *m*, Hörer *m (Tel.)*
handshake procedure Quittungsbetrieb *m (Bus)*
handshaking method Quittungsverfahren *n (PCM-Daten, -Sprache)*; Beginnabgleich *m*
hang up aufhängen, einhängen, auflegen *(Hörer)*
hangover Abfallverzögerung *f (PV)*; Überhang *m (von Sprachblöcken)*
  h. (time) Nachwirkzeit *f (Gegenteil von Antwortzeit, Modem)*
hard-wired program (fest)verdrahtetes Programm *n*, verdrahtungsprogrammiert
hardcopy output Protokollausgabe *f*, Ausdruck *m*
hardware Gerätetechnik *f*, Hardware *f* (HW), Technik *f*
  h. check system Inbetriebnahmesystem *n*
  h. fault Gerätefehler *m*
harmonic distortion Klirrverzerrung *f*
  h. ratio Klirrdämpfung *f*
harmonics: generation of h. Klirrproduktion *f*
hashing Hashing *n (binäre Bitsuche)*
  h. function Hasch- *oder* Streufunktion *f*
HCS s. Hundred Call Seconds
HDLC s. High-level Data Link Control
HD-Mac s. high-definition MAC
HDOP (horizontal dilution of precision) horizontale Präzisionsverringerung *f*
HDPCM (hybrid DPCM) Hybrid-DPCM *f (HD-MAC)*
HDTV s. high-definition TV
HDX s. half duplex
head end Empfangsstelle *f (Gemeinschaftsantenne)*
  h. station Kopfstation *f*, Kopfstelle *f (Kabel-TV)*
header Zellkopf *m (ATM)*, Blockkopf *m (TDM, ATM)*; Datenkopf *m*
heat shrink Schrumpfschlauch *m*
  h. sink Kühlkörper *m (Halbleiter)*
held belegt *(Leitung)*
  h. call gehaltene Verbindung *f (Tel.)*
helical scan recording Schrägspuraufzeichnung *f (MAZ)*
HEMT s. high electron mobility transistor
hermaphrodite *oder* **hermaphroditic (sexless) connector** Hermaphrodit-Kupplung *f*, Zwitterkupplung *f*
hermetically sealed luftdicht
heterodyning Überlagerung *f (Frequenzen)*
hierarchical level Hierarchieebene *f (Prozess)*
high-bit-rate modulation hochratige Modulation *f*
  h.-calling-rate subscriber Vielsprecher *m*
  h.-capacity station Hochgeschwindigkeitsstation *f (LAN)*
  h. definition MAC (HD-Mac) hochauflösendes Mac *n (HDTV-Standard, Zeitmultiplex-*

high 184

technik)
h. definition TV (HDTV) Hochzeilenfernsehen *n (Eu-95, 1250 Zeilen, Seitenverhältnis 16:9, progressive Abtastung 1:1)*
h.-density bipolar (HDB3) Dreiercode *m (CCITT Rec. G.703, Annex A.)*
h. electron mobility transistor (HEMT) Transistor *m* mit hoher Elektronenbeweglichkeit
h. frequency hohe Frequenz *f*, hohe Frequenzlage *f*
h.-impedance hochohmig
H.-level Data Link Control (HDLC) bitorientiertes Übertragungssteuerungsverfahren *n (synchrones Schicht-2-Protokoll im LAN, ISO 3309, 4335, DIN 66221)*
h.-level communication protocol höheres Kommunikationsprotokoll *n*
h. noise immunity logic (HNIL) störsichere Logik *f*
h. power amplifier (HPA) Hochleistungsverstärker *m (Sat.)*
h.-priority call instruction priorisierte Anforderung *f*
h.-resistance hochohmig
h.-speed channel Breitbandkanal *m (ISDN-H-Kanal)*
h.-speed user information channel (H channel) H-Kanal *m*, Breitband-Informationskanal *m (ISDN, H_0 = 384 kB/s, H_{11} = 1,536 MB/s, H_{12} = 1,92 MB/s, H_2 = 30-45 MB/s, H_4 = 120-140 MB/s, für Videokonferenzdienst usw.)*
h.-speed hochratig *(Strecke)*
h.-usage line (HUL) Querleitungsbündel *n* (Ql) *(Netz)*
h.-usage route Direktweg *m*, Querweg *m* (QW)
h.-voltage HRC-type fuse HH-(Hochspannungs-Hochleistungs)-Sicherung *f*
highly ramified weitverzweigt
h. resistive hochohmig
highway Leitung *f*, Vielfachleitung *f*, Zeitmultiplexleitung *f (PCM)*; Schiene *f*
super-multiplex h. Supermultiplexschiene *f*
Hilbert transformer Hilbert-Transformator *m*
hinged-frame construction Schwenkrahmenbauweise *f (Gestell)*
h.-frame panel Schwenkrahmenfeld *n (Gestell)*
history Lebenslauf *m (eines Teils)*
hit Störung *f*, Störungsspitze *f*, Nadelspitze *f*, Spannungsstoß *m*
impulse h. Impulsstoß *m*
line h. Leitungsstörung *f*

phase h. Phasensprung *m*
HLR s. home location register
HNIL s. high noise immunity logic
hold a display eine Anzeige *f* festhalten
h. for inquiry rückfragen *(Tel.)*
h.-in range Haltebereich *m (VCO)*
h. latch Haltespeicher *m (Verm.)*
h. period Wartezeit *f*
h. toggle makeln
holding (a call) (Ruf *m*) parkieren, in Rückfrage halten
h. circuit Warteschaltung *f (EWS)*
h. time Belegungsdauer *f (ununterbrochene Belegtzeit des Abnehmers, Tel.-Anl.)*; Belegungszeit *f (Fernwirktechnik)*
home banking elektronischer Bankverkehr *m*
home location register (HLR) Heimatdatei *f (GSM)*
homefax private Telefaxnutzung *f*
hook switch Gabelumschalter *m* (GU) *(Tel.)*
hook-up wire Schaltdraht *m*
hop Sprung *m*; Frequenzsprung *m*; Funkfeld *n*; Richtfunkstrecke *f*
double-h. link Zweisprungverbindung *f (VSAT)*
single-h. link Einsprungverbindung *f (VSAT)*
hopper Frequenzsprungsender *m*
hopping Frequenzspringen *n oder* -hüpfen *n*
horizontal dilution of precision (HDOP) horizontale Präzisionsverringerung *f (GPS)*
host Großrechner *m*
h. computer Dienstleistungsrechner *m (ZGS.7 UP)*; Verarbeitungsrechner *m*
hot line Direktruf *m*
h. standby Betriebsbereitschaft *f* (BB)
housing Gehäuse *n*
HPA s. high power amplifier
HRC s. hypothetical reference connection
hub Zentralstation *f (VSAT-Netz)*
shared h. geteilte Zentralstation *f (VSAT-Netz)*
HUL s. high-usage line
Hundred Call Seconds (HCS) *(Verkehrswerteinheit, = 1/36 Erl)*
hunt group Sammelgruppe *f*, Sammelanschluß *m*, Sammelrufnummer *f*
hunting Pumpen *n (Oszillator)*; Pendeln *n*; Suchen *n (Tel.)*
group h. Gruppenwahl *f*, gruppenweise Nummernsuche *f*, Sammelruf *m*
HW (hardware) Hardware *f*, Gerätetechnik *f* Technik *f*
hybrid circuit Hybridschaltung *f*, Gabel *f (Tel.)*

h. **DPCM** (HDPCM) Hybrid-DPCM f *(HD-MAC)*
h. **network** Gabelschaltung f *(Tel.)*
h. **termination** Gabelnachbildung f *(Tel.)*
h. **transformer loss** Gabelübergangsdämpfung f

h. **transition** Gabelübergang m *(Tel.)*
hypothetical reference connection (HRC) Bezugsverbindung f
HX (half duplex) Halbduplex n

I

I Series of CCITT Recommendations I-Serie f der CCITT-Empfehlungen *(betrifft ISDN, s. Tabelle III)*
I420 interface Teilnehmer-Netz-Schnittstelle f *(BT ISDN, 192 kB/s, entspricht S_0-Schnittstelle, nach BTNR 191)*
IA5 (International Alphabet No.5) internationales (Telegraphen-) Alphabet n Nr.5
IAOG (International Administrative management domain Operators Group) Internationale Verwaltungsgruppe f von Betreibern im Versorgungsbereich
Iasnet sowjetisches paketvermitteltes X.25-Netz n *(UdSSR, DNIC 2501)*
IBC (Integrated Broadband Communications) integrierte Breitbandkommunikation f
IBC (International Broadcasting Convention) Internationale Rundfunk-Konvention f
IBCN (Integrated Broadband Communications Network) integriertes Breitband-Kommunikationsnetz n
IBM International Business Machines Corp.
IBS (Intelsat Business Service) Intelsat-Geschäftsdienst m *(Sat.)*
IBU (International Broadcasting Union) Weltrundfunkunion f
ICM (internal communication matrix) Internverkehrvielfach n
icon Piktogramm n *(PC)*
ICS (ISDN communication system) ISDN-Kommunikationssystem n
ICT (in-circuit test) In-Circuit-Test m
IDA (Integrated Digital Access) integrierter digitaler Anschluß m *(BT-BA)*
IDAphone BT-Digitaltelefon n *(unterstützt V.24)*
IDAST (Interpolated Data and Speech Transmission) Übertragung f mit Daten-/Sprachinterpolation
identification Kennzeichnung f
  i. code Kennung f *(Nachrichtenkopf)*
  number i. Rufnummernanzeige f *(ISDN)*
identifier Bezeichner m *(DV)*
IDF (intermediate distribution frame) Zwischenverteilergestell n *(Tel.)*
idle belegungsbereit, frei *(Kanal, Leitung)*
  i. call Leerruf m
i. channel unbelegter Kanal m
i.-channel noise Grundgeräusch n, Ruhegeräusch n *(Tel.)*
i.-circuit condition Freileitungszustand m; Schreibruhezustand m *(FS)*
i. code word Ruhecodewort n *(PCM)*
i. condition Freizustand m, Ruhe f, Ruhezustand m *(Übertragungskanal)*
i. cycle Ruhezyklus m
i. state Ruhezustand m *(Hörer)*
i. status indication Freimeldung f
i. status signal Freizustandssignal n
IDN (Integrated Digital Network) integriertes Text- und Datennetz n
IDR (Intermediate Data Rate) mittlere Übertragungsgeschwindigkeit f *(Intelsat-Dienst nach IESS 308, Fernsprechübermittlung)*
IDTF (inverse discrete Fourier transform) diskrete Fourier-Rücktransformation f
IDTV (improved definition TV) Fernsehen n mit verbesserter Auflösung *(US)*
IEC (Interexchange Carrier) Querverbindungsnetzbetreiber m *(US)*
IEC (International Electrotechnical Commission) Internationale Elektrotechnische Kommission f
IEC (ISDN echo canceller) ISDN-Echolöscher m
IEEE (Institute of Electrical and Electronic Engineers) Verband m der Elektroingenieure und -techniker *(US-Netzstandards 802.x)*
  IEEE 488 *IEEE-Parallelbus (Meßtechnik)*
IFIP International Federation of Information Processing *(Genf)*
IFRB (International Frequency Registration Board) Internationaler Ausschuß m für Frequenzregistrierung
IH s. In-House application *(RDS)*
ILC (ISDN link controller) ISDN-Übertragungssteuerung f
ILD (injection laser diode) Injektionslaser m *(-diode f) (FO)*
illegal unzulässig, ungültig
illuminated switch Leuchtschalter m
illumination (level) Beleuchtungsstärke f *(FO, in lx)*
IM s. independent maintenance

image 188

image Bild *n*; Abbild *n*, Darstellung *f*
i. phone Bildtelefon *n*
i. regeneration Bildwiederholung *f*
imaging path Abbildungsweg *m (FO)*
IM/DD (intensity modulation with direct detection) Intensitätsmodulation *f* mit Direktdetektion *(FO)*
immunity to line-induced interference Einströmungsstörfestigkeit *f*
i. to radiation-induced interference Einstrahlungsstörfestigkeit *f*
impact button Schlagtaste *f*
impairment Güteabfall *m*
impairments Störbelag *m*
impedance Impedanz *f*, Scheinwiderstand *m*
implementation Realisierung *f*
improved definition TV (IDTV) Fernsehen *n* mit verbesserter Auflösung *(US)*
impulse hit Impulsstoß *m (Tel.)*
impulsive noise kurzzeitiges Geräusch *n*
IM3 (3rd order intermodulation product level) Intermodulationsprodukt *n* 3. Ordnung *(in dBm, CT1)*
IN (intermediate node) Transitknoten *m*
in-band signalling Imband-Signalisierung *f*
in-car telephone Autotelefon *n (Mobilfunk)*
in-channel echo Rückhören *n* im eigenen Kanal
in-circuit test (ICT) In-Circuit-Test *m*
In-House (IH) **application** Eigenanwendung *f (RDS)*
in-house network hauseigenes Netz *n*, Hausnetz *n*
in-house wiring Endstellenleitung *f*
in-phase channel I-Kanal *m (FO, Homodynempfänger)*
in-phase signal Gleichtaktsignal *n*
in-quad near-end crosstalk attenuation Imvierernahnebensprechdämpfung *f*
in-quad crosstalk Imvierernebensprechen *n*
in service in Betrieb
in-service monitoring (ISM) Betriebsüberwachung *f (ISDN)*, Überwachung *f* ohne Betriebsunterbrechung
in-service test Betriebsmessung *f*
in-slot signalling Imband-Signalisierung *f*, Zeichengabe *f* innerhalb der Zeitlagen
inactive passiv, un(an)gesteuert
inband Inband-, Imband-
inbound kommend; (in) Sammelrichtung *f (VSAT)*
INC s. INcoming Call
incidence time Einfallzeit *f (PV)*
incoming ankommend, kommend *(Ruf)*
  i.-call protection Anrufschutz *m*
  i. call set-up Verbindungsaufbau *m*
kommend (VAK) *(C-Netz)*
INcoming Call (INC) Ankommender Ruf *m (V.25 bis)*
incorrect fehlerhaft *(Daten, Blöcke usw.)*
increment erhöhen; fortschalten *(Zähler)*
independent maintenance (IM) unabhängige Wartung *f*
i. station selbstgespeistes Amt *n*
i. subscriber search unabhängige TN-Suche *f*
independently powered versorgungsunabhängig, speisungslos *(Tel.)*
index of cooperation (IOC) Modul *n* der Auflösung *(Fax, Verhältnis Trommeldurchmesser/Zeilenabstand)*
i. page Programmvorschauseite *f (Fernsehtext)*
indexed sequential index-sequentiell
indication Meldung *f (FW)*; Hinweis *m*
i. message Meldetelegramm *n (FW)*
i. store Meldespeicher *m (FW)*
indirect exchange access Halbamtsberechtigung *f*
individual type approval Einzelzulassung *f (ZZF)*
i.-route store richtungsindividueller Speicher *m*
induction Beeinflussung *f (z.B.* elektromagnetischer Störung*)*
ineffective erfolglos *(Belegungsversuch)*
i. access Leergriff *m*
infinite server Bedienstation *f* mit unendlich vielen Bedienern *(Netzübergangsfunktion, Sat.)*
influencing characteristic beeinflussende Kenngröße *f*
i. variable Einflußgröße *f*
informatics Informatik *f*, Nachrichtentheorie *f*
information Daten *npl*, Information *f*, Meldung *f*
i. and communications equipment Informations- und Kommunikationsgeräte *npl* (I+K-Geräte)
i. content Aussagefähigkeit *f*
i. exchange Nachrichtenaustausch *m*
i. frame Informationsblock *m (ISDN)*
i. message Übertragungszeichenfolge *f*
i. on available legal remedies Rechtsbehelfsbelehrung *f*, Rechtsmittelbelehrung *f*
i. provider (IP) Informationsanbieter *m* Netzwerkrechner *m* (NR), Teilnehmerrechner *m* (TR) *(Vtx.)*
i. provider database externer Rechner *m* (ER) *(Vtx.)*
i.-related service attribute Informa-

tionsdienstmerkmal *n*
i. specialist Informatiker *m*
i. technology (IT) Informationstechnik *f*, Informatik *f*
i. tone Bescheidzeichen *n*
i. transfer capability Dienstnutzung *f*, Nutzung *f (Transportdienst)*
i. transfer rate Übertragungsrate *f (Transportdienst)*
inherent distortion Apparateverzerrung *f*
i. noise Eigenrauschen *n (Gerät)*
system-i. systemgebunden
inhibit anhalten *(Takt)*; sperren *(Daten, Impulse)*
initial capacity stage Erstausbau *m*
i. parameter Ausgangsgröße *f*
i. section Anlauffeld *n (Fernspeisung)*
i. service request message (ISRM) Dienst-Erstanforderungssignal *n*
initialization mode Vorbereitungsbetrieb *m (Modem)*
initialize definiert starten *(Mikroprozessor)*, einrichten *(SW)*
initiate einleiten, anstoßen, auslösen
initiation message Anreiztelegramm *n (FW)*
inject einspeisen *(Signal)*, stopfen *(PCM)* einblenden *(Signal, PCM)*; einspielen *(Musik)*
i. a signal into a time slot Zeitkanal *m* mit einem Signal beaufschlagen
injection laser diode (ILD) Injektionslaser *m* (-diode *f*) *(FO)*
injector circuit Gebührenweiche *f* (GBW)
INMARSAT (International Maritime Satellite Organisation) Internationale Seefunk-Satelliten-Organisation *f*
inoperable arbeitsunfähig, fehlerhaft
input Eingabe *f*, Eingang *m*, Eingangssignal *n*
i. attenuation Vordämpfung *f*
i. backoff Eingangssignalabstand *m* vom Sättigungspunkt *(TWT, in dB)*
i. circuit Vorkreis *m*
i. current Stromaufnahme *f*
i. filter Vorsatzweiche *f (GGA)*
i. line Zubringer *m*
i./output code converter *(EDS)* Ein-/Ausgabe-Codewandler *m* (EACW)
i.-output controller Datenkonzentrator *m* (DKZ) *(Mobilfunk-FuKo)*
i./output coupler Ein-/Auskoppler *m* (VBN)
i. power flux density (IPFD) Eingangsleistungsflußdichte *f (Sat.)*
inquiry Anfrage *f*, Auskunft *f (Tel.)*
i. call Anfrageruf *m*

i. sequence Abfragefolge *f*
i. set Abfrageapparat *m*
insert einblenden *(Signal, PCM)*; einkoppeln *(FO)*; einordnen, einreihen *(in eine Folge oder Warteschlange, PCM-Daten, -Sprache)*; stopfen *(PCM)*; weiterleiten *(Daten in MUX)*
insertion Anschaltung *f (HW)*; Einblendung *f*
i. loss Einschaltdämpfung *f*, Einfügungsdämpfung *f*, Grunddämpfung *f*, Restdämpfung *f*
i. signal test set Prüfzeilenmeßplatz *m (TV)*
inset Einsatz *m*
i. location Einsatzplatz *m* (EPL) *(Gestell)*
i. section Einsatzfeld *n*
inside wiring Teilnehmereinrichtungsverdrahtung *f*
Install Registrieren *n (Benutzer in MHS-Namensverzeichnis)*
i. a program ein Programm *n* einrichten *(DV)*
installation Neueinrichtung *f (einer TLN-Einrichtung)*
i. barring level Anlagenberechtigung *f*, Nicht-Anlagenberechtigung *f*
i. kit Montagesatz *m*
i. pitch Einbauteilung *f*
Institute of Electrical and Electronic Engineers (IEEE) Verband *m* der Elektroingenieure und -techniker *(US)*
instrumented van Meßbus *m*
integral integral, stoffschlüssig
integrated integriert, Einbau-
i. automatic dialling facility integrierte automatische Wähleinrichtung *f* für Datenübertragung (iAWD)
I. Broadband Communications (IBC) integrierte Breitbandkommunikation *f (RACE-Projekt)*
I. Broadband Communications Network (IBCN) integriertes Breitband-Kommunikationsnetz *n (besteht aus TLN-Netz und PTT-Netz)*
i. broadband telecommunication network integriertes Breitband-Fernmeldenetz *n* (IBFN) *(DBP, FO)*
i. data network (IDN) zusammengefaßtes Daten- und Textnetz *n*
I. Digital Access (IDA) integrierter digitaler Anschluß *m (BT, baut das IDN zum TLN hin aus, um damit das ISDN bereitzustellen;* $B_{64}+B_8+D_8$)
I. Digital Network (IDN) integriertes digitales Text- und Datennetz *n (digi-*

integrated 190

tales Fernsprech-, Text- und Datennetz mit analoger Zugriffsweise)
i. optical circuit (IOC) integrierte optische Schaltung *f*
I. Services Digital Network (ISDN) diensteintegrierendes Digitalnetz *n* (IDN mit Digitalzugriff; auch: "Ist So- was Denn Nötig?")
i. sidelobe ratio (ISLR) integrierter Nebenzipfelabstand *m* (Sat.-Antenne, in dB)
I. Trading System (ITS) integrierte Makleranlage *f (BT-NStAnl. für Börsen- makler)*
i. voice/data terminal (IVDT) Mehr- dienstterminal *n (Multikom-Gerät, US)*
integrating Einbinden *n (Teilnehmer)*
i. period Integrierintervall *n*
intelligibility Hörbarkeit *f (Tel.)*; Ver- ständlichkeit *f (Sprache)*
INTELSAT (International Telecommunica- tions Satellite Organisation) Interna- tionale Gesellschaft *f* für den Betrieb von Nachrichtensatelliten
I. Business Service (IBS) Intelsat-Ge- schäftsdienst *m (Sat., IESS 309)*
intensity-dependent helligkeitsabhängig *(FO)*
i. modulation Intensitätsmodulation *f* (IM) *(FO)*
i. modulation with direct detection (IM/DD) Intensitätsmodulation *f* mit Direktdetektion *(FO)*
inter-arrival time Einfallabstand *m (War- tesystem)*
i.-network call Querruf *m*
i.-PBX tie line Querverkehrsleitung *f*
i.-quad crosstalk Nebenviernebenspre- chen *n*
interactive capability Dialogfähigkeit *f*
i. operation dialoggeführte Bedienung *f*
intercell handoff externes Umschalten *n (Mobilfunk)*
intercept erfassen *(Radar)*
i. announcement Bescheidansage *f*
i. announcement unit Hinweisansagegerät *n*
i. service Bescheiddienst *m*, Bescheid- verkehr *m*, Hinweisdienst *m*
i. tone Hinweiston *m*
interchange circuit Schnittstellenleitung *f* (DIN 44302)
i. point Übergabestelle *f (Tel.)*
interchanging Austauschen *n (Dateien)*
interchannel gap Kanallücke *f*
i. signal/crosstalk ratio Kanalisolation *f*
intercom Reihenanlage *f (Tel.)*, Gegen- sprechanlage *f*
intercommunication Übergang *m (zw. Diens- ten)*; Zusammenarbeit *f*
i. between service attributes Dienstüber- gang *m (Transportdienst)*
interconnected zusammengeschaltet, ver- netzt
interconnecting cable Schnittstellenkabel *n*
interconnection Verschaltung *f (Chips)*, Zusammenschaltung *f*; Netzverbund *m*
i. level Anschaltepegel *m*
i. option Anschlußmöglichkeit *f*
i. panel Anschaltfeld *n*
i. support equipment Verbindungsunter- stützungseinrichtung *f* (VU-E)
i. support system Verbindungsunterstüt- zungssystem *n* (VU-S)
interdigital pause Zwischenwahlzeit *f (Tel.)*
interested party Bedarfsträger *m*
Interexchange Carrier (IEC) *(US)* Querver- bindungsnetzbetreiber *m*
i. circuit Externsatz *m* (ES)
i. signalling externe Leitungszeichen- gabe *f*
i. traffic Externverkehr *m*
i. trunk Verbindungsleitung *f* (Vl) *(Tel.-Anl.)*
interface Schnittstelle *f*, Anschluß *m* (DK); Übergangsstelle *f*, Übergabestelle *f (Tel.)*; Anschaltstelle *f*, Koppelstelle *f*
i. adapter Datenumsetzer *m* (DU) *(für Digitalbetrieb)*
i. attenuation Schnittstellendämpfung *f*
i. circuit Anpassungsschaltung *f*
i. loopback Prüfschleife *f*
i. module Nahtstellenbaustein *m*
interference Störbeeinflussung *f*, Beein- flussung *f (z.B. elektromagnetischer Störung)*, Störung *f*
i. immunity Interferenzfestigkeit *f (FO, Sat., in dB)*
i. suppression filter Entstörfilter *m*
interfering field beeinflussendes Feld *n*
interleave verschachteln *(Pakete)*; ver- zahnen *(Programmteile)*, verkämmen *(TDM)*
interleaved channel arrangement Doppel- raster *m (Mobilfunk)*
i. signals verschachtelte Signale *npl* (TDM)
interleaving Verschachtelung *f (von Pake- ten)*; Code-Spreizung *f (Sat.)*
cell i. Zellenmultiplexierung *f (ATM)*
interlocking Verriegelung *f*; Blockierung *f*

Intermediate Data Rate (IDR) mittlere Übertragungsgeschwindigkeit *f (Intelsat-Dienst nach IESS 308, Fernsprechübermittlung)*
 i. **distributor** Zwischenverteiler *m* (ZV) *(Vermittlung)*
 i. **distribution frame** (IDF) Zwischenverteilergestell *n (Tel.)*
 i. **level** teilzentral, teilzentrale Ebene *f (Vermittlung)*
 i.**-level processor** Teilsteuerwerk *n*
 i. **node** (IN) Transitknoten *m (PCM-DFÜ)*
intermittent operation Aussetzbetrieb *m*
intermodulation noise Klirrgeräusch *n*
 i. **noise measurement** Rauschklirrmessung *f*
 i. **ratio** Intermodulationsabstand *m* (IMA)
internal communication matrix (ICM) Internverkehrvielfach *n*
 i. **noise** Eigenrauschen *n (Gerät)*
 i. **test** Eigentest *m*
International Alphabet (IA) internationales (Telegraphen-) Alphabet *n*
 I. **Administrative management domain Operators Group** (IAOG) Internationale Verwaltungsgruppe *f* im Versorgungsbereich *(von Postverwaltungen zum Verwalten des E-Mail-Protokolls X.400)*
 I. **Broadcasting Union** (IBU) Weltrundfunkunion *f*
 i. **call** Auslandsverbindung *f*
 I. **Electrotechnical Commission** (IEC) Internationale Elektrotechnische Kommission *f*
 i. **exchange** Auslandsamt *n*
 I. **Frequency Registration Board** (IFRB) Internationaler Ausschuß *m* für Frequenzregistrierung
 i. **gateway centre** internationales Kopfamt *m*
 i. **gateway exchange** internationales Kopfamt *n*
 I. **Organisation for Standardisation** (ISO) Internationale Organisation *f* für Normung
 I. **Standard** (IS) internationale Norm *f* *(ISO)*
 I. **Switching Centre** (ISC) internationales Vermittlungsamt *n (internationaler Gateway)*
 I. **Telecommunication Union** (ITU) Internationale Fernmeldeunion *f*
internet protocol Übergangsprotokoll *n (OSI-Schicht 3 und höher)*
 i. **traffic** Querverkehr *m*

interoffice trunk Querverbindung *f (US)*
interoperation Zusammenarbeit *f (zw. Anlagenteilen)*
interpersonal messages (IPM) interpersonelle Mitteilungen *fpl (CCITT X.400)*
interphone Interphonanlage *f*, Türsprechanlage *f*
interpin space Polteilung *f (Verbinder)*
Interpolated Data and Speech Transmission (IDAST) Übertragung *f* mit Daten-/Sprachinterpolation *(GB, Datenpaketübertragung auf Sprechwegen)*
interregister signal Registerzeichen *n (dig. Tel.)*
interrogate abfragen *(Adressen, Tasten, rufenden TLN)*
interrogation Stationsaufforderung *f*, Abfrage *f (Tel., Daten)*
 i. **and information** Abfrage- und Auskunftsystem *n*
interrupt ausschalten, schalten *(Leitung)*
interrupted ringing signal periodischer Ruf *m*
intersatellite link (ISL) Satelliten-Querverbindung *f (Sat.)*
intersymbol interference Impulsnebensprechen *n (FO)*, Nachbarzeichenstörung *f*
intervening time Zwischenschaltzeit *f*
interworking Anbindung *f (von Netzen)*, Übergang *m*, Verbund *m*; Zusammenwirken *n*
 i. **service** (IWS) Übergangsdienst *m*
intonation Sprachmelodie *f*
intra-exchange circuit Internsatz *m (Vermittlung)*
 i.**-exchange signalling** Inneramtssignalisierung *f (Tel.)*
 i.**-office call** internes Gespräch *n*
 i.**-quad crosstalk** Imviererrnebensprechen *n*
intracell handoff internes Umschalten *n (Mobilfunk)*
intrinsic error Grundfehler *m (PCM)*
intrusion Aufschalten *n (NStAnl.)*
 i.**-protected call** Datenschutzverbindung *f (Tel.)*
 i. **protection** Anklopfschutz *m*, Aufschalteschutz *m* (AS) *(Tel.)*
 i. **tone** Aufschalteton *m*
INV s. INValid
invalid (INV) Ungültigkeit *f (V.25 bis Meldung)*; fehlerhaft *(Daten, Blöcke)*
invalidate verfälschen *(Datensatz)*, ungültig machen
invasive eingreifend
inverse discrete Fourier transform (IDTF) diskrete Fourier-Rücktransformation *f*

inverter 192

inverter Inverter *m*, Umkehrverstärker *m*
inverting amplifier Umkehrverstärker *m*
invitation of tender Ausschreibung *f*
invoke aufrufen *(Code)*
i. priority Priorität *f* in Anspruch nehmen
I/O port E/A-Port *n*, E/A-Anschluß *m*
IOC (index of cooperation) Modul *n* der Auflösung *(fax)*
IOC (integrated optical circuit) integrierte optische Schaltung *f*
IOT (in-orbit test) Prüfung *f* im Orbit *(Sat., vor Inbetriebnahme)*
IP (information provider) Informationsanbieter *m (Vtx.)*
IPAT ISDN Primary Access Transceiver *(HW)*
IPFD (input power flux density) Eingangsleistungsflußdichte *f*
IPM s. interpersonal messages
IPM service IPM-Dienst *m (CCITT X.400)*
IPM transfer service IPM-Übermittlungsdienst *m (CCITT Rec. X.400, P2; Schicht 7 OSI-Modell)*
IRIG Inter-Range Instrumentation Group *(US, Standards für Datenerfassung und -aufzeichnung)*
irradiance Bestrahlungsstärke *f (FO, in W/cm^2)*
ISC s. International Switching Centre
ISDN (Integrated Services Digital Network) diensteintegrierendes Digitalnetz *n*
ISDN communication system (ICS) ISDN-Kommunikationssystem *n (bis 70 Anschlüsse)*
ISDN echo canceller (IEC) ISDN-Echolöscher *m*
ISDN image transmission ISDN-Bilddienste *mpl*
ISDN link controller (ILC) ISDN-Übertragungssteuerung *f*
ISDN PBX (ISDX, ISPBX) ISDN-Nebenstellenanlage *f*; Telekommunikations-Anlage *f* (TK-Anl.). *(neue TKO-Definition)*

ISDN-UP s. ISDN user part
ISDN user part (ISDN UP) ISDN-Anwenderteil *m (ZGS.7, CCITT Q.761...764)*
ISDN 2 BT-BA-Anschluß *(2x B+D-Kanäle)*
ISDN 30 BT-PA-Anschluß *(30x B+D-Kanäle, früher Multiline IDA)*
ISDX s. ISDN PBX
ISL s. intersatellite link
ISLR (integrated sidelobe ratio) integrierter Nebenzipfelabstand *m (Sat.)*
ISM (in-service monitoring) Betriebsüberwachung *f*
ISO (International Standardisation Organisation) Internationale Organisation *f* für Normung
ISO 8877 ISO-Norm *f* für ISDN-Steckverbinder
isochronous isochron *(in Echtzeit)*
isolate entkoppeln; abriegeln; eingrenzen, lokalisieren *(Fehler)*
isolated network Inselnetz *n*
isolating diode Trenndiode *f*
isolation Freischalten *n (Geräte)*, Isolieren *n*, Trennen *n*, Entkoppeln *n*
ISPBX (ISDN PBX) ISDN-Nebenstellenanlage *f*, Telekommunikationsanlage *f (TK-Anl.)*
ISRM (initial service request message) Dienst-Erstanforderungssignal *n*
ISUP s. ISDN user part
IT (information technology) Informationstechnik *f*, Informatik *f*
itemized charge account Einzelgesprächsnachweis *m*; Einzelgebührennachweis *m* (EGN) *(ISDN)*
ITS (Integrated Trading System) integrierte Makleranlage *f*
ITU (International Telecommunication Union) Internationale Fernmeldeunion *f* (IFU)
IVDT (integrated voice/data terminal) Mehrdienstterminal *n*
IWS s. interworking service

J

J.17 Audio-Preemphase *f* für C-MAC/Paket und D2-MAC/Paket *(CCITT-Empf. J.17)*
jack panel Klinkenfeld *n*
   j. plug Klinkenstecker *m*
jackfield Klinkenfeld *n*
   j. distributor Schnurverteiler *m*
jitter Aperturunsicherheit *f (ADU)*; Impulszittern *n (PCM)*
   j. tolerance Jitterfestigkeit *f (PCM)*
   phase j. Phasenjitter *m (DFÜ)*
joint Kabelverbindung *f*
   j. loss Übergangsdämpfung *f (FO)*
   j. manhole Kabelbrunnen *m*
jointing Spleißen *n (FO)*
JPL Jet Propulsion Laboratories *(UCLA, US)*
JRTIG Joint Radiophone Technical Interfaces Group *(GB, Urheber von TACS)*
jumper Verbindungsdraht *m*, Brücke *f*
   j. module Schaltelement *n*
   j. wire Rangierdraht *m*
jumpering rangieren
junction Knoten *m (Netz)*; Übergangszone *f (Halbleiter)*
   j. exchange Knotenamt *n*
   j. line Verbindungsleitung *f* (VI) *(Tel.-Anl.)*, Anschlußleitung *f*
justification bit Füllbit *n*, Stopfbit *n (PCM)*
   j. service bit Füllinformation(sbit) *n*
justify ausrichten, füllen *(PCM)*

K

Ka band Ka-Band *n* (20 - 30 GHz, Sat.)
Kalman filter Kalman-Filter *n* (Zustandsschätzer)
KBS s. knowledge-based system
keep clear frei halten
  k. time Takt *m* halten
  k. watch empfangsbereit sein
key array Tastenfeld *n* (VDU)
  k. click filter Schaltknackfilter *n*
  k. in eintasten
  k. lock Tastensperre *f*
  k. on hochtasten *(Sender)*
  k.-operated switch Schlüsselschalter *m*
  k.-operated telephone Tastfernsprecher *m*
  k. switch Taster *m*
  k. (telephone) system (KTS) Büro-Nebenstellenanlage *f*, Teilnehmereinrichtungs-Nebenstellenanlage *f*
keyboard Tastatur *f* Tastenfeld *n* (Terminal usw.)
  k. transmitter Handsender *m*

keying filter Tastfilter *n*
KeyLine BT-Punkt-zu-Punkt-Datenverbindung *f* (X.21, 48 u. 64 kB/s)
KEYLINK-D Textspeicherdienst *m* (AUS-MHS nach CCITT Rec. X.400, entspricht TELEBOX)
keylock switch Schlüsselschalter *m*
keypad Tastatur *f*, Tastwahlblock *m* (TWB), Wahlblock *m*, Bedienfeld *n* (Tel.)
  12-button k. 12er Wahlblock *m*
keysending Tastung *f*
keyword Kennwort *n*
kilometric cable attenuation Kabeldämpfung *f* in km, kilometrische Kabeldämpfung *f*
KiloStream BT-Punkt-zu-Punkt-Analog-Datenverbindung *f* (bis 14,4 kB/s)
kink Kennlinienknick *m*
knowledge-based system wissensbasiertes System *n* (KI)
KTS s. key (telephone) system
Ku band Ku-Band *n* (10 - 12 GHz, sat.)

L

L2R s. layer 2 relay
L-shaped upright L-profiliger Gestellholm m *(Gestell)*
LA (line access module) Leitungsanschlußmodul n
label Marke f *(DV)*; Kennsatz m *(Daten)*, Nachrichtenkopf m
  l. mounting Schildträger m
lacing cord, string *oder* **thread** Kabelformgarn n
lamp array Lampenfeld n
  l. test Lampenkontrolle f
LAN (local area network) Grundstücknetz n, lokales Netz n *(Datagramm-orientiertes Privatnetz)*
land (mobile) radio service Landfunkdienst m, landmobiler Fundienst m
  l. mobile satellite service (LMSS) satellitengestützter Landfunkdienst m *(VSAT)*, Satelliten-Mobilfunk m
LAP (link access procedure) Übertragungssteuerungsverfahren n, Leitungszugangsverfahren n *(ISDN)*
  LAPB (LAP for balanced mode) LAP für gleichberechtigten Spontanbetrieb *(X.25 LAP, ISO 6256, DIN 66222 Teil 1)*
  LAPD (LAP for ISDN D channel) LAP für ISDN-D-Kanal *(X.32, X.75 LAP, CCITT Rec. I.440,441, FTZ 1R6D)*
  LAPM (LAP for modem error control) LAP für Modem-Fehlerüberwachung *(basiert auf CCITT LAPD, V.42, einschl. MNP)*
large-capacity disk storage unit Großplattenspeicher m
laser disk Bildplatte f
  l. shutdown Laserabschaltung f (LSA) *(FO)*
  l. turn-on signal Laserstartsignal n *(FO)*
last-choice route Letztweg m (LW)
  l.-number (automatic) redialling Wahlwiederholung f *(K.-Tel.)*
LATA Local Access and Transport Area *(lokaler, gewöhnlich regionaler Telefonanschlußbereich, US)*
latch Signalspeicher m, Haltespeicher m, Auffang-Flipflop m *(Signal)*; auffangen, speichern; verriegeln *(z.B. FF-Ausgang)*

latching block Rastblock m *(X.21, ISO 4903)*
latency Latenzzeit f *(DV, enthält Wartezeit)*
lateral section Seitenteil n
lattice filter Kreuzglied n *(dig. Audio)*
launch einkoppeln *(Signal, FO)*
layer Schicht f *(im OSI 7-Schicht-Referenzmodell (RM))*; Lage f *(Wicklung)*
  l. 1 B channel protocol B-Kanal Schicht 1 (B1) *(ISDN)*
  l. 2 relay (L2R) Schicht-2-Brückenfunktion f *(GSM)*
  l. 3 signalling protocol Schicht-3 Signalisierungsprotokoll n
  l. protocol Schichtenprotokoll n *(ISDN)*
layout Disposition f; Bestückung f; Lage f; Anordnung f
  l. character Formatsteuerzeichen n
  l. drawing Ansichtsplan m, Übersichtsplan m
LD (loop disconnect) Impulswählverfahren n (IWV)
LDL (long-distance loop) Weitverkehrsschleife f
LDM s. limited distance modem
lead-in (character) Antext m *(PCM-Daten)*
lead time Vorlaufzeit f *(bei langem Code, PCM)*; Vorhaltezeit f
leading base station Bezugs-Funkkonzentrator m *(Mobilfunk)*
  l. contact voreilender Kontakt m *(Schalter)*
  l. edge voreilende Impulsflanke f
leakage resistance Ableitwiderstand m
leakance Ableitung f, Ableitungsbelag m *(Kabel, in kOhm/km)*
leaky undicht, leck
  l. feeder signal transmission Übermittlung über Leckleitung f *(Mobilfunk)*
  l. mode Leckwelle f *(FO)*
  l. wave Leckwelle f *(Kabel)*
learning tool Einarbeitungshilfe f
leased line Mietleitung f, Standleitung f
least significant bit (LSB) niedrigstwertiges Bit n
leave the connection up die Leitung f stehenlassen

LEC (local exchange carrier) Ortsnetzbetreiber *m (Tel.)*
left hand circular polarisation (LHCP) linkszirkulare Polarisation *f (Sat.)*
leisure electronics Unterhaltungselektronik *f* (UE)
length indicator (LI) Längenindikator *m (ZGS.7)*
  l. of lay Schlaglänge *f (Kabel)*
word l. Wortlänge *f*, Wortbreite *f*
LET s. link establishment time
letter of intent Absichtserklärung *f*
  l. shift Buchstabenumschaltung *f* (BU) *(Tx.)*
letterbox format Breitbildformat *n (TV, 16:9)*
lettering Beschriftung *f*
level Ebene *f (Software, Netz)*; Stufe *f (FS)*; Höhe *f*, Pegel *m*, Stand *m*
  l.-change value Sprungwert *m*
  l. matching circuit Logikadapter *m*
  l. response Pegelverlauf *m*
  l.-1 distributor Verteiler *m* 1. Ordnung *(elektronischer oder aktiver Verteiler)*
  l.-2 distributor Verteiler *m* 2. Ordnung *(elektromechanischer oder passiver Verteiler)*
  l.-3 distributor Verteiler *m* 3. Ordnung *(Schnurverteiler)*
LHCP s. left hand circular polarisation
LI s. length indicator
licence Genehmigung *f (ZZF)*
LIDS (listener idle state) Ruhezustand *m* des Hörers
lift Hub *m (mech.)*; abnehmen *(Hörer)*
light sensor Lichtempfänger *m (FO)*
  l. intensity Lichtstärke *f (FO, in cd)*
  l. signal equipment Lichtzeicheneinrichtung *f* (LZE)
  l. transmission Lichtleitung *f (FO)*
LIM s. line interface module
limit Grenzwert *m*; Eckwert *m*
  l. frequency Eckfrequenz *f (FO)*; Grenzfrequenz *f*
limited distance Kurzdistanz *f (Modem)*
  l. distance modem (LDM) Modem *m* für begrenzte Leitungslänge
line Leitung *f (Stromkreis zwischen TLN-Anschluß und Vermittlung)*; Strang *m (Gestelle)*; Strecke *f*
  l. access module (LA) Leitungsanschlußmodul *n*
  l. adapter Netzanpassung *f*, Netzvorsatz *m (SV)*
  l. amplifier Leitungsverstärker *m (Sat.)*
  l. attenuation Leitungsdämpfung *f*
  l. backing Zeilenhintergrund *m (Vtx.-Mon.)*
  l. balance Leitungsnachbildung *f*
  l. balancing network Nachbildung *f* (Nb)
  l. building-out network Leitungsnachbildung *f*
  l. card Leitungsanschlußkarte *f* (LAK) *(VBN, 140 MB/s)*
  l. category (Anschluß-)Klasse *f*
  l. circuit Übertragung *f (Tel.-Signalisierung)*
  l. clock Schrittakt *m (Übertragung)*
  l. code Leitungscode *m (Übertragung)*
  l. coded leitungskodiert *(Datenstrom)*
  l. concentrator Teilnehmerkonzentrator *m*; Wählsternschalter *m (Tel.)*
  l.-conducted leitungsgebunden *(Signal)*
  l. designation Leitungszugname *f*
  l. driver Leitungstreiber *m*
  l. equipment linientechnische Einrichtung *f*
  l. error control Leitungssicherung *f (Sat.)*
  l. filter Netzfilter *n* (NFI) *(SV)*
  l. finder Anrufsucher *m*
  l. grouping Mehrfach-TN-Anschluß *m (Tel.)*
  l. hit Leitungsstörung *f*
  l. holding time Verbindungszeit *f*, Verbindungsdauer *f*
  l. interface Leitungsschnittstelle *f (ISDN)*
  l. interface module (LIM) Vermittlungsschrank *m (DFS-Bodenstelle)*
  l. jack unit (LJU) Leitungsanschlußeinheit *f*, Teilnehmeranschlußeinheit *f*, Übergabestelle *f (nach BS6506 für NStAnl., entspricht DBP TAE)*
  l. lockout technisches Fangen *n (TLN-Anschlußzustand, nachdem der Antwortzustand eine vorbestimmete Zeitdauer statisch geblieben ist)*
  l. loss Leitungsdämpfung *f*
  l. losses Leitungsverluste *mpl*
  l. protection Teilnehmerschutz *m*
  l. section Teilstrecke *f*
  l. selector Leitungswähler *m* (LW) *(Tel.)*
  l. shuffling Zeilenumordnung *f (HDTV-Abtasttechnik, Eu-95)*
  l. side Kabelseite *f*
  l. spectrum Spektrallinienabstand *m*
  l. switch Netzschalter *m (US, SV)*; Anrufsucher *m (Tel.)*
  l. switching Durchschaltevermittlung *f*
  l. terminating equipment Leitungsendeinrichtung *f* (LE), Leitungsempfänger *m*

(LE)
l. **terminating unit (LTU)** Leitungsendgerät n
l. **termination** (LT) Leitungsabschluß m; Übertragungseinheit f (TÜE, jetzt TÜ) (TEMEX); Leitungsanpassung f (ISDN); Leitungsendeinrichtung f (LE)
l. **transformer** Leitungsübertrager m, Fernmeldeübertrager m
l. **turnaround** Umschaltezeit f (RS232C-Verbindung, halbduplex)
l. **trunk group** Anschlußgruppe f
l. **unit** (LU) Anschlußeinheit f (AE) (PCM-Daten); Beschaltungseinheit f
l. **verification** Anschlußerkennung f
linear predictive coding (LPC) lineare Prädiktions-Codierung f
link Anschluß m (Computer); Brücke f (HW); Strecke f, Verbindung f, Übertragungsstrecke f; Zwischenleitung f (Verm.); Zugangspfad m (PAD)
l. **access procedure** (LAP) Leitungszugangsverfahren n; Übertragungssteuerungsverfahren n (ISDN)
l. **budget** Streckenbilanz f (Sat.)
l. **by link** abschnittweise (ZGS.7-Netz)
l. **establishment** Verbindungsaufbau m
l. **establishment time** (LET) Verbindungsaufbauzeit f (Bündelfunk)
l. **group** Zwischenleitungsbündel n
l. **management** Streckenmanagement n (ZGS.7 MTP)
l. **plug** Verbindungsstecker m (Verteiler)
l. **protocol** Übermittlungsvorschrift f
l. **section** Funkfeld n
list of circuit connections Verbindungsliste f
listen before and while transmitting in den Kanal hineinhören (PCM)
l. **in** mithören
listener Hörer m, Nachrichtenaufnehmer m (Meßgerät)
l. **idle state** (LIDS) Ruhezustand m des Hörers (Meßgerät)
listening device Protokollgerät n
l. **protection** Abhörsicherheit f (Tel.)
LJU s. line jack unit
LL s. local laser
LLC (logical link control) Steuerung f der logischen Verbindung
LMSS (land mobile satellite service) satellitengestützter Landfunkdienst m (VSAT)
LNA (low noise amplifier) rauscharmer Verstärker m

LNB (low noise block converter) rauscharmer Blockwandler m (Sat.)
LNC (low noise converter) rauscharmer Empfangsumsetzer m oder Konverter m (Sat.)
load Last f, Belastung f; Auslastung f, Beschaltung f, Verbraucher m (el.); Senke f (Daten); belasten; belegen (Speicherbereich)
l. **conductance** Lastleitwert m (FO)
l. **input** Verbraucheranschluß m (el.)
l.**-invariant** belegungsunabhängig
l. **measurement** Belastungsmessung f
l. **of traffic carried** Belastung f (Verkehrswert des abgewickelten Verkehrs)
l. **sharing** Lastteilung f
loaded belastet; bespult (Leitung); eingeschrieben (Pufferspeicher, PCM-Daten)
l. **cable** Pupinkabel n
loading Belastung f; Belegung f (Kanal); Füllstand m (Speicher)
l. **coil** Pupinspule f
electric l. Strombelag m
local lokal, örtlich, Orts-
l. **area network** (LAN) lokales Netz n, Nahbereichsnetz n, Grundstücknetz n (Daten); Ortsnetz n (ON) (Tel.)
l. **battery** Ortsbatterie f (OB)
l.**-battery set** Ortsbatterie-(OB-)Apparat m (Tel.)
l. **bus** Nahbus m
l. **call** Ortswählverbindung f (Tel.), Innenübertragung f
l. **code** Ortscode m
l. **computer** Teilnehmerrechner m (TR, TNR) (Vtx.)
l. **exchange** (LX) Ortsvermittlungsstelle f (OVSt)
l. **exchange carrier** (LEC) Ortsnetzbetreiber m
l. **(exchange) line** Hauptanschlußleitung f (HAsl)
l. **junction line** Ortsverbindungsleitung f (Ovl) (Tel.)
l. **laser** lokaler Laser m (LL) (optischer Heterodynempfänger, FO)
l. **loop** Ortsanschlußleitung f
l. **message** eigenes Telegramm n; interne Nachricht f
l. **network** Ortsnetz n (ON) (Tel.)
l. **time offset** (LTO) lokale Uhrzeit f (VPT, = Ortszeit - UTC)
localized ortsgebunden, punktuell
l. **stress** punktuelle Beanspruchung f
locating part Paßteil n (Verbinder)

locating

l. wedge Polungskeil *m (Verbinder)*
location Steckplatz *n (Baugruppenträger)*; Aufenthaltsort *m (GSM)*
   l. update Aktualisierung *f* der Aufenthaltsregistrierung *(GSM)*
lock Sperre *f*, Verriegelung *f*; Synchronismus *m*, Synchronzustand *m (PCM, Signal)*
   l. (together) verkoppeln
   l. key Schloßtaste *f*
   l. on (to) einrasten (auf), aufsynchronisieren *(Träger)*
   l. out sperren *(Tastatur)*
   l.-out Abwerfen *n*
   l.-out time Sperrzeit *f*
   l. switch Schloßtaste *f*, Schlüsselschalter *m*
   loss of l. Synchronisierungsausfall *m*
locked eingerastet *(Signal)*, verriegelt; synchronisiert
   l. in phase phasenstarr
   l. range Haltebereich *m (VCO)*
   l. to im Rhythmus *m* der/des ..., mit ... verrastet
locking-in range Fangbereich *m (z.B. PLL)*
   l. part Rastteil *n (Verbinder)*
   l. pulse *(PCM-Daten)* Verkopplungsimpuls *m* (V-Impuls)
log Protokoll *n (DV, Fax)*; protokollieren
   l. of incoming calls Anrufliste *f*
   l. off sich abmelden
   l. on sich anmelden
logging device Protokollgerät *n*
logic array Gatternetzwerk *n*
logical channel logische Verbindung *f (ISDN)*; virtueller Kanal *m (Sat.)*
   l. connection logische Verbindung *f (ISDN)*
   l. link control (LLC) Steuerung *f* der logischen Verbindung *(Schicht-2-Protokoll im LAN, IEEE 802.2)*
long-, medium-, short-wave signal Lang-, Mittel-, Kurzwellensignal *n* (LMK-Signal) *(Hörfunk)*
   l.-distance communication Fernverkehr *m*
   l.-distance exchange Fernvermittlung *f* (FVSt)
   l.-distance exchange trunk Fernamtsleitung *f*
   l.-distance field cable Feldfernkabel *n* (FFK) *(NATO)*
   l.-distance loop (LDL) Weitverkehrsschleife *f*
   l.-distance switching system Fernamtstechnik *f*
   l.-distance traffic Fernverkehr *m (Tel., PCM)*

l.-haul modem Fernverkehrsmodem *m (s.a. LDM)*
l.-haul network Fernnetz *n*, überregionales Fernnetz *n (Tel.)*; Fernverkehrsnetz *n (FO)*
l.-range communications network Weitverkehrsnetz *n*
l.-term fading Dauerschwund *m*
l.-term prediction (LTP) Langzeitprädiktion *f (GSM)*
longitudinal longitudinal, Längs-
   l. balance Unsymmetriedämpfung *f (PCM-Daten)*
   l. conversion loss Unsymmetriedämpfung *f (Kabel, Schnittstelle)*
   l. induced voltage Längsspannungsbeeinflussung *f (Tel.)*
   l. redundancy check (LRC) Blockprüfung *f*, Längsprüfung *f*
   l. support Längsholm *m (Gestell)*
look up einsehen
   l.-up table Nachschlagetabelle *f*
loop Schleife *f*; Regelkreis *m*
   l.-back command Schleifenbefehl *m (NT)*
   l. closure Schleifenschluß *m (Tel.)*
   l. closure on a/b wires Belegung *f* (Bel)
   l. delay Schleifenimpulslaufzeit *f*
   l. (disconnect) dialling (LD) Impulswahlverfahren *n* (IWV) *(Tel.)*
   l. in idle condition Ruheschleife *f*
   l. network Ringleitungssystem *n (FO)*
   l. output circuit Wahlnachsendesatz *m* für Schleifenkennzeichen (WNSS)
   l. plant Leitungsnetz *n*, Teilnehmerleitungsnetz *n*
   l. signalling Hauptanschlußkennzeichengabe *f* (ZGS.7 UP)
   l. through durchschleifen
loopback Prüfschleife *f*; Nahe Prüfschleife einschalten *(nicht standardisiert, V24, Pin 9/10)*
looping Schleifenbildung *f*
loose wiring fliegende Verdrahtung *f*
LOS s. loss of signal
loss Dämpfung *f*, Verlust(e) *m(pl)*
   l./frequency distortion Restdämpfungsverzerrung *f*
   l. of lock Synchronisierungsfehler *m*
   l.-of-service time Dienstunterbrechungsdauer *f*
   l. of signal (LOS) Signalverlust *m*; Synchronisierungsausfall *m (Sat.)*
   l. of synchronism Synchronisierungsfehler *m*, Synchronisierungsausfall *m*
   l. system Verlustsystem *n (Vermittlung, eine angebotene Belegung wird bei Blokkierung abgewiesen, geht verloren)*

l. **voltage** Verlustspannung *f*
lossy verlustreich, verlustbehaftet
lost call Verlustbelegung *f (zu Verlust gehender Verbindungswunsch, Tel.-Anl.)*, nicht zur Verbindung führender Anruf *m*
 l.**-call principle** Verlustprinzip *n*
 l. **time** Verlustzeit *f*
 l. **traffic** Verlustverkehr *m (Tel.-Anl.)*
loudspeaker monitoring Lauthören *n*
 l. **intrusion protection** Ansprechschutz *m (dig. K-Tel.)*
loudspeaking Lautsprechen *n* (LS) *(K.-Tel.)*
low-calling-rate subscriber Wenigsprecher *m*
 l.**-noise amplifier** (LNA) rauscharmer Vorverstärker *m (Sat.)*
 l.**-noise block converter** (LNB) rauscharmer Blockwandler *m (Sat.)*
 l.**-noise converter** (LNC) rauscharmer Empfangsumsetzer *m*, rauscharmer Konverter *m (Sat.)*
 l.**-speed** niedrigratig *(Strecke)*
lower (half) band Unterband *n (Mobilfunk)*

 l. **sideband** Unteres Seitenband *n* (USB)
 l. **special channel band** Unterer Sonderkanalbereich *m* (USB) *(TV)*
lozenge key Rautentaste *f (Tel.)*
LPC (linear predictive coding) lineare Prädiktions-Codierung *f*
LRC s. longitudinal redundancy check
LSA s. laser shutdown
LSB (least significant bit) niedrigstwertiges Bit *n*
LT (line termination) Leitungsabschluß *m*; Übertragungseinheit *f (TEMEX)*
LTO (local time offset) lokale Uhrzeit *f*
LTP (long term prediction) Langzeitprädiktion *f (GSM, Sprachcodierung)*
LTU (line terminating unit) Leitungsendgerät *n*
LU (line unit) Anschlußeinheit *f* (AE); Beschaltungseinheit *f*
luminance Leuchtdichte *f (FO, in cd /cm^2)*
LX (local exchange) Ortsvermittlungsstelle *f* (OVSt)

M

M.1020 CCITT Empfehlung für internationale Mietleitungen
MAC (Media Access Control) Endgeräte-Anschlußsteuerung f (FDDI)
MAC (monitoring, alarm and control facility) Überwachungs-, Alarm- und Kontrolleinrichtung f (Sat.)
MAC (Multiplexed Analog Components) gemultiplexte Analog-Komponenten fpl (TV-Übertragungsprotokoll, CCITT Rep. 1073, Zeitmultiplextechnik)
machine-aided oder **-assisted** rechnerunterstützt oder -gestützt
   m.-assisted translation (MAT) rechnergestützte Übersetzung f
   m.-readable maschinenlesbar
mail box Mailbox f, Textspeicherdienst m, verzögerte Weitersendung f (MHS, CCITT Rec. X.400, AT&T-E-Mail-Dienst)
main (station) Hauptstelle f (NStAnl. oder Centrexeinrichtung, an die andere NStAnl. angeschlossen sind)
   m. center office Knotenamt n (KA) (US)
   m. distribution frame (MDF) Hauptverteiler m (HV,HVT), Hauptverteilergestell n (HV,HVT) (Verm.)
   m. exchange (MX) Hauptvermittlungsstelle f (HVSt), Vollamt n; Hauptzentrale f (THZ) (TEMEX)
   m. line Anschlußleitung f (Asl)
   m. memory Arbeitsspeicher m
   m. program Rahmenprogramm n, Leitprogramm n
   m. route Grundleitung f
   m. station Fernsprechhauptanschluß m (FeHA), Hauptanschluß m (HAs) (TLN), Hauptapparat m; Hauptstelle f
   m. station for fixed connections Hauptanschluß m für Direktruf oder Direktverbindung (HfD) (DBP-Datex)
   m. station for tie lines Hauptanschluß m für Direktruf oder Direktverbindung (HfD) (DBP-Datex)
   m. station identification Hauptanschlußkennzeichen n (HAK,HKZ) (Tel., für nicht-Durchwahl)
   m. station line Einzelanschluß m (EA)
   m. traffic burst (MTB) Bündelburst m (Sat.)

mains control relay Netzkontrollrelais n (NK-Relais) (NStAnl.)
   m. filter Netzfilter n (NFI) (SV)
   m.-independent netzlos (PV)
maintenance Unterhaltung f, Wartung f
   m. centre Wartungszentrale f, Entstörungsstelle f, Kundendienststelle f
   m. panel Wartungsfeld n
make einschalten (Schalter, Stromkreis)
   m.-busy key Sperrtaste f
male positiv (Verbinder)
malfunction test Fehlfunktionstest m
malicious böswillig
   m. call hold Fangzustand m (Tel.)
   m. call identification data Fangdaten npl (Tel.)
   m. call tracing Auffangen n des Anrufers bei böswilligem Anruf
MAN (metropolitan area network) Stadtnetz n (IEEE 802.6)
man-machine interface (MMI) Benutzerschnittstelle f, Mensch-Maschine-Kommunikation f (MMK)
   m.-made noise technisches Geräusch n
management Verwaltung f (Daten, Programme)
   m. data network service (MDNS) Netzdienst m für Managementdaten
   m. domain Versorgungsbereich m (MHS)
   m. entity Versorgungsinstanz f
   m. information service (MIS) Management-Informationsdienst m (VAS)
   m. system Leitsystem n
manager/secretary function Chef-Sekretär-Funktion f (Tel.)
   m./secretary station Chef-Sekretär-Anlage f (Tel.)
Manchester code Manchester-Code m (Ethernet, IEEE 802.3)
mandatory verbindlich vereinbart, zwingend
manhole Kabelschacht m, Kabelbrunnen m
Manned Spaceflight Network (MSFN) Funkverbindungsnetz n für die bemannte Raumfahrt (weltweites JPL-Bodenstellennetz)
manual answering service Dienstplatz m (ISDN)
   m. calling Handruf m
   m. mode handvermittelt (Tel.)
   m. operation Rufbetrieb m (Vermittlung)

m. ringing Handruf *m*
m. switching position (MSP) Vermittlungsplatz *m*
m. trunk operator position Nachvermittlungsplatz *m*
Manufacturing Automation Protocol (MAP) Fertigungsautomationsprotokoll *n (General Motors, OSI bis Schicht 5)*
MAP s. Manufacturing Automation Protocol
mapping Abbildung *f (logische Zuordnung von Werten, wie Adressen in einem Netz, zu Werten, wie Vorrichtungen, in einem anderen Netz)*
MAR (miscellaneous apparatus rack) Universalgestell *n*
MAR (mobile access radio) Mobilanschluß-Funkgerät *n*
margin Abstand *m*, Reserve *f*
maritime mobile service beweglicher Seefunkdienst *m*
  m. radio Seefunk *m (INMARSAT)*
  m. radionavigation service Seenavigationsfunkdienst *m*
mark Marke *f*, Kennzeichen *n*; Einsbit *n*, Zeichenschritt *m*
  m. frequency Zeichenfrequenz *f (FS)*
marking Markieren *n*, Kennzeichnen *n*
  m. condition Signalzustand "Eins"
MAS (mobile access system) Mobilfunk-Anschlußsystem *n (an das Netz)*
MASCAM (masking pattern adapted subband coding and multiplexing) Mithörschwelle *f (Toncodierung-Prozedur)*
mask Maske *f*; Schema *n (am KO- bzw. Monitor-Bildschirm, nach CCITT G.712 u.a.)*; verdecken, überdecken
  m. out ausblenden *(Jitter)*, aussparen *(Bit)*
masking Verschleierung *f*, Verdeckung *f (dig. Audio)*; Maskierung *f*
  m. pattern (threshold) Mithörschwelle *f (MASCAM, dig. Sat.-Sprachkanal)*
  m. sound Maskierer *m (dig. Audio)*
master antenna TV (MATV) Gemeinschaftsantennenanlage *f (TV)*
  m. clock Mutteruhr *f*
  m. computer Führungsrechner *m*
  m. frequency Steuerfrequenz *f*
  m. pulse Leitimpuls *m*
  m. set Hauptapparat *m*
  m. station Sendestation *f*; Hauptanlage *f*, Erstnebenstellenanlage *f (Tel.)*, Erstanlage *f (Konferenzkreis)*; Leitstelle *f* (LSt) *(TEMEX)*
mastership Herrschaft *f (bei Busvergabe)*
matching network Leitungsanpassung *f*

m. option Anpaßmöglichkeit *f*
m. pad Anpaßglied *n*, Anpassung *f (Test)*
m. unit Anpassungseinrichtung *f*
materials Sachmittel *npl*
mating contact Gegenkontakt *m (Verbinder)*
matrix Matrix *f*; Kreuzschienenverteiler *m (Audio, Video)*; Verteiler *m*, Vielfach *n*
  m. board Lochrasterplatte *f*
  m. distribution panel Kreuzschienenverteiler *m*
  m. plug Koordinatenstecker *m (Signalverteiler)*
  m. scan recording Blockaufzeichnung *f (MAZ)*
  m. spacing Rastermaß *n*
  m. system Vielfachsystem *n*
  connecting m. Anschalte-, Zugangskoppler *m*
  switching m. Koppelfeld *n*, Koppelvielfach *n*
MATS (mobile automatic telephone system) Selbstwähl-Funktelefonsystem *n*
MATV s. master antenna TV
MAU s. medium attachment unit
MAU (multistation access unit) Mehrfachendgeräte-Anschlußeinheit *f (LAN)*
maximum capacity Maximalausbau *m*
  m. group delay distortion maximale Gruppenlaufzeitverzerrung *f (Symb.: Tg)*
  m. load Belastbarkeit *f (Übertragungsstrecke)*
  m. power Spitzenleistung *f*, Höchstleistung *f*, Dachleistung *f*
MC s. measurement & control
MCL Mercury Communications Ltd. *(2. Netzbetreiber in GB)*
MCMI (modified coded mark inversion) modifizierte codierte Schrittinversion *f (FO)*
MDF (main distribution frame) Hauptverteiler(gestell) *n* (HV, HVT)
MDNS (management data network service) Netzdienst *m* für Managementdaten
mean gain Mittenverstärkung *f*
  m. interconnecting number Mischungsverhältnis *n* (Q) *(Tel.-Anl.)*
  m. signal Gleichsignal *n*
  m. subjective opinion score (MOS) mittlerer Beurteilungs-Punktestand *m (Audio)*
  m. time between failures (MTBF) mittlerer Ausfallabstand *m*
  m. time to failure (MTTF) mittlere Zeit *f* bis zur (ersten) Störung, mittlere Funktionsdauer *f*
  m. time to repair (MTTR) mittlere Repa-

raturzeit *f*
m. value analysis Mittelwertverfahren *n (math.)*
means of authentication Berechtigungsmittel *n*
measurand Meßwert *m*, Meßgröße *f*
measure messen, erfassen; Maß *n*
measured value Meßwert *m*, Meßgröße *f*
measurement & control (MC) Messen, Steuern, Regeln *n* (MSR); Messen und Regeln *n* (MR)
measuring error Meßungenauigkeit *f*
mechanical design Aufbau *m*
Media Access Control (MAC) Endgeräte-Anschlußsteuerung *f (FDDI-Teilprotokoll nach IEEE 802, ergänzt LLC)*
medium attachment unit (MAU) Endgeräte-Anschalteeinheit *f*, Medium-Anschlußeinheit *f (Sende-/Empfangseinheit, LAN)*
m.-dependent interface Medium-Schnittstelle *f (LAN)*
m. discontinuity Medienbruch *m (DFÜ)*
m.-power satellite (MPS) Satellit *m* mittlerer Sendeleistung
m.-rate speech coding (MSC) mittelratige Sprachcodierung *f (dig. Audio, US)*
m.-sized concentrator mittlerer Konzentrator *m* (MKT)
MegaStream BT-Punkt-zu-Punkt-Digitalverbindung *f (2 MB/s, unterstützt G.703 und HDB3)*
membrane keypad Folientastatur *f*
memory Speicher *m*
m. content Speicherfüllung *f*
m. loading Speicherfüllstand *m*
menu Menü *n (Benutzeroberfläche zur Programmanwahl)*
m. page Programmvorschau-Seite *f (Fernsehtext)*
m. prompt(ing) Bedienerführung *f*
MES s. micro earth station
MESFET metal semiconductor FET *(Halbl.)*
meshed network Maschennetz *n*
message Nachricht *f*, Meldung *f*; Telegramm *n (TEMEX)*
m. block Funkblock *m (Mobilfunk)*
m. buffer Nachrichtenverteiler *m (dig. Vermittlung)*; Zwischenspeicher *m (Verm.)*
m. channel Nutzkanal *m*
m. discrimination Nachrichtenunterscheidung *f (ZGS.7 Schicht 3)*
m. handling service (MHS) Mitteilungsdienst *m*, mitteilungsfähiger Dienst *m*, Mitteilungs-Übermittlungs-System *n (CCITT Rec. X.400, ISO MOTIS)*

m. handling system (MHS) Nachrichtenübertragungssystem *n (CCITT Rec. X.400)*
m. header Nachrichtenkopf *m*
m. oriented signalling (MOS) Mitteilungssignalisierung *f*
M.-Oriented Text Interchange Standard (MOTIS) Mitteilungsdienst *m (ISO, entspricht CCITT Rec. X.400)*
m. preamble Nachrichtenkopf *m*
m. recording mode Nachrichtenablegebetrieb *m (Tel.)*
m. segment Teilnachricht *f (PCM-Daten, -Sprache)*
m. service Benachrichtigungsdienst *m*, Speicherdienst *m*
m. signal unit (MSU) Nachrichtenzeicheneinheit *f (ZGS.7)*
m. store (MS) Nachrichtenspeicher *m (CCITT Rec. X.400)*
m.-switched system nachrichtenvermitteltes System *n (Speichervermittlung)*
m. switching Sendungsvermittlung *f*; Nachrichtenvermittlung *f (TWX, Telex)*
m. telephone service (MTS) Ferngesprächsdienst *m (US, amtliche Bezeichnung)*
m. transfer agent (MTA) elektronisches Postamt *n (MHS SW, CCITT Rec. X.400)*; Mitteilungsaustausch-Systemteil *m*
m. transfer part (MTP) Nachrichtentransferteil *m*, Nachrichtenübertragungsteil *m (ZGS.7, CCITT Rec. Q.701...707)*
m. transfer service (MTS) Mitteilungs-Transfer-Dienst *m* (MT-Dienst) *(CCITT Rec. X.400, P1, OSI Schicht 7)*
messaging Mitteilungsübermittlung *f*, Nachrichtenübermittlung *f (CCITT X.400)*
messenger call Botenruf *m (Chef-TelAnl.)*; Gespräch *n* mit Herbeiruf
meter Meßinstrument *n*; Zähler *m (Gebühren)*
m. clock pulse Gebührentakt *m*
m. comparison Zählvergleich *m*
m. status log Zählwerkprotokoll *n*
metering Zählung *f (Tel.)*, Zeitzählung *f (Tel.,DK)*
m. fault Zählstörung *f*
m. pulses Gebührenimpulse *mpl*
metropolitan area network (MAN) Stadtnetz *n*, Regionalnetz *n (1 - 200 MB/s, IEEE 802.6, ANSI X3T9.5)*
MF (multiframe) Mehrfachrahmen *m*, Überrahmen *m (TDM)*
MFC (multifrequency code) Mehrfrequenz-Code *m*
MFLOPS million floating point operations per second
MHS s. message handling service

micro earth station (MES) Kleinstation f
(Sat., Ku-Band)
microcell Kleinzelle f (Mobilfunk)
Microcom Networking Protocol (MNP)
Microcom-Netzverbindungsprotokoll n
microinstruction Mikrobefehl m
microterminal Kleinstation f (Sat., Ku-Band)
microwave link Richtfunkstrecke f
   m. video distribution service (MVDS) Mikrowellen-Videoverteildienst m (GB)
mid-talkspurt clipping (MTC) Sprachausblendung f (PCM-Sprache)
midpoint of bit Bitmitte f
miniature fuse Geräteschutzsicherung f (G-Sicherung)
minicell Kleinzelle f (zellularer Mobilfunk)
MIS (management information service) Management-Informationsdienst m (VAS)
miscellaneous apparatus rack (MAR) Universalgestell n
mismatch Fehlabschluß m
mix mischen; hinterlegen (Vtx.-Mon.)
mixed communication Verbundkommunikation f (Daten/Sprache)
   m. configuration Mischbestückung f (Gestell)
   m. network Verbundnetz n
   m.-services communication Mischkommunikation f
mixing Überlagerung f (Frequenzen)
MJB (multi-joint box) Verbindungs- und Verteildose f (VVD) (Tel.)
MMI (man-machine interface) Mensch-Maschine-Kommunikation f
MNP s. Microcom Networking Protocol
mobile beweglich, mobil
   m. access radio (MAR) Mobilanschluß-Funkgerät n
   m. access system (MAS) Mobilfunk-Anschlußsystem n (an das Netz)
   m. automatic telephone system (MATS) Selbstwähl-Funktelefonsystem n
   m. base station Funkfeststation f (Mobilfunk einschl. C-Netz)
   m. radio Mobilfunk m
   m. (radio) concentrator Funkkonzentrator m (FuKo) (C-Netz)
   m. satellite service (MSS) mobiler Satelliten-Funkdienst m (CCIR)
   m. station Mobilstation f (MS) (C-Netz); Teilnehmer m, Teilnehmergerät n (TG) (Mobilfunk)
   m. subscriber Funkteilnehmer m
   m. switching centre (MSC) Funkvermittlungsstelle f (FVSt) (C-Netz);

Überleiteinrichtung f (ÜLE) (Mobilfunk)
   m. telephone Funktelefon n
   m. telephone service Funktelefondienst m
   m. terminal (MT) mobiles Endgerät n (GSM)
   m. (unit) Mobilteil m, Mobileinheit f
mode Modus m, Betriebsart f (BA)
   m. selection switch Funktionsschalter m
model Modell n; Ausführung f, Bauform f
modem (modulator/demodulator) Modem m, Anpassungseinrichtung f, Datenumsetzer m (DU), Umsetzer m (Datenübertragung auf analogen Leitungen)
   m. bypass Modem-Eliminator m, Nullmodem m (0-Modem)
   m. eliminator Modem-Eliminator m, Nullmodem m (0-Modem); Kreuzkabel n (DEE-DEE-Direktverbindung)
   m. socket Modemdose f (TAE 6 bzw. ADo 8)
modification wiring list Nachlegeliste f
modified monitored sum code MMS43-Code m (DBP BA-Leitungscode, 43 = 4B3T-Codierung)
   m. Palm Jacobus formula MPJ-Formel f
modulation rate Schrittgeschwindigkeit f, Schrittrate f
modulator Sendeumsetzer m (dig. TV)
   m. and demodulator stages Umsetzerstufen fpl
module Baugruppe f, Print n
   m. extractor Baugruppenziehwerkzeug n
   m. extractor tool Ziehwerkzeug n
   m. frame Baugruppenrahmen m
   m. group Großmodul n
   m. handle earth Blendenerde f
   19" rack size m. 19"-Raster-Modul n
modulo N Modulo-N n (eine Anzahl N von z.B. Telegrammen oder Rahmen, die vor Rücksetzen des Zählers bzw. erforderlicher Bestätigung hochgezählt werden kann)
MOH (music on hold) Wartemusik f
molested subscriber belästigter Teilnehmer m
monitor erkennen; mitlesen (Kanal), überwachen; Monitor m (Anzeige); Wächter m (Alarm)
monitored section Überwachungsabschnitt m
monitoring Ablaufüberwachung f, Ablaufverfolgung f, Aufschalten n, Beobachtung f, Überwachung f, Verfolgung f
   m., alarm and control facility (MAC) Überwachungs-, Alarm- und Kontrolleinrichtung f (Sat.-Bodenstation)
   m. decoder Meßdekoder m (RDS)
   m. detector Meßempfänger m (Funkruf)
   m. protection Aufschalteschutz m (Tel.)

m.-protected call Datenschutzverbindung f *(NStAnl.)*
monomode fibre Einmodenfaser f *(FO)*
MOS (Mean (subjective) Opinion Score) mittlerer Beurteilungs-Punktestand m
MOS (message-oriented signalling) Mitteilungssignalisierung f
MOSFET metal oxide silicon FET *(Halbl.)*
most significant bit (MSB) höchstwertiges Bit n
MOTIS (Message-Oriented Text Interchange Standard) Mitteilungsdienst m *(ISO, entspricht CCITT Rec. X.400)*
mounting adapter Einbausatz m
  m. hardware Befestigungsteile npl
  m. location Einbauplatz m
  m. rail Tragschiene f
movable ortsveränderlich, beweglich
MPLPC (multipulse linear predictive coding) Multipuls-LPC n
MPS (medium power satellite) Satellit m mittlerer Sendeleistung
MPT Ministry of Posts and Telecommunications *(GB)*
MPT 1327 *DTI Signalisierungsstandard für Bündelfunk (zufallsmäßiger Zugriff in S-Aloha-Technik mit dynamischer Rahmenlänge, Philips)*
MPX (multiplex) Multiplex n
MRJE (multileaving remote job entry) verschachtelte Jobfernverarbeitung f
MRS s. multi-role switch
MS (message store) Nachrichtenspeicher m *(CCITT Rec. X.400)*
MS s. mobile station
MS (music/speech switching) Musik-/Sprache-Umschaltung f *(RDS)*
MSB s. most significant bit
MSC Matrix Systems Corporation
MSC (Medium-rate Speech Coding) mittelratige Sprachcodierung f
MSC (mobile switching centre) Funkvermittlungsstelle f, Mobilkommunikations-Vermittlungsstelle f *(GSM)*
MSFN (Manned Spaceflight Network) Funkverbindungsnetz n für die bemannte Raumfahrt
MSK (minimum shift keying) Mindestwertumtastung f, Minimum-Frequenzumtastung f
MSP (manual switching position) Vermittlungsplatz m
MSS (mobile satellite service) mobiler Satelliten-Funkdienst m
MSU (message signal unit) Nachrichten-Zeicheneinheit f
MT s. mobile terminal

MTA (message transfer agent) elektronisches Postamt n
MTB (main traffic burst) Bündelburst m
MTBF (mean time between failures) mittlerer Ausfallabstand m
MTC (mid-talkspurt clipping) Sprachausblendung f
MTP (message transfer part) Nachrichtenübertragungsteil m
MTS (message telephone service) Ferngesprächsdienst m *(US)*
MTS (message transfer service) MT-Dienst m
MTTF (mean time to failure) mittlere Zeit f bis zur (ersten) Störung, mittlere Funktionsdauer f
MTTR (mean time to repair) mittlere Reparaturzeit f *oder* Reparaturdauer f
MULDEX s. multiplexer/demultiplexer
multi-access line Mehrfachanschluß m
  m.-access point Mehrfachanschluß m
  m.-address branching gefächerter Sprung m
  m.-address calling Rundsenden n
  m.-addressing device Rundsendeeinrichtung f
  m.-call Vielfachanruf m
  m.-endpoint connection Mehrpunktverbindung f
  m.-homing Teilnehmerdoppeleinbindung f *(Tel.)*
  m.-joint box (MJB) Verbindungs- und Verteildose f (VVD) *(Tel.)*
  m.-line IDA Multiplexanschluß m *(ISDN, BT PA, 2 MB/s, Kapazität 30xB_{64}+D_{64})*
  m.-role switch (MRS) Koppeleinrichtung f für Mehrfachnutzung
  m.-services terminal Mehrdienstterminal n *(Tel.)*
  m.-terminal installation Mehrfachendgeräte-Anschluß m
multibeam coverage Vielstrahlbedeckung f *(Sat.)*
multicoupler Antennenweiche f
multidrop Mehrpunktverbindung f *(MUXs, gemeinsamer Kanal für Mehrfachanschlüsse)*
multiframe (MF) Mehrfachrahmen m, Überrahmen m *(TDM)*
  m. alignment Überrahmensynchronisierung f *(PCM)*
  m. alignment signal Signalisierungs-Rahmenkennungswort n *(PCM)*
  m. frame alignment signal Mehrfachrahmen-Rahmenkennwort n (M-RKW), Multiframe-Rahmenkennwort n (M-RKW)
multiframing Mehrfachrahmensynchronisierung f

multifrequency code (MFC) Mehrfrequenz-Code *m (Zeichengabe)*
m. code signalling Mehrfrequenz-Code-Zeichen *n (PCM)*
m. receiver Mehrfrequenzempfänger *m* (MFE) *(NStAnl.)*
m. transmitter Mehrfrequenzsender *m* (MFS) *(NStAnl.)*
multifunction terminal Mehrdienstterminal *n (Tel.)*
multifunctional communication device Multikom-Gerät *n (ehem. Ceptel, Vtx-Terminal mit Telefonoption)*
multileaving remote job entry (MRJE) verschachtelte Jobfernverarbeitung *f*
Multiline BT-Primärratenanschluß *m (ISDN-S_{2M}, 2 MB/s, 30xB+D-Kanäle, heute ISDN 30)*
multimode dispersion Intermodendispersion *f (FO)*
multipath fading Mehrwege-Fading *n (Mobilfunk)*
multiple bit error Bit-Vielfachfehler *m*
m. access Vielfachzugriff *m*, Mehrfachzugriff *m*
m. polling Mehrfachabruf *m (Fax.)*
m. routing Mehrwegeführung *f*
multiplex Multiplex *n* (MPX); bündeln *(FO)*; zusammenstellen, zusammensetzen, multiplexen *(TDM)*
multiplexed analog components (MAC) gemultiplexte Analogkomponenten *fpl (TV)*
m. channels Kanalbündel *n*
m. D channel Multiplex-D-Kanal *m* (Dm) *(ISDN)*
multiplexer (MUX) Multiplexer *m*, Vielfach *n*, Vielfachübertrager *m*, Verteiler *m*

m./demultiplexer (MULDEX) Multiplexer/-Demultiplexer *m*
multiplexing Bündelung *f*, Multiplexierung *f*, Multiplexbildung *f*, Verschachtelung *f*, Vielfachübertragung *f*
multiplication Überlagerung *f (Pulsmodulation)*
multipoint conference system Mehrpunkt-Konferenzeinrichtung *f* (MKE)
m. network Knotennetz *n*
m.-to-point service Datensammeldienst *m*, Sammeldienst *m (VSAT)*
multipulse linear predictive coding (MPLPC) Multipuls-LPC *f*
multiservice communication Mehrfachkommunikation *f*
multistation access unit (MAU) Mehrfachendgeräte-Anschlußeinheit *f (LAN)*
Muse Multiple Sub-Nyquist Sampling Encoding *(NHK-HDTV-Codierungsmethode)*
music injection Musikeinspielung *f (Tel.)*
m. on hold (MOH) Wartemusik *f*; Musikeinspielung *f*
m./speech switching Musik-/Sprache-Umschaltung *f* (MS)
m.-while-you-wait Wartemusik *f*
mutilate verfälschen *(Zeichen)*, verstümmeln
muting elektronische Störaustastung *f* (ESA) *(FM-Rundfunk)*; Stummschaltung *f*
MUX s. multiplexer
MVDS (microwave video distribution service) Mikrowellen-Videoverteildienst *m (GB)*
MX (main exchange) Hauptvermittlungsstelle *f*

N

N-PSK (N phase shift keying) N-Phasenumtastung *f*
N-QAM (N quadrature amplitude modulation) N-Quadratur-Amplitudenmodulation *f* *(zellularer Mobilfunk)*
NAB National Association of Broadcasters *(US)*
NABTS North American Basic Teletext Specification *(US)*
NACK s. negative acknowledgement
nailed connection (NC) Langzeitverbindung *f (Hilfsdienstkanal, ISDN)*
name key Namentaste *f*, Zieltaste *f (K.-Tel.)*
   n. server (elektronisches) Namensverzeichnis *n (MHS SW, CCITT Rec. X.400)*
   n. server system elektronisches Verzeichnissystem *m*
NAP s. network access point
NAPI (Numbering and Addressing Plan Identifier) Numerierungs- und Adressierungskennung *f (ISDN)*
NAPLS (North American Presentation Layer Protocol Syntax) nordamerikanische Protokollsyntax *f* für die Präsentationsschicht *(AT&T/ANSI-Vtx-Standard, nach Telidon, Kanada)*
narrow-band (NB) Schmalband *n* (SB)
   n.-band FM (NFM) Schmalband-FM *f*
national code Landeskennzahl *f (Tel.)*
NB s. narrow band
NBDT (nadir bulk data transmission) Massendatenübertragung *f* im Nadir *(Sat.)*
NBS National Bureau of Standards *(US)*
NC s. nailed connection
NC s. network congestion
NCC s. network control centre
NCP s. network control program
NCP s. network control protocol
NCTA National Cable Television Association *(US)*
NCU s. network control unit
near-end echo Nahecho *n*
   n.-end crosstalk (NEXT) Nahnebensprechen *n*
   n.-instantaneous companding (NIC) echtzeitnahe Kompandierung *f (A/D-Quantisierung*
   n.-instantaneously companded audio multiplex (NICAM) echtzeitnah kompandiertes Tonfrequenz-Multiplex *n (digitales TV-Stereotonverfahren, DQPSK, 728 KB/s, GB)*
   n.-real-time echtzeitnah
negative acknowledgement (NACK) negative Bestätigung *f*; Schlechtquittung *f*
   n. phase relationship Gegenlauf *m (Filter, Phase)*
negatively acknowledged (N-ACK) unbestätigt
NEMP (nuclear electromagnetic pulse) nuklearer elektromagnetischer Impuls *m*
nested eingelagert, geschachtelt
NET (Norme Européenne de Télécommunication) Europäische Telekommunikationsnorm *f* CEPT standard *(s. Tabelle II)*
net bit rate Nutzbitrate *f (Übertragung)*
   n. loss *(US)* Restdämpfung *f*
network Netz *n (vernetzte Gruppe von Knotenpunkten - ISO TC97)*
   n. access Netzanschaltung *f* (NA) *(Funkruf)*
   n. access point (NAP) Anschlußpunkt *m* zu anderen Netzen
   n. architecture Netzarchitektur *f (Vtx.)*
   n. capabilities Netzeigenschaften *fpl*
   n. change-over system Netzersatzschaltung *f*
   n. computer Verbundrechner *m* (VR) *(Vtx.)*
   n. congestion (NC) Netzüberladung *f (Netzmeldung)*
   n. control centre (NCC) Netzkontrollzentrale *f* (NKZ)
   n. control program Netzsteuerprogramm *n* (NCP)
   n. control protocol Netzsteuerprotokoll *n* (NCP)
   n. control unit (NCU) Netzsteuereinheit *f (VSAT)*
   n. controller Einsteller *m* (EN)
   n.-dependent service attribute netzgestütztes Dienstmerkmal *n*
   n. entity Netzinstanz *f*, Vermittlungsinstanz *f*
   n. gateway (NG) Netzübergang *m* (NÜ) *(für DEE)*
   n.-independent netzunabhängig, endgeräteautark
   n.-independent service attribute autarkes Dienstmerkmal *n*

network

n. **interface card** (NIC) Netzschnittstellenkarte *f*
n. **interface unit** (NIU) Netzschnittstelleneinheit *f*
n. **interworking (unit)** Netzübergang *m*
n. **layer** Netzwerkebene *f*, Vermittlungsschicht *f (CCITT I.450 und I.451, Schicht 3, OSI 7-Schicht-Referenzmodell)*
n. **level** Netzebene *f (z.B. untere, obere N. im Fm-Netz)*
n. **management processor** (NMP) Netzführungsrechner *m*
n. **management system** Netzkontrolleinrichtung *f*
n. **node** Netzknoten *m (eine VSt.)*
n. **operator** Netzbetreiber *m*
n. **out of service** (NOS) Übertragung *f* im Netz gestört *(Schleifenprüfung)*
n. **service access point** (NSAP) Netzdienst-Zugriffspunkt *m (ZGS.7, CCITT Rec. Q.761...764)*
n. **status display** Netz-Zustandsanzeige *f*
n. **terminal selection** Polvorgabe *f (bei Schaltungsentwurf)*
N. **Terminating Equipment** (NTE) Netzabschlußeinrichtung *f (BT ISDN)*
N. **Terminating Unit** (NTU) Netzabschlußeinheit *f (BT ISDN)*
n. **termination** (NT) Netzabschluß *m*, teilnehmerseitiger Leitungsabschluß *m (ISDN, CCITT Rec. I.112)*; TEMEX-Netzabschluß *m* (TNA) *(TEMEX)*
N. **Termination and Test Point** (NTTP) Netzabschluß- und Meßstelle *f (BT)*
n. **termination point** (NTP) Hauptanschluß *m*
n. **timing** Synchronisation *f* durch das Netz
n. **user address** (NUA) Netzanschluß-Rufnummer *f (Paketvermittlung)*
n. **user identification** (NUI) Teilnehmerkennung *f (DBP DATEX-P, X.25)*
n. **voice protocol** (NVP) Netz-Sprachübertragungsprotokoll *n*
networked vernetzt
networking Netzverbindung *f*, Vernetzung *f*
new call Neubelegung *f*
N. **Line** (NL) Neue Leitung *f (V.25 bis)*
NEXT s. near-end crosstalk
NFM (narrow-band FM) Schmalband-FM *f*
NG s. network gateway
NHK (Japan Broadcasting Corp.) japanische Rundfunkgesellschaft *f*
nibble 4-Bit-Wort *n*, Tetrade *f*
NIC s. near-instantaneous companding
NIC s. network interface card

NICAM s. near-instantaneously companded audio multiplex
night service extension Nachtabfragestelle *f*, nachtgeschalteter NStA *m*
n. **service key** *or* **switch** Nachtschalter *m*; Vertretungsschalter *m (Chef-Sekretär-Anlage)*
NIU s. network interface unit
NL s. New Line
NMP s. network management processor
NMT 450, 900 Nordic (cellular) Mobile Telephone system *(450, 900 MHz)*
No (answer) Tone detected (NT) Keine Antwort *(V.23-Signal)*
no-current bit stromloser Schritt *m (FS)*
no loop closure on a/b wires Keine Belegung *f* (K.Bel.)
no-message state telegrammloser Zustand *m*
no-operation call Leerruf *m* (LR) *(C-Netz)*
no-reply call unbeantworteter Anruf *m*
No Signal signal "kein Signal" (KS)
nodal equipment Knoteneinrichtung *f*
n. **switching centre** Knotenvermittlungsstelle *f* (KVSt)
node Netzknoten *m*, Knotenpunkt *m*
noise Rauschen *n*; Signalgemisch *n*
n. **burst** Bündelstörung *f*
n. **component** Störanteil *m*
n. **generator** Quasizufallsgenerator *m* (QZG); Rauschsender *m*
n. **level** Stromrauschen *n*
n. **power ratio** (NPR) Rauschleistungs-(dichte)abstand *m* (RLA)
n. **spectrum** Störspektrum *n*
n. **window** Störtor *n (Schirmwirkung, Frequenzbereich)*
nominal loss Nenndämpfung *f*
non- -fremd, nicht ...
n.-**blocking** blockierungsfrei *(Koppelfeld)*
n.-**centralized control** dezentrale Steuerung *f*
n.-**chargeable subscriber** gebührenfreier Anschluß *m*
n.-**decreasing** nichtfallend *(Funktion)*
n.-**dialling** nicht wählfähig
n.-**increasing** nichtwachsend *(Funktion)*
n.-**linear distortion** Steilheitsverzerrung *f*
n.-**metering relay** Zählverhinderungsrelais *n*
n.-**operate current** Fehlstrom *m*
n.-**packet-mode DTE** Start-Stopp-DEE *f (asynchron arbeitende DEE mit Start- und Stoppbit)*
n.-**power-fed station** selbstgespeistes

Amt *n*
n.-preemptive priority nicht unterbrechende Priorität *f*
n. return to zero (change) (NRZ(C)) **code** Richtungsschrift *f (PCM-Code)*
n. return to zero inverted (NRZI) **code** Wechselschrift *f (PCM-Code)*
n. return to zero (mark) (NRZ(M)) **code** Wechselschrift *f (PCM-Code)*
n.-secure nicht verschlüsselt
n.-switched connection fest geschaltete Verbindung *f*; Festverbindung *f*; Festanschluß *m*
n.-urgent alarm (signal) Nicht-Dringend-Alarm *m* (N-Alarm) *(FS)*
n.-volatile memory Festspeicher *m*; Haftspeicher *m (DDR)*
n.-volatile RAM (NVRAM) nichtflüchtiger Direktzugriffsspeicher *m*
normal call number Langrufnummer *f*
n. disconnected mode abhängiger Wartebetrieb *m*
n. response mode (NRM) Aufforderungsbetrieb *m (HDLC)*
n. state Ruhestellung *f (Flipflop)*
n. use bestimmungsgemäßer Betrieb *m*
normalize normieren
norms Richtwerte *mpl*
NOS (network out of service) Übertragung *f* im Netz gestört
notch out aussparen *(Bits)*
notebook Terminregister *n (K.-Tel.)*
notepad Terminregister *n (K.-Tel.)*
NPR s. noise power ratio
NRM s. normal response mode
NRZ(C) s. non-return to zero (change)
NRZ(M,I) s. non-return to zero (mark, inverted)
NSAP (network service access point) Netzdienst-Zugriffspunkt *m (ZGS.7)*
NT s. No (answer) Tone detected
NT (network termination) Netzabschluß *m (ISDN)*; teilnehmerseitiger Leitungsabschluß *m*
NT1 *(NT mit Schicht-1-Funktionen, OSI-RM)*
NT2 *(NT mit Schicht-1-bis-3-Funktionen, OSI-RM)*
NT12 *(NT1 + NT2)*
NTE (Network Terminating Equipment) Netzabschlußeinrichtung *f (BT ISDN)*
NTP (network termination point) Hauptanschluß *m*
NTSC National Television System Committee *(Original-FBAS-TV-Codierungssystem, Frequenzmultiplexübertragungstechnik; auch: "Never Twice the Same Color", US)*
NTTP (Network Termination and Test Point) Netzabschluß- und Meßstelle *f (BT)*
NTU (Network Terminating Unit) Netzabschlußeinheit *f (BT ISDN)*
NU s. number unobtainable
NUA (network user address) Netzanschluß-Rufnummer *f (CCITT X.25)*
nuclear electromagnetic pulse (NEMP) nuklearer elektromagnetischer Impuls *m*
NUI (network user identification) Teilnehmerkennung *f*
nuisance caller Klingelstörer *m (Tel.)*
null character Nullzeichen *n*, Füllzeichen *n*
n. modem Nullmodem *m*, Modem-Eliminator *m*, Kreuzkabel n *(DEE-DEE-Direktverbindung)*
nulling Nullabgleich *m*
number conversion Rufnummernumsetzung *f (Nummern im Register)*
n. directory Rufnummernregister *n*
n. of incoming calls Belegungsangebot *n*
n. of seizures Belegungszahl *f*
n. of transmission channels Bündelstärke *f*
n. unobtainable (NU) Nummer *f* unbeschaltet (NU)
n. unobtainable tone NU-Ton *m*
Numbering and Addressing Plan Identifier (NAPI) Numerierungs- und Adressierungskennung *f (ISDN I.450)*
numeric mode Ziffernmodus *m (EWS)*
NVP (network voice protocol) Netz-Sprachübertragungsprotokoll *n*
NVRAM s. non-volatile RAM
Nyquist theorem Nyquist-Theorem *n*, Abtasttheorem *n*

O

O & M service (operation and maintenance service) Betriebsdienst *m*
OBN (optical broadband network) optisches Breitbandnetz *n*
observational switchboard Beobachtungsplatz *m*
obtainable erreichbar *(Teilnehmer)*
OC-1 (optical channel) optischer Kanal *m* (50 MB/s, SONET-Standard)
occupied besetzt, belegt *(Leitung)*
octet Oktett *n* (8-Bit Byte)
   o. timing Bytetakt *m (X.21)*, Worttakt *m (TE)*
ODA s. Office Document Architecture
ODA s. Open Document Architecture
ODIF s. Office Document Interchange Format
OEIC (optoelectronic IC) optoelektronische Schaltung *f (FO)*
OEM (original equipment manufacturer) Originalgerätehersteller *m*
off-air call set-up Verbindungsaufbau *m* ohne Sprechkanal *(C-Netz-Merkmal)*
   o.-hook abhängen, abheben, aushängen
   o.-hook detection Anreizerkennung *f*
   o.-hook program Aushängeprogramm *n*
   o.-hook state Beginnzustand *m (Tel.)*
   o.-line lokal *(FS-Betrieb)*; nicht angeschlossen
offered call angebotene Belegung *f*, Verbindungswunsch *m*, angebotene Belegung *f (Tel.-Anl.)*
   o. load Verkehrsangebot *n*, Angebot *n* *(Verkehrswert des angebotenen Verkehrs, Tel.-Anl.)*
offering Anbieten *n (eines Gesprächs nach Aufschalten)*, Anklopfen *n*
   o. signal Meldezeichen *n (von der Vermittlung)*; Aufschaltezeichen *n*
   o trunk group Zubringerbündel *n*, Zubringerleitung *f (Tel.-Anl.)*
office *(US)* Vermittlung *f*, Amt *n*
   o. communication Bürokommunikation *f* (BK)
   o. computers mittlere Datentechnik *f* (MDT)
   O. Document Architecture (ODA) Dokumentenarchitektur *f (ISO DIS 8613)*
   O. Document Interchange Format (ODIF), Dokumenten-Austauschformat *n (ISDN,* *CCITT Rec. I.415, ISO DIS 8613)*
   o. selector Amtswähler *m*
offset Versatz *m*
   o. current Fehlstrom *m*
OFTEL Office of Telecommunications *(GB)*
OIC (optical IC) optischer Baustein *m (FO)*
OMC (operation and maintenance centre) Betriebs- und Wartungszentrum *n (GSM)*
OMT (orthogonal mode transducer *oder* orthomode transducer) Polarisationsweiche *f*
ON (Other Networks) andere Programme *npl (RDS)*
on demand nach Teilnehmerwahl *f (Transportdienst)*
on duty diensthabend
on-hook aufhängen, auflegen *(Handapparat)*
on-hook dialling Wahl *f* bei aufliegendem Hörer, Wählen *n* mit aufgelegtem Handapparat (WaH) *(K.-Tel.)*
on-hook pulse (negative) Einhängeminus *n*
on-hook pulse (positive) Einhängeplus *n*
on-hook state Schlußzustand *m (zeigt Auflegen des Handapparats in Rückwärtsrichtung an)*
on hot standby in Betriebsbereitschaft *f* stehen
on-line (aktiv) angeschlossen, On-line
on-line monitoring Betriebsüberwachung *f*, Überwachung *f* ohne Betriebsunterbrechung
on-line user Teilhaber *m (Tel.-Anl.)*
on/off colour effect Farbschwindeffekt *m*, Ein-/Auseffekt *m (Folientastatur)*
ONA s. Open Network Architecture
one-way gerichtet
   o.-way propagation time einfache Echolaufzeit *f (PCM)*
   o.-way service Einwegdienst *m (z.B. Teletext oder Funkruf)*
ONP s. Open Network Provision
open offen, getrennt *(Schaltung)*
   o.-circuit voltage Leerlaufspannung *f*
   o. competitive tender offene Ausschreibung *f*
   O. Document Architecture (ODA) Dokumentenarchitektur *f (CCITT Rec. I.410)*
   o.-ended line leerlaufende Leitung *f*
   o. listening Lauthören *n (K.-Tel.)*
   o. listening key Lauthörtaste *f (K.-Tel.)*

open 214

o.-loop control Steuerung *f*
O. Network Architecture (ONA) Offene Netzarchitektur *f (FCC)*
O. Network Provision (ONP) Richtlinien *fpl* für offene Netze *(EG)*
O. System Interconnection (OSI) Offene Kommunikation *f (ISO DIS 8613, US-Netzstandard)*
o.-wire circuit *oder* line Freileitung *f*
opening flag Beginn-Flagge *f (ZGS.7)*
operability Funktionsfähigkeit *f*
operable arbeitsfähig, funktionsfähig, funktionstüchtig
operate bedienen, betätigen, betreiben
  o. time Ansprechzeit *f (Relais)*
operating Bedienen *n*, Betreiben *n*
  o. aisle Bedienungsgang *m (Gestell)*
  o. and maintenance panel Bedienungs- und Wartungsfeld *n*
  o. and monitoring centre Betriebsführungs- und überwachungszentrale *f* (BÜZ)
  o. channel Betriebskanal *m* (BK) *(Richtfunk)*
  o. condition Betriebszustand *m*
  o. cycle Arbeitstakt *m*
  o. data acquisition (unit) Betriebsdatenerfassung *f* (BDE)
  o. data entry (unit) Betriebsdatenerfassung *f* (BDE)
  o. error Gebrauchsfehler *m*, Fehlbedienung *f*
  o. experience Betriebserfahrungen *fpl*
  o. frequency Arbeitsfrequenz *f*, Betriebsfrequenz *f*
  o. hardware Betriebstechnik *f*
  o. life Betriebslebensdauer *f*
  o. manual Betriebshandbuch *n*
  o. mode Betriebsart *f* (BA)
  o. panel Bedienfeld *n*
  o. personnel Bedien(ungs)personal *n*
  o. state Betriebszustand *m*; Arbeitslage *f (einer Triggerschaltung)*
  o. system (OS) Betriebssystem *n (SW)*; Bedienungsrechner *m* (BR) *(Tel.)*
  o. threshold Ansprechwert *m (Schaltung)*
  o. time Eigenzeit *f*, Ansprechzeit *f (Relais)*; Einschaltdauer *f*; Betriebzeit *f*, Betriebsdauer *f*, Laufzeit *f*
operation Betrieb *m*, Bedienung *f*; Gang *m*, Funktion *f*
  O. and Maintenance (O&M service) Betriebsdienst *m*
  o. mode indication Anwendungskennung *f (Übertragungssignal)*
  description of o. Funktionsbeschreibung

f
operational data Betriebsdaten *npl*
  o. task betriebstechnische Aufgabe *f*
operator Bediener *m (DEE)*; Betreiber *m (Netz)*; Platzkraft *f (Tel.)*
  o.'s answering delay Warten *n* auf Abfragen
  o. assistance Wahlhilfe *f*
  o.-assisted calls Handvermittelung *f*
  o. interface Bediener-, Benutzer-Oberfläche *f*
  o.'s position Vermittlungsplatz *m (NStAnl.)*
  o. prompt(ing) Bedienerführung *f*
  o. recall Eintreteaufforderung *f*, Platzherbeiruf *m*
  o.'s station Bedienplatz *m*
  o. support system Platzkraftunterstützungssystem *n* (PLUS) *(Funkruf)*
  o.-switched handvermittelt
  o.'s telephone set Abfrageapparat *m*
OPLL s. optical phase-locked loop
opposite-seizing signal Gegenbelegzeichen *n (Tel.)*
optical optisch, Licht-
  o. broadband network optisches Breitbandnetz *n* (OBN)
  o. grating optischer Raster *m*
  o. heterodyne receiver optischer Überlagerungsempfänger *m (FO, $f_{ZF}>0$)*
  o. homodyne receiver optischer Überlagerungsempfänger *m (FO, $f_{ZF}=0$)*
  o. IC (OIC) optischer Baustein *m (FO)*
  o. phase-locked loop (OPLL) optischer Phasenregelkreis *m (FO)*
  o. receiver optischer Empfänger *m* (OE)
  o. transmitter optischer Sender *m* (OS)
  o. waveguide (OWG) Lichtwellenleiter *m* (LWL)
  o. waveguide transition Querschnittswandler *m (FO)*
-optimized -freundlich
optional priority freier Vorzug *m*
options Bestückung *f (Geräte)*
optoelectronic IC (OEIC) optoelektronische Schaltung *f* (FO)
O/R name s. originator/recipient name
orbit Umlaufbahn *f*, Umlauf *m (Sat.)*
ordinary subscriber Normalteilnehmer *m*
original address Ausgangsadresse *f*
  o. equipment manufacturer (OEM) Originalgerätehersteller *m*
originate a call Ruf *m* beginnen, einleiten
  o. mode Sendemodus *m*
originated traffic erregter Verkehr *m*
originating exchange A-Vermittlungsstel-

le f (A-VSt.), Ursprungsvermittlung f
originator Urheber m (einer Verbindung), Quellstation f
o./recipient name (O/R name) O/R-Name m (CCITT Rec. X.400, MHS)
orthomode transducer (OMT) Polarisationsweiche f (Sat.)
OS (operating system) Betriebssystem n
oscillation Schwingung f
OSI (Open Systems Interconnection) Offene Kommunikation f
OSInet NBS-Prüfnetz n für OSI-konforme Produkte (US)
OSITOP (international association of OSI users) OSITOP-Anwendervereinigung f (OSI + TOP)
OTC Overseas Telecommunications Commission (AUS)
Other Networks (ON) andere Programme npl (Dienstinformation, RDS)
out-band signalling Signalisierung f ausserhalb des Bandes, Außerband-Signalisierung f, Outband-Signalisierung f
o.-of-area equipment Vorfeldeinrichtung f
o. of lock ausgerastet, außer Tritt m
o. of order gestört (Verbindung)
o. of phase phasenverschoben, asynchron
o. of service außer Betrieb
o.-slot signalling Außerband-Signalisierung f, Zeichengabe f außerhalb der Zeitlagen
outage Ausfall m, Stillstand m, Nichtverfügbarkeit f
outbound Verteilrichtung f (VSAT)
outgoing abgehend, gehend, Abgangs-
o. access abgehender Zugang m (von einem Netz zu einem Teilnehmer in einem anderen Netz, CCITT)
o. call abgefragte Verbindung f, gehende Verbindung f
o.-call barring facility gehende Sperre f (Tel.)
o. call set-up Verbindungsaufbau m gehend (VAG) (C-Netz)
o. circuit gehender Satz m (GS)
o. conductor section Leiterabgang m (Folientastatur)

outlet Austritt m, Anschluß m; Steckdose f
3-wire power o. Terko-Steckdose f (Gestell)
outletbar Suchbrücke f (zu einem freien Anschlußweg/-satz, Tel.)
output Ausgabe f, Ausgang m, Ausgangssignal n, Leistung f
o. circuit Wahlnachsendesatz m (WNS)
o. frequency Ausgangsschwingung f (als Signal)
o. line Abnehmer m (PCM-Daten/Sprache)
o. switching network Auskoppelfeld n
outside line Amtsleitung f, Amtsverbindung f (NStAnl.)
outstanding charge data Schuldnerdaten npl
outstation Unterstation f (TEMEX)
overall attenuation Restdämpfung f
o. decoupling capacitor Summenentkopplungskondensator m
o. delay Gesamtlaufzeit f
o. loss Restdämpfung f
overflow call Überlaufbelegung f (Tel.-Anl., auf ein anderes Abnehmerbündel überlaufende angebotene Belegung)
o. traffic Überlaufverkehr m (Tel.-Anl.)
overhead Kopfteil m (TDM); Zusatzaufwand m (Steuerung, Wiederholungen)
o. information Paketkopfinformation f
o. line Freileitung f (el.)
path o. (POH) Pfadkopfteil m (TDM)
section o. Abschnittsrahmenkopf m (STM-1, CCITT G.70X)
transport o. Übertragungskopfteil m (TDM)
overlap signalling Einzelwahlziffern-Wahlverfahren n (ZGS.7 MTP)
overload capability Überlastbarkeit f
o. level Betriebsgrenze f (Datenblatt)
overshoot Vorläufer m (Puls)
oversized überdimensioniert
OWG (optical waveguide) Lichtwellenleiter m (LWL)
own facility eigene Einrichtung f
own-number dialling Eigenwahl f (NStAnl.)

P

P code (precision code) P-Code *m (GPS)*
PA (primary rate access) Primärmultiplexanschluß *m* (PMXA) *(ISDN)*
PA system (public address system) ELA-Anlage *f*, Beschallungsanlage *f*
PABX (private automatic branch exchange) Nebenstellenanlage *f (nach BS6301, 6324, nur Sprachband)*; Wählnebenstellenanlage *f*; bedienungslose Wählunteranlage *f* (WU-Anl.) *(veraltet)*
PABX line group Sammelanschluß *m*
PACE (paging access control equipment) Funkrufleitzentrale *f (BTMC, Sat.-Paging)*
packet Datenpaket *n*, Paket *n (diskrete Datenbitvollgruppe mit Nutzinformationssegment, Wegeleit-, Folgesteuerungs- und Fehlersicherungsinformationen)*
   p. assembly facility Paketierer *m* (PAK)
   p. assembly/disassembly facility (PAD) Paketierer/Depaketierer *m (DEE, die nicht-X.25-Terminals mit einem X.25-Netz verbindet. PAD-Protokoll-bezogene Standards sind X.3, X.28, X.29)*
   p. body Paketrumpf *m*
   p./circuit interface (PCI) Datenpaket-Leitung-Schnittstelle *f*
   p. disassembly facility Depaketierer *m* (DEPAK) *(PCM-Daten)*
   p. group Paketbündel *n*
   p. interleaved paketweise verschachtelt
   p. handler (PH) Paketsteuerung *f (ISDN)*
   p. length in bits (PLB) Paketlänge *f* in Bit
   p. loss rate Paketverlustrate *f* (PVR)
   p. losses Paketverluste *mpl*
   p.-mode paketorientiert
   p.-mode DTE Paket-DEE *f*
   p.-oriented interexchange trunk paketorientierte Verbindungsleitung *f* (VI-P)
   p. radio (PR) Paketradio *n (paketvermittelter Funkdienst, AX25 - Amateur-X.25, VHF)*
   p. radio unit (PRU) Paketradioeinheit *f*
   p. rate (PR) Paketrate *f* (PR) *(Pakete/Sek.)*
   p. retransmission Paketwiederholung *f*
   p. sequencing Paketreihung *f*
   p. stream Paketblock *m*
   p. switch (PS) Paketvermittlung *f (US)*
   P. Switch Stream (PSS) paketvermittelter Dateldienst *m (BT, entspricht Datex-P)*
   p. switched paketvermittelt
   p.-switched connection Wählanschluß *m* der Gruppe P (Datex-P) *(DBP)*
   p.-switched data exchange (network) paketvermitteltes Datennetz *n* (Datex-P, Dx-P) *(CCITT X.25)*
   p.-switched data network (PSDN) paketvermitteltes Datennetz *n* (Datex-P, Dx-P)
   p.-switched public data network (PSPDN) paketvermitteltes öffentliches Datennetz *n*
   p. switching network Paketvermittlungsnetz *n* (PV-Netz)
   p.-terminal customer Paketteilnehmer *m*
   p. utilization ratio Paketnutzungsgrad *m*
   p. voice terminal (PVT) Sprechstelle *f* für Paketvermittlung
Packetized Ensemble Protokoll (PEP) Protokoll *n* für die paketierte Datengesamtheit *(Datenkompressionsprotokoll für hochratige Modems)*
pad stopfen *(Zeichen, EWS)*
   p. (character) Füllzeichen *n*
PAD s. packet assembly/disassembly facility
padding (stop) element Stopfschritt *m*, Füllschritt *m (Geschwindigkeitsanpassung)*
PAG s. paging
page Seite *f*, Tafel *f (Vtx.)*
   p. layout Seitengestaltung *f (Vtx.-Mon.)*
pager Pager *m*, Personenrufempfänger *m*, Personenrufendgerät *n*, Nur-Ton-Empfänger *m (Funkrufdienst)*; Anrufmelder *m (Mobilfunk)*
pages per hour (pph) Seiten pro Stunde *(Drucker)*
paging (PAG) Funkruf *m (RDS)*; Personenruf *m*
pair Doppelader *f (Tel.)*
PAL (phase alternation line) zeilenweiser Phasenwechsel *m (FBAS-TV-Codierung, Frequenzmultiplexübertragungstechnik auf Basis des NTSC-Systems)*
PAM (pulse amplitude modulation) Pulsamplitudenmodulation *f*
PAMR (public access mobile radio) öffentlicher beweglicher Landfunk *m* (öbL),

öffentlicher mobiler Landfunk m (ömL)
Pan European Paging service (PEP) Europäischer Funkrufdienst m (EFuRD)
panel Platte f, Feld n, Tafel f
  p. jack Einbaubuchse f
panic button Not-Aus-Druckknopf m; Schlagtaster f
paper alignment Papieranpassung f (Fax.)
  p. tape Lochstreifen m (LS) (FS)
  p. tape reader (PTR) Lochstreifenleser m
P/AR s. peak/average ratio
parallel computer Mitrechner m
  p. input/output (PIO) Parallel-Ein-/Ausgabe f (Port)
  p. input/output bus paralleler Ein-/Ausgabebus m (PEAB)
  p. (telephone) set Nebenapparat m
parent exchange Hauptvermittlung f
parity bit Paritätsbit n (Übertragungssignal)
  p. check Paritätskontrolle f
  p. check bit Kennschritt m (FS)
parked position Parkstellung f (Tel.)
parking Parken n, Parkierung f (Ruf)
partial authorization Teilberechtigung f
partially selected teilbewählt (Leitung)
particularize instanzieren (einen Logikzustand mit 'H' oder 'L' i.)
partition noise Verteilungsrauschen n (FO)
partner Teilnehmer m (Konferenz)
party Konferenzteilnehmer m, Teilnehmer m (Tel.)
  p.-line Gemeinschaftsleitung f (Tel.)
pass Durchlauf m (Programm, Band); Durchgang m, Überflug m (Sat.)
  p.-band attenuation Durchlaßdämpfung f, Grunddämpfung f (Filter)
  p.-band loss Grunddämpfung f
passive optical network (PON) passiv übermittelndes optisches (Fernmelde-)Netz n (FO)
  p. station Wartestation f
password Kennwort n, Paßwort n
patch through durchschalten, verbinden
patching Rangieren n, Schalten n
  p. error Steckfehler m (Kreuzschiene)
path Gang m (optisch); Weg m, Zweig m
  p. finding Wegermittlung f
  p. loss Funkfelddämpfung f (Sat.)
  p. overhead (POH) Pfadkopfteil m (TDM)
  p. selection Wegermittlung f, Wegesuche f
pattern Muster n, Raster m (Frequenz), Takt m (Impuls)
pause indication Pausenmeldung f (EWS)

pay TV Gebührenfernsehen n
  p.-per-view TV Gebührenfernsehen n
payload Nutzlast f (Nutzsignalteil des PCM-Rahmens, ATM)
PBX (private branch exchange) Nebenstellenanlage f (NStAnl)
PBX main line Nebenstellen-Anschlußleitung f
PBX-to-Computer-Interface (PCI) Nebenstellenanlage-Computer-Schnittstelle f (US)
PBX with dialling capability Wählanlage f (W-Anl.)
PCB (printed circuit board) Print(platte) f, Leiterplatte f
PCB module Kartenbaugruppe f (KBG)
PCC (protocol communications controller) Protokoll-Übertragungsablaufsteuerung f
PCI (packet/circuit interface) Datenpaket-Leitung-Schnittstelle f
PCI s. PBX-to-Computer-Interface
PCM (pulse code modulation) Pulscodemodulation f
PCM30 (primary rate TDM system) Primärmultiplexsystem n (DBP, 2 MB/s, 30 Kanäle Kapazität)
PCN (personal communication network) persönliches Kommunikationsnetz n (DTI-Konzept als Telepoint-Nachfolgedienst, DCE + GSM, 1,7-2,3 GHz)
PCR (preventative cyclic retransmission) vorbeugende zyklische Wiederholung f
PDAU (physical delivery access unit) Anschlußeinheit f für physikalische Zustellung
PDC (Programme Delivery Control system) Programm-Zustellungssteuersystem n (TV)
PDM (pulse duration modulation) Pulsdauermodulation f
PDN (public data network) öffentliches Datennetz n
PDOP (position dilution of precision) Positions-Präzisionsverringerung f (GPS)
PDU (protocol data unit) Informationseinheit f (Vtx.)
PDX (private digital exchange) private Telekommunikationsanlage f
peak code Aussteuergrenze f, maximale Codeaussteuerung f (PCM)
  p./average ratio (P/AR) Spitze-Mittelwert-Verhältnis n (analoge Leitungsmessung)
peakedness factor Spitzigkeitsfaktor m (Stat.)
peer entity Partnerinstanz f (OSI)
  p. protocol Verständigungsprotokoll n

PEL (photographic element) fotografisches Element n (Fax.)
PELV (protected extra low voltage) geschützte Kleinspannung f (Tel.)
PEP (Packetized Ensemble Protocol) Protokoll n für die paketierte Datengesamtheit
PEP (Pan European Paging service) europäischer Funkrufdienst m (jetzt Euromessage)
performance Leistung f
  p. check Funktionsprüfung f
  p. criterion Leistungsmaß n
  p. index Gütekriterium n (Reg.)
period Ablaufzeit f (Verzögerungsglied); Periode f, Zeitdauer f
  p. under review Berichtszeitraum m
periodic ringing Weiterruf m
peripheral interface adapter (PIA) Peripherie-Adapter m
permanent bleibend, fortdauernd, permanent
  p. circuit fest geschaltete Verbindung f
  p. connection Festanschluß m
  p. node ortsfeste Knotenvermittlung f (ofKnV)
  p. switch ortsfeste Knotenvermittlung f (ofKnV)
permanently installed fest eingebaut
persistence check Wiederholungsprüfung f (eine bitweise Prüfung von PCM-Empfangsdaten)
personal call Gespräch n mit Voranmeldung
  p. earth station (PES) persönliche Erdfunkstelle f (VSAT)
  p. identification number (PIN) persönliche Kennummer f (Telepoint-System, elektronischer Bankverkehr)
  p. mobile communicator (PMC) persönliches mobiles Kommunikationsgerät n (Mobilfunknetz PCN im Bereich 1,7-1,9 GHz)
  p. portable telephone (PPT) persönlicher Funkfernsprecher m (GB)
PES s. personal earth station
PFM (pulse frequency modulation) Pulsfrequenzmodulation f
PH (packet handler) Paketsteuerung f
phase Phase f; Strang m (E-Mot.); Takt m
  p. angle Phasenwinkel m, Phasenlagenabstand m
  p.-angle controlled phasenangeschnitten (SV)
  p. displacement Phasenverschiebung f, Phasenabweichung f
  p. encoding Richtungstaktschrift f
  p. front Phasenfläche f (FO)

  p. hit Phasensprung m (CCITT Rec. 0.95)
  p. jitter Phasenjitter m, Phasenzittern n (DFÜ)
  p. modulation (PM) Phasenmodulation f
  p. region Phasenbereich m (PCM)
  p. segregation Phasenisolation f
  p. shift Phasenverschiebung f; Phasensprung m, Phasendrehung f, Phasenabweichung f
  p. shift keying (PSK) Phasenumtastung f
  p. space Phasenraum m (PCM)
phone plug Klinkenstecker m
phonecard Berechtigungskarte f (ÖKartTel.)
  p. telephone öffentliches Kartentelefon n (ÖKartTel.) (DOV-Technik)
  p. telephone access unit Anschalteeinheit f Kartentelefon (AEK) (amtsseitig, DOV-Technik)
phoneme Phonem n, Lautform f
phonepoint Phonepoint m (öffentliche Telepoint-Feststation, BT CT2, Reichweite 200 m, nicht DECT-kompatibel)
photographic element (PEL) fotografisches Element n (Fax.)
physical delivery access unit (PDAU) Anschlußeinheit f für physikalische Zustellgeräte (z.B. Drucker, CCITT Rec. X.400)
  p. delivery device physikalisches Zustellgerät n (CCITT Rec. X.400)
  p. layer physikalische Schicht f, Bitübertragungsschicht f; (CCITT I.430, Schicht 1, OSI-Referenzmodell); Hardwareschicht f (FDDI)
  p. line wirkliche Leitung f
  p. service Bitübertragungsdienst m
PI (Programme Identification) Programmketten- oder Senderkennung f (SK) (RDS)
PIA s. peripheral interface adapter
pick-up Heranholen n (Ruf, Tel.)
picture element Bildpunkt m, Pixel n (TV)
  p. mail Bildspeicherdienst m
  p. phone Bildtelefon n
  p.-signal encoding Bildcodierung f
pigtail Anschlußfaser f (FO)
pilot lamp Kontrollampe f, Meldelampe f, Betriebsanzeige f
  p. broadband network Breitbandvorläufernetz n (BVN), Vorläufer-Breitbandnetz n (VBN) (DBP, FO, 565 MB/s)
pin Anschluß m, Stift m
  p. assignment Anschlußbelegung f
  p. configuration Anschlußanordnung f (IC)
  p.-contact and receptacle strip Stift-

und Federleiste f
-pin -polig *(Verbinder)*
2-p./3-wire power outlet Schuko-Steckdose f *(HW)*
8-p. connector plug 8-poliger Anschlußdosenstecker m (ADoS8) *(ISDN, X-Schnittstelle)*
PIN s. personal identification number
PIN (positive-intrinsic-negative) positiv dotiert - eigenleitend - negativ dotiert *(Photodiode)*
PIN (Programme Identification Number) Programm-Reihenfolge f *(RDS)*
PIN/TAN (personal identification number/- transaction number) persönliche Kennummer/Transaktionsnummer f *(Bankverkehr-Paßwortcode)*
ping pong method Ping-Pong-Verfahren n *(Vollduplex-Zeitgetrenntlageverfahren, Übertragungsrichtung gleichfrequenter Signale wechselt, z.B. im 8-kHz-Rhythmus)*
PIO (parallel input/output) Parallel-Ein-/ Ausgabe f
PIO (programmable input/output) programmierbare Ein-/Ausgabe f
pitch Teilung f; Raster m *(Verbinder-Stifte)*; Schlaglänge f *(FO)*
pixel Bildelement n, Bildpunkt m, Pixel n *(pl: Pixeln, TV)*
planar cable shelf Flächenkabelrost n *(Gestell)*
p. waveguide Schichtwellenleiter m *(FO)*
plane Ebene f *(Verteiler)*
planning Planung f, Projektierung f
p. regulations for telecommunications equipment Fernmeldebauordnung f (FBO) *(DBP)*
PLB (packet length in bits) Paketlänge f in Bit (PLB)
plesiochronous plesiochron *(freilaufend)*; unabhängig getaktet
PLMN (public land mobile network) öfffentliches Landfunknetz n, Funkfernsprechnetz n
plug-in device Steckgerät n
  as a p.-in device in Einschubtechnik f
p.-in jumper Steckbrücke f
p.-in location Einbauplatz m
p. storage *oder* **panel** Steckerdepot n, Steckerablage f *(Verteilerstecker)*
PM (phase modulation) Phasenmodulation f
PM (processable mode) Nachverarbeitungsmodus m
PMC (personal mobile communicator) persönliches mobiles Kommunikationsgerät n

(Vorschlag für 1,7-1,9-GHz-Mobilfunknetz, GB)
PMR (private mobile radio) privater Mobilfunk m, nicht öffentlicher beweglicher *oder* mobiler Landfunk m (nöbL, nömL)
PMR chipcard Telekarte f *(nömL)*
PMXA (primary rate access) (PA) Primärmultiplexanschluß m *(ISDN)*
PN (pseudo noise) Pseudozufallsfolge f
PN generator (pseudo noise generator) Pseudozufallsfolgen-Generator m
POCSAG Post Office Standardisation Advisory Group *(GB; alphanumerische Signalisierungsnorm für Funkruf, vom CCIR als 'Radio Paging Code No.1' übernommen)*
POH (path overhead) Pfadkopfteil m *(TDM)*
point of entry Zugriffspunkt m; Ankerpunkt m *(Datennetz)*
p. of origin Ausgangspunkt m, Ursprung m
p. of sale (POS) Kassenterminal n *(elektron. Bankverkehr)*
p. of sale terminal Kassenterminal n *(elektron. Bankverkehr)*
p.-to-multipoint Punkt-zu-Mehrpunkt *(Verbindung)*
p.-to-multipoint network Punkt-zu-Mehrpunkt-Netz n, Punkt-zu-Multipunkt-Netz n (PMP-Netz) *(VSAT)*
p.-to-multipoint switch Verteilvermittlung f
p.-to-point (PTP) Punkt-zu-Punkt *(Verbindung)*
p.-to-point circuit Standleitung f *(Mobilfunk)*
p.-to-point communication Standverbindung f
p.-to-point connection fest geschaltete Verbindung f, Festverbindung f, Festanschluß m; Zweipunktverbindung f *(RS232)*
p.-to-point link Standverbindung f
Pointel französisches Telepoint-System n *(öffentliches Funkfernsprechen)*
pointer Hinweismarke f
polarizer Polarisator m *(Sat.)*
policing Überwachung f *(Bitrate, ATM)*
polling Abfrage f *(Daten, Terminals, Telefaxstationen)*, Fernabfrage f; Abruf m, Fernabruf m *(Fax.)*; Aufrufverfahren n, Sendeaufruf m; abfragen
p. call Sendeaufforderung f, Lockruf m
p. method zyklisches Zuteilungsverfahren n *(Zugriffssteuerung)*
p. primary centre zyklusführende Haupt-Z-Station f

p./**selecting mode** Aufrufbetrieb *m*
p. **unit for telephone connections with data service** Abfrageeinrichtung *f* für Telefonanschlüsse mit Datenverkehr (AED) *(FTZ)*
polluted verseucht *(Rauschen)*
PON (passive optical network) passiv übermittelndes optisches (Fernmelde-)Netz *n (FO)*
port Port *m*, Anschluß *m (MUX)*; Eingang *m*, Ausgang *m*; Kanal *m*
portable transceiver tragbares Funktelefon *n (Mobilfunk, auch: 'Schleppy')*
p. **VF test set** Fernmeldemeßkoffer *m*
POS s. point of sale
position Einbauplatz *m*, Lage *f*; -polig *(Schalter)*, Stelle *f (DV)*
p. **dilution of precision** (PDOP) Positions-Präzisionsverringerung *f (GPS)*
p. **point** Wegpunkt *m (Navig.)*
positive phase relationship Mitlauf *m (Filter, Phase)*
post-dialling delay Rufverzug *m*
p.-**processing of call data** Rufdatennachverarbeitung *f*
POTS (plain old telephone system) das einfache alte Fernsprechsystem *n ("Dampftelefon")*
power Energie *f*, Kraft *f*, Leistung *f*, Strom *m*, Vermögen *n*
p. **connection** Netzanschluß *m*
p. **consumption** Leistungsaufnahme *f (in W)*
p. **density spectrum** Leistungsdichtespektrum *n (Sat.)*
p.-**down mode** Ruhezustand *m (HW)*
p. **down switch** Sparschalter *m (Mobilfunk)*
p. **failure mode** Netz-Ausfallbetrieb *m*
p.-**fed** fernspeisbar
p.-**fed station** ferngespeistes Amt *n*
p. **feeding** Speisung *f (von DEE)*
p.-**feeding ...** (RPF) Fernspeise- (FSP) *(Tel.)*
p. **level difference** Leistungspegelabstand *m*
p.-**on reset** Einschaltrückstellung *f*
p. **rating** Leistungsaufnahme *f (in W)*
p. **supply (unit)** (PS, PSU) Stromversorgung *f (STRV, SV)*
p. **switching** Fernschaltsystem *n*
p. **system frequency** Betriebsfrequenz *f*
p.-**up mode** Betriebszustand *m (HW)*
PPC (program-to-program communication) Programm-Programm-Verbindung *f*
pph (pages per hour) Seiten pro Stunde

(Drucker)
PPM (pulse phase modulation) Pulsphasenmodulation *f*
PPT (personal portable telephone) persönlicher Funkfernsprecher *m (GB)*
PR (packet radio) Paketradio *n*
PR (packet rate) Paketrate *f*
PR (private) privat *(Tel.)*
pre-drilled gebohrt *(Chassis, Print)*
pre-mating pins voreilende Stifte *mpl (Verbinder)*
precedence Vorrang *m*, Priorität *f*
p. **handling system** Vorrang-Handhabungssystem *n*
p. **level** Vorrangstufe *f*
precision code (P code) P-Code *m (GPS, Zyklusperiode 7 Tage)*
predicted value Prädiktionswert *m (Bildcodierung)*, Schätzwert *m*
preemphasis Vorverzerrung *f*, Voranhebung *f*; Akzenturierung *f*, Preemphase *f*
preemption Prioritäts-Unterbrechung *f*, Prioritätsverkehr *m (Tel.)*
p. **tone** Unterbrechungsankündigungston *m*
preemptive priority unterbrechende Priority *f*
preference Priorität *f*; Anhalt *m*
prefix Zugangskennziffer *f*, Präfix *m*; Verkehrsausscheidungsziffer *f*
preliminary regulation vorläufige Regelung *f*
prescaler Vorteiler *m (Synthesizer)*
preselection code Vorwahlkennzahl *f (Tel.)*
p. **stage** Vorwahlstufe *f (Verm.)*
presentation layer Darstellungsschicht *f*, Präsentationsebene *f (Schicht 6, OSI 7-Schicht-Referenzmodell)*
p. **standard** Darstellungsstandard *m (für Vtx-Terminals, CEPT-Profil 1...3)*
press button Druckknopf *m (Verbinder)*
Prestel *(Videotex-Standard in GB, Belgien; Cept-Profil 3, s. Tabelle VIII)*
preventative cyclic retransmission (PCR) vorbeugende zyklische Wiederholung *f (Fehlerkorrekturverfahren, ZGS.7)*
primary Leitsteuerung *f (Funktion der Kommunikationssteuerung)*
p. **(master) station** Erstanlage *f (Konferenzkreis)*; Erstnebenstellenanlage *f*, Hauptanlage *f*
p. **frequency control** Leitfrequenzsteuerung *f*
p. **information** Hauptinformation *f*
p. **line switch** erster Anrufsucher *m*
p. **protection (circuit)** Grobschutz *m*
p. **rate access** (PA) Multiplexanschluß *m*, Primärmultiplexanschluß *m* (PMXA), Primärratenanschluß *m (ISDN S_{2M}, 2 MB/s,*

Kapazität 30xB_{64}+D_{64}-Kanäle, CCITT Rec. I.421)
p. station Leitsteuerungsstation f (HDLC)
primitive Dienstelement n (DIN), Meldung f, Primitive n, Schnittstellenelement n (ZGS.7, Elementarnachricht für die vertikale Verständigung zwischen Schichten; Grundeinheit des Maschinenbefehls)
graphical p. Darstellungselement n (Kreis, Linie usw., Vtx.)
principal Auftraggeber m (AG)
printed backplane gedruckte Rückverdrahtung f (GRV) (Gestellverdrahtung)
p. circuit board (PCB) Leiterplatte f, Printplatte f
printer terminal Schreibstation f
printing speed Zeichengeschwindigkeit f
printout Druckprotokoll n
prioritize priorisieren
priority Priorität f; Bevorrechtigung f, Vorrang m
p. A A-wertig (AIS, Fehlermeldung)
p. grading Prioritätsstaffelung f
p. level Prioritätsstufe f
p. number Prioritätsziffer f (Mobilfunk)
p. return information Schnellrückmeldung f
assign p. priorisieren
with emergency p. katastrophenberechtigt
with p. A A-wertig (AIS, Fehlersignal)
privacy Abhörsicherheit f, Mithörsicherheit f (Tel.); Geheimhaltung f; Vertraulichkeit f
protected-p. call Datenschutzverbindung f (NStAnl.)
data p. Datenschutz m
private (PR) privat (Tel.)
p. automatic branch exchange (PABX) Nebenstellenanlage f (NStAnl) (wählfähig), Wählnebenstellenanlage f
p. branch exchange (PBX) Nebenstellenanlage f (NStAnl) (nach BS6450)
p. circuit Festanschluß m (BT)
p. digital exchange (PDX) private Telekommunikationsanlage f
p. key privater Schlüssel m (symmetrisches Verschlüsselungssystem mit begrenzter Gültigkeit, Chipkarten)
p. management domain (PRMD) privates MHS-System n; privater MHS-Versorgungsbereich m (CCITT Rec. X.400)
p. mobile radio (PMR) privater Mobilfunk m (DTI, UK), nichtöffentlicher beweglicher oder mobiler Landfunk m (nöbl,nömL) (gewöhnlich Simplex, umfaßt Teilnehmerbetriebsklasse, Bündelnetze)
p. network Hausnetz n, hauseigenes Netz n
p. transatlantic telephone cable (PTAT) privates transatlantisches Telefonkabel n
privately owned PBX private Fernsprech-Nebenstellenanlage f
PRMD s. private management domain
PRN s. pseudo-random noise
probability of delay Wartewahrscheinlichkeit f
proceed-to-send signal Abruf m
p. to dial signal Wahlaufforderungszeichen n (Tel.)
process verarbeiten (Ruf); bedienen (Signal); abarbeiten (Blöcke)
processable mode (PM) Nachverarbeitungsmodus m (Teletex, CCITT Rec. X.200)
processing equipment Aufbereitungseinrichtung f (ABE) (ISDN-Vtx)
processor Prozessor m, Rechenwerk n (DV); Steuerwerk n, Verarbeitungsschaltwerk n, Schaltwerk n (Vermittlung)
profile Profil n, Kontur f
low p. niedrige Bauform f
potential p. Potentialverlauf m
program programmieren; belegen
p. bit Nutzbit n
p. control unit Programmsteuereinheit f (PE) (EWS)
programmable input/output (PIO) programmierbare Ein-/Ausgabe f
programme delivery control system (PDC) Programm-Zustellungssteuersystem n (TV-Rundfunkdienst)
P. Identification (PI) Programmkettenkennung f, Senderkennung f (SK) (RDS)
P. Identification number (PIN) Programm-Reihenfolge f (RDS)
p. line Modulationsleitung f (Rundfunk)
p. organiser Veranstalter m (Rundfunkdienste)
P. Service (PS) Programmname m (RDS)
p.-to-program communication (PPC) Programm-Programm-Verbindung f
P. Type (PTY) Programmartenkennung f (RDS)
progress Fortschritt m; Verlauf m
p. signal Dienstsignal n
p. tone Warteton m (Tickerzeichen)
progression Verlauf m; Polygonzug m (Vektor)
p. matrix Weiterschaltmatrix f
progressive fortschreitend, allmählich; sukzessive
p. error kontinuierlicher Fehler m

prompts Sprachansagen *fpl (in Sprachspeicherung)*
propagation Ausbreitung *f*, Fortpflanzung *f*
  p. angle Führungswinkel *m (FO)*
  p. coefficient Gangkonstante *f*
  p. constant Übertragungsmaß *n (Kabel)*
  p. delay Ausbreitungslaufzeit *f (von Paketen)*
  p. time Laufzeit *f (von Paketen)*
proper delay system reines Wartesystem *n*
protect sichern *(Übertragung)*
protected geschützt; gesichert *(Daten)*
  p. extra low voltage (PELV) geschützte Kleinspannung *f (Tel.)*
  p.-privacy call Datenschutzverbindung *f (NStAnl.)*
protection class Schutzart *f*
protective ground Schutzerde *f (V.24/-RS232C)*
protocol Protokoll *n*, Vereinbarung *f (Satz von Datenübertragungsregeln)*
  p. communications controller (PCC) Protokoll-Übertragungsablaufsteuerung *f*
  p. data unit (PDU) Informationseinheit *f (Vtx.; ISO, ein zwischen Netzinstanzen ausgetauschtes Datenpaket)*
  p. discriminator Protokolldifferenzierung *f*, Protokollkennung *f (ISDN ZGS.7)*
prototype approval Versuchszulassung *f (ZZF)*
  p. construction Musterbau *m*
proving Probebetrieb *m*; Garantienachweis *m*
provisional recommendation vorläufige Empfehlung *f (CCITT)*
PRU (packet radio unit) Paketradioeinheit *f*
PS (packet switch) Paketvermittlung *f (US)*
PS s. Programme Service
PSDN (packet-switched data network) paketvermitteltes Datennetz *n*
PSDS s. Public Switched Digital Service
pseudo-noise (PN) Pseudozufallsfolge *f (PZF) (Code)*
  p.-noise generator Pseudozufallsfolgen-Generator *m*
  p.-random noise (PRN) Pseudozufallsfolge *f (PZF)*
PSK (phase shift keying) Phasenumschaltung *f*, Phasenumtastung *f*
  4PSK Phasenumtastung *f* mit vier Zuständen
PSM (pulse step modulation) Pulsstufenmodulation *f*, Treppenstufenmodulation *f*
PSPDN (packet-switched public data network) paketvermitteltes öffentliches Datennetz *n*
PSS (Packet Switch Stream) paketvermittelter Dateldienst *m (BT, entspricht Datex-P, X.25)*
PSTN s. public switched telephone network
PTAT (private transatlantic telephone cable) privates transatlantisches Telefonkabel *n*
PTO s. public telecommunications operator
PTP (point-to-point) Punkt-zu-Punkt *(Verbindung)*
PTR (paper tape reader) Lochstreifenleser *m*
PTT (Postal, Telegraph and Telephone administration) Postverwaltung *f*
PTT-owned circuits posteigene Stromwege *mpl*
PTY s. Programme Type
public access mobile radio (PAMR) öffentlicher beweglicher Landfunk *m (öbL)*, öffentlicher mobiler Landfunk *m (ömL)*
  p. address system (PA system) ELA-Anlage *f*, Beschallungsanlage *f*
  p. CT2 service Telepoint-Dienst *m (öffentlicher Funktelefondienst)*
  p. data network (PDN) öffentliches Datennetz *n*
  p. key öffentlicher Schlüssel *m (asymmetrisches Verschlüsselungssystem, bei dem ein Teil des Schlüssels veröffentlicht wird, Chipkarten)*
  p. land mobile network (PLMN) Funkfernsprechnetz *n*, öffentliches Landfunknetz *n*
  p. maritime radio service Seefunkdienst *m*
  p. phonecard phone öffentliches Kartentelefon *n (ÖKartTel) (BT)*
  p.-service broadcast station öffentlich-rechtliche Rundfunkanstalt *f*
  P. Switched Digital Service (PSDS) öffentlicher digitaler Vermittlungsdienst *m (BOC-Dienst, AT&T-CSDC, US)*
  p. switched telephone network (PSTN) Drahtnetz *n*, Selbstwählfernsprech-Drahtnetz *n*, öffentliches (Post-)Netz *n*, Postnetz *n*, öffentliches Fernsprechwählnetz *n*
  p. telecommunications operator (PTO) Anbieter *m* öffentlicher TK-Dienste *(z.B. Mercury, GB)*
  p. videotex terminal öffentliches Btx-Terminal *n (Ö-Btx) (DBP)*
pull nachziehen *(Frequenz)*
  p.-in period Einschwingzeit *f (PLL)*
  p. into synchronism in Tritt ziehen *oder* fallen
  p. out of lock außer Tritt ziehen *oder* fallen, kippen
  p.-out range Ausrastbereich *m (Signalsynchronismus)*

pulling into lock Intrittfallen *n*;
Aufsynchronisieren *n*, Intrittziehen *n*
pulse Impuls *m*, Puls *m*
  p. action Impulswahl *f*
  p. amplitude modulation (PAM) Pulsamplitudenmodulation *f*
  p. code modulation (PCM) Pulscodemodulation *f*
  p. dialling Impulswahl *f*
  p. dialling (loop disconnect) method Impulswahlverfahren *n* (IWV) *(Tel.)*
  p. duration modulation (PDM) Pulsdauermodulation *f*
  p. duty ratio *oder* **factor** Impulstastverhältnis *n*, Tastverhältnis *n*
  p. fault location Pulsfehlerortung *f (PCM-Daten)*
  p. frequency modulation (PFM) Pulsfrequenzmodulation *f*
  p. period Pulsperiode *f*, Schrittdauer *f*
  p. phase modulation (PPM) Pulsphasenmodulation *f*
  p. signal Impulskennzeichen *n* (IKZ) *(Tel., für Durchwahl)*
  p. spacing Taktzeit *f*
  p. speed Wahlfrequenz *f (Tel.)*
  p. step modulation (PSM) Pulsstufenmodulation *f*, Treppenstufenmodulation *f*
  p. tail Nachschwinger *m*
  p. time delay Impulslaufzeit *f (Kabel)*
  p. train Impulsserie *f*, Pulsfolge *f*, Impulsfolge *f*
  p. width modulation (PWM) Pulsbreitenmodulation *f*
pulsed gepulst, getaktet, getastet
punched-card reader Lochkartenleser *m* (LKL)
  p. tape Lochstreifen *m* (LS) *(FS)*
  p.-tape reader (PTR) Lochstreifenleser *m*
pure-chance traffic (reiner) Zufallsverkehr *m*
push-fitting Anschlagen *n (Kabel)*
pushbutton dialling Tastwahl *f (Tel.)*
  p. dialling receiver for malicious call identification Fangtastenwahlempfänger *m* (FTE) *(Tel.)*
  p. signal Tastwahlzeichen *n*
  p. telephone Fernsprecher *m* für Tastwahl, Tastfernsprecher *m*
put through durchstellen *(Ruf)*
putting into service Inbetriebnahme *f (Einrichtung)*
PVT (packet voice terminal) Sprechstelle *f* für Paketvermittlung
PWM s. pulse width modulation

Q

Q bit s. qualifier bit
Q-CIF ş. quarter CIF
Q-series of CCITT Recommendations Q-Serie *f* der CCITT-Empfehlungen *(betrifft das Zeichengabesystem Nr.7)*
QA s. quality assurance
QAM s. quadrature amplitude modulation
QASK s. quadrature amplitude shift keying
QMF s. quadrature mirror filter
QOS s. quality of service
QPSK s. quadrature phase-shift keying
QPSK s. quaternary PSK
QPSX s. queued packet synchronous switch
QRN s. quasi-random noise
QSAM s. quadrature sideband amplitude modulation
QTAM s. queued telecommunications access method
quad bit coding Quadbit-Codierung *f* (2^4 = 16 Bit, QAM)
quadrature amplitude modulation (QAM) Quadratur-Amplitudenmodulation *f*
   q. amplitude shift keying (QASK) Quadratur-Amplitudenumtastung *f*
   q. mirror filter (QMF) Quadratur-Spiegelfilter *n (dig. Audio-Teilbandfilter, DAB)*
   q. phase-shift keying (QPSK) Quadratur-Phasenumtastung *f*
   q. sideband amplitude modulation (QSAM) Quadratur-Seitenbandamplitudenmodulation *f*
qualification test Typenprüfung *f (FTZ)*
qualifier bit (Q bit) Q-Bit *n*, Unterscheidungsbit *n (ISDN NUA)*
quality Qualität *f*; Güte *f (Filter)*
   q. assurance Qualitätssicherung *f* (QS)
   q. of service (QOS) Dienstgüte *f*
   q. per unit length Belag *m*
quantization Quantisierung *f*, Rasterung *f*, Stufung *f*, Schrittweitenbestimmung *f*; Signalraster *m*, Signaltiefe *f*
   q. size Quantisierungsstufe *f*

quantize quanteln, quantisieren
quantizing level Quantisierungspegel *m (Sprachcodierung)*
quarantine service Zurückstellungsdienst *m*
quarter CIF (Q-CIF) gemeinsames Zwischenformat *n* mit Viertel-Pixelzahl *(CCITT-Bildtelefonstandard mit 38016 Pixeln)*
quartet Tetrade *f (4-Bit Byte)*
quasi-full availability quasivollkommene Erreichbarkeit *f*
   q.-random (bit) sequence Quasizufallsfolge *f* (QZF)
   q.-random noise (QRN) Quasizufallsfolge *f*
quaternary PSK (QPSK) Vierphasen-Modulation *f (Sat.)*
query Abfrage *f (Daten)*
queue Warteschlange *f (PCM-Daten, Sprache)*
   q. discipline Abfertigungsreihenfolge *f (Wartesystem)*
   the block has reached the head of the q. der Block *m* is an der Reihe
queued access method erweiterte Zugriffsmethode *f*
   q. packet synchronous switch (QPSX) synchrone Koppeleinrichtung *f* mit Paketwarteschlangenbetrieb *(FDDI, MAN)*
   q. telecommunications access method (QTAM) erweiterte TK-Datenzugriffsmethode *f*
queuing Warten *n*, Reihen *n*, Staffeln *n*; Parken *n (Ruf)*; Warteschlangenbetrieb *m*
   q. buffer Wartespeicher *m*
   q. delay Wartezeit *f*
   q. device Reihenordner *m*, Warteordner *m*
   q. network Warteschlangennetz *n (PCM-Daten, Sprache)*
   q. time Staffelzeit *f*
quiescent state Ruhezustand *m (EWS)*
quint bit coding Quintbit-Codierung *f* (2^5 = 32 Bit, hochratige Modems)
quote tone Ansage-Anfangston *m (Tel.)*

R

R-TDMA (reservation TDMA) TDMA *m* mit Buchung *(Sat.)*
RA s. rate adaptation
RACE Research and development for Advanced Communications in Europe *(Eureka-Projekt, FO-Netz, HDTV)*
rack Gestell *n*, Gestellrahmen *m*
r. **base** Gestellsockel *m*
r. **equipment** Gestellbelegung *f*
r. **face layout** *oder* **plan** Gestellbelegung *f*
r. **frame** Gestellrahmen *m* (GR)
r. **front layout** *oder* **plan** Gestellbelegung *f*
r. **row** Gestellreihe *f*
r. **row base** Gestellreihenfuß *m*
r. **shelf** Gestellrost *m*, Rost *m* *(Kabel)*, Etage *f*, Baugruppenträger *m*
r. **suite** Gestellreihe *f*
r. **unit** (RU, U) Höheneinheit *f* (HE) *(1 HE = 1 3/4", 44,45 mm; Gestell)*
19" r. 19"-Gestell *n*, Großrahmen *m*
radial network Strahlennetz *n*
radiance Strahldichte *f (FO, in N)*
radiant emittance Leuchtdichte *f (FO, in cd/m^2)*
r. **intensity** Strahlstärke *f (FO, in W/sr)*
radiated interference Störstrahlung *f*
radiation centre Antennenschwerpunkt *m*
r. **pattern** Antennendiagramm *n*, Antennencharakteristik *f*
radio Funk *m*, Rundfunk *m*, Rundfunkgerät *n*
r. **(relay) link** Richtfunkstrecke *f*, Richtverbindung *f* (RV)
r. **access point** (RAP) Funkanschlußpunkt *m (zum Netz, Tel.)*
r. **checks/measurements office** Funkkontroll-Meßstelle *f*
r. **communication service** Funkdienst *m*
r. **data system** (RDS) Radio-Datensystem *n (EBU-Spezifikationsdokument Tech. 3244-E)*
r. **data transmission** Datenfunk *m*
r. **determination satellite service** (RDSS) Satelliten-Ortungsfunkdienst *m (US)*
r. **frequency** (RF) Hochfrequenz *f* (HF) *(gewöhnlich ab 150 kHz)*
r. **frequency interference** (RFI) Funkstörung *f*
r. **hop** Richtfunkstrecke *f*; Funkfeld *n*

r. **interface** Luftschnittstelle *f (Tel.)*
r. **interference suppression** Funkentstörung *f*
r. **link** Richtfunkstrecke *f*
r. **link protocol** (RLP) Funkverbindungsprotokoll *n (GSM, mit ARQ)*
r. **PABX** Funk-Nebenstellenanlage *f* ; mobile Nebenstellenanlage *f*
R. **Paging Code No.1** Funkrufcode *m* Nr.1 *(vom CCIR übernommener POCSAG-Code)*
r. **paging service** Funkrufdienst *m*
r. **paging switching centre** Funkrufvermittlungsstelle *f* (FuRVSt) *(Cityruf)*
r. **relay** Richtfunk *m* (RiFu)
r. **relay section** Richtfunkabschnitt *m*
r. **relay (station)** Funkvermittlung *f*
r. **relay station cable network** Zubringersystem *n* für Richtfunk
r. **relay (switching centre)** Funküberleitstelle *f (C-Netz)*
r. **relay system** Richtfunknetz *n*
r. **signalling system** Funkmeldesystem *n* (FMS)
r. **supervisor** (RSV) Funküberwachung *f*
r. **telefax** Funkfax *n*
r. **telegraphy** Tastfunk *m*
r. **telephone** Funktelefon *n*
r. **telephony** (RT) Sprechfunk *m*
r. **teleswitching** Funk-Fernschaltsystem *n (GB; FW - Nachtstrom-Fernschaltung)*
r. **teletype** (RTTY) Schreibfunk *m*
r. **text (service)** Radiotext *m (RDS)*
r. **trunking** Bündelfunk *m (nömL)*
Radiocom 2000 *(zellulares Mobilfunksystem, FR, 200 u. 400 MHz)*
radiodetermination service Ortungsfunkdienst *m*
radiofax Funkfax *n*
radiolocation service nichtnavigatorischer Ortungsfunkdienst *m*
radiotelephone Funkfernsprecher *m*
radiotelephony (RT) Funkfernsprechen *n (Mobilfunk, nömL)*
r. **service** Funkfernsprechdienst *m*
radioteletype (RTTY) Funkfernschreiben *n*
radius of propagation Ausstrahlungsradius *m (Sat.)*
rain attenuation Regendämpfung *f (Sat., Mikrowellen)*

rainfall rate Regenintensität *f (Sat., Mikrowellen)*
ramification Verästelung *f (Netz)*
random broadcast zufallsmäßiger Rundruf *m*
  r. multiple access (RMA) zufallsmäßiger Vielfachzugriff *m (Sat.)*
  r. noise stochastisches Rauschen *n*
  r.-number generator Zufallsgenerator *m*
range Bereich *m (Meßgerät)*, Entfernung *f (Radar)*, Hub *m (Spannung, Signal)*, Reichweite *(Sender)*
  r. of expected values Erwartungsbereich *m (Bildcodierung)*
  r. of faulty operation Abschaltebereich *m (Zeichengabestrecke)*
  r. of power supply Speisereichweite *f (Fernspeisung, in Ohm)*
  r. predictive code modulation bereichsprädiktive Codemodulation *f (Bereich von Erwartungswerten, Bildcodierung)*
  r. switch Bereichsumschaltung *f* (BU)
RAP s. radio access point
RARE (Réseaux Associés pour la Récherche Européenne) Vereinigung *f* der Netzbetreiber für europäische Forschung
raster Raster *m*, Bildraster *m (Anzeige)*; Abtastfeld *n*
  r. image processor (RIP) Rasterbildprozessor *m (DTP)*
rate Geschwindigkeit *f*, Rate *f*, Tarif *m*
  r. adaptation (RA) Geschwindigkeitsanpassung *f (GSM)*
  r. of a clock Gang *m* einer Uhr *(in ns/d für Atomuhr)*
  r. of change Gradient *m*, Steilheit *f (Wert, z.B. Spannung)*, zeitliche Änderung *f*
  r. of impairment Störbeeinflussung *f (ISDN)*
  r. of phase change Phasensteilheit *f*
  r. of voltage change Spannungssteilheit *f*
  at a 10-ms r. im 10-ms-Zeitraster *oder* Rhythmus
rated range Nennbereich *m*
  r. working voltage Isolationsspannung *f* (FO)
ratings Betriebsdaten *npl*, Nennwerte *mpl*
ratio Verhältnis *n*, Abstand *m*
raw data Ausgangsdaten *npl*
RB (return to bias) Rückkehr *f* zur Grundmagnetisierung, Rückkehr *f* zum Ausgangszustand
RBOC Regional Bell Operating Company *(US)*
RC (access computer *oder* local *oder* regional computer) Teilnehmerrechner *m* (TR,TNR) *(Vtx.)*
RC s. Receive Clock
RC (regional centre) Fernamt *n*
RC (regional computer) Teilnehmerrechner *m* (TR, TNR) *(Videotex)*
RC (resistor-capacitor circuit) belasteter Kondensator *m*
RD s. Receive Data
RDS s. radio data system
RDS (running digital sum) laufende Digitalsumme *f*
RDSS s. radio determination satellite service
re-call Zweitanruf *m*, Wiederanruf *m (K.-Tel.)*
re-storing Wiedereinschreiben *n*
read addressing Ausleseadressierung *f*
reading Anzeige *f (Meßgerät)*, Stand *m (Uhr)*
ready status Betriebsbereitschaft *f*
  r. criterion Bereitschaftskriterium *n (EWS)*
  r. to send ausgabebereit, sendebereit
real component Wirkanteil *m*
  r.-time clock (RTC) Echtzeituhr *f*
  r.-time kernel Echtzeitkern *m (Steuer-Software)*
  r.-time monitoring Echtzeit-Ablaufverfolgung *f*
reassign wiedereingliedern *(TLN in Warteschlange)*
recall neu rufen; abrufen *(Meldungen in E-Mail)*; Neuruf *m*; Wiederherbeiruf *m*; Herbeiruf *m*, Rückruf *m (von Platzkraft)*
Recallcard Recallcard *f (laseraktualisierbare Speicherkarte, BT, mit WORM-Laufwerk)*
receive aufnehmen, empfangen
  R. Clock (RC) Empfangsschrittakt *(V.24/-RS232C)*
  R. Data (RD) Empfangsdaten *(V.24/RS232C)*
  r. identifier Empfangsadresse *f (PCM-Daten)*
  r. loudness rating (RLR) Empfangslautstärke-Index *m (Tel.)*
  r. module Empfangsbaustein *m (PCM)*
  r. not ready (rnr) keine Empfangsbereitschaft *f (Vtx.)*
  r. only (RO) Nur-Empfang *m (Sat.-TV)*
  r. only satellite (ROS) Satellitenempfangsantenne *f (Antenne)*
  r. path Empfangszweig *m*
  r. ready (rr) Empfangsbereitschaft *f (Vtx.)*
  r. requests for connection Verbindungswünsche *mpl* aufnehmen
  r. terminal Empfangsendgerät *n (Mobil-*

funk)
receiver Empfänger *m* (E); Aufnehmer *m*, Wandler *m*
  r. capsule Hörkapsel *f (Tel.)*
receiving channel Empfangskanal *m*, Empfangszug *m*
  r. level equivalent Empfangsbezugdämpfung *f (FO, Tel.)*
receptacle (strip) Federleiste *f*
recirculating Wiederholung *f (Pakete)*
recognized private operating agency (RPOA) Betriebsgesellschaft *f*
reconnect wiedereinschalten, entsperren
reconnection Freigabe *f (eines TLN-Anschlußes)*
reconstructed sample zurückgebildeter Abtastwert *m*
record aufzeichnen, erfassen; Satz *m (DV)*
recorded announcement equipment Ansagegerät *n (Tel.)*
  r. announcement service Ansagedienst *m*
recorder trace Schreiber-Mitschrift *f*
recording Aufzeichnung *f*, Registrierung *f*, Mitschnitt *m*, Mitschrieb *m*
  r. chart Meßstreifen *m*
  r. field trip Meßkampagne *f*
  r. device Protokollgerät *n*
  r. oscilloscope Registrieroszillograph *m*, Oszilloreg *n*
  r. programme Meßkampagne *f*
recovery Einschwingen *n (Transienten)*, Wiedergewinnung *f (Daten)*
  r. point, Rückzugspunkt *m*
  r. procedure Wiederherstellung *f*
  r. voltage einschwingende Spannung *f*
rectified current Richtstrom *m (TDM, Richtfunk)*
redial neu wählen
redialling Wahlwiederholung *f (WW)*
2nd-exchange r. Nachwahl 2. Amt *(nur MFVF-Vermittlungen)*
redirection Umlenkung *f*, Weiterleitung *f*, Weiterschaltung *f (Ruf)*
reduce vermindern, abbauen
reduced accuracy bedingte Genauigkeit *f*
  r. instruction set computer (RISC) Computer *m* mit verringertem Befehlsvorrat
redundancy Redundanz *f*
reel Spule *f (Band)*
reference Bezug *m*, Referenz *f*, Hinweis *m*
  r. configuration Bezugspunktkonfiguration *f (CCITT Rec. I.112)*
  r. equivalent Bezugsdämpfung *f (PCM)*
  r. model (RM) Referenzmodell *n* (7-Schicht OSI-Modell, s. Tabelle I)
  r. point Bezugspunkt *m (CCITT Rec. I.*

112)
  r. shaper Führungsformer *m (Reg.)*
  r. signal Sollwert *m (KO)*, Vergleichssignal *n*
  r. to something auf etwas abstützen *(Werte)*
  r. tone Normalton *m*
reflection loss Stoßdämpfung *f (FO)*
  r. point Stoßstelle *f (FO)*
reflective mixer Reflexionsmischer *m (FO)*
reflector Antennenspiegel *m*
refraction Brechung *f (FO)*
refresh rate Bildwechselfrequenz *f*, Bildelement-Wiederholfrequenz *f (Monitor)*
regeneration Aufbereitung *f (Impulse)*; Störbefreiung *f (von Signalen)*
regenerative repeater Zwischenregenerator *m* (ZWR) *(Tel., ISDN BA)*
regenerator section Regeneratorfeld *n (Tel.)*
regime Betriebszustand *m (System)*
regional Bezirks-, regional
  r. centre (RC) Fernamt *n*
  r. computer (RC) Teilnehmerrechner *m* (TR,TNR) *(Vtx.)*
  r. exchange (RX) Knotenvermittlungsstelle *f* (KVSt)
  r. postal district administration Oberpostdirektion *f* (OPD) *(DBP)*
  r. radio-paging service Stadtfunkrufdienst *m* (SFuRD, Cityruf) *(DBP, nach POCSAG-Standard)*; Ortsruf B *(Schweiz, nach POCSAG-Standard)*; Piepserl *m (Österreich)*
register erfassen, aufzeichnen
  r. finder marker Registersuchermarkierer *m* (RSM)
registered mobile subscriber beheimateter Funkteilnehmer *m*
regular directory number Langrufnummer *f (K.-Tel.)*
reject abweisen, unterdrücken; Wiederholungsaufforderung *f (Netzbetrieb)*
rejection device Abweisvorrichtung *f (Verkehrssteuerung)*
related bezogen; Abbild-
relation Beziehung *f (z.B. Zeichengabebeziehung im Netz)*; Verknüpfung *f*
relay Relais *n* (HW); Brückenfunktion *f* (GSM); Richtfunkverbindung *f*
release Auslösung *f*, Freigabe *f (für Weitergabe)*; freigeben *(Signal, Verbindung)*
  R. Complete Auslösebestätigung *f (ZGS.7 SCCP)*
releasing delay Abfallverzögerung *f (Re-*

lais)
reliable sicher, verläßlich, funktionssicher
RELP (residual excited linear predictive coding) RELP-Codierung *f*
remote abgesetzt, entfernt, fern
  r. access Fremdanschluß *m*, Ausnahmeanschluß *m (an ISDN-Vermittlung in nicht-ISDN-Vermittlung)*
  r. (circuit) management Fernverwaltung *f (Konferenzkreis)*
  r. concentrator vorgezogener Konzentrator *m (für Fremdanschluß)*
  r. control unit Fernschaltgerät *n (Datex, TEMEX)*
  r. data communications controller Datenfernübertragungssteuerung *f*
  r. data processing Datenfernverarbeitung *f* (DFV)
  r. data switching unit Datenfernschaltgerät *n* (DFG(t) *(Sat.)*
  r. data transmission Datenfernübertragung *f* (DFÜ)
  r. equipment Vorfeldeinrichtung *f (ISDN)*
  r. power feeding (RPF) FSP Fernspeisung *f (Tel.)*
  r. replay Fernabfrage *f (Anrufbeantworter)*
  r. screening Fernvorabfrage *f (Anrufbeantworter)*
  r. station fernes Amt *n*
  r. supervision (system) Fernüberwachung *f*
  r. (telecontrol) terminal unit (RTU) Fernwirk-Unterstation *f*, Unterstation *f* (US) *(FW)*
remotely located vom Amt *n* abgesetzt, herausgezogen *(HW)*
removal Herausnahme *f*; Rücknahme *f (TEI-Zuordnung)*
remove the handset abheben, abhängen, aushängen
repair order Instandsetzungsauftrag *m* (IA)
  R. Service Centre (RSC) Reparaturdienstzentrale *f (BT-IDA)*
repeat last call Wahlwiederholung *f*
  r. distance Wiederbelegungsentfernung *f (Gleichkanal, Mobilfunk)*
  r. printing Doppeldruck *m (Fax.)*
repeatability error Wiederkehrfehler *m*
repeater Zwischengenerator *m (Tel.)*; Satzübertrager *m*
  r. section Verstärkerfeld *n*
  r. station Verstärkeramt *n*, Verstärkerstelle *f*, Zwischenstelle *f (Übertragungsstrecke)*
repeating coil Übertrager *m (Tel.)*

repertory dialler Namentaster *m*, Speicherwähleinrichtung *f (K.-Tel.)*
  r. dialling Anrufwiederholung *f (K.-Tel.)*
repetition frequency Folgefrequenz *f*
  r. period Folgezeit *f (Pulse)*; Wiederholdauer *f*
repetitive metering Mehrfachgebührenerfassung *f (Tel.)*
replace anhängen, aufhängen, auflegen *(Hörer)*
  r. a defective amplifier einen defekten Verstärker austauschen *oder* havarieren
replacement assembly *oder* **module** Ersatzbaugruppe *f*
replenishment Austauschen *n (Bildcodierung)*
replugging of terminals Umstecken *n (am Bus)*
report Bericht *m*, Meldung *f*
representative repräsentativ, typisch
  r. voltage Abbildspannung *f (eines Stromes)*
reproducibility Vergleichbarkeit *f (QA)*; Wiederholgenauigkeit *f*
request Anforderung *f*; Aufforderung *f*; Befehl *m (ein Primitive von einer höheren an eine niedrigere Schicht)*; anfordern; abrufen *(Meldung in E-Mail)*
  r. for connection Verbindungswunsch *m (Tel.-Anl.)*
  R. for Information (RFI) Antrag *m* auf Auskunftserteilung *(vor Beschaffung)*
  r. key Abfragetaste *f*
  R. for Price Quotation (RPQ) Preisangebotsanforderung *f*
  R. for Proposal (RFP) Angebotsanforderung *f*
  R. for Quote (RFQ) Ausschreibung *f*
  R. To Send (RTS) Sendeteil einschalten *(V.24/RS232C)*
requirement specification Pflichtenheft *n*, Lastenheft *n*
rerouting Neuwahl *f*; Rückführung *f (nach Verbindungswiederherstellung)*; Umlenkung *f (Verkehr)*; Umwegsteuerung *f*, Umsteuerung *f (PCM-Daten, Sprache)*, Leitungsumschaltung *f*
  r. of traffic Lastübernahme *f*
reservation TDMA (R-TDMA) TDMA *m* mit Buchung *(Sat.)*
reserved-access method Reservierungsverfahren *n (PCM-Sprache)*
reset rücksetzen, löschen *(Zähler)*; normieren
residual restlich, remanent
  r. attenuation Grunddämpfung *f (FO)*; Restdämpfung *f*

r. **error rate** Restfehlersatz *m (in %)*
r. **error ratio** Echorestabstand *m (Echo-löscher)*
r. **parameter** Schaltwert *m*
r. **sideband modulation** (RSB) Restsei-tenbandmodulation *f* (RM)
resistance Widerstand *m*
r. **characteristic** Widerstandsprofil *n*
r. **per unit area** Flächenwiderstand *m*
r. **per unit length** Widerstandsbelag *m (Kabel, in Ohm/km)*
resistive reell *(Widerstand)*
resistor-capacitor (RC) circuit belasteter Kondensator *m*
resistor coding RKM-Code *m (z.B. 4R7,47K, 4M7)*
resolution Auflösung *f,* Auflösungsvermögen *n (TV)*; Rastermaß *n (Fax.)*
r. **in bits** Bittiefe *f,* Signaltiefe *f (Videocodierung, z.B. 8 Bit/Pixel)*
r. **of access contentions** Zugriffssteuerung *f*
r. **selector** Rasterschalter *m (Fax.)*
resolve collisions Kollisionen *fpl* auflösen
resolving capability Auflösungsvermögen *n*
resource Betriebsmittel *n*
response Verlauf *m,* Gang *m (Frequenz)*; Meldung *f (HDLC)*; Antwort *f (Puls)*
r. **block** Antwortblock *m (PCM)*
r. **time** Antwortzeit *f (Modem)*; Antwortverzug *m,* Beantwortungszeit *f (Abfrage)*; Meßzeit *f* ; Einschwingzeit *f (Tel., MFV)*; Ansprechzeit *f,* Reaktionszeit *f*
restart Neuformierung *f (Programm)*
restoral attempt Wiederaufprüfung *f (Sat.)*
restoration of the call *oder* **connection** Wiederherstellung *f* der Verbindung
restoring Wiederherstellen *n (Information)*
restricted gesperrt *(Anschluß)*
r. **powering** Notspeisung *f,* Notstromversorgung *f (Fernspeisung)*
restriction Begrenzung *f*; Sperre *f*
resynchronisation Resynchronisierung *f*
r. **of a connection** Rücksetzen *n* einer Verbindung *(ISDN)*
retransmission Nachsendung *f,* Wiederholung *f,* Wiederholungssendung *f (Pakete)*
retrieval Abfrage *f (Daten),* Rückholen *n (eines umgelegten Rufes)*
r. **mode** Abfragebetrieb *m,* Nachrichtenabfragebetrieb *m*
retrieve wiedergewinnen; abfragen *(Mitteilungen)*
retry Wiederholung *f*
retune nachsteuern *(Filter)*
return zurückführen, zurückkehren

r. **control channel** Antwortkanal *m (Bündelfunk)*
r. **current** Strom *m* ableiten *(zu Masse)*
r. **loss** Reflexionsdämpfung *f*, Rückflußdämpfung *f (Verteiler, FO)*; Rückhörbezugsdämpfung *f (Tel.)*
r. **to bias** (RB) Rückkehr *f* zum Ausgangszustand, Rückkehr *f* zur Grundmagnetisierung *(Daten-Aufzeichnungsmethode, PCM)*
r. **to zero** (RZ) Rückkehr *f* nach Null *(PCM)*
reuse distance Wiederbelegungsentfernung *f (Gleichkanal, Mobilfunk)*
reversal to normal polarity Rückpolung *f (Tel.)*
reverse umsteuern; umlegen *(Relais)*
r. **charging** Gebührenübernahme *f*
r. **direction** Sperrichtung *f (Halbl.),* Gegen- *oder* Rückwärtsrichtung *f (Übertr.)*
r. **frequency operation** Gegenfrequenzbetrieb *m (Feststation, Bündelfunk)*
r. **polarity** umpolen
r. **voltage** Sperrspannung *f*
reversed polarity gekreuzt *(Tel.-Stromspeisung)*
r. **trunking scheme** Umkehrgruppierung *f*
r. **wires** Adernvertauschung *f*
revolution Umlauf *m (Sat.)*
rewind rückspulen *(Lochstreifenleser)*
RF (radio frequency) Hochfrequenz *f* (HF)
RF block Hochfrequenzabriegelung *f*
RF distribution matrix HF-Verteilungsmatrix *f* (HVM) *(HF-Sender)*
RF interference (RFI) regulations Funkschutzbestimmungen *fpl*
RF voltmeter Diodenvoltmeter *n*
RF-screened door HF-dichte Tür *f*
RFI (radio frequency interference) Funkstörung *f*
RFI (Request for Information) Antrag *m* auf Auskunftserteilung
RFP (Request for Proposal) Angebotsanforderung *f*
RFQ (Request for Quote) Ausschreibung *f*
RHCP s. right-hand circular polarization
Rhine radio-telephone service Rheinfunkdienst *m (international)*
RI s. Ring Indicator
ribbon cable Flachkabel *n*
right to transmit Senderechte *npl (PCM-Datenblöcke)*
r.**-hand circular polarization** (RHCP) rechtszirkulare Polarisation *f (Sat.)*
ring down junction Abfragebetrieb *m,* Nachrichtenabfragebetrieb *m*
r. **down line** Rufleitung *f*
R. Indicator (RI) Ankommender Ruf *m*

ring 232

(V.24/RS232C)
r. tripping Rufabschaltung *f*
ringer Tonruf *m (Tel.)*
  r. volume Tonruflautstärke *f*
ringing Tonruf *m (Tel.)*
  r. and signalling generator Ruf- und Signaleinrichtung *f* (RSE)
  r. cadence Ruftakt *m*
  r. (current) source Rufstromquelle *f*
  r. cycle Ruftakt *m*
  r. generator Rufgenerator *m*
  r. relay Anrufrelais *n*
  r. signal Freiton *m* (F-Ton), Ruf *m*
  r. time Rufzeit *f*
  r. time supervision Rufzeitüberwachung *f* (ZGS.7)
  r. tone Anrufton *m*; Freiton *m* (F-Ton), Rufton *m (Tel.)*
RIP (raster image processor) Rasterbildprozessor *m (DTP)*
rise Anstieg *m*; Hub *m (Spannung, Signal)*
  r. time Flankensteilheit *f (Puls)*; Einschwingzeit *f*
RM (reference model) Referenzmodell *n* (7-Schicht OSI-Modell)
RM (residual sideband modulation) Restseitenbandmodulation *f (TV)*
RMA (random multiple access) zufallsmäßiger Vielfachzugriff *m (Sat.-Zugriffsverfahren, z.B. ALOHA)*
RMS meter Effektivwertmesser *m*
RMVD (running majority vote detection) Erkennung *f* durch laufende Mehrheitsentscheidung
RNIS (Réseau Numérique à Intégration des Services ("numeris")) diensteintegrierendes Digitalnetz *n* (ISDN) *(in FR)*
RO (receive only) Nur-Empfang *m*
roaming Wandern *n*, Bereichswechsel *m*, Ruf- *oder* Verkehrsbereichswechsel *m*; Gesprächsweitergabe *f*
  (FuKo-Bereichswechsel, Mobilfunk)
ROS (receive only satellite) Satellitenempfangsantenne *f*
rotary dialling Nummernschaltwahl *f (Tel.)*
  r. out-trunk *oder* **outgoing selector** Ausgangsdrehwähler *m*
round-trip delay Antwortzeit *f* (= 2 x Signallaufzeit, Sat.), gesamte Echolaufzeit *f (PCM)*
  r.-trip time Umlaufzeit *f*
route Leitweg *m*, Trasse *f*; Strecke *f*; Richtung *f (Tel.-Anl.)*; Linienzug *m (Tel.)*; Kabelverbindung *f*; leiten *(Zeichengabe)*, steuern *(Signale)*
  r. allocation Leitwegzuteilung *f (Tel.)*

r.-idle-marking relay Bündelfreimarkierungsrelais *n*
r. management Wegemanagement *n (ZGS.7 MTP)*
r. name key for exchange lines Bündelzieltaste *f* (BZT) für Amtsleitungen
r. section Streckenabschnitt *m*
r. segregation Richtungsausscheidung *f*
r. tap Richtungsabgriff *m (Verzoner)*
r. translation Richtungsumwertung *f*
router Adreßumsetzer *m* und Nachrichten-Weiterleitgerät *n (LAN)*
routing Leitwegführung *f*, Leitweglenkung *f* (ZGS.7); Wegelenkung *f (Verm.)*; Rangieren *n (Signale)*
  r. assignment Belegungsplan *m* (Blp)
  r. centre Leitvermittlungsstelle *f*
  r. digit Leitziffer *f*
  r. label Nachrichtenkopf *m*
  r. page Leitseite *f (Vtx.)*
row Reihe *f (Anzeige)*; Zeile *f (Verteiler)*
  r. blocking contact Zeilensperrkontakt *m*
  r./column clearance Putzen *n (Koppelfeld)*
  r. rest-condition marking Zeilensummenmarkierung *f*
RPE (regular pulse excitation) RPE-Code *m*
RPF (remote power feeding) Fernspeisung *f* (FSP) *(HW)*
RPOA (recognized private operating company) anerkannte private Betriebsgesellschaft *f*
RPQ (Request for Price Quotation) Preisangebotsanforderung *f*
rr (receive ready) Empfangsbereitschaft *(Vtx.)*
RS code (Reed Solomon code) RS-Code *m* (Fehlerkorrektur)
RS232 EIA-Standard für serielle Datenkommunikation mit bis zu 20 kB/S und NRZ-Signalisierung (0 = +3 bis 25V, 1 = -3 bis -25V; in CCITT-Empfehlungen V.24, V.28 und DIN 66020 aufgenommen)
RS232A *RS232-Schnittstelle mit 20mA-Stromsteuerung*
RS232C *RS232-Schnittstelle mit 5V-Spannungssteuerung*
RS232D *RS232C-Revision für vollständige Übereinstimmung mit V.24/V.28*
RS422, RS423 *entspr. RS232D-Logik, für hohe Datengeschwindigkeit und Weitverkehr*
RS485 *entspr. RS422, als Bussystem*
RSA (Rivest-Shamir-Adleman) RSA-Verfahren *n (asymmetrische 'public-key'-Verschlüsselung für Chipkarten)*
RSB (residual sideband) Restseitenband *n*

(TV)
RSC (Repair Service Centre) Reparaturdienstzentrale *f (BT-IDA)*
RSV (radio supervisor) Funküberwachung *f*
RT (radio text (service)) Radiotext *m (RDS)*
RT (radiotelephony) Funkfernsprechen *n (Mobilfunk, nömL)*
RT (receive terminal) Empfangsendgerät *n*
RTC (real time clock) Echtzeituhr *f*
RTS (Request To Send) Sendeteil einschalten *(V.24/RS232C)*
RTTY (radio teletype) Funkfernschreiber *m*
RTU (remote terminal unit) Fernwirk-Unterstation *f*
RU (rack unit) Höheneinheit *f* (HE) *(Gestell)*

rule system Regelwerk *n*
run ablaufen (lassen), abarbeiten, fahren, aufrufen *(Programm)*; Ablauf *m*, Durchlauf *m*
running digital sum (RDS) laufende Digitalsumme *f*
   r. majority vote laufende Mehrheitsentscheidung *f*
   r. majority vote detection (RMVD) Erkennung *f* durch laufende Mehrheitsentscheidung
runway Rost *m (Gestell)*
   r. support Roststütze *f*
RX (regional exchange) Knotenvermittlungsstelle *f* (KVSt)
RZ (return to zero) Rückkehr *f* nach Null *(PCM-Code)*

S

S-ALOHA (slotted ALOHA) segmentiertes Aloha n (Sat.)
S-interface circuit (SIC) S-Schnittstelle f (Teilnehmerschnittstelle, Vierdraht-Leitung, ISDN)
S$_0$ interface S$_0$-Schnittstelle f (S-Schnittstelle für ISDN-BA)
S$_{2M}$ interface S$_{2M}$-Schnittstelle f (S-Schnittstelle für ISDN PA)
SAA (Systems Applications Architecture) SAA-Architektur f
SAD (signalling converter. A/D) Analog-/Digital-Zeichen-Umsetzer m
SAF (store-and-forward (S&F,SF)) Speichervermittlung f (Vermittlung)
safety margin Sicherheitsabstand m
  s. precautions Schutzmaßnahmen fpl (Datenblatt)
Samaritans' call service Telefonseelsorge f
sample Abtastwert m (AW); abtasten (digital)
  s. and hold circuit Abtast-/Halteschaltung f, Abtastumschaltung f, Abtaster m, Tastspeicher m, Abfrage- und Speicherglied n; Halte- und Entnahmekreis m (ADU)
sampled-data system Abtastsystem n (Reg.)
sampling Abtastung f, Probenahme f
  s. cadence Abtasttakt m (Tel.)
  s. interval Abtastabstand m
  s. pattern Abtastraster n
  s. rate Abtastfrequenz f
  s. theorem Abtasttheorem n, Nyquisttheorem n
SAP (service access point) Dienstzugriffspunkt m (ZGS.7)
SAPI (service access point identifier) Dienstzugriffspunktkennung f (ZGS.7)
p-SAPI (SAPI for packet data) SAPI f für Paketdaten
s-SAPI (SAPI for signalling data) SAPI f für Signalisierungsdaten
SAR successive approximation register) Iterationsregister n (IC)
SARCOM (search and rescue communication) Seenotfunknetz n (BRD, FM-Seefunkdienst)
SAT (supervisory audio tone) Überwachungston m (Mobilfunk)
satellite circuit Satellitenstromweg m
  s. data distribution service Satelliten-Verteildienst m
  s. link protocol Satellitenkommunikationsprotokoll n
  s. master antenna TV (SMATV) Fernsehen n mit Satelliten-Zentralantenne (Gemeinschafts-TV)
  S. Multiservice System (SMS) Satelliten-Mehrdienstesystem n (Eutelsat)
  s. switched TDMA (SS-TDMA, SSTDMA) TDMA m mit Vermittlung im Satelliten (Sat.)
  S. Tracking and Data Network (STADAN, STDN) Satellitenverfolgungs- und Datenerfassungsnetz n (NASA)
saturation routing Verkehrslenkung f mit Zielsuche
save speichern; abspeichern, sichern (Daten nach Bearbeitung)
  s. point Rückzugspunkt m (Programm)
SAW (surface acoustic waves) akustische Oberflächenwellen fpl (AOW)
SC (service channel) Dienstkanal m (DK)
S/C (spacecraft) Raumfahrzeug n (Sat.)
scaling Skalierung f; Normierung f, Schrittweitenbestimmung f, Stufung f (Bildcodierung)
  signal s. Signalraster m (Quantisierung)
scan abfragen (Adressen, Tasten, Zeichengabe); abtasten (analog); absuchen (Sat.)
scanner Abtaster m; Fühlerschaltung f (PCM-Daten)
scanning Abfragen n, Abtasten n
  s. and distribution circuits Fühler- und Geber(schaltungen) fpl (dig.Tel.)
  s. cadence Abtasttakt m (Tel.)
  s. circuit Fühlerschaltung f (PCM-Daten)
  s. density Zeilendichte f (Fax.)
  s. pattern Rasterung f (Videoanzeige)
  s. point Abfragestelle f (dig. Verm.)
scatter Streuung f
  s. band Streubreite f
scattered light Streulicht n (FO)
SCCP (signalling connection control part) Steuerteil m für Zeichengabeverbindungen (ZGS.7)
SCPB (single channel per burst) Einzelkanalburst m (Sat.)
SCPC (single channel per carrier) Ein-Kanal-pro-Träger-System n (Sat.)
SCPT (single channel per Transponder)

scrambler 236

Ein-Kanal-pro-Transponder-System *n* (Sat.)
scrambler Verwürfler *m*
screw assembly Kombiverschraubung *f (Kabelkupplung)*
SCVF (single channel voice frequency) Einkanal-Niederfrequenz-Verfahren *n*
SCU (service channel unit) Dienstkanal-Einheit *f*
SCU (subnetwork control unit) Unternetz-Steuereinheit *f (VSAT)*
SDA (Signalling converter, Digital/Analog) Digital-/Analog-Zeichenumsetzer *m*
SDD (state description diagram) Zustandsbeschreibungsplan *m (CCITT)*
SDH (synchronous digital hierarchy) **bit rate** SDH-Bitrate *f (155 MBit/s, RiFu)*
SDL s. Specification Description Language
SDLC (synchronous data link control) synchrone Übertragungssteuerung *f (IBM)*
SDM (space division multiplex) Raummultiplex *n*
SECAM (séquentiel à mémoire) sequentielle Übertragung *f* mit Zwischenspeicherung *(FBAS-TV-Codierung auf Basis des NTSC-Systems, FR)*
search and rescue communication system Seenotfunknetz *n*
  s. operation Suchvorgang *m*
second (third, fourth ...) **station** Zweit-, Dritt-, Viert- usw. anlage *f (Konferenzkreis)*
  s. usw. choice routing alternatives Bündel *n*
secondary Folgesteuerung *f (Kommunikationssteuerungsfunktion)*
  s. alarm Folgemeldung *f*
  s. information Nebeninformation *f*
  s. line switch zweiter Anrufsucher *m*
  s. operator's console Nebenbedienungsplatz *m* (NBP)
  s. protection (circuit) Feinschutz *m*
  S. Received data (SRCV) Hilfskanal Empfangsdaten, Rückkanal Empfangsdaten *(V.24/RS232C)*
  s. station Zweitnebenstellenanlage *f (Tel.)*;
  Folgesteuerungsstation *f (HDLC)*;
  Gegenstation *f*
  S. Transmit data (SXMT) Hilfskanal Sendedaten, Rückkanal Sendedaten *(V.24/-RS232C)*
secrecy of telecommunications Fernmeldegeheimnis *n*
secretarial function transfer Vertretungsschaltung *f (K.-Tel.)*

section Abschnitt *m*; Feld *n (Verstärker, Gestell)*; Teilstrecke *f (Tel.)*
  s. attenuation Teilstreckendämpfung *f*
  s.-by-section switching Teilstreckenvermittlung *f*
  s. control unit Arbeitsfeldsteuerwerk *n* (AST) *(EWS)*
  s. overhead Abschnittsrahmenkopf *m (STM-1, CCITT G.70X)*
secure gesichert; verschlüsselt *(Daten)*
  s. dial-back Sicherheitsrückruf *m*
security level Sicherheitsstufe *f*
  s. unit Abschaltebereich *m (von Einrichtungen in Vermittlung)*
seize belegen *(Leitung)*
  s. outgoing exchange line Amt *n* gehend belegen (AG)
seized belegt *(Leitung)*
seizure Belegung *f (Leitung, Kanal)*
  s. of exchange line Amtsbelegung *f*, Amtsanlassung *f*
SEL (SELect data signal rate) Übertragungsgeschwindigkeit *f (V.24/RS232C)*
select auswählen, anwählen, bewählen *(Leitung)*; ansteuern *(Adressen)*
  s. lines and poke points Anwahlzeilen *fpl* und -punkte *mpl (Sichtgerät)*
  s. transmit frequency Sendefrequenz *f (V.24/RS232C)*
selectable einstellbar *(Adressen)*
selection Anwahl *f (Dienst)*; Auswahl *f*
  s. code Kennung *f (ZGS.7 MTP)*
  s. signal Wählzeichen *n (X.21)*
selective answering gezielte Abfrage *f (Tel.)*
  s. call facility (SELCALL) Selektivrufeinrichtung *f*
  s. calling Selektivruf *m (Tel.)*
  s. detector Meßempfänger *m (Richtfunk)*
  s. polling Selektivabfrage *f*
  s. repeat (SR) selektive Wiederholungsaufforderung *f (ARQ-Prozedur, Sat.)*
  s. ringing Einzelanruf *m (Gemeinschaftsleitung)*
  s. serial repeat (SSR) selektive serielle Wiederholung *f (ARQ)*
selector Wähler *m*, Wahlstufe *f (Vermittlung)*
  s. logic Auswahllogik *f*
  group s. Gruppenschalter *m* (GS) *(Fax.)*
self-check Eigenprüfung *f*
  s.-routing switching network selbststeuerndes Koppelnetz *n (ATM)*
  s.-service terminal Selbstbedienungsterminal *n* (SB-Terminal)
  s.-test Selbsttest *m*, Eigentest *m*
semaphore *oder* **semaphore counter** Koordinationszähler *m*, Semaphor *n*

semigraphic symbols halbgraphische Symbole *npl (Anzeige)*
semirestricted halbamtsberechtigt, halbgesperrt *(Nebenstelle)*
send by fax faxen, wegfaxen *(Dokumente, Graphik)*
  s. loudness rating (SLR) Sendelautstärke-Index *m (Tel.)*
  s. terminal (ST) Sendeterminal *n (DK)*
sending call waiting tone Anklopfen *n*
  s. reference equivalent Sendebezugsdämpfung *f (FO)*
sensing Abfrage *f*, Erfassen *n (HW)*
sensitivity Empfindlichkeit *f*; Steilheit *f (Verstärker)*
separate system Inselnetz *n*
  s. the channels in the frame Rahmen *m* auflösen
separating filter Weiche *f*, Auftrennweiche *f*; Trennweiche *f (GGA)*; Impulsweiche *f*
separation Trennung *f*, Abstand *m*; Frequenzraster *m*, Kanalraster *m*
sequence Folge *f*; Ablauf *m (Prozess)*
  s. calling Rundsenden *n (ISDN-Tel.)*
  s. conformity Reihenfolgetreue *f (von Blöcken, Sat.)*
  s. control Ablaufsteuerung *f (Vermittlung)*
  s. number Reihenfolgenummer *f* (RFN) *(von Blöcken, Sat.)*, Laufnummer *f (ZGS. 7)*
  s. of operations Funktionsablauf *n*
  s. supervisor Ablaufüberwachung *f*
sequenced protocol class sequenzgesicherte Protokollklasse *f (ZGS.7)*
sequencing Folgesteuerung *f*; Sequentialisierung *f (ISO - Aufteilung der Nutznachricht in Rahmen, Blöcke oder Pakete mit Folgenumner)*
serial input/output (SIO) serielle Ein-/Ausgabe *f (Port)*
  s. network Liniennetz *n (FS)*
series Folge *f*, Reihe *f*, Serie *f*
  s. circuit Serienschaltung *f*, Vorkreis *m*
  s. mode rejection range (SMRR) Serientakt-Unterdrückungsmaß *n*
  s. resistance Längswiderstand *m* (LW)
  s. resonant circuit Saugkreis *m*
  s. telephones Reihenanlage *f (Tel.)*
  s.-connected vorgeschaltet *(Bauteil)*
server Server *m*; Abnehmer *m*, Abnehmerleitung *f (Tel.-Anl.)*; Bediener *m*, Bedienstation *f (Sat., Netzübergangsfunktion)*; Dienstleistungsrechner *m*;

administration and data s. (ADS) Betriebs- und Datenserver *m (ISDN)*
busy s. belegter Abnehmer *m (Tel.)*
communication s. (CS) Verbindungsabnehmer *m*
name s. (elektronisches) Namensverzeichnis *n (MHS SW, CCITT Rec. X.400)*
service Dienst *m*, Dienstleistung *f*; abarbeiten, bearbeiten *(Programm)*
  s. access point (SAP) Dienstzugriffspunkt *m (ZGS.7 Schicht-Zugriff, CCITT Rec. Q.761...764)*
  s. access point identifier (SAPI) Dienstzugriffspunktkennung *f*
  s. alarm signal Störungsmeldung *f (PCM-Daten, CCITT Rec. G.704)*
  s. area Anschlußbereich *m (Tel.)*; Versorgungsbereich *m (TV)*
  s. attribute Dienstmerkmal *n (ISDN, CCITT Rec. I.112)*; Merkmalsattribut *n (CCITT X.32)*
  s. centre Leitzentrale *f (Vtx.)*
  s. channel (SC) Betriebskanal *m* (BK) (TF), Dienstkanal *m* (DK), Nutzkanal *m*
  s. channel below message unterlagerter Betriebskanal *m*
  s. channel network Betriebskanalnetz *n* (BK-Netz)
  s. channel unit (SCU) Dienstkanaleinheit *f*
  s. code Hinweisgabe *f (BT, FS)*, Dienstsignal *n (FS)*
  s. computer Bedienungsrechner *m* (BR) *(Tel.)*
  s. denial Anschlußsperre *f*
  s. facility Leistungsmerkmal *n* (LM) *(Tel.)*
  s. feature Leistungsmerkmal *n* (LM) *(Tel.)*
  s. file Betriebsdatei *f*
  s.-independent dienstneutral
  s. indicator Dienstekennung *f (ISDN)*
  s. indicator octet (SIO) Dienstkennung *f (ZGS.7 MTP)*
  s. information channel (SIC) Dienstinformationskanal *m (ATM)*
  s. intercommunication Dienstübergang *m*
  s. level Betriebspegel *m (DÜ)*
  s. life Lebensdauer *f (eines Bauteils)*
  s. management system (SMS) Dienstverwaltungssystem *n (GSM)*
  s. processor Servicerechner *m* (SVR) *(Vtx.)*
  s. provider Dienstleistungsanbieter *m (Vtx., Mobilfunkzellennetz, Temex)*; Dienstträger *m*
  s. provider interface Anbieterschnitt-

service 238

stelle f *(TEMEX)*
s. radio Betriebsfunk m *(nömL, Teilnehmerbetriebsklasse)*
s.-related dienstorientiert
s. signal Dienstsignal n *(FS)*; Nutzsignal n, Netzmeldung f
s.-specific terminal Einzeldienstendgerät n *(ISDN)*
s. station Bedienstation f *(Netzübergangfunktion, Sat.)*
s. time Abfertigungszeit f
s. unit (SU) Servicegerät n (SG) *(FO-Dienstkanal)*
s. word Meldewort n (MW) *(PCM-Daten)*
putting into s. Inbetriebnahme f *(Einrichtung)*
services Dienstleistungen fpl *(Schicht-Schicht)*
serving Abnehmer-; Bedienen n
s. delay Bedienzeit f *(Netzübergangsfunktion)*
s. line Abnehmer m *(PCM-Daten/Sprache)*
s. time slot Abnehmerkanal m
s. trunk Abnehmerleitung f *(Tel.-Anl.)*
s. trunk group Abnehmerbündel n *(Tel.-Anl.)*
session establishment Sitzungsaufbau m
s. layer Kommunikationssteuerungsschicht f, Sitzungsebene f *(Schicht 5, OSI 7-Schicht- Referenzmodell)*
s. service (SS) Kommunikationssteuerungsschichtdienst m, Sitzungsdienst m
set Satz m; Block m *(PCM-Rahmen)*
s. a signal to Low, to High ein Signal n tieflegen, hochlegen
s. of curves Kennfeld n
s. of expected values Erwartungsmenge f *(Bildcodierung)*
s. up a connection Verbindung f aufnehmen, Verbindung f herstellen
setpoint Sollwert m *(Regelung)*
setting accuracy Treffunsicherheit f *(Meßgerät)*
s. instruction Einstellbefehl m
s. up Aufbau m, Einrichtung f *(Verbindung)*
s.-up time Aufschaltezeit f
settle ausregeln, einschwingen; einpendeln *(Oszillator)*
setup message Verbindungsaufbaumeldung f *(ISDN)*
severe conditions rauhe Bedingungen fpl
s. errored seconds stark gestörte Sekunden fpl *(CCITT G.821)*
sexless connector, adapter Zwitterkupp-

lung f *(Kabel)*
SF, S&F (store-and-forward (switching) (SAF)) Speichervermittlung f
SG (Study Group) Arbeitsgruppe f *(CCITT)*
shape Verlauf m *(Kurve)*; Form f
shaper Former m *(Frequenzgang)*
shareable mehrbenutzbar *(SW)*
shared hub geteilte Zentralstation f *(VSAT)*
s. line Gemeinschaftsanschluß m, Zweieranschluß m *(Tel.)*
s.-line equipment Gemeinschaftseinrichtung f
shedding Abwerfen n *(Rufe)*
shelf Baugruppenträger m, Etage f, Rost m *(Kabel)*, Gestellrost m *(Gestell)*
19" s. 19"-Etage f
shell Gehäuse n, Riegelwanne f *(Verbinder)*
SHF (super high frequency) superhohe Frequenz f *(Sat., 3-30 GHz)*
shielding efficiency Schirmdämpfung f
shift Verschiebung f *(Phasen)*, Hub m *(FSK, PSK)*
shock-proof plug CEE-Stecker m, Perilex-Stecker m
short-haul modem Modem m für begrenzte Leitungslänge *(s.a. LDM)*
s.-haul network regionales Fernnetz n, Bezirksnetz n *(Tel.)*
s.-path switching Kurzwegdurchschaltung f
s.-time kurzzeitig *(Spitzen)*
s.-wave band Kurzwellenbereich m, K-Bereich m, KW-Bereich m
shortcode dialling Kurzwahl f (KW) *(K.-Tel.)*
s. dialling position Kurzwahlplatz m *(K.-Tel.)*
shot(-effect) noise Schrotrauschen n *(FO)*
shunt bracket Nebenschlußbügel m
shutdown sequence Abschaltkette f *(Prozess)*
SIC s. service information channel
SIC (S-interface circuit) S-Schnittstellenschaltung f *(ISDN)*
side circuit Stammkreis m *(PCM-Daten, Sprache)*
s. tone Mithörton m *(Tel.)*
s. tone masking rating (STMR) Rückhördämpfung f *(Tel., CCITT Rec. P.10)*
s.-lobe attenuation oder **gain** Nebenzipfelabstand m *(Antennen)*
sign off sich abmelden
s. on sich anmelden
signal mitteilen, melden, signalisieren; Signal n, Zeichen n, Kennzeichen n;

signalling

Meldung f, Nachricht f
s. change Signalverlauf m
s. channel Meldekanal m (FS)
s. conditioning Meßwertaufbereitung f, Signalumformung f, Signalaufbereitung f
s. contribution Signalzuführung f (TV-Studios)
s./crosstalk ratio Signal/Nebensprechverhältnis n (Tel.); Isolationsabstand m (Koppelfeld, in dB)
s. crushing Signalstauchung f (GGA, Schwarzwert)
s. delay Signallaufzeit f
s. distance Hamming-Abstand m
s. distortion Zeichenverzerrung f
s. distribution Signalausbreitung f (TV-Rundfunk)
s. distributor Signalverteiler m (Audio, Video)
s. duration Zeichenlänge f (Tel.)
s. element Schritt m; Bit n (bei Binärmodulation); Signalzeichen n, Zeichenschritt m (ZGS.7)
s. element timing Schrittakt m (X.21)
s. end Rufende n (PCM-Daten, Sprache)
s. flow Signalverlauf m
s. flow diagram Signalzug m
s. generator Signalgeber m, Meßsender m
S. Ground (GND) Betriebserde (V.24/RS232C); Funktionserde f, Signalerde f
s. level Nutzpegel m
s. levels Signalbelegung f
S./Noise and Distortion ratio (SINAD) Störabstand m einschließlich Verzerrungen
s./noise-density ratio S/R-Leistungsdichte-Verhältnis n
s./noise ratio (SNR, S/N) Rauschabstand m, Rauschverhältnis n, Signal-Geräusch-Abstand m (SGA), Signal/Rausch-Abstand m (SRA), Signal-Rausch-Verhältnis n (SRV), Störabstand m
s. path Signalweg m, Signalzug m, Signalverlauf m
s. power Nutzleistung f
s. processing Signalaufbereitung f
S. Quality detect (SQ) Empfangsgüte (V.24/RS232C)
s./quantization noise ratio (SQNR) Quantisierungsrauschabstand m
s./quantizing distortion ratio (S/Q) S/Q-Verhältnis n (ADU)
s. resolution Signaltiefe f (Videocodierung, z.B. 8 Bit/Pixel)
s. range Meßspanne f
s. shape Signalverlauf m

s. space diagram Strahlendiagramm n
s. speed Signalgeschwindigkeit f (Übertragung, in Mikro-Sek./km)
s. tag Lötstift m
s. tone Rufton m (Daten)
s./tone converter Zeichentonumsetzer m (ZTU)
s./total distortion ratio Gesamtverzerrung f
s. trace Signalverlauf m (KO)
s. tracking the input voltage nachgeführtes Signal n, Nachlaufsignal n
s. transit time Signallaufzeit f (2 x = Antwortzeit)
s. transmission Signal-Führung f
s. unit Zeicheneinheit f (ZGS.7 MTP-Rahmen)
s. variation Signalverlauf m
s. waveshape Signalform f
signalling Rückmeldung f, Kennzeichengabe f, Signalgabe f, Signalisierung f; Zeichengabe f (CCITT Rec. I.112)
s. channel Kennzeichenkanal m, Signalisierungskanal m
s. code Kennzeichen n (PCM)
s. connection control part (SCCP) Transportfunktionsteil m (TF) (ZGS.7, CCITT Rec. Q.711...714; FTZ)
s. converter Kennzeichenumsetzer m (KZU) (Tel.-Zeichengabe); Signalisierungs-Umsetzer m, Signalumsetzer m
S. converter, Analog/Digital (SAD) Analog-/Digital-Zeichenumsetzer m, Zeichenumsetzer m (Analog-/Digital)
S. converter, Digital/Analog (SDA) Digital-/Analog-Zeichenumsetzer m
s. current Zeichenstrom m (Tel.)
s. data Kennzeicheninformation f (PCM)
s. data link Kennzeichengabekanal m, Zeichengabeübertragungsstrecke f, Zeichengabestrecke f, Zeichenstrecke f (ZGS.7 MTP); Kennzeichenabschnitt m
s. link Zeichengabestrecke f, Zeichenstrecke f (ZGS.7 MTP)
s. link selection code Zeichengabestrecken-Kennung f (ZGS.7 MTP)
s. link set Zeichengabestrecken-Bündel n (ZGS.7 MTP)
s. message Kennzeichennachricht f (ZGS.7)
s. multiplexer Signalisierungs-Multiplexer m (SMUX) (DK)
s. opportunity pattern (SOP) ausgewähltes Bitmuster n, Signalisierungsgelegenheitmuster n

signalling 240

s. **point** (SP) Zeichengabepunkt *m (Netzknoten im ZGS.7-Netz)*
s. **processor** Signalisierungs-Prozessor *m* (SPROZ) *(DK)*; Zeichengaberechner *m* (ZGR) *(VBN, FO)*
s. **route set** Zeichengabewegebündel *n (ZGS.7)*
s. **set** Wahlsatz *m (Vermittlung)*
s. **system** (SS) Signalverfahren *n*, Zeichengabesystem *n (CCITT Rec. Q.700 ff, FTZ RL 1TR6)*
S. **System No.7** (SS7) Zeichengabesystem Nr.7 (ZGS 7) *(ISDN, CCITT Rec. Q.701 - 764, FTZ RL 1R7)*
s. **time slot** Kennzeichenwort *n*
s. **wire** Signalader *f (FS)*
signals Signale *npl*, Kennzeichen *npl*, Informationen *fpl*
s. **which change abruptly with time** Signale *npl* mit Unstetigkeitsstellen
signature Signalkombination *f*, Bitkombination *f*
significant condition *oder* **state** Kennzustand *m (FS)*
silence Pausenblock *m (PCM Sprache)*
s. **duration** Pausenblocklänge *f*
s. **period** Pausenlänge *f*
silent reversal Weichumtastung *f (der Leitungspolung, Tel.)*
silicon Silizium *n*
silicone Silikon *n*
simplex Wechselsprechen *n (Tel.)*; Simplex *n* (SX) *(Modem)*
s. **dialling** Simultanwahl *f (NStAnl.)*
s. **signal** Eintaktsignal *n (Datenübertragung)*
s. **transmission** Richtungsbetrieb *m*
SINAD (Signal to Noise and Distortion (ratio)) Störabstand *m* einschließlich Verzerrungen
singing Pfeifen *n (Tel.)*
single Ein-, Einfach-, Einzel-
s.**-channel FDM data transmission system** Ein-Kanal-Datenübertragungssystem *n* mit Frequenzmultiplex (EDF) *(Tx.)*
s. **channel per burst** (SCPB) Einzelkanalburst *m (Sat.)*
s. **channel per carrier** (SCPC) Ein-Kanal-pro-Träger-System *n (Sat.)*
S. **channel per carrier PCM multiple Access Demand assignment Equipment** (SPADE) Vielfachzugriff *m* im Frequenzmultiplex mit Kanalzuteilung nach Bedarf *(Sat.)*
s. **channel per transponder** (SCPT) Ein-Kanal-pro-Transponder-System *n (Sat.)*

s. **channel voice frequency** (SCVF) Einkanal-Niederfrequenz-Verfahren *n (Telex-Signalisierung)*
s.**-ended, outer conductor grounded** einseitig geerdet
s.**-ended feeding** einseitige Einspeisung *f*
s.**-fee metering** Einzelgesprächszählung *f*
s.**-hop link** Einsprungverbindung *f (VSAT-Sternnetz, Einwegverbindung)*
s.**-length start element** einfacher Startschritt *m*
s. **line** Einzelanschluß *m*
s.**-line IDA** Basisanschluß *m* (BT-ISDN, 80 kB/s, Kapazität $B_{64}+B_8+D_8$)
s. **message** Einzelmeldung *f (Telefax-Protokoll)*
s. **metering** Einfachzählung *f*
s. **parity check** (SPC) **code** SPC-Code *m (Fehlerkorrekturcode mit 1 Bit Redundanz)*
s. **sideband** (SSB) Einseitenband *n* (ESB)
s.**-sideband modulation** (SSB) Einseitenbandmodulation *f* (EM)
s.**-sided clamp** Einfachklammer *f*, Halbklammer *f (Gestell)*
s.**-terminal access** Einzelendgeräte-Anschluß *m*
s.**-terminal configuration** Einzelkonfiguration *f*
sink Senke *f*, Verbraucher *m (Datenaufnehmer)*
SIO (scientific and industrial organisation) wissenschaftlich-technische Organisation *f*
SIO (serial input/output) serielle Ein-/Ausgabe *f (Port)*
SIO (service indication octet) Dienstindikator *m*, Dienstkennung *f (ZGS.7 MTP)*
SITA Societé Internationale Télécommunication Aeronautique *(internationales Datennetz für die Luftlinien)*
size Maß *n*; Mächtigkeit *f (Speicher, Kanal)*
skew Schieflage *f (Taktanpassung)*, Schieflauf *m (Fax.)*; Bitversatz *m*
skip überspringen, überlesen; ausblenden *(Programmteile)*
skirt: attenuation s. Dämpfungsflanke *f (Sat.)*
Skyphone Passagiertelefondienst *m (GB, INMARSAT-unterstützt)*
slave station Zweitnebenstellenanlage *f*
SLC (subscriber line circuit) Teilnehmersatz *m* (TS)
slew rate Nachführgeschwindigkeit *f (IC)*
SLIC (subscriber line interface circuit) Teilnehmeranschluß-Schnittstellenbaustein *m (Tel., K-Anl.)*

slide-in unit Einbausatz *m*, Einschub *m*
slim design schmale Bauform *f*
slope Abfall *m*, Steigung *f (Charakteristik)*, Steilheit *f (Kurve)*
  s. overload Überschwingen *n (DPCM-Video-Codierung)*
  s. rate Flankensteilheit *f*
slot Einbauplatz *m*; Abschnitt *m*, Segment *n (Zeitschlitz)*; Steckplatz *m (Baugruppenträger)*
  s. in einstecken
slotted ALOHA (S-ALOHA) segmentiertes Aloha *n (Sat., RMA-Verfahren der University of Hawaii)*
  s.-core cable Kammerkabel *n (FO)*
slow scan TV (SSTV) Schmalband-Fernsehen *n* (SB-TV)
SLR (send loudness rating) Sendelautstärke-Index *m (Tel.)*
smart card Speicherkarte *f*, Chipkarte *f*
  s. terminal programmierbare DEE *f*
SMATV (satellite master antenna TV) Fernsehen *n* mit Satelliten-Zentralantenne
SMD (surface mounted device) oberflächenmontiertes Bauelement *n*
SMP bus (Siemens microprocessor bus) Siemens-Mikroprozessor-Bus *m* (SMP-Bus)
SMPS (switched-mode power supply) Schaltnetzteil *n*
SMRR (series mode rejection range) Serientakt-Unterdrückungsmaß *n*
SMS (Satellite Multiservice System) Satelliten-Mehrdienstesystem *n (Eutelsat)*
SMS (service management system) Dienstverwaltungssystem *n (GSM)*
SMT (surface mounting technology) Oberflächenmontagetechnik *f*
SMUX (signalling multiplexer) Signalisierungsmultiplexer *m (DK)*
SN s. source node
SNA (Systems Network Architecture) SNA-Architektur *f (IBM)*
snap closure Schnellverschluß *m*
  s. disc Schnappfeder *f (Folientastatur)*
SNG (satellite news gathering) **terminal** SNG-Terminal *n (VSAT)*
SNR (signal/noise ratio) Signal-Geräuschabstand *m* (SGA), Rauschverhältnis *n*
socket (strip) Buchsenleiste *f*, Federleiste *f*
softkey Softtaste *f (programmierbare Taste)*
software provider Software-Anbieter *m (Vtx.)*
solder lug Lötöse *f (DIN)*
  s. tag Lötfahne *f (DIN)*
soldering side Leiter-, Lötseite *f* (L-Seite) *(Print)*

solid massiv, starr, fest;
  s. circle ausgefüllter Kreis *m*, Kreisfläche *f*
  s.-state drive (SSD) Festkörperansteuerung *n*
  s.-state power amplifier Halbleiterleistungsverstärker *m*
  s.-state relay (SSR) Festkörperrelais *n*
  s.-state switch elektronischer Schalter *m*
SONET (synchronous optical network) synchrones optisches Netz *n (FO)*
SOP (signalling opportunity pattern) Signalisierungsgelegenheitsmuster *n*, ausgewähltes Bitmuster *n*
sound component Begleitton *m (TV)*
  s.-powered speisungslos *(Seefunk-Tel.)*
  s. recorder Tonschreiber *m*
source node (SN) Quellensystem *n*
SP (signalling point) Zeichengabepunkt *m (Netzknoten im ZGS.7-Netz)*
space Leerzeichen *n*, Leerschritt *m*; Pause *f (Takt)*
  s. (division multiplex) stage Raumstufe *f*
  s. division multiplex (SDM) Ortsmultiplex *n*, Raum(lagen)vielfach *n*, Raummultiplex *n*
  s. division multiplex switching element Raumkoppelelement *n*
  s. division multiplex switching network Raumvielfachkoppelnetz *n*
  s. division (switching) network Raumkoppelnetz *n (je Ruf wird ein getrennter physischer Weg durch die VSt. aufgebaut)*
  s. frequency Trennfrequenz *f*
  s. switch Raum(lagen)vielfach *n*
  s. switch module Raumstufenmodul *m*
  s. switching Raummultiplexdurchschaltung *f (EWS)*
  s./time switch Raum-/Zeitlagenvielfach *n*
spacing Abstand *m*; Teilung *f (Verbinder)*, Raster *m (Frequenz, Takt(-impuls))*, Frequenzraster *m*, Kanalraster *m*
  s. condition Signalzustand *m* "Null"
  s. stop bit stromloser Sperrschritt *m (FS)*
  pulse s. Taktzeit *f*
SPADE (Single channel per carrier PCM multiple Access Demand assignment Equipment) Vielfachzugriff *m* im Frequenzmultiplex mit Kanalzuteilung nach Bedarf *(Sat.)*
SPAG (Standards Promotion and Applications Group) Arbeitsgruppe *f* zur Förderung und Anwendung von Standards *(im EG-Esprit-Programm)*

spare control capacity Stellreserve *f*
  s. part Ersatzteil *n* (ET)
SPC (stored program control) speicherprogrammierbare Steuerung *f* (SPS)
SPC code (s. single parity check code)
SPE (synchronous payload envelope) synchrone Nutzlast-Bitvollgruppe *f (TDM)*
speaking circuit Sprechkreis *m (Tel.)*
  s. clock service Zeitansage *f (Tel.)*
  s. key Abfragetaste *f (NStAnl.)*
  s. pair Sprechadern *fpl (Tel.)*
  while s. sprachbegleitend, gesprächsbegleitend *(TK-Anl., bei Benutzung anderer Dienste)*
SPEC s. Speech Predictive Encoding Communication
special channel Sonderkanal *m (Kabel-TV)*
  s.-purpose key Sondertaste *f*
  s.-purpose telephone Sonderfernsprecher *m*
  s.-service circuit Sonder(dienst)satz *m* (SDS)
Specification Description Language (SDL) *(CCITT-Programmierungssprache)*
specifications Lastenheft *n*, Spezifikationen *fpl*
spectrum oscillator Rasteroszillator *m*
spectral window Übertragungsfenster *n (FO)*
speech Sprache *f*
  s. activity Sprachaktivität *f*
  s. circuit Sprechkreis *m*
  s. detector Sprachdetektor *m*
  s. encoding Sprachverschlüsselung *f*
  s. interpolation Sprachpausennutzung *f (TASI)*
  s. path Sprechweg *m*
  S. Predictive Encoding Communication (SPEC) Kommunikation *f* mit Sprachprädiktionscodierung
  s. wire Sprechader *f*
SpeechLine BT-Analog-Festverbindung *f (Sprachband, 2-drahtig)*
speed dialling Zielwahl *f (zu externem TLN, mit Zieltasten, Tel.)*
spikes Nadelspitzen *fpl (auf Impulsen)*
splicing Spleißen *n (FO)*
split frequency Spaltfrequenz *f (Meßtechnik)*
  s.-screen monitor Eigenbildmonitor *m (Videokonferenz)*
splitter Verteiler *m (GGA)*
splitting jack Trennbuchse *f (Tel.)*
  s. up Abbereitung *f (Trägerfrequenztechnik)*
spot beam scharfgebündelte Abwärtsübertragung *f*, Bündelstrahl *m (Sat.)*
spot frequencies Festfrequenzen *fpl (Meß-*

technik)
spread Streubereich *m*, Streuung *f*; spreizen
  s. spectrum multiple access (SSMA) Spreizspektrumzugriff *m (VSAT)*
  s. spectrum technique Spreizspektrum-Verfahren *n*
spring contact pins federnde Kontaktstifte *mpl*
  s.-loaded key federnde Taste *f*
sprocket wheel Stiftenwalze *f (Bandleser)*
spurious switch-off (SSO) ungewollte Abschaltung *f (Sat.)*
SQ (Signal Quality (detect)) Empfangsgüte *f (V.24/RS232C)*
S/Q (signal/quantizing distortion ratio) S/Q-Verhältnis *n (ADU)*
SQNR (signal/quantization noise ratio) Quantisierungsrauschabstand *m (ADU)*
square-root calculator Quadratwurzelbildner *m*
SR (selective repeat) selektive Wiederholungsaufforderung *f (ARQ-Prozedur, Sat.)*
SRCV (Secondary ReCeiVed data) Hilfskanal-Empfangsdaten *npl (V.24/RS232C)*
SS (session service) Kommunikationssteuerungsschichtdienst *m*, Sitzungsdienst *m*
SS (signalling system) Signalverfahren *n*, Zeichengabesystem *n (CCITT Rec. Q.700 ff, FTZ RL 1TR6)*
SS7 (Signalling System No.7) Zeichengabesystem Nr.7 (ZGS.7) *(ISDN)*
SS-TDMA (satellite switched TDMA) TDMA *m* mit Vermittlung im Satelliten *(Sat.)*
SSB (single-sideband (modulation)) Einseitenband *n*
SSD (solid-state drive) Festkörperansteuerung *n*
SSMA s. spread spectrum multiple access
SSO s. spurious switch-off
SSR (selective serial repeat) selektive serielle Wiederholung *f (ARQ)*
SSR (solid-state relay) Festkörperrelais *n*
SSTDMA (satellite switched TDMA) TDMA *m* mit Vermittlung im Satelliten *(Sat.)*
SSTV (slow scan TV) Schmalband-Fernsehen *n*
SSU (Step-by-Step exchange, Unbalanced signalling) Schrittschaltesystem *n*, unsymmetrische Zeichengabe *(analog)*
ST (send terminal) Sendeterminal *n (DK)*
stabilisation characteristic Einlaufverhalten *n*
stability Stabilität *f*, Konstanz *f (Frequenz)*; Kippsicherheit *f*, Pfeifsicherheit *f*

stacked terminal block Schichtverteiler *m*
STADAN (Satellite Tracking and Data Acquisition Network) Satellitenverfolgungs- und Datenerfassungsnetz *n (NASA)*
stage-by-stage control system schritthaltend gesteuertes System *n*
  s. of completion Ausbaustufe *f*
stairstep generator Treppen(stufen)generator *m (TV)*
standard standardmäßig, einheitlich, genormt, serienmäßig, handelsüblich
  s. abbreviated call number Einheitskurzrufnummer *f* (EKR)
  s. abbreviated directory number Einheitskurzrufnummer *f* (EKR)
  s. cable equivalent Leitungsdämpfung *f*
  s. frequency inset Normalfrequenzeinsatz *m* (NFR)
  s. grading Normmischung *f (TelAnl.)*
  s. mismatch Fehlernormal *n (Meßtechnik)*
standardisation Standardisierung, *f*, Normierung *f*; Typisierung *f*
Standards and Codes Regelwerk *n*
standby Reserve *f*, Bereitschafts-
  s. operation Ersatzbetrieb *m*, Ersatzschaltung *f*
  s. power system switching Netzersatzschaltung *f*
  s. processor Reserveprozessor *m*
  s. system Bereitschaftssystem *n*
stand-in (selection) switch Vertretungsschaltung *f (Chef-Sekretär-Anlage)*
star-type network Sternnetz *n*
start Beginn *m*, Anfang *m*, Start *m*
  s. bit Anlaufschritt *m (FS)*
  s. delay Anlaufverzögerung *f*
  s. element Startbit *n*
  s. record Anfangssatz *m (PCM-Daten)*
  s. signal Anlaufschritt *m (FS)*
starting direction Angriffsrichtung *f (Impuls)*
  s. delimiter Anfangsfeld *n (FDDI)*
state Zustand *m*; Stand *m (Uhr)*
  s. description diagram (SDD) Zustandsbeschreibungsplan *m (CCITT)*
  s. of loading Belegung *f (Bus)*
  s. of occupancy Belegung *f (Bus)*
  s. switching Stufenkippen *n*
statement of compliance Konformitätserklärung *f*
  s. of services provided Leistungsbeschreibung *f*
static communication area statischer Verständigungsbereich *m (SVB) (SW)*
station answerback Anschlußkennung *f (Tx.)*
  s. battery Amtsbatterie *f*, Zentralbatterie *f* (ZB), Ortsbatterie *f* (OB) *(Vermittlung)*
  s. control equipment Betriebssteuereinrichtung *f* (BSE) *(Sat.)*
  s. wiring Amtsverdrahtung *f*
statistical time division multiplexer (STDM) statistischer Multiplexer *m*
status description Zustandsbeschreibung *f (ARQ)*
  s. request Statusabfrage *f*
STD (subscriber trunk dialling) Selbstwählferndienst *m* (SWFD)
STD (synchronous time division multiplex) synchrone Zeitvielfachtechnik *f (STM)*
STDN (Satellite Tracking and Data Acquisition Network) Satellitenverfolgungs- und Datenerfassungsnetz *n (NASA)*
steady-state condition eingeregelter Zustand *m*, eingeschwungener Zustand *m*
  s.-state distribution stationäre Besetzung *f (FO)*
steepness Steilheit *f (Impuls)*, Anstiegssteilheit *f*
step Arbeitsschritt *m* (AS); fortschalten *(Zähler)*
  s.-by-step (SXS) selector Schrittschaltsystem *n (analog)*; Step-by-Step-Wähler *m*
  s. change Sprung *m (Spannung)*
  s.-function excitation Sprunganregung *f (FO)*
  s. load change Lastsprung *m*
  s. size control Skalenfaktor *m (ADM, CCITT Rep.953)*
stepping pulse Fortschaltimpuls *m*
  s. speed Schrittgeschwindigkeit *f (Relais)*
STM (synchronous transfer mode) synchroner Übertragungsmodus *m*
STM-1 (synchronous transport module) synchroner Transportmodul *m*
STMR (side-tone masking rating) Rückhördämpfung *f (Tel.)*
stop band Sperrbereich *m (Filter)*
  s.-band attenuation Sperrtiefe *f*
  s. bit Sperrschritt *m*
  s. element Stoppschritt *m (Geschwindigkeitsanpassung)*
  s. signal Sperrschritt *m*
storage bus interface unit Speicherleitungsanschluß *m* (SLA)
  s. cycle Speichertakt *m*
  s. space Speicherraum *m*
  s. unit Speichereinheit *f* (SE) *(EWS)*
store Speicher *m (allgemein: eine Hilfsspeichervorrichtung)*; speichern
  s.-and-forward (SF,SAF,S&F) switching

stored position — 244

Teilstreckenvermittlung f, Speichervermittlung f; Zwischenspeicherung f *(MHS)*
stored position Ablageposition f
s.-program control (SPC) speicherprogrammierbare Steuerung f (SPS)
straight-through reception Geradeausempfang m
s.-through trunking scheme gestreckte Gruppierung f
strain relief Entspannungsbogen m *(Kabel)*
s.-relief element Zugorgan n *(Kabel)*
strap überbrücken, rangieren
stream Strom m *(Daten)*, Folge f *(Bits)*
string Strang m *(Laufwerke)*; Kette f *(Zeichen)*
strobe Abtastimpuls m, Ausblendimpuls m; ausblenden; freigeben, öffnen *(Gatter)*
s. pulse Takt-, Leit-, Öffnungsimpuls m
structogram Ablaufdiagramm n
structural part Konstruktionsteil n
s. unit Baueinheit f
structure Gebilde n *(Kabel)*, Aufbau m *(Feld, Rahmen)*; Anordnung f
Study Group (SG) Arbeitsgruppe f *(CCITT)*
stuff einblenden *(Bit, Blockbegrenzer)*; stopfen *(PCM, Geschwindigkeitsanpassung)*
stuffable stopfbar *(PCM-Daten)*
stuffing word Füllwort n, Stopfwort n *(PCM)*
style Bauform f, Ausführungsform f
SU (service unit) Servicegerät n
sub-centre Teilvermittlungsstelle f
sub-nyquist sampling method Unterabtastverfahren n *(Bildcodierung)*
subassembly Baugruppe f *(in einem Modul)*
subband coding Teilbandcodierung f (TBC) *(dig. Audio)*
subchannel Unterkanal m
subclass of service access level Teilberechtigung f
subgroup Teilgruppe f *(Tel.-Anl.)*
subject to notification anzeigepflichtig *(z.B. HF-Geräte, ZZF)*
s. to permit *oder* **approval** zulassungspflichtig
submarine cable Seekabel n
subnetwork Teilnetz n; Inselnetz n
s. control unit (SCU) Unternetz-Steuereinheit f *(VSAT)*
subrack Baugruppenträger m, Etage f
19" s. 19"-Etage f
subscriber Teilnehmer m (TN, TLN) *(Tel.)*
s.-activated change-over Selbstumschaltung f
s.-activated service features Selbsteinschreiben n von Betriebsmöglichkeiten

s.'s check meter Gebührenanzeige f, Mitlaufgebührenanzeiger m für Hausanschluß *(Tel.)*
s. dialling Selbstwählverkehr m *(Tel.)*
s.'s directory number Fernsprechnummer f
s. installation Teilnehmereinrichtung f
s.'s line Hausanschluß m, Anschlußleitung f (Asl) *(Tel., FTZ)*
s. line category Teilnehmerklasse f
s. line circuit (SLC) Teilnehmersatz m (TS); Teilnehmeranschlußschaltung f
s. line interface circuit (SLIC) Teilnehmeranschluß-Schnittstellenbaustein m *(Tel., K-Anl.)*
s. line network Liniennetz n *(Tel.)*
s. line testing network Wählprüfnetz n
s.'s main station Hauptapparat m, Hauptanschluß m
s.'s meter Gebührenzähler m *(Tel.)*
s. module Teilnehmerbaugruppe f (TB)
s. off-hook program Teilnehmeraushängeprogramm n
s. premises network Teilnehmernetz n (LAN)
s.'s private meter Mitlaufgebührenanzeiger m für Hausanschluß
s. terminal Teilnehmerendeinrichtung f (TEE) *(FTZ)*
s. terminal data Anschlußdaten npl
s. trunk dialling (STD) Selbstwählferndienst m (SWFD)
called s. B-Teilnehmer m
calling s. A-Teilnehmer m
subscription time: at s. bei Einrichtung f, zum Zeitpunkt der Antragstellung f *(Dienstleistung)*
substitute message Leertelegramm n *(Übertragungsstrecke)*
subsynchronous untersynchron
successful DCE Gewinner m *(DÜE in Buszuordnung)*
successive approximation register (SAR) Iterationsregister n
suffix (digit) Nachwahlnummer f, Suffix m *(K.-Tel.)*
s. dialling Nachwahl f *(K.-Tel.)*
sum former Summenbildner m
s.-forming circuit Summen-Bildner m
summation alarm Summenalarm m
s. call metering Summengebührenzählung f, Summengesprächszählung f *(Tel.)*
s. meter Summenzähler m
summing circuit Summierer m
s. integrator Summator m *(diskretes Analog des Integrators)*
super high frequency (SHF) superhohe Fre-

quenz f (Sat., 3-30 GHz)
super-multiplex highway Supermultiplexschiene f
superaudio channel Überlagerungskanal m (TEMEX, Centrex, ÖKartTel)
superframe Überrahmen m (PCM)
superheterodyne receiver Überlagerungsempfänger m (HF)
superimpose einblenden (Signal, FO)
superimposed feedback Rückwirkungsüberlagerung f
supervision Überwachung f (Ü) (PCM-Einheit bzw. Einrichtung); Kontrolle f
  s. circuit Überwachungssatz m
  s. threshold Überwachungseinsatz m
supervisory Steuer-, Überwachungs-
  s. audio tone (SAT) Überwachungston m (Mobilfunk)
  s. channel Steuerkanal m
  s. control in networks Netzleittechnik f
  s. control system Fernwirksystem n (FW) (allgemein); Leitsystem n (Prozess)
  s. frame Überwachungsrahmen m; Steuerblock m
  s. function Überwachung f, Überwachungsaufgabe f
  s. network control system Netzführungssystem n
  s. sequence Übertragungssteuerzeichenfolge f
supplementary zusätzlich, ergänzend
  s. circuit Zusatzschaltung f
  s. service Dienstmerkmal n (ZGS.7, CCITT Rec. I.451)
  provide a s. service Dienstmerkmal n durchführen
  s. service attributes Zusatzdienste mpl (ZGS.7)
  s. services Teilnehmerdienstmerkmale npl, teilnehmerbezogene Dienstmerkmale npl (ZGS.7)
supplier Auftragnehmer m (AN)
supply Versorgung f, Zufuhr f; Ablauf m (Kabel, Band)
  s. conditions Anschlußbedingungen fpl
  s. voltage conversion Speisespannungsaufbereitung f (Tel.-Anl.)
support unterstützen; absichern (Ergebnisse)
  s. plate Stützblech n
supraregional überregional
surface Oberfläche f, Fläche f
  s. acoustic waves (SAW) akustische Oberflächenwellen fpl (AOW) (Filter)
  s.-bonded oder **-connected** stoffschlüssig
  s. impedance Flächenwiderstand m

  s. mounted device (SMD) oberflächenmontiertes Bauelement n
  s.-mounting Aufputz-... (AP) (Steckdose)
  s. mounting technology (SMT) Oberflächenmontagetechnik f
surge voltage Stoßspannung f
surplus length bent inwards Ausgleichsknick m nach innen (Drahtbrücke)
  s. load Mehrbelastung f
  s. wire Aderplus n
suspension strand Tragorgan n (Kabel)
SVC s. switched virtual channel
SW (synchronization word) Synchronwort n
swap Dienstewechsel m (ISDN-Tel./Daten, BT-DPNSS)
swath Bodenstreifen m (Erderkundungssat.)
  s. width Streifenbreite f (Erderkundungssat.)
sweep Ablenkung f, Hub m (KO), Durchlauf m; abtasten
  s. amplifier Kippverstärker m
  s. generator Wobbelgenerator m, Wobbelsender m
  s. speed Ablaufgeschwindigkeit f (KO)
  s. range Kippwahl f (KO)
SWIFT Society for Worldwide Interbank Financial Telecommunications
swing Ausschlag m; Hub m (Messwert, Logik)
switch Schalter m, Schaltteil n; Vermittlung f (US), Wählanschluß m (NStAnl.); Koppeleinrichtung f; kippen (Flipflop)
  s. element Schaltteil n
  s. terminal Vermittlungsterminal n
  s. through durchschalten (Tel.)
switchable link Schaltbrücke f (DIP FIX-Schalter)
switchboard Vermittlungstisch m
  s. position Vermittlungsplatz m
switched geschaltet, gekoppelt, vermittelt, vermittelnd
  s. broadband network vermittelndes Breitbandnetz n (VBN)
  s. circuit Wählleitung f
  s. coaxial jack koaxiale Schaltbuchse f
  s. connection Wählverbindung f (WV) (Dienstmerkmal)
  s. data exchange (network) Wählnetz n für Datenaustausch (Dx)
  s. distribution network Verteil-Koppelnetz n
  s.-distribution service verteilvermittelter Dienst m (TV usw.)
  s.-mode power supply (SMPS) Schaltnetzteil n
  s. network Wählnetz n

switched 246

s. **path** Schaltweg *m*
s. **satellite connection** vermittelnde Satelliten-Datenverbindung *f*
s. **virtual channel** (SVC) geschalteter virtueller Kanal *m*
switching Schalten *n*, Kopplung *f*, Vermittlung *f*, Vermittlungstechnik *f*
s. **action** Schaltgefühl *n (Folientastatur)*
s. **amplifier** Schaltverstärker *m*
s. **array**, Koppelfeld *n*
s. **centre** Vermittlungsstelle *f* (VSt)
s. **device** Schalteinrichtung *f*
s. **element** Koppelpunkt *m (Signalverteiler)*
s. **equipment** Vermittlungseinrichtung *f* (VE); Anpassungseinrichtung *f* (ANPE) *(Sat.)*
s. **from door intercom to telephone** mode Apothekerschaltung *f (K.-Tel.)*
s. **matrix** Koppelfeld *n*, Koppelvielfach *n*
s. **matrix row control units** Koppelvielfachreihen-Steuerteile *npl*
s. **module** Koppelbaustein *m*
s. **network** Koppeleinrichtung *f*, Koppelnetz *n*, Koppelanordnung *f (Tel.-Anl.)*, Koppelfeld *n*
s. **network section** Teilkoppelfeld *n*
s. **node** Vermittlungsknoten *m*
s. **point** Koppelpunkt *m (aktiver Signalverteiler)*; Koppelstelle *f (D-Netz)*
s. **processor** Vermittlungsrechner *m* (VR), (TVR) *(TEMEX-VR)*
s. **response** Schaltgefühl *n (Folientastatur)*
s. **sequence** Ansteuerfolge *f*; Schaltfolge *f*
s. **signal** Schaltkennzeichen *n (Vermittlung)*
s. **signals** Kennzeichen *n (Tel.)*
s. **stack** Schaltpaket *n (Folientastatur)*
s. **stage** Koppelfeld *n*, Wahlstufe *f (Vermittlung)*
s. **system** Durchschaltevermittlungseinheit *f*, Vermittlung *f*, Vermittlungsrechner *m* (VR)
s. **task** vermittlungstechnische Aufgabe *f*
s. **time** Aufschaltezeit *f (Tel.)*
s. **unit** (SWU) Durchschalteeinheit *f*, Schaltwerk *n*; Vermittlungseinheit *f (ISDN)*; Koppelgruppe *f* (KG) *(Tel.)*
s. **value** Schaltwert *m*
SWU s. switching unit
SX (simplex) Simplex *n (Modem)*
SXMT (Secondary transmit data) Hilfskanal Sendedaten *(V.24/RS232C)*

SXS (Step-by-Step (selector) exchange) Schrittschaltsystem *n (analog)*
symbol error Schrittfehler *m (Übertragung)*
s. **rate** Schrittfolgefrequenz *f (Bitstrom)*, Schrittrate *f (Übertragung)*
symmetry Symmetrie *f (PCM-Codierer)*
sync (character) trap Synchronfalle *f (FS)*
synchronism Gleichlauf *m (Signale)*, Synchronzustand *m*
in s. **with** ... im Takt *m* des/der ...
synchronization Synchronisierung *f*
s. **time** Einschwingzeit *f*
s. **word** (SW) Synchronwort *n*
synchronized flashing Einphasenblinken *n (Vtx.-Monitor)*
synchronizing character Synchronzeichen *n (FS)*
s. **to** Aufsynchronisieren *n (z.B. Anschlußzustand)*
synchronous synchron, gleichlaufend
s. **data link control** (SDLC) synchrone Übertragungssteuerung *f*
s. **optical network** (SONET) synchrones optisches Netz *n (FO, US, ANSI-Standard T1X1)*
s. **payload envelope** (SPE) synchrone Nutzlast-Bitvollgruppe *f (TDM)*
s. **supervision** mitlaufende Überwachung *f*
s. **time division** (STD) **multiplex** synchrone Zeitvielfachtechnik *f (STM)*
s. **transfer mode** (STM) synchroner Übertragungsmodus *m (FO, leitungsvermittelte PCM-Datenübertragung, wobei 'synchron' auf die Information und nicht die Bitsynchronisation bezogen ist)*
s. **transport module** (STM-1) synchroner Transportmodul *m (Pulsrahmen, CCITT Rec. G.70X)*
synthesis Synthese *f*
word s. Wortaufbereitung *f*
synthetic speech generator Sprechmaschine *f*
syntonisation Frequenzabstimmung *f*, Frequenzvergleich *m*, Abstimmung *f*
syntonize abstimmen *(Frequenzen)*
system barring level Anlagenberechtigung *f*
s. **complex** Systemverband *m*
s. **deadlock** Systemverklemmung *f (Netzknoten)*
s. **earth** Betriebserde *f*
s.-**linked** systemgebunden
S. Network Architecture (SNA) SNA-Architektur *f (IBM-LAN)*
s. **specification** Kenndaten *npl*

s. user Teilnehmer *m (off-line, Datenkanal)*
S. X digitale Vermittlungsanlage *f* System X *(Plessey, GB)*
Systems Applications Architecture (SAA) SAA-Architektur *f (IBM-LAN)*

T

T series of CCITT Recommendations T-Serie *f* der CCITT-Empfehlungen *(betrifft Faksimile der Gruppe 1,2,3, Telematik-, Teletex-, Telex- und Videotex-Dienste)*
T1 *(digitales Übertragungsmerkmal mit Imband-Zeichengabe, AT&T, 1,544 MB/s)*
T3 *(T-Netzträger mit Summenbitrate 44,736 MB/s, US)*
TA (terminal adapter) Endgeräteanpassung *f (ISDN)*
TA-A (TA for manual calling) Endgeräteanpassung *f* für Handruf *(leitungsvermittelt, CCITT Rec. I.463, V.110)*
TA-B (TA for automatic calling) Endgeräteanpassung *f* für automatische Wahl *(leitungsvermittelt, CCITT Rec. I.463, V.25, V.25 bis)*
TA (Traffic Announcement) Verkehrsdurchsagekennung *f (RDS)*
table of pages (TOP) Seitentabelle *f (Vtx., entspricht FLOF)*
t. set Tischapparat *m*
tablet Tablett *n (Tastenfeld)*, Tableau *n (z.B zum Fernzeichnen)*
TACS (Total Access Communications System) Kommunikationssystem *n* mit Totalzugriff *(GB 'Cellnet' u. 'Vodaphone', JRTIG, mobiles Analog-Fernsprechsystem auf Basis von AMPS (US), 900 MHz)*
E-TACS (extended TACS) erweitertes TACS *n (GB, plus 720 Kanäle)*
tactile response Tastgefühl *n (Folientastatur)*
tail hintere Flanke *f (Welle);* Anschlußfaser *f (FO)*
take off-line deaktivieren *(DEE)*, passivieren
takeover circuit Einspringschaltung *f (FS)*
t. priority Einspringberechtigung *f (FS)*
talking circuit Sprechkreis *m (Tel.)*
talkspurt Sprachblock *m (PCM Sprache)*
t. compression Sprachblockstauchung *f (PCM Sprache)*
t. duration Sprachblocklänge *f (PCM Sprache)*
TAN (transaction number) Transaktionsnummer *f*
tandem exchange Durchgangsamt *n (verbindet OVSt.)*, Durchgangsvermittlungsstelle *f*
t. dialling Durchgangswahl *f*
t. memory Staffelspeicher *m*
t. switching Knotenvermittlung *f* (KnV)
tape bin Streifenbehälter *m (Bandleser)*
t. punch Lochstreifenlocher *m*, Lochstreifenstanzer *m (FS)*
t. reader Lochstreifenleser *m*
t. take-up system Streifenaufnahme *f (Bandleser)*
t. tension Streifenzug *m (Bandleser)*
TASI (time-assigned speech interpolation) zeitmultiplexierte Sprachübertragung *f*
TAT-x (Transatlantic Telephone cable No. x) transatlantisches Telefonkabel Nr. x *(TAT8 in FO-Technik)*
TAU (terminal adapter unit) Engeräteanpassungseinheit *f (K-Anl., US)*
TAU-P (terminal adapter unit for PCs) Endgeräteanpassungseinheit *f* für PCs
TAU-T (terminal adapter unit for telephone) Endgeräteanpassungseinheit *f* für Fernsprecher
TC (time code) Zeitcode *m*
TC (transformation coding) Transformationscodierung *f (dig. Audio)*
TC (transmission control) Übertragungssteuerung *f*
TC (Transmit Clock) Sendeschrittakt *(V.24/RS232C)*
TCM (time compression multiplex) Zeitkompressionsmultiplex *n*, Burst-Übertragung *f*
TCP (transmission control protocol) Übertragungssteuerungsprotokoll *n*
TCP/IP (Transmission Control Protocol/Internet Protocol) Übertragungssteuerungsprotokoll/Querverkehrprotokoll *n*
TD (Transmit Data) Sendedaten *npl (V.24/RS232C)*
TDC (Data Channel) Datenkanal *m (RDS)*
TDD (time division duplex) Zeitduplex *n;* Zeitgetrenntlageverfahren *n*
TDF1 Télédiffusion de France 1 *(französischer DBS, D2-Mac)*
TDM (time division multiplex) Zeitmultiplex *n*
TDM data transmission Zeitmultiplex-Datenübertragung *f* (ZD)
TDM switching matrix Zeitkoppelfeld *n*

TDMA (time division *oder* domain multiple access) Vielfachzugriff *m* im Zeitmultiplex *(VSAT)*
R-TDMA (reservation TDMA) TDMA *m* mit Buchung *(Sat.)*
SS-TDMA (satellite-switched TDMA) TDMA *m* mit Vermittlung im Satelliten
TDPSK (three-level differential PSK) dreiwertige Differenz-Phasenumtastung *f*
TDRSS (Tracking and Data Relay Satellite System) Bahnverfolgungs- und Datenübermittlungssatellitensystem *n (NASA)*
TE (terminating exchange) Endamt *n*
TE (terminal *oder* terminating equipment) Endeinrichtung *f (ISDN)*
TE1 (ISDN terminal equipment) ISDN-Endeinrichtung *f*
TE2 (non-ISDN terminal equipment) Endeinrichtung *f* ohne ISDN-Schnittstelle *(benötigt TA für ISDN-Zugriff)*
technical and office protocol (TOP) Bürokommunikationsprotokoll *n (OSI)*
t. information Gebrauchsunterlage *f*
T. Requirements Technischer Leitfaden *m* (TL)
t. service position Betriebsdienstplatz *m*
technique Technik *f*, Verfahren *n*
technology Technologie *f*, Technik *f*
TEI (terminal endpoint identifier) Endgeräte-Endpunktkennung *f*
teleaction Fernwirken *n (DBP-TEMEX-Dienst; NTG Rec. 2001)*, Fernwirk- (Fw)
t. link Fernwirk-Verbindung *f*
t. master station Fernwirk-Leitstelle *f* (FwLSt)
t. service provider Fernwirk-Dienstanbieter *m*
t. station Fernwirk-Stelle *f* (FwSt)
t. terminal Fernwirk-Endgerät *n* (FwEG)
t. terminal equipment Fernwirk-Endeinrichtung *f* (FwEE)
telebanking elektronischer Bankverkehr *m*
Telecom Gold BT-Textspeicherdienst *m (MHS nach CCITT Rec. X.400, entspricht DBP TELEBOX)*
Telecom Silver BT-Transaktions- und Kreditüberprüfungsdienst *m (PSS und X.400)*
telecommanding Fernschalten *n (TEMEX)*
telecommunication Fernmelde- (Fm), Übermittlung *f*, Fernmeldewesen *n*
t. company Fernmeldeunternehmen *n (in BRD z.B. Siemens)*
t. equipment Fernübertragungseinheit *f* (FÜ) *(FS)*
t. line unit (TLU) Telekommunikations-Anschlußeinheit *f*, Teilnehmer-Anschlußeinrichtung *f* (TAE) *(FTZ) heute:* Übergabestelle *f (ISO-Standard IS 8877)*; Universalanschluß *m (ISDN)*
T. Management Network (TMN) Fernmelde-Kontrollnetz *n (CCITT)*
t. socket Fernmeldesteckdose *f (ISDN)*
telecommunications Fernmeldewesen *n*, Telekommunikation *f*
t. maintenance district Fernmeldeunterhaltungsbezirk *m* (FEUBZ)
t. satellite Fernmeldesatellit *m*, Nachrichtensatellit *m*
telecontrol (system) Fernwirksystem *n* (FW)
telecopier Fernkopierer *m*, Telefaxmaschine *f*
telefax machine Fernkopierer *m*, Telefaxmaschine *f*
teleindication Fernanzeige *f*
telematics services Telematikdienste *mpl (Masseninformatik, Textkommunikation, Datenfernverarbeitung, Videokonferenz, TV usw.; FR télématique)*
telemetry data Telemetriedaten *npl*
t. equipment Fernmeßeinrichtung *f*
telephone fernsprechen, telefonieren; Fernsprech- (Fe)
t. accounts service Fernmelderechnungsdienst *m* (FRD)
t. construction district Fernmeldebaubezirk *m* (FBBZ)
t. directory Fernsprechbuch *n*, Telefonbuch *n*
t. fault clearance Fernsprechentstörung *f* (FeE)
t. network Fernsprechnetz *n*
t. ringer Weckeinrichtung *f*
t. set Fernsprecher *m*, Fernsprechapparat *m* (FeAp)
t. station Sprechstelle *f*
t. subscriber line Fernsprech-Anschlußleitung *f* (FeAsl)
t. user part (TUP) Anwenderteil *m* für Fernsprechen *(ZGS.7, CCITT Rec. Q.721 - 725)*
t. voice service Telefonsprachdienst *m*
telephony Fernsprechübertragung *f*
telepictures Fernzeichnen *n*
Telepoint Telepoint *m (öffentliches Funktelefon-System, BT, umfaßt Handapparat, Haus-Feststation und Zugriff zum öffentlichen 'Phonepoint', CT2, nicht zu DECT kompatibel)*
teleport Teleport *m ('Medienpark', Gebäude (-komplex) mit Telematik-Verbund für mietende Unternehmen, ggf. mit IBS/IDR*

bzw. SMS)
teleprinter Fernschreiber *m*, Fernschreibmaschine *f*
telescript Fernzeichnen *n*
teleservice (telecommunication service) standardisierter Dienst *m (CCITT Rec. I.112, I.210)*
Teletel *(Videotex-Dienst in Frankreich, CEPT-Profil 2, s. Tabelle VIII)*
teletex Teletex *n* (Ttx), Bürofernschreiben *n (2400 Bit/s, leitungs- oder paketvermittelt, nach OSI-Standard)*
t./telex converter (TTC) Teletex-Telex-Umsetzer *m* (TTU)
teletext (txt) Fernsehtext *m*, Videotext *m (nicht dialogfähiger Videotextdienst im Rundfunk-TV)*
teletype (TTY) Fernschreib- (Fs), Fernschreiben *n* (FS)
telewriting Fernschreiben *n*, Fernzeichnen *n*
telex (teleprinter exchange (tx)) Telex *n*, Fernschreiben *n* (FS) *(ASCII)*
temporal resolution Zeitauflösung *f*, zeitliche Auflösung *f (Bildcodierung)*
temporary line bewegliche Leitung *f*
  t. meter comparison befristeter Zählvergleich *m*
  t. signalling connection temporäre Zeichengabetransaktion *f* (tZGT) *(ZGS.7 MTP, CCITT Rec. Q.711...714)*
  t. storage Zwischenspeicherung *f*
tender specifications Leistungsverzeichnis *n* (LV)
tension arm Spannarm *m (Bandleser)*
tentative specification vorläufige Spezifikation *f*
  t. standard Vornorm *f (DIN)*
Ter, ter *(einem CCITT-Netzstandard nachgefügt, wird damit seine dritte Version identifiziert, z.B. V.27 bis)*
terminal (TE) Endeinrichtung *f* (EE), Endgerät *n*; Terminal *n*, Außenstation *f*; Anschluß *m (Bauteil)*; Anschlußpunkt *m (Netz)*; -polig *(Klemmenblock)*
  t. adapter (TA) Endgeräteanpassung *f (ISDN, für (TE2-)Einrichtungen ohne ISDN-Schnittstelle)*
  t. adapter unit (TAU) Engeräteanpassungseinheit *f (K-Anl., US)*
  t. assignment Anschlußbelegung *f*
  t. block Reihenklemme *f*, Anschlußverteiler *m*, Klemmenblock *m*, Verteiler *m*
  t. box Klemmenkasten *m*; Endverzweiger *m* (EVz) *(Tel.)*
  t. clip Polklemme *f*, Anschlußlasche *f*

  t. conditions Anschlußbedingungen *fpl*
  t. device Endgerät *n*; Anschlußstelle *f*
  t. disconnect patchboard Trennsteckverteiler *m*
  t. endpoint identifier (TEI) Endgeräte-Endpunktkennung *f*
  t. equipment (TE) Endeinrichtung *f* (EE) *(ISDN, CCITT Rec. I.112)*
  t. exchange (TX) Endvermittlungsstelle *f* (EVst), Endamt *n*
  t. for data channel Anschluß *m* für Datenkanal
  t. line Endstellenleitung *f* (EndStLtg.) *(Tel.)*
  t. link Querverbinder *m (Verbinder)*, Klemmenbrücke *f*
  t. module Klemmenbaustein *m*
  t. node controller (TNC) Netzknotensteuerung *f (PR)*
  t. office Endamt *n*
  t. operating elements Bediener-, Benutzer-Oberfläche *f*
  t. regenerator Endregenerator *m*
  t. restriction data Anschlußsperre *f*
  t. station Endstelle *f (PCM-Daten, Sprache)*; Anschlußstation *f* (AS) *(Sat.)*
  t. strip Klemmenleiste *f*, Verteilerleiste *f*
terminate abschließen
  t. in characteristic impedance wellenrichtig abschließen
terminating Abschluß-, End-; abschließend
  t. cable Schaltkabel *n*
  t. criteria Endebedingungen *fpl*
  t. equipment (TE) Endeinrichtung *f* (EE) *(ISDN, CCITT Rec. I.112)*
  t. exchange (TE) Endamt *n*
  t. rack Endgestell *n*
  t. subscriber Endteilnehmer *m*
  t. traffic Endverkehr *m*
termination Abschluß *m*, Endverschluß *m*; Anschluß *m (Festverbindung)*
  t. circuit Anschlußschaltung *f*
terms of reference Aufgabenstellung *f*
ternary ternär *(mit drei diskreten Werten)*
tertiary exchange Zentralvermittlungsstelle *f* (ZVSt)
test Prüfung *f*, Test *m*; aufprüfen *(einen Draht auf z.B Belegung)*, prüfen, messen;
  t. accessories Meßzubehörkoffer *m*
  t. assembly Meßplatz *m*
  t. call generator automatischer Teilnehmer *m*
  t. circuit Prüfkreis *m*, Prüfsatz *m*
  t. desk Prüftisch *m*; Meßplatz *m*

t. environment Testumgebung f *(Programm)*
t. in the field Betriebsversuch m
t. indicator Prüfzustand m *(nicht standardisiert, V.24/RS232C)*
t. interface Meßebene f
t. jack Prüfbuchse f
t. kit Meßzubehörkoffer m
t. panel Meßfeld n
t. planning Prüfvorbereitung f
t. position Meßplatz m, Prüfstellung f
t. rack Meßplatz m
t. rig Meßplatz m
t. room Prüfraum m, Prüffeld n
t. set *oder* **set-up** Meßplatz m
t. tone receiver Meßtonempfänger m (MTE)
testing Prüfen n, Prüftechnik f
text/fax server (TFS) Text-Fax-Server m *(ISDN)*
TFS s. text/fax server
THD (total harmonic distortion) Klirrfaktor m
third-party maintenance (TPM) Herstellerwartung f für Eigen- und Fremdsysteme
threaded ferrule Schraubstutzen m *(Kabel)*
three-level differential PSK (TDPSK) dreiwertige Differenz-Phasenumtastung f
t.-party call Dreierverbindung f
t.-port coupler Y-Verzweigung f *(FO)*
t.-tone caller Drei-Ton-Ruf m *(K.-Tel.)*
t.-tone ringing Dreiklang-Tonruf m *(Tel.)*
threshold period Zeitschwelle f
t. voltage Einsatzspannung f
through-connection Durchschaltung f
t.-connection gate Durchschaltegitter n (DG) *(PCM, Tel.)*
throughput Durchsatzrate f *(Pakete/Sek.)*, Durchsatz m
ticking tone Tickerzeichen n *(Warteton, Tel.)*
TICOG Texas Instruments Communications Grid *(US)*
TID (touch input device) Tasteingabevorrichtung f *(DSG)*
tie line Querverbindung(sleitung) f *(zw. privaten Vermittlungen)*; Standleitung f, Festanschluß m, Festverbindung f; Direktanschluß m, Nachbarverbindung f, Mietleitung f
t. trunk Querverbindungsleitung f *(zwischen NStAnl.)*
tieing-in Einbinden n *(Teilnehmer)*
tilt Schräge f, Dachschräge f, Abfall m, Dachabfall m *(Impuls)*

time announcement Zeitansage f
t.-assigned speech interpolation (TASI) zeitmultiplexierte Sprachübertragung f
t. characteristic zeitlicher Verlauf m, Zeitverlauf m
t. code (TC) Zeitcode m (ZC) *(FS)*
t. compression multiplex (TCM) Zeitkompressionsmultiplex n, Burst-Übertragung f *(Ping-Pong-Verfahren, mit wechselseitiger Übertragung von hochratigen Datenpaketen)*
t. congestion Zeitsperrung f *(Tel.-Anl.)*
t. correlation Zeitbezug m
t. deviation Standablage f *(Uhr)*
t. discriminator Zeitentscheider m
t. division duplex (TDD) Zeitduplex n; Zeitgetrenntlageverfahren n *(Ping-Pong-Verfahren für Ortsanschlußleitung, ISDN-B-Kanal)*
t. division method Zeitgetrenntlageverfahren n *(allgemein)*
t. division multiple access (TDMA) Vielfachzugriff m im Zeitmultiplex *(VSAT)*, Zeitmultiplexzugriff m; Zeitvielfachzugriff m
t. division multiplex (TDM) Zeitlagenvielfach n, Zeitvielfach n; Zeitmultiplex n, Zeitscheibenteilung f *(bit- oder byteweise Verschachtelung mehrerer Nutzdatenströme in Zeitschlitzen auf einem seriellen Kommunikationskanal)*
t. division multiplexer Zeitmultiplexer m, Zeitvielfach n
t. domain multiple access (TDMA) Vielfachzugriff m im Zeitmultiplex *(VSAT)*
t. interval Zeitabschnitt m
t. measurement Zeitmessung f
t.-of-day program Uhrzeitprogramm n
t. of origin (TOO) Sendezeit f
t. of reception (TOR) Empfangszeit f
t. of the wake-up call Weckzeit f *(Tel.)*
t.-out Zeitüberwachung f *(SW)*; ablaufen *(Zeitüberwachung)*
t. pattern Zeitraster m
t. pulse counter Zeittaktzähler m
t. reference Zeitbezug m
t. reserve Zeitrückhalt m
t. sharing user Teilnehmer m *(Netz)*
t. shifted zeitversetzt
t. slice Zeitscheibe f *(Teilmenge der Gesamtrechenzeit in Multitasking)*
t. slot Zeitabschnitt m, Zeitlage f (PCM); Zeitschlitz m, Zeitkanal m *(ein bzw. mehrere Oktette)*

t.-slot pattern Kanal-Zeitlage *f*
t.-space-space-time structure Zeit-Raum-Raum-Zeit-Struktur *f*
t. stamp Zeitmarke *f*
t. supervision Zeitüberwachung *f (HW)*
t. switch Zeit(lagen)vielfach *n*
   as a function of t. zeitlich
   at the correct t. zeitgerecht
   in the correct t. relationship zeitgerecht
   in t. with ... im Rhythmus *m* der/des ...
   over t. zeitlich
   with respect to t. zeitlich
timed taktgesteuert; zeitlich gesteuert *oder* erfaßt *oder* überwacht
timeout Zeitsperre *f*, Zeitauslösung *f*
timer Zeit(takt)geber *m*; Zeitüberwachung *f* Verzögerungseinrichtung *f*
timing Taktung *f*, Takt *m*, Takten *n (PCM-Daten)*; Synchronisierung *f*; Zeitmessung *f* ; Raster *m (z.B. Abtastwerte)*
   t. chart Ablaufdiagramm *n*
   t. diagram Taktdiagramm *n*, Pulsplan *m*
   t. (difference) Stand *m (Uhr)*
   t. error Rasterverzerrung *f (EWS)*
   t. extraction Taktableitung *f*
   t. generator Synchronisiereinheit *f*
   t. information Taktgehalt *m*
   t. pattern Rasterung *f* , Zeitraster *m*
   t. program Zeitprogramm *n*
   t. relationship Zeitlage *f (PCM)*
TLU (telecommunication line unit) Telekommunikations-Anschluß-Einheit *f (TAE)*
TMN (Telecommunications Management Network) Fernmelde-Kontrollnetz *n (CCITT)*
TNC (terminal node controller) Netzknotensteuerung *f (PR)*
TOH (transport overhead) Übertragungskopfteil *m (TDM)*
token Token *m*, Belegungs-Steuerblock *m*, Zugangs-Steuerblock *m (steuert den Zugang zu einem Token-Ring-Netz)*, Sendeberechtigungsmarke *f*
   t. bus interface Token-Bus-Schnittstelle *f (IEEE 802.4)*
   t. passing Berechtigungsweitergabe *f (LAN)*
   t. ring network Token-Ring-Netz *n (LAN nach IEEE 802.5, in dem ein Token der Reihe nach von Anschlußpunkt zu Anschlußpunkt weitergegeben wird)*
tolerance band Toleranzschlauch *m (Kabel)*
toll centre Knotenvermittlungsstelle *f (DBP, Mobilfunk)*
   t. office Fernamt *n*
   t. restriction Fernsperre *f*

t. traffic Fernverkehr *m*
t. trunk Fernleitung *f*
tone caller Tonruf *m (K.-Tel.)*
tone-dialling telephone Fernsprecher *m* für Mehrfrequenzwahl
   t.-off condition Pausenzustand *f*
   t./two-party circuit Ton-Zweiersatz *m (TZS)*
TOO s. time of origin
TOP (table of (preview) pages) Programmvorschau-Seitentabelle *f (Vtx.)*
TOP (technical and office protocol) Bürokommunikationsprotokoll *n (OSI)*
topology Topologie *f*; Lagebeziehung *f*, Lage *f (IC)*
TOR s. time of reception
total failure Totalausfall *m*, Vollstörung *f*
   t. harmonic distortion (THD) Klirrfaktor *m*
   t. traffic intensity Summenverkehrswert *m*
touch area Tastfläche *f (auf Taste)*
   t. display berührungssensitive Anzeige *f*
   t. input device (TID) Tasteingabevorrichtung *f*, berührungssensitive Eingabeeinrichtung *f (DSG)*
   t. panel Tastenfeld *n*
   t. sensitive berührungssensitiv
   t.-sensitive coding switch Tastkodierschalter *m*
   t.-tone dialling Tastaturwahl *f*, Tastaturtonwahl *f*, Tastenwahl *f (Tel.)*
TP s. Traffic Programme (identification)
TPM (third-party maintenance) Herstellerwartung *f* für Eigen- und Fremdsysteme
TPON (telephony over passive optical networks) Fernsprechbetrieb *m* über passiv übermittelnde optische Netze *(FO, BT)*
trace Mitschrift *f*, Mitschrieb *m*, Linienzug *m (Schreiber)*;
verfolgen, abfahren *(Kabel, Leiterzüge)*
tracer gas Spürgas *n (Kabel)*
track side Leiter-, Lötseite *f* (L-Seite) *(Print)*
tracker ball Steuerkugel *f*, Rollkugel *f (DSG)*
tracking Verfolgung *f*, Nachführung *f*; Nachlauf-, nachlaufend; Gleichlauf *m (Bauteileigenschaften)*
   t. accuracy Nachführgenauigkeit *f*
   T. and Data Relay Satellite System (TDRSS) Bahnverfolgungs- und Datenübermittlungssystem *n (NASA)*
   t. filter Mitlauffilter *n*
   t. range Haltebereich *m (VCO)*
   t., telemetry and command (TTC) Bahnver-

trade 254

folgung, Telemetrie und Befehlsgabe *f (Sat.-Bodenstation)*
trade makeln *(Tel., Schalten zwischen zwei bestehenden Verbindungen)*
trading facility *oder* **station** *oder* **system** Makleranlage *f*
traffic Verkehr *m*
 T. **Announcement** (TA) Verkehrsdurchsagekennung *f*, Durchsagekennung *f* (DK) *(RDS)*
 t. **(broadcast) programme** Verkehrs(rund)funk *m* (VRF)
 t. **capacity** Leistungsfähigkeit *f (Tel.-Anl.)*
 t. **channel** Verkehrsweg *m*; Sprachkanal *m (Bündelfunk)*
 t. **circuit** Dienstleitung *f*
 t. **components** Teilverkehre *mpl (Tel.-Anl.)*
 t. **density** Verkehrsstärke *f (Tel.-Anl.)*
 t. **discrimination code** Verkehrsausscheidungsziffer *f*
 t. **distributor** Anrufverteiler *m*
 t. **handling capacity** Verkehrsleistung *f*
 t. **intensity** Verkehrslast *f*; Verkehrswert *m (dimensionslos, in Erlang)*
 t. **list** Anrufliste *f*
 t. **load** Verkehrswert *m (allgemein)*, Verkehrsumfang *m*
 t. **management** Verkehrsmanagement *n (ZGS.7)*
 t. **mode** Verkehrsart *f*
 t. **padding** Scheinverkehr *m*, Störverkehr *m*
 t. **processor** Funkprocessor *m (Bündelfunk, nömL)*
 T. **Programme Identification** (TP) Verkehrsfunkkennung *f (RDS)*
 t. **relation** Partnerbeziehung *f (ISDN)*
 t. **routing** Verkehrsführung *f*
 t. **section** Betriebsdienst *m*
 t. **unit** (TU) Verkehrseinheit *f* (VE) *(= 1 Erl)*
 t. **variance method** Streuwertverfahren *n*
 t. **volume** Verkehrsaufkommen *n*, Verkehrsumfang *m*
 to suit t. **conditions** verkehrsgerecht
train Folge *f*, Zug *m (Impulse, Wellen)*
 t. **of ones, zeroes** Dauereins-, -nullsignal *n*
 t. **of pulses** Impulsreihe *f*, Impulsfolge *f*
 t. **tannoy** Fahrgastinformationssystem *n* (FIS) *(GB)*
transaction number Transaktionsnummer *f* (TAN)
transceiver (transmitter/receiver) Sender/Empfänger *m* (S/E); Buskoppler *m*
transconductance Steilheit *f (Verstärker)*

transducer Wandler *m*, Umsetzer *m*, Signalgeber *m*
transfer Übertragung *f*, Weitergabe *f*, Weiterleitung *f*, Weiterschaltung *f*, Umlegung *f (Ruf)*, Übergabe *f*; Anschaltung *f*; überkoppeln *(Licht)*; überspielen *(Daten)*
 t. **exchange** Überleitungsamt *n (Tel.)*
 t. **facility** Überleitungseinrichtung *f* (ÜLE)
 t. **impedance** Kopplungswiderstand *m (Kabel)*
 t. **traffic** Überweisungsverkehr *m* (NStAnl.)
transferring a call Ruf *m* umlegen *(K.-Tel.)*
transformation coding (TC) Transformationscodierung *f (FS)*
transhybrid loss Gabelübergangsdämpfung *f*
transient Wischer *m*, Übergangsvorgang *m*, Einschwingvorgang *m*; kurzzeitig *(Spitzen)*
 t. **response** Einschwingverhalten *n*
 t. **response time** Einschwingzeit *f*
transit Durchgang *m*, Übergang *m*, Durchlauf *m*
 t. **exchange** Transitamt *n*, Durchgangsvermittlungsstelle *f*, Durchgangsamt *n*
 t. **network** Durchgangsnetz *n*
 t. **store** Durchlaufspeicher *m (FIFO-Prinzip)*
 t. **switching** Durchgangsvermittlung *f* (DV)
 t. **time** Laufzeit *f (von Paketen)*
 t. **traffic** Durchgangsverkehr *m*
transition Übergang *m*, Sprung *m*
 t. **count** Flankenzählung *f*
 t. **to idle state** Außerbetriebnahme *f*
 t. **traffic** Übergangsverkehr *m*
optical waveguide t. Querschnittswandler *m (FO)*
zero t. Nulldurchgang *m*
translator Zuordner *m (NTG 0902)*; Umwerter *m*, Umwertespeicher *m (Signalisierung)*, Umsetzer *m*, Kanalumsetzer *m*
transmission Übertragung *f*, Übermittlung *f*
 t. **bandwidth** Übertragungsbereich *m*
 t. **bit rate** (TBR) Übertragungsbitrate *f*
 t. **burst** Trägerpaket *n (Sat.)*
 t. **capacity** Übertragungskapazität *f*
 t. **coefficient** Kopplungsgrad *m (FO)*
 t. **control** (TC) Übertragungssteuerung *f* (FS)
 t. **control protocol** (TCP) Übertragungssteuerungsprotokoll *n (Schicht 4, OSI-*

Modell; DARPA)
t. distance Übertragungslänge *f*
t. frequency Durchgangshäufigkeit *f (Signale)*
t. line termination übertragungstechnischer Kabelanschluß *m (ISDN U-Schnittstelle)*
t. loss Betriebsdämpfung *f*, Dämpfungswert *m*, Durchgangsdämpfung *f (FO, Tel.)*
t. mode Durchstrahlungsmodus *m*
t. module Übertragungsbaugruppe *f* (TÜB) *(TEMEX)*
t. on demand Abfragebetrieb *m (FW)*
t. path Übertragungsweg *m*
t. plan Dämpfungsplan *m (Fernsprechnetz)*
t. sequence control Übertragungsablaufsteuerung *f* (UEAS) *(EWS)*
t. speed Taktgeschwindigkeit *f (FS)*
t. surveillance centre zentrale (Betriebs-)Beobachtung *f* (ZBBeo) *(FO)*
t. system design Übertragungstechnische Planung *f (DBP, FTZ 1TR800)*
t. test equipment Pegelsende- und Meßeinrichtung *f* (PSME)
t. test equipment connecting matrix Sende- und Meßkoppler *m* (SMK)
transmissive mixer Durchgangsmischer *m (FO)*
transmit übertragen, senden, abliefern, absetzen *(Signal)*
t. block Sendesperre *f*
t. clock (TC) Sendeschrittakt *(vom DÜE, DEE, V.24/RS232C)*; sendeseitige Taktzentrale *f*
T. Data (TD) Sendedaten *(V.24/RS232C)*
t. identifier Sendeadresse *f (PCM-Daten)*
transmitter Sender *m* (S); Geber *m*
TRANSPAC *(paketvermitteltes Datennetz, FR, unterstützt X.25, X.3, X.28 und X.29 DÜEs und DEEs, 72 kB/s-Kanäle)*
transparent transparent, durchlässig *(allgemein mit Außerbandsignalisierung)*
t. connection Transportverbindung *f*
transponder Transponder *m (Sat.)*
transport connection Transportverbindung *f*
t. layer Transportebene *f (Schicht 4, OSI 7-Schicht-Referenzmodell)*
t. overhead Übertragungskopfteil *m (TDM)*
t. protocol Transportprotokoll *n (ISO, Sat.)*
transporting information Nachrichten *fpl* befördern
transversal filter Transversalfilter *n (Übertragung)*
transverse support Querholm *m (Gestell)*
travel Weglänge *f*, Hub *m (mech.)*; Lauf *m*

travelling clock Transportuhr *f (Uhrensynchronisation)*
t. wave tube (TWT) Wanderfeldröhre *f (Sat.)*
t. wave tube amplifier (TWTA) Wanderfeldröhrenverstärker *m (Sat.)*
tray Ablage *f*, Trog *m (Batt.)*, Rost *m (Kabel)*
trial approval Erprobungszulassung *f (FTZ)*
triangular-wave generator Dreieckgenerator *m*
tributary bits Nutzinformation *f (TDM)*
trigger anstoßen, kippen, auslösen
trip auslösen *(Relais)*
true earth radius natürlicher Erdradius *m*
trunk bündeln *(Funkkanäle)*; Leitung *f (ein Kommunikationskanal zwischen 2 Vermittlungseinrichtungsreihen derselben Vermittlungsstelle oder zwischen 2 Vermittlungsstellen)*, Verbindungsleitung *f* (Vl); Übertragungsstrecke *f (Tel.-Anl.)*; Vielfachleitung *f*
t. access (level) Fernberechtigung *f*
t.-barring level Nicht-Amtsberechtigung *f*, Amtsberechtigung *f (Tel.)*
t. busy fernbesetzt
t. cable Programmzuführungskabel *n (Kabel-TV)*
t. circuit Fernleitung *f*
t. circuit with dialling facility Fernwahlleitung *f*
t. coding equipment Bündelschlüsselgerät *n (Tel.)*
t. exchange Fernvermittlung *f* (FVSt.), Fernamt *n*
t. exchange access Vollamtsberechtigung *f*
t. group Bündel *n (Tel.-Anl., Bündelung von Übertragungswegen einer Strecke)*
t. group layout Bündelführung *f (Tel.)*
t. junction exchange Fernknotenamt *n*
t. network Verbindungsleitungsnetz *f*
t. offering Aufschalten *n* (AS)
t.-offering tone Aufschalteton *m*
t. position B-Platz *m*, Fernplatz *m*
t. prefix Verkehrsausscheidungszahl *f*
t. subscriber's line Fernanschluß *m*
t. terminating unit Fernleitungsabschluß *m*
t. unrestricted subscriber fernamtsberechtigter Teilnehmer *m*
trunked channels Kanalbündel *n (nömL)*
t. mobile radio network Bündelfunknetz *n (regionaler ömL-Dienst 'Chekker')*
t. radio channels gebündelte Funkkanäle *mpl*
trunking Bündelfunk *m (nömL, Organisa-*

tionskanäle, Warteschlangen, DTI-Standard MPT 1327)
t. **arrangement** Gruppierung f (TelAnl.)
t. **diagram** Übersichtsplan m, Verkehrswegeschaltbild n (Tel.-Vermittlung)
t. **scheme** Fernleitungsschema n
t. **system** Bündelnetz n (nömL)
t. **system control** (TSC) Bündelnetzsteuerung f (nömL)
t. **term** gruppentechnischer Begriff m (TelAnl.)
TSC s. trunking system control
TTC (tracking, telemetry and command) Bahnverfolgung, Telemetrie und Befehlsgabe f (Sat.)
Ttx (teletex) Teletex n
TTY (teletype) Fernschreiben n
TU (Traffic Unit) Verkehrseinheit f (VE)
tune abgleichen (Frequenz); abstimmen (Empfänger)
tunnelling mode Leckwelle f (FO)
TUP (telephone user part) Anwenderteil m für Fernsprechen (ZGS.7)
turn off abschalten; sperren (Transistor)
t.**-off voltage** Einsatzspannung f
t. **on** einschalten (Bauteil), durchschalten (HW); durchsteuern (Halbleiter)
t. **on harder** mehr durchsteuern
t.**-on voltage** Einsatzspannung f
turnaround time Durchlaufzeit f (für ein Job, DV), Verweilzeit f
line t. Umschaltezeit f (RS232-Verbindung, halbduplex)
turnkey system schlüsselfertiges System n
TVRO (TV receive only) Fernsehempfang m, Fernsehempfangsstation f (Sat.)
TV-SAT TV-Satellit m (deutscher DBS, D2-Mac)

TV-top unit Beistellgerät n (Sat.-Heimempfänger)
twin connector zweipoliger Verbinder m
t. **contact** Doppelkontakt m
twisted-pair paarverseilt (Kabel)
t.**-quad** viererverseilt (Kabel)
two-frequency recording Wechseltaktschrift f (Magnetstreifenkarte)
t.**-party line** Gemeinschaftsanschluß m (GAS), Zweieranschluß m (Tel.)
t.**-party subscriber** Zweieranschluß m
t.**-port** zweitorig
t.**-way** doppeltgerichtet (Abnehmerleitung, Tel.)
t.**-way alternate** halbduplex
t.**-way service** Zweiwegdienst m (z.B. Btx.)
t.**-way simultaneous** vollduplex
t.**-way trunks** wechselseitig betriebene Leitungen fpl
t.**-way videotext** Videotex n, Bildschirmtext m (BTX)
t.**-wire** ... zweidraht ... (zdr.)
t.**-wire trunk** Zweidrahtleitung f
TWT s. travelling wave tube
TWTA s. travelling wave tube amplifier
TWX (teletypewriter exchange) Fernschreibvermittlung f (ASCII, Western Union, US)
tx (telex) Telex n
TX (terminal exchange) Endvermittlungsstelle f (EVSt)
txt (teletext) Fernsehtext m
Tymnet (paketvermitteltes US-Netz, X.25/X.75)
type Typ m, Bauform f, Bauart f, Ausführung f
t. **approval** Zulassung f (FTZ)
t. **approval number** DBP-Zulassungsnummer f (FTZ)
t. **test** Typenprüfung f

U

U (rack unit) Höheneinheit *f* (HE) *(1 HE = 1 3/4", 44,45 mm)*
U-interface circuit (UIC) U-Schnittstelle *f (netzseitige Schnittstelle für Zweidraht-Anschluß, ISDN)*
U$_{2M}$ interface U$_{2M}$-Schnittstelle *f (netzseitige U-Schnittstelle für ISDN-PA)*
UA (user agent) Benutzer *m*, Benutzermittel *n*, elektronischer Briefkasten *m (CCITT Rec. X.400)*
UART s. universal asynchronous receiver/-transmitter
UC (Unit Call) *(Verkehrseinheit, = 1/36 Erl)*
UCNR s. UnControlled Not Ready
UIC s. U-interface circuit
U$_{ko}$ interface U$_{ko}$-Schnittstelle *f (U-Schnittstelle für ISDN-BA-Kupferleitungen zur ISDN-OVSt)*
unassigned (exchange line) answer allgemeine Amtsabfrage *f* (AA), offene Amtsabfrage *f*
unattended unbeaufsichtigt, unbesetzt *(Fernstation)*; unbedient, bedienungslos *(NStAnl., Modem)*
unauthorized unzulässig, unberechtigt
unbalanced Einader- *(Zeichengabe)*
   u. interference unsymmetrische Überlagerung *f (PCM-Daten)*
unblanked hellgetastet, sichtbar *(Vtx. Mon.)*
unblanking Helltastung *f (Vtx.. Mon.)*
uncanted ungeneigt *(Niederschlag)*
unconnectorized fibre unkonfektionierte Faser *f (FO)*
UnControlled Not Ready (UCNR) nicht betriebsfähig *(X.21)*, DÜE nicht betriebsfähig *(Schleifenmeßtechnik)*
underrun unterschreiten *(Zeit)*
undersea cable Seekabel *n*
undershoot Unterschwingen *n*, Nachläufer *m (Impuls)*
UNI (user-network interface) Teilnehmerschnittstelle *f* S$_0$, Teilnehmer-Netz-Schnittstelle *f (ISDN)*
unified S-band (USB) kombiniertes S-Band *n (Sat.)*
uniformly illuminated aperture homogen belegte Apertur *f (Sat.)*
unilateral einseitig
   u. conductivity unipolare Leitfähigkeit *f (Kabel)*
uninterruptible power supply (UPS) unterbrechungsfreie Stromversorgung *f* (USV)
unipolar operation Einfachstromtastung *f*, Unipolartastung *f (NTG 1203)*
uniselector with gold-plated contacts Edelmetallmotordrehwähler *m* (EMD)
unit Einheit *f*, Einrichtung *f*;
   (U) Einheit *f*, Höheneinheit *f* (HE) *(Gestell, 1 HE = 1 3/4", 44,45 mm)*;
   (E) Teileinheit *f* (TE) *(Gestell, 1 TE = 0.2", 5,08 mm)*
   u. front Frontplatte *f*, Bedienfeld *n*
   u. interval Schrittlänge *f*, Einheitsschrittlänge *f*
   u. location Einschubplatz *m* (EP) *(Gestell)*
   u. pulse response Stoßantwort *f (r(t))*
   u. under test (UUT) Prüfling *m*
   seven u. high 7HE hoch *(Gestell)*
universal asynchronous receiver/transmitter (UART) universeller asynchroner Empfänger/Sender *m*
   u. night service (extension) allgemeine Nachtschaltung *f (Tel.)*
   u. synchronous/asynchronous receiver/-transmitter (USART) universeller synchroner/asynchroner Empfänger/Sender *m*
   u. synchronous receiver/transmitter (USRT) universeller synchroner Empfänger/Sender *m*
   u. telecommunication socket einheitliche Fernmeldesteckdose *f*, Universalanschluß *m (ISDN)*
   u. time (UT) Weltzeit *f (= GMT)*
   u. time coordinated (UTC) koordinierte Weltzeit *f*
   u. transaction monitor (UTM) universeller Transaktionsmonitor *m (Vtx., DP SW)*
unlisted number Geheimnummer *f (Tel.)*
unloaded VF line unbespulte NF-Leitung *f*
unoccupied unbesetzt, frei *(Leitung)*
unquote tone Ansage-Endton *m (Tel.)*
unrestricted amtsberechtigt *(Nebenstelle)* berechtigt *(TLN)*
unselected unbewählt *(Leitung)*

unshielded twisted pair (UTP) unabgeschirmte verdrillte Doppelleitung f
unsuccessful erfolglos *(Belegungsversuch)*
unused jack unbelegte Buchse f
unvoiced stimmlos
unwanted störend, unzulässig
unweighted unbewertet
  u. noise voltage Fremdspannung f
UP s. user part
up-converter Aufwärtsumsetzer m *(VSAT)*
up-link Aufwärtsstrecke f *(Sat.)*; Aufwärtsverbindung f *(Mobilfunk, Mobilstation — Feststation)*
update ändern n, aktualisieren; nachführen *(Datei, Anzeige)*
  u. level Ausbaustufe f *(SW)*
upgrading Verbesserung f, Ausbau m
  u. options Ausbaumöglichkeiten fpl
U$_{PO}$ interface U$_{PO}$-Schnittstelle f *(U-Schnittstelle für ISDN-BA Zweidraht-Leitung, für Ping-Pong-Übertragung zu/von der OVSt, de facto TK-Anl.-Standard in der BRD 1989)*
upper sideband (USB) oberes Seitenband n
upper special channel band Oberer Sonderkanalbereich m (OSB) *(TV)*
  u. specification limit Grenzwert m nach Datenblatt
upright Gestellholm m
UPS s. uninterruptible power supply
upstream: in the u. link from the user im Upstream m vom Teilnehmer
uptime Verfügbarkeitszeit f *(Netz, Computer)*, Betriebszeit f
urgent alarm (Signal) D-Alarm m (Dringend) *(FS)*
US socket (USOC) US-Steckdose f *(Standard)*
usage Belegung f *(Kanal)*
  u. factor Belegungsfaktor m
USART s. universal synchronous/asynchronous receiver/transmitter
USB (unified S-band) kombiniertes S-Band n *(Sat.)*
USB s. upper sideband
used to full capacity voll ausgelastet
useful wirksam, nützlich, brauchbar
  u. life Betriebslebensdauer f
  u. signal Nutzsignal n
  u. video bandwidth Bildnutzbandbreite f *(TV)*
user Benutzer m, Anwender m, Teilnehmer m; Bedarfsträger m
  u. agent (UA) Benutzer m, Benutzermittel n, elektronischer Briefkasten m *(Box in TELEBOX, MHS-SW, CCITT Rec.* *X.400)*
  u. class of service Benutzerklasse f
  u. connection device Teilnehmeranschlußeinrichtung f (TAE) *(DBP ISDN-Steckverbinder)*, Übergabestelle f *(ehem. TAE)*
  u. facility Leistungsmerkmal n *(Tel.)*
  u.-friendly anwenderfreundlich, komfortabel
  u.-individual presentation control benutzergesteuerte Präsentation f
  u. information Nutzinformation f
  u. information channel Informationskanal m, Nutzkanal m
  u. information (channel) connection Nutzkanalverbindung f
  u. (information) signal Nutzsignal n
  u. interface Bediener-, Benutzeroberfläche f; Nutzerschnittstelle f *(TEMEX)*
  u. line circuit Teilnehmeranschlußschaltung f (TAS)
  u. module Teilnehmeranschlußmodul n (TAM) *(DBP BIGFON)*
  u. (network) access Anwenderzugriff m *(CCITT I.112)*
  u.-network interface (UNI) Teilnehmerschnittstelle f S$_0$, Teilnehmer-Netz-Schnittstelle f *(ISDN, B+B+D$_{16}$)*
  u. organisation Bedarfsträger m *(Betriebsfunk)*
  u.-oriented anwenderfreundlich
  u. part (UP) Anwenderteil m *(ZGS.7)*
  u. program Anwenderprogramm n
  u. prompt(ing) Benutzerführung f
  u. prompts Benutzerführung f
  u.-specific projekt-spezifisch
  u. terminal Teilnehmeranschlußgerät n (TAG) *(DBP BIGFON)*
  u.-to-user protocol Anwender-Anwender-Protokoll n *(CCITT I.112)*
  u. traffic Nutzkanalverkehr m
USOC s. US socket (standard)
USRT (universal synchronous receiver/transmitter) universeller synchroner Empfänger/Sender m
UT (Universal Time) Weltzeit f *(= GMT)*
UTC (Universal Time Coordinated) koordinierte Weltzeit f
utilization rate of capacity Auslastung f
  u. ratio Nutzungsgrad m *(PCM-Daten, Sprache)*
UTM (universal transaction monitor) universeller Transaktionsmonitor m
UTP s. unshielded twisted pair
UUT (unit under test) Prüfling m

V

V series of CCITT Recommendations V-Serie f der CCITT Empfehlungen (s. Tabelle IV)
VADS s. value-added data service
VAL s. Valid
valid gültig; fehlerfrei *(HW)*; Gültigkeit f *(V.25 bis Nachricht)*
validity Gültigkeit f, Bestandsfähigkeit f
  v. check Plausibilitätskontrolle f
value-added data service (VADS) Mehrleistungs-Datendienst m *(ein MDNS)*
  v.-added network (VAN) Dienstleistungsnetz n, Mehrwertnetz n
  v.-added network services (VANS) Dienstleistungsnetzdienste mpl
  v.-added service (VAS) Mehrwertdienst m *(ISDN)*
VAM/VAD (variable asynchronous multiplexer and demultiplexer) variabler asynchroner Multiplexer/Demultiplexer m *(FO, ATM)*
VAN s. value-added network
VANS s. value-added network services
VAP s. videotex access point
variable attenuator steuerbarer Teiler m, Regler m; Eichleitung f *(FO, tel.)*
  v. quantizing level (VQL) variabler Quantisierungspegel m *(Sprachcodierung, nom. 32 kB/s)*
variance Streuung f; Wechselleistung f *(des Quantisierungsfehlers, ADU)*
  v. coefficient Streuwert m *(Verkehr)*
variation Abweichung f, Schwankung f; Verlauf m; Streuung f
  v. due to temperature Temperaturgang m
vary gradually feinstufig verändern
VAS s. value-added service
VC s. video conference
VC (virtual channel) virtueller Kanal m *(Sat.)*
VC (voice channel) Sprechkanal m
VCXO (voltage-controlled X-tal oscillator) spannungsgesteuerter Quarzoszillator m
VDA s. video distribution amplifier
VDOP s. vertical dilution of precision
VDU s. video display unit
vector quantization Vektorquantisierung f (VQ)
Venn diagram Euler-Diagramm n *(Statistik)*
verify prüfen, nachweisen; bestätigen
version Ausführung f, Variante f,
Bestückungsvariante f
vertical senkrecht, vertikal
  v. communication vertikale Verständigung f *(zwischen OSI Schichten)*
  v. dilution of precision (VDOP) vertikale Präzisionsverringerung f *(GPS)*
  v. frequency Bild(wechsel)frequenz f *(TV)*
  v. interval test signal (VITS) Prüfzeilenmeßsignal n *(TV)*
  v. redundancy check (VRC) Querprüfung f, Vertikalprüfung f
very small aperture terminal (VSAT) Bodenstelle f mit sehr kleinem Öffnungswinkel, Kleinstation f *(Sat., Ku-Band, Hughes)*
VF s. video frequency
VF (voice frequency) Niederfrequenz f (NF)
VF level NF-Lage f
VF path Sprechweg m
VFT (voice-frequency telegraphy) Wechselstrom-Telegraphie f
VHSIC (very high-speed IC) integrierte Schaltung f mit sehr hoher Arbeitsgeschwindigkeit
VI s. videotex interworking (protocol)
viable funktionsfähig, -tüchtig
video communication system Videokommunikationsanlage f (VKA)
  v. conference (VC) Videokonferenz f (VK)
  v. conference party VK-Teilnehmer m
  v. conference room Videokonferenzraum m (VKR)
  v. data bits lineare Datenbits npl *(dig. TV)*
  v. disk Bildplatte f
  v. display unit (VDU) Sichtgerät n (SG), Datensichtgerät n (DSG)
  v. distribution amplifier (VDA) Video-Verteilverstärker m *(TV)*
  v. frequency (VF) Videofrequenz f
  v. signal/noise ratio (A) Videostörabstand m
  v. tape recording (VTR) Magnetbandaufzeichnung f (MAZ)
  v. teleconferencing service Videokonferenzdienst m *(CCITT Rec. H.261, 41,920 MB/s)*
  v. terminal Datensichtgerät n (DSG)
videophone Bildtelefon n, Bildfernsprecher m *(ISDN 64 kBit/s, Bewegtbildübermitt-*

videorecorder programming system

lung)
videorecorder programming system Video-Programm-System *n* (VPS) *(TV-Rundfunkdienst)*
v. programming by teletext (VPT) Videorecorder-Programmierung *f* mit Fernsehtext *(TV-Rundfunkdienst)*
VideoStream BT-Punkt-zu-Punkt-Videokonferenz- und Bildtelefondienst *m (64 kB/s, 2 MB/s)*
videotelephone Bildfernsprecher *m*
videotex Videotex *n* (Vtx) *(dialogfähiger Videotext, international, auf Prestel-Basis, s. Tabelle VIII),* Bildschirmtext *m* (BTX, Btx)
v. access point (VAP) Videotex-Anschlußpunkt *m (internationaler Vtx.)*
v. access unit Btx-Anschlußbox *f (an ISDN)*
v. computer centre Bildschirmtextzentrale *f* (BTZ), BTX-Zentrale *f*
v. E-mail service Btx-Mitteilungsdienst *m*
v. interworking (VI) **(protocol)** Videotex-Verbund *m (internationaler Vtx)*
v.-ISDN access Btx-ISDN-Anschluß *m (BA, später PA)*
v. message handling service Btx-Mitteilungsdienst *m*
v. service centre Bildschirmtext-Leitzentrale *f* (Btx-LZ)
v. switching centre Bildschirmtext-Vermittlungsstelle *f* (Btx-VSt)
v.-telex converter Bildschirmtext-Telex-Umsetzer *m* (BTU)
v.-telex service Bildschirmtext-Telex-Dienst *m* (Btx-Tx) *(bietet Telex-Zugriff für Videotexbenutzer)*
v. terminal for Teletel Minitel *n (FR)*
viewdata Bildschirmtext *m* (BTX, Btx) *(GB Prestel, BT, s. Tabelle VIII)*
viewphone teleservice Bewegtbilddienst *m (CCITT)*
violation bit Verletzungsbit *n (TDM)*
v. of range limits Überschreiten *n* der Einstellbereiche, Bereichsüber-/Unterschreitung *f*
virtual channel (VC) virtueller Kanal *m (Sat.)*
v. circuit (VC) virtuelle Verbindung *f* (VV) *(PVN)*
v. networking service (VNS) virtueller Vernetzungsdienst *m (Privatnetze)*
visited network Aufenthaltsnetz *n*, Fremdnetz *n (Mobilfunk)*
visitor location register (VLR) Besucherdatei *f (GSM)*

visual display Visualisierung *f;* Sichtanzeige *f,* Bildschirmanzeige *f,*
v. call signalling optische Anrufsignalisierung *f (K.-Tel.)*
v. display unit (VDU) Sichtgerät *n* (SG), Datensichtgerät *n* (DSG)
VITS (vertical (blanking) interval test signal) Prüfzeilenmeßsignal *n (TV)*
VLR s. visitor location register
VMS s. voice mail server
VNS s. virtual networking service
VOCODER (voice code to recreate) Vokoder *m*
voice Sprache *f;* Gesprächszustand *m (z.B. 'Gesprächszustand hergestellt')*
v. channel (VC) Sprachkanal *m* (SK); Sprechkanal *m* (SpK) *(C-Netz),* Sprechkreis *m*
v. circuit Sprechkreis *m,* Sprechwegeführung *f*
v. communication Sprechverkehr *m*
v./data mailbox Sprach-/Datenspeicher *m*
v.-frequency tonfrequent
v. frequency (VF) Niederfrequenz *f* (NF), Tonfrequenz *f (Tel.)*
v. frequency telegraphy (VFT) Wechselstrom-Telegraphie *f* (WT)
v. guidance akustische Bedienerführung *f (ÖKartTel)*
v. input Spracheingabe *f (Mobilfunk, Freisprechen)*
v. link Sprechweg *m,* Sprechverbindung *f*
v. mail Sprachbox *f,* akustische Telegramme *npl*
v. mail server (VMS) Sprachinformationsserver *m (TK-Anl.);* Sprachspeicherdienst-Bediener *m (ISDN)*
v. mail service Sprachspeicherdienst *m (AUDIOTEX)*
v. messaging service Sprachspeicherdienst *m (AUDIOTEX)*
v. output buffer Sprachausgabepuffer *m*
v. packet transmitter Sprachpaketsender *m* (SPS)
v. terminal Sprachterminal *n (TK-Anl.)*
v. transmission Sprachübertragung *f*
voiced stimmhaft
voltage coefficient Spannungsabhängigkeit *f*
v.-controlled crystal oscillator (VCXO) spannungsgesteuerter Quarzoszillator *m,* nachgeführter Quarz-Oszillator *m*
v. excursion Spannungshub *m*
v. resistance level Spannungswiderstand *m*
v. source drive Spannungssteuerung *f* (RS 232)

v. swing Spannungshub *m*
VPN (virtual private network) virtuelles Privatnetz *n (Vermittlungsdienst)*
VPS (videorecorder programming system) Video-Programm-System *n*
VPT (videorecorder programming by teletext) Videorecorder-Progammierung *f* mit Fernsehtext
VQ (vector quantization) Vektorquantisierung *f*
VQL (variable quantization level) variabler Quantisierungspegel *m*
VRC (vertical redundancy checking) Querprüfung *f*, Vertikalprüfung *f*
VSAT (very-small aperture termminal) Bodenstelle *f* mit sehr kleinem Öffnungswinkel, Kleinstation *f (Sat., Ku-Band, Hughes)*
VTR (video tape recording) Magnetbandaufzeichnung *f* (MAZ)
Vtx (videotex) Videotex *n*

W

WACK (Wait before positive ACKnowledgement) Meldung *f* der momentanen Nichtempfangsbereitschaft
waiting wartend
   w. **call** wartende Belegung *f (Tel.-Anl.)*
   w. **loop** Warteschleife *f*
   w. **traffic** Wartebelegung *f*
wake-up call Weckruf *m*
   w.**-up signal** Wecksignal *n (HW-Aktivierung)*
walkie-talkie Handfunke *f*, Handfunksprechgerät *n*
wall-mounted set Wandgerät *n (Tel.)*
WAN s. wide area network
WAN-CTS s. Wide-Area Networks Conformance Testing
wanted band Nutzband *n*
   w. **signal** Nutzsignal *n*
waste traffic Blindverkehr *m*
watch receiver Wachempfänger *m (Seefunk)*
watchdog Überwachungseinrichtung *f (Computer)*
WATS s. Wide Area Telephone Service
WATTC World Administrative Telegraph and Telephone Conference
wavelength division multiplex (WDM) Frequenzbandmultiplex *n (FO)*; Wellenlängenmultiplex *m* (WD-Multiplex) *(Multi-Laser FO-Anwendung)*
waveshape Wellenform *f*; Kurvenform *f (eines Signals)*
WB s. wideband
WDM s. wavelength division multiplex
weighted noise Ruhegeräusch *n (PCM)*
weighting factor Bewertungsfaktor *m*
   w. **program** Wägeprogramm *n*
west beam Westschiene *f (Sat.-Programme)*, Westkeule *f (Sat.-Ausstrahlung)*
while speaking sprachbegleitend, gesprächsbegleitend *(TK-Anl., bei Benutzung anderer Dienste)*
white noise loading sprachähnliche Belastung *f*
   w.**-paper edition** Weißdruck *m (DIN)*
Who-are-you (WRU) Werda *(Tx.)*
whole-page scanner Ganzseitenabtastung *f (Fax.)*
wide area network (WAN) Fernverkehrnetz *n*; Weitverkehrsnetz *n*;
Langstreckennetz(werk) *n*
W.-Area Networks Conformance Testing Services (WAN-CTS) WAN-Konformitätsprüfungsdienste *mpl (EG, Prüfhäuser für X.21-, X.25- und ISDN-Terminals)*
   w. **area radio paging** großräumiges Personenrufsystem *n*
W. Area Telephone Service (WATS) Fernsprech-Fernverkehr *m (zu Festgebühr bzw. Nulltarif für A-Tln, US, entspricht dem DBP-Service 300)*
wide screen format Breitbildformat *n* (16:9, HDTV)
wideband (WB) Breitband *n* (BB) *(meist analog)*
   w. **cable system** Breitbandkabelanlage *f* (BK-Anlage)
   w. **switching point** (WSP) Breitbandkoppelstelle *f (D-Netz)*
width modulated längenmoduliert *(Impuls)*
   w. **unit** (E) Teileinheit *f* (TE) für die Breite (1 TE = 0.2", 5,08 mm)
window Fenster *n*; Öffnung *f (Tor)*
noise w. Störtor *n (Abschirmung)*
winner Gewinner *m (bei Buszuordnung)*
wire Draht *m*, Ader *f (Kabel)*; beschalten, verdrahten
   w.**-wrap block** Wrapfeld *n*
2-w. 2-Draht-, Zweidraht-
wired telecommunications installation Drahtfernmeldeanlage *f*
   w.**-AND** verdrahtete UND-Verknüpfung *f*
wirewrap connection Wickelanschluß *m*
   w. **method** Drahtwickeltechnik *f*
wiring Verdrahtung *f*; Beschaltung *f*
   w. **compartment** Verdrahtungsraum *m (Gestell)*
   w. **diagram** Bauschaltplan *m*, Leitungsplan *m*, Montageschaltbild *m*, Montageschaltplan *m*
   w. **grid** Verdrahtungsraster *m*
   w. **list** Beschaltungsliste *f*
   w. **run** Leitungszug *m*
   w. **tool** Beschaltwerkzeug *n*
word interleaving wortweise Verschachtelung *f*
   w. **length** Wortbreite *f*; Bittiefe *f* (Bildcodierung, z.B. 8 Bit/Pixel)
   w. **synthesis** Wortaufbereitung *f (PCM-*

Sender)
working frequency Betriebsfrequenz *f*
  w. voltage (WV) Betriebsspannung *f*
workshop Werkstatt *f*, Workshop *m (Seminar)*, Kampagne *f*
workstation Bedienplatz *m*
WORM s. write once, read many
write in einschreiben, einlesen, einspeichern
  w. once, read many (WORM) einmal beschreiben, mehrmals lesen *(CD-R)*

wrong connection Fehlverbindung *f*
  w.-number call Fehlverbindung *f*, Falschanruf *m*
WRU s. who-are-you
WSP s. wideband switching point
WST (World System Teletext and Data Broadcasting System) weltweiter Teletextstandard *m*
WV s. working voltage
WYSIWYG what-you-see-is-what-you-get *(DTP-Methode)*

X

X interface X-Schnittstelle *f (Achtdraht-ISDN-Anschlußvorrichtung zwischen Fernsprecher und Zusatzeinrichtung, analog)*
X series of CCITT Recommendations X-Serie *f* der CCITT-Empfehlungen *(betrifft leitungs- und paketvermittelte digitale Datenübertragung, Mitteilungsdienstleistungen, Dokumentübermittlung, s. Tabelle V)*
XB (crossbar) Kreuzschiene *f*
XB(X) (crossbar (selector) exchange) Koordinatenschalteramt *n (analog)*
XBU (crossbar exchange, unbalanced signalling) Koordinatenschalteramt *n*, unsymmetrische Zeichengabe
Xon/Xoff Handshakeverfahren *n* für Peripheriegeräte *(SW)*
X/OPEN Vereinigung *f* von Computerherstellern für Softwarestandardisierung *(RARE)*
X.PC Tymnet-Fehlersicherungsprotokoll *n (bis zu OSI-Schicht 3)*
XPD (cross polarisation discrimination) Kreuzpolarisationsentkopplung *f (Sat.)*

Y

Y interface Y-Schnittstelle *f (Vierdraht-ISDN-Anschlußvorrichtung zwischen Fernsprecher und Zusatzeinrichtung, digital)*

Y junction Y-Verzweigung *f (FO)*
yellow-paper edition Gelbdruck *m (DIN)*

Z

Z interface Z-Schnittstelle *f (am Fernsprechterminal, z.B. X.21, S_0, ISDN)*
ZC s. zone centre
ZC0 s. zero character impedance
zero character (line) impedance (Z_{C0}) Zeichenimpedanz *f (ZZ) (Tel.)*
   z. crossing Nulldurchgang *m*
   z.-movement bit rate Ruhebitrate *f (Bildcodierung)*
   z. sidetone (line) impedance (Z_{S0}) Rückhörimpedanz *f (ZR) (Tel., CCITT Rec. P.10, Impedanz zw. 300-3400 Hz)*
   z.-signal current Ruhestrom *m*
zone centre (ZC) Zonenzentrum *n (Vermittlung)*
   z. of dispersion Streubereich *m*
zoner Verzoner *m (Vermittlung)*
zoning Verzonung *f (Vermittlung)*
ZS0 s. zero sidetone impedance

ANHANG: Tabellen

Tabelle I: Schichten im Referenzmodell für offene Kommunikation

Tabelle II: European Telecommunication Standards NET

Tabelle III: I Series of CCITT Recommendations

Tabelle IV: V Series of CCITT Recommendations

Tabelle V: X Series of CCITT Recommendations

Tabelle VI: V.24/RS232C-Schnittstelle

Tabelle VII: TEMEX-Schnittstellen

Tabelle VIII: Europäische Videotexnetze

Tabelle I: Schichten im Referenzmodell für offene Kommunikation
Layers in the OSI 7-layer reference model

1. **Schicht**: physikalische Schicht, Bit-Übertragungsschicht	layer 1: physical layer *(CCITT Rec. I.430)*
2. **Schicht**: Sicherungsschicht	layer 2: data link layer *(CCITT Rec. I.440 and I.441)*
3. **Schicht**: Netzwerkebene, Vermittlungsschicht	layer 3: network layer *(CCITT REC. I.450 and I.451)*
4. **Schicht**: Transportebene	layer 4: transport layer
5. **Schicht**: Sitzungsebene, Kommunikationssteuerungsschicht	layer 5: session layer
6. **Schicht**: Präsentationsebene, Darstellungsschicht	layer 6: presentation layer
7. **Schicht**: Anwendungsebene, Verarbeitungsschicht	layer 7: application layer.

Tabelle II: European Telecommunication Standards NET*

NET 1	X.21 Access	relates to CCITT Rec. X.21 *(1984)*; X.21 access by terminal equipment to a PSTN and point-to-point or multipoint leased circuits
NET 2	X.25 Access	relates to CCITT Rec. X.25 and CEPT Rec. T/CD 08.01 access by terminal equipment to a PTN
NET 3	ISDN Basic Access	relates to CCITT Rec. I.420 *(1984)* and CEPT Rec. T/GSI 04.01, 04.02,1,2,3 access by terminal equipment to a PTN at an ISDN BAP
NET 4	PSTN Basic Access	relates to access by analog voice or non-voice terminals *(modems)* to a PSTN
NET 5	Digital Telephony	additional to NET 3, relates to telephony via a PTN
NET 6	Analog Modem	relates to access to a PSTN, initially for CCITT Rec. V.32
NET 7	Group 3 Fax	relates to CEPT Rec. T/SF 21, connection to a PSTN
NET 8	Teletex	relates to CEPT Rec. T/SF 22, connection to a PSTN
NET 9	ISDN Terminal Adaptor	DCE-DTE BA interface to a PTN, relates to CCITT Rec. I.460, 461, 462; additional to NET 3
NET 20	PSTN Access	Requirements for Category I *(non-CCITT, PEP-type and V.26 bis, V.26 ter, V.27 ter)* and Category II *(V.21, V.22, V.22 bis, V.23, V.32)* modems

*(Quelle u.a.: Telecommunications Approvals Handbook, British Telecom 'Teleprove', Ausgabe 1988/89)

Tabelle III: I Series of CCITT Recommendations, relating to ISDN*

I.100 series	relates to the general ISDN concept, definitions, terminology, descriptions of ISDNs, general modelling methods
I.200 series	relates to service aspects of ISDNs, telecommunications services, bearer services, teleservices supported by an ISDN
I.300 series	relates to network functional principles, modelling, numbering
I.400 series	relates to ISDN user-network interfaces
I.410 family	relates to general aspects and principles, reference configurations, interface structures
I.420 family	relates to the application of I-Series Recommendations to ISDN user-network interfaces
I.420	basic user-network interfaces
I.421	primary rate user-network interfaces
I.430 family	relates to ISDN layer 1 recommendations
I.430	basic user-network interfaces
I.431	primary rate user-network interfaces
I.43x	higher-rate user-network interfaces
I.440 family	relates to ISDN layer 2 recommendations
I.440 (Q.920)	general aspects of the data link layer
I.441 (Q.921)	data link layer specifications
I.450 family	relates to ISDN layer 3 recommendations
I.450 (Q.930)	general aspects of the network layer
I.451 (Q.931)	network layer specifications
I.460 family	relates to multiplexing, rate adaptation and support of existing interfaces
I.461 (X.30)	relates to support of X.20 bis, X.21 and X.21 bis-based DTEs by an ISDN
I.462 (X.31)	relates to support of packet mode DTEs by an ISDN
I.463 (V.110)	relates to the interface adaptation of DTEs with a V interface to S interfaces
I.464	relates to rate adaptation and multiplexing
I.500 series	relates to internetwork interfaces and interworking
I.600 series	relates to maintenance principles and user-related testing

*(Quelle: CCITT Red Book, Volume III - Fascicle III.5 - INTEGRATED SERVICES DIGITAL NETWORK, 1984)

Tabelle IV:
V Series of CCITT Recommendations, relating to telephone networks[*]

V.3	defines IA *(q.v.)* 5 and national variations
V.4	defines binary 1s and 0s, parity bit use, start/stop bits *(corresponds to DIN 66022)*
V.7	defines terms concerning data communications over the telephone network
V.10	defines electrical characteristics for unbalanced double-current interchange circuits (X.26) *(DIN 66259 Part 2, EIA RS423)*
V.11	defines electrical characteristics for balanced double-current interchange circuits (X.27) *(DIN 66259 Part 3, EIA RS422)*
V.15	relates to the use of acoustic couplers for data transmission
V.20	relates to parallel data transmission modems *(DIN 66021 Part 10)*
V.21	relates to 200/300 bps asynchronous modems, full duplex, FSK *(corresponds to DIN 66021 Part 1)*
V.22	relates to 600,1200 bps synchronous and asynchronous full duplex modems for 2-wire circuits, PSK
V.22 bis	relates to 2400 bit/s duplex dial-up modems, QAM
V.23	relates to 600,1200 bps synchronous and asynchronous half duplex/full duplex modems for 2-wire and 4-wire circuits, FM *(DIN 66021 Part 2)*
V.24	relates to DCE/DTE serial data communication interfaces *(corresponds to EIA RS232C, DIN 66020, Part 1)*
V.25	relates to automatic calling and answering equipment and procedures for 2-wire dial-up systems *(DIN 66021 Part 4)*
V.25 bis	relates to automatic diallers and answering machines in a PSTN, PSK
V.26	relates to 2400 bps synchronous modems for 4-wire circuits, full duplex, PSK *(DIN 66021 Part 3)*
V.26 bis	relates to 1200/2400 bit/s half duplex modems for PSTNs, PSK
V.26 ter	relates to 2400 bit/s full-duplex modems with echo cancellation for PSTNs, PSK
V.27	relates to 4800 bps synchronous modems, PSK
V.27 bis	relates to modems for 2- and 4-wire leased circuits, PSK
V.27 ter	relates to modems for 2-wire dial-up circuits, *PSK (V.27, V.27 bis, V.27 ter correspond to DIN 66021 Part 7 and DIN 66259 Part 3)*
V.28	relates to the electrical characteristics of V.24 *(DIN 66259 Part 1; RS232C)*
V.29	relates to 9600 bps modems for synchronous use on point-to-point 4-wire leased telephone circuits, half duplex, PSK, QAM *(fax, DIN 66021 Part 8)*
V.30	relates to 50-110 bps FSK-type modems for 2-wire circuits
V.31	defines electrical characteristics for single-current interchange circuits *(corresponds to DIN 66021 Part 10)*
V.32	relates to 9600 bps modems for 2-wire circuits, full duplex, QAM
V.35	relates to 48000 bps modems for 4-wire wideband circuits
V.36	relates to modems for synchronous data transmission *(DIN 66021 Part 9)*
V.42	error correction method for modems with asynchr./synchr. conversion *(derived from Microcom MNP (Microcom Networking Protocol))* for 2-wire circuits, also covers LAPM
V42 bis	relates to data compression for modems
V.50	defines standard limits for the transmission quality of data transmission
V.54	relates to loop testing of modems and circuits between modems
V.100	relates to adaptive modems
V.110	relates to the interface adaptation of terminals with V interface to S interfaces *(CCITT Rec. I.463)*

[*](Quelle u.a.: Funkschau 3/1990)

Tabelle V: X Series of CCITT Recommendations, relating to data networks

X.3	relates to the PAD facilities of a packet switching network *(PSN; DIN 66258 Parts 1, 2; 66348 Part 1)*
X.4	relates to International Alphabet 5 code signals for character oriented data transmission *(DIN 66022)*
X.20	defines the interface between DTE and DCE for start-stop transmission on PDNs *(DIN 66244 Part 6)*
X.20 bis	relates to DTE for asynchronous duplex V-series modems on PDNs *(DIN 66021 Part 6)*
X.21	defines the interface between DTE and DCE for synchronous operation on PDNs *(DIN 66244 Parts 2, 5, for IDN)*
X.21 bis	relates to DTE for synchronous V-series modems on PDNs *(compatible with V.24; DIN 66021 Part 5, 6)*
X.24	defines DTE/DCE interchange circuits on PDNs *(DIN 66020 Part 2, EIA RS449)*
X.25	relates to the interface between a PSN and a synchronous packet-mode DTE in ISO OSI layers 1,2,3 *(DIN 66244 Part 3; DIN 66258 Part 1, 2; DIN 66348 Part 1; DBP protocol P10, LAP B)*
X.26	relates to electrical characteristics for unbalanced double-current interchange circuits (V.10)*(DIN 66029; DIN 66259 Part 2; EIA RS423)*
X.27	relates to electrical characteristics for balanced double-current interchange circuits (V.11)*(DIN 66029; DIN 66259 Part 3; FIA RS422)*
X.28	relates to the interface between the PAD facilities of a PSN and an asynchronous DTE *(DIN 66258 Part 1, 2; DIN 66348 Part 1; DBP protocol P20A)*
X.29	relates to the interface between the PAD facilities of a PSN and a packet-mode DTE *(DIN 66258 Part 1, 2; DIN 66348 Part 1; DBP protocol P20B)*
X.30	relates to support of X.20 bis, X.21 and X.21 bis-based DTEs by an ISDN *(CCITT Rec. I.461)*
X.31	relates to support of packet mode terminals by an ISDN *(CCITT Rec. I.462)*
X.32	relates to the interface between packet mode DTEs and DCEs accessing a PSPDN or CSPDN
X.71	relates to interexchange signalling
X.75	relates to interexchange packet-oriented trunks, signalling between public packet-switched networks
X.81	relates to interworking between an ISDN and a CSPDN
X.121	international numbering plan for packet-switched public data networks
X.150	relates to loop testing of data terminal stations with X interfaces *(X.20, X.21 etc.)*
X.200	OSI reference model for CCITT applications, ISO 7498
X.300	relates to the interworking between public data networks
X.400	relates to message handling services (MHS), OSI application layer *(S&F)* standard, ISO 10021-x
X.500	OSI directory services *(for X.400 addressing)*
X.509	relates to encrypted data transmission and authentication of electronically transmitted documents, directory

Tabelle VI: V.24/RS232C-Schnittstelle*

Pin No.	CCITT V.24	EIA RS232C	Designation		DIN 66020	Bezeichnung
1	101	AA	Protective Ground, Frame Ground		E1	Schutzerde
2	103	BA	Transmit Data	(TD)	D1	Sendedaten
3	104	BB	Receive Data	(RD)	D2	Empfangsdaten
4	105	CA	Request to Send	(RTS)	S2	Sendeteil einschalten
5	106	CB	Clear to Send	(CTS)	M2	Sendebereitschaft
6	107	CC	Data Set Ready	(DSR)	M1	Betriebsbereitschaft
7	102	AB	Signal Ground	(GND)	E2	Signalerde Betriebserde
8	109	CF	Data Carrier Detect	(DCD)	M5	Empfangssignalpegel
9	141		Loopback		PS3	Nahe Prüfschleife einschalten
10	"		"		"	
11	126	CK	Select Transmit Frequency		S5	Sendefrequenz
12	122	CF	Secondary DCD		HM5	Rückkanal Empfangssignalpegel
13	121	CB	Secondary CTS		HM2	Rückkanal Sendebereitschaft
14	118	SBA	Secondary TD	(SXMT)	HD1	Rückkanal Sendedaten
15	114	DB	Transmit Clock	(TC)	T2	Sendeschrittakt von DÜE
16	119	SBB	Secondary Receive Data	(SRCV)	HD2	Rückkanal Empfangsdaten
17	115	DD	Receive Clock	(RC)	T4	Empfangsschrittakt
18	142		Test Indicator		PM1	Prüfzustand
19	120	SCA	Secondary RTS	(BRTS)	HS2	Rückkanal Sendeteil einschalten
20	108.1		Connect Data Set to Line		S1.1	Übertragungsleitung anschalten
	108.2	CD	Data Terminal Ready	(DTR)	S1.2	Endgerät betriebsbereit
21	110	CG	Signal Quality	(SQ)	M6	Empfangsgüte
22	125	CE	Ring Indicator	(RI)	M3	Ankommender Ruf
23	111	CH	Select Data Signal Rate (from DTE)	(SEL)	S4	Übertragungsgeschwindigkeit *(von DEE)*
	112	CI	Select Data Signal Rate (from DCE)	(SEL)	M4	Übertragungsgeschwindigkeit *(von DÜE)*
24	113	DA	Transmit Clock		T1	Sendeschrittakt von DEE
25	142		Test Indicator		M1	Prüfzustand

*(Quelle u.a.: Elektronik-Sonderheft Nr.56 "Datenkommunikation", 2. Auflage)

Tabelle VII: TEMEX-Schnittstellen*
TEMEX Interfaces

TSS 11 *(TNA-Schnittstelle)* — input interface for bivalent information *(to CCITT V.31 bis)*

TSS 12 *(TNA-Schnittstelle)* — output interface for bivalent information *(to CCITT V.31 bis)*

TSS 13,14,15 — input/output interfaces for bivalent information *(to CCITT X.21)*

TSS 17 *(LSt-LSt-Schnittstelle)* — input/output interface as for TSS 13 to 15 *(to CCITT X.21)*

TSS 19 *(TNA-Schnittstelle zum angeschlossenen Fernsprechapparat)* — network termination/connected telephone set interface

TSS 31 *(LSt-Schnittstelle zu HfD bzw. Datex-L)* — input/output interface for serial data transmission *(to CCITT X.20 for asynchr. mode, to X.21 for synchr. mode, communications protocols to DIN 66019 4A/B (byte-oriented) or to DIN 66222 Part 1 (bit-oriented))*

TSS 32 *(LSt-Schnittstelle, Modem/Telefonnetz-Verbindung)* — input/output interface for serial data transmission *(to CCITT V.24; call setup to V.25 bis, communications protocols to DIN 66019 (byte-oriented))*

*(Quelle u.a.: TEMEX - a new telecommunication service of the Deutsche Bundespost, H. Lydorf, 1986)

Tabelle VIII: Europäische Videotexnetze (Stand Dezember 1988)*

Country	Service	Gateway protocol	Presentation standard
FRG Denmark Sweden	Bildschirmtext Teledata Videotex Datavision	EHKP	CEPT Profile 1 (alphageometry)
Belgium GB Italy Netherlands	Videotex Prestel Videotel Viditel	Prestel and modifications of Prestel	CEPT Profile 3 (Prestel)
Austria Switzerland	Bildschirmtext Videotex		CEPT Profile 1 (alphageometry)
Norway	Teledata	Teletel	Profile 1 ... 3
France	Teletel	Teletel	Profile 2 (Antiope)
Spain	Ibertex	Ibertex	Profile 1 (alphageometry)

*(Quelle u.a.: Funkschau 12, 3. Juni 1988)

Erich Bürger

Fachwörterbuch Informatik

Deutsch – Englisch – Französisch – Russisch

Hüthig

1989, 2 Bände, 903 S., geb.,
DM 138,—
ISBN 3-7785-1586-1

Dieses zweibändige Fachwörterbuch enthält Termini der allgemeinen Informatik, aus der EDV-Technologie und aus den Bereichen CAD und CAE. Bei der Auswahl der Fachwörter wurden die allgemeinen Grundlagen der Informatik, wie beispielsweise Rechnerarchitektur, Hard- und Softwarekomponenten, Systemtechnik, Dialog- und Stapelverarbeitung sowie Grundlagen der Programmierung, die Softwareentwicklung, wie Entwurfsvorbereitung, programmtechnische Realisierung, Datenerfassung und -verwaltung, Hardwarekomponenten, wie Schaltungen, Speicher, Ein- und Ausgabevorrichtungen, Interfaces, Datenerfassungsterminals, Sensoren und Aktoren, Übertragungsmedien und Netzkontroller, Systemzuverlässigkeit, Anwendungen der Informatik in Industrie und Wirtschaft, wie CIM, CAD, CAM, künstliche Intelligenz, Expertensysteme, Datenbasen usw. berücksichtigt. Dadurch wird dem Informationsbedürfnis der Fachleute und Studenten auf diesem wissenschaftlich-technischen Gebiet entsprochen.

Hüthig Buch Verlag
Im Weiher 10
6900 Heidelberg 1

Hüthig

Peter-Klaus Budig (Hrsg.)

Fachwörterbuch Elektrotechnik/Elektronik

Englisch-Deutsch

5., ergänzte Auflage 1989,
803 S., geb., DM 138,—
ISBN 3-7785-1724-4

In diesem Fachwörterbuch sind mehr als 60 000 Fachbegriffe, davon 6 700 neue, aus den Gebieten Theoretische Grundlagen der Elektronik einschließlich der elektrischen Meßtechnik, der Starkstromtechnik mit den Sachgebieten elektrische Maschinen und Antriebe sowie die gesamte Nachrichtentechnik und Informatik enthalten. Bei dem Zusammenstellen der Stichwörter wurde bewußt davon ausgegangen, daß Fachwörter sowohl der klassischen als auch der Supraleitung, Lasertechnik, Optoelektronik, Hochspannungsmeßtechnik aufgenommen wurden.

Besonders hervorgehoben sei, daß die Fachbegriffe, alphabetisch nach dem Nestsystem geordnet, in der englischen und deutschsprachigen Fachliteratur belegt sind. Viele Wörter sind mit besonderen Hinweisen und Erklärungen versehen, die die Anwendung, d. h. die Übersetzung, wesentlich erleichtern.

In den letzten Auflagen wurden neben Korrekturen und Ergänzungen vor allem neue Termini, die durch die kurzen Innovationszeiten der Fachgebiete und der fortschreitenden internationalen Standardisierung in der Zwischenzeit entstanden sind, aufgenommen. Damit wurde das Wörterbuch wieder wesentlich verbessert und entspricht dem neuesten Stand der Technik.

Hüthig Buch Verlag
Im Weiher 10
6900 Heidelberg 1

Bernhard Walke

Hüthig

Datenkommunikation I

Teil 1: Verteilte Systeme ISO/OSI-Architekturmodell und Bitübertragungsschicht.
1987, 225 S., 95 Abb., kart., DM 44,—
ISBN 3-7785-1565-9

Teil 2: Sicherungsprotokolle für die Rechner-Rechner Kommunikation. Lokale Netze und ISDN-Nebenstellenanlagen.
1987, 235 S., 92 Abb., kart., DM 44,—
ISBN 3-7785-1566-7

Datenkommunikation steht in diesem Werk als Oberbegriff für Bereiche wie:
- Übertragung digitaler Signale über bandbegrenzte Kanäle
- Architektur von Kommunikations- und Übermittlungssystemen
- Dienste und Protokolle für transport- und anwendungsbezogene Funktionen
- verteilte Verarbeitung

Das Buch besteht aus zwei Teilen. Die Stoffdarbietung folgt dem ISO/OSI-Architekturmodell für die Kommunikation zwischen herstellerunabhängigen (offenen) Systemen. Anhand verteilter Systeme werden die Funktion und Bedeutung von Kommunikation erläutert und dann das ISO/OSI Basismodell eingeführt.
Teil 1 enthält weiter die notwendigen theoretischen Grundlagen der Datenübertragung (Signale, Pulse, Basis-, Träger/Breitbandübertragung, Modulations- und Zeitmultiplexverfahren) und behandelt die üblichen Protokolle und Leitungsschnittstellen zum physischen Übertragungsmedium gemäß Schicht 1 des ISO/OSI Modells.
Teil 2 beschreibt Protokolle und Dienste der Schicht 2 und stellt alle bekannten Steuerungs- bzw. Sicherungsverfahren nebeneinander wie sie bei Punkt-zu-Punkt und Mehrpunktverbindungen bzw. Zeitmultiplex-Übermittlungssystemen benutzt werden. Zeichen- und bitorientierte Protokolle, die Beherrschung von Übertragungsfehlern und die vergleichende Bewertung von lokalen Netzen und datenvermittlungstüchtigen digitalen ISDN-Nebenstellenanlagen sind weitere Schwerpunkte. Das Buch hat besondere Aktualität durch die Behandlung aller wesentlichen, in den letzten Jahren neu standardisierten Protokolle und Dienste für den Datentransport zwischen Rechnern im Nah- wie Fernbereich. Die Darstellung ist so gewählt, daß ein Student der Elektrotechnik oder Informatik ab dem 3. Hochschulsemester den gebotenen Stoff im Selbststudium erarbeiten kann. Er wird dabei durch Selbsttestaufgaben und zugehörige Lösungen und eine für das Fernstudium erprobte Darbietungsform unterstützt.

Hüthig Buch Verlag
Im Weiher 10
6900 Heidelberg 1

Hüthig

Andreas Kanbach, Andreas Körber

ISDN – Die Technik

1990, X, 276 S., 240 Abb., 101 Tab., geb., DM 78,—
ISBN 3-7785-1781-3
Reihe: Telekommunikation
Band 9

Mit dem ISDN wird die bisher größtenteils analoge Übertragungstechnik vollständig durch eine digitale Technik abgelöst, wobei für jeden ISDN-Teilnehmer bereits in der Grundausführung (Basisanschluß) zwei Nutzkanäle zur Verfügung gestellt werden, so daß z. B. gleichzeitig telefoniert und fernkopiert werden kann. Die bereits millionenfach vorhandenen Teilnehmeranschlußleitungen werden weiterhin genutzt.

Das vorliegende Buch führt in die Technik des ISDN ein, wobei vorwiegend auf die Realisierung des Teilnehmeranschlusses von den Endsystemen bis zu den teilnehmerbezogenen Einrichtungen der Vermittlungsstellen eingegangen wird.

Das erste Kapitel beschreibt den Weg der Fernmeldetechnik vom herkömmlichen Fernsprechnetz und den heutigen Rechnernetzen zum ISDN. Kapitel 2 erläutert das Bezugsmodell für die Verbindung offener (herstellerunabhängiger) Systeme, das sowohl für die ISDN-Zeichengabe, als auch für die Realisierung der ISDN-Anwendungen von größter Bedeutung ist. Die Bitübertragungsschicht des Teilnehmeranschlusses wird im Kapitel 3 behandelt. In den beiden anschließenden Kapiteln werden die Schicht 2 bzw. 3 der ISDN-Zeichengabe erörtert. Das Kapitel 6 widmet sich der Realisierung einiger ausgewählter Dienstmerkmale und Kapitel 7 befaßt sich mit dem Aufbau von ISDN-Endsystemen. Kapitel 8 behandelt schließlich die spezifischen Hardware-Komponenten von ISDN-Endsystemen und sonstigen Einrichtungen am Teilnehmeranschluß.

Dieses aus einer Vorlesung am Institut für Fernmeldetechnik der TU Berlin entstandene Buch soll alle diejenigen ansprechen, die sich mit der modernen Kommunikationstechnik vertraut machen wollen. Es soll den technisch Interessierten ebenso informieren wie den Studenten der Informatik und Nachrichtentechnik sowie den Anwender in der informationstechnischen Industrie und in den Fernmeldeverwaltungen.